BRET
HART
HITMAN

EBURY
PRESS

5 7 9 10 8 6

First Published in Canada by Random House Canada in 2007
This edition published 2009 by Ebury Press, an imprint of Ebury Publishing
A Random House Group Company

The Random House Group Limited Reg. No. 954009

Addresses for companies within the Random House Group can be found at
www.randomhouse.co.uk

A CIP catalogue record for this book is available from the British Library

The Random House Group Limited supports The Forest Stewardship Council (FSC),
the leading international forest certification organisation. All our titles that are printed
on Greenpeace approved FSC certified paper carry the FSC logo. Our paper
procurement policy can be found at www.rbooks.co.uk/environment

Mixed Sources
Product group from well-managed
forests and other controlled sources
www.fsc.org Cert no. TT-COC-2139
© 1996 Forest Stewardship Council

Printed and bound in Great Britain by Clays Ltd, St Ives PLC

Hardback ISBN 9780091932855
Trade paperback ISBN 9780091933036

To buy books by your favourite authors and register for offers visit www.rbooks.co.uk

HITMAN

This book is dedicated to the memory of my loving mom,
Helen "Tiger Belle" Hart

ACKNOWLEDGEMENTS

I want to thank my children for giving me the time and space to write this book, especially after sacrificing so much of our time together during my pro wrestling career. Thanks to David Moraniss and Joe Fiorito for their encouragement throughout. Thanks also to Bruce Westwood and his staff at Westwood Creative Artists; and to Anne Collins at Random House Canada for an absolutely brilliant editing job, and for helping me to pull it all together. Thanks to all Hart family members, especially Ross and Alison; and to Julie, for putting up with me for as long as she did. I need to give special thanks to Marcy Engelstein for her amazing and tireless devotion to helping me write this book, which would never have been written without her. That's the plain truth of it. Thank you my friend. I'll never forget the time and energy you've given me through some very difficult times. Thanks to Dave Meltzer and Bob Leonard for preserving history. Thank you to all my fans around the world: I hope I haven't disappointed too many of you by being as truthful as I've been in these pages. Lastly, to every wrestler mentioned in this book—the good, the bad and the ugly—and even more so to all the wrestlers I worked with from the start, I thank each and every one of you for working with me, and for trusting me like a brother and a friend. I'm free at last.

CONTENTS

One thing you will discover is that life is based less than you think on what you've learned and much more than you think on what you have inside you from the beginning.

— MARK HELPRIN, *Memoir from Antproof Case*

PREFACE

It seemed like an eternity until the pastor called me to the podium. I rose slowly from my seat, away from the insulation of loved ones—Julie, our four kids, my friend Marcy and Olympic wrestling champion Daniel Igali. I felt them all take a deep breath as I made my way to the aisle.

My father's funeral service was held on October 23, 2003, at the biggest church in Calgary, yet it overflowed with an eclectic throng of thousands who came to pay their respects to the legendary Stu Hart, old-time pro wrestling promoter extraordinaire.

I moved slowly, a silent prayer resounding in my head, "Please, God, help me make it through." I am an experienced public speaker, but my confidence had been shattered by a major stroke.

It hadn't been that long since I'd been trapped in a wheelchair, paralyzed on the left side, unsure whether I'd ever walk again. Since then I'd been having emotional meltdowns triggered by the most unlikely things; this is common among stroke victims. I didn't know how I was going to deliver a eulogy worthy of my father and not break down. It was also hard for me to walk tall when I felt so many eyes measuring the difference between what I was now—my body stiff, the chiselled edges softened—to what I'd been.

But when I walked past the pew where my brothers and sisters sat—my limp more noticeable than I wanted—I sensed, perhaps for the first time in our lives, that they were all behind me, even those with whom I'd had differences. *Do it for Dad, Bret. Do it for all of us. Do us proud.* There'd been twelve Hart kids, and now there were ten. Our beloved mother, Helen, had died just two years earlier. We'd all been through so much, travelled such a long, long road.

This wasn't just the end of my father's life, this was something deeper, and I think we all felt it. So many times over so many years I truly thought this godforsaken business was dead to me, but this was the day pro wrestling died for me—for good.

In the front pew sat Vince McMahon, billionaire promoter of the WWE (once the WWF), who'd made a failed attempt to steal my dignity, my

career and my reputation. Beside him sat Carlo DeMarco, my old friend
turned loyal McMahon lieutenant. They were doing their best to look dignified, but I knew—and they knew I knew—that McMahon's presence at
Stu Hart's funeral was more about image than anything else. It only made
me more determined to climb the steps with my head held high. *You don't
matter to me any more, Vince. I survived you, and everything else too.* I had
thought it was wrestling's darkest hour when I'd had my heart cut out in the
middle of the ring by that son of a bitch. Then the Grim Reaper of wrestling
took my youngest brother, Owen, and that was the blackest day.

Keep walking, I told myself, for Davey, Pillman, Curt, Rick, Liz . . . so
many of us are gone, so young, and directly on account of the wrestling life.
Hell, even Hawk. People told me he had wept like a baby when he heard
Stu had died of pneumonia at eighty-three . . . and then Hawk died that very
night. One more for the list. And surely not the last.

I reached into my breast pocket and took out my notes, carefully
unfolding them on the slippery, polished surface of the oak podium. I sur-
veyed the crowd, my gaze stopping at the young apprentices, Chris
Benoit, Edge and Storm, who looked back at me with respectful anticipation. Next I glanced at a company of stalwart ring veterans—The Cuban,
Leo, Hito, even Bad News—all more ruminative and melancholy than I'd
ever seen them. I read it in their faces, the unspoken truth that burying a
man like Stu Hart was truly the end of what we had lived for—and too
many had died for.

And then the sight of old Killer Kowalski, in his good suit, transported
me back four decades, to before Owen was even born.

I am a survivor with a story to tell. There's never been an accurate account
of the history of pro wrestling. All the public knows is what is packaged and
sold to them by the industry. Since I'm no longer in the business, I'm in a
decent position to tell the truth, without fear of recrimination. With this
book, which is based on the audio diary I kept through all my years in
wrestling, starting in my early twenties, I want to put you in my shoes so you
can experience what pro wrestling was like in my era, through my eyes. It's
not my intention to take needless jabs at those who made the journey with
me, but I'll pull no punches either. Not here.

Wrestling was never my dream, and all too often it was my nightmare.
Yet ingrained in me from birth was the instinct to defend it like a religion.
For as long as I can remember, my world has been filled with liars and
bullshitters, losers and con men. But I've also seen the good side of pro
wrestling. To me there is something beautiful about a brotherhood of big,
tough men who only pretend to hurt one another for a living instead of

actually doing it. I came to appreciate that there is an art to it. In contrast to my father, who loved to proudly tell people who the real tough guys, or shooters, of his generation were, I can just as proudly tell you who the great workers, or pretenders, of my generation were. Unlike so many wrestlers with their various made-up names and adopted personae, I was authentic, born Bret Hart into a wrestling world I couldn't escape. I can't say life's been easy, but I can say it's been interesting.

I've always thought of myself as a quiet, easygoing kind of guy, and I believe I was well respected by most of my peers. Some have labelled me as arrogant, and others say I lacked charisma. Admittedly, I wasn't the best talker or mic man in the business, but I more than made up for it with my technical proficiency in the ring. I don't think anyone can rightly dispute that I was a wrestler who put the art first and gave everything I had to the business—and to the fans.

I've always been grateful to have been a world champion who actually did travel the world. People from all walks of life, from New York to Nuremberg, from Calgary to Kyoto, have told me that I inspired them in some way and that I represented everything that was decent about pro wrestling, the way it used to be, when there was still honour in it. It seems like all the world loves an honest battler.

I worked hard to bring out the best in my opponents. I gratefully acknowledge the hundreds of wrestlers I worked with in thousands of matches over twenty-three years, and am proud that I never injured another wrestler to the point that he couldn't work the next day. Regrettably, I can't say the same about some of those who worked with me. I took it as a challenge to have a good match with anybody. I respected both the green-horn jobbers, whose role it was to lose or put me over, and the old-timers, the big tough men of wrestling who allowed me the honour of standing over them with my hand raised. I refused to lose to a fellow wrestler only once in my career, and that was because he refused to do the same for me and others.

The public record is filled with false impressions of me from those who think they know me. Sadly, that includes some members of my own family. My youth wasn't as loving and sweet as the fable that's been perpetuated in wrestling lore. I've been hurt and betrayed by some of my brothers and sisters, yet I don't feel I ever let them down. Some of them sometimes behave as though they begrudge what I've achieved, even though I've paid my dues in ways they can't even imagine. The truth is, my family knows very little about me.

It wasn't easy growing up the eighth of twelve kids, with seven brothers and four sisters. As a child I was drawn to my sweet mother and intimidated by my gruff father. Stu had a temper so fierce that some would consider his corporal punishment child abuse. Too many times I limped around bruised and battered, my eyeballs red and ruptured because of his discipline. On more than a few occasions I thought I was going to die before he was done with me. Often, as I was on the verge of blacking out from some choke hold of Stu's, he'd huff, "You've breathed your last breath."

My father was two different people. At an early age I began to call one of them Stu, and I was terrified of him. Dad was the father I loved. When I was little I used to think Stu overlooked the bad behaviour of his favourite kids and ignored the goodness in the kids who didn't matter as much to him. Looking back I can see that he was hardest on the ones he thought had the most potential. He instilled in me a tenacious drive to succeed by implanting in me his own strong fear of failure. For most of my youth, he teetered on the brink of bankruptcy while I feared becoming the first Hart kid to fail a grade in school. My empathy with his fear connected us.

Like my father, I developed at least a couple of alter egos. At home I kept to myself and generally did whatever my older brothers told me to do; it was just easier that way. At my father's wrestling shows every Friday night, I played Joe Cool, popular with the girls and on top of the world—all part of the show. At school I was shy, but the fights were real. All the Hart kids were bullied for wearing hand-me-downs, and I was always scrapping to defend the family honour. The wrestling fans on Friday nights had no idea that I often attended school wearing shorts in the winter because that's all I had, or that I got my first pair of new runners when I was fourteen.

Later on in life I was one guy on the road, another at home and yet another in the ring. Which one is truly me? They all are.

PART ONE

STAMPEDE DAYS

I

HART BOY

MY EARLIEST MEMORY OF WRESTLING goes back to 1960, when I was three years old. There were nine Hart kids then, and we were huddled in the kitchen on a Friday night, watching my dad's TV show on a flickering black-and-white screen. My mom, pregnant with Ross—it seemed like she was always pregnant then—held my baby sister Alison in her arms. Though back then she never liked to watch wrestling, she, too, was riveted to the TV as Sam Manacker, the wrestling announcer, repeated frantically, "Kowalski has broken Tex McKenzie's neck! He's broken his neck!" My eyes popped out of my head and my mouth hung open. I was watching my very first wrestling angle.

Tex was a handsome, dark-haired cowboy. I loved cowboys, and I was wearing my Roy Rogers holster and six-shooters at that very moment. Killer Kowalski was an agile, baldheaded brute with an angry scowl on his face. Just as I was wondering what kind of man calls himself Killer, Kowalski climbed to the top of the corner ring post and leaped off, high and hard, driving his knee into Tex's neck. Now Tex lay there quivering, his cowboy boots shaking and kicking.

We watched the ambulance attendants load Tex tenderly onto a stretcher, sliding him out and under the bottom rope. Manecker said Tex might be paralyzed. I asked my ten-year-old brother Bruce, my most reliable source of information, what that meant. Bruce stared hard at the television. "It means he'll never, ever walk again."

Suddenly Killer was back up on top of the turnbuckle, and he jumped off and landed on Tex, knocking him off the stretcher and onto the floor. The audience screamed, and the stretcher-bearers ran for cover. I was terrified. Kowalski really was a damn killer!

It didn't occur to me to wonder why Smith, my oldest brother, who was twelve at the time, had such a big grin on his face. He remarked on how well Tex was selling it. From what I could tell, poor Tex wasn't selling anything. And I couldn't understand why my tender-hearted mom seemed more concerned about how well the match came across on TV than

7

whether Tex would ever walk again. Only much later did I realize that she was happy my dad's TV show was back on the air; they could catch up on the bills again.

That night the Hart brothers stayed up into the wee hours of the morning, talking about the match. Even though it was all so frightening, it was very exciting too! I was relieved to hear my older brother Dean say that my dad was not only the toughest, greatest wrestler of them all, but that he could tie that Killer Kowalski up into knots any time he wanted. Our dad was utterly invincible.

I shared a bed with Bruce, who looked after me most of the time back then. When he got up early every morning to milk Daphne the cow, I'd sit on the warm radiator and watch him from the big picture window of the boys' room, walking down past the front of the house in his blue-checkered flannel jacket, swinging the milk pail. In the distance, I could see the sprawling city of Calgary glinting in the early-morning light and the Bow River winding through the valley. I knew even at that young age that way out there past those lights was New York City, where our mom came from. New York City was where our mom met Stu.

My dad was born in Saskatoon in 1915 and grew up in Edmonton in extreme poverty. He managed to lift himself up out of poverty through his drive to succeed and his athletic ability. He spent a lot of time hanging around the YMCA in Edmonton and got into amateur wrestling and football. He was a kicker and defensive tackle with the Edmonton Eskimos in the late thirties. But what he really excelled at was wrestling.

When the Second World War broke out, Stu Hart was the undefeated Canadian heavyweight amateur wrestling champion, and if the war hadn't intervened, he might have won an Olympic medal for Canada. Instead, he joined the navy. When the war ended, he went to New York, where a tough old promoter with cauliflower ears by the name of Toots Mondt hired him to wrestle in the New York territory. Being an Olympian was a dream he had said good-bye to forever. But Stu never said goodbye to his dreams easily.

He was thirty-one years old when he met Helen, on a beach in Long Island in the summer of 1946. She was one of the five daughters of Harry J. Smith, a famous 1908 Olympic marathon runner, and his Greek wife, who was known to us only as Gah-Gah. Helen married my dad on New Year's Eve 1947, even though her mother didn't care too much for him. It didn't help that all five of her girls paid Stu a lot of attention, which he enjoyed. Helen was beautiful and intelligent and could have married someone of higher social standing, but she was smitten with my dad, even though he was a little rough around the edges and she thought wrestling was a dirty business. She'd quip, "We got married in a snowstorm, and I've been snowed under ever since!"

My dad saved his money, and he and Helen left New York in 1948, headed for Montana, where he started a pro wrestling circuit. During the next few years he bought out and took over all the wrestling businesses around him. Then in 1951 they sold their house trailer in Great Falls, Montana, and moved to Calgary with everything they had, including their two boxer dogs, Bing and Demitasse, and their three young sons, Smith, Bruce and Keith.

Television, a recent invention, was just starting to become widespread. Since wrestling (along with boxing) was easier to light and film than team sports such as football or baseball, it was suddenly very popular on the tube. Across North America, wrestlers such as Gorgeous George Wagner, Lou Thesz, Whipper Billy Watson, Pat O'Connor, Argentina Rocca and Verne Gagne became household names. Mirroring the tensions in the world at the time, the villains were called the Kalmikoffs, Fritz Von Erich and Shinji Shibuya. There were midget wrestlers such as Sky Low Low and Little Beaver, a French Canadian with a Mohawk who wasn't even a real Indian. And there were the giants: Haystacks Calhoun, a big, fat farm boy, and the former World Heavyweight boxing champion Primo Carnera. There were lady wrestlers too. I remember one called The Lady Angel, who was bald and had her teeth filed down to points. In those days most of the ladies of wrestling were anything but beautiful. I never found much enjoyment in watching them drag each other around by the hair.

With TV, and the start of his *Big Time Wrestling* show, my dad had fallen into a gold mine. Throughout the 1950s the Hart family prospered and he bought land. We grew up in a big, red-brick, twenty-one-room Victorian mansion high on a hill in the desirable southwestern outskirts of Calgary, with pointy-finned Cadillacs parked all over the yard.

In Calgary, Helen had another baby boy, Wayne, and then another, Dean, before my dad finally got what he wanted most of all—a baby girl. Ellie was followed by Georgia, and then me, on July 2, 1957. My dad said that when he saw me for the first time, he looked at my hands, with long fingers like my mother's yet thick like his, and knew I would be the biggest of his sons. I lost my glow as the new baby pretty quickly because Alison soon followed, and then Ross. Ross once climbed all over my mom's desk while she was working and tipped over a bottle of ink, earning him the nickname Inky. Ross never strayed very far away from my mom and that desk. After him came another sister, Diana, and finally my baby brother, Owen.

By the time I was born, interest in wrestling had waned, and things weren't quite so rosy at Hart house any more. My dad had made some poor investments and was barely making ends meet. Then wrestler Iron Mike DiBiase said something bad about Canadians on my dad's TV show: "If nickels were brains and ten cents could get you around the world, the average Canadian wouldn't be able to get across the street." That was all it took for the TV bosses to take *Big Time Wrestling* off the air. By 1962, the days of the Hart boys wearing new Hush Puppies and matching sweaters embroidered with our first names were over. My parents endured, running live wrestling cards throughout Alberta and Saskatchewan and down into Montana, working a thousand-mile circuit out of Calgary. But without TV, it was all they could do to hang on.

I was four when I learned about death for the first time. I was in the kitchen with my mom when someone knocked on the door to tell her that a wrestler called Riotcall Jim Wright had died. Riotcall had looked like a giant version of Walt Disney, and I'd liked talking with him whenever he came to our house.

My mom was upset by the news and, while I tried to comfort her, she explained what death was. She told me Riotcall had gone up to heaven and would never be back again, and that sooner or later everyone dies, including her and even me. God decides when your time is up. Good people go to a good place called heaven, and bad people go to a bad place called hell. She said nobody was really sure that heaven or hell existed. Maybe when you died, it was just plain over. She said she believed in heaven, but that I could believe whatever I wanted.

My parents were free thinkers; they never tried to force religion on us kids. Once, when we were given some hand-me-down dress clothes, my parents rounded us up and herded us off to church on Sunday morning wearing suit jackets and ties. It was a parents' nightmare: kids teasing, fighting and crying throughout the service. They never tried it again. I've had little or nothing to do with organized religion, although I've always felt God's presence.

Hart house was a cross between a big hotel where the housekeepers had quit, a cat and dog refuge and an orphanage for troubled children. My five older brothers spent a lot of time toughening me up for my life ahead. Bruce guided me along, but the biggest influence in my life was the runt of the litter, Dean, who was three years older than I was. We nicknamed him Bizz because he was always up to some sort of business. He was as mischievous as he was dishonest, but I loved him; he was my hero. He taught me to stand up for myself and, above all, to remember that I was one of the Hart boys. All my brothers were handsome, but Dean was the best looking, with a big white smile and dark brown eyes. I was proud to be his sidekick, especially in the never-ending guerrilla war with the two sisters who were right between us in the sequence of Hart kids.

Ellie, the first-born daughter, was the apple of my father's eye. She was small, like Dean, with the same dark hair and eyes, and she had a ferocious temper. Georgia bore a striking resemblance to my dad, with blond hair, blue eyes and strong chin. Georgia took up for Ellie the way I took up for Dean.

You might figure that, with so many unruly brothers, the girls would have had a tough go of things, but my dad thundered to their rescue like an angry bear at the slightest sound of a wail. I spent a great deal of my young life sticking up for Dean, standing my ground against Ellie and Georgia and answering to my dad for it.

My dad was a shooter, or submission wrestler, and he loved to stretch anyone who dared to show up at his door. I remember him stretching the daylights out of Father Roberts, the Catholic priest who baptized all the Hart kids. Father Roberts got closer to God in my father's basement dungeon than he felt comfortable with. But Stu was non-denominational; he stretched a rabbi once too.

The dungeon was a cramped room with sweat- and blood-soaked canvas mats covering a thinly padded floor. There were big holes in the low ceiling made by the heads and feet of wrestlers. Stu trained and broke in his wrestlers down there, hooking on like an octopus, squeezing hard enough that the screams of his victims would echo eerily through the rest of the house. I used to wander outside on Saturday mornings with Dean and peer into the window to watch a dozen or so big-necked Goliaths sweating and groaning while they lifted weights and fooled around on the mat, testing each other, until my dad finally came down and pulled on his black trunks. Soon enough they'd be gawking in amazement as he stretched them, one after another. When they were done, they'd shower and drink bottles of the homemade beer Stu stored in the fridge next to the basement shower. He rarely drank himself but made beer for his wrestlers.

My mom was tiny, just five-foot-two, but she was the only one who could make Stu run for cover. She took out her frustrations on him constantly. Sometimes when they'd argue she'd break down in tears and threaten to leave him and go back to New York. This, of course, meant that she was leaving all of us. She'd pack her suitcase while my dad repeated submissively, over and over, "Please, dear, please." I'd go to bed crying, afraid that she'd be gone forever. My older brothers, long used to these fights, would tell me not to worry, it was just a big act. By the following morning my parents would be drinking coffee in the kitchen and laughing like nothing had happened. This scene played out so many times that I sometimes found it hard to forgive my mom for making such threats when she didn't mean them. At least my dad never talked of quitting on us kids.

By the time I came along, my mom had given up on housework. There were always mounds of clothes, broken toys and old sports equipment scattered everywhere, and the kitchen was always stacked with dirty cups and dishes. She was pretty reclusive, I realize now. You could usually find her in one of three places: her bedroom, the kitchen or the office, where she worked all week preparing ads, doing the payroll and answering the never-ending ring of the two black phones on her desk.

Stu was almost always out of town on the wrestling circuit, gone every night of the week to Saskatoon, Regina, Edmonton, Lethbridge, Red Deer and into Montana. Friday night was the Calgary stop, and Saturday morning was my parents' one day to sleep in. When my dad did work at home, he was usually leaning back in his leather office chair with his big forearm across his forehead, talking to some promoter or wrestler on the phone while my mom toiled away at her typewriter.

Stu did all the shopping, a little cleaning, most of the cooking, and all of the driving. When my mom was pregnant with Bruce, my parents were in a car accident in Montana that made her afraid to learn to drive. An escapee from an asylum was driving down the wrong side of the highway and crashed into my parents' car. My mom went teeth-first into the dashboard and head-first into the windshield, shattering her Rita Hayworth looks. It took some time before she recovered, and she was so afraid she'd lose her baby that when Bruce was born, safe and sound, she forever had a soft spot for him. Stu survived because of his big, thick chest.

Our backyard was an obstacle course littered with old cars, ancient farm equipment, wrestling rings and junk. Wandering around in the midst of it all were Daphne the cow, two goats, hundreds of hens and Mighty the rooster, named for the Mexican wrestler Mighty Ursus.

Crew cuts, brown shorts and T-shirts were standard summer issue for all the boys. I wore a straw cowboy hat that I rarely took off. Most of us went barefoot, at least until school started. We were always cutting our feet on broken glass, and we were lucky if we were able to scrounge up a bandage; such things were considered extravagant at Hart house. And we rarely had luxuries such as toothbrushes, unless you count the two crusty ones in the boys' bathroom cabinet, along with the tin of tooth powder that'd been around longer than I had. I brushed my teeth with my finger.

On school days my dad made a big pot of oatmeal for everyone. On weekends it was up to us to feed ourselves. I learned early on to stand on a chair, light the stove with a match, boil eggs, make toast and cut cheese and fruit with a ridiculously large butcher knife; it was that or go hungry.

As far back as I can remember I was called on to defend the family honour. At three or four years old, I was coached by my brothers in what must have been my first match. I took on one of the Tag Team Champion Scott brothers' kids, who happened to be the same age as I was. Down by the pasture gate where Daphne grazed we rolled around on top of prickles and cow pies. I lost a close one.

Dean and I collected glossy photos of all the top wrestlers of the time. I was fascinated by the toothless behemoth Antonio the Great, with his long, mangy hair and scraggly beard. But I really loved the masked wrestlers, Dr. Death, Mr. X, The Destroyer and my favourite, The Zebra Kid, with his black and white striped mask. My dad's championship belts were made of gold and silver, with real gemstones on them; my brothers and I made our own belts of gold and silver Christmas wrapping paper, with pieces of broken bottle glass as gems.

One day Dean and I were playing in the barn behind the house. He was pulling me up to the roof on a bale of hay attached to a pulley. As I neared the roof, the rope broke and I came crashing down, whacking my head on the brick floor. I lay there groaning and dazed as a huge bump began to grow on my forehead. A tearful Dean promised to give me a picture of Antonio the Great if I promised not to tell, so we made up a story about how I'd tripped and hit my head on a rock. Dean was good at making up stories. My parents were worried when they saw the purple-blue goose egg, and they fussed over me for several days, but they didn't take me to the doctor. My reward for silence was the prized photo of Antonio the Great pulling a big bus on a chain.

A lot of the time it was like a scene from *Lord of the Flies* around my house, and we were left to our own devices. We were so unruly that the neighbours—and at that time there were only two families living close to us in Patterson Heights—rarely allowed their kids to play with us. One of the good things about being from a big family was that there were always enough players for baseball and football games. Now and then my dad would come out and punt a football over the trees and into the neighbour's yard.

Smith and Bruce were like pint-sized mobsters, usually up to no good. They seemed to have it in for Keith and Wayne. Stocky Keith had no problem standing up for himself, but Wayne, who was small, was usually made into the fall guy.

We all wrestled one another often, and I can remember times when Smith or Bruce inadvertently knocked the wind out of me. Stu would storm in demanding to know, "Who did it?" but I never wanted to see Stu get mad at anyone. I'd be bawling my eyes out while trying very hard not to. Then I'd hesitate to answer out of pure fear, and he'd get angrier. Smith would position himself directly behind Stu, glaring at me while hoisting up a closed fist. He'd point across the room at Wayne, mouthing, "Say Wayne did it." Wayne would be playing with his Dinky toys, minding his own business. Caught between Dad and Smith, I had no choice but to finger Wayne, who'd look up just in time to see Stu stomping over to throttle him. Smith and often Bruce would both promise me total protection from a seething Wayne. Sooner rather than later Wayne would beat me up, and as punishment they'd beat up Wayne. This was routine life at Hart house.

If Wayne was overlooked, he wasn't the only one. Alison, who was the easiest of the Hart kids to get along with, never got anywhere near the love heaped on her two older sisters. Like me, she just seemed to operate better by herself.

I recall one time being cuffed by Stu and then being yelled at by both him and my mom for something I hadn't done. I decided to punish them by running away. I planned everything out. I lopped off a piece of cheddar cheese, gathered up some apples in a bag and left home around noon, heading west past CFCN hill, hiking all the way up to Mr. Ferguson's house. He was the school-bus driver, and his big yellow buses reminded me of my block of yellow cheese, so I stopped there, stretching out on the dry grass, taking in blue skies and white clouds. I daydreamed, picturing my mom crying and asking my dad, "What have we done?" I imagined my dad, with a grim expression, talking to two policemen, one of them scribbling on a pad while the other talked about using dogs to pick up my scent.

I wanted them to suffer for being so tough on me, but then I had a change of heart. I thought about Stu's annoyed expression in the daydream, and I knew I was in heaps of trouble. On top of everything else, cheese and apples weren't enough to sustain me. It was a long way back, but I double-timed it, only slowing down when I drew close enough to see that there weren't any police cars or bloodhounds waiting for me.

I braced myself as I entered the kitchen. My mom and dad were reading the paper, and the TV was on with the sound low. The table was the usual mess of dirty dishes, except for one giant plate of spaghetti. My mom said, "Hello, dawling"—her New York accent was distinct—but Stu didn't look up. Nobody had even noticed that I was gone. I sat down and ate my cold spaghetti and never thought about running away again.

I always looked forward to Sundays. That's when my parents cooked the biggest dinner of the week. After dinner my dad would take us boys down to the basement and let us wrestle one another, teaching us the basics. Then he would get us to run around in a circle on the mat and, in a strange version of dodge ball, try to knock our feet out from under us using one of his heavy leather medicine balls. I used to love this game and was often the last one standing.

Then it was time to hit the shower. Dean and I usually ended up crying because Smith and Bruce would pee in our mouths or blast us right in the eyes, which burned. The best we could manage was pee on their legs. There was no point telling on them because in the Hart house you were only guilty of something if you got caught.

Afterwards, we'd all put on our pyjamas and watch *Bonanza,* which came on at nine o'clock. I liked to imagine we Harts were like the Cartwrights.

I was four years old when my brothers succeeded in talking my mom into letting me go with them to the Calgary matches, reassuring her that they'd all watch over me. Only the boys were allowed to go. On Friday nights we'd zoom down to what was then called the Victoria Pavilion with my dad in his long black Chrysler transport limo, which had four rows of seats, four doors on each side and a big luggage rack on top. He'd give us the wrestling programs wrapped in brown paper, and in the limo we'd all clamber to tear the bundle open. I still recall the smell of fresh ink and the feel of the smooth paper. The older boys would sell the programs, but my first job was pulling lucky numbers out of a big steel box during intermission. That job was short-lived; soon, I was replaced by cute, curly-haired Inky. After that I earned a few bucks a week selling programs. That's how I learned how to count, but more importantly that's how I learned that if I really hustled, I could earn enough money to buy toy soldiers or cowboys and Indians.

During the winter it was tough work standing in the bitter cold. And as soon as Ross grew old enough to start selling programs, he cut into my market because the fans liked to buy from the smallest Hart kid.

I met all kinds of crazy characters: real cowboys and real Indians; big, fat, friendly older women; and a few younger ones who smoked cigarettes and were dolled up in red lipstick, cheap perfume and high hairdos, squeezed into short dresses and fishnet stockings like cut-rate versions of Marilyn Monroe. Then there were even younger ones who my dad referred to contemptuously as arena rats, but I kept my thoughts to myself, remembering a saying Bruce taught me: "All the world loves a lover and that's why the world loves me." I thought, Yeah, that'll be me some day!

During the matches, Dean and Ross and I would sit at the timekeeper's table at ringside. Sometimes my dad had really interesting attractions. I recall Cowboy Carlson climbing up and down a ladder with a horse slung over his shoulder. At least once a year, Terrible Ted The Wrestling Bear came to town for a couple of months. Terrible Ted lived in a mesh cage under our back porch. Dean, Ellie, Georgia and I would dangle our bare feet through the slats in the porch steps and drip Fudgesicles on our toes for Ted to lick.

Once I was invited to a neighbouring kid's birthday party. His parents took us just up the hill to the CFCN TV studio to attend a live kid's program called *The Headhunter Show*. Out came Ted, playfully wrestling with Gene Dubois, his handler, to help publicize that week's wrestling show. After Ted had been led away, Headhunter came around asking all the kids questions. Strangely enough, he asked me whether I wished I had a bear like that in my backyard. Of course he had a great laugh when I insisted that, in fact, I did have exactly that bear living under my back porch. He kept winking at the camera until I actually got annoyed with him. My mom gave me the biggest, sweetest hug when I got home. She'd seen the whole thing. "You were so right, dawling. At least you tried, and you never backed down."

When Dean and I got bored at the matches, we'd go out to the front of the pavilion, where there were always lots of kids from the nearby neighbourhood of Victoria Park. The kids were as poor as we were, so we blended right in. We'd wrestle them on a small patch of grass, and Dean was always quick to boast that we were Stu Hart's kids, but no one would believe him. We'd take our shirts off and an hour or so later we'd be drenched in sweat, having taken on all comers, one after another. I never lost one of those matches, and neither did Dean. It's as beautiful a memory as wrestling ever gave me.

When the show was over, my dad would bring the car around front and honk the horn, and we would scramble to get in. The Victoria Park kids would look on in wonder. "Wow, they really are Stu Hart's kids." On the drive home I looked forward to the Jell-O or chocolate pudding that my mom, Ellie and Georgia always had waiting for us. Sometimes on the way home, my dad would slow down and point at a giant chandelier hanging in the window of a lighting store on Eleventh Avenue, saying how he wanted to buy it. I think everyone in the car was dreaming about what they wanted in life. I was happy on these drives simply because my dad was happy.

Being a middle kid was like being stuck in nowhere land. Smith was a bully who didn't want to grow up—much as my parents tried to mould him into being our leader. I could never figure Smith out, and only in the last couple of years did one of my mother's sisters fill me in on what had happened to

Smith before my parents moved to Calgary. When Stu and my mom had that near-fatal car accident, Gah-Gah took Smith so that my mom would have time to recuperate. But then she wouldn't give him back; she and mom's four sisters doted on him and spoiled him until he was four years old.

When they were about to move to Calgary, Stu decided that enough was enough and demanded that Gah-Gah give Smith back, but she still refused. Stu had to drive all the way to New York to get him. That would have been an abrupt change in Smith's life, going from being doted on by five loving women to living in Stu's world of discipline, with two little brothers and another sibling on the way. When we were kids, all we knew was that for some reason, we weren't likely to see Gah-Gah or our aunts. Our only contact with them was the family Christmas card, including photo, that my mom sent back east each year.

Bruce, on the other hand, was sometimes too clever for his own good. He was a tremendous influence on me, teaching me all about sports, Mickey Mantle, Babe Ruth, Johnny Unitas and Gordie Howe. He also taught me the Lord's Prayer and added to my sense of what God was—and then balanced it out by also teaching me all about girls. At night I'd go through his yearbook with him and pick out the prettiest ones. I wasn't fussy. I loved blonds, brunettes and redheads too.

Dean had a vivid imagination and was fascinated by cars and by characters from the Old West, especially Davy Crockett, Daniel Boone, General Custer and Wild Bill Hickock. He encouraged me to be charming to girls and taught me to kiss, using our pillows as imaginary girlfriends. One day he was playing up on the abandoned, closed-off top floor of the house with a toy campfire set he'd been given for his birthday. It came with plastic frying pans, plastic logs and a fake fire. Around three in the morning, my mom woke us up one by one and calmly told us not to panic and to follow her outside because the house was on fire.

We walked behind her in a line, with blankets wrapped around us. Looking up I could see a smouldering red square on the ceiling. Dean had started a real fire up there and, unable to put it out, he'd pushed a big old mattress over it thinking that would smother it. In the frigid January night, we all stood huddled with my mom, watching the growling red fire trucks and the firemen hosing down the roof. Stu was out of town but due back in the morning, and every one of us knew there was going to be hell to pay.

As soon as he walked through the front door, Stu ordered everyone upstairs to the attic and angrily told us the dangers of what might have happened. Then he grabbed Dean by the hair and hurled him head-first down the stairs. I was terrified. Then, because he'd caught Bruce and Wayne playing with matches only days before, he snatched both of them and threw them down the stairs for good measure. As they tumbled, I prayed I wouldn't be next.

Eventually Smith, Bruce, Keith and Wayne were all moved out of the boys' room and up to the attic after it had been repaired to prevent them from poisoning the minds of their little brothers, but by then it was already too late.

Every year back then my dad would close down the wrestling circuit for the summer in mid-July. At the time, the annual Calgary Stampede was called the Greatest Outdoor Show on Earth, and each July people from all over the world flocked to the fairgrounds. There were cowboy hats everywhere, Ferris wheels and roller coasters, the smell of cotton candy mixed with the stink of manure. While the rodeo kicked off next door, my dad ran his biggest show of the year, a supercard on par with the biggest midway attractions. In 1964, he brought in the newly crowned World Wide Wrestling Federation (WWWF) World Champion Bruno Sammartino, who'd only just defeated the great Nature Boy Buddy Rogers, rated by many as the best wrestler of all time. Stu also brought in the undefeated boxing champion Rocky Marciano to be the special guest referee for the main event. After the Stampede parade, all of us Hart kids were posing alongside the big, long transport limo with Marciano when a tiff broke out between Dean and Ellie. Stu cracked Dean hard on the ear just seconds before the photo was taken, yet we all look happy in that picture, even Dean.

I'd learn years later that Marciano was a horrible cheapskate; when he left town he intentionally misled Stu into writing him two cheques, each for the whole fee. Even knowing how badly my dad needed the money, he cashed them both. Despite my dad's attempts to get him to send the money back, he never did. About a year later, Marciano died in a plane crash. My mom didn't shed any tears.

That year my dad gambled whatever savings he'd scrimped together to purchase a hundred-and-sixty-acre man-made sandbar called Clearwater Beach, seven miles outside of the city. The idea was that it would help him make ends meet in the summers, when he shut down his wrestling territory. Clearwater Beach consisted of two man-made lakes, picnic tables, barbecue pits, a canopied dance floor and one concession building. The idea was that the Hart kids would work out there in the summer, and then a new and better batch of wrestlers would arrive to turn things around when my dad's circuit started up again in September.

The beach became a horrible place for me. Far too often, it was my responsibility to man the dreaded toll booth, no wider than a telephone booth. I'd sit out there for countless hours, barefoot, in cut-offs, swatting horseflies and collecting five bucks a car. I often had three or four hundred bucks crammed into my pockets, and it's no small miracle that I wasn't robbed, out there all alone. Sometimes it was just too much for me to take, sitting all day in the heat with no bathroom, water or food. It was about a five-minute walk to the concession building and the lakes, where I'd find most of my older brothers swimming and splashing around pretending to be lifeguards, flirting with girls, never once giving any thought to their promise not to leave me out at the booth.

One morning Stu loaded us all up in his latest acquisition, a beautiful round-curved purple 1959 Hudson, and drove us out to the beach, and I complained all the way there that I didn't want to go back to the booth. Of course, when we got there, Wayne immediately ordered me back to the booth. When I angrily refused, Stu grabbed me by the hair and flung me into the backseat of the car, busting my forehead open just above my right eyebrow. On the drive back home, I pressed my T-shirt to my eye to stop the blood from dripping all over his new car. He asked me to please not say anything to my mom, and, feeling sorry for him, I promised I wouldn't say a word. He asked me what he could get for me to make up for splitting my head open. I told him a bike; I was the only brother who didn't have one yet. As soon as we got home, he told my mom exactly what had happened anyway. As always, there wasn't a bandage to be found, so my dad used Scotch tape to hold the two-inch gash on my forehead together. Then we left to go to the doctor.

On the way, Stu stopped at the house where the producer of his TV show lived and said he had to go in to talk to him. So I sat in the hot car, hanging my head out the open window. Three hours later Stu came out and took me for my stitches. As for the promised bike, he bought it for me—seven years later. Tough times were ahead, and after his meeting that day, I was the least of his problems.

Life at school was an entirely different, drearier kind of hell. Hart house was a terrible environment for studying. Because Smith was so much older, my mom would volunteer him to help me with my homework. He was no scholar, so his method consisted of him knuckling me hard on the head when I didn't know the right answer, which was more often than not. In time, I realized it was smarter to follow Dean's approach and lie to my mom about even having homework. In fact, I learned to just lie whenever it made things easier. At Hart house, a lie was only a lie if you got caught.

My dad was generally late for everything, and he passed that trait down to us kids. When we missed the school bus, which was most of the time, he would load us up in the transport limo and race us off to school, skidding to a halt on the gravel parking lot of Wildwood Elementary. All the doors would fly open and a handful of Hart kids would pile out just as the bell was sounding. Then the car would take off again, throwing more gravel on the way to the next school, and the next.

My Grade 2 teacher, Miss Mitchaluk, reminded me of those pretty ladies at the wrestling matches. She wore nylons and dresses, and even at that age I felt an uncontrollable urge to look up her skirt. One day she announced to the class that there was going to be a school play and we would dress up as elves. She told us to bring green leotards to school. Now I had a kind of phobia not only of leotards, but of bras, panties and stockings. Whenever my pants were intertwined with Ellie's or Georgia's leotards in the big clothes dryer at home, I cringed at the thought of even touching them. I was sick at the notion of pulling those horrible things on.

Every day Miss Mitchaluk reminded me to bring my green leotards, and every day I purposefully forgot. Finally, she ordered me not to dare show up without them. The next morning when my dad herded us into the limo, I lagged behind, pretending to be sick. Stu demanded to know what the hell my problem was. I broke down in tears. "I don't want to wear leotards!" I pleaded my case on the way to school with little hope, but after we pulled up, my dad climbed out and came with me to see Miss Mitchaluk. When he told her how strongly I felt about wearing leotards, she said, "You'll regret this, Bret. You'll have to sit out the entire play." I was happy my dad stuck up for me. Little did I know that someday I'd make my living wearing leotards—pink ones at that!

It was around that time that I took up drawing cartoons, probably the only constructive thing Smith taught me. If I couldn't have the toys I wanted, I'd draw them instead. With my tongue twisting up over my top lip, I drew Frankenstein versus Werewolf, and Wolfe and Montcalm on the Plains of Abraham, but what I always drew best were the ugly faces of my favourite wrestlers. I was torn between Snoopy and the Red Baron, between *Hogan's Heroes* and Waldo Von Erich, a baldheaded wrestler who was terrorizing my dad's territory as a pretend Nazi thug. Waldo billed himself as a brother of another supposed Nazi, Fritz Von Erich. Thirty years later, Waldo laughed like it was the funniest thing in the world when he told me about a joke he'd pulled on my dad. He'd stolen Daphne the cow and sold her to a slaughterhouse. Then he generously presented Stu with a rack of beef, saying a farmer friend had given it to him. With my dad having so many kids, he said, he wanted him to have it instead. Poor old Daphne. Some joke.

In 1963, my sister Diana was born, a breech delivery that was really rough on my mom; the doctor had insisted that Diana be Helen's last child. But my mom was as stubborn a Hart as there ever was and made up her mind to have just one more, to make it an even dozen. In May 1965, my mom came home from the hospital with the last Hart baby, my youngest brother, Owen.

Ellie and Georgia raced to get home so they could see him first, but I overtook them in the final half mile, bounded up the steps and was the very first Hart kid to welcome Owen Hart into the fold. From the moment I saw him, I wanted to be the best brother to him he'd ever have.

As soon as he was out of the crib, Owen was taken in by the girls, and he lived in their room until he was three. He looked like the little bird Woodstock from the *Peanuts* cartoon, with a beaky nose, a tuft of blond hair and big blue eyes. Living with Ellie and Georgia, Owen became quite the tattletale, telling on the boys for everything.

Then one night my mom casually announced that Owen would be moving into the boys' room. Panic washed over his face, and his eyes grew wide. Dean and I glared over at him, and he knew exactly what those glares meant. A few hours after Owen's bed had been moved, a heated argument broke out between Dean and Ellie. Stu was out of town, so my mom intervened, demanding to know who started it. Little Owen stood, holding his blue furry blanket, and said matter-of-factly, "Ellie started it, Mom." It was true, but more importantly it was smart: he won over all the boys in an instant. Welcome to the club, brother. Much like Bruce had taken care of me, it became my responsibility to dress Owen, comb his hair, tie his shoes and teach him how to be a Hart.

That summer of 1965, at my dad's Stampede show, I'd watched the smooth and graceful former champion Pat O'Connor take on Gene Kiniski, a wrestler whom Stu had started out years before and who was the current National Wrestling Alliance (NWA) World Champion. Since 1948, the NWA had been an affiliation of North American wrestling promotions who voted every year to pick one wrestler as the NWA champion—a fellow who could really draw—and then let him defend the title in all the territories. I was fascinated by how real the match seemed, but at the same time I wondered how it was possible for someone to do this or that move or break that hold. Without knowing it, I was making a thorough study of pro wrestling. But I was failing at just about everything else.

Once my dad had shut down for the season, my focus became surviving another summer out at Clearwater Beach. Dean had an extra bike, obtained through questionable means, that he let me ride on my own, as far as I could go. After we got back home from the beach, or on rare weekend days at home, I'd get on that bike and take off. It was my first taste of freedom, my escape from everybody at the house. I found that I enjoyed being alone with my daydreams about cowboys, soldiers, girls and wrestling, away from the noise and fighting.

I generally did all that I could to avoid Ellie and Georgia. The biggest problem in my life at that point was how easily I was drawn into Ellie's ongoing quest to see Stu punish me for being born. Feisty and hot-tempered, Ellie regularly managed to provoke fights with me in which Stu usually intervened on her side and administered a shitkicking to me. On top of that, Georgia, her loyal supporter, couldn't resist tattling on me, which also got me into trouble with Stu.

I also tried to stay clear of Ross, who was a strange little fellow. He had problems with his ears and had to have tubes put in, which automatically excluded him from Stu's punishing left hand. He was very smart and could read the entire lineup on the back of the programs when he was still in diapers. He had a stubborn temper and hated to lose at anything, which was tough on me, because when I was growing up I'd been made to understand that little brothers were supposed to do what their big brothers told them to do. Ross wouldn't answer to me or to anyone else, and if you got into a conflict with him, he would never back down.

Dean felt much the same about Ellie and Georgia as I did; a fight with either of them would cost us severely. We distracted ourselves by playing a lot of football and baseball with the McDonald kids—Johnny, Karen and Cameron—who lived next door. The hatchet was much easier to bury when we needed the girls to help make up teams. These games are easily my favourite memories of growing up—an escape where I found team spirit, order and rules that made sense.

The last weekend of the summer before school started, my dad arrived home with boxes of apples, bananas, oranges and all kinds of vegetables tied to the roof of the car. Safeway regularly gave him all the distressed produce he could take. I eagerly helped unload the heavy cardboard crates, stacking them under the porch where the bear used to live. I couldn't have been happier lifting all those boxes of nice yellow bananas. I loved bananas.

When we grumbled about hand-me-downs and such, my mom would speak of how tough times had been for my father when he was a kid living in poverty with his two sisters and his parents on the unforgiving Alberta prairie, sometimes with only a canvas tent and an open fire to keep them warm, eating rabbits and birds that Stu hunted with a slingshot. My paternal grandmother had died before I was born, and Stu never talked about his sisters. We never met any of our aunts. The only link to those times on the prairie was Stu's father, Edward, who'd had nowhere to go and had recently moved into a room next to the gym in our basement, together with his

Dalmatian, Zero. My grandfather was nice enough to me, but he was a religious zealot and perhaps a bit nutty: He used to take his dog on long walks of thirty miles or more. His attitudes and habits drove my mother crazy.

Stu kicked off the new wrestling season with a better crew than he'd had for a while and with a new TV show, *Wildcat Wrestling*, which aired on Saturdays. He had started major renovations on the house, but they were left unfinished when the money from Clearwater Beach fell short that summer. The brickwork around the big picture windows was missing and the old house grew colder as the days grew shorter. At night I'd go looking for one of our many cats to put under my blanket as a way to keep warm.

There was a new villain working the territory, one who would make a lasting impression on me. Sweet Daddy Siki strutted into the ring with snow-white hair and white sunglasses, a black Adonis in white trunks with red pinstripes and a fancy red-sequined robe. He carried two white hand-mirrors just so he could admire himself. He was too handsome, too smart, too cocky and too cool. He was also an innovator and a great showman. Regi Siki, out of Houston, Texas, was probably a bigger influence on Muhammad Ali than Gorgeous George, whom Ali would later credit as being his greatest inspiration. But Sweet Daddy Siki was also deeply influenced by Gorgeous George, so I guess it all comes to the same thing.

Later, Sweet Daddy would tell me that he was the first black man to wrestle for the NWA world title, against Nature Boy Buddy Rogers in Greensboro, South Carolina, back in the 1950s. The Ku Klux Klan had ringside seats for the fight. They all stood up in unison, arms crossed, letting Siki know he'd never walk out of the building as world champion. Sweet Daddy feared for his life that night. He was wrestling as the babyface, or good guy, and the ref told him not to even think about closing his hand into a fist. Siki let Rogers call every move and take the whole match too. This wasn't just wrestling, it was a matter of life or death.

I remember crowding close to our old black-and-white TV, which had a bent coat hanger for an antenna, watching Stu's new ring announcer, Ed Whalen, introduce Siki. Whalen was tall and slender, balding on top, wearing black-framed glasses and a nice suit and tie. "Ladies and gentlemen, do not adjust your sets," he said dryly. In the interview that followed, they both played their roles brilliantly. Siki talked about driving all the ladies insane, then denounced a local favourite named Dave Ruhl, a black-bearded, pot-bellied version of Ulysses S. Grant, who was the territory's version of a Canadian champion. Ruhl was billed as being a farmer from Hanna, Alberta. He was as respected as any wrestler who ever worked for my dad, not so much for his mat skills, but because he came across as a salt-of-the-earth guy in whom fans in Alberta and Saskatchewan desperately wanted to believe.

In those days our fans were likely to be farmers, ranchers and labourers who needed to let their aggressions out by watching a form of staged violence. From the early days of pro wrestling, these fans had been educated to believe in the strategies of varying styles and finishing holds. Ruhl's finish was a basic, boring full nelson, a submission hold that I never saw get over anywhere else. But in Calgary the fans had no doubts—once Ruhl had it on you, you were finished.

The person who puts together the matches and determines their basic content—how long the match will last, who will win and what the storyline will be—is called the booker. Stu had the final say on booking the territory and was always in charge of his wrestlers. When a wrestler got disgruntled or angry, my mom had a way of sweet-talking him back into the fold. At the time, Dave Ruhl was Stu's "pencil." He could write guys into the storyline, or just as easily erase them.

Throughout my life in wrestling, I never once saw a script for a pro wrestling match. It was up to the wrestlers to figure out how to tell the story that the booker wanted. The booker only controlled the last three seconds—the finish. Good booking is essential to the success of a promotion, no matter how talented the roster is. Fan enthusiasm is heightened by combining athletic skill with a dramatic story that is exciting and plausible. For fans to willingly suspend their disbelief, they have to think that what they're watching *could* be real.

Every week, as Sweet Daddy ridiculed Ruhl, calling him a pig farmer and a chicken plucker, humiliating him by blindsiding him in match after match, eventually leaving a dead chicken tied around his neck, Stu's business got better. At long last, while Whalen was interviewing Siki, a furious Ruhl hit the ring like a tornado, and the pavilion came unglued, exploding as everyone rose to their feet to watch the pig farmer, goaded beyond reason by the arrogant Black pretty boy. Spilling out onto the floor, Ruhl chased after Siki, tore the robe off his back and peppered him with lefts and rights. Stu was in the middle, acting out his part, trying to keep control. Barely noticeable were the two young Hart boys, Dean and I, trailing the action. Dean snatched the sequined robe from the floor as swarms of hands tried to yank it from him; this was Sweet Daddy Siki's costume, worth more than gold. Whalen declared in his usual nasal near-panic pitch, "There's absolute bedlam in here."

The following Monday, Dean brought Siki's torn-up robe to school, and all the kids clambered over one another just to touch it. Wrestling was cool again—and more importantly so were we.

A month later I had a freckle-faced kid named Brett MacFarlane clamped in a headlock out in the field by the soccer posts at Wildwood School. He was a grade above me and bigger than I was. I still don't know what his problem was, but he kept making fun of how poor I was, wearing pants with knees that'd been patched so many times that my dad couldn't patch them any more. He wouldn't stop pulling my tail.

Once I had him, I didn't want to let him go, and he wouldn't give up even though his face was scarlet. In the distance I heard the sound of my dad's car horn. I flashed Dean a worried look. He scanned the street in front of the school. "Keep going, it's not him." But we both knew that horn and who was pushing it. I wrenched MacFarlane's head, ordering him through clenched teeth to give up. "No way," he fired back. Dean finally made the decision, "We'd better go." I released the hold, and the two of us took off toward the front of the school. I could hear MacFarlane yelling, calling me a chicken shit. Tears welled up in my eyes, and Dean comforted me. "We both know you had him; don't worry, Bret." When my dad asked what happened, Dean said, "Bret got into a fight."

My dad caught my eye in the rear-view mirror. "How'd you do?" I didn't know what to tell him. He was far more intimidating than that kid. Finally Dean told him that I had the bigger boy, but that we broke it off when he got there.

At home, Dad took me aside to give me some pointers. "First, take 'em down, and never forget this important rule—where the head goes, the body follows. If you find yourself in a real bind, pull him in close, like you're gonna kiss him, and use your back teeth if you can—bite him right on the tip of the nose. He won't bother you too much after that." Then he said, "Just remember who you are, Bret." He stroked the top of my head with his hand, and I knew then just how much I loved him.

Behind our house was a carriage house that my dad rented out to an artist, Katie Ohe. She had a studio and barebones living quarters in there, but she travelled a lot for her art and so was often not home. She had a white Volkswagen Beetle that seemed like it was intimidated, being parked among the black-eyed, bloodied Cadillacs all around the yard. One morning it was so cold that my dad loaded everyone up in one car after another and each one sputtered and died as he turned the ignition key. With an exasperated "Christ Almighty," Stu slammed his fist into windshield after windshield, teeth bared and eyes ablaze, leaving spiderweb cracks in the glass. Finally, he stuffed us into Katie's Beetle, like so much cord wood, and we all fought to suppress giggles as he ground the gears all the way to school.

In December, my dad realized he couldn't patch the holes in our jeans any more and ordered Dean and me to wear pathetic brown Boy Scout shorts to school. It was thirty below zero when we climbed out of the limo, embarrassed as we stood in the cold with our pale white legs. By the end of the week, Stu had rounded up some horrible green pants with elastic in the waist, known to the kids at school as twangs. We might as well have worn a sign: too poor for real pants.

The best place to get warm was at the pavilion on Friday nights. I felt at home there because the other kids were just as poor as I was. Sweet Daddy Siki continued to draw big crowds for my dad for a while, even taking on Terrible Ted, the wrestling bear, one night. But there was never enough money. One day my mom got so angry that she stormed down to the basement and threw a shoe through the window of the room my grandfather Edward lived in. For a reason known only to himself, my grandfather was suing my dad over some property in Edmonton that was never his in the first place, even while Stu was letting him live in our house and knowing that my dad could barely feed and clothe his kids. (When he eventually died, Edward Hart left a small fortune to the Oral Roberts Ministries.)

The bank was forever foreclosing on Hart house, and every time the bank's "FOR SALE" sign went up in front of our place, my dad would take it down and hide it.

2

LOVES ME LIKE A ROCK

BY THE SUMMER OF 1967, my parents were more broke than they'd ever been. My dad had to swallow his pride and borrow money from his accountant in order to place an ad in the *Calgary Herald* to let people know the newly renamed Stampede Wrestling was starting back up for the fall season. On Friday night, September 15, Stu calmly floored the limo down to the pavilion for what very well might have turned out to be both opening and closing week.

Bruce tore open the bundle of programs and there, on the cover, I saw a brooding bullet head atop a muscled frame. He was the answer to our prayers: Archie The Stomper Gouldie.

The Stomper was the best wrestler I ever watched, and he was the one I studied the most. He turned my father's fortunes around that year, selling out week after week against all kinds of different wrestlers, including Stu himself. But digging ourselves out of the hole took time. That Christmas I didn't get any presents except for a red plastic bubble-bath gorilla and a small blue plastic American revolutionary soldier. I was hurt until I saw my mom smile and offer us coffee with cream and sugar to dip our chocolate chip cookies in. I named my toys King Kong and Montcalm and played with them for the rest of the day, waiting for the turkey that was roasting in the oven. At least we had that.

Over the next three years, with the help of The Stomper, Stampede Wrestling became cutting edge in Calgary and across Canada, and through TV its popularity spread to far-off places around the world. Most wrestling shows were shot under hokey lighting in TV studios, with a scattering of fans on three benches on each side of the ring. My dad's live wrestling show, filmed in front of capacity crowds at the pavilion, with Ed Whalen masterfully commentating, made wrestling seem real, gritty, exciting. My parents pulled themselves out of debt, us kids finally had nice clothes, and Stu bought a new big black Cadillac limousine to haul us around in — and, in secret, the chandeliers he'd had his eye on. He hid them from my mom for a while under blankets in the closets.

One night The Stomper attacked Stu, stomping his arm over and over until he broke it. Stomper shouted in a rage that he was going to come and tear our house apart brick by brick and even piledrive my mom! I was really scared—I still hadn't been smartened up. Stu had to wear a cast, but strangely enough he'd take it off when nobody else was around, or when he was cooking dinner.

The Stomper and Stu show sold out for six straight weeks. And then, one Saturday afternoon, I saw Stomper climb out of his Corvette and come up the back steps. I didn't know what to do. Mom greeted him with a hug. "Aw, hi, Arch." She handed him his cheque. I still wasn't sure what was going on, but I never viewed wrestling in quite the same way after that.

Stomper left us in June 1969 after a new British wrestler named Billy Robinson, who was a noted shooter, tried to get cute with him in the ring. At the Stampede supercard that summer, I watched Robinson work with the newly crowned NWA champion, Dory Funk Jr. I watched their every move, two of the greatest, blending both the American and British styles together in a match that was ahead of its time. But what stands out in my mind the most about that Stampede week was holding my breath as my dad wrestled a Bengal tiger. I'll never forget how, only days later, we were all watching *The Untamed World* and the voiceover told us that a tiger could break the neck of a yak with one swipe of its mighty paw. My mom slapped Stu hard on the arm with her own paw, and it was right around that time that my dad nicknamed my mom Tiger Belle.

When my dad opened back up the next September without The Stomper, his ace heel, business was horrible right up until Christmas Day. Then Stu lucked out, bringing in a three-hundred-pound black school janitor out of Windsor, Ontario, who called himself Abdullah The Butcher and was billed as hailing from Khartoum. I watched this monster, unlike any I'd ever seen in wrestling, sell out week after week telling violent, bloody stories. Around the house, we called him Abbie.

Abbie jumped Stu one night at the pavilion, and my brother Smith bravely came to his rescue. Abbie quickly decked Smith, leaving him out cold with blood pouring everywhere. Ed Whalen actually received a letter from Idi Amin inviting him, Abdullah and the entire cast and crew to perform in Uganda. It wasn't hard for me to envision Idi Amin getting off on Abdullah The Butcher biting the bloody forehead of Dave Ruhl!

In March 1971, Stu persuaded The Stomper to come back to the territory to battle Abdullah in what was billed as the fight of the century. It was a feud that gave Stu the biggest gate so far in the history of the company but, unfortunately, Archie and Abdullah had a titanic clash of egos and only fought once.

That year, I was in grade eight, and Georgia was being teased by bullies from the grade nine in-crowd about how she dressed and about how fake her dad and wrestling were. They goaded her relentlessly, often to the point of tears. One day during lunch hour one of my dad's Cadillacs pulled up to the front of Vincent Massey Junior High and out jumped Bruce and Dean.

Dean was a tough little scrapper, the first Hart to win the city high-school amateur wrestling championship. The big bully of the in-crowd tried to flee the scene, but Georgia pointed him out. Dean grabbed him, took him down and taught him a lesson.

Out of the mob that pressed in for a closer look came Brett MacFarlane, the same bully I had released from a headlock back in grade three. He tried to start up with me, but Bruce gave him a shove. Then, like a bunch of victorious gangsters, we climbed into the Cadillac and sped home for lunch.

My best friend from school was Dean Wilkinson, a skinny blond kid with glasses nicknamed Wilk, who often came home for lunch with me. That day when we got back after lunch, Brett MacFarlane, backed up by four or five of his Grade 9 buddies, challenged me to a fight out in the alley after school. I accepted. All afternoon, while my classmates looked at me with sympathetic eyes, I thought about how I could beat this kid. The words of my friend Mike Bracko echoed in my head: "Yer gonna get killed!" If there had been tickets, they would have sold out: Everyone wanted to cheer for the underdog.

When the bell sounded at three-thirty, I walked out of the school visualizing what was going to happen, just like I would do later before my pro wrestling matches. A few girls pleaded with me not to fight. My science teacher, Mr. Daniels, wished me luck. I peeled off my green tank top to "ooh"s from the crowd gathered in the teachers parking lot. We went to an alley just off the school grounds, and the fight was on.

I knew I couldn't box, but I could wrestle. I began throwing high, wild punches, and MacFarlane put his fists up, just as I expected. At the right moment I dove for his legs and took him to the ground, getting behind him and clamping on a sleeper hold as hard as I could. I would have choked him out right there, but a kid from senior high made me break it. When we got to our feet again, I stuck with my plan, throwing high punches and then wrestling him to the ground, pinning him with my knees on his shoulders. I remembered the way he'd made fun of how poor I was, and I rained fists into his face, not stopping until he gave up not once, but twice.

All the kids who, just minutes before, were so sure I was going to lose hoisted me on their shoulders. I'll never forget watching Brett MacFarlane run down the street crying with his head down.

About that time I had my first girlfriend, Marla, a cute blond I met at the matches. We'd sit in the stands together, but her catcalls were so dirty and vulgar that fans down front would look up at us in disgust. I had no choice but to stop seeing her.

At fourteen, I could better appreciate Clearwater Beach because of the pretty girls from all over the city who came out there to strut their stuff in their bikinis. I was tanned and muscular in cut-offs, with long brown hair. I was scared to get in the water—when I was younger, so-called swimming lessons from Smith and Wayne, during which I had nearly drowned more than once, had pretty much turned me off—but I didn't hesitate to climb the big tree that leaned against the side of the concession building with some fresh new acquaintance to make out on the roof.

In late July 1971, Bruce and Dean invited me along on a drive to Amarillo, Texas, to visit Dory Funk Jr. Because Dory Funk Sr. was a respected tough guy, the territory had always featured one of the more realistic fighting styles, and since both Dory Funk Jr. and his younger brother Terry had been world champions and had learned their stuff there, wrestlers worked hard at keeping it real. The psychology and feel of the Amarillo territory was in many ways similar to that of Calgary, even down to its long, exhausting road trips. I took advantage of the opportunity to study the realistic Amarillo style and get a deeper understanding of what would ultimately become my life. It was also the first time I saw America with my own eyes. I was thrilled to pose with Dean as Bruce snapped a picture of us at the site of Custer's last stand.

By the time I hit high school that fall, I was determined to study hard, get better grades and make something of myself, but I couldn't seem to get on track. Dean, Owen and Ross kept me up every night with their talking. I quit the football team after a week because the early-morning practices and the long walk home after the afternoon practices were just too hard on little sleep.

On top of that, my guidance counsellor told me that I would never go to university and urged me to spend the rest of high school taking vocational courses. With that, what little motivation I had left went down the drain. The biggest support I received in almost everything came from my mom. She always took time to talk with me, and I realized I had a unique ability to make her laugh. I'd find her in her office after school and tell her about my day. And she always said little things that made me feel that one of these days I would amount to something that would make my parents proud.

For the rest of the year I goofed off academically, but I did join Dean on the wrestling team. I only had three matches. The night before the provincials my mother suggested that Stu give me some pointers. I should have known better. He stretched me for hours and the next morning I was so sore I couldn't even raise my arms up over my head. I lost so miserably that I considered quitting wrestling entirely.

Smith and Bruce were both pro wrestling now for my dad, but in the spring Bruce separated his shoulder and had to have surgery. I was determined to make the football team when school started in September, so I made a point of running CFCN hill and doing leg presses in the dungeon with Bruce. It clearly bothered him that I'd become stronger in the legs than he was. Bruce and Dean were also more than a little perturbed that I'd grown taller than them. When Dean's girlfriend once made the mistake of teasing him about it, he decked her.

Meanwhile, Smith had been seeing my old girlfriend, Marla, who was a year younger than I was. In June, she had his baby. The baby girl, Toby, was the first Hart grandchild. But nobody was allowed to know; if word had got out about the illegitimate baby, it would have completely shattered the wholesome image my parents worked so hard to perpetuate. (To this day, no one is quite sure how many kids Smith has fathered.) Stu's temper and Marla's dirty mouth were like fire and gasoline. She was basically excommunicated and, after she left, taking the baby with her, Smith assumed no responsibility for the child.

That summer, my grandfather passed on. I knew it was going to be a lot of work to make the football team, so I asked my mom whether I could move into his room in the basement so I could sleep. It was cold, unfinished and unheated, and nobody else wanted it. It became my refuge.

I fondly remember my dad waking me up for my oatmeal and driving me to my early-morning practices with the orange glow of the sun just beginning to rise and Paul Simon's "Loves Me Like a Rock" playing on the radio. It was during those drives that I finally began to bond with my dad. We'd talk about all kinds of things, his life and his disappointments, in particular Smith, a total sore point because of the baby and because he seemed to screw up every chance my dad gave him to be our leader. It was during these intimate talks that I sensed he saw something in me.

Of course, there were still times when our relationship was complex, even volatile. One night during football season, I was watching *The Merv Griffin Show* with my mom, and Ellie wouldn't stop whistling a jingle from a TV commercial. When I asked her to quit it, she whistled as loudly as she could until even my mom became annoyed and told her to stop. Ellie flew into a rage, smashed a dish on the kitchen floor and tore into my mom for taking my side.

Seconds later, Stu stomped down the stairs and tackled me to the floor, mauling me like he'd done countless times before. After several minutes of my mom screaming in his ear that I'd done nothing wrong, he let up and got off me. I went down to my room in the basement and punched the walls, promising myself I would never let him do that to me again. Stu, Ellie and my mom carried on arguing noisily and then I heard a knock on my door. My dad had come to apologize to me. It was the last time he ever laid a finger on me.

That fall, Stampede Wrestling became interesting again with the arrival of a masked British wrestler called Kendo Nagasaki, who bore an uncanny resemblance to The Cool Cool Killer, one of the imaginary wrestling characters I liked to draw. I was no longer selling programs; I'd grown big enough to join Wayne as a bouncer at the front door. I was girl-crazy, bursting with testosterone. I'd grown up, probably too fast.

My brothers had taught me all there was to know about sex before I knew the truth about Santa Claus. Smith had a movie projector and showed hard-core porn flicks on the wall of the attic bedroom. Young trollops at the wrestling matches, many of whom I'd known since I was little, eagerly opened my eyes to what I'd seen playing out on the attic wall. By the time I was sixteen, I was sneaking them down the dungeon steps at night and into my little lair, where I lost my virginity to a cute, dark-haired, blue-eyed ring rat named Sheila. On weekends I'd cruise down to Victoria Park in my dad's van along with several buddies, with Steve Miller playing on the radio, singing about the midnight toker getting some lovin' on the run. Three or four ring rats would climb in, and we'd head out to Clearwater Beach. Heads bobbed up and down in every seat. With Smith's example in front of my eyes, I was always careful not to get anyone pregnant.

Once the football season ended, wrestling started. Dean had graduated from high school and was still the only Hart kid to ever win a wrestling medal at the city championships, two years earlier. I decided it was my responsibility to pick up where Dean left off. Though he was always working and never got to see a match, I knew my involvement in amateur wrestling made my dad happy. That year all I could think about was winning a gold medal. With the help of an injured teammate by the name of Brian Hatt, who motivated me to train hard, I burned off ten pounds to drop to under 145 pounds—and a lower weight class, where I stood a better chance of winning.

The Friday night of the city championships was the first time that I didn't go to the matches at the pavilion. My dad gave me an encouraging pat on the back as he was leaving, but I sensed he didn't think I could win. I beat everyone in my weight class, including Bob Eklund, who would eventually become the Canadian National Amateur Wrestling Champion. I carried on winning into the second day of the tournament. When my brother Keith showed up that Saturday afternoon to give me a ride home, he didn't hide his surprise that I'd won. On the way, we spotted Stu filling up at the usual gas station for the weekly Saturday drive to the show in Edmonton. We stopped, and when I got out of the car, he asked, looking ready to be disappointed, "How'd you do?" I opened my hand, showed him my gold medal and said, "I won." His face lit up like I'd never seen it before. He may even had tears in his eyes. And maybe I did too.

One week later I competed for the provincial championships. While collapsing on top of my opponent in a double-leg takedown, I managed to break my collarbone on his jaw. My season ended with no provincial medal. I don't know who was more disappointed, me or my dad.

Ellie, Georgia and I had all just got our driver's licences. Georgia's boyfriend had a car, so that left Ellie and me vying for the use of Stu's old gold Brougham. As a reward for winning the city championships, my dad gave me full use of it, which infuriated Ellie to no end.

I remember the first day I ever saw that car, parked in the backyard, shiny and new. Eight years and hundreds of thousands of miles later, Stu handed me the keys and said, "Go ahead, but don't drive it like Smith!" Smith was responsible for the death of far too many of the Cadillacs scattered like tombstones in the yard. If only those cars could talk, they'd tell horrific stories of Stampede Wrestling's giants and midgets, strongmen and freaks, packed in like sardines, racing down western highways in what was usually a hellish ride. It didn't matter to me that the Brougham now shuddered at what it'd been through. I was seventeen, and the car got me to the movies with my first serious girlfriend, Sue McClelland, who had long blond hair and blue eyes, was an honours student and also one of the best athletes in the city. Just having her on my arm gave me all the confidence in the world.

In the fall of 1974, I was doing fine playing varsity football until the new coach, Dale Parsons, learned that I was Stu Hart's kid. Parsons despised pro wrestling and from that point on he never played me again. Even in the last game of the season, when it looked unlikely that we would make the playoffs, Parsons played everyone but me.

Despite being undefeated all season in amateur wrestling, I had a less than stellar performance in both the city and the provincial championships and was soundly out-pointed by Bob Eklund. A lousy school year was capped off when my English teacher failed me by one per cent because she didn't think I was doing my own work. I was, but she'd had Dean in her class, and she knew that he'd got an older brother to do his assignments, so she assumed I was doing the same thing. Failing English meant I would have to go back to school for another semester in the fall.

That summer, Sue and I broke up, basically because her mother felt I wasn't worthy of her. All I could do was accept it and move on. I got a summer job bending rebar at Russell Steel. It was hard work, but I was saving up to buy a car of my own: Dean had offered to sell me his Eldorado convertible. Dean had decided he was a rock music promoter and had brought some bands out to Clearwater Beach, but it had rained nearly every weekend. He couldn't afford to pay the musicians, so he wrote bad cheques. One of the many pissed-off bands that never got paid burned the place to the ground. Stu couldn't afford to rebuild it, and had no choice but to sell the beach for a fraction of what it was worth: He had to pay his wrestlers. (Today that land is worth well over $125 million, and is the site of pricey estate homes.)

I gave Dean $1,500 for the Eldorado, but he never gave me the car, and my dad never did anything about it. When I confronted Dean, he burst out laughing and told me not to worry, he'd pay me back. He never did. It broke my heart. What made it even worse was that times were hard enough for my dad that he needed the old beat-up Brougham back for his own use. I ended up walking home from school all winter while Dean drove right past me with a different girl each time. I was never close with Dean after that.

I figured I'd make the best of being stuck in school for an extra half-year by playing senior football, but Coach Parsons kicked me off the team at the first practice. My dad went to straighten things out with him, but unfortunately Parsons disliked Stu even more than me.

But Parsons couldn't stop me from wrestling. Our team had no real coach; the teacher in charge didn't know the ins and outs. Then I found out that in the city championships I would have to wrestle a blind teammate named Larry Rinke, who was loved by the media even though he'd already been eliminated. Some coaches decided that Larry should wrestle me so that if he won and I lost, one of their wrestlers could go to the provincials instead of me. This was decided even though the mats had already been rolled up and parents, students, coaches and wrestlers were milling about waiting for the medals to be handed out. For our match, one mat was unrolled, and a lone spotlight shone down on it, reminding me of the ring at the pavilion. For the first time, I strode out like a heel pro wrestler, to a chorus of boos. Of course Larry got a thunderous babyface ovation. I came to life and beat him in forty seconds.

The following week, on the bus ride to Camrose, Alberta, for the provincials, I took considerable razzing from the entire Calgary contingent about how phony pro wrestling is. I redeemed myself by beating two good wrestlers from Edmonton in the best amateur wrestling matches I ever had. But my coveted gold medal was a disappointment to me, a flimsy coin from the tourist bureau that said nothing about wrestling. Then Coach Parsons excluded the wrestling team from the school sports dinner because it was only a club, not a sport. Amateur wrestling, I concluded, was a pursuit with little appreciation and even less reward.

3

LEARNING THE ART

In February 1976, I finally got my English credits, grabbed my diploma and got the hell out of high school. With all my older brothers now involved in Stampede Wrestling, it would have been the most natural thing in the world for me to work for my dad, but I didn't want that life. I always had quite an imagination, and the little wheels in my head never stopped turning. I thought the only wheels that turned for my dad were the ones on the road.

Dean hung around the business but was too small. Wayne was a ref, and became famous as a great wheelman who could drive through the most godawful weather and get the wrestlers to the shows, alive and on time. Bruce was taught the art by an old Mexican hand; despite being too small and light, he had a fever for wrestling, and at that time, he may well have been the Hart who wanted most to succeed in the ring. As hard as he tried, Bruce just was not a good worker. When he broke his shoulder, Keith, who was bigger than Bruce and an amateur on the University of Saskatchewan wrestling team, stepped into Bruce's spot until he recovered. Keith turned out to be a decent worker, with a better sense of the business than Bruce, and ended up taking a year off from university to wrestle full-time. Keith ran things for Stu, while Bruce tagged up with Smith, who, in many ways, had more natural ability as a worker than either Keith or Bruce. But Smith lacked the drive to put in a real effort and squandered every chance my parents gave him. I didn't want to follow in any of their footsteps.

Having unloaded Clearwater Beach, my dad now had to sell the prime acreage in front of Hart house, out of necessity, for $1.5 million. We took the news with mixed emotions; our childhood surroundings would be changing, but it was one more chance for the Harts to get out of the poor house.

By April I was working at Occidental Petroleum, and I had a plan. My friend Jim Cummings and I wanted to go to film school together and start a movie production company; we were both accepted to Mount Royal College in Calgary for the term that started in February 1977.

That summer Jim and I bought a Eumig 8 mm movie camera. One of our pre-college epic action features was a spoof of monster flicks called *The Lizard*, which starred my pet iguana Snyder, some model cars that we painted to match the ones in Stu's yard and a Chihuahua named Spike. I bought a beat-up old Ford Falcon and we got a simple-minded guy named Eugene, whom we knew from hanging out at the pavilion, to drive it, screaming in mock terror, "Oh no! It's the lizard!" Production came to a screeching halt when Snyder suddenly died.

The night before the first day of film school, Jim backed out. Construction was booming in the province, and he decided it would be more practical for him to keep working with his dad at a surveying job.

When college started in February, I had a hard time staying focused. At the tail end of the wrestling season that spring, I was summoned by the coach and asked to pull off a win at the collegiate amateur wrestling championships. Somehow, even after a two-year layoff, I succeeded, but my grades were in the toilet. After one semester I abandoned my dream of making movies. I got a job raking leaves and digging graves at Queen's Park Cemetery and contemplated what I wanted to do with my life.

That July, at my dad's Stampede show, I watched the new NWA Champion Harley Race defend his title against seven-foot-four André The Giant. Both Harley and André were friendly to me. They could see I was going to be the biggest of Stu's boys and had wrestling in my blood: Soon Verne Gagne, visiting kingpin of the rival American Wrestling Association (AWA), who was an old friend of Stu's, invited me to Minneapolis so he could personally train me, and I began rethinking a career as a pro wrestler. My brothers were making out okay. Surely I could be as good as them, or better. I told myself to take Verne Gagne up on his offer. I decided to moonlight as a referee a couple of nights a week for my father, who was now running Stampede Wrestling year-round; I'd work the short trips and keep my day job to save up money to go down to Minneapolis in the spring.

I finally got smartened up to the business by Keith and the rest of the boys on a drive up to Red Deer. Certainly I'd suspected that on some level there was unreality in wrestling, but I'd never really clued in. That's how careful the wrestling profession was back then with keeping the illusion alive for the fans.

When my cemetery job was over for the season, I became a full-time referee and driver. Business was awful, but I was getting my first real taste of wrestling life, driving the whole circuit, listening to rock 'n' roll and drinking beer with the wrestlers, setting up the ring and giving the wrestlers the finishes of their matches as told to me by the booker, Leo Burke, a great French-Canadian wrestler out of the Maritimes.

Leo became a huge influence on me, teaching me right from wrong when it came to booking. He stressed the simple things, like when it made sense for a wrestler to bleed, or get juice; how to work a match, an angle, a program; when to do a count-out or a disqualification; who should go over and who shouldn't; and not to repeat the same things week after week and risk boring the fans.

A kid named Jimmy Rougeau (who, years later, would be known as The Mountie in the WWF) had just begun to work the territory. For working a fifteen-minute match every night, he was making double the money I was. I still intended to go to Minneapolis and break in, and then come back to work for my dad. But then, on a long, snowy drive home from a show, two well-respected Japanese wrestlers offered to teach me pro wrestling. I figured, why wait for Minneapolis?

Katsuji Adachi (who worked as Mr. Hito) and Kazuo Sakurada kindly began instructing me in the dungeon at Hart house. I thought I could learn this wrestling stuff in a week or so, but they continued to show up every morning, week after week, putting me through basic training for three or four hours a day. I realized that I'd been studying the art of pro wrestling my whole life, analyzing the moves of every wrestler I ever saw: Canadians, Americans, Japanese, Mexicans, Puerto Ricans and Brits; big and small, real and unreal; the high flyers, the tough guys, the greenhorns and the great champions. Though I had a lot to learn in terms of the mechanics, it began to dawn on me that maybe, just maybe, pro wrestling had been my destiny all along.

Hito looked Inuit and had a long, shaggy mane of black hair. Sakurada reminded me of a grey seal, with a shaved head and a thin moustache. Both men had been sumo wrestlers who weighed more than 350 pounds each, but they'd trimmed down to an agile 250 pounds. Were they tough? One night Hito and Sakurada mopped the floor with an entire hockey team at the Diamond Head lounge in Saskatoon, kicking bodies in the air like soccer balls. But they were never troublemakers, unless given reason to be.

I was a skinny kid then, with shoulder-length brown hair, six feet tall and weighing 198 pounds. I took to the training like a fish to water. A great many wrestlers boasted about coming out of Stu's dungeon, and I would too. My father taught me submission wrestling down there, but Hito and Sakurada taught me pro wrestling. I owe them everything. I learned to perfect my balance; how to lock up, which is when wrestlers first make physical contact during a match; how to throw and be thrown; how to make the desired sound when hitting the mat; and how to break my fall using my feet and hands, head tucked. I knew that a good worker never makes contact with bone, never forces things. I learned to protect knees, shoulders, hips, teeth and eyes. The most important rule of all was to protect my opponent, not myself, because he was putting his trust, his life, in my hands. If someone got hurt, there was usually no compensation, no matter whose fault it was.

I ended each training session with Hito and Sakurada by taking fifty slams in a row. With every one I was taught simple things some wrestlers never learn, like how to get up from lying flat on my back by throwing out my leg and using my elbows to roll to my knees.

At the end of each session I'd put on some tea, and my dad would join us in the dining room. Hito would enthusiastically tell him that I was very good, that I had a natural, cat-like instinct when it came to falling. "This one I'm never see, him besto one, him fan-tas-tic bump. Stu, this one you see. Him become your best son!"

My dad would smile and tell him that I was a good amateur too, that I could turn around in my own skin. He never pushed me to become a pro; he believed I could still go to the Olympics or the Commonwealth Games if I wanted. He once put it to me this way, "Don't you want to walk down the street and hear people say, there goes Bret Hart; he won a gold medal in wrestling?" I replied, "I'd rather drive by those very same people in a brand-new car."

Apart from training, my life in those days consisted of driving the wrestlers and refereeing matches. We'd do a Friday-night show in Calgary, then make the three-hour drive to Edmonton on Saturday, driving back after the show in the middle of the night. We'd be home in Calgary for Sunday, when we'd have our booking and general business meeting at Hart house. On Monday, we'd drive 400 miles to Saskatoon, staying in a sleazy hotel every Monday night, where the wrestlers got drunk and picked up middle-aged women, some of whom had been sleeping around with wrestlers for years. On Tuesday, we'd drive the 180 miles from Saskatoon to Regina. Sometimes we'd stay over, but often we'd drive the 500 miles back to Calgary after the show, arriving with the sunrise on Wednesday morning. Wednesdays it was 150 miles north to Red Deer, then back after the show. Thursdays, 225 miles south to Lethbridge and back. This went on every week of the year. And we could just as easily find ourselves adding spot shows in Montana, British Columbia or way up north.

In Saskatoon, I usually ended up playing rummy in John Foley's room. John was from Wigan, England. He wasn't a big man, but he'd been a feared shooter and a bully in his day. Story had it that, somewhere down south, as he was roughing up the two Poffo boys, Randy and Lanny, their dad, Angelo, hit the ring, and the three of them beat Foley senseless for real. It was one story this old shooter couldn't seem to live down. He was now a harmless, jolly old boozer with a little pot-belly and a cigarette hanging out of his mouth. He loved singing old songs as we drove and telling the same tired old jokes every night.

I was the only Hart making road trips at that time; Stu didn't travel any more, except for the hop up to Edmonton. Bruce and Keith had gone back to university, Wayne was in art school and Smith and Dean were too busy scheming and dreaming to actually work at anything.

That April, snowstorms buried houses all across the Prairies. One night the van sputtered to a stop in the middle of nowhere, thirty miles outside of Regina. A full crew was packed in like sardines: Hito; Sakurada; Little Tokyo, a midget wrestler whose usual good nature took a turn to the dark side when he drank; several black wrestlers, including Kasavubu, a big friendly kid out of Akron, Ohio, who talked and acted like a giant-sized Gary Coleman; Jerry Morrow, a hardworking French-speaking wrestler from Martinique who could sell a beating so well that it would bring tears to your eyes; George Wells, a natural athlete who was one of the best CFL tackles to ever play and a star with the Saskatchewan Roughriders; and the quiet, easygoing, hairy-faced Cuban Assassin who worked hard, never complained and carried a knife tucked in his boot in case anybody decided to get cute with him in the ring. Then there was Oki Shikina, a fat, bald, over-the-hill Mexican with a Fu Manchu who was pretending to be Manchurian. And four midgets, including the Haiti Kid, who looked like a tiny Lou Rawls. The midgets slept on the floor or on top of the bags stacked in the back of the packed van because that was the only way to fit them in.

I had no idea why we'd broken down but knew that if we didn't make it to Regina, we'd lose the gate money. It was damp and cold as we all climbed out of the van. I was sure that nobody in their right mind was going to stop for us. I asked everyone to huddle down in a ditch at the side of the road while I tried to wave down a passing motorist. Finally an ancient black car that may actually have been a Model T eased over to the side of the road, and I ran up and opened the door. Inside was a smartly dressed old white-haired couple who looked as if they were just coming back from church. Before I could explain my predicament, the wrestlers rose up out of the ditch like the ragged ghosts of Genghis Khan's army and began to run toward the car. It was scary even for me—and I knew who they all were! The old woman nearly fainted as her husband clenched his teeth in fear and floored it, with me hanging on to the open door, running alongside the car, trying to tell them not to worry.

It was hard not to laugh as they sped off, leaving a crowd of midgets and giants shouting and shaking their fists. I managed to get everyone to stay hidden in the ditch long enough so that I could explain things to the next car that pulled over. Miraculously, we made the town, and the van was ready to go again by the time the show was over.

Back in Calgary, Hito and Sakurada explained to me that because of the low ceiling and the fact that there was no ring, ring posts or ring ropes in the dungeon, there was nothing more they could teach me. I protested: "When do I learn how to do drop kicks and throw punches, do all those fancy moves?" Hito grinned. "The rest you learn by yourself. You learn as you go."

They thought I was ready, and I knew I wasn't. But fate stepped in.

4

PUERTO RICO

I GOT TALKED INTO making my unofficial debut in Saskatoon on May 2, 1978. Stu was one wrestler short, and it was as simple as that. Being green here wouldn't hurt the ring rep I needed to build as a Hart in Calgary; I'd appear before the usual crowd of about one hundred fans, which consisted mostly of busloads of mentally challenged kids, a handful of diehards and a few drunks. I would tag up with an old veteran wrestler named Paddy Ryan, a thick, rugged mick, as big and round as a cement truck. All I really needed to do was sell—make it look like my opponents were getting the better of me—which would be easy since Paddy and I would be working with Hito and Sakurada. I walked out that night pale, skinny and cold, and Hito and Sakurada kicked and slammed me so hard I thought I'd really pissed them off. After the match they praised me, explaining, "Stiff okay!" For the handful of dedicated fans who knew I was normally just a referee, and that I was a rookie, it was necessary to protect the business, keep it real. Stiff was as real as it got.

After the matches that night, I relaxed at the hotel bar drinking draft with Paddy Ryan and was more than proud of myself. It meant a lot to me when an old fan came by and said, "Hey, Hart, you done good out there tonight!"

That same trip, a new wrestler from England was making his first loop around the territory. Bruce had discovered Tom Billington, raving that he was the most incredible wrestler he'd ever seen. Billington called himself The Dynamite Kid.

At that time, the business was filled with big, heavy men. Dynamite stood a mere five-foot-eight and was lucky if he weighed 170 pounds. He was two years younger than I was, with a pale, angular face and sandy blond hair. Out of the ring, he wore mod Brit clothes. In the land of ring giants, he suffered from small man's complex, which would haunt him for the rest of his life. He was clean cut and he didn't smoke or drink, yet. None of the big heels wanted to work with him, let alone put him over, and he looked like he was sorry he'd ever let Bruce talk him into coming to work for our dad. But he said nothing.

Always the professional, The Cuban finally obliged and put Dynamite over for his debut week, a favour Tom would never forget. I watched him do a match filled with fancy flips and rolls, stuff that I doubted I could ever do, and thought I'd like to work with him one day and learn what I could. But he kept his distance.

A week later, Keith made the trip to Regina and asked me whether I could fill in again, working a simple babyface match against Paddy Ryan. Knowing Paddy's experience and style, I had little to worry about. But the card was switched around at the last minute because Dynamite's opponent, Steve Novak, a big, bearded 280-pound slob, refused to work with him, let alone put him over. Keith had no choice but to match me up with Dynamite. I had already worked out a nice paint-by-numbers match with Paddy and knew I was nowhere near experienced enough to go out and do Dynamite's Brit style of flips and rolls. "Keith, you promised me Paddy. Maybe you should wrestle Dynamite. You have a lot more experience than I do." Dynamite took it the wrong way, thinking I didn't want to work with him either. And Keith stood firm.

I laced up my bright red boots and pulled on my red trunks, all the while talking to Dynamite about the one or two things that I did know how to do. If I thought he was grateful for my honesty, I was wrong. Dynamite stiffed me from bell to bell, to the delight of the fans. For no apparent reason, he elbow-smashed me in the face and broke my nose. The blood probably saved the match. I blamed the bad match on the situation, not on myself, but I also felt that he was less than professional and vowed to be a bit more careful the next time we worked together.

A couple of days later, Smith and Bruce were talking over their upcoming trip to Puerto Rico. Bruce suddenly had a change of heart about going with Smith, but the plane tickets had already been purchased by the promoter, and they were both expected to be there.

What I didn't know was that my parents had arranged the trip to get Smith out of their hair for a while. A few years earlier they'd sent him off to Japan to learn how to wrestle; they thought a good dose of Japanese discipline wouldn't hurt either. He lived in a dojo and was forced to train hard: The Japanese were the toughest, most serious teachers in wrestling. He was ordered to clean and scrub down the mats and to wash the backs of his superiors, who beat the backs of his legs with a bamboo stick when he failed to do a thousand squats as ordered. Every time he called begging to come home, my parents told him to hang in there. Nine months into it, Smith had got really drunk on sake and run buck-naked through a Japanese hotel lobby and crashed right through a plate-glass window. The Japanese police were looking everywhere for him as two equally crazy wrestlers from New Zealand, known as The Kiwis, hid him in their hotel room. Smith was shipped home the next day. He couldn't have been happier. My parents couldn't have been unhappier; they'd wanted Smith out of their hair a while longer.

I think that one trip to Japan destroyed what little spirit was left in Smith's tortured soul. He was never really the same after that.

Bruce didn't trust the set up in Puerto Rico. So he suggested I take his place. Times were simpler then and the plane tickets simply said S. Hart and B. Hart. I'd heard the Puerto Rican horror stories. A kid from Edmonton called Kim Klokeid, who broke in with my older brothers, had a black belt in karate. He went to Puerto Rico as a big, blond 250-pound heel, and when he made his debut, the crowd went berserk and rioted. Kim wasn't afraid of much. He climbed the corner post and dove into the fans only to have one of them carve a giant *L* in his guts with a knife. He was lucky to leave there with his life, and he never wrestled again.

Smith pleaded with me to go. A few hours later we were on a plane heading for Puerto Rico.

My dad had given the Puerto Rican promoters, Carlos Colón and Victor Jovica, their first break in the business, and they'd stayed with him for five years. Colón was a great worker and had a good mind for the business. Once upon a time he'd been a handsome kid; now his forehead was scarred with thousands of razor cuts, and he was as ugly as they came. I vividly remembered the great bloody matches he had with Abdullah The Butcher.

Colón's business partner, Victor Jovica, was a horrible wrestler, but he'd built up a nest egg from various investments. The two of them had put their heads together and hatched a dream of opening their own wrestling company in Puerto Rico, Capital Wrestling. They were on the brink of folding for good when they shot an angle using a veteran Stampede wrestler from Thunder Bay called Bad Boy Gilbert Hayes, pitting him against Terrible Ted, the wrestling bear. To their utter amazement it popped the territory, and Bad Boy Gil became their hottest heel. They never looked back after that, and Puerto Rico became a gold mine. Once they started making money, the WWWF tried to steal the territory away from them, but eventually they feared no one, not even WWWF owner Vince McMahon Sr. Then Gil, who had more balls than brains, had a falling out with Colón and threatened to walk. Carlos beat him nearly to death in the dressing room.

Puerto Rico was a dangerous place to work if you were a heel because the fans were so hot-blooded. The promotion employed mostly Latin American and American wrestlers who couldn't get booked stateside, or anywhere else, along with the occasional big-name WWWF headliner. Stu often traded talent with Jovica and Colón because neither he nor the Puerto Ricans paid much; Puerto Rico could be murderous, while Calgary could be murderously cold. But we thought Carlos and Victor would take good care of Stu's boys.

There was no one to greet us when we arrived in San Juan. We had little money and no idea where to go until the Capital Wrestling office opened in the morning. Smith and I slept on the filthy airport floor using our bags as pillows.

Once we checked in with the office, we ended up at the Tanama Hotel, a dump where only the bottom-end wrestlers stayed. Smith and I were each making U.S.$300 a week, and I was intent on getting back to Calgary with enough money to put a down payment on a house of my own.

The Tanama was a real shithole, situated across a river from an over-crowded prison full of violent criminals. The air conditioning in our room didn't work, and we were too naive for it to occur to us to change rooms. We relied on the ceiling fan, which didn't work too well either, so we opened our windows and slept fitfully every night in the sweltering heat, listening to sirens from the prison and vicious fights among the prostitutes on the street below our windows. The very first night we heard what sounded like gun-shots and somebody groaning—I was too scared to look. All the while the steady thumping beat of salsa music and Barry Manilow singing "Copa Cabana" drifted up from the disco joints. What had I got myself into?

My second mistake, after the one about agreeing to come, was thinking I should stay away from Latin food and water. I walked down to a Burger King to get some American food, where I met a friendly Puerto Rican kid who introduced himself as Kikay. He spoke good English and he wanted to take me to a fiesta. I told him I couldn't leave my brother behind, so he came back to the Tanama with me. Off we all went to a small carnival with Ferris wheels. Smith said Kikay was dying to get into my pants, but I should be nice to him because it might be useful to know someone who had a car. I didn't believe it.

Our room was an oven, and by morning I was drenched in sweat—and sick with the runs. By the time our ride picked us up for our first show, I was weak and dizzy. Luckily, Chief Thundercloud and his son Chewie both spoke English and had a cheap but reliable car. Chewie was a few years older than I was, but he was too small to wrestle. All the way to Ponce I fought not to shit my pants right there in the car. To my dismay, the highways were littered every hundred feet or so with dead dogs that had their legs pointing straight up in the air. The narrow, winding road added to my nausea.

My match was with a big American by the name of Mike York, a heavy-set clodhopper of a wrestler who had a thick, black beard and hair all over his body. The ring wasn't covered with canvas but with cheap, slippery blue vinyl, made more hazardous by puddles of sweat mixed with baby oil, the residue of previous matches. Mike was a clumsy freight train, but he did all he could to take care of me. Hito had been right. I just started doing all the moves I'd seen, including an explosive comeback. But as I found myself jumping up to hit Mike with a drop kick, my feet hit a slippery spot and I crashed down on my shoulder. "I'm hurt, Mike," I said. "We better go home."

To end the match, he got me onto my feet, grabbed me, spun me upside down and gave me a shoulder breaker across his knee. I knew I was in good hands because he dropped me on my good shoulder. Then he covered me and panted in my ear, "Sorry, brother, thanks for the match."

I headed back to the dressing room, holding my shoulder, as the crowd gave me a round of applause. Dammit! What lousy luck to get hurt my first night! When I told Carlos, he simply said, "You're tough," as he chomped on a cigar. He expected Smith and me to hit the ring in the main event that night to help save him and another Puerto Rican wrestler from some heels. I said I'd do whatever I could, and I wandered out to the concession stand to find some ice for my shoulder.

Stu Hart's kid or not, nobody gave a damn about me here. I clamped a leaky bag of ice to my shoulder and was standing in agony next to Smith when somebody yelled, "Andale! Andale! Andale!" The place suddenly went insane. I started for the ring, and then I stopped. "I'm not getting killed out there!" Smith agreed.

The arena floor was a tangle of rioters and police beating them back with batons. Chairs flew through the air like rain, and Carlos and his partner were covered in blood, begging for mercy as they were clobbered by two heels, Frenchie Martin and Fidel Castillo, who had steel chains wrapped around their fists. People were crying real tears. Finally, to everyone's relief, The Masked Invader arrived on the scene, and in seconds he was helping Carlos and his partner fight their way back through the sea of people.

As Frenchie and Fidel came toward me, their eyes were wild and filled with terror. They held metal chairs over their heads like shields as irate fans lunged at them. I didn't see any knives, but I knew they were out there, and I could hear metal clanging off the chairs as the fury of the fans boiled over.

In the midst of the riot, I noticed a young, blond American couple wearing Bermuda shorts and golf shirts, and holding hands, immobilized by the fights raging around them. The referee, a quiet little fellow called Hammer, was also fighting for his life, blindly swinging a steel chair, deflecting unidentified flying objects and attacking fans. He was backing his way toward the two Americans. My first instinct was to intervene, but they were more than thirty feet away, and I would never have made it. Hammer swung full force as he turned, smashing his chair over the blond man's head. The man fell to the floor, his girl beside him, helpless and terrified. Now I understood why Bruce had stayed home.

Back in the hotel room, Smith was sick too, and we took turns racing to the toilet and sweating on our grungy beds. My shoulder was killing me, and I couldn't raise my arm. Tiny gnats landed on us incessantly; they seemed harmless enough, so we just rubbed them out. The street sounds filtered up, sirens wailed, and it turned out the little gnats weren't so harmless after all: For weeks we were covered in festering boils. Smith and I took turns with a pair of tweezers plucking at the eruptions on our arms and chests, leaving big pink craters.

Because of my shoulder, I had no choice but to miss a full week of bookings until I recovered. Smith went on alone. I went one more time to the farmacia. I'd already tried everything they'd told me to do, and I pleaded with the chemist, saying that I was very ill. I was skin and bones compared to when I'd left home. He felt sorry for me and gave me some white pills in a small paper bag, enough for Smith and me. I thanked him and paid him. I have no idea what kind of pills they were, but I was so desperate I took them anyway.

When the week was over, I had no choice but to go to work again. I told Smith to let Jovica and Colón start booking me, but only in tag matches for now. Smith found some marijuana, which helped our dysentery. High as a kite, I drew caricatures of some of Smith's fucked-up friends from back home; it felt good to see him laugh.

We hit the beach in our free time, and stayed in the sun too long. We were ill, we were taking bumps every night, we couldn't sleep; the sunburn was just one more thing.

But we didn't take any more chances with food. The upscale La Concha Hotel, a few blocks away, catered to American tourists. They had an all-you-can-eat buffet that opened at noon. At U.S.$18 a head, it was pricey for us, but the food was worth every penny. Every day, we'd wait until they opened, and we'd gorge. Smith would stuff himself. For my amusement he'd struggle to his feet holding his hand to the seat of his pants, then stagger to the men's room while the tuxedoed waiters fell over laughing. He would come out smiling ten minutes later, flailing his arms and doing deep knee bends, and then he'd grab another plate, load it up and head back to our table. The waiters and I would be in tears.

Soon Smith met a beautiful, hot-tempered Puerto Rican girl named Maria, after she cursed him out in Spanish one day on the beach. Before long he was talking to her, drawing diagrams in the sand, explaining how there were ten Cadillacs parked around the big house where he lived with his rich and famous father. Maria warmed to him, but of course he failed to tell her that most of the Caddies didn't run, and that none of them were his.

I had a nice dark tan now, and I wore my black bullrider cowboy hat everywhere I went. At night, I'd wander past the prostitutes as I headed for the beach. The moon lit my way as I followed the black rocks that stretched out into the ocean. Waves washed over little crabs scurrying on the sand, and big ships blinked their red lights in the distance. I'd sit out on the rocks, drink a carton of orange juice, treat myself to a chocolate bar, eat bananas and wonder what my friends back home would think of what I was doing. I'd been doing a great job of pretending to get the shit kicked out of me, rolling around in pain, reaching out desperately to Smith, fighting back just enough to get cheers from the fans. I realized that I had a knack for it, and I was determined to be the best loser Puerto Rico had ever seen. I could be great if I wanted to be—the fans told me so with their eyes. The truth about these fans is that they had great sympathy and emotion because they really believed. They loved their wrestling so much that they could—and would—kill you without remorse if you offended them or let them down.

I had the pleasure of meeting the legendary Bruno Sammartino, the former WWWF Champion. He was really nice and even posed for a picture with Smith and me. But I have to say that I didn't think he was anywhere near the worker that Dory Funk Jr. or Harley Race were. I was disappointed in the cage match he had with Gorilla Monsoon; if the same match had played out in front of the Calgary fans, they would have booed the two of them out of the building. In their defence, I was well aware that Sammartino's New York wrestling style sold out Madison Square Garden every month, but it was probably the phoniest wrestling anywhere. To see realistic wrestling, you went to Japan, or to Calgary, St. Louis, Kansas City, Amarillo, Minneapolis, even Portland or Louisiana. I didn't know how or when or where I learned these things, but I knew they were true.

Gorilla Monsoon was a nice guy. His real name was Robert "Gino" Morella, and he had the kindest things to say about Stu. When I mentioned this to Stu on the phone, he told me he had trained the 350-pound Gorilla in the dungeon back in 1961. Gino had been undefeated as an amateur wrestler, and was the only wrestler on the U.S. national team whom the Russians couldn't take off his feet. Stu chuckled about how he had cross-faced Gino down in the basement, locking his arm and pressing down on his shoulder, forcing the Gorilla to the mat and bloodying his nose. "The big bastard was pretty hard to contain after that," Stu said.

I was learning that pro wrestling wasn't all fake and could be very painful. I had a match with King Kong, a five-foot- two, 350-pound human boulder from Argentina, who did a belly flop and landed on me like a slab of concrete, knocking all the wind out of me. To him, I was just a piece of meat. I never gave him the satisfaction of letting him know he had hurt me.

Afterwards, in the dressing room, King Kong shook my hand and said, "Gracias." He stood as high as my nipples. I smiled down at him, thinking, Fuck you, fatso. It was all part of paying my dues.

In Puerto Rico, I understood for the first time the creativity and the drama required to be a great worker: the art of making it all seem real and telling a story using my body. I would show them all . . . someday.

Out on the rocks, I made a pact with the full moon, asking God to watch over me as I decided to dedicate my life to this crazy profession.

Smith began socializing with a notorious New York wrestler by the name of Dick Steinborn. He was the son of Milo Steinborn, a wrestler from my father's era. Dick was to his respected father as Smith was to Stu. As a wrestler, Dick bordered on genius and at the time was rated as the best junior heavyweight in the business. But he was equally renowned for sketchy manoeuvres. Dick took Smith under his wing, and the two of them sat for hours drinking beer, conjuring up scams.

Kikay came around from time to time. One night he took Smith, Maria and me to a strip bar. A beautiful bronze dancer came over to me and she seemed very interested. I was bedazzled by her long hair and the dark curves of her body. I asked Kikay to tell her that I thought she was beautiful. His face turned red and he rattled on in Spanish. She left the table abruptly and never returned. Months later, Maria told me Kikay had made it clear that I was taken—by him. Kikay never tried anything, but I always sensed that he wanted to ask me something but couldn't quite bring himself to do it.

Back in the lobby at the Tanama, Smith was propositioned by two teenaged prostitutes who were sucking red lollipops and wearing tight red dresses. He was happy courting Maria so, like a good big brother, he negotiated on my behalf. I wasn't sure I was interested, although they were very pretty. Smith haggled and said, "I got her down to ten bucks." I dug into my jeans. "All I've got is eight."

We called home every Sunday. I told Stu how much I hated it, and he told me to ride it out. Smith and I decided to leave at the end of June, stopping in New York to visit my mom's sister, Aunt Joanie, before going back to Calgary. When Smith broke the news to my mom, she asked him to put me on the phone and promptly broke down in tears. "Please, dawling, you can't let Smith get anywhere near your Aunt Joanie! Please promise me." My mom's relatives thought their Canadian cousins were the picture-perfect family, the Kennedys of Canada. Mom thought that Smith would expose in a few moments an image that had taken years to cultivate.

Without giving her away, I said, "Don't worry, Mom. I'll take care of it. I promise."

That night there were too many heels winning matches, so the hapless Hart brothers were going to go over. It didn't mean much to anyone else, but I was excited, especially because it was an honour for me to wrestle at Roberto Clemente Stadium. The Pittsburgh Pirate had been a sports hero of mine until he died in a plane crash when I was fifteen. I thought this night would be one that I'd tell my children about some day.

The stadium was packed, and the buzz of the crowd was electric. As we waited to make our entrance, I noticed two pea-sized spiders, red as little tomatoes, perched above me on opposite sides of the doorway, having a stare-down. Suddenly they charged each other, colliding and dropping in front of me on a single thread, dangling and spinning furiously. I said to Smith, "Maybe they're fucking." And then I realized it was a fight to the death. It lasted a full minute, until one spider wrapped the other in a silk coffin. Those two spiders turned into a symbol of my time in Puerto Rico, where death was always hanging in the air.

Smith scored the win with a sloppy sunset flip in front of a sold-out stadium full of roaring fans. I was surprised when they rose to their feet, jumping and cheering for us. Smith really overdid it, throwing his fist high in the air and shouting like a girl, jumping around me, humping my leg. "We won! We won!" He was a nut, but I loved him for it.

We would leave Puerto Rico on July 2, my twenty-first birthday. Victor insisted that because of everything Stu had done for him and Carlos, he would treat Smith and me to lunch before we left. I wouldn't know until I got home that I'd lost twenty-five pounds in Puerto Rico; all I knew is that I was grateful for his offer.

I'd been trying to talk Smith out of visiting Aunt Joanie, so I was relieved—and amused—when he came to me with a plan. He'd met a pasty-faced platinum blond out by the small, filthy hotel swimming pool, which had a dead rat floating in it the whole time we were there. She invited Smith and me to stay at her well-to-do parents' dairy farm, just outside Chicago. So, instead of New York it would be Chicago—and I kept my promise to my mom, sort of.

Smith and I arrived by taxi in time for lunch with Victor. We were famished, because we'd skipped our usual feast at the La Concha. After we'd waited for nearly an hour, Victor came out of his office with his car keys jingling in his hand. "Sorry, boys, no time today. We'll do it another time. I'm busy. Got to go." We walked all the way back to the hotel, missed the buffet and never did eat that day.

On the Wednesday before we were to leave, we did TV tapings at a studio in Bayamón. It always seemed to be pouring down buckets of rain, yet it was never cool, always hot and sticky. The town reminded me of a short, wet crying scene from *The Good, the Bad and the Ugly*. There was a six-year-old albino kid who hung around the studio with sad, hungry eyes. I remember him running away as fast as he could, screaming, being chased by a cockroach as big as a mouse; it seemed to be gaining on him as they ran down a muddy street.

I was sick and tired of the heat and the squalor. I vowed never to complain about the Calgary cold again and began counting the seconds until the flight. Then Smith had a change of heart. He'd fallen in love with Maria and was going to hang on for a while longer. I was happy for him, but I was out of there.

Smith and I teamed up for a six-minute TV match with Frenchie Martin and Michel Martel, the hottest heel team the territory had ever known. We were going to get squashed, which was fine by us. I liked Frenchie and Michel, and I was happy to do my small part in helping them get over.

I took my usual shit kicking and tagged in Smith. He was hoping to shine ever so slightly in case Maria saw the match on TV, though I doubted she could afford a TV. Michel and Frenchie ate Smith alive, slapping and kicking him, leaving red marks all over his chest. Smith was annoyed at their obvious potatoes, and they could barely refrain from laughing as they tagged in and out to dish out more punishment. Smith sulked about it for the rest of the night.

I was standing in the dugout in Ponce watching when Michel Martel dropped to one knee and gripped his chest. Something was wrong, for real. Frenchie worked the rest of the match and took the fall. He slung Michel's arm over his neck and carried him back to the heel dressing room, doing his best to protect Michel from the flying debris. Frenchie laid him out in the shower, letting the cold water run over him, and he suddenly sat up and said he was fine, chalking the episode up to indigestion from some Chinese food he'd eaten too close to match time. They dressed and hurried to beat the crowd. They were heels, so they had to park far away from the building or their car would have been destroyed. They slipped out of the building, running with their bags, zigzagging the fifteen blocks to their car. Michel felt sick again as they were driving. Frenchie pulled over to the side of the road so Michel could stick his finger down his throat in order to throw up. But he collapsed again. Frenchie lifted him back into the car and raced to the nearest hospital. The orderlies who put Michel on a gurney told Frenchie, "Your friend is dead." Michel Martel was thirty-four years old, and his heart gave out. He was the first of my wrestling brothers to die. I was proud that he had his last real match with me, and that he smiled all the way through it.

It was my twenty-first birthday, and I was finding out that the wrestling business would always be about the things I learned along the way.

I had a non-refundable plane ticket to Chicago, so I left with the farmer's daughter. On the flight, she said her purse was in the overhead bin and asked, "Hon, would you mind buying me a drink?" I figured, What the heck, I'd be staying at her house and eating her food. She had plenty of drinks. When we landed in Chicago she said, "Wait here and I'll see if my dad's out front."

I never saw her again.

I had $2,000 in my pocket to show for what I went through in Puerto Rico, and I was afraid I'd be robbed in Chicago: The only images I knew of the city were of Elliott Ness and *The Untouchables*. I remembered that Keith always said that if I was ever in a bind, I should go to the YMCA. I asked for directions at the airport, and I ended up at 2 a.m. on a train along with street urchins and the night shift. I guess I was a midnight cowboy, with my bullrider hat pulled down over my eyes.

I got off at Wabash Avenue at 3 a.m. and carried my bags through deserted streets to the Y. The guy at the desk said check-in was in three hours and that the cheapest room was eight bucks. I paid him and took the key, only to find the furniture was smashed, the mattress was slashed, and there was blood splattered everywhere! I went back downstairs and asked, "How much is your best room?" He said $24. I said, "Fine," and asked him to hold my bags. I backtracked a few blocks to a fancy hotel where I stretched out on a couch in a side lobby for a few hours until I could check in at the Y.

I had a couple of days to kill in Chicago before my flight back to Calgary. On my first Fourth of July in America, I ended up down by the railroad tracks behind the Y, with no shirt on, just my jeans and cowboy hat, trying to keep my tan and listening to hoboes playing harmonica and singing the blues. I found a place where I could peek between tall buildings to see just enough of the fireworks to be impressed.

On my last day, I bought a small portable TV. I thought I'd bring it back with me to plug it into the cigarette lighter of Stu's van so the whole Stampede crew could watch *Hockey Night in Canada* as we zoomed across the Prairies. I was on my way to my room with the TV when I was approached by a strange little guy who looked like Scrooge McDuck.

Out of nowhere he started to tell me that I had a beautiful voice, and he kept insisting that he wanted to come to my room and teach me how to sing. I didn't want Scrooge McDuck, or anyone else, to know what room I was in because I was worried the TV would be stolen, but I was still too good-natured to be rude. I thought the only way to get rid of the guy was to follow him to his room, where he wanted to show me his scrapbooks.

I could tell that he lived in that tiny room; there was a shelf full of dog-eared paperbacks mounted on the wall over his bed. We sat down on the bed and I was looking for my first opening to get out of there, images of Chicago serial killer John Wayne Gacy floating in my head. Scrooge plopped three big scrapbooks down on our laps and began flipping through pages of clippings and programs; much to my surprise he actually had been a singer, when he'd had a life. He seemed harmless enough now, but when I opened up the third scrapbook I was stunned to see two men screwing on the cover of a gay magazine. He gently put his hand on my knee and asked, "Do you like?" In a recoil reaction, my fist smashed him right in the face, knocking him against the wall, bringing down the bookshelf and covering him with books! He lay there twitching, pretending to be out cold, with a deep, ugly cut oozing under his right eye. I felt bad that I hit him so hard, but I was never going to sing the way he wanted me to. I picked up my TV and left.

The next day I was standing at the foot of the steps in front of Hart house, glad to be home in one piece.

A few days later I was in Stu's kitchen when Aunt Joanie phoned. Surprise, Smith and Maria were there! And surprise, again, they were married! My whole detour to Chicago turned out to have been for nothing after all. The look on my face didn't even come close to my poor mother's aghast expression!

5

BIG-HEARTED BRUTES

I GOT HOME FROM PUERTO RICO just in time to see Dynamite work with Nelson Royal, the NWA Junior Heavyweight Champion during Stampede week. Watching Royal in action lit me up; I wanted to be doing what he was doing, and to be doing it with him. But first I needed to put some weight back on for my Calgary debut in September, and so I took most of the summer off. Smith got back to town with his new bride, moving Maria into the attic of Hart house; it must have been a real shock to her to see that the Cadillacs in the yards were all wrecks.

That year Keith and I were the older brothers introducing thirteen-year-old Owen and Diana to the annual summer pilgrimage to visit Dory and Terry Funk in Amarillo. Dory was considered the best wrestler in the business, and Terry was as good in many ways but was the more wildly unpredictable of the two. Now that I was determined to become a really good wrestler in my own right, the opportunity to learn from the Funks took on a whole new significance for me.

The Funks let me referee a couple of nights, and they even threw me into a couple of job matches with a big Japanese guy named Tetsuo Sekigawa and a local named Dennis Stamp. I attempted to throw a punch to Stamp's gut but accidentally smashed him in the groin. A lot of wrestlers would have been angry, but Dennis forgave me for my greenness and gave me a good match. (Twenty years later, Terry Funk would pick me, of all people, to work his retirement match with him, and Stamp was the referee.)

Stu's business got worse that summer. A match between Mike York and The Magnificent Zulu at the tail end of August was so terrible that at the ten-minute mark a fan in the front row stood up and yelled, "Hey, come on, Stu! What is this shit?" Stu cringed and watched for another thirty seconds and then walked up to ringside, pounded his hands on the apron and ordered, "Go home! Go home!" After the match, barely out of the fans' view, he scolded Mike and Zulu for putting on such a phoney performance.

I really wanted to have my own place, away from the chaos at Hart house, and Smith suggested a fixer-upper that I could resell quickly for a modest profit. He pointed out that it was by investing in houses such as this that Jovica made the money to start up the Puerto Rico territory. That was how I ended up living in a dilapidated part of town known as Ramsay, in a lopsided grey shack with leaky ceilings that seemed to have been decorated by a colour-blind lunatic.

Then Smith left to work in Germany with Bruce, Dynamite and Hito. Stu also lost most of the rest of his roster to the Maritimes. It was good for wrestlers to give their faces a rest in front of regional fans so promotions regularly exchanged talent, but this time the roster was really thin. That was how I became a temporary booker for Stampede Wrestling, working with Ross to make up the cards. Neither of us felt we were qualified, but Stu seemed to think we were doing a fine job, so he let us book the whole territory.

Ross was a walking encyclopedia of wrestling. He collected and studied everything he could get his hands on: magazines, programs and publicity photos sent to Stu from territories far and wide. He could recite from memory who fought whom, when and where they fought, and how the finish went for any card from most of the territories around the world back to the 1940s. Even as a kid, Stu would ask Ross's advice on who could get over. He had such a keen eye that when he critiqued young, green wrestlers with brutal honesty, they accepted his opinion because he was rarely wrong. Ross at twelve got so upset over the booking of a Stampede week card that he got into a heated argument with Stu and ended up popping him square on the chin! Stu was stunned, but it turned out that Ross was right.

I made my official Stampede Wrestling debut in Calgary on September 1, 1978, and I was proud that the match with Mike York passed muster with Stu, who watched the whole thing nervously, probably because he was curious to see how bad it might be.

I spent most of that month with the skeleton crew on an old Greyhound bus Stu bought with money he could ill afford. The referee, Sandy Scott, was also the driver, a heavy-smoking Scot in his mid-forties who could pass as a much younger man. With his little red Afro, neatly trimmed beard and false teeth, Sandy resembled an elkhound.

Kasavubu liked to mellow us out on the night drives by getting us to sing The Temptations' "Papa Was a Rolling Stone." Norman Frederick Charles III was also a regular. He had been one of the Royal Kangaroos, a top tag team, but he'd had a falling out with his partner. Now in his late forties, he was thin and frail with bandy legs and a scruffy beard. We often joked about how he'd lost his ass in a card game because his outfit hung on him like a pair of old long johns, but he was the British Commonwealth Junior Heavyweight Champion nonetheless, having taken the belt from Dynamite just before Tom left for Germany, in an angle where Norman destroyed Tom's knee.

Jimmy Rougeau was a stark contrast to our tired old North American Champion, Paddy Ryan. Paddy, like so many of Stu's Calgary crew, was the last to know that the sun was setting on his career. I could see the light dim in his eyes when I gave him his finishes, and after he worked he'd sit red-faced and out of breath. It didn't help that he weighed four hundred pounds and smoked like a chimney.

I soon got used to long drives, listening to music, singing, going from town to town, finding camaraderie in this strange mix of humanity. The bus would pull over in the middle of nowhere for a piss stop and that was a sight unto itself: Men of all different sizes and colours pissing at the side of the road while gazing up at the northern lights.

I worked my first program with Norman, who had been around long enough that he wasn't keen on taking a lot of bumps. He knew plenty of short cuts, and he knew exactly how to settle me down and make me look good enough. On September 26, 1978, he pulled a chair up beside me in the dressing room in Regina, sipping coffee from a foam cup and smoking a cigarette. "Well, kid," he said in his raspy Aussie accent, "looks like there might be a decent house coming in. Maybe this would be a good time to work a title change. What do you think about getting a little juice?"

Getting a little juice meant deliberately cutting my head with a razor blade. I felt butterflies in my stomach at the thought of it. As a referee I'd seen it done lots of times, close up; blading was practically a rite of passage in Puerto Rico. I told Norman I'd consider it, then went to check on the other matches, peeking out of a little hole in the wall, to give myself time to think. If I was going to make it to the top in wrestling, this moment was bound to come sooner or later. But that didn't make it any easier. I wanted to believe that, in some pathetic way, this might help me get over and help my father at the same time.

The plan had been for Dynamite and Norman to pick up where they left off when Dynamite came back from Germany in December, but when I called Stu about all this, he liked the thought of me working title matches with Dynamite, rather than Norman. If I was going to cut myself, it was best to keep it near the hairline. I didn't want to end up looking pocked and pitted like so many wrestlers. I found Norman and told him, "You better show me how to make a blade."

He looked over my shoulder as I snipped a quarter section of razor blade. I cut the top corner at an angle, taped all but the exposed point and then taped the blade onto the wrist tape on my left arm.

Despite being known as a despicable heel, Norman settled into a basic babyface match with me and, after fifteen minutes of clean wrestling, the crowd started to buy it. As we broke clean on the ropes, Norman said, "Are you ready, kid?"

"Yeah."

As I came at him, he side-stepped me and threw me out onto the floor. He followed me out of the ring and reached into his trunks and slid on his brass knuckles; which were really just paper napkins, tightly taped together.

He nailed me. Down I went.

I had the blade in my hand now. I rolled onto my stomach, jabbed it deep into my head and cut.

Nothing.

I cut again.

Still nothing.

And then, suddenly, blood poured all over my face. Hot blood. My blood.

I heard Norman say, "Jesus Christ, kid, it's a good one." He dragged me back to the ring. Because the crowd had fallen for his babyface act, they were livid. As I desperately fought back, the fans got behind me even more because in their hearts they knew it'd been their fault for encouraging me to trust him. I staggered through the match with blood running down my face until Norman said, "Let's go home, kid."

On my knees and totally at his mercy, we locked hands as Norman planted some last kicks to my ribs. Suddenly I rolled onto my back, prying Norman's legs apart with my feet, tucking his head and collapsing him into a sunset flip out of nowhere.

The ref counted one . . . two . . . three!

The crowd jumped to its feet with a roar as Norman sat up with a stunned look on his face. As the referee handed me the belt, Norman jumped me from behind, knocked me flat and stomped out of the ring. After he left, I got up slowly and raised the British Junior Heavyweight belt over my head. I walked down the aisle to pats on the back and words of praise from the fans.

In the dressing room, Norman congratulated me, then inspected the cut on my forehead, which was an inch long and right to the bone: "Nice job, kid." Then, with a goofy grin, he said, "Now I better show you how to make a butterfly bandage." And off we went to the sink.

What a strange business.

That November, Ross thought it might be interesting to throw my brother Keith and me together as a tag combo, since Stu's tag champs, the Castillo

Brothers, had nobody to work with, and I had no real opponents as Junior Heavyweight Champ. When I walked into the dressing room in Edmonton on the day of our first match, I found Ross talking to Raul Castillo. Ross turned to me to say, "Raul has a family emergency. They're going back to Puerto Rico. Dad says you and Keith will have to take the tag belts tonight."

And that's how I became the holder of not one but two title belts so early in my career. I knew that both were not likely to be mine for long, but Stu, Ross and I decided that it might do good business for me to hold on to the title for a little while after Dynamite got back, so he could go after Norman, defeating him to avenge the knee injury. Then he'd come after me. I wanted desperately to work with Tom, learn from him and maybe even impress him with how much I'd improved since our last struggle of a match back in May. I wanted to put Tom over so that he could see clearly that he was our champion and that I was only holding the belt for him; it never occurred to me that Tom might assume that I was just another spoiled promoter's kid, out for easy glory.

Anyone watching Dynamite and me wrestle for the three weeks leading up to our Boxing Day match in December 1978 would have had plenty of reasons to think it was real. Under the guise of "working," Tom stiffed me, over and over, until I just did the same back to him. One minute he'd smash me right in the face or kick me as hard as he could or simply throw me with complete disregard and then, just as suddenly, he'd be working again, calling spots and taking bumps for me. I've always felt wrestling was a lot like figure skating, but when your pairs partner is trying to throw you on your head, it stops being art.

When we got back to the dressing room after our first title match, I wasn't sure whether Dynamite was stiff or if he had it in for me. I didn't realize it at the time, but I had actually just learned what would become my signature moves: my pile driver, back breaker, German suplex and what was initially a pretty weak Dory Funk Jr.–style elbow smash, or lifter. They all came from running out of things to do in the face of Dynamite's onslaught and trying everything I could think of.

We sort of worked all the following week and then duelled it out in Calgary in a return title match that was televised. Even though Dynamite had been stiffing me every night, I was still giving him the benefit of the doubt. I finally realized that Tom was intentionally stiffing me when he intentionally soccer-kicked me in the face just as I was cutting myself. The kick alone was bad enough, but because of the blade, he could have severely injured me. I still can't think of anything more unprofessional.

The match became a working brawl. Wayne was the referee, and after trying to regain control, he gave up and headed back to the dressing room. There was one little problem. Stu barked at both of us, "We need eight more minutes for TV, goddamn it, right now!"

I was slumped in a turnbuckle, regretting that I'd ever stepped in the ring with The Dynamite Kid. He walked across the ring and offered to shake my hand. I extended my hand despite my doubts, only to have him kick me in the ribs as hard as he could. And just like that we were off again, with Stu filling in as the referee until we gave him his eight more minutes.

When we got back to the dressing room, I made a weak attempt to confront Tom, who was glaring at me, wanting me to. Hito held me back, and I sank into my chair, thinking, What the hell is his problem?

In our third and final week together, we had the only match in which I was going over, in Calgary. Dynamite broke into an impressive series of cartwheels and a handstand, and then he picked me up, I thought, to slam me. Instead, he slowly fell to the mat with me on top of him, pinning himself for the one . . . two . . . three. The crowd groaned its disapproval at the obvious dive, and I was embarrassed to have my hand raised. The following night I dropped the belt back to Dynamite in Edmonton.

Dealing with Tom was like dealing with a bad-tempered pit bull. I just never knew when he'd take a bite out of me, or why, but I knew that as talented as he was, sooner or later we'd have to make a truce. I was relieved to be done with him, yet sorry he felt the way he did about me.

I was too sore that year to notice Christmas. I could barely move, every bone in my body hurt, I had two black eyes, my lips were cut and swollen and I had a scar on my forehead near the hairline. I'd recently bought this great new invention called a VCR and, on New Year's Eve 1978, I sat watching a tape of myself for the first time, the televised match where Dynamite and I beat the hell out of each other. Ed Whalen, who'd become the most realistic play-by-play announcer of them all, said, "I am going to apologize to you right here and now. I have been sitting here for forty-eight minutes with my mouth open, watching one of the finest fights I have ever seen. I do not exaggerate." He wasn't. If only Tom would work with me, it'd be magic. Stu was still losing money. Unlike many of the other promoters, he was sincerely devoted to the talent: He always paid his wrestlers, no matter what. And if one of his rising stars got a break elsewhere, he'd encourage him to go, even if it meant that the Stampede territory limped along. For the most part, this earned Stu the loyalty and respect of his crew, who in turn tolerated the brutal weather, being packed in like sardines on seemingly endless drives and being paid in Canadian dollars. But by this point in his life, I think Stu was always hoping that his sons would step up and take over. Which is the only way I can explain the fact that after Smith got back from Germany, he persuaded Stu that he needed to hire a real booker: his old pal from Puerto Rico, Dick Steinborn. I don't know how Stu managed to overlook Dick's track record outside the ring; desperate men do desperate things. Dick started work on New Year's Day 1979.

Steinborn was a clever operator with survival on his mind: He was walking into a minefield of brotherly rivalries between the real siblings and among the brotherhood of the ring. He clearly checked out all of Stu's sons and soon saw that Helen still had a huge soft spot for Bruce, and that Bruce, also back from Germany, truly believed that we could book the territory ourselves and resented anyone else being brought in. Before long, Dick was describing to Bruce how he would build him into a superstar beyond his wildest dreams, the centrepiece of richly layered angles, and victory after victory. Dick knew that all it would take to get Bruce's support was to promise that he'd make him a star. And that flattering Bruce would get him good with my mom too.

As for me, Dick told me straight out that even though I was a better worker than Bruce, I was younger. From now on I'd be playing the role of the weak little brother. "It's just business, kid," is how he put it to me. I didn't see how it would help business to turn me into a jobber, but what did I know?

It turned out Dick had some pretty good ideas. He had Keith and me lose to my old teachers, Hito and Sakurada, in Edmonton: We all agreed it would make sense to put the tag belts on a heel team. He reinvented John Foley as J.R. Foley, a corrupt millionaire manager character who could buy anyone's loyalties—or could he? It turned out to be a great boost to all the angles.

Dick's next brainstorm was to turn Tom heel, have J.R. manage him and have him work against Bruce. Tom almost fell off his chair when, despite the fact that for the past three weeks his matches with me went thirty minutes to an hour, Dick told Bruce to pin The Dynamite Kid in less than five seconds with a simple, small package. I saw some sense in it because it was so unexpected that the fans would really pop—which they did. But Tom was furious. I didn't think he could get any angrier—until the next week, when Dick had Bruce do it again!

We couldn't afford to lose Dynamite, so Ross brought Marty Jones into the territory to appease him. Marty came from Manchester, and he had been Tom's chum and mentor. But when he got to Calgary, Steinborn told him he wanted him to be an Australian Kangaroo.

"A fookin' Australian what?" I heard from the other end of the dressing room in Marty's thick Manchester accent.

I didn't think it would be so bad to be a Kangaroo, and I thought it was funny watching Marty walk around the dressing room wearing an extra set of Norman's gear, that silly hat folded up on one side and carrying a boomerang. When Keith and I wrestled against this reincarnation of the Royal Kangaroos, Marty and I clicked, and between the four of us we tore the house down.

My back was killing me while working this match with Marty, and as a result I happened into a move that would become an intricate part of my wrestling for the rest of my career. As Marty threw me hard into the turnbuckle, I couldn't will myself to turn into it with my sore back, so instead I hit it full force with my chest and bounced back to the middle of the ring. The crowd gasped! It looked like I had broken my neck, and even Marty bent over and asked me whether I was okay. I was more amazed than he was to say yes. To the best of my knowledge, this move had never been done before. From that point on, I used it all the time to change the momentum of my matches. Nobody could take a front turnbuckle like I could. Nobody.

Despite being peeved about the Kangaroo gimmick, when we got back to the dressing room that night, Marty was lit up. So was I, especially when a tall, lanky kid from Louisiana approached me and drawled, "Unbelievable, brother. Y'all had a helluva match. Solid as hell." His name was Jake The Snake Roberts. For any young guy in the business it meant a lot when anyone took the time to watch your match, especially one of the American wrestlers. I took an immediate shine to his sly air and his smooth-talking demeanour and soon invited him to stay at my place. Jake could pay a little rent and it would be cheaper and better for him than staying at the Regis Hotel, where the rest of the wrestlers always stayed when they were in Calgary. He moved in with me the next day.

In Regina the next night, Keith and I were getting worked over good by Hito and Sakurada. As I waited to tag in, I twisted my head around to stare at a pretty girl in the front row. Even Hito and Sakurada were surprised when I launched into an exceptionally long and explosive comeback. When the match was over, I couldn't take my eyes off the girl as I walked past. The head security guard, Gil, a big old friendly guy, brought her back to the hall by the babyface dressing room so I could meet her. She was even prettier up close, with light-brown, shoulder-length hair and greenish-brown eyes. She told me her name was Julie, and she seemed excited to talk to me . But not as excited as I was to talk to her.

That night as I took over the wheel of the bus for a while, the moon was full, high and white, and as the snow streaked by I felt like I was piloting a spaceship in hyperdrive. The miles passed easily as sleepy, snoring heads rolled from side to side behind me. I thought about the girl named Julie and felt glad that I'd be back in Regina again next week. I almost didn't recognize my own face in the rearview mirror, I'd changed so much in one year. I hardly saw my old high school friends any more. Either they weren't interested in wrestling, or they sensed it was awkward for me to talk about it. My life was full of the strangest characters now, and it was all so oddly inviting. I was beginning to understand why all my big brothers were involved in wrestling; the camaraderie, mutual respect and sense of belonging did wonders to mend lost and battered souls. But what I didn't see, as I followed the broken white line home, is that life as a pro wrestler is highly addictive. Once you get a taste for it, your old life fades away and disappears.

Dick Steinborn now began building Jake The Snake for main events with Big Daddy Sylvester Ritter, who later became known as The Junkyard Dog in the WWF. Smith and I first met Ritter when we were working Puerto Rico. He looked like a friendly black bull mastiff, and although his work was really green, as a heel he was good enough on the mic to become our North American Champion. I was shy in front of a microphone, but I understood all too well that I'd have to become a better talker if I was going to make it to the top.

Then, just three months after he arrived, Dick was suddenly gone: His ideas were good, but the gates hadn't come up. I can't say that I was sorry to see Dick go; I was more than happy to say goodbye to the little brother role he'd stuck me in. And despite the potato harvest when we'd worked those three weeks together, I wanted to be put with Dynamite again.

There was the possibility that could happen, as he was getting fed up working with Bruce, who was wild and stiff and all too often exploded with reckless abandon, without consideration for the guy he worked with. When doing his finishing move, the flying clothesline, he would hook your head on delivery, which made it impossible to take without bouncing your skull off the mat. Dynamite was stiff on purpose, whereas Bruce never had a clue. It was only because Bruce was Stu's kid that most wrestlers took their lumps from him without complaint.

Finally, Tom watched me work a terrific match with Marty Jones and realized what I already knew, that he and I could have the best matches in the territory.

All that winter and into the spring of 1979, Stu was personally breaking in a kid named Jim Neidhart, who had come to Calgary from the United States clutching Stu's phone number in his hand. He was a high school all-American shot-putter and football player, rumoured to have been the final guy cut from tryouts with the Dallas Cowboys. Stu had a passion for turning athletes into wrestlers, especially when they were bigger than him, and he took a liking to Neidhart right away.

Though he didn't travel the circuit any more, Stu always came to the Edmonton show on Satruday night. The first time Jim came with us, Stu detected the aroma of marijuana on the bus. He jumped up out of a dead sleep and barked, "Who the hell is burning tea leaves?"

It was never a good idea to get Stu mad, and Wayne and I exchanged glances that said, Better Jim than us! Jim, having no idea of the lion he'd just unleashed, casually answered, "Oh, I sometimes like to smoke a small amount of marijuana to relax me, Stu." My dad made him throw the joint out the window, then gave Jim the first of many lectures about how an athlete shouldn't pollute his body with drugs.

Wayne and I were surprised Jim got off so easily. But the next day we heard poor Jim, as big as he was, screaming for his life down in the dungeon. It was a good thing Stu liked him!

Neidhart was one of the many to get his first break from my dad, but one of only a few who can honestly say that Stu Hart taught him how to wrestle. He spent a lot of time on his belly in the bowels of Stu's dungeon, as the old octopus squeezed the life out of him. When they were done, Jim would shower, then come upstairs and hang out with the Hart brothers. Though we soon realized it was my sister Ellie he was hoping to see.

Jim and I were talking in the living room once when Smith sat down and yanked Heathcliff the Siamese cat up into his arms by the tail. Heathcliff screeched, but Smith continued to agitate the cat. Ellie yelled from upstairs, "Whoever is hurting the cat, leave him alone." Smith carried on, and we all knew where this was going, except for Jim. Sure enough, before long Ellie stomped down the stairs in a rage, yelling, "Leave the goddamn fucking cat alone!" Smith, with perfect timing, tossed Heathcliff into Jim's arms just as Ellie burst in.

"Listen here, you stupid son of a bitch, leave the cat alone!" she yelled at him.

Jim's mouth fell open, Heathcliff leapt to freedom, Ellie stomped off and the rest of us howled in laughter. Big Jim had just got his first dose of Ellie's temper.

On the next trip, we had to go by old Caddie and van again because the bus got totalled in a run-in with a moose. I was driving the van, with none other than the legendary Gene Kiniski up front, right next to me. Long retired, Kiniski was still a large man and in great shape, and famous for being one of wrestling's best blabbermouths. He sported a flat-top, and his gnarly face and big, round nose were framed by two large, floppy ears.

The Calgary territory held many memories for Kiniski. And I remembered him having some rugged matches with O'Connor, Thesz and The Stomper when I was a kid. Gazing out the van window, he had to be thinking about his days growing up in Edmonton. He'd met my dad there playing Canadian football, and it was Stu who helped break him into pro wrestling, where he eventually rose to the top, winning the NWA World title from Lou Thesz.

Someone yelled from the back of the van, "Has Gene ever seen the statue of Stu?"

For as long as I'd been making this trip, the statue had been a rib on the rookies. The small town of Drumheller, in a deep, desert-like valley, had become world-famous for some of the world's greatest dinosaur finds. "Stu was actually born down here," I bullshitted Gene. "Then his family settled up in Tofield. They built a statue of Stu in the Drumheller town square in recognition of all the work he's done in the community."

Gene was flabbergasted, "Well, after all these years, your dad never told me that! Have I got time to take a picture?"

"Sure, Gene, we'll be seeing it just up around the bend . . ."

The van rounded the corner. "There he is, Gene!"

Everyone exploded in laughter, especially Gene.

With the same big eyes that stare right into you, glaring teeth and huge legs braced like a rotund wrestler, there stood a thirty-foot-tall Tyrannosaurus rex—looking eerily like my dad. From the back, Wayne piped in a superb imitation of Stu, "Eh, c'mon, ya big bastard!"

The ribbing moved on to Jim, packed in the backseat with Norman, J.R. and The Cuban.

"Hey, Jim," I said innocently. "What the hell did you do to Stu's cat?" All ears went up.

Jim, defensive, said it was Smith who had stuck his finger up the cat's ass, not him.

The Cuban paused a beat and said that Stu worshipped Siamese cats, especially Heathcliff. Dynamite added that Stu had once fired a wrestler simply because the guy was allergic to cats. J.R. said that when he'd spoken with Stu that morning, he'd never heard him so angry.

By the time we got to Saskatoon, Jim was convinced that Stu thought he'd mistreated the cat and that his days were numbered. And what was Ellie, the object of his desire, thinking? It made him very grumpy.

The next morning we were working out in the weight room at the University of Saskatchewan. It was poorly equipped, but it was the only gym in town. When Jim strolled in, his shades were pushed back on top of his head, and he was wearing a T-shirt and a pair of Stu's long, black wrestling leotards. He proceeded to stack plates and more plates onto the bench-press rack. I looked at Jake.

"He's got to be kidding. That's over five hundred and fifty pounds."

Jim pulled his shades down, leaned back, slammed the weight up and down three times and then said, "This bench press is bullshit." And he walked out, leaving everyone stunned.

I'd already heard about his potential for wildness. When Jim was a shot-putter at UCLA, he went berserk one night on alcohol and downers, tore up his motel room, tied some bedsheets together, strapped a fire extinguisher on his back and leaped off the fourth-floor balcony like a gorilla, swinging down three floors and crashing through the windows of his coach's room.

The next day we went south across the border to work in Billings, Montana. On Thursday, the van broke down on the way to Butte, which put us all in a bad mood. Making the five hundred miles back to Calgary on Friday in time for the TV show was a white-knuckle drive, and by the time we got to the dressing room everyone was especially tired and ornery. That all changed when Big Jim walked up to Stu and politely set the record straight: "Stu, I just want you to know that it wasn't me who was sticking his finger up the cat's ass!" Stu stood there with a baffled look on his face as a dressing room full of tired guys erupted into laughter.

It was Friday night at the pavilion, March 23, 1979. Jake The Snake would finally face Big Daddy for the North American Championship belt. And Tom, tanned and fit from a working vacation in Hawaii, was going to defend the British Commonwealth belt against me. Hito and Sak had the tag belts up. And Stu wore a satisfied smile: It was the first sellout of 1979.

This time things were different with Tom and me. Our work was solid, not stiff, and we protected each other with mutual respect. In the dressing room afterwards, Tom smiled as he shook my hand, and for the first time, he thanked me for a match. I also noticed that he was growing thicker, and I'd soon learn he was getting steroids from the Boxing and Wrestling Commission doctor in Edmonton to build muscle on his 170-pound frame.

When Jake beat Ritter for the North American title, the fans really popped, and we knew they would be coming back for more. But the next night at a spot show on a little Native reserve in Wetaskiwin, our North American Champion couldn't even stand up in the dressing room without grimacing in pain: He'd badly wrenched his knee. It's always hard to guess how serious a knee injury is or how long it'll take to heal. Our hopes of breaking even or maybe even making some money centred on the Jake and Ritter angle playing out over several weeks. The look on Stu's face said it all.

A few days later, Tom pulled me aside in Regina. "You know, we're going to have to carry things until Jake gets back, so let's show 'em we can be the main event." We posed for a *Body Press* cover shot, each of us holding one end of the belt in mock tug o' war. To me that meant, I'll carry my end if you carry yours.

The plan that night was for me to put Dynamite over, with Marty Jones helping him. Then Bruce would come out of nowhere and save me. Together we'd clean house and come back in some tag matches, ultimately leading to a steel cage match with Bruce and Marty. Marty would put Bruce over and then head home to England. It was rare for Tom to screw up a finish, but that night he did. In a simple dive off the top rope that he should have kicked out on, he didn't. Wayne had no choice but to raise my hand and declare me the winner. Tom admitted the title change was his fault, and we agreed I'd drop it back to him in a few weeks. I kept it to myself that I was grateful for the twist of fate. Getting a win over The Dynamite Kid was no small thing. The fans considered it a huge upset, and it helped them forget the useless-little-brother image that Steinborn had saddled me with.

Jake stayed out longer than anyone expected. When Bruce picked me up in the van for the weekly drive to Saskatoon, just after Good Friday that year, it had been five weeks since Jake had worked, and he stood in the doorway of my house leaning on his crutches to wave goodbye. We hadn't gone far when I realized I'd left the Junior Heavyweight belt on the dining-room table, so we went back to get it. As we came up the walk, we could see Jake strolling around my kitchen without so much as a limp, cooking a hearty meal for himself. But when we knocked, he opened the door on crutches with what I now knew was a phoney pained expression on his face. I didn't confront him about it, just grabbed my belt and left. But we filled Stu in right away. He was none too happy, but he reasoned that it wouldn't do any good if Jake left town on us and asked us to keep it under our hats.

The one real boost to the territory, and to overall morale, at this time was the return of the Kiwis, Crazy Nick and Sweet William, later known as the Bushwhackers in the WWF. The two New Zealanders, who'd worked the Stampede territory back in 1975, came to help Stu out for six weeks and make a few bucks. Tom teamed up with them, and together they took on me, Bruce and Keith in some tremendous six-man tag matches. The Kiwis were brilliant as heels. They came across as lunatics, with their bleached-blond hair, dark beards, missing teeth and bug eyes twitching every which way. They called great spots for me, and I surprised myself by being able to do everything they called. Crazy Nick once complimented me in front of all the boys in the dressing room, "You're by far the best one of the Hart kids, mate!"

Meanwhile, Stu put subtle pressure on Jake to get back in the ring, allowing him to believe that coming back would be valiant and courageous. Wrestlers often portray promoters as scoundrels, but here was a good example of it being the other way around. Jake finally decided to come back to work in May, on the Kiwis' last day. They rode in his car with him, and when they passed us in the van, both Crazy Nick and Sweet William had their butt cheeks pressed to the side windows: a full moon in broad daylight. Not to be outdone, we passed them a few minutes later with a wide assortment of big hairy asses stuck to the van windows. Several miles later, Jake overtook us again. This time the trunk popped open and there was Crazy Nick bent over on his knees, with Sweet William pretending to shag him from behind. The crazy Kiwis made wrestling fun, and I was sorry to see them go.

The boys had become family to me. New brothers showed up all the time, forming just as real a bond, in some cases even more so. Just as suddenly, they'd move on to the next territory, and I never knew if or when I'd see them again. There were way too many goodbyes for a bunch of big-hearted brutes, so we just said, See ya, somewhere down the road.

Dynamite and I worked with each other regularly now, and even skeptical fans were convinced our rivalry was a shoot. We were young, fast and seriously intent, right down to our facials. We were always adding new moves spliced with long, flowing high spots. We'd build higher and higher, climaxing with a finish that was always fresh and believable. The wrestling business had grown stagnant, with most wrestlers repeating the same old tired routines from one territory to the next. Tom and I each had a unique, diversified background, and that's how we set ourselves apart from other wrestlers. In order to get the Junior belt back on Tom in our return match, and to give the fans something different, we decided to do the match in rounds, like in boxing, which was the way wrestling matches played out in England. I came up with a wild finish that I ran by Tom, playing it in our heads like a movie. We found that we both had the rare ability to visualize a match way before we ever did it.

Tom, staying heel, made a point of having shoving matches and punch-ups with various fans, only to be restrained by Stu and security. So the fans really wanted me to teach him a lesson. We were tied at one fall a piece. I was pacing in my corner between rounds, like I was going to kill him. Dynamite sat on his stool, looking totally knackered, with J.R. Foley sponging him down. At the bell, J.R. took a bucket of water and threw it in Dynamite's face as a last desperate attempt to revive him. I came charging in, lifting Dynamite off the ground with an elbow smash as the fans cheered me on. I ran him across the ring to the opposite corner and bounced his head off the turnbuckle. "Be careful, it's slippery," he said. I spun him around and threw him back toward the far corner. He reversed and I slipped magnificently on the water, sliding under the corner rope, wrapping my back around the steel post. The crowd cringed at the realism. Tom dragged me promptly to the middle of the ring and twisted me up in a vicious-looking one-legged crab. I submitted instantly, pounding my hands on the mat in agony. As some of the wrestlers and the ushers crowded in to help me, Tom was strapping on the junior belt. Not even Tom knew whether I was really hurt. I squinted into the scared face of fourteen-year-old Owen, who'd been sitting with Tommy Carr at ringside. "You okay, Bret?" he whispered softly.

With my mouth hidden by my forearm, I reassured him. "Yeah, how'd it look?"

Owen sighed. "It looked like he killed you."

At the Calgary Stampede parade that July, André the Giant, Harley Race and a handful of midgets piled into several convertibles to get maximum exposure. André had been born with acromegaly. At seven-foot-four, he reminded me of a huge mound of rocks; his protruding jaw and forehead, topped off with a big Afro, added to his unique appeal.

Harley was one of the legit tough guys in wrestling and one of the best bump-takers of all time. He was born with tendons twice as strong as a normal man's, his hands were like Vise-Grips and he enjoyed bringing blowhards to their knees. Harley lived hard, drank hard and had survived countless near-fatal car wrecks. He had a steel plate in his forehead and another piece of metal pinning his forearm together. Nobody commanded more respect within the wrestling business than Harley, especially from the Hart family. And the respect went both ways. Nobody but my dad could ask the great champions to show up for a parade at 5:45 a.m. and have them happy to oblige.

That night the pavilion was packed. With all the extra overhead, airfares, hotels and name attractions, Stu would lose money, as usual, but he was content to put on a great show for the fans.

I stood by the back doors watching the midgets go into their finish when some guy came strolling through the front gates with a chimpanzee cradling his neck. He walked up the aisle toward the ring just as the midget Cowboy Lang launched into his comeback. I wondered whether the guy with the chimp was part of their match. He let the chimp off on the apron and into the ring as all four midgets were running every which way. The chimp joined in like he'd done it a thousand times before. They fell together in a pile of little legs and arms, with the chimp on top screeching and jumping up and down. Sandy Scott dove down to the pile for the one . . . two . . . three as the crowd exploded in laughter. I shook my head, amazed that they got a chimp to do all that.

Back in the dressing room, the boys were still laughing when li'l Cowboy Lang came in, slammed the door and angrily hopped on one leg as he pulled his cowboy boot off and threw it as hard as he could against the wall.

"What's the matter, Cowboy?" I asked.

"The goddamn monkey fucked the finish!"

Turned out the guy was the handler of the chimp from the TV show *B.J. and the Bear*. A friend of André's, he'd just stopped by to say hello. I didn't have the heart to tell Cowboy it was one of the funniest things I'd ever seen. Cowboy just couldn't understand that midget wrestling was supposed to be funny. He was tired of being laughed at and wanted to be taken as seriously as the rest of us.

"Hey, boss," André said, "you're much bigger now." André called every-one boss, and I was flattered he remembered me. "Not as big as you are," I said and shook his huge hand. André always had a couple of bottles of red wine close by as he dressed for his match. He was the man to beat in the twelve-man battle royal, a match in which all the wrestlers try to throw one another over the top rope; the last man standing wins. André's gimmick was that he never lost battle royals.

By the time I wrestled Dynamite, the crowd was tired after having watched so many matches, but we gave them all we had, every high spot, every bump we knew, ending with a double disqualification or DQ. When we came back to the dressing room, Hito was the first to say, "Fan-tas-tic. This one I never see. No joke." Tom and I both beamed with pride.

Then Harley came up to us, "You two had a great match, but if you go on taking all those bumps, you'll both end up in wheelchairs." With a smirk, Tom said, "You're one to talk, yo' old fook," and we all had a good laugh.

The next morning the crew would be heading to Montana, and there were enough wrestlers that I could have a rare couple of days off. I have no idea how I ended up with Smith, driving André to the Calgary airport. His original flight had been cancelled, which was fine with André, as he didn't mind missing a sold-out show in Butte to have a couple of days off either. But Smith had found a seat on another flight: The problem was that the plane took off in twenty-two minutes, and the airport was forty minutes away. I was in the passenger seat when we picked André up at the hotel, and he squashed himself into the back, rightly protesting, "I'll never make it, boss." Smith stubbornly replied, "We can still give it a try!"

That's when I buckled my seatbelt. Smith drove like an absolute lunatic at speeds in excess of a hundred miles per hour through city traffic. We made the sharp curve into the airport with the speedometer pinned and the car tilted up on two wheels, a hair's breadth away from careening forty feet down off the elevated departure ramp! My yell was drowned out by André's loud roar. When we screeched to a stop, Andre, his big eyes bulging out of his head, was about to explode. I watched my brother march him into the terminal, thanking God I was alive.

"Put your hands up over your head, you crazy son of a bitch!"

I looked up from the passenger seat to see a scowling Mountie with his gun drawn! I slowly put my hands up, then told the officer a slightly embellished story about how my dad had finally let Smith be in charge of some shows and how he had everything riding on getting André on that plane. Then Smith came out, followed by one very angry giant. Smith simply held his hands out to be cuffed.

"On account of what your brother just told me, I'm going to let you off, but so help me God, if I ever . . ."

André's stare burned straight through Smith, and me too, and he never forgave my dad for letting Smith take him to the airport that day.

Meanwhile, the NWA Championship ended up being fought on a high-school wrestling mat in Butte, Montana, that night because the ring never showed up. It was Smith's job to hitch the ring trailer to the van before it left. He forgot. Few champions would've worked without a ring, but Harley didn't complain, he had that much regard for Stu.

After only a few weeks, the big-name attractions of the Stampede card were just a memory, and a good portion of the crew were making plans to try their luck working in other territories. Big Jim Neidhart was playing football again and had been signed by the Oakland Raiders.

At the A4 Club in Saskatoon, a slightly more upscale night spot a few blocks from the Baldwin Hotel, where we usually stayed, I sat down to some beers with Jake, Wayne and a new kid by the name of Terry Sawyer. He was an affable Virginian, a reputable amateur, compactly built, with short arms and legs and neatly trimmed blond hair. He'd done a tour as a medic at the close of the Vietnam War, and when he told me he'd held soldiers in his arms and watched them die, I believed him. Sometimes he'd just stare out the van window into the black night, clearly reliving some hell he couldn't forget.

A scrawny kid approached Jake. "North American Champion, my ass! You don't look so tough to me! I got a hundred bucks says I can take you right now!"

This kind of thing happened to wrestlers all the time, and it was seen as disgracing the territory for the champion to get his ass whipped by anybody, no matter what the excuse. If the situation was unwinnable, a wrestler needed to bluff or call for backup. Jake never pretended to be a tough guy, but we all thought he could make quick work of this kid. Soon enough the kid was following Jake outside to have it out. Wayne, Terry and I didn't bother to get up. "Be over before we get out the door," I said.

Then curiosity got the best of us. We found them in an alley, where our North American Champion was in the process of begging off. Terry grabbed the kid and head-butted him square in the nose, knocking him out cold!

"It's called protectin' the business, Jake!" he said.

After blowing hot and cold for a while, I was now seeing Julie, the girl from Regina, regularly. But because we didn't often stay over there, I could only get together with her at the building while the show was going on. We'd find some quiet place out back. She was nineteen and never wore makeup, and her colouring was spectacular: shaded brown Romanian eyelids from her dad's side and high Assiniboine cheekbones from her mother's side. She blushed like those toy Indian dolls that you see for sale at the airport.

Julie also started bringing her sixteen-year-old sister, Michelle, to the matches. Michelle was tall and thin with those same striking eyes and pouting curl to her lip. The only family members Julie felt really close to were Michelle and Mark, their seventeen-year-old brother. Julie told me that her mother, Marge, had been divorced twice and that their house was filled with lots of half-sisters and half-brothers. She wanted to get out of Regina and maybe look for work in Calgary. One night that summer I told her she was welcome to stay with me if she came, and then Wayne called out, "Bret, you're up." Julie looked like a sad little girl as I got up to leave her.

Tom had booked himself to work a tour for International Wrestling, which was the number-three wrestling office in Japan. Antonio Inoki's New Japan was number two, and the number-one company was All Japan, run by Giant Baba. At the time, he had no way of knowing that Stu was working with New Japan to put together a jointly promoted card to take place in Calgary on August 17, 1979, which was to be broadcast in Japan as a TV special. Tatsumi Fujinami was New Japan's WWF World Junior Heavyweight Champion (the WWWF had just dropped a W for cosmetic reasons), and the plan was for Dynamite to work with him. Now that Tom had booked himself with rival promoters, that couldn't happen. Hito was pushing hard for me to get the big match with Fujinami instead, and I appreciated it. It would open doors for me, and I was confident I could rise to the occasion.

I had this weird dream in black and white. I was wrestling Dynamite at Madison Square Garden. For some reason the roof had caved in. It was pouring down rain, lightning flashed, thunder clapped. The crowd stood drenched, pressed in close, cheering loudly, nobody leaving. Tom and I were dripping with sweat, rain and black trickles of blood. We leaned on each other to hold ourselves up. I threw a hard lifter, and Tom staggered, almost falling. He spun back and slammed one right back into me. The ring had long since collapsed. Ring posts jutted out at odd angles, with the ropes hanging loose. This fight was unstoppable.

A call from Ross jolted me from my sleep. Much to my disappointment, he told me New Japan bought out Tom's International contract, and they wanted Tom to wrestle Fujinami at the show in Calgary. All I could do was hope something else would open up for me.

Tom had a terrific match with Fujinami. Mr. Shimma, a small, Jiminy Cricket–looking guy who was the New Japan moneyman, immediately signed him for a tour of Japan starting in September. The money was great, triple what he was earning with us, and Tom would finally get the big break he deserved. Despite his size, The Dynamite Kid was being touted as the next big sensation in wrestling. I was both proud and envious; what I needed now was an opportunity to prove what I could do outside of my dad's territory.

Then Stu came back from the annual NWA convention, which was attended by promoters from all over the world, with the news that Jim Barnett, out of Atlanta, wanted me to work down there. Stu told him I was keen, but weeks went by with no word, so I began to lose hope that I'd be going anywhere.

Heading into September, Hito and Sakurada got booked to work in Florida. There was no other established tag team for them to drop the straps to before they left, so Keith and I suddenly found ourselves with the belts again. At the same time I was involved in a heated singles feud with Terry Sawyer over the British Commonwealth Junior Heavyweight title. Terry had been a good babyface, but he surprised everyone, especially himself, by being even better as a heel. The storyline was that I accidentally cost him his hair in a match he had with Dynamite—the gimmick of that match being that the loser gets shaved bald—and he turned on me with a vengeance.

Finally Stu heard from Barnett and told me that I was set to start in Atlanta in October. He also put in a call to Peter Maivia, the promoter in

Hawaii, and just like that I was booked for a one-week working vacation before Atlanta—mostly to work on my tan.

But I needed a dramatic exit from my dad's territory; the fans always needed an explanation to cover the wrestlers' comings and goings. So we cooked up the idea that I would drop the British Commonwealth Junior Heavyweight belt to Terry Sawyer in a "loser leaves town" match.

Just as I was getting ready to leave, Julie called. She and Michelle had hitchhiked in from Regina and were at a pay phone by a motel at the edge of town. I was grateful that Jake The Snake had moved out and I had room. On the way over to pick them up, it hit me that I couldn't smarten Julie up as to what was about to happen in the ring because I didn't know what she might tell people. I was so old school, I couldn't bring myself to explain to anyone not inside the business what was going on. The code among pro wrestlers at the time was to kayfabe, which is wrestling jargon for babyfaces and heels not being seen together in public and doing whatever it takes to perpetuate the idea that wrestling is real. It was thought that if the fans knew the matches were a work, it would destroy the business, along with the livelihood of everyone in it.

So when Julie and Michelle climbed into my shitbox grey Caddy, I told Julie that I was about to fight a "loser leaves town" match the next day. I was sure to win, I said, "But if I do lose, somehow, then I might have to leave town for a while." The look on my face said, "I wish I could tell you everything." But I kept my mouth shut. She didn't say a whole lot after that, and she and her sister crashed on my couch like stray kittens.

The following night, I was lying on my belly on the mat at the pavilion with a deep cut above my eyebrow and drops of blood splashing on the canvas. Fans were standing and shouting, some of them telling me to stay down and others urging me to get up. I was thrilled about getting out of town, but I had no idea what lay ahead for me: It was going to be my first time away from home all by myself. On the other hand, I felt terrible leaving Julie, especially leaving her in the dark. The referee knelt beside me and asked, "Is it time?" I looked out at rows of loyal Calgary fans, many of whom I'd known since I was small. "Yeah, stop the match, Sandy. It's time."

6

NOT A BIG ENOUGH NAME

WHEN I LANDED IN HONOLULU, the airline had lost my luggage. I had managed to lose my plane ticket to Atlanta too and had to spend the cash I had to buy a new one. I wasn't about to call my dad and ask him to wire me money; I prided myself on being a son my parents didn't have to worry about. But I did have the phone number of a genuine Samoan prince in my pocket, and I called him from the first pay phone I saw. No answer. Now what? I hung up the phone only to turn and find Prince Sui standing there smiling at me like an answered prayer.

Dean had befriended Sui on one of his many mysterious trips to Hawaii, and then Sui had come up to Calgary to break into the business. He was easily big and muscular enough to become a wrestler, but it turned out he was happier being around the business than in it. In a Hawaiian shirt and a brand-new cherry-red El Camino, Sui reminded me of a happy Neanderthal. As soon as we pulled away from the curb, he handed me a joint. "Light this up, brudda, you're safe with me." I didn't want to offend him . . .

When we got to his place, Sui loaned me shorts, flip flops and a Clark Hatch muscle shirt. Thanks to the Don Ho buffet and training every day, I got up over two hundred pounds for the first time ever. At the end of a week by the blue Pacific, I was relaxed and carefree, skin bronzed and hair wild. On the way to my match, Sui made me promise to have a good one because his entire family and all his friends would be there. He had promised them I was tough, and I sure as hell better be.

In the dressing room I met the legendary Samoan High Chief Peter Maivia, who ran the territory with his wife, Leah. Their son-in-law, Rocky Johnson, was one of my favourite wrestlers when I was a kid. Rocky's young son, Dwayne, hung around just outside the dressing room. Dwayne was destined, twenty years later, to become The Rock, one of the biggest stars in the history of wrestling.

Peter wanted a twenty-minute draw and felt awkward asking me whether I'd mind working heel, but I thought it was a great opportunity. My partner was Kurt Von Steiger, another wrestler I had watched when I was growing up, who was still doing his Nazi gimmick. We were up against Buck Zumhoff and Greg Gagne, son of Verne Gagne. Greg was a decent worker, although — just as they did with me — people said that he got ahead because he was a promoter's son. I set a blistering pace, doing most of the work, much to the relief of Von Steiger. In front of a loud and easy crowd, I discovered how much fun it is to play the part of a hotheaded jerk, and I made the babyfaces work even harder to keep up with me. Back in the dressing room, between gasps for breath, Greg told me I needed to slow down. I went off to shower, smiling.

As I was lathering up, I was startled by Ripper Collins, a squat, pig-faced wrestler with slicked-back white hair. I hoped he was just admiring my tan, but he asked me straight out if I was gay. He shuffled off after I bluntly told him I wasn't. I remembered a sordid incident when he worked Stu's territory a few years back. Halfway through a show in Fort McMurray, he left the building to get gas for Stu's van and picked up a teenaged hitchhiker whom Ripper allegedly sexually molested. The boy managed to fight him off and get away. As Stu described it, "Ripper damn near bit the poor kid's prick off." Ripper was arrested but somehow managed to persuade his naive landlady to bail him out, explaining that it was all a dreadful mistake. She used her house to post his bail bond, but he skipped over the border and was gone by morning. The poor lady lost her house. Ripper died of AIDS in 1991.

Judging by the grin on Sui's face when I came out of the dressing room after the match, he was pleased with how I'd done. I left Hawaii the next day. I often wonder what became of Sui — I have never seen him again. *Mahalo*, brudda.

I walked into the dressing room in Atlanta on October 5, ready to make my mark. Abdullah The Butcher turned in his chair and shot me a look. "I remember you."

As I shook his heavily-jewelled hand, I asked, "Remember the T-shirt I silk-screened for you in art class? Stu let me give it to you as a present, out behind the dressing rooms back in Calgary."

"That was you?"

What I didn't tell him was that when I was twelve years old I was so terrified of him that I couldn't look him in the eye. Abdullah was heavier and older now, but back in 1970 he had moved like a three-hundred-pound cat, flying through the air to deliver an elbow drop that looked like it would kill you. Not long after I'd given Abdullah the T-shirt, I'd sat with my friend Wilk next to the timekeeper watching this giant monster sink his teeth into my dad's bloody head. I'd kicked him as hard as I could, leaving the imprint of my running shoe on the seat of his white karate pants. He had turned his bald, scarred head, rolled his eyes right at me—and had let me live. Wilk just stared at me, horrified.

While I was still talking with Abbie, a wrestler known as Superstar Billy Graham came over to me: Wayne Coleman was six-foot-three, with twenty-four-inch biceps. I remembered him in the dungeon on the mat, where Stu had him clamped in a thread-through with his arms twisted up behind his head, as he was screaming for his life. "Please say hello to your dad," he said. "I'll never forget how much he did for me."

Just then, Ole Anderson, the Atlanta booker, introduced himself and said he needed me for a twenty-minute draw with a French-Canadian wrestler, Rene Goulet. Goulet was working a French Foreign Legionnaire heel gimmick and stood sour-faced with his arms crossed as Ole explained that he needed to see what kind of worker I was. I told myself that I'd get all my moves in, whether Rene liked it or not. He didn't appreciate the liberties I took bumping him all over the ring, but when the bell rang, I knew I'd had a good match.

As I sat undoing my boot laces, I heard Ole's voice on the other side of the dressing-room wall. "Did anyone see Hart's match? Damn, I really wanted to see him work."

The fall weather in Hapeville, a seedy suburb of Atlanta, was beautiful, but I spent most of the time I wasn't working in a basic, furnished room at the notorious Falcons Rest apartments, watching TV. I remember watching every moment of the coverage of the United States embassy hostage taking in Teheran by followers of the Ayatollah Khomeini. I was making less money than I had been at home, even though the houses we played to were full, but all the wrestlers seemed to be in the same boat, most of us staying at the Falcons Rest, sharing rides to the venues when we could.

I was depending on Buzz Sawyer (no relation to Terry), a short, thick, bald kid, my age, with similar ambition, to get me to the shows. At first he'd been helpful, assuming that since I was a promoter's kid I had some clout, but when it became obvious how untrue that was, I'd had to keep my door propped open to catch him as he jogged by my door to the parking lot: He'd intentionally leave me behind just to make me look bad. The last time he'd left me stranded I missed my first town ever. Ole was mad, but not madder than I was.

Suddenly, one day Buzz flashed by my doorway yelling, "C'mon!" and tore off down the hall. I grabbed my bag and ran as fast as I could, but all I found was an empty parking lot—again. I headed over to the phone booth, digging through my pockets for the phone number of Candy, a cute cheerleader who seemed nothing but innocent to me but turned out to be one of a horde of ring rats who hung around the Falcons Rest and came to my room like it was a revolving door, eager to please. I asked her for a ride, and she was only too happy to help me out. When she got there, she insisted that I drive, and at the edge of town, she slid my zipper down and lowered her head. I was twenty-one and single, and I was no more innocent than she was. I tried to keep my eyes on the road.

The next day I was in that phone booth again calling around for a ride. I wasn't supposed to ride with the heels, and none of my fellow babyfaces ever seemed to have room for me. Just as I'd run out of people to call, a Lincoln Town Car pulled up behind me. Ernie Ladd with his big red Afro was hunched over the steering wheel. "You stuck again, kid? C'mon, jump in!" I've always thought it was strange that the heels were usually nicer people than the supposed good guys.

Ernie was a six-foot-nine pale-skinned black man, one of the greatest defensive tackles to ever play in the NFL. Up front next to Ernie was Bobby The Brain Heenan, a fast-talking, crazy-bumping manager with a shock of bleached-white hair. I climbed in back with The Russian Bear, Ivan Koloff, famous for being one of the few guys to beat Bruno Sammartino for the WWWF World title. Ivan said hello in a heavy Russian accent.

"I remember you," I said. "You're Red McNulty from Winnipeg. I watched you have your first match, with Firpo Zybysko, up in Calgary."

He was stunned. Later, he pulled me aside and politely asked me to never tell anyone about that. "Everyone believes I'm Russian." In those days a wrestler became his gimmick. He lived it.

A few blocks from the building, Ernie slowed down to let me out so I wouldn't be seen with the heels, and as I walked along the street, the babyfaces drove past me in their empty cars.

Inside I was surprised to see André the Giant, playing cards with his usual two big bottles of red wine on the table beside him. I extended my hand and said, "Hey, boss!" He ignored me like I was invisible. Thanks, Smith.

That night I was working with Ernie, who said, "Okay, kid, we'll see-saw, seesaw, do the waltz across Texas and then you slip on a banana peel, one . . . two . . . three, ya got it?" What a simple analogy for a wrestling match. Ernie Ladd did all right by me.

When Harley Race came to Atlanta to defend the NWA World Heavyweight title, he took me under his wing, insisting I ride with him. He always bought me a few beers for the drive, and he never let me pay for meals. Buzz couldn't believe his eyes when he saw me riding with the World Champion, and after that I was treated well by everyone. Though, as far as I was concerned, it was too late. I wanted to go home—I wasn't earning enough, wasn't being pushed by Ole and Barnett.

When I called Stu, he told me he could use me any time. He also had news: Big Jim, who had been injured in the pre-season and had yet to set foot on the field for the Raiders, had flown Ellie down to visit him in Reno, Nevada, and he'd proposed. When she said yes, he bartered his Raider helmet for a bottle of Dom Perignon. They were set to tie the knot at Hart house on December 26 unless the Raiders made the playoffs.

As soon as I hung up the phone I called Jim Barnett, who agreed to let me go—a little too quickly, I thought. We decided I'd finish up in early December.

Then Ole's budding star, Buzz, held up the office for more money and when Ole said no, he walked out on him. Afterwards, Ole told me what I already knew. "We had to decide on your first night whether to push you or Buzz, and damned if I didn't miss your entire match. So I went with Buzz and now look!"

That night in the dressing room, Bobby Jaggers, a harmless but outrageous bullshitter and heel, cornered a large rat in the dressing room and happily stomped it to death, which, trust me, was harder than one might think! The Masked Superstar, Bill Eadie, went off on him: "I suppose you're just going to go in the ring now with dead rat germs all over your boots, ya moron."

I'd never seen a rat before, and I don't think I was the only one, judging by the way so many big, tough wrestlers jumped up on chairs!

After the rat stomping, Ole introduced me to Sterling Golden, the territory's newest big blond heel. He had quite a presence about him, standing a massively muscled six-foot-nine and sporting the biggest arms I'd ever seen. As soon as I saw him, I thought, Boy, my dad would love to get his hands on *this* guy! Ole told me to make it short and simple because Golden was green. I hit the ropes, and when I crashed into him it felt like I'd hit a brick wall. I charged again, right into his waiting arms. He squeezed me like an anaconda while I screamed uncle and writhed in agony. After almost being disqualified for not releasing me, he dropped me limp to the mat, dead, like Bobby Jagger's rat.

His real name was Terry Bollea, soon to become Hulk Hogan.

When I was on my way home to Calgary, Hito tracked me down in Chicago, where I'd stopped to visit a friend. He called with big news: Dynamite had been scheduled to wrestle Fujinami for the WWF Junior Heavyweight Championship at Madison Square Garden the next day, but his papers weren't in order; the New Japan office would be grateful if I could take his place. My mind raced: Here was my big break—a chance to wrestle at Madison Square Garden, on a card that would be broadcast across the eastern United States and throughout Japan.

I'd never been to New York before. As the yellow taxi made its way through the crowded, noisy streets it looked pretty much like I had expected it would from TV. I got out of the cab in front of the Statler Hilton hotel, across the street from Madison Square Garden, to find Hito waiting for me. We were immediately surrounded by a mob of Japanese reporters. Hito pulled me close and advised me to be intimidating; being a heel was the best way to get over with the Japanese press. Any fears I'd had vanished, and I was the picture of confidence as I waded into them.

I did one interview after another, posing for photos with a fixed glare on my face and my fists balled up in anger.

When Hito suggested that I go up to my hotel room and rest before the match, I was too pumped up to lie down, thinking about different strategies and moves for my debut in the greatest wrestling hall in the world.

When it was time, I came out of the elevator and strode across the lobby riding high and ran straight into Hito. From the look on his face, I could tell something was wrong.

"You off. No work Fujinami. Vince McMahon say you no big name to work Madison Square Garden. Me sorry." And he handed me an envelope with $500 in it from New Japan.

I was crushed, and Hito felt almost as badly as I did. He invited me to the dressing room, but I didn't want to hang around like a pathetic wannabe. Instead, I went back up to my room, ate some Chinese take-out and flew home in the morning.

Later I found out it wasn't Vince McMahon Sr. who'd given me the thumbs down, it was his son. Not a big enough name to wrestle at MSG? I made a promise to myself that someday I'd go back there and change Vince Jr.'s mind for him.

7

KEEPING IT REAL

WHEN I GOT HOME, everyone was busy planning Ellie and Jim's wedding. Hart house had never looked so grand as it did on their wedding day. The chandeliers were polished and shone so brightly that you could see their glow all the way from the highway. Outside, snow hid the skeletons of the dead Cadillacs. Inside, logs crackled in the fireplaces, a teenaged musician strummed her acoustic guitar, a hired hand in a tuxedo tended bar, and the dining-room table was piled high with hors d'oeuvres. Owen entertained everyone, sprawled on the carpet in the living room, pitting Heathcliff the cat against his arch-nemesis, a stuffed monkey. The three of them put on a fine show, reversing in and out of holds, with Heathcliff's tail pounding on the rug as he tried to think up a countermove.

At last Stu escorted Ellie down the main stairs, and she looked resplendent. When the reverend asked whether there was anybody who objected to the marriage, none of us were going to pipe up: We thought Jim was a perfect match for Ellie, as he was the only man we knew with a personality just as combustible as hers. But Shep, our old, half-blind bearded collie, barked frantically, and everyone laughed. Maybe Shep knew something we didn't.

The whole time I'd been gone, business had been horrible. Art Nelson, from Amarillo, had been doing the booking, and the most boring wrestler on the planet, a big, slow, and arrogant old-timer named Larry Lane, was headlining. They were soon unceremoniously ushered out of the territory. By a process of elimination, I ended up the booker again—Keith and Bruce had gone back to school to get teaching degrees and could only work for the promotion on the weekends. I took it as a personal challenge to get my dad's business back on its feet. Wayne and I worked together on the road, and Ross and my mom ran the office; Helen actually seemed to have built up a tolerance for the business, and was often in the best of moods, fascinated by the day-to-day mishaps and funny stories I loved to tell her. We knew who was coming in and who was going out, and I'd sit with Ross and Stu and book three weeks in advance. It felt like we got the territory organized, for the very first time.

Dynamite was back for a little bit. In Japan he'd shaved his head and built himself an even more chiselled physique. I thought he looked like Pee-wee Herman with muscles. The original British punk had taken Japan by storm, but he wasn't going to be around much for the next while, having been booked for several tours in Japan. Stu had grown extremely fond of Tom, and gave him all the leeway he needed to work in Japan; and Tom repaid him by working harder than anyone else when he was in Calgary. I also couldn't help but notice that Tom was relying heavily on steroids, taking a lot of pills and polishing off a case of beer a night, but in the ring he was magnificent.

Ross frantically searched for talent anywhere and managed to book Steve Wright, a thin, balding English wrestler who had a reputation as a shooter. He'd been taught by Ted Betley, who'd also taught Tom, and we hoped that Wright might be the second coming of The Dynamite Kid. When Tom went to England to work a few shows before heading off to Japan for another three-week tour, he helped us out by booking Giant Haystacks for us, whose real name was Martin Ruane. The seven-foot, 550-pound behemoth, billed as England's version of André the Giant, was due to arrive in February, along with Wright.

I was back in Regina again for the first time at the end of the first week of January 1980. The fans seemed to have missed me, and I realized that I had missed them too. The show was over, and I was zipping up my bag when Gil, the old security guard, leaned his head in the dressing room to tell me Julie was waiting for me. My first reaction was to sneak off. She and her sister had stayed on at my house when I'd left for Hawaii, but they went back to Regina after only a week, and I hadn't heard from her since. After all the girls in Atlanta, I couldn't see that Julie and I had much future, so I decided to tell her to her face that it was over.

The arena was completely empty, and most of the lights were turned off. Julie was sitting on the ring apron. She smiled at me, and I found myself thinking that I didn't need to make any rash decisions.

"So, did you want to see me still, or are we done?"

Someone leaned on the horn of the van to hurry me up.

"If you want to pick up where we left off, we can," I said.

"But I have to go. We'll be staying over next week. We can talk better then."

We did. She told me her life story and I told her mine. Like a Mafia man, I told her to never ask me questions about the business; it was easier for me not to explain and better for her not to know.

The territory was slowly improving. Keith and I held on to the tag belts; Leo Burke, a respected veteran in his early thirties, was our North American Champion, and we'd turned our referee, Sandy Scott, into a great heel, which worked really well because the fans could be easily encouraged to hate a ref. Like a snide headmaster who relished his authority, Sandy was never wrong, even when he was. He never saw the obvious, yet he was a stickler for the slightest infraction. He'd level fines and threaten suspensions, pursing his lips and wagging his finger in your face. The fans grew to totally despise him. Was Sandy on the take, they'd speculate, or was he just a horse's ass? Any reaction from the fans was a good reaction.

Then our two British wrestlers arrived. Steve Wright did have a repertoire of flips and rolls, but unfortunately he was no Dynamite.

Giant Haystacks was a hairy beast, grizzled and ruddy, a grump with a short fuse and a sharp wit. He'd been gawked at his whole life, and he was sick of it. I changed his name to The Loch Ness Monster, and we started to build him. He didn't do much in the ring, but he was hard to take off his feet, and when he laid out one of the Japanese wrestlers with a massive belly flop, the crowd gasped.

One of the cardinal rules for a booker is never to book yourself on top, but we needed someone to pit against Leo Burke for the North American belt: It was me or nobody. Leo was ruggedly handsome in a Burt Reynolds kind of way, and the grin on his face told me he was looking forward to working with me.

In our first match I listened to every word he said: Leo Burke was a wrestler who could elevate me from being a good worker to a great one. We went a full hour, and we both got a bit of a scare when I accidentally almost put him to sleep for real. Stu was all smiles when I came back to the dressing room. A sweat-drenched Leo gave me a happy hug and said, "Beautiful, it was beautiful."

A couple of days before Valentine's Day, I climbed into the van heading for Regina carrying a five-foot-tall Pink Panther, which I set on top of all the bags so it wouldn't get dirty. The boys ribbed me about it all the way across the Prairies. Once the matches were on, Julie and I went out back. I'd wanted to give her a better gift, but she really loved it. At the end of the night when the van pulled away, I had a pang in my heart as she disappeared in my rearview mirror; waving goodbye, holding the big toy like a little girl.

The following Friday, in Calgary, I thought Leo was kidding when he said, "Get your second wind, kid. The fans will never expect us to go an hour again." At the fifty-two-minute mark the fans were standing on the seats cheering us on: the veteran and the youngster in a scientific struggle. The waltz was about over when I slipped on Ernie Ladd's proverbial banana peel. Leo caught me out of nowhere in his finishing move, the sleeper. I slowly sank to my knees and faded into black. The drama was endearing to both the young fans and the old-timers. Harts didn't lose, and when I did it gave me all the credibility in the world.

Meanwhile, Tom had injured his knee in Japan and had come home to heal. When he was working again, I naturally booked him against Steve Wright, thinking the fans would love it, though outside of the ring there was a noticeable coolness between them. Tom seemed more than a little nervous about working with him. Apparently, when Tom was a kid, Steve had made a steady habit of stretching and hurting him. I wasn't sure if Tom was afraid that Steve would mop the floor with him or of what he would do to Steve if he tried. Maybe his biggest fear was of the disappointment that Ted Betley would feel either way. Regardless, we needed the match.

But it ended up being a disaster. For most of it, Steve hooked into Dynamite while he was on all fours; Tom looked bored and made no attempt to even fight back. It was easy to see the immense pleasure Steve took in hurting Tom. At one point, he applied a surf board, a move that consisted of him standing on the back of Tom's knees and hooking his legs, then grabbing Tom's wrists, falling onto his own back and hoisting Tom up in an arch above him. Steve may just as well have taken a sledgehammer to Tom's just-healed knee. Stu angrily approached the apron, pounding his hands on the mat, "I'm paying you to work, not to shoot, damn it!"

We'd been building Loch Ness into a monster heel. He'd had nothing but short, decisive wins and was now beating two wrestlers at a time in handicap matches. He was over with the fans, but not with the wrestlers. A couple of French Canadians griped that they didn't want to work with him because he was too stiff, too clumsy and he smelled bad. I tried to reason with them, explaining that we were short on talent and we'd paid a lot to bring him in, but then had no choice but to tell them if they didn't work with him, they could finish up. I gambled that a hard line would put an end to their complaints—we couldn't afford to lose them either—and it did.

Loch Ness *was* stiff, and he did smell a bit ripe, but it didn't make things any easier when he was constantly beaned with gum wrappers and bottle caps by the wrestlers seated behind him on the long rides. He'd sit there steaming mad, smoking his cigarettes right down to the filter; I felt like a school-bus driver hopelessly trying to keep the kiddies in line.

At one point Loch Ness finally snapped. "I'll kick the shit out of the whole lot of you," he threatened, and he turned, pointing his huge fat finger at everyone in the back row. The Cuban, who hadn't done anything, quickly had his knife out and ordered the van to a stop. In the nick of time, Loch Ness apologized to The Cuban, and that was the end of it.

Then Big Jim came back, billed as the strongest lineman in the NFL. I had kept Loch Ness invincible—until Jim knocked him flat on his ass with some football tackles. It blew the roof off the pavilion.

On the way to Regina, one night at the beginning of March, the wind was sharp as a knife, and the temperature had fallen to forty below. We sputtered to a stop in the middle of nowhere, with a frozen gas line.

I got out and stood in the cold, flagging down cars and trucks. As Wayne got a ride to a gas station to get some line de-icer, I managed to find volunteers to take every wrestler into town but Loch Ness. I could see he was starting to panic, thinking I would leave him on his own to freeze to death. So I stayed, a captain going down with his ship; no heat, no light, waiting for rescue.

To take our minds off the cold, I told him a story about the world famous McGuire twins, more than seven hundred pounds each, who'd come up one Stampede week a few years back. As the story goes, it was a hot summer morning, just after sunrise, when the school bus my dad rented broke down. All the wrestlers climbed out, including the midgets, and pushed the bus down the highway while the driver popped the clutch trying to get the engine to catch. All except Billy and Benny McGuire who, at their size, didn't have the stamina for bus pushing. They were left standing at the side of the road with "Don't worry, we'll be back for you."

The other wrestlers pushed the bus all the way to a truck stop five miles up the road and then went into the café for coffee while the mechanic sorted out the problem.

At that hour, the long-distance truckers were just coming off overnight hauls. One by one they pulled into the truck stop, shaking their heads: "You're not going to believe what I saw back there on the road!" It must have been an eyeful to come upon this massive blob of humanity standing there in the heat, and then a quarter mile down the road, an identical blob!

My breath froze in the air as I said, "That's one good thing, at least we don't have to stand in the hot sun!" And Loch Ness laughed.

He said, "Bret, I just want you to know I appreciate how you stood up for me with those French lads. I won't forget it."

Then a car pulled up and Wayne jumped out, and a few minutes later we took off through the snow, just in time to make the show.

That night, just before the van left Regina for the nine-hour drive to Billings, Julie gave me a kiss goodbye. Tom watched from the van window, and after we drove off, he asked, "What's with that?" I braced myself for the inevitable off-colour remark, but when it didn't come, I told him the truth: that Julie and I sort of hit it off. "I like her a lot, Tom."

I was surprised to hear him say, "I know what you mean. I wish I could find a girl like that."

In Billings, I'd be working with Harley Race, setting him up to defend his World Heavyweight title against Leo throughout the territory when we did the loop in the coming week. (Little did I know at the time that this would be the one and only time I'd ever wrestle for the NWA World Heavyweight title.) For some reason it was assumed I'd go an hour with him, but the question was whether I could, after a five-hundred-mile drive. When Harley and I locked eyes in the dressing room, I could see he was just as beat as I was.

"Don't tell me we're going for a fuckin' hour?"

I smiled and said, "Harley, it's whatever you want." He wanted ten minutes, which was fine with me.

By Friday night of that circuit, the pavilion was completely sold out: everyone wanted to watch Harley successfully defend his title. Business had been steadily climbing. To capitalize on Loch Ness's last two weeks, Keith and I dropped the tag straps to him and Dynamite. For the finish, Sandy Scott restrained Keith as Dynamite dove like a bird across the ring wearing a rugby helmet, no doubt filled with titanium steel, and crashed head-to-head with me. I lay there flat on the mat watching as Loch Ness collapsed on top of me like a house. Not being able to breathe, I felt a sense of panic, and the thought crossed my mind that this is what the French boys had been complaining about. After what seemed like an eternity Sandy dove down to the mat and counted one . . . two . . . three.

The next week the pavilion thundered as Keith and I battered Loch Ness with a barrage of lefts and rights until he flopped into his corner. I headed back to Dynamite in the far corner just as Loch Ness recovered enough to charge across the ring like a runaway train. Tom told me the exact second to move and Loch Ness squashed him like a grape. The crowd became unglued, Keith fell in on all fours behind Loch Ness and I delivered a nice high, drop kick to his chest. Loch Ness reeled, his arms flailing like giant windmills. I hit him with another drop kick and he toppled backwards over Keith, with me diving on top for the pin.

Afterwards, in the dressing room, it was all hugs and handshakes. Loch Ness had worked hard and had a huge grin on his face. Even Tom was pleased.

The next week, with Loch Ness and Wright gone, Stu had a cavalry of American wrestlers arriving, including Kasavubu, The Ugandan Giant. He suffered from diabetes and kidney disease, and every few days he needed to hook himself up to a dialysis machine. Sometimes he was very tired, but he kept it to himself and never complained. He would often relieve Wayne or me for a spell at the wheel, pop in a Marvin Gaye tape and sing softly in perfect harmony. When Kas was with us, he made a habit of looking after J.R. He couldn't stop him from taking the odd nip, but he kept J.R. busy playing cribbage and diverted him with bad jokes, making sure he wasn't quite so drunk every night come match time.

The spring snow was replaced by rain. One night, as the wipers kept time with a Motown beat, Wayne fell into a conversation with the midget wrestler, Cowboy Lang. Cowboy could do great drop kicks and all the other moves just like the big guys, but midgets had always been slapstick. Cowboy said, "We were gonna do a title change, but we couldn't find a promoter who would let us do it." I asked him if there was a belt and he told me Little Tokyo had it in his bag. Wayne and Kas kidded him that maybe Stu would let them switch the title. Cowboy's eyes grew wide when I agreed to actually take it up with Stu.

That Friday night as I drove to the pavilion, I thought about how happy Cowboy would be, winning that tiny World Midget Championship belt. I stopped and bought a couple of bottles of cheap champagne. When he won, all the boys charged into the ring and showered Cowboy with it. He cried during his interview with Ed Whalen, and he was so ecstatic that he poured champagne over his own head.

And there had to be at least one fan who went home thinking, Wow, the World Midget title changed hands tonight!

Each night I wrote out detailed accounts of every match in a small orange notebook; I thought it would be invaluable to be able to look up what worked, what didn't and why and especially to keep a record to make sure I didn't repeat the same outcomes every week. I was really beginning to understand how to structure a card. Never have two disqualifications back-to-back. Keep the broadways, or draws, to a minimum. Go easy on the gimmicks. Use juice only when necessary. Not too many low blows. Never let the fans guess the outcome. Keep it real. Book at least three weeks in advance. Above all, make sure nobody gets hurt for real.

The territory was now filled with a nice mix of old-timers and rookies who enjoyed bringing out the best in one another. Because there wasn't much difference in pay between top and bottom, egos were kept in check, and the dressing room was pretty relaxed. I never asked anyone to do what I wouldn't do myself. I worked hard every night and was honest and direct, and the wrestlers treated me the same.

There were pitfalls to booking, especially as the son of the promoter. People would often put down to ego moves that were really simply protecting Stu's business.

It was Leo who came to me and told me I needed to take the North American Heavyweight title from him, insisting it was in Stu's best interest. The Edmonton fans were on the edge of their seats for the whole match. At the forty-minute mark, I had Leo in a headlock. He called for a reverse abdominal stretch and fired me hard into the ropes. As I came back at him, he threw his arm up to get around me, and elbowed me squarely at the base of my nose. I fell flat on the canvas and rolled slowly over on my stomach, blood flooding from both nostrils. Leo rolled me back and said, "Don't move," and dropped a knee into my face. The beauty of a really great pro like Leo was that all I felt was the faintest touch, and I sold the hell out of it. At the sight of blood in a babyface match, the crowd rallied behind me. Leo worked my nose for the rest of the match, but never once did he hurt me.

When the time was right, he called for the finish. I reversed him into the ropes and he dove over top of me attempting a simple sunset flip, but I fought off falling backwards and dropped to my knees. I hooked his legs and there was no escape. What a beautiful finish, one that I would keep in the back of my mind forever for something special.

In the dressing room afterwards, I looked in the mirror and saw that my top lip was detached from my mouth on the inside. I was worried that I'd lose my front teeth. The commission doctor was useless. He was a little old German guy who picked his nose until his fingernails were caked with blood, and yet he thought wrestlers were uncouth. All he ever did was take your blood pressure to make sure you were fit enough to get in the ring. How you came out of the ring was no concern of his.

At the show in Calgary the following Friday, my eyes were circled with black rings and my lips and nose were puffed out, giving me the profile of a B-52 bomber. It hurt like hell.

I was supposed to have a match with a guy I'd never met. When I first looked at Duke Myers, from Portland, he struck me as a big Elmer Fudd, sitting there smoking a cigarette, wearing some old beat-up white boots and a pair of blue trunks that looked like old underwear. He had a beer belly and a head like a watermelon. When I asked him how long he'd been working, he confessed that he'd recently got out of prison. As it turned out, he was a good worker, with just a bit of ring rust, and we did just fine. I had him in an abdominal stretch, with Sandy Scott ready to ring the bell, when, right on cue, Kas charged in wearing his street clothes, viciously attacking me and slamming me to the mat. He hit the ropes to deliver his flying elbow drop, but his foot caught in his pant cuff and he crashed down, right on top of my face! By the time I was helped back to the dressing room, there was Kas hanging his head while Stu berated him in front of all the boys for not being careful enough. In Kas's defence, I said it was an accident. Stu left it at that. Kas felt awful. A few days later he confided to me that he was having a hard time working; his kidneys were getting worse and he might need to return home soon for a transplant. I was worried about him.

When the van pulled up to the back of the building in Regina, I noticed that Julie's sister, Michelle, was working security for Gil. She was tall and looked way too appealing for her age—she wasn't even eighteen yet—as she opened the big sliding doors at the back and waved us in. Tom mumbled, "I'd shag that." With Tom, it was easier to let remarks like that pass.

Julie and I were at the point where we couldn't stand seeing each other only once a week, and I'd just talked her into moving in with me. I had no idea whether it would last a day, a week or forever. Living with me in my little house in Ramsay didn't mean she'd see me all that much more, when you got right down to it. And Stu had just booked Keith and me over to Japan; I may have been doing well by the family business, but Stu would sacrifice his own interests if there was a chance for his sons to earn more money and make their mark.

I never met a wrestler who didn't believe that the big break was just around the corner, even though for most of us that break would never come. I believed that my best chance was waiting for me in Japan, where it didn't matter how good you were on the mic.

And I guess I hoped that Julie would be able to handle my being gone so much.

8

JAPAN AND THE RISING SON

KEITH AND I WERE PICKED UP at Narita airport in a sleek blue bus emblazoned with a lion's head, the logo of New Japan wrestling. On the bus already was Tiger Jeet Singh, a Punjabi wrestler with menacing eyes, a trim beard and a turban. He was carrying a sword. Keith and I also met a baldheaded black wrestler from New York called Bad News Allen Coage. He'd won a bronze medal in judo at the Montreal Olympic Games in 1976, but he was more famous for once stopping the New Japan bus after André the Giant made an off-colour racial remark and calling André out. The Giant looked out the window and never made a move. Bad News had been trained in Japan and worked there exclusively. He had no sense of American-style wrestling, but there was no denying that even at forty-five years old, he was a lean, mean fighting machine.

We tripped along for an hour in the heat and exhaust fumes, and finally arrived at the Keio Plaza Hotel. The lobby was swarming with reporters and teenaged fans, mostly boys, who seemed terrified of us *gaijin*. Nevertheless, they managed to bow and politely ask for photos and autographs on placards of white cardboard.

My room was on the thirty-second floor and had a magnificent view of the Shinjuku district, Tokyo's bustling centre of business, shopping and entertainment. I slid Julie's picture out of my wallet. She had also given me a small, plush Pink Panther doused in her perfume. I didn't feel the least bit awkward about pressing my face into it every chance I got.

The first show was to be broadcast live on TV all over the country. When we arrived at the venue, which was located many floors above a big department store, the mob pressed in for a closer look. Suddenly Tiger Jeet and Bad News charged the fans and reporters. Tiger Jeet was smashing people over the head with the flat part of his sword, and Bad News was knocking down anyone and anything that stood in his way. No one was actually hurt, though a few cameras got knocked over, and some reporters had to look around for their broken eyeglasses. I got the feeling this scene wasn't unusual, and that the reporters loved their part in the drama because it would be a good story, which was the whole point.

While few of the Japanese wrestlers I met could speak any English, they all understood the English terms for moves and high spots, and they could all call a drop kick or a sunset flip in English; when they worked with Mexican wrestlers, they could even do it in Spanish.

Peter Takahashi, the Japanese referee in charge of foreign crews, was thick and stocky, with a fish face and a flat-top. He was almost obsequious with the big names such as Tiger Jeet and Bad News, but he seemed mildly annoyed by the rest of us. I felt unmistakable dislike for me, or maybe for all big, white North Americans, emanating from behind his eyes as he took me to meet my opponent, a very short, five-foot-three, thick-legged wrestler named Hoshino. Even though I was going over, Hoshino seemed friendly enough. Takahashi told me to go as heel as possible.

Just before the first match, a group of young girls in kimonos climbed into the ring to present us with flowers. Peter ordered me to charge over, rip the flowers apart and chase the girls out of the ring. I did as I was told. And I'd just fallen for an old Japanese ploy designed to tire me out before I'd even started my match. I looked out at the hushed audience, sitting there in silence. Tough crowd, I thought.

I found out in short order what the Japanese wrestlers were all about: Give them an inch and they'd take a mile. Hoshino didn't sell anything for me, and he didn't co-operate with me on anything either. The crowd barely made a sound other than the occasional cough or yell from way up high. I could hear the TV announcers talking a mile a minute at a long table right in front of me. At the end I was so blown up I thought I'd trip over my tongue as I struggled to get Hoshino up for my pile driver. I was merely the first of the sacrificial lambs that night. With the exception of Bad News, the rest of the foreign crew didn't fare any better than I did. I knew I was in for a long six weeks.

The rivalry between the two major pro wrestling companies in Japan—New Japan, headlined by Antonio Inoki, and Giant Baba's All Japan—was fierce. They timed their TV and house shows to compete with each other, and with both promoters in starring roles as top babyfaces, they contracted monster heels from around the world at unprecedented salaries. Both men were considered good and fair promoters. Baba, who was seven-feet tall, was a well-loved but terrible worker, but I never met a classier wrestler than Antonio Inoki. He was a legitimate tough guy, respected by fans and wrestlers alike.

Keith breezed through main event six-man tags working with the top Japanese wrestlers, men who did understand that it was much easier to work with their opponents. I had to deal with the less experienced hands, in Japan collectively called Young Boys. They sported their cauliflower ears as if they were a badge of honour and thought it was good business to break some teeth or wrench a knee. All the better if the broken bits belonged to a *gaijin* like me.

I soon began to catch on. I approached every match as a half-shoot, refusing to sell, and I'd make them look stupid by moving if one of them threw a big drop kick. I was as stiff as I could be. The problem was that the Young Boys were in superb condition because they trained year-round, like members of a professional sports team. Even their sparring sessions were closely covered by the media.

That first week, John Wayne's recent passing was still big news in Japan. They were playing a lot of his movies on TV, and as I watched him swagger across the screen speaking perfect Japanese I wondered what he would have thought of that. One night the phone bleeped. It was Yani, a young friend of Hito's. "Hito ask me show you Tokyo," he said. I grabbed my black cowboy hat just as The Duke was firing back from behind a wagon wheel.

Yani was in his late twenties, and thin with neatly permed hair. He wore a dark blue silk suit, and he bowed slightly as he greeted me, then opened the door to his black Mazda sports coupe. In Japan, the practice seemed to be to drive tiny, shiny cars, very fast in heavy traffic, on the left side of the road. I felt like I was on a spaceship in a *Jetsons* cartoon as we flew past trucks and small taxis, whose drivers wore white masks over their faces to protect them from exhaust fumes. We drove past the Imperial Palace of Emperor Hirohito, a beautiful grey brick castle with a moat, which stood out in stark contrast to the neon that was everywhere. Yani took me to a sushi bar, where we watched sumo on TV. As I watched, I realized it was about more than two fat guys pushing each other out of a circle. It took more skill than I'd thought. For the first time since I got to Japan, I had thoroughly enjoyed myself. I thanked Yani for his generosity by giving him my black cowboy hat.

We were heading north toward Sakata on the bullet train when Bad News announced, "That's Mount Fuji." It was sort of a shock to hear his voice, he was such a loner. I don't think he isolated himself for racial reasons, although he made it clear that he was very Black in his politics and orientation.

Some of the wrestlers were having a kind of cultural discussion across the aisle from me. "I heard they have these bath houses where these gorgeous geishas soap you down and wash you clean with their pussies. They'll suck you and fuck you and do whatever you want." Somebody else added that they were very expensive; whether that knowledge was from personal experience, we didn't know.

After we checked into our hotel, Keith and I went with a Japanese heel wrestler named Waida to a noodle shop. The proprietor was a friend of his, and all the chefs and mama-sans fussed over us while we autographed their white cardboards. There were some turtles as big as army helmets in the restaurant's aquarium. As the owner proudly showed them off to us, I wasn't quite sure what he was saying, but I assumed he was asking me which one I thought was the most beautiful, so I pointed to the biggest one. When we were seated, the beautiful turtle was brought to our table, its legs and head tucked inside its shell. The owner coaxed the turtle to stick his head out, and then, quick as lightning, a cook seized the turtle's head with a pair of tongs, yanked its neck out as far as it could stretch, and cut its throat close to the shell.

Then the owner dribbled blood out of the hose-like neck into a shot glass, edged it toward me and said, "Kampai." I said, "No, thanks." The cooks and the owner laughed and said it was good for "fuckie-fuckie," and they raised their forearms with clenched fists.

"A lot of good it'll do us over here," Keith shook his head.

But Waida smiled, hoisted the glass and downed the blood in one gulp. As for the turtle, they pried it open right in front of us, cut it up and slapped the slices on the grill. I declined my portion.

When I turned twenty-three that July in Japan, Keith told everyone it was my birthday, so all the boys took me out. Tiger Jeet knew a restaurant within walking distance of the hotel, a cozy little place. Before long Waida had the staff surround me, clapping and singing "Happy Birthday" in Japanese. Tiger Jeet handed me a warm, clear drink. It went down easy. My first sake. They told me it wasn't as strong as beer, and so I had another, and another, tossing them back until all I could see were the brown, yellow, and white laughing, spinning faces of Tiger Jeet, Waida and Keith. The next morning I woke up with all my clothes on and my head pounding. An angry Peter Takahashi stood over me telling me I was holding up the whole bus.

We celebrated my birthday four nights in a row.

Every night we worked in a different town, some big, some small, but always sold out. The Japanese I met on the main island were leery of North Americans. If a wrestler asked for directions, people would turn and run away as if he were Godzilla.

We took the ferry to Hokkaido, the north island. Not only were the people there much bigger, they weren't nervous of us in the least. The countryside was also different, with such thick forests that it reminded me of Canada.

We pulled into a tourist stop where they sold carved wooden bears, which are considered to be a sacred animal in that part of Japan. I wondered what they would have thought of Terrible Ted. Outside the shop, I stared into the sad eyes of a miserable Asiatic black bear confined to a small cage. He certainly wasn't being treated as sacred. I also noticed a totem pole, and I felt a kind of kinship with the angry face on the bottom: I was the low man on the pole in Japan. I was glad for Keith when he got the world title shot with Fujinami, in Sapporo, but every night I had my usual struggle. I still couldn't understand why the young Japanese boys couldn't just work. On top of that I was so homesick I was going out of my mind.

One night I went with all the boys to a fuck show. A Japanese girl came out and, when she'd taken her clothes off, she picked a nervous young man out of the audience. She laid him out on a rug and gave him a blow job, to the enthusiastic applause of the crowd. The young man lasted about ten seconds. He'd been sitting with an older man, probably his father, who looked awfully proud. In the main event, a beautiful American girl danced around until her partner, a slender Japanese man, shorter than she was, screwed her on the runway. It shocked me to think what some people will do for a living.

Ever since my birthday hangover, Peter Takahashi went out of his way to find an excuse to ride me about something, but the next day he was even more irritable than usual. When I went up to the front of the bus to ask him whether there might be a chance to pay our respects at the memorial site in Hiroshima, he angrily told me no. Bad News told me Peter's father had been killed in Okinawa during the Second World War, but whether this was the reason for his dislike of his foreign crew, I don't know.

On the surface, Hiroshima seemed no different than the rest of Japan, with fish shops and pachinko parlours where old women sat on stools, tirelessly catching baskets of tiny steelies. But it seemed to me that the blankness in their faces and the coldness in their eyes as they watched the wrestlers rolling by was a cross between sorrow and hate.

The days passed slowly. After long hauls by bus and train from one end of Japan to another, we'd all clump into the dressing room. Bad News would read the lineup sheet taped to the wall and sum up each opponent. "He's good. He's the shits."

One night he casually announced to me, "You've got Fujinami." He was the one Japanese wrestler I'd been longing to work with. Tatsumi Fujinami was well built, with boyish good looks and terrific skills. But the show was outdoors, and the weather was overcast, which made for the tour's first and only dismal crowd. Fujinami told me, "No people today; easy, okay?" And so we went through the motions, doing a short, simple match. The bright lights over the ring attracted huge flying insects, and as we wrestled I could feel them crunching under my back, smearing on my skin like yellow mustard. At one point a giant bug crawled between my boots and in a panic I slammed Fujinami, crushing it flat! We swapped arm bars, and after ten minutes he pinned me.

After that we were back in Tokyo, with a few days off. I was tired of watching samurai soap operas, wacky game shows and vividly violent kids cartoons, so one night Keith and I went to an American movie and feasted on Kentucky Fried Chicken. We saw posters plastered everywhere promoting the big showdown between Tiger Jeet and Inoki at the Sumo Palace, the most sacred wrestling hall in Japan. The posters were typical of the first-rate way that wrestling was promoted in Japan. Often a truck with sirens and music would cruise the streets, barking out the matches on a loudspeaker. (I imagined a time when war propaganda had been broadcast the same way.) The promotion's buses and ring trucks were always immaculate. Shows were on time and well planned. And the wrestling coverage in the daily papers and weekly magazines was an industry unto itself.

Tiger Jeet and Inoki were quite believable together, down to the smallest details of facials, mixing realistic selling with real fury and tight work. Inoki had gained worldwide attention as a result of his boxer/wrestler match with Muhammad Ali in 1975. Ali thought it was a work, but Inoki took it as a shoot. That idea went out the window fast. The black Muslims who were backing Ali made it clear that if Inoki laid a finger on their champ, they would kill him. That's why Inoki lay on his back for fifteen rounds, kicking Ali in the shins so as not to use his hands.

The phone bleeped. I was desperate to hear Julie's voice, and I'd been anxiously waiting for an English-speaking operator. When the call went through, my heart was racing, but when Julie answered I knew right away that something was wrong. It turned out that Keith's girlfriend, Leslie, had implied that Julie was the butt of some sort of inside joke, one that all the Harts were in on, and then proceeded to enlighten her about the true nature of the business—which I had never done, at least not in so many words. And I'd left for Japan so soon after Julie arrived in Calgary that there had been no chance to take her over to Hart house to spend time with my family. As far as Julie knew, Leslie could be right. She was angry and hurt, and no matter how I tried to convince her to stay, she said she'd be gone before I got home. We were through.

An hour later the phone rang again. I hoped it might be Julie, but it was Yani.

Five hours later I was drunk and tripping through the Soapland district of Tokyo with Yani, who was wearing my cowboy hat and grinning from ear to ear. Before I knew it I was lying naked on an inflated mattress, drinking cold beer, watching as a cute, naked Japanese girl lathered herself in soap and slid all over me, washing me with her pussy. I'd set out for adventure, and that it was, but deep in my heart I just didn't give a damn.

When we arrived at the Sumo Palace I was too depressed to appreciate the climax of the tour, even though there was a huge crowd and several TV trucks waiting for us. Since he needed something from me, Peter was suddenly nice to me. He explained that Fujinami had vacated the World Junior title and was moving up to the heavyweight class. I was to put over a rising Korean star, Kengo Kimura, making him the new World Junior Champion. I was disappointed not to be working with Fujinami, but I was flattered that they thought enough of my work to give me a big match. Mr. Shimma hinted at a possible cash bonus.

Kimura was tall and handsome, an Asian Elvis in white trunks who could really work. As for me, after six weeks of hard wrestling, I was as fit as I had been when I trained in the dungeon with Hito and Sakurada. I realized how important the match was when Peter told me not to chase the flower girls out of the ring. A dignitary read from a scroll, and the crowd threw streamers that unravelled in streaming tangles all across the ring. I gave Kimura all I had. In the end, he pinned me with a perfect German suplex, and for once the cheers were loud. As I walked back to the dressing room, Keith patted me on the back and Tiger Jeet winked. "You showed them."

I felt better knowing I'd saved a little face.

Throughout the evening, the Japanese wrestlers kept sneaking over to our dressing room to thank us. After the end of the show—Tiger Jeet and Inoki had a great match—a tall wrestler named Sakaguchi came into the dressing room to pay me: $7,050 in crisp U.S. bills. I was pleased at myself for somehow managing to live for six weeks on an advance of only $450. Sakaguchi congratulated me, laughing and putting his hand over his mouth. "You fight hard, good style, say hi to your father." Mr. Shimma didn't give me a bonus, but he hinted that I would come back.

On the bus after the show we celebrated the end of the tour with giant bottles of Kirin beer, and I pretended to be as happy as everyone else.

Back in my room I felt as forlorn as the little Pink Panther slumped over in my suitcase. I was waiting for Keith to call, but when the phone bleeped it was Julie, telling me that she was sorry.

Just after we hung up, Keith called. "Did you feel that tremor? We just had a mild earthquake."

I had a feeling this wouldn't be the last time Julie would shake up my world.

9

"OH, DAWLING, NOT YOUR NOSE!"

IT WAS TIME FOR JULIE TO MEET MY FAMILY—a big deal for us all because it was the first time in years I had brought a serious girlfriend to Hart house for Sunday dinner, let alone a girlfriend who was now living with me.

After six weeks in Japan I was starving, and as if in answer to my prayer, Stu was cooking prime rib. My mom was in the kitchen wearing glasses and funny pink slippers and a red cotton dress embroidered with small strawberries; the dress had big pockets, one of which contained the huge flat pencil she always kept in her pocket to take messages (the phones never stopped ringing in Hart house).

Mom greeted me with a big hug, "Oh, dawling!" And then she put Julie at her ease and warned her, "Never mind the cats, they're every-where." Stu was leaning into the oven putting the finishing touches on the enormous roast. He wiped his hands on a cloth and made his way over to say hello. I could see him checking her out appreciatively. And I laughed to myself, wondering what Julie must have thought of Stu, who was wearing a bright orange T-shirt that read Maui Waui above a giant cannabis plant. He wore that shirt every Sunday for a year because it was big and comfortable to cook in, and had no idea what kind of plant it was, or what the words meant. When someone finally smartened him up, he never wore it again.

I showed Julie around before dinner, Mom trailing behind us, pleading with me not to show her any of the messy rooms. There were big rugs and heavy maroon leather couches in the living room, and mounted high above the dark wood panelling hung framed black-and-white portraits of every Hart kid taken when we each turned five-and-a-half years old. Wiped clean shiny noses, as cute as could be, the five eldest boys hung over the fireplace. On another wall hung Ellie and Georgia. I was the only kid on a small wall by himself, a picture of pure innocence in a striped T-shirt and cute smile. On the wall to the left of me came Alison and Ross, and farther down the next wall were Diana and Owen.

I scooped up Heathcliff, carried him upstairs and showed Julie what had been the boys' bedroom. Next door, my mom's office was piled high with papers, phone books, the two black telephones, a typewriter and filing cabinets crammed with pictures of wrestlers going back forty years. Then we went down the heavy steel stairs to the basement, and the dungeon, where dumbbells engraved with HART were stacked up along the planked walls. When Julie asked me why there were holes in the ceiling, I said, "If this room could talk—nah, if this room could scream . . ."

We took our places at the dinner table. My mom and dad sat at opposite ends, with all the siblings who were in town, and their significant others, ranged along each side. The prime rib looked perfect, there were bowls of mashed potatoes sprinkled with parsley, fresh green peas and salad. The salad went around first, but I passed on it and reached for the meat. Julie followed my lead.

Ellie sniped at her. "So you're too fucking precious to eat the fucking salad?"

Julie didn't know what to say, and Ellie didn't know when to shut up. I stood up abruptly and said, "We're outta here." As Julie followed me to the car, Georgia was right behind, begging us to stay, then stood in front of my car so I couldn't drive off. After a few minutes, I had calmed down, and the three of us went back inside, took our places and picked at what was left of the meal. My mom apologized to Julie, then said, "Well, now you've met Ellie."

When I'd left for Japan, I'd relinquished the responsibility of booking to Bruce. I'd given him my orange notebook with all the finishes in it, wanting to help him in every way I could. Bruce didn't feel he'd had enough time, or the roster, to show what he could do as a booker in the six weeks I was gone, so I offered to let him keep running things, even though Stu intimated to me that he wanted me to be in charge. Only intimated, because when it came to his children, once they were grown up, Stu rarely came out and told us the way he wanted things to go. But Stu was never too thrilled about the way Bruce ran the show, since Bruce wasn't the most organized guy in the world and he didn't take criticism very well either.

But he did have a vivid imagination, and some of Bruce's ideas worked well. For instance, my brother was the first to introduce theme music for the main matches, picking The Eagles' "Heartache Tonight" to intro himself, Keith and me. Keith, Ross and I all got behind him, hoping he'd surprise us; part of me hoped he'd managed things so well that it would free me up to work elsewhere and make it on my own.

The roster that summer didn't give Bruce much to work with, at least until the Maritimes territory shut down at the end of August. Keith was only working the Friday and Saturday shows, having been accepted to start with the Calgary fire department in January 1981. And with Dynamite out now for knee surgery, Bruce was wearing his World Mid-Heavyweight belt, while I still held the North American Championship, with no real prospects to contend for it.

Bruce's idea of how to carry the territory was to rename Sandy Scott, our heel ref, Alexander, and make him even more of a heel; every night Alexander restrained Bruce by the hair while J.R. and all the heels overpowered him five on one. Bruce ultimately made his own comeback, cleaning house. Stu was stuck out there at ringside gritting his teeth: He didn't have an answer for the incensed and frustrated fans, who couldn't understand why he was letting a ref get away with doing this to his own son. I can only compare it to Ben Cartwright from *Bonanza* standing idly by while Little Joe gets the tar beaten out of him. It was no less awkward for Keith and me to stand uselessly on the apron watching Bruce single-handedly fight off an army of heels. The ref had all the heat, and the biggest reaction every night came from Bruce barely holding himself back while Alexander Scott poked him in the chest.

Each week the calls would come from the accountant letting my mom know they'd lost the usual $5,000, and she'd become distressed all over again at the thought of the family fortune senselessly disappearing into a bottomless pit. There were numerous tearful episodes when she'd plead with Stu to get out of the business, arguing that we had enough to live comfortably. Stu would remind her with quiet sternness, "All the boys, even Ellie and Jim, are making a living in the business. How can I fold up my tent?" After raging back and forth with Stu, she'd take to bed and bottle, and the next week, they'd go through it all over again.

The truth was, my mom was right. Stu had become the conductor of a giant toy train, a runaway locomotive with his sons stoking the furnace. Still, it was the only life my father knew, and he loved it, and he wanted all his sons on board, even at the risk of losing everything. But the money he made from selling Clearwater Beach and the acreage around the house was paying for the whole ride, and soon enough we'd all be broke. Stu contended that he'd bought the land in the first place with money earned from wrestling, and he always reasoned that things would turn around, and when they did there would be plenty for everyone.

I thought the obvious solution was to make Stampede Wrestling pay its own way. I saw this as a pivotal time for all the Hart boys to pull together and save Stu's business, and did my best to back Bruce up.

I was into wrestling now as deep as the razor cuts on my forehead. I worked a series of bloody matches with Duke Myers, doing well enough to carry the territory until some new talent came in. The only other thing that was working was Bruce's frustrating altercations with Alexander Scott. I wanted to do more for my dad, but all I could see was doom and gloom ahead. It didn't help when I pulled up to my ugly house and yanked my bag out of the van one morning that August only to see the mangled remains of the orange notebook I'd given to Bruce scattered all over the floor, covered with chicken bones and garbage. Loose pages blew away right in front of me.

Julie and I were in deep now, but sometimes she'd lash out at me. I thought it was because I was gone so much, so I suggested that her little sister move into my house to keep Julie company. Michelle got a job waitressing at a diner a couple of blocks away, but Julie never got a job, which might have gotten her out of the house and made her feel less lonely when I was away.

By October I finished a good five-week run with Duke Myers, who had turned out to be a hell of a good hand. I stood by the back doors as Bruce defended his World Junior belt against Dynamite, who was back from knee surgery. For the finish, Alexander Scott fast-counted Bruce, costing him the title. Bruce became so enraged, he finally hauled off and decked Alexander. The pavilion shook with the explosion, and Alexander suspended Bruce indefinitely. Even Ed Whalen got all worked up and almost came to real blows with Alexander during their TV interviews.

Finally, by Halloween, we got the dressing room restocked with some fresh faces. David Schultz smiled as he pressed his hand firmly into mine. He was six-foot-four, with a curly blond Afro and a goatee, a slender upper body and big, thick legs. He looked fiery, but his Tennessee drawl was laid-back. "Nice ta meet you, Brit. I'm Dave, but you can call me the Doctor. Doctor D." According to Leo, Schultz was a top heel who could work and talk. For a while Schultz would tolerate taking a back seat to a heel ref who couldn't wrestle, as long as he got his guarantee. And then he would contend with me for the North American belt.

I was working my first match with Iron Mike Sharp. I've dealt with some real crowbars in my time, but Mike was the stiffest wrestler of them all. Of course, he was six-foot-four and he weighed three hundred pounds, so there wasn't a whole lot I could do about it. When he moved on to work with Big Jim, I was more than relieved.

J.R. and Iron Mike did an angle where they challenged Big Jim to a test of strength, with a set of weights that looked heavy but were in fact four-inch-thick circles of particle board encased in rubber. As they pretended to struggle with various lifts, Jim kept winning and J.R. kept scolding Mike. Finally, when Jim went for an overhead lift, Mike attacked him viciously, knocking him backward onto the mat so the "weights" pinned him. Then he clubbed him with a series of forearm smashes that were brutally stiff—it was Jim's turn to find out that Mike was no fun. Several babyfaces came to the rescue, and Iron Mike and J.R. fled the ring; a stretcher was called for, and Jim was carried out. I still laugh when I think about how one scrawny usher hoisted up the stack of bogus weights like pizza boxes and casually walked them back to the dressing room. He looked like the strongest guy in the world, but no one even noticed.

That same night, Kas came by to say goodbye. He told me his brother was going to donate a kidney so he could have his transplant. He asked me to keep an eye on J.R. for him and said he'd call as soon as he could work again. We shook hands. I told him, "Take care, Kas. You've always got a place here." "I know."

That same night the buildup between Bruce and Scott was almost complete. Bruce flew in a lawyer friend of his from Vancouver and gave him the made up name Tyrone McBeth so he could play the role of the President of the NWA. McBeth was planted in the audience awaiting just the right moment to make his move. Scott was poking Bruce in the chest, provoking and daring him in every conceivable way. Bruce was restraining himself, damned if he did and damned if he didn't. The crowd was dangerously close to boiling over when McBeth suddenly climbed into the ring and not only disciplined Scott but lifted Bruce's suspension and ordered Scott to face Bruce in the long-awaited grudge match next Friday. The pavilion went nuts!

Two days before Christmas that year, I silk-screened a bunch of T-shirts to give away as gifts. On the front was a drawing of Hart house and a caption that read, "United we stand, divided we fall." Then I went to a mall and bought Julie a promise ring. I wasn't sure whether I was promising to quit wrestling, stay home, marry her or all three. I've never seen Julie happier than when I gave her the ring that Christmas morning. Then we all headed up to Stu's for turkey dinner.

The world was changing, turning colder, darker, hawks eating doves. John Lennon had been shot, Ronald Reagan was soon to be sworn in as the fortieth U.S. president, new wave was changing to punk and the Hart family was changing too. Ellie was now holding her first-born, a beautiful month-old baby girl with huge brown eyes named Jenny. Dean was back from one of his Hawaii trips; he seemed different, detached and spaced out, but none of us paid that much attention. Keith had started at the fire department, Ross was still working in the office, Wayne was refereeing. Diana and Owen were growing up. Smith was dreaming of promoting a black Antiguan wrestler named Charlie Buffong into a big star of Stampede Wrestling. Our TV show aired in Antigua, and Smith's plan was to launch a wrestling promotion there on Buffong's back, the only trouble being that

Smith didn't have two cents to rub together; Antigua was dirt poor. And worst of all, poor Charlie could barely walk and chew gum at the same time. But over all the Harts were fairly happy that year, and my mom and dad beamed proudly.

Bruce was anxious about his big match with Alexander Scott on Boxing Day, and at Christmas dinner Ross led the charge from the business standpoint that it made sense to somehow let Scott go over. The rivalry was simply way too hot not to capitalize on, and we could easily bring them back for another big show later on, when Bruce would go over. Bruce stubbornly resisted, but was eventually talked into it. The problem was that Alexander's dreadful lack of wrestling ability would be difficult to cover up. Nevertheless, after a year of buildup, thousands of fans had to be turned away at the sold-out pavilion that cold Boxing Day.

Bruce had Sandy, whoops, Alexander, pull out all the stops, including nailing Bruce with brass knucks. Bruce was bloody and unbowed as he battled back. Then J.R. distracted the match ref, which allowed Alexander to boot Bruce in the groin and beat him.

The fans were stunned. I could feel the urge to riot hanging heavy in the air, and we were lucky to get Alexander out of the ring, let alone out of the building. It was as hot as it gets, and we were all proud of Bruce for pulling it off.

"Brit Hart, you punk, boy! You a dog. Your whole family's dogs, gonna git your whole family, one-two-three at a time. I'm callin' you names, boy, but you just sit back hidin.' I'm the greatest rassler to ever walk the face of the Earth, gonna keep walkin' keep talkin' till I walk all over you!"

That was the sound of David Schultz calling me out. Schultz was exactly what the territory needed. He had an intense look that suggested a temper best left undisturbed. Unlike that of the majority of Southern wrestlers, his work was realistic. But his strongest asset was his ability to talk. With never a slip or a stumble, he just drawled right under the fans' skins: "Listen here, Mr. Whalen, I'm the answer to every woman's dream. I'm the Tennessee stud, Mama!"

I straddled a chair in the dressing room and offered to put Dr D. over any way he wanted. "You should leave me laying," I said, but he shook his head.

"Brit, I won't get no heat doing that. I get my heat by barely staying alive, just hanging on. Everyone in the building will know you whupped my ass. That's when I'll screw you. That's how I'll get heat." This was a simple lesson in ring psychology.

Bruce and I worked with Schultz and Dynamite on January 16, 1981, with Alexander Scott as the referee. The match consisted of Bruce desperately fighting back only to have Scott hook his arms so Dynamite could beat him down again. It was getting beyond embarrassing for me to stand in the corner looking useless while Bruce was dying in the heel corner. Bruce finally tagged me in, but not before erupting into his own comeback. I salvaged what I could, and together we hurled Dynamite upside down into Scott's backside. The pavilion came unglued. Schultz and Dynamite both went down, selling, but Alexander was already up screaming at Bruce when I nailed him with a drop kick for another huge pop. J.R. tossed Schultz his thick walking stick and Schultz decked me and Bruce. I could see he hated to toss the stick back to Alexander, but he did what he was supposed to do. Alexander whacked Bruce across the chest. Keith ran in and Stu was quick to follow, but all the Harts were soon overpowered. That was enough for the hard-core fans, having watched us Hart boys since we were kids: They hit the ring one after another.

Suddenly it all got very real. Dynamite drilled one fan squarely in the eye, lunging at him like a pit bull. Schultz was a flurry of fists, seizing the stick from the terrified Scotsman and clubbing fans over the head with it until it broke in half. The Harts fought the heels off, the ushers shielded Alexander, while Dr. D. and Dynamite stood back to back using what was left of the stick to fend off the mob!

By the time I got to the dressing room, Sandy was white as a ghost and a pissed-off Schultz was telling Stu that if Bruce potatoed him one more time, he'd knock his lights out. It was plenty hot both in and out of the ring! I felt bad about the fans getting hurt, but as far as the heels were concerned, they were only acting in self-defence.

That fall Tom had moved in with Wayne, who'd bought into a fourplex only three blocks from my house. Wayne moved into the basement and rented Tom the more spacious upper level. The new place was conveniently only one block from the diner where Michelle waitressed, and Wayne and Tom took to eating there regularly. All it took was one look at Tom's face as he gazed up at Michelle to see he wasn't there for the food. As I gave Wayne a lift home one night, he let slip that seventeen-year-old Michelle was coming around to their place to see Tom.

When I got home I told Julie, who became distraught, since she was fully aware of Tom's proclivities. She was afraid Tom would use Michelle and then toss her in the discard pile. Before I knew it, I was standing on Wayne's doorstep in the cold of night ringing the bell, while Julie waited in my car. When Wayne answered, I could see Tom and Michelle sitting together on the couch watching TV. I met Tom's stern look with one of my own, and we had a heart-to-heart on the porch. When he told me he really liked her and his intentions were good, I believed him.

Tom was looking as fit and strong as I'd ever seen him, 210 pounds, with hard ripped muscles that twitched as he laced up his boots. Now that his knee had healed, he was getting ready to re-establish himself in Japan. No matter how good he was, Dynamite suffered horribly from small-man complex: He was touchy about his position and always eager to make the point that he was the toughest and meanest of us all. And he was jealous of the attention that Alexander was getting from the fans.

So Tom had Sandy over for dinner and spiked his hot chocolate with ExLax. By Monday morning our top heel was too sick to travel, and he phoned Stu and told him that Tom had shoo-flied him. Tom was furious that Sandy had grassed on him. Two days later, when Sandy was getting into the van, Tom drilled him in the mouth, breaking his false teeth. More hurt than angry, Sandy blinked back tears, got in his car and drove off. Sandy never got over being attacked by Tom, and within a few months he was gone from the promotion, never giving Bruce his rematch.

Physically, Tom ended up coming out much worse than Sandy, breaking two knuckles in his right hand. As well put together as Tom was, he had brittle bones.

That night in Red Deer, Schultz was in a jovial mood after decisively beating almost everyone in the dressing room at arm wrestling, even Iron Mike and Big Jim. Then Tom casually flicked a cigarette across the room and said, "I'll try ya, David, but it'll have to be left-handed." Some of the world's ugliest mugs circled the table as Tom and Schultz took forever posturing for a fair grip. "Go!" J.R. shouted. Their faces twisted red, blue veins popped, flexed arms locked in struggle. To everyone's disbelief, Tom slowly forced Schultz's hand to the table. Schultz begged him for a rematch, but I could tell by the smirk on Tom's face that it would never come.

The following week, I was standing at the dressing-room door watching the matches with Stu. A tall, wiry kid from Edmonton came up to him and enthusiastically inquired whether Stu would consider teaching him to wrestle. Stu sized him up and actually took some interest in him. The kid went on to explain how he knew he had what it took, and then, out of nowhere, he wound up and drilled himself right in the face, collapsing to the floor in front of us, catching both me and Stu off guard! Just as suddenly, the kid jumped back up to his feet grinning, "See, I can act! I can really act!" From the way he licked his lips it was obvious that Stu would love to get his hands on this smartass.

"If you're interested," Stu said, "you could come see me in Calgary." The next day that's exactly what the kid did.

After Stu, Ross, Bruce and I had wrapped up the usual Sunday booking session, I headed to the basement, where I found Tom working out. Just then Owen brought the kid from Edmonton down to the dungeon, and Tom and I immediately kayfabed each other. I backed away from Tom, making it clear that I wasn't about to turn my back on my old enemy, but that sometimes enemies do cross paths. Things as subtle as that were all it took to keep a mark from getting smart.

Then Stu came in wearing his baby-blue wool trunks, and his eyes lit up like an old lion seeing his quarry. The kid called out with a goofy grin, "Ready for me, Stu?"

Soon they were bulling around on the mat. "Drive!" Stu ordered. The kid pushed as hard as he could, but Stu was still pretty tough to move. Then suddenly Stu pulled him down to the mat with a thud and a groan. Even at sixty-six, Stu still weighed easily 250 pounds, and once he was on your back, good luck getting him off.

Owen wandered in with an old tape recorder and recorded the young guy's horrific pleading screams. The tape remains as a testament to how real it was down in Stu's basement. To say that Stu was annoyed with this pushy kid would be an understatement. He punished him so severely that when the bawling started, I'd seen enough and went to chat with my mom and Diana. We could still hear the screams from Mom's office, two floors up, though Diana seemed oblivious to them. She was shuffling through photos of a handsome young wrestler from England who wanted to come over, mesmerized by the sight of him.

"He's Dynamite's cousin," she sighed, a teenager with a crush. "I can't wait until he gets here!"

When the screaming stopped, I went back down to the basement and found only Tom, who'd thoroughly enjoyed the show.

"So, your cousin is coming over?"

"Is he what? If you got that fook comin' over here, maybe you can do without me." I was surprised that Tom was so opposed to Davey Boy Smith coming to Calgary.

When I went upstairs, there sat Heathcliff on the back porch, feasting on a mouse he'd caught. It struck me that his expression was curiously similar to Stu's, who was at the kitchen table stirring a cup of tea. All that was left of that little mouse were the back legs. At least Stu let the kid crawl out on his hands and knees.

Tom phoned asking whether he could catch a lift from Calgary to Regina in my car, instead of us all going in the van. He was leaving for Japan soon, and he thought it might be nice if we brought Julie and Michelle along. On that thousand-mile drive, we all got a little closer, I thought. Michelle brought out a playfulness in Tom that I'd never seen.

When we pulled up to the back of the building in Regina, Tom ducked down and hid under our coats so none of the fans caught us together. There was going to be a decent house on hand to see me exact some revenge on him for costing me my belt. It would be our first "ladder match." The concept was actually conceived by Dan Kroffat, a smooth-talking protege of Stu's who had Robert Redford looks. He and Tor Kamata, a pear-shaped wrestler who was born in Hawaii and whose parents were Mexican and Chinese, sold out the pavilion with the first ever ladder match in the summer of 1975. The current storyline between me and Dynamite was that J.R had wagered the sum of $5,000, which would be hung in a canvas bank bag high above the ring. Whoever could climb the ladder and grab the money first would be the winner.

When the bell rang, Dynamite and I tore into each other so ferociously we soon spilled out onto the floor. I slammed his head into a steel chair, and although he had his hands out for protection, he hit that chair a lot harder than I thought he would. His head bounced back. I tried to turn away, but our heads smashed together, splitting open the back of Tom's head and shattering my face. I knew it was bad when I was able to poke my baby finger through a gaping hole in the side of my nose!

Dragging him by the hair, I tossed him back into the ring and pounded him down to his knees with my fists. He clung there, like in a real fight, helpless and reeling. I always thought I threw realistic working punches, but the art was also in the believable way Tom sold them.

I asked him how bad my nose was as I pulled him up from the floor.

"Ooh fook, it's bad!"

So much for my promise to my poor mother that'd I'd never break my nose. The wrestling business was filled with broken promises.

Both of us were covered in crimson, and the frenzied crowd was filled with blood lust. I remember Tom jumping up high, gripping that heavy steel ladder and coming straight down on my head. I froze. The crowd gasped. Tom was such a pro that the ladder had only lightly brushed my forehead. Naturally I sold the hell out of it. Over and over we tried to climb up the ladder only to come crashing down. Finally, I had him right where I wanted him. We timed one of our collisions with the ladder to knock out the ref. I struggled up to my feet ahead of Dynamite, but then Foley whacked me across the back with his heavy walking stick. The ref came to as Dynamite crawled to the ladder. The crowd noise was ear-splitting. Tom climbed to the top, his fingers about to grab the money, when I threw a perfect desperation drop kick, just like he'd asked me to do. "Just barely touch the ladder with your toes, I'll control how I go over."

Sure enough, the ladder wobbled and tipped. and with perfect timing. Dynamite leapt off, straddled the top rope and bounced up and out of the ring, landing right on top of Foley. I stood that big steel ladder up and began my slow climb to the money, wondering why I was doing all this for a lousy fifty dollars. With every step I realized that the blurred mass of faces screaming as one truly believed in me, and that's when it struck me—this is why I do it. With blood dripping from my nose, I yanked the sack down and blew the roof off the place. It was so loud that I could not hear a single sound but the beating of my own heart. People forever ask me what my greatest match was. It may very well have been the night of the ladder match in Regina, Saskatchewan, in 1981.

Tom and I got stitched up at the Pasqua Hospital, which was only a block away. Then we drove home with the radio down low so Julie and Michelle could sleep in the backseat. Each time I glanced into the rearview mirror, the black around my eyes was bigger and darker. Every once in a while Tom and I would look at each another with a silent acknowledgement that we had just worked our greatest match. When I think of it now, a quote from Georges Braque comes to mind: "Art is a wound turned to light." To my mind, that is also the beauty of pro wrestling.

When I went to pick up my weekly cheque from my mom the next day, I was doing my best to hide my face, keeping my baseball cap pulled low. But she broke into tears, "Oh, dawling, not your nose!" All I could do was wrap my arms gently around her and promise that it would be all right.

The New Zealand promoter Steve Ricard had seen a tape of the one match I had in Hawaii and had raved about me, back in December, to Leo. Leo thought it would be a good place for me to go to work, and said he could get me a guarantee of U.S.$1,000 a week, with all my transportation paid. He said I'd stay in the same hotel in Wellington the whole time I was there and that the longest drive to each of the venues was no more than a couple of hours. Part of me longed to get Julie away from Calgary to someplace where we could spend more time together, and I thought in New Zealand I could make that happen. I'd asked Leo to call Ricard on my behalf, and then I bought Julie her plane ticket; she'd arrive two weeks after me, giving me enough time to find us a little apartment and scope out the scene. I was booked for six months.

The night before I was to leave, as we lay together in bed, she kissed the stitches on the bridge of my swollen, puffy nose. My eyes were encased in black fading to purple and yellowish brown. Dried blood soaked through a bandage covering that night's razor slice on my forehead, like an empty box frame for X's and O's. I had this fantasy that maybe Julie and I would never come back from New Zealand.

In the dressing room in Wellington, just off a twenty-one-hour flight, I met Steve Ricard, a stocky, middle-aged man with curly orange-and-grey hair. "I know you're tired," he said, "but I need to see how good you are, mate, now, before I do my TV." He said I'd be wrestling him for a one-hour draw in that evening's semi-main event; like my dad, he liked to assess his talent first-hand. By the end of the match, a beaming Ricard hugged me and welcomed me aboard. He told me I was going to be a top babyface and that they'd build their TV shows around me. Ricard was the only promoter who ever saw anything in me the first time he laid eyes on me, and, strangely, he's the only promoter I ever walked out on.

A week into the tour, I realized that I'd seriously misunderstood Leo and that, though the drives between venues were never more than two hours, there was no home base, no place where I could come back every night and be with Julie. I called her and told her to forget it: I had to be there for six months, but there was no point in her even making the flight. "Just stay home," I told her, and listened to her stunned silence.

Would she even be there by the time I got back? Who could blame her if she wasn't?

A week later, the tour came through Auckland. I pulled aside a bushy-haired Greek kid named Con, who wrestled for the promotion, and asked him to drive me to the airport. He hesitated, fearful he might get fired, but we piled into his car and I made my escape just as the door of the plane was closing. I hated to run out on Steve, but I decided to put my love for Julie first. I left him my cheque for the two weeks work I'd done and hoped he'd understand.

I rang my front doorbell. When Julie pulled the door open, she wore the biggest smile I'd ever seen and wrapped her arms around me like she'd never let me go.

The following night I decided to drop in at the pavilion while the show was on to say hello. To anyone who asked, I simply said that things didn't work out for me. Smith appeared in the dressing room with Charlie Buffong; the poor guy had wrestled with Dynamite a couple of weeks back, and Tom had soccer-kicked his head for real and broken his jaw. Charlie had just had his jaw wired and was out of commission for a while. He was carrying a strange little figure with him. It had red sewing pins stuck in the eyes and bits of actual hair, clothing and wrist tape stuck on it—all Dynamite's as it turned out. Charlie had wrapped bright orange electrical wire around the legs, and impaled one knee with a giant diaper pin. He painfully mumbled to me that this was a voodoo doll and he'd put a curse on Tom to injure his knee.

The next morning, Tom called from Japan looking for Michelle, and was surprised to hear my voice on the line. "What are you doin' back so fast?"

I told him it was a long story and asked him how things were going for him in Japan. I could hear the pain in his voice when he told me that he had blown his other knee out the night before. I decided not to mention Charlie Buffong's voodoo doll.

10

THE COWBOY SEES THE WORLD

TOM DIDN'T GET BACK FROM JAPAN until May 1, 1981. He not only managed to finish the tour, but he stole the show. He worked on live TV with a small, sensational masked wrestler, Satoro Sayama, known as Tiger Mask. Between the two of them they set new standards of fast-paced, high-flying razzle-dazzle. Shimma not only gave Tom a nice fat bonus and booked him for more tours, but he also paid him in cash for his knee surgery (which Tom then had done for free in Canada). Compared to the rest of us, Tom was rich.

A few days after Tom got home, Julie and I looked out the front window as a not-quite-new olive-green Eldorado pulled up in front of our place. Out stepped Michelle, decked in black leather boots that came to mid-thigh and a mini skirt. She was growing up fast.

Tom's cousin Davey had arrived from England and was staying at Tom's place. When Michelle told me that Tom was shoo-flying Davey and all he did was run to the toilet, I knew that I had to go rescue him. Davey was a shy, skinny, simple-hearted kid with big dimples. Only eighteen years old and lucky if he was 170 pounds, he was handsome; I could see why Diana gushed all over his pictures. His first mistake was assuming Tom would treat him like a little brother. When I got over to Tom's place, I told him that Stu wanted Davey to stay with me since he and his cousin would be working together and they needed to kayfabe.

That Sunday all the wrestlers played a charity baseball game with a local radio station in exchange for a couple of free plugs. Tom explained it as best he could to Davey: "It's, erm, like rounders, Bax," calling the kid by his childhood nickname, short for Baxter.

Tom, not surprisingly, played well while seemingly not even trying. Davey blindly struck out every time up. It would have been hard not to notice Diana cheering him on from the bleachers, and when he glanced up at her as he came up to bat the next time, I realized he really didn't want to strike out in front of her. Davey looked down at the bats lined up on the grass, unsure which to choose. Bruce raised an eyebrow and in an encouraging voice said,

"Why don't you try one of these left-handed bats, Davey," as if there was a difference because of the way they were facing. Davey grabbed one of the bats, thinking he finally had the right one, marched up to the batter's box and blasted the first pitch out of the park! As he rounded third grinning from ear to ear, he yelled in amazement, "It was the fooking bat the whole time!"

That was just how Davey Boy was.

But one thing was for sure; you only had to show him how to do something a couple of times for him to get the hang of it. He was an excellent athlete and a fast learner. Now that he was living with me, his weight was coming up, and he was smiling all the time. This naive little kid from northern England had found a home.

"Hey, Bret," he said after the game, "I'm goin' to catch a lift with yer sista, Diana."

At the end of May, Davey Boy was to wrestle Dynamite for the World Mid-Heavyweight title in Regina. Though Davey was living with me, Tom had earned Davey's trust by giving him some old gear he didn't need any more, and as the days had gone by and Davey saw what his cousin could do in the ring, he was more and more in awe of him. Sometime during that month, Tom also turned Davey on to steroids.

Tonight Tom decided it was Davey's time to get some juice.

Davey said, "I've never done it before."

Tom blew him off like it was no big deal. "Fook, I'll do ya. You'll not feel a thing, just a pin prick."

I pulled Davey aside and said, "Never let anyone cut you, ever. Do it yourself, or don't do it at all. This business is all about trust, and you can't trust him." Davey went back to Tom and told him I said he shouldn't do it. When they both came to me, I reluctantly told them it was up to them. Davey looked back and forth between us. Finally he said to Tom, "You won't hurt me, right?"

I watched them from the back wall by the dressing-room door. They were fantastic together. Davey, also taught by Ted Betley, had already picked up a lot of Tom's moves, and they were bursting into beautiful English-style routines, leaping and diving over and under each other until Dynamite stopped Davey cold with a stiff knee in the gut. He tossed Davey out of the ring, ran him into the wall not ten feet away from me, reached into his trunks and pulled out wrestling's newest novelty item, a scalpel blade. When Davey rightfully panicked, Tom grabbed him in a choke hold, and with Davey fighting and squirming to get away, he drove the blade into Davey's head, cutting him to the bone. Davey jerked to one side and the blade sliced halfway around the top of his skull! It looked like someone poured a bucket of thick red paint over his head. I was certain that without immediate medical attention, he'd bleed to death. I dashed over and threw Davey's arm over my shoulder, first running with him and then carrying him the short distance to Pasqua Hospital. The familiar doctor hurried to stitch him up, asking in a disgusted tone how it happened. Davey started telling him about brass knucks, but I cut him off with the truth. "The wrestler he worked with took a razor blade and tried to cut the top of his head off."

In the van on the way home, Tom and Davey sat together drinking beer. "You shouldna fookin' moved, Bax!" Tom said.

"Sorry, Tom."

The simple truth is, Tom got away with a lot because he was good for business.

Stu was the longest still-active member of the NWA, having signed up back in 1948, but nevertheless at the end of May that year, he got a call from the organization informing him that their newly crowned champion, Dusty Rhodes, couldn't be spared for Stu's annual Stampede show. Needless to say, Stu was disappointed; he'd always got the champion before. But he put in a call to Verne Gagne and booked the AWA World Champ, Nick Bockwinkle, instead.

Schultz should have been the one to take on Bockwinkle, but he argued that it made no sense for him to lose all his heat to a champion from another territory who'd basically beat him and leave. So Stu, Ross and I decided I'd get to work with Bockwinkle instead. This was fine with me, as it was a childhood dream come true for me to work with the World Champion on the big Stampede supercard.

In the weeks leading up to my big match with Bockwinkle, I was filled with nervous anticipation. On the night, with no parking on the Stampede grounds, I simply walked over to the venue from home with Julie, Michelle and Wilk. I'd come in late from the previous night's road trip, having celebrated my twenty-fourth birthday in the van, with nobody making any fuss. I'd had to be up by 5:30 a.m. to be in the Stampede Parade, where I sat between Bruce and Keith, along with Owen and Georgia, in an open convertible waving at people lining the streets on an unusually hot morning. Most of the day was taken up with media events, where my father proudly introduced me and announced that I'd be taking on the World Champion.

By the time I'd carried my bag and Stu's famous black-and-red ring robe up the steep steps of Scotsman's Hill, the temperature had soared well into the nineties. I stood at the top soaked in sweat and smiling at the view of Stampede Park as a rush of memories came back to me. The whole carnival scene of swirling neon took on a magical feeling as I told myself it was time to live a dream. I had a lot on my mind as I descended the steps toward the pass gate. At the bottom, suddenly Julie was really upset with me, she said, because I was walking too far ahead of her. I was thinking, Please, not now.

Before I knew it, she'd pulled off her promise ring, threw it past me and stormed off, Michelle behind her. Wilk and I looked at each other dumbfounded as I scanned the area trying to find the ring. I knew Julie would later be upset with herself for acting this way; she always was. With people wandering all around me, I took note of the precise area. I'd have to look for the ring after the show.

The dressing room reeked of bullshit from some of the finest beef in the world—and I don't mean the wrestlers. The big Brahma bulls were stabled in the same building as us for the Stampede. Heinrich Kaiser, a German promoter, was there scouting new talent to work for him in September. Stuffy and autocratic with neatly trimmed silver hair and thick tortoiseshell glasses, Kaiser sported the biggest diamond ring I've ever seen.

Tom was talking over his title match with Keith. Davey Boy looked like he was ready to burst into tears, crushed to find that he was wrestling a pal of Bruce's whom Bruce had dubbed Mandingo The Wildman of Borneo; he was barely a wrestler at all and came into the ring devouring raw beef kidneys. Bruce chatted with Jochem, a friend he'd met in Hanover. Six-feet tall and wiry with long, dark hair and a squared-off beard, Jochem bore a distinct resemblance to a Civil War general. His profession was no less colourful—he was a homicide detective who happened to be a big wrestling fan. He had a deceptively friendly and unimposing face, which, I suspected came in handy for a cop. Jochem was on vacation, but Bruce was about to put him to work.

Since Sandy's departure, Bruce had become obsessed with trying to recreate another heel ref. It didn't matter to him that Jochem had no ring experience whatsoever. He called him Jergin Himmler, and just like that the eager and willing fan was now a heel referee.

I smiled on seeing the midgets again. Sky Low Low, now sixty-five, was surely the greatest midget wrestler of all time. He stood thigh-high as I shook his hand, his stubby fingers like tiny sausages. Sky's face was that of a baby combined with an old man; he looked exactly like he did when I was a kid. When I was about five years old, my dad stopped on the way to the matches to pick the midgets up at the Royal Hotel. They climbed into the back seat of the big limo, where Dean and I were sitting. I asked an ugly guy called Little Irish Jackie whether he wanted to wrestle me. He quickly clamped his short fat fingers on my knee really hard, and I cried out. Dean slipped on a friendly headlock, which only got Irish Jackie madder. Jamaica Kid, a black midget, nudged me with his knee to try Jackie one more time, while Sky Low Low and Little Beaver laughed their heads off.

Lou Thesz, six-time NWA World Champ, was standing talking to Nick Bockwinkle. Thesz was sixty-five too and looked great, though his black hair was thinning and his cauliflower ears were the size of doorknobs. He was the special guest ref for the world title match. Bockwinkle, more than twenty years older than I was, looked smooth and athletic just lacing his boots up.

I sat down with him to give him the outline of the match. We'd basically do a sixty-minute draw, or broadway, with Foley sneaking out in the dying seconds and ringing the bell with his steel-tipped cane, costing me the world title. The next week Nick and I would come back for a rematch with a ninety-minute time limit. Nick said fine.

The crowd was surprisingly vocal considering the suffocating heat, and the fact that there had been eleven matches ahead of us. I was more than grateful for the thunderous ovation they gave me when I came out wearing my father's robe.

I'd given him the outline, but as a bona fide World Champ, Nick called the match. A champion never allowed a greenhorn to take control. To a champion, the belt was more than real. With his reputation at stake, he needed to always be braced to protect and defend it at all times during a match, whatever the cost. Things can happen. Wrestling legend had it that Bruno Sammartino tossed Buddy Rogers over his shoulder in an upside down bear hug only to have them ring the bell on Rogers, screwing him out of the title. Of course, Bruno always professed that Rogers was in on it, but even to this day, I'm not sure.

After fifty-eight minutes I was sunk in deep with an abdominal stretch, with no chance that Nick could reach the ropes. Every fan was standing, and it didn't hit them at first when J.R. rang the bell, ending the match. When J.R. entered the ring, Thesz peeled off his striped ref's shirt, knocking J.R. on his ass with a nice elbow smash for the easy pop.

In the dressing room I dripped a huge puddle of sweat, praying I'd have enough energy to do it all again the next night in Edmonton.

Julie was there with Wilk to walk me home. Who could figure her out? I was too tired to be mad and just wanted to go home. When we got to where she'd thrown the ring away, she frantically clawed through the grass. I was amazed to see a glint in the grass and nonchalantly bent to pick the ring up. I actually wasn't sure what I wanted to do with it, and didn't mention that I'd found it. But Julie was so depressed on the rest of the way home I finally handed it back to her.

I made the drive up to Edmonton the next day with Davey Boy and went another full hour in the ring with Bockwinkle.

Lou Thesz asked whether he could ride back with us, and we had a long and fascinating talk. He told me that the business was a total shoot until about 1925. At a time when Jack Dempsey was knocking everyone out in a couple of rounds and Babe Ruth was smashing the home run record in baseball, the average world title match often lasted five or six hours and ended in a stalemate. Ed Strangler Lewis, Thesz's mentor, was impossible to beat, so he eventually worked a title loss just to pump some new blood into the business and make a nice payoff—and that was when it had all changed.

Lou told me that every wrestler on a card in those days knew how to wrestle. The difference in the business was that the wrestlers always had respect for each other based on their actual wrestling ability and toughness, but nowadays the fans, promoters and too many of the wrestlers didn't even care about that. By the time we hit Calgary at around four in the morning, I was toast yet totally full of excitement. Then a car was coming at us, hard. In order to avert a broadside collision, I slammed on the brakes, missing the other car by inches. By the time we pulled up to a red light, there were six guys drunkenly sneering at us.

Davey called out, "Where'd you fooking learn to drive?"

That was all it took. In seconds Davey and I were out of the car teaching these drunks a lesson. As we sped away afterward, I felt a thump under the back left tire and hoped I hadn't driven over somebody's leg.

I apologized to Lou, but he wouldn't hear it. Instead he told me he was sorry for not helping us. "Sorry, boys. These days I fight with my head, not my fists."

Throughout the rest of the summer of 1981, I had some fantastic bloody brawls with Schultz, who was kind enough to take me under his wing and teach me all he could about heel psychology. Schultz would barely stagger back to the dressing room, his blond hair streaked red, clutching the belt in victory, leaving me standing in the ring, having lost yet again—with every fan in the building believing I was the rightful champion. I was over strong thanks to Schultz.

Mr. Shimma wanted me in Japan again, with Dynamite, for six weeks starting the next January. And Kaiser, the German promoter, was so impressed with my matches with Bockwinkle that he booked me, Big Jim Neidhart and Adrian Street, a five-foot-six, stocky, bleached-blond wrestler who worked a fag gimmick with his valet-girlfriend Linda, to work a sixty-day tournament in the fall for U.S.$1,000 per week. Tom told me he was going to head home to England in November and said he'd call Max Crabtree, the

U.K. promoter, and book us there after Germany; the money wasn't great in England, but we could bring Julie and Michelle with us.

As the summer of 1981 came to a close, I recall a bunch of us working out in Stu's basement after the usual Sunday booking meeting. Jim was dripping with sweat. Tom and Davey were lifting really heavy now. Tom could easily bench press 450 pounds, and "little Davey," who was spotting him, wasn't little any more. With the help of steroids he'd gained twenty-five pounds in a few months and was now more than two hundred pounds.

Stu brought Karl Moffat down to the basement, a baldheaded biker who'd jumped out of the crowd to attack Adrian Street at one of the matches a while back. Stu reminded me of an old lion bringing a rabbit to his cubs to practice on. Karl wanted to break in to the business. Stu left to take a phone call and Jim eagerly clamped Moffat in a headlock, rolled up against the wall and nearly pulled his screaming head right off his shoulders.

After we'd had our fun, Karl crawled out of there, and I remember thinking on that particular afternoon, we were all happy. There were decent crowds that gave the illusion that business was good despite the fact that the overhead was so high that there was no profit. Still, there was a sense that things would get better. Bruce had what he always wanted: control of the book. Everyone was paired off. Tom was in love. Diana was head over heels for Davey. Even Jim and Ellie were close. As for me, I was about to see the world, with Julie by my side.

Julie and I flew to Hanover along with Jim, Ellie, and ten-month-old baby Jenny in October. Jochem, the steely homicide detective with the big heart, met us when we landed. He'd fallen in love with Canada, Stampede Wrestling and the Hart family and he had gone to great lengths to make arrangements to look after us. He set the Neidharts up in the apartment of a police informant who'd had some trouble with the law and was now stuck in a Hungarian jail cell. Julie and I would stay with Jochem, his wife, Heidi, and their three-year-old son, Dennis. As Jochem drove us down cobblestone streets on the way to their apartment, he proudly pointed out stoic cathedrals and beautifully restored buildings. I was surprised to learn that much of Hanover had been destroyed during the Second World War; the unforgettable evidence of artillery was engraved in pockmarked viaducts. As we passed the soccer stadium, there were posters up promoting everything from rock concerts to wrestling. Jochem pointed out the Schutzenplatz, where a huge circus tent was erected. Tucked neatly in the rear were several small trailers where some of the wrestlers lived. Out front, a billboard boldly announced, Catch Welt-Cup! Every night for the next six weeks we would work in that tent, and I was anxious to show the German fans what I could do.

On the first night of the tournament Heinrich Kaiser directed us to his right-hand man, Peter William, who had white hair and was built like a stork. He smiled, clicked his heels together and said, "Nice to meet you, gentlemen. How is your brother Smith?" He told us how, when Smith had been in Germany, all the wrestlers would parade out at the beginning of the show, marching around the ring and then climbing into it to the sound of marching music. "It was quite amusing," he said. "Sometimes Smitty would walk backward, or hop on one leg, or wear his boots on the wrong feet. The best one was the time he did Charlie Chaplin. He brushed his hair to one side, trimmed his moustache, stuffed a ball of socks down the front of his trunks, and goose-stepped to the ring, complete with a one-armed salute. We all had such a laugh." He wasn't smiling when he said it, and I took it as a warning.

The wrestlers came from all over the world: Russians, Brits, Frenchmen, Spaniards, Africans, Japanese, Americans. The top babyface in the tournament was a German named Axel Dieter; he looked about sixty years old, with a face like an axe, and wore his stringy hair in a comb-over. It occurred to me that all the German wrestlers were at least fifty years old, while all the guys they'd be beating every night were the young stars from everywhere else.

After the parade I watched one match after another. The old men wrestled in a slow, stiff style that was almost comical, yet the German fans whistled and cheered enthusiastically. The more I watched, the more I saw how easy it would be to impress these fans with how well I could work.

On that first night in Germany, I was wrestling Bob Della Serra, a thirty-year-old French Canadian who worked under a mask as UFO. He was an established star, and my job was to put him over. I entered the ring to a German pop song, which signalled to the fans that I was a babyface. UFO was eager to work, and we gave them a splendid old-time match with him calling all sorts of high-flying drop kicks and slick roll-ups before catching a quick fall on me. The crowd was easy to please, typical of wrestling fans all over Germany.

After intermission on the first night, they posted the next night's match-ups on the billboard. Jim was working, but I was off. And that became the pattern. I'd made a mistake, having a good match that first night; the old German wrestlers couldn't follow it. I was considered a threat to the old established order, so the promoters made it clear, both to the fans and to me, that I wasn't going to contend. After that, I rarely worked, and when I did, I was disposed of in short matches by jobbers.

Big Jim, on the other hand, was being built as a top heel so that he could eventually be thumped by Axel. He worked hard every night, usually going a minimum of four rounds. Jim couldn't understand why I was unhappy about not working, since my pay was the same either way. But I was thinking of the future, and I was sure that I wouldn't be invited back the next year.

I liked Germany, the people, the food, the open-mindedness. Jochem arranged for Jim and me to have the use of a cheap car, so every day we went to the co-ed Sport Fitness Zentrum, where we sweated out the previous night's alcohol. When we showered, hard-bodied Fräuleins with unshaven armpits would eagerly soap our backs. We'd return the favour, laughing and giggling like little kids. After a few days it didn't seem unusual to us any more.

Every night after the show, Jochem took Jim and me to sex clubs, lesbian bars and brothels where he conducted undercover police work. I imagined myself as some sort of a shadowy player in the world of international intrigue, which served to distract me from my bruised ego. I plopped down on a stool with a beer in front of me, always the best and always compliments of the owners, busy talking to Jochem. On many of these outings, Jim seemed lost in thought, having learned that Ellie was pregnant again. Eventually Jochem would give us a nod: Time to move on to another club. By 3 a.m., I was drinking apple Schnapps in the best brothel in Hanover, debating the differences between American and German culture with the owner. I couldn't get over the fact that prostitution was legal in Germany. Then the proprietor offered Jim and me the girls of our choice, compliments of the house. Jim declined with a sheepish look, saying, "Umm, I'm married. To Bret's sister."

"And what about you?" the owner smiled at me.

I said, "My girlfriend is here."

"Girlfriends, they do not count!"

Before I knew it I was being led through six floors of hallways, trying to choose among at least three hundred good-looking girls, wearing everything from lingerie to leather. I kept reminding myself that I wasn't married, and a chance like this wasn't likely to come again, and besides, who would know?

And then I thought of Julie. Perhaps it was the booze, or the fact that I couldn't begin to pick just one girl. "Maybe some other time," I said.

I resigned myself to my role as a jobber and actually had some good matches. As a special treat one night, I rode in an unmarked police cruiser with Jochem while he worked. A call came in over the radio that shots had been fired, and I ended up hunched down in the car while Jochem and his partner chased a killer, who they eventually caught hiding in a tree!

I returned to the apartment drunk, with visions of sex and violence spinning in my head. I crawled quietly into the little bed that Jochem had provided—one for me and one for Julie—when she suddenly slammed her fist hard into my face. In whispered shouts she tore into me: "I can smell perfume on you a mile away."

"It's just some soap-on-a-rope that I borrowed from this Spanish wrestler. I've been out with Jochem all night chasing killers!"

It occurred to me, even as I said it, that as excuses go, it was a pretty strange line. Even stranger because it was true. Julie gave me the cold shoulder for several days. As the weeks went by it really began to bother me that Julie kept accusing me of something I didn't do, to the point that sometimes I wished I had. Of course it never occurred to me to go home to her right after the matches.

Meanwhile, Jim and Ellie had alienated everyone at their apartment complex with ear-shattering shouting matches.

On the final day of the tour I stopped by Adrian Street's trailer and met a well-dressed, stern-looking man who introduced himself as Adrian's father. He had been one of the British army's most highly decorated heroes during the Second World War and had escaped twice from his Japanese captors.

I sat lacing my boots up in the dressing tent when the flap opened and in stumbled a dazed German wrestler named Dahlburg. There was blood pouring out of his mouth and spilling down his chin, and he was holding three teeth in his open hand. My music played and minutes later I was in the ring with Adorable Adrian Street riding me around like a pony and spanking me on the ass while the crowd roared with laughter. At least I still had my teeth.

Naturally, Axel Dieter won the tournament and was bedecked in wreaths of flowers and awarded a big silver cup.

Julie and I were off to England, where Tom and Michelle were waiting for us. We stayed with Davey's mom and dad in the small town of Golborne, in the north country, not far from Wigan, renowned within wrestling circles for its shooters. Tom and Michelle were staying at Tom's parents' place, about a minute's walk down the street.

Davey's parents were in their fifties. Sid was handsome, with jet-black hair and a thin moustache. Joyce was a sturdy woman who didn't say a lot. Davey had an older brother, Terrance, who no longer lived at home, and two young sisters. Joanne looked like Davey, and Tracey was a frail but adorable blond born with brain cancer who'd gone through years of painful surgeries that left her mentally challenged. She always wore a big, bright smile. Julie and Michelle had plenty to catch up on, which was just as well, since Tom and I had a full calendar of bookings.

Tom had got me a guarantee of U.S.$500 a week, which was good by British wrestling standards. Max Crabtree, the promoter, was the cleverest of the three Crabtree brothers who controlled wrestling in the U.K. The boys thought of Max as a penny-pincher who talked out of both sides of his mouth, a tendency common to wrestling promoters, although he was fair and honest with me. I had a hunch that, like my dad, Max probably wasn't making as much as the boys imagined. But nobody argued that he didn't have a brilliant mind for business. Running five or six different shows a night all over the U.K., he managed to pack the halls even though he was running some of the sorriest-looking wrestlers to ever suit up—although that's not to say that there weren't some great British wrestlers. Max and his smaller brother, Brian, who was his emcee, had at one time been workers, but it was the oldest brother, Shirley Big Daddy Crabtree, who was the biggest attraction in Great Britain. He was a year older than Max, had a sixty-five-inch chest and weighed more than five hundred pounds. His white hair poked out under a red, white and blue top hat; he reminded me of a friendly polar bear. One of his biggest fans was Prime Minister Margaret Thatcher. Big Daddy's finishing move was to fall backward and crush his opponent flat. Few men could handle the impact, but all it took was for Max to wave a few extra quid in a wrestler's face, and he'd put his life on the line.

Nobody gave a wank about who was winning or losing. If anything, the Brits preferred to wrestle first so they could dash back home, since most of them had day jobs. There were silly gimmicks everywhere in the dressing room and a variety of accents, from Cockney to Yorkshire, and all the wrestlers, from sixteen to sixty, spoke English rhyming slang fluently. There was Steve Logan, a small, sixteen-year-old kid. Another guy, a bit older but just as slender, clomped around dressed up as a firefighter, dragging a four-foot length of fire hose. A short East Indian called The Prince was easily as hairy as a gorilla. Tarzan Johnny Hunter, a big bodybuilder, wore a leopard-skin singlet. Then there was strongman Alan Dennison, a kind, middle-aged, baldheaded wrestler wearing silver arm bands. Dennison had a nice physique for his age, but his strongman bit was all show. There was Mick McManus, a small, crusty wrestler who had to be sixty years old, the greatest villain of U.K. wrestling, whom the boys still tip-toed around. King Kong Kirk stood six-foot-four and 350 pounds, with a shaved head and one ugly mug. I remembered him briefly working for my dad in the early 1970s.

King Kong was my opponent the first night. Max told me I would work as the blue-eye, as the Brits called a babyface, and I was to put him over in five rounds. Tom was working with none other than Mark Rollerball Rocco, considered one of the best grafters, or workers, in Britain at the time. He was small and dapper with dark hair and a trim moustache. At thirty, Rollerball was a second-generation heel, as much loved by his peers for his hard work in the ring as for his knack for telling colossal bullshit stories.

The British wrestling style was gymnastic and choreographed, and the rules were a bit like boxing. If a wrestler was down, his opponent had to back off while the referee gave him a ten count. I went out wearing my silly cowboy hat to an enthusiastic cheer. Kirk stood sneering in the middle of the ring, which was big and bouncy and surrounded by old-time fans, hat-pin types. Kirk turned out to be a great worker and bump-taker, and when he collapsed on top of me, he was as light as if he'd covered me with a blanket. King Kong loved the match and so did Max, who booked me to work with Tom in his home town the next night.

The following morning at Tom's place, I was introduced to his mentor, Ted Betley. It was strange to think that this short, balding, softspoken old farmer in a tweed coat was tough as nails. And Tom acted like a choir boy around him: no swearing, no smoking and no boozing.

In the packed hall that night in Warrington, I was whipping forearm smashes across Dynamite's lower back. With every blow the crowd grew more incensed, and when I forgot to break for the count, the crowd wanted my head. I was black-hatted Cowboy Bret Hart the baddy.

Tom was taking such high back drops that I feared his feet would hit the ring lights overhead. I knew this match meant the world to him. He wanted to show what he could do to the other wrestlers, his old mates, friends who had ridiculed his choice of career, and especially his old mentor, Ted Betley, all of whom were looking on from the stands. Tom's dad was also there, small and hard, like his son.

We weren't giving the crowd the usual flips and rolls; we were giving each other an absolute physical thrashing. Dynamite jammed his thumb up his nose and blood poured, smearing the lower half of his face. When I finally went for my side backbreaker, he kicked his legs up and turned a complete circle in the air, landing on his feet in perfect position to piledrive me. I lay flat on my back and stared up at the ring lights, happy to have had a great match. The thought disappeared when the lights were blocked by the flying body of Dynamite, who had launched himself off the top turnbuckle and crashed head to head with me. The crowd screamed as I twisted in pretend agony. I never felt a thing. Dynamite hooked my leg for the one . . . two . . . three.

When we returned to the dressing room, the boys were in awe. Later Tom pulled me aside and told me that Max was so thrilled that he'd added me to the last card ever at the Kings Hall at Belle Vue Stadium in Manchester to work with Marty Jones, the Lancashire Lion.

"It's like Madison Square Garden. It's had wrestling and boxing since forever, and they're tearing the building down," Tom said. I heard later that many of the boys approached Max wanting to take my place on the bill, even offering to work for free, but Max stood by me. I think the fan in him wanted to see The Cowboy tangle with The Lion.

Kings Hall was packed to overflowing with 7,500 enthusiastic fans. All the wrestling legends of the past came by for one last visit. The mood in the dressing room was melancholy as wrestlers pieced together the last bouts they'd ever have in that historic old building. All the Brits had fond memories of the place, as did all the fans, and when the night was over things wouldn't be the same for wrestling in England.

Marty and I worked a hard, solid match in which the crafty Brit beat me with a fancy double roll-up. I'm still honoured to have worked that final show.

Julie and I took the train to Liverpool to see the Cavern Club, where the Beatles first played; it wasn't much more than a hole in the wall selling souvenirs. On the train back, she brought up the whole thing about being unfaithful in Germany again and said that when we returned home we should go our separate ways. I was angry and hurt that she'd put me through all this again, so I decided to take her at her word and accept that she was really leaving this time.

I was single again.

Royal Albert Hall. I couldn't help but whistle "A Day in the Life." I was supposed to put Pat Roach over, who was a strict blue-eye in England. He was awfully big, but I said I'd do all that I could. Tom grabbed me just before the match and took me upstairs where there were stacks of long tables and chairs piled up next to a small janitor's room. He nodded toward the door.

"Open it."

When I did, I saw a girl, slightly older than I was, with dirty-blond hair and a slim but busty figure in a black leather miniskirt. "This him?" she asked coyly. Tom had already disappeared. The girl tugged me inside, pushed the door shut and fumbled with my zipper in the dark. Before I could stop myself things were already out of hand. Now I know how many holes it takes to fill the Albert Hall. I could hear Tom laughing in the distance.

In the ring I hit Pat Roach with everything I had, gouging his eyes, whaling away on him with a barrage of punches and kicks. Every time I pounded him down, he jumped back up in his boxer's stance, and we'd have to start building the match all over again. Oddly, I thought how it wasn't a whole lot different from how I kept pulling myself back up, again and again, to start all over with Julie.

And it was the fact that many British houses had no central heating that may well have saved me and Julie. Just before we were to go home, England was hit with the worst winter snowstorm of the century, but there was no army of snowplows like we had back home. It was twenty-five below zero; we'd go to bed not talking to each other, wearing all our clothes, including our coats. Even in the midst of breaking up we saw the humour, waking up in each other's arms, stuck together like icicles. We just sort of made up.

When we finished up with Max, I took Julie to London for a few days, bought her a new winter coat and lots of new clothes. She chose trendy punk styles and Doc Martens boots, and I hoped it would make her happy to show Michelle what I'd had bought for her. In the evening, we rode to the theatre in a shiny black London cab and found *Evita* nothing short of awe-inspiring. Afterwards we ate at a pricey seafood restaurant across the street, sucking down raw oysters on the half-shell and sipping shark fin soup. Finally, Julie poured out how sorry she was. Although the royal wedding of Charles and Diana inspired young couples everywhere, my thoughts on getting more serious were lukewarm. Instead I was satisfied knowing I'd at least given Julie the memory of strolling arm in arm past the storied statues of Trafalgar Square and watching the changing of the guard at Buckingham Palace.

II

PUZZLE RINGS

I SPENT CHRISTMAS EVE at Stu's with all the Harts, including Alison's new boyfriend, Ben Bassarab, a good-looking bodybuilder who seemed just as much in love with Davey as he was with Alison. Much to Alison's horror, Jim and Davey helped Ben get so bombed that he couldn't get up off the floor. Welcome to Hart house, Ben!

In January, I set off for the land of the rising sun, where Tom and I were met by the usual horde of reporters and fans. It was obvious that he was over big in Japan, but I was worried about him. There were times when I had to shoot him up with his steroids because his butt was so knotted up he couldn't inject himself.

We soon got familiar with the rest of the foreign crew. In what was almost like a big-time sports trade, Tiger Jeet and Abdullah had swapped places. Abdullah sat grinning like a big fat cat, wearing wraparound shades and glittering with diamonds and gold. "What's up, champ?" he waved to me. There was ex-NFL all-American Wahoo McDaniel, a Choctaw-Chickasaw from Oklahoma who, like Ernie Ladd, was one of the toughest tackles in the NFL. Rounding out the crew were Superstar Billy Graham, who wasn't looking forward to the tour; S.D. Jones, a big, friendly black wrestler from Antigua working out of New York; and two short Mexicans.

In a dressing room in a town somewhere outside Tokyo, I paced around with my cowboy hat on while TV sets all over Japan were set to carry our opening match live. I gained real respect for one of the Japanese wrestlers, Tiger Mask, that night. He wore a black and gold mask with little teddy bear ears and stood short and thick in blue and gold tights, but he moved with lightning speed, diving into somersaults, exploding into spinning back kicks, leaving the crowd speechless, like the Bruce Lee of wrestling. Shimma was desperately in need of wrestlers who could work with Tiger Mask. A much friendlier Peter Takahashi explained that because I was going to be Dynamite's sidekick, they'd be building me up for a World Junior Heavyweight title shot with Tiger Mask in Sapporo on February 5. Then Tom would face him on February 12, in a triple main event at the

Sumo Palace in Tokyo, under Inoki and Abdullah. I was grateful that Tom let me ride his coattails. The biggest pop every night came when Dynamite marched out.

We bused from town to town, selling out everywhere, suffering through lousy food and hard matches. I missed Julie, and Tom missed Michelle, even though he'd never admit it. Like I had the last time I was in Japan, I propped up my perfumed Pink Panther on the dresser and wrote long, sappy letters home.

I became Tom's drinking buddy, often protecting him from himself. Without me around he grew lonely, dangerous and occasionally cruel. One morning as we waited to leave on the bus, Tom opened the window, calling and waving over a poor vagrant. I thought Tom was going to toss a few coins out the window to him, but instead he spit right in his face and said, "Fuck you, you dirty yellow bastard." I felt bad for both of them, but more for Tom, because the last lesson a bully ever learns is that what goes around always comes around.

When I called home, Julie was packing it in and going back to Regina, just like the last time I was in Japan.

On the bus I was absorbed in the James Clavell novel *Shogun*. I imagined myself as a Barbarian pirate in medieval Japan, not so much raping and plundering, but maybe seducing the Orient. When I gazed around, taking in the twitchy, anxious eyes of S.D. Jones; Abdullah's fat, round head;, Bad News's one gold earring and the assorted tics and affectations of Tom, Wahoo, Billy Graham and the two little Mexicans, the bus itself felt like a modern-day pirate ship.

After a month in the country, we boarded a ferry for the overnight ride up the coast to Hokkaido, which I think is the most beautiful part of Japan. Inoki, wearing a full-length fox-fur coat, disappeared into his first-class cabin while everyone else crashed on the floors of the various decks. Everyone, that is, except for me, Tom and Wahoo. By 4 a.m. we were stumbling drunk. Wahoo had stripped down to his socks and shorts and was lying on a rubber female mannequin that was intended for use in CPR instruction. Tom was wearing my cowboy hat. I was wearing Wahoo's headdress. By the time the boat docked, we were slumped and snoring. Inoki, fully rested and robust in his fox fur, stepped out of his cabin and practically tripped over Wahoo, still half-naked, nuzzling a rubber girl. Inoki cracked a smile and stepped over him, followed by an outraged Peter. All the foreign boys stood around Wahoo, laughing hard, as he woke up.

Arriving for the last week of the tour was the legendary Dusty Rhodes, to replace Superstar Billy Graham. Dusty, a large, heavyset west Texan with curly blond hair and deep-set eyes that were always ringed with dark circles, sat in the bar with a big smile and blade marks all over his forehead. He and Wahoo swapped war stories all night long. When we all fell out of the elevator on the way to our rooms, two cute Japanese girls approached us nervously and asked for autographs. When I got to my door at the end of the hall, I could hear the thud of the other doors closing and I looked back. The girls didn't seem to have anywhere to go. The trains stopped running around 2 a.m., and most fans were never out this late.

I waved the girls over, and it turned out I was right: They were stuck. I decided to be helpful. "You can stay my room, okay?" We sat up for a while, laughing and talking in broken English. Then I stretched out across my bed, wearing only my jeans. They crept in beside me like kittens, in white cotton bras and panties. They took turns kissing me gently on the cheek, and on my puffy lip, then began to tug at my jeans. I arched my back, thinking none of the other wrestlers would believe this. Sorry, Jules. Then I clicked off the light. I wasn't going to say no any more: a pirate in paradise.

The pine trees were frosted with snow as the train rocked north toward Sapporo. Wahoo, Dusty and Abdullah came into the dining car for something to eat. Before long they were bragging about the money they'd made in Florida, Charlotte and Japan—jewellery, Rolexes, fancy cars, fur coats—each topping the other in a grand bullshit contest. Tom and I listened quietly until they broke it up and went back to their seats, all except Abdullah, who winked at us over his shades: "They bullshit me, I bullshit them. It's all just bullshit." I appreciated the humour and the honesty, but Tom muttered that it wasn't fair that they made all the money while, in his view, wrestlers like us did all the work.

I could already hear the packed crowd in Sapporo as Tiger Mask and I met with Peter secretly between the dressing rooms before our match. Satoro Sayama was likable and polite as we worked out numerous complicated high spots, with Peter dictating the finish.

At the twenty-three-minute mark, I had Tiger Mask clamped in a rear chin lock. Peter was on his knees encouraging us both on. We'd set a blistering pace, and my lower back was killing me. Suddenly, another spin kick. I bumped down hard, but was right back up, only to be drop-kicked out between the narrow rubber ropes, to the floor. Tiger Mask sailed high over the top rope and I moved out of the way at the last second. He crashed to the padded floor, and the stunned crowd became concerned. I climbed back into the ring, and when Tiger Mask tried to come under the ropes I met him with a barrage of punches. Then I tore off across the ring, and Tiger Mask one-jumped it perfectly, perching himself on the top turnbuckle. He caught me coming off the ropes with a stiff drop kick, and the crowd exploded! As I staggered to my feet I could feel that the inside of my mouth was shredded—I was lucky I didn't lose any teeth! Gripping me around the waist, Tiger Mask suplexed me backward for the win.

In the dressing room, Tom and Abdullah congratulated me on a great match, as I sat, exhausted, watching the TV monitor as Tiger Mask bowed and accepted his World Junior Heavyweight belt along with a five-foot-tall trophy that was only a few inches shorter than he was.

At the Sumo Palace in Tokyo, Dynamite and Tiger Mask tore the house down, but from the way Dynamite limped back to the dressing room it was clear that the match took a physical toll on him.

As Shimma paid me on the final night, he congratulated me on a great match and rewarded me with a five-day, U.S.$3,000 tour to the United Arab Emirates in April with Dynamite, and a Japanese tour in the summer, with a raise. Before the main match, Abdullah's massage guy worked on him and then an ancient-looking Japanese doctor injected him with adrenalin. Tom and I watched, like two weary soldiers from the front line, as Abdullah and Inoki squared off. Before they even touched each other, Abdullah abruptly broke into a karate stance, yelling, "Wooo!" and that was all it took to bring the house down. Some guys just had the look. Tom rolled his eyes, thinking of how he killed his body to get the same reaction. But despite our skepticism, Abdullah and Inoki had a great match that went well over twenty real and intense minutes. Both of them were bleeding by the time Inoki back-kicked him in the head for the win. After the match, Abdullah lay on the dressing room floor hyperventilating as the nervous doctor held an oxygen mask over his face. I can only imagine what alarms were going off in his massive chest, and I feared he might die right there on the spot. But Abbie left Japan in one piece.

The good news when I got back was that Julie was still there. And there were some pluses now to my personal position: I was still steroid-free when so many weren't. Blessed with my dad's great legs, I filled out my six-foot frame with a thick back and neck, round shoulders and a muscled chest; I was lean at 235 pounds. And my mom insisted I take a raise in pay to $600 a week, since that was what they were paying Bruce.

But the territory was out of control. The shows started late, there were lots of lame finishes and then there were the ball shots. Nothing infuriated Stu more than watching one wrestler after another spread his opponent's legs and drill him right in the balls. Every night he ordered that it be stopped, but it wasn't.

I immediately set about fixing things. Whenever I confronted anybody on it, they always said, "That's what Bruce told me to do." I'd shake my head and tell them not any more. Another problem was blood in the early matches: How were the main events supposed to top that?

The one big plus was David Schultz, whose hilarious banter with Ed Whalen made him an immensely entertaining character. Foley and his heel thugs double-crossed Schultz on TV, turning him into the babyface star the territory so desperately needed. Tom and I had only been back for ten days when he blew out a knee again. When wrestlers were injured, Stu kept them on the payroll, which said a lot about his generosity and good faith, especially since Tom's injury was probably a direct consequence of his last match with Tiger Mask.

Meanwhile, in the rundown Ramsay district of Calgary, love seemed to be everywhere. Diana and Davey had become inseparable. And one day Tom pulled me aside to tell me that he and Michelle were getting married, and asked if I would be his best man.

The day they picked was March 25, 1982—Julie's birthday. I had told Julie I didn't intend to follow Tom's example any time soon, and it was a bit awkward as I drove the four of us down to city hall. In the parking lot a bum drunkenly challenged Tom, who bristled to put him in his place. Michelle pleaded, "Please, Tom, not on our wedding day!" He smiled and laughed it off. A small victory for Michelle in a war that was already lost. I was relieved, but I thought she had better get ready for a lifetime of collaring this bad dog.

I knew it hurt Julie to see her younger sister married while she and I floated along on a sea of uncertainty.

Though Tom was still hampered by his knee surgery, in April he decided he would come to the Middle East with me anyway. After a day-long layover in New York, we boarded a Pakistan International Airlines flight to Dubai. When I looked closely at my ticket, I realized we'd be making stopovers in Paris, Frankfurt and Cairo: Shimma had purchased the cheapest coach tickets possible. Tom was furious. We stayed on the same plane through all the stops. It was packed, and my seat didn't recline. For sustenance, we were served only a small paper cup of Kool-Aid and some pasty curried chicken. By the time we stopped in Cairo, I was dead-tired and drenched in sweat.

Then the plane sat on the runway for four hours for security reasons; armed soldiers would not allow anyone to disembark. Finally, we were permitted to take off, but as we neared Dubai, the pilot announced that there was a sandstorm obscuring the runway. We were diverted to Karachi. Two full days of flying to end up—where?

At 2 a.m., Tom and I got off the plane delirious with fatigue. He limped, favouring his sore knee. We found a lone baggage office employee, who told us we couldn't get to Dubai until the ticket counter opened in the morning. We were hustled off in a tin van to the Karachi Airport Hotel, and we checked into the only room they had.

I lay awake for a while on my half of the bed while Tom snored like a chainsaw on his. My eyelids grew heavy and soon Julie was in my arms, her head on my chest, and I was telling her about a nightmare in which Tom and I were stuck in Karachi, Pakistan, and—wait a second. We *were* in Karachi, and the morning sunlight was streaming through the windows! I blinked my eyes open to find Tom cuddled up next to me. I started to laugh. He opened his eyes, blinked and I gave him a light elbow to the head. "What are you doing, Tom?" He was back on his side of the bed in a flash.

The International Hotel in Dubai was better than a mirage in the desert. Tom emerged from Mr. Shimma's palatial suite with a cold look in his eye. "He wants to see you."

Shimma explained that the tour had been shortened from five days to three, and he could only pay me half the money he'd offered. I closed the door as I left him, cursing under my breath. I told Tom I'd been short-changed, and his eyes got wide. "He just gave me your $1,500 as a bonus." I marched right back into Shimma. "If you can afford to give Dynamite a bonus, then you can afford to pay me as promised." The nervous worm acted like it had been a joke and paid me in full.

I was surprised to find that I had some degree of notoriety in Dubai; apparently, Stampede Wrestling had been the highest-rated TV show there for years. At the press conference the next day, I answered several questions about my famous father, and when attentions turned elsewhere, I casually doodled a cartoon of Mr. Azeem, one of the promoters, a small man with a big, long nose and huge bulging eyes who looked like an East Indian version of the Pink Panther. I slid the doodle to Tom, who buried his face in his elbow to hide his laughter. It was passed around and soon every wrestler was laughing, even Inoki. Somehow it was passed to Azeem while he was standing at the podium addressing a reporter. He stopped mid-sentence and held it up, asking, "Who is this?" The wrestlers exploded in hysterics, and the reporters never knew why.

Later that day, I sat around the hotel pool watching the Japanese wrestlers having piggyback fights in the water. With no Japanese media to impress, they were actually laughing and goofing around: It was the first time I saw them as just young men, like me.

That first night of the Grand Prix—a special tribute to Inoki at Al Maktoum Stadium, where the promoters were expecting at least 30,000 people to attend on each of the three nights—the ringside seats were filled with billionaire sheiks. They'd paid fortunes for huge reclining leather easy chairs, each equipped with a small, closed-circuit TV and a tray of cold cuts and fresh fruit. But, by show time, it was clear the event was a disaster: There were fewer than five hundred people in the stadium.

Still, Tiger Mask and I had a terrific match: realistic, tight and fast-paced. When it came time for the finish, he dove off the turnbuckle on top of me. Peter Takahashi signalled for the bell, and I exploded into a temper tantrum, complaining that it was only a two-count. The small crowd rose up in my defence, booing Peter, the biased Japanese referee. I was cheered all the way back to the dressing room. There was such a protest in the newspapers the next day that Shimma altered the final night's lineup to give us a rematch.

That last night, Inoki was going to dispose of the top American on the card, Dirty Dick Murdoch, whom I hadn't seen since he dropped a knee on Bruce back in Odessa, Texas. Dick had a fat face, no chin and a much-loved golly-gee sense of humour. "Hey, I'm a goin' out there and work New York style," he joked as he walked past me toward the toilets, buck-naked except for high black socks and dress shoes, a new colour newspaper called *USA Today* tucked under his arm.

As the wrestlers made small talk, I noticed a pair of shit-stained white underwear under my bench, long abandoned by one of the young soccer players who also used the stadium. Dick's clean, white briefs were hanging from a hook by his bag. For Tom's amusement, I switched them, tweezer-like, with the dirty ones. After I came back from another good match with Tiger Mask, I stood with Tom and Dick to watch the matches from the dugout. Dick was looking around anxiously. Finally he blurted, "All I know is there must be a shit freak running around here, because somebody shit in my underwear, and I'm dang sure it wasn't me!" When he walked off scratchin' his butt, Tom and I collapsed laughing.

Before we left for home, Tom and I visited the "gold mine"—tented shops where gold jewellery and keepsakes glittered everywhere. The proprietors had no fear of shoplifters because if they caught you stealing they'd chop your hand off. Tom loaded up on gold trinkets for Michelle. I bought Julie a gold medallion with a map of the world on it and a set of white gold puzzle rings.

Our love was a puzzle.

12

MARRIAGE AND FATHERHOOD

SINCE TOM AND MICHELLE HAD TIED THE KNOT, I felt subtle but constant pressure from Julie to do likewise. But I resisted: Being a wrestler meant being away from home a lot, and the temptations on the road were too great for me to withstand. Maybe I'd have felt differently if Julie hadn't spent too much of what little time we had together being angry at me; most of the time I didn't have a clue why. But when I got back from the Middle East that spring, she'd clearly lost hope that our relationship would grow into more than what it was and gave up. She said she needed a bit of time to get a job and arrange to move in with a friend but that she would be gone by July 1.

I got back from a night drive from Saskatoon at dawn on June 30, 1982. The sky was already blue and smeared with white clouds. I sat on the edge of the bed watching Julie sleep. The window was propped open, and a soft breeze stirred. What did I really have to lose by marrying her? A shitty house in Ramsay and an old Caddy? If I promised to do my best to care for her, could I somehow be forgiven for knowing already that on the road, I would be unfaithful? I didn't know the answers, but in that moment I felt that God was giving me permission to do whatever was necessary to be myself. Mind you, if I asked her, I'd also have to deal with Stu, who'd slammed his fist down on my mom's desk and told me I was too damn young when I'd first approached him on the subject. But one step at a time.

I gently shook Julie awake and asked her to marry me. She hugged me and pulled me down into the bed. And she didn't move out the next day.

On July 8, 1982, we were married at city hall. Just before the service, I discovered we needed two witnesses, and I quickly recruited Wilk and my friend George, who operated a Greek restaurant just down the street. For the time being, I asked Julie, Wilk and George to keep it a secret.

It was Stampede week, and that night the pavilion was sold out for what was billed as a world title double main event; my match was, once again, with reigning AWA Champ Nick Bockwinkle. Near the end of a long, hard-fought classic, I spilled out onto the floor, and out of the shadows came our soon-to-be top heel, Bad News Allen, who attacked me and ran my head into the dressing-room door. I coughed out the blade I was carrying under my tongue and cut. The thought struck me that I'd had to give less blood to get married to Julie; I was already married to the business. But which was my mistress?

After the show Julie and I celebrated at our house. To our unknowing guests, it was billed as a week-late party for my birthday.

Some honeymoon. For the next few weeks I rode buses and trains all over Japan. Nobody there knew my secret, not even Tom.

The foreign crew on this trip was mostly from New York, and they were a new breed. Vince McMahon Jr. had now taken over from his father and was moving away from the slow, ponderous giants and to wrestlers who had a faster, harder style.

Greg Valentine bore a striking resemblance to his legendary father, Johnny Valentine, having the same blond hair and turtlelike face. Broad-chested Adrian Adonis stood on two thin legs like a June bug. His face, which often bore a sneaky grin, looked like Grandpa from *The Munsters*, and he was always up to something. He was also one of the hardest-working big bump men in the game. Classy Freddie Blassie, an old-timer about Stu's age, managed Adrian. Freddie had been one of the great wrestlers of his day; in Japan he'd become infamous in the 1950s when he filed his teeth into points and bit the heads of his opponents. The sight of blood on TV caused a startling number of deaths among the elderly throughout the country. Almost a quarter-century had passed and Freddie, this smiling old man with white hair combed straight back from his tanned and leathery face, was still remembered by the Japanese fans as a terrifying wrestling legend.

Rick Quick Draw McGraw stood only five foot four, but he was thickly muscled. Seconds after they met for the first time, Quick Draw and Tom were trading pills like kids trading candies on a playground. I'd been concerned that Tom might be developing a drug problem—but Q.D. clearly already had one. Every night he'd swallow a handful of Placidyls and wind up passed out face down in his dinner. Peter Takahashi hated him on sight.

Just before I had my big match with Tiger Mask at the end of July, I called Julie: All I could think of was getting home to her. She sounded nervous and excited, and what she had to say caused my head to spin. "Bret, I think I'm pregnant." I'd always been in love with the idea of having a child with her, but not this soon; we'd only been married three weeks. I didn't know what to say.

And then she broke the news to me that Kas had died on the operating table during the kidney transplant. Jimmy Banks, the kid from Akron with the big smile and the big heart, was gone. God opens one door while closing another, I thought.

Back in my hotel room after my match with Tiger Mask, I thought about Kas. And I thought about Julie. A baby would change everything. The marriage couldn't stay our little secret for long. I'd have to think of a way to tell Stu. I was putting the finishing touches on a letter to Julie when Tom called and invited me to Rick McGraw's room. Rick had taken enough downers to tranquilize an elephant, and he stood in front of the bathroom mirror, his eyes half open, cutting his forehead with a razor blade as Tom laughed and egged him on.

I felt sad for Rick. I wasn't worried about the cuts, I was worried that he'd overdose on downers. When Rick eventually passed out, Tom dumped him outside Peter Takahashi's room in a wheelbarrow, and then had the front desk call Peter to say there was a problem with one of the wrestlers. Rick never got booked to Japan again. Too many times Tom didn't take into account the consequences of his ribs.

We weren't going home just yet. Stu told me that he needed Tom and me to fly directly from Japan to Antigua, where Smith was putting on a show. I pointed out that this was not necessarily a smart thing to do, as Smith was unlikely to pay us. My dad said he'd pay us himself. I never knew whether he was still trying to give Smith the benefit of the doubt or whether he was willing to pay to get Smith out of Hart house and out of his and my mom's hair for a while.

I was surprised when hundreds of smiling fans greeted Tom and me at the airport in St. John's, Antigua. We were whisked off to a second-rate deserted resort that had a flickering black-and-white TV and a fully stocked self-serve bar in the lobby. Like an Etch-a-Sketch, visions of Japanese neon vanished, replaced by the absurd sight of poor old J.R. Foley, whom Bruce had ordered to shave his moustache so he looked like Hitler. There he was in Antigua, wearing boxers, a white undershirt and a yachting cap, standing between a couple of palm trees, surrounded by turquoise waves and white sand in the blazing Caribbean sun. He chuckled, saying to Tom, "Fookin' hell, Tommy, what am I doing 'ere?"

At the stadium there were fifteen thousand cheering fans: It looked like Smith was really going to pull this off. Tom and I were the main event, and I had to laugh at both him and J.R., so drunk that they could barely stand, holding each other up. For the finish I saw J.R. on the apron and took a wild swing at him. He ducked and grabbed me. Dynamite charged with a high knee and I moved and out of the corner of my eye I saw J.R. sail upside down into the front row. Tom was laughing uncontrollably as I covered him for the pin. Then J.R. and Tom staggered for the dressing room, an old pug and a pit bull, an over-the-hill bully and one in his prime.

In the end, Stu did have to pay us. The local fans had pulled the fences down, and no one had been able to collect the gate. It had turned into a free show.

Bad News had done good business for the territory all summer long, working his way through the entire roster of babyfaces, eating them up and spitting them out. When I got back in late August, we worked a three-week program; I dropped the North American belt to him on September 3 and won it back two weeks later. He ate me up so badly that I was seen as a guy who was lucky to be alive, let alone be the champion. He left me in a bloody heap every time. I was Stu's top babyface now. When News left, there weren't any big heels for me to work with so, once again, I found myself holding the North American belt yet only wrestling tag matches.

By the end of October, Smith had put together another tour to Antigua; this time Smith's old pal, Dick Steinborn, was helping him out. And he talked Stu into coming along. I couldn't believe Stu was going along with it. Tom refused to go this time because he didn't want his cheque coming from Stu again. But Bruce, Big Jim, half the crew from Calgary and even Ed Whalen decided to go, while the rest of the boys stayed behind to cover the Friday-night show in Calgary. I went too, thinking the trip would be a good chance to get my dad alone and tell him not only that Julie and I were married, but also that we were going to make him a grandfather.

We stayed at the same hotel as last time, with the open bar, and Big Jim decided to play bartender, doling out rum and Cokes as if they were water. Well, after all, we'd been warned against drinking the water—so we drank everything else! A catchy local reggae number called "Stampede Wrestling"—written to celebrate us—played on the radio in the bar; in my head I saw the strange band of wrestling characters I usually associated with freezing snowstorms wrestling to a tropical beat. Ed Whalen was a bigger star down here than any of the wrestlers, and he couldn't get over being mobbed for autographs everywhere he went.

Jim insisted to Stu that there was no alcohol in the drinks he kept handing him. Stu thought he was downing Cokes—until he stood up and swayed out into the steamy tropical heat. When he came back into the bar sunburned and not in a very friendly mood either, Jim offered to fix him a cold one, and Stu barked, "Go to hell, you bastard! I'll get my own!" and wandered off to his room. It was the first and only time I ever saw my dad tipsy.

One afternoon I seized the opportunity to take Stu for a walk on the beach and tell him about me and Julie. My plan was foiled when two girls walked by. Stu's eyes grew wide with disbelief. He'd never in his life even heard of a topless beach, and in his wildest dreams he couldn't imagine what had got into these women. But it turned out he didn't mind it any more than I did. Somehow it didn't feel like the most appropriate time to mention that I was married.

Stu ended up not making a dime on Smith's adventure. He ended up having to pay for everything, including the bar tab. Smith and Steinborn had both gone on to Puerto Rico, taking the proceeds with them, where they were planning to invest in a questionable deal together. By Smith's way of reasoning, he would turn a nice profit and no one would be the wiser. The problem was that Steinborn ended up with all the money. Smith called the police to get it back. No such luck, and Smith returned home empty-handed.

By November, Julie was four months pregnant and beginning to show. I cautiously penned a letter to my mom and dad that included these lines: "I hope you'll forgive me for going about this the way I have. I never intended on hurting you or disrespecting you. On July 8th Julie and I were married. Sadly, I never felt anyone in the family would be too thrilled with that announcement so therefore they didn't need to know. If the bases were loaded, with Ellie and Jim on 3rd, and Georgia and B.J. on 2nd . . . I guess I'd have to be on 1st. Julie is 4 months pregnant." I taped the letter to my mother's pillow. Unbeknownst to me, my mom went to bed in the dark that night, turning her pillow over, and didn't find the letter for six days! When she found it and told the others our news, Georgia was the first to call to say congratulations. My mother said she understood. Stu never brought it up with me.

That New Year's Eve, Keith and Leslie got married at Hart house, the first of a long line of can-you-top-this weddings. Five hundred guests we hardly knew stubbed out their cigarettes on the oriental rugs and slapped Stu on the back offering him drinks, which he refused. I was glad I had eloped! At Keith's wedding, Alison and Ben announced that they'd be getting married in May. Bruce had brought as his guest his new young girlfriend, Andrea. A few days later my mom suddenly announced that they'd be getting married too, in June.

Being the North American champion but never once defending the title didn't sit well with me, especially since, as of January 4, 1983, I was set to drop it to Leo in a few weeks. I got the idea that it would be a terrific opportunity to have a match with Davey. He and I had spent a lot of time in my living room during the past year watching videos of our matches: a teacher and his student. Davey could copy any move and was great at doing what he was told, but, unlike Tom or myself, he had little clue how to call a match on his own. He desperately wanted to work in Japan, and I thought I could do for him what Leo had done for me.

Davey and I were both very popular in Regina, which I thought would be the perfect setting for our match. I gave Davey the finish and worked out six complicated high spots that I'd call out by number only and drilled them into his head.

In the ring, wearing a red singlet, Davey stood nervously staring back at me while I took in the cheering crowd. With no real issue between me and Davey Boy, it was beginning to dawn on the fans that they really weren't sure who would win. I outweighed Davey by fifteen pounds, so he'd surely be the underdog. The match built slowly. At one point, after breaking on the ropes, we erupted into a heated scuffle that grew tense after I gave Davey a hard slap. Some of the fans thought it was a cheap shot while others thought he needed it. A minute later, by design, Davey hauled off and slapped me right back. Then we got serious.

Fifteen minutes of heavy action later, Davey had to hide his head under the ring so he could throw up, while I covered for him by breaking the count. I eventually settled him down, and soon we had everyone standing. Davey tore into the ropes and dove out onto me, on the floor. The fans popped at the high-speed collision. Cedrick Hathaway, the ref, began to count, and the fans assumed it was all over, so they circled around us. I pulled Davey up and we cut a swath through them, and then I rolled him back into the ring. The fans stayed, pounding their hands on the mat, cheering us on. I held Davey in a rear chin lock, glancing out to Gil, who was trying to maintain security. He looked back apologetically because now it would be impossible to get the fans back in their seats. But I wasn't worried, it was a babyface match.

But I was glad I'd worked out all the high spots by number—instead of having to blab a long sequence of moves with the fans so close, all I did was hiss out the next number. It worked like a charm. I got a rush from the realism. For a moment it felt like I was wrestling Davey in the dungeon at Stu's house, and then I thought that this must be what it was like fifty or even a hundred years ago, wrestling in mining camps, at rodeos and at carnivals. I could see the faces of the fans I'd known for years pressing in around us, not knowing which of us to root for.

With less than a minute remaining, Davey rifled me into the corner, following close behind me, but when I got to the corner I jumped up, dropped behind him and waist-locked him with a perfect German suplex for the one . . . two . . . three.

As the drama had unfolded, I could feel Davey's heart break. But I understood the art of losing: What he didn't know was that this match would make him. The claps turned to thunder as we hugged and shook hands. These were some of my most treasured moments in the ring.

An hour later, at the Plains Hotel bar, Davey and I clinked beer bottles to one beautiful match: a great and total work. Smiling that toothy grin, he said, "Err, it was fookin' good un, Bret. Thanks."

"My pleasure, Dave."

Much to Alison's chagrin, Hito and I began breaking in her fiancé down in the dungeon. Owen would come downstairs to watch. Following in my footsteps, he had won the provincial amateur wrestling championships, and he'd started coming around my place a lot because his new girlfriend, Martha Patterson, lived a few blocks from me in Ramsay. I was glad to hear him talk of going to university and a world as far away from pro wrestling as possible. Maybe Owen would be the one Hart to escape.

I dropped the North American belt to Leo, who was now our top heel. My mind was a million miles away. All I could think about was the baby. As far as Julie and I were concerned, it was still part prayer and part promise that ours would be a love that lasts. She had grown huge and had ruddy-red cheeks. I'd lie with my head on her belly at night and hear the beating of our baby's heart.

At 7 a.m. on March 31, 1983, Michelle woke me in the waiting room at the hospital holding a tightly wrapped bundle in her arms. I turned back a fold of cloth and saw a pair of beautiful dark eyes blinking back at me. My heart filled with joy. We named our little girl Jade.

"This is it, the night of nights. No more rehearsing and nursing a part. We know every part by heart . . ." the boys sang in the van as we pulled up to the Saskatoon arena. It would no doubt be cold and empty like it was every week. The gate was never more than a few hundred bucks, and it made me wonder why we kept going back. But "on with the show, this is it."

The usual Saskatoon crowd consisted mostly of mentally challenged fans who were brought to the matches by bus every week and then left unsupervised. They bragged to us that they often went high up into the dark seats and fornicated; the proof was that several babies were born, and named Bret or Bruce in what was intended to be a compliment.

Ben was along for his first road trip. He'd already fallen for the statue of Stu in dinosaur land, but we were only just getting started. Since it was such a dead town, more thought went into the ribs than the matches. We all smiled and winked as Ben nervously laced up his boots for his first match, with Animal Manson, a dead ringer for the scruffy little drummer from *The Muppets*. Manson was an ex-con with a rap sheet as long as your arm, and I suspect it would have taken all of ten minutes to talk him into robbing a bank. As planned, Ben went for a leapfrog and "accidentally" got clipped by a shoulder to the groin. Three or four goonlike ushers and a storklike St. John's Ambulance attendant, who seemed to be mentally challenged too, helped him back to the dressing room. They entered to shouts of "make room" and "kayfabe" as Ben was laid out on the floor, still writhing. The medic, who had a tendency to pop his false teeth in and out when he got excited, crouched down to tend to Ben. "Let's have a look, son," he said as he jammed his hands down Ben's trunks and gently squeezed his balls. "Easy boy!" All Ben could do was keep selling as we all struggled to keep from laughing. Ben wasn't the first to be ribbed this way—and he wasn't the last.

Ben married Alison at Hart house on May 21, with Davey as best man. He and Diana got caught up in the romantic atmosphere and promptly announced their own engagement. My poor mother, another daughter lost to a wrestler!

After a party that went all night, the whole crew flew to Vancouver the next morning to do a couple of shots that Stu had put together with music promoter Bruce Allen. On the ferry to Victoria, Stu and Gene Kiniski reminisced, while I was mesmerized by blue whales that raced alongside us. The Stampede Wrestling style was much more real than what the fans in B.C. were used to. We sold out Victoria, and for Vancouver I booked myself, with Davey as the main event, knowing we'd steal the show. In Vancouver, Bruce Allen came into the dressing room and Kiniski threw him down a flight of stairs. Gene was old school: no outsiders allowed.

That night when I slapped Davey across the cheek and he slapped me right back, he broke my eardrum. It hurt like hell. My balance was off, but we kept on. Then when Davey dove out on top of me, on the floor, he cracked his ribs and sprained my ankle in what turned out to be an extremely painful match.

Later that night I once again carried Davey into an emergency room. When the nurse asked us what was wrong, he groaned, "It's me ribs!"

She looked at me, "And you?"

"I think my eardrum is broken, and my ankle is sprained."

"Who did this?" she asked with a concerned look.

We pointed a finger at each other and in perfect unison replied, "He did!"

Then we flew back to Calgary, which was no fun with a busted eardrum either. Stu gave Davey some time off because of his ribs but asked me, "Can you make it? It won't be much of a show if you're both off."

I limped into the van. Anything for the business. And for Stu.

The old bus had been resurrected and in June, Wayne steered it east out of town for the run to Saskatchewan. With us were two newly arrived midgets, an adorable Hawaiian called Coconut Willie, who was as agile as a monkey, and Kevin, a scruffy, troll-like kid who had long, jagged teeth that looked like spikes that'd been pounded through the top of his head. Kevin liked to perch himself on the front steps of the bus and sing hit songs from the 1960s. I guess in any other circumstance a bongo-playing midget singing "do wah diddy diddy" would be considered unusual; to me this was normal.

I found myself staring out the window at a road that had become all too familiar. I also knew big changes were ahead. Tom had given his notice, and he'd be leaving in July, this time for good. New Japan had called him to work with Tiger Mask at Madison Square Garden for just one show; a blown-away Vince McMahon Jr. did the commentary. The wrestling world in North America was catching on to what I already knew: The Dynamite Kid was ahead of his time.

We turned Tom babyface so he could work with Bad News, building News up for a feud with me that would climax with a blow-off during Stampede week. I was trying to find the right time to approach Bad News about giving me a little more in our matches. News was a decent worker and a hard one, but he had no psychology: He just ate up anyone in his path. He refused to cut himself, while I stupidly cut myself freely for him. Most nights, in the middle of my comeback he'd scoop my legs out from under me, grab me by the throat and tell me, "If you touch my head again I'll kill you, mo'fucker." Every match, I went in looking like a nine and, after he was done, came out looking like a three.

Meanwhile, Kevin the midget actually wiped tears from his eyes when I explained to him that we simply couldn't have a midget babyface match: "One of you guys has to be a heel." Kevin had a terrifying mouth full of teeth that looked like giant crooked spikes, while Coconut Willie was so cute and adorable you'd want to take him home: It was pretty clear who would have to be the heel. When I heard Kevin singing "Monster Mash," it dawned on me to call him Little Wolfie. "C'mon, it won't be so bad." Kevin stood blinking at me like a ghoul and blubbered right up until match time, even as J.R. dragged him out to the ring by a long chain. The second he was in front of the crowd he was fine though, and he played the role perfectly. Afterwards, in the bus, he acted like it never happened, and sang all the way to Regina.

The next night, when Wayne and I cut through the horse stalls in the back of the venue, I noticed a spray can that read "horse hair adhesive" and turned to Wayne with a playful smirk. "Are you thinking what I'm thinking? It says it washes out with water."

In the dressing room Wayne and I stood over Kevin as I chided, "You know that little wolf-man gimmick is great, but something is missing, don't you think?"

Kevin perked up, hoping we might change it.

Wayne offered, "The teeth are great, but you're just not hairy enough. If there was only some kind of way we could glue hair to you . . ."

Eager to please, Wolfie absent-mindedly blurted out, "Well you know, I'll do anything to make it work."

Wayne held up the can. In seconds we'd sprayed Kevin's back and chest with the glue and stuck clumps of horsehair that we'd picked up from the floors of the stalls all over, even on his face, where we glued hair to his eyebrows. When he innocently asked me how he looked, I couldn't stop laughing long enough to answer him.

Kevin climbed up on a chair to look in the mirror and broke down crying again, same as the night before, right up until match time.

"I wonder if he'll sing on the bus tonight," Wayne said.

"It's a good thing it'll wash off," I replied.

But, it didn't! Whoever wrote that on the can must have been an even bigger ribber than we were. After his match Little Wolfie scrubbed for more than two hours, but those black smudges just wouldn't come off. For the first thirty miles out of Regina, he sulked with his arms crossed, looking like a cartoon character that'd been singed in a fire. We all began calling his name, whistling and clapping, "Wolfie! Wolfie!" I even gave him a big send up, and in no time the mini wolf-man was back, slapping those bongos and giving us the show of his life.

13

THE DEEPEST POCKETS

IN THE TENTED BARN behind the pavilion, the bleachers were full for our Stampede show as I laced up my boots. I looked up to see Bad News approaching, with Bruce close behind.

In a stern, almost argumentative tone, News gave me a speech about not letting my ego stand in the way of what would be good for Stu's business, while Bruce stood behind him smirking. News's idea was that I should drop the championship belt to him and then chase him for it, not the other way around. Before I had a chance to say that I had intended to do that all along, News went on to tell me that all our previous, terribly one-sided matches were, in his view, beneficial to me. "All that sympathy," he said, "that's all Bruno Sammartino ever did, and he sold out Madison Square Garden for years!"

I couldn't believe what I was hearing! News slaughtered me every night, which was not good for Stu's business at all, since there was a difference between a beloved underdog and a doormat. And Bruce, not my biggest fan lately because I objected to a lot of the calls he made about the business, couldn't wipe the smile off his face.

"Fine, News, you want the belt, you can have the belt."

As a reward for being a good sport, I guess, News suggested that in the match I grab the bamboo stick from his spastic Japanese manager, Wakamatsu, and whack News with it. "But don't touch my head!" he warned.

As instructed, during the match, I flattened Wakamatsu and picked up the bamboo stick. Instead of backing away as if he were afraid, News looked more like he was going to burst out laughing. I had bladed again, and blinking the blood from my eyes I looked for a place to hit him that wasn't his head, but he put his arms up defensively. Since he had left me no other place to hit him, I cracked him right on the skull. He stood there frozen and, in that split second, I felt like Bugs Bunny in that old cartoon where he hits a daddy gorilla in the head with a baseball bat.

News took me down with a judo leg sweep and gripped me by the throat—and he wasn't working! My comeback went straight out the window, as did our match, and as a result, all the business we were expected to do for the rest of the summer.

Too many times that summer, I'd walk back to the dressing room and see the disappointed look in my dad's eyes. I felt like everything was spiralling down around me, and Stu was losing everything too. Also too many times that summer, in the wee hours of the dejected mornings, blood seeped through the bandages on my forehead and dripped onto our bedsheets. And often I could hear Julie sniffling, worried about the toll the business was taking on me, and I'd lie there silent: I'd never really come clean with her as to all the ins and outs of keeping the wrestling "real," and my silence stood between us like a wall. Finally, one night I sat up in the dark and told her everything there was to tell about the business. Julie felt better knowing the score and was finally able to sleep at night.

With Jade on her hip, Julie hugged Michelle in an emotional goodbye on the street in front of our house. In the dry August heat, I leaned against the fender of Tom's loaded-down green Eldorado, while Duke, his bull mastiff, hung his head out the back window. Tom took a last drag of his smoke and tossed it out on the road. He was huge, bigger than ever before—his skin looked ready to burst. His head was shaved again, and he had deep razor marks on his forehead from his matches with News. They were headed to Portland—his way into the lucrative American market, and a place where he could get his green card—and my gut told me Tom might never be back this way again.

In a serious tone, Tom warned me that I had to watch my back when it came to some of my siblings. Bruce, he said, had sold Diana a story that I was doing all I could to keep Davey from getting ahead, and had warned her to keep an eye on me. He apparently had told her that it was more than a coincidence that I made a point of booking myself with Davey, and that I had wanted to beat him because I thought he was getting over too strong. For Tom to be telling me this, it was clear that Davey had bought into Bruce's interpretation too.

I was disappointed, but I couldn't say I was really surprised. Davey had lived with me rent-free for more than two years. After Jade was born, since I now had a family to support, I had asked whether he'd mind chipping in. He promptly moved into a spare bedroom at Stu's place, where he could continue to live for free. But it hurt to realize that he had turned against me. I always tried to pass on to him any wrestling wisdom I could, and for him to believe otherwise was due to his own poor judgment.

It felt like we were all breaking up. Big Jim had just got booked to work for Bill Watts in the Louisiana territory. Jim now weighed about 285 pounds and was strong as an ox. At the Stampede, he competed in a strongman contest and managed to throw an anvil twenty-two feet, setting a rodeo record. He, too, would soon be loading up the Eldorado that Stu gave him as a wedding present; Jim, Ellie and their three girls would make the long drive south to Bayou country.

Before he left, though, Jim The Anvil worked one last match with Bad News, which got completely out of hand when News used a dinner fork on Jim's already bloody head to get more heat. The wrestling commission was furious and fined both Stu and News for excessive violence and levied a six-month suspension on News.

My boyhood enigma, Archie The Stomper Gouldie, now fifty years old, was coming back. Bruce discounted him as too old, but Leo said he was fit as ever, and Stu had great faith in him. Ross came to me and said that what with Bad News being suspended, they'd have to rely on me and Archie to carry the territory. I told him that it wouldn't be easy now that News had practically killed me off.

Davey, Jim, Tom and I—all of us were now signed on for the whole ride down the rough roads of pro wrestling, a pack of wild stallions, each taking chances and praying we wouldn't get lost along the way. At that time I had no way of knowing that we'd end up together again, in a completely different place. And in this stampede of wild horses, it felt to me like I was the darkest one.

On Sunday afternoon, when I walked into Stu's kitchen, the house seemed oddly quiet and empty. Stu was bent over the sink scouring one of his cooking pots, and he stopped long enough to ask me how the show went in Edmonton the night before. I never lied to my dad, especially about his business. The boxing and wrestling commissions in both Calgary and Edmonton were coming down hard on him for the shows being too violent both in the ring and with the crowd. Reluctantly, I told him that yet again almost every bout concluded with some sort of a low blow to the groin. Stu slammed down the pot, splashing himself with water. "That damn Bruce! Why can't he ever listen?"

Then he noticed Diana, eavesdropping behind me. When she raced off, he cautioned me that she'd been singing Bruce's praises all morning. He was almost whispering, and when I asked him why, he said he didn't want my mom to hear. They'd had a monumental blow-up a couple of days earlier that was still cooling down. But Stu couldn't help himself, and soon he was ranting about how Bruce was going to cost him his licence and put him out of business. Then Bruce appeared out of the shadows of the basement steps, glaring at me, not his father. "You don't have to talk behind my back, Bret. You can say it to my face!"

"Bruce, I say it to your face every night," I replied, "and Dad says it to you every week, and I'll say it to you again. Why were all those matches ball shots last night? You don't have enough respect for Dad to simply do as he asks, whether you like it or not!"

It soon erupted into a heated shouting match, with Stu pleading for us to quiet down: "I don't want to upset your mother!" But it was too late. Suddenly, my mom was in the thick of it, tired, fed up and so right.

"Stu! Please, please I'm begging you to get out of the lousy business; every damn week we're losing everything we worked so hard for!" And she stormed back up to her bedroom, Stu trailing her, calling back to Bruce and me, "I hope you're both happy!"

Just then Diana slipped by, making her getaway out the back door. I decided I wanted to know what her problem was with me, direct from the horse's mouth, so I raced down the back steps and caught her by the sleeve. I started to say, "Do you see what you started . . ." but she spun around and punched me square on the chin! With tears streaming down her face, she kept on punching me. I had no intention of hitting her, but I was still hold-ing her by the arm as she kept crying and hitting me. Out of nowhere Ross appeared, yelling at me to let her go, and then he tackled me around the legs. I could easily have pancaked his face into the pavement, but at the last second I surrendered my legs to him: How could I hurt Ross for trying to protect his sister? Then Ellie was into it too, screaming at me to let Ross go, right fucking now. I was too busy to tell her that she had it backward: Ross was the one who needed to let me go. Then Jim came charging out, beating his chest like Tarzan, with Davey right behind him. I was sur-rounded, and could easily end up fighting everybody.

Out of the corner of my eye, I saw Bruce's Riviera burn rubber down the front driveway. Then came Stu's booming voice, more than a tinge of heart-break in it: "Break it up!" All of them backed away as he gently pulled me by the arm back into the house. With an expression that was both sad and somehow fearful, Stu told me he'd never seen any situation among his chil-dren with the potential to get *that* ugly. Then he patted me on the shoulder and told me that I was right, that he appreciated all I did for his business, and that he especially appreciated my restraint. As I left, I could hear my mom behind their bedroom door wailing like she was at a funeral.

Las Vegas was some kind of a strange dream illuminated in flashing neon. I flew down on August 22 to attend the thirty-fifth National Wrestling Alliance convention, an annual ritual that my father relished. This year

Bruce was going with him, but, perhaps as a way of saying sorry about what happened to me in the driveway a few days earlier, my mom had insisted that I should go too.

Professional wrestling promoters throughout North America had founded the National Wrestling Alliance in 1948 in order to avoid stringent U.S. anti-trust laws. Since then the organization had expanded to become international in scope. Although promoters ran their own territories, which had their own borders that all the other promoters respected, they agreed to work with one another under the NWA banner. Each territory had its own champion, but every one of them recognized the NWA champion as the one true world champion. Ideally, the idea was that the NWA World Champion would visit all the territories and take on the top guys in hot main event matches everywhere. There were agreed-upon exchanges of talent to keep the cards fresh, but nobody ran in another man's backyard.

The alliance had worked surprisingly well until now. What was shaking it up was the advent of cable TV. Suddenly, the local wrestling shows that served each market were popping up everywhere. Promoters who had got along on mutual respect and a handshake were now competing with one another, unintentionally, because their shows aired in whatever markets the cable systems happened to expand into. In 1982, Vince McMahon Jr. bought his father's promotion and then, despite his father's warnings, began an expansion process that fundamentally changed the business. Though his base was the northeastern U.S., Vince Jr. syndicated the WWF TV shows to markets across America and then used the profits to raid the talent rosters of the regional promotions. By 1983, it was a serious enough problem that every promoter from every territory around the world descended upon the Flamingo Hotel in Vegas to hash it out. It was like a meeting of Mafia dons protecting their turf.

Stu introduced me to the Crocketts, direct descendants of Davy Crockett, who ran the Carolinas, to Eddie Graham from Florida and Don Owens from Portland. Paul Boesch, who ran out of Houston, was also there.

The Nature Boy Ric Flair made a grand entrance into the hotel lobby, strolling by in a sharp light-blue suit and perfect shoulder-length white hair, escorted by a dozen girls, one of whom he was carrying. He did a silly little jig and yelled out what was to become his trademark, "Wooooo," sounding a lot like a siren revving up. Flair had recently dropped the NWA World belt back to Harley Race, but the star from the Carolinas was still considered by many to be the hottest American wrestler in the business at that time.

Harley stood talking quietly with Dory and Terry Funk; in another corner, seated in a wingback chair and sucking on a big cigar, Baba talked cordially with Inoki. A few feet away from them, Jim Barnett and Ole Anderson were in intense conversation. Kaiser, Jovica and Colón were there, too, all with big fat cigars. It was a bit awkward seeing Steve Ricard; I made a point of sitting down with him over a beer to explain why I left New Zealand and how much I truly appreciated what he would have done for me. "No worries," he said, "sometimes a man's gotta do what he's gotta do."

The formality of the meeting room, bedecked with long polished wood tables, plush carpeting and a podium, signalled the serious business that was about to unfold. Stu brought Bruce and me in with him as the doors were closing. Outsiders and hangers-on were definitely not welcome. Everyone had a kink in their tail because Verne Gagne, of the rival AWA, had been spotted in the lobby. I was half expecting them to round up a posse to go out and lynch him.

There were sixty of us in the room listening to a lot of boring speeches, which went a long way to explaining why my mom had stopped coming to these things. Everyone skirted around the real issue until Ole Anderson got up and got right to the point, talking about how the New York territory ran their TV in his Ohio markets. Ole stared hard at Vince Jr., but Vince remained impassive.

"If you want war, McMahon, I'll give you war! I'll run in your Pennsylvania towns."

Everyone started arguing, and there were cries of order. Then Vince stood up in the midst of the commotion and simply walked out. In that moment, I was witness to the beginning of the end of promoters such as my dad and regional territories such as Stampede—though none of us recognized that at the time.

But Stu did tell Bruce and me that now there was going to be a three-way pissing match between Vince, the Crocketts and Verne Gagne, and all three had enough money to piss for a long time. I asked him who'd win. After careful consideration, he said, "I'll put my money on Vince. With that New York TV, he'll have the deepest pockets."

Stu was reminiscing about when he first met The Stomper, back in 1959. He told me that I would've still been crawling around in diapers when a young brute named Archie Gouldie drove up from a small town called Carbon, seventy-seven miles southeast of Calgary, to seek him out. A complete mark, he was brawny, strong and confident that he could beat Stu's top guy, or anyone else on the card. He entered the pavilion and started to climb right into the ring. Stu grabbed him by the arm and somehow managed to persuade him to come up to the house and work out with him instead.

"I kicked the shit out of him," Stu said. "Head between the knees, hip to head, the bastard kept trying to scoot on his ass until he had nowhere to go." Stu gave him "all the ugly stuff after that. Everything!"

He showed up at the house again the next day and was humble enough to say, "Sir, I want you to teach me how to wrestle."

That's how he became The Stomper, and he rescued Stampede Wrestling.

Now, some twenty-four years later, the past and present swirled together as I clamped Archie in a headlock while he angrily stamped his feet, trying to escape. My heart raced at the thrill of working with the man who had put fear in my heart when I was a kid. He was still intense, still believable, and he hadn't lost a step. The crowd in Regina was standing as we brawled back and forth. When I kicked him, he shook from the pain of the blow. I spun him and slammed a lifter into his chest, and he hit the mat and rolled out, holding his jaw. He retreated to the dressing room and the ref counted him out. When I got there, I was surprised to see that Archie was in an angry sulk. It turned out that although I thought it had all gone perfectly, I'd chipped his tooth with the lifter. He was packing his gear and going back to Knoxville because he thought I'd potatoed him on purpose. I apologized. I told him how well I thought we worked together and how badly we needed him. I offered to get him a good dentist in Calgary and pay for it.

He showed a trace of a smile. "It was a helluva match, wasn't it?"

I extended a hand, and we shook. "Yeah, Arch, it really was."

The greatest thing about working with Archie The Stomper Gouldie was that he was everything he pretended to be.

Since News was still under suspension, we needed an angle that would carry us through to spring. Soon Archie suggested that he team up with J.R. Foley to work against Stu and me. Everyone loved the idea, especially my sixty-eight-year-old father, so that's what we did.

One of my greatest memories ever is teaming up with my dad. I'd have thought that having J.R. in there would have added a bit of humour to the mix, but when you throw two old shooters together, things are bound to get out of hand. Stu broke J.R.'s dentures in half, and somehow J.R., who was working in real cowboy boots, stomped my dad so hard that he broke a few ribs. Needless to say, every time he crossed my dad after that, J.R. had a malfunction at the junction.

As for me, Archie gave me back the confidence that I'd lost with Bad News.

The bus headed east in late October for another trip to Saskatoon. I sat next to Bruce, and across the aisle sat Karl Moffat. That baldheaded biker had passed his auditions down in the dungeon, having become good enough, quite good actually, that he was eagerly making his very first road trip. Also back was a newly reinstated Bad News, who was still on very thin ice with the commission. Moffat was still a mark, and gushed about Bad News, or should I say, "Mr. Allen," just loud enough for News, seated near the back of the bus, to hear every word of it. News could barely keep a straight face, except when Karl turned to look back at him. Karl expected an appreciative nod and instead got only an icy cold stare, and he swallowed and turned away.

The wink went out. Bruce nonchalantly let slip that News's four-year-old daughter had just been accepted into Juilliard as the youngest piano player ever in the history of New York. Karl hung on every word, but we acted like we didn't notice. Bruce then suggested to me that it might be a good idea to congratulate News. As I purposely hesitated, Karl bolted out of his seat and headed down the aisle, all eyes on him. Karl approached News, cautiously smiling, "Well congratulations, Mr. Allen! I hear your daughter is quite the talented piano player!"

"You fucking asshole," News yelled in a deep, angry voice. "My daughter lost both her hands in a boat accident! I oughta cut your heart out!" He stood up and pulled out his knife. "Get the fuck away from me before I change my mind!"

The Cuban and Davey attempted to calm Bad News down as Karl abruptly turned around, whiter than a ghost, shaking. When the big biker took his seat, he burst into tears, mumbling for the next three hundred miles that Bruce had sent him on a suicide mission. If Karl had only looked back, he might have seen all the boys bustin' their guts laughing. Karl may have survived Stu's dungeon, but he cracked on his first rib.

By the time we headed back to Calgary, we'd all grown sick of hearing Karl's bawling about how he could have been killed. News couldn't take it any more so he confessed to Moffat that he didn't even have a four-year-old daughter. Karl was so relieved he immediately embarked on an all-out drinking binge, which only made it worse for everybody because now he kept on laughing deliriously about how we really got him.

In the darkness of early morning, in that last hundred miles home, there was old J.R. snoring under another mound of shaving cream, while Little Wolfie tirelessly pounded on the bongos, singing; it did help Wayne stay awake at the wheel.

And then Moffat, so drunk he could barely stand, suddenly announced that he'd decided to "bust my cherry." Nobody knew what the heck he was talking about, until he braved a visit to the godforsaken, foul-smelling toilet and emerged minutes later holding a blade in his hand with blood dripping down his forehead. "Look, Mr. Allen, I can do it!" The dumb ass accidentally dripped blood on News, who always wore nice duds. As we pulled into town, News was up and threatening to kill Moffat, for real this time, which started the endless bawling all over again.

Little Wolfie sat on the steps, blinking back tears as he stared up at Moffat. "It's okay, Karl," he said. Wolfie was such an emotional fellow.

A couple of nights later, just outside the Calgary city limits, two guys in a black Camaro ran a red light, and Wayne narrowly avoided a nasty crash. As they flew by us, one of them hurled a beer bottle at the bus. The enraged wrestlers broke into cheers when a little farther up the road the Camaro was pulled over by a cop for speeding, and we stopped because some of the wrestlers wanted to tell the cops about how crazily the Camaro had been driving. But nobody could believe what happened next. Davey jumped off the bus, shoved the cop out of the way and grabbed the driver through his half-open window. The cop tried to restrain Davey by choking him with a flashlight. In the blink of an eye Davey hip-tossed him into the middle of the road!

The Camaro booted it, never to be seen again. We all sat in the bus in disbelief staring at Davey, now handcuffed in the back of the cop car. He was looking at a whole world of trouble; if he was convicted of assaulting a police officer he'd be kicked out of the country. I didn't want to be the one to tell Diana.

I finally got some great news. Leo was off working for the Crocketts down in the Carolinas and had put in a good word for me. The Crocketts sent wrestlers up to the Tunneys in Toronto every second Sunday for a big show, and as a result I got a call from the booker, Johnny Weaver, asking me to start in Toronto on December 4. There was one small hitch. There was a guy calling himself Bret Hart who had done nothing but jobs on the Crocketts' TV show, which aired all over the South—and also in Toronto. I wouldn't be able to wrestle as Bret Hart. So Weaver gave me the moniker Buddy The Heartthrob Hart, a name I loathed. But still, this could well be the break I'd been praying for. Buddy The Heartthrob I would be.

Before I left the territory for Toronto in December, we planned to shoot the biggest angle since Abdullah fought The Stomper back in 1971: a six-man tag pitting Davey, Sonny Two Rivers and me against Bad News, The Stomper and a green kid from Tennessee named Jeff, who was pretending to be Archie's son. The crowd sensed that something big was about to happen, knowing that Bad News and The Stomper had monster egos that were bound to collide.

Gord Grayston, the head of the Calgary Boxing and Wrestling Commission, was in the crowd looking for any excuse to make trouble. He had a serious dislike for Bad News. I heard Bruce warn News, "Don't use a fork or anything tonight." News agreed.

The "Theme from Shaft" played as News made his way to the ring. A little old man whacked him as he went by and News jerked him out of his chair and held him up by his hair. Ed Whalen was livid. Then, during the double-cross, in full view of a horrified Ed and a contemptuous Grayston, Bad News attacked The Stomper with his fork and then piledrived The Stomper's supposed kid into the cement. Bad News had to fight his way to the dressing room. He used to say, "The only thing I like to do more than fuck is fight, and not necessarily in that order." This time, he'd done them both simultaneously.

Ed held the mic for Archie, who cut one of the most powerful promos I've ever watched, decrying what had happened in the ring. Fans and ushers milled about, sad and scared. This one seemed all too real. Even Ed marked out when he saw Archie, looking deathly pale, climbing into the ambulance as it took Jeff away. But when the smoke from this perfect work had cleared, there was nothing but real bad news: News was suspended, Stu had his Calgary licence taken away and Ed Whalen quit the show, saying things had become too violent.

Incredibly, Bad News still didn't understand what he'd done wrong. After the match in Edmonton the very next day, a fan tried to trip him, and News beat the man with a steel chair. In the rampage a pregnant woman was injured, and News lost his wrestler's licence in Edmonton too. Luckily, there were no lawsuits.

The angle should have been a big moneymaker, sweet relief for my mom and some long-awaited peace for my dad. Instead, the reckless actions of Bad News knocked the territory off course and, in my opinion, after that it never fully recovered.

Stu was forced to pack up his ring for the length of his suspension and move it to the Seven Chiefs Arena, on a Native reserve just outside the city limits. The Sarcee Indians (now known as the Tsuu T'ina Nation) were kind enough to help Stu out, but things looked bleak. The weather turned horrible, almost as bad as the press. We had no main event and, most noticeable of all, no Ed Whalen, who had been, in a lot of ways, the star of the show.

The whole family wore blank, empty stares, except for my mom, who was on a full-blown rampage, pleading with Stu to give up on the business.

14

WAR BREAKS OUT

As my flight took off for Toronto on December 3, 1983, I looked out the window half expecting to see a mushroom cloud hovering over Hart house. TV news crews had positioned themselves outside looking for a big story, ready to play up the violence of wrestling and accusing Stu of hiding from them instead of coming out to face them like a man. In fact, Stu was over at the Whalens' house, trying to talk Ed into coming back.

I stepped out of the cab at the back door of Maple Leaf Gardens and explained to the security guards that I was Buddy the Heartthrob and I was here to wrestle. They took me straight to the promoters, Jack and Ed Tunney. Jack was large and jovial, and Ed was small and friendly. Johnny Weaver, their booker, was a floppy-eared old-timer. In the dressing room, Greg Valentine grunted and smiled my way. He was talking over his dog-collar match with a regular-looking guy in a kilt and a tight T-shirt called Rowdy Roddy Piper. What struck me about Roddy was his politeness as he shook my hand.

I stunned the crowd with an upset victory over a top heel called The Great Kabuki, a Japanese wrestler with long hair who wore black karate pants and blue face paint. Just beyond the curtain, Johnny Weaver greeted me with a huge smile. As I unlaced my boots Johnny promised that, as soon as I got back from my next trip to Japan, Leo Burke and I would work a long program in the territory, with Leo as the heel, and that I would eventually win their version of the North American belt. I couldn't help but smile — finally a break.

I was in Tokyo when I learned that Julie was pregnant again. I still didn't know where I stood with wrestling, and another baby on the way only made me fear even more for the future. I felt better when Julie put Jade on the phone and she talked baby-talk to me. She had four teeth now and when I was gone, Julie told me, she crawled around kissing my picture.

In Japan, Abdullah was back as the main attraction, looking bigger, rounder and richer than ever. There was Playboy Buddy Rose, a fat blond,

Winnie the Pooh–shaped wrestler from the Oregon territory who was a surprisingly good worker. Rollerball was over from England. And Sterling Golden was due to arrive in February for the last two weeks of the tour, only now he was known as Hulk Hogan. And Davey was there on his first Japanese tour, trailing along behind his cousin. Sadly, under Tom's influence, Davey was developing a bit of a mean streak. The two of them reminded me of a set of genetically altered, raging pit bulls. They revelled in blasting long, stinky farts in the crowded elevators of the luxury hotels where we stayed. At every opportunity Davey belched loudly right into my face, and when I'd had it up to here, we nearly came to blows.

On this trip the promoters had me losing to everybody, and I took it as a bad sign. When it came time to work with Davey, I thought it would be easy to simply do the same matches that we'd done in Canada, except reverse the outcome. But Davey was just as awkward as any of the Japanese Young Boys, and on the finish he drove me as hard as he could into the mat, jamming my neck like I was a bag of garbage.

One night a Japanese old-timer called Rusher Kimura invited Tom, Davey and me out to an expensive night club; despite our differences, we all went. Three small shot glasses appeared on the bar in front of us, containing Japanese vodka. Floating in each was what looked like a long-stemmed white mushroom. Kimura explained that each drink cost more than U.S.$400, that the Japanese fellow seated in the corner had sent them over and that it would be an insult if we didn't *kanpai*. Tom noticed he was missing his baby finger, so we figured he must be a big-time Japanese gangster. We all toasted the man, barely choking down what felt like a piece of rubber. Dynamite only pretended to drink his, and, never one to turn down a $400 drink, I downed his too! Then, Kimura slapped me on the back really hard and said, "Turtle penis. Good for fuckie fuckie." He was right. For the next week, all I wore were sweat pants, and it got a little embarrassing every time I stood up.

Tom, Davey and I stood with Abdullah in the dressing-room door watching Hulk Hogan wrestle: still the same massive blond, with the biggest arms I'd ever seen. He was never too fancy, and was smart enough to stick to the moves he did well, but his physique more than made up for his limited ability in the ring. Hulk had come a long way since I'd seen him in Atlanta.

He had been doing huge business with Dr. D. for Verne Gagne and the AWA in Minneapolis. Then, at the TV studio where they did their tapings, Verne, who still believed he was as tough as he'd been in his old shooting days, lost his temper and dove at Hogan. Hulk snatched him in a front face lock and choked the sixty-one-year-old promoter out on the floor. Verne was humiliated. Vince McMahon Jr., ever poised to strike, swooped in and financially lured both Hulk and Schultz over to the WWF, even taking Verne's announcer, Mean Gene Okerlund. The war was on.

The day before Hulk arrived in Japan, he'd won the WWF World Heavyweight title and still seemed overwhelmed by it. It was the most financially rewarding belt in the business, even more so than the NWA or AWA, despite the fact that the NWA title commanded more respect. When Hulk had got to the WWF, Bob Backlund had begrudgingly refused to drop it to him, demanding that whomever beat him had to have at least some kind of legit wrestling background. So The Iron Sheik took the belt from Backlund and immediately dropped it to Hogan.

As we watched, Tom flipped his butt onto the floor and ground it out. "So that's the big sensation," he said. "Can't work much, can he?"

Abdullah lowered his shades.

Davey stared out at the ring nearly lovesick, fantasizing about being as big and built as Hulk.

On the final night of the tour, February 10, 1984, the climax of the tournament was a three-way run off for the World Junior belt at the Budokan Hall in Tokyo. I stood watching from the dressing-room door as Dynamite took on Davey in their highly anticipated showdown. At the end, Davey hoisted Dynamite up in a standing suplex in the middle of the ring. Teetering from exhaustion, they both tipped over the top rope with Tom landing painfully hard on the corner of the ring apron. Although he was hurt, Tom managed to crawl back in, beating the count to win. He could barely walk, but he went right back out and had another bruising match.

When it was over, the Young Boys helped Tom back to the dressing room, gently laying him down on the floor. Hulk stepped around him as he tore out of the dressing room for his match with Inoki: his first ever WWF World title defence. The Young Boys pressed ice packs into Tom's lower back as he moaned in agony, gripping the World Junior belt tightly.

Titles. It would be wrong for anyone to think they didn't mean anything, that it's all fake. I knew, on that night, the title meant the world to Tom, but at a price even he couldn't begin to imagine.

When I collected my money for the tour that night, I wasn't surprised to learn that Tom and Davey would be coming back to Japan in July without me, but I understood why. Tom and Davey were both thick and chiselled; though I was every bit the wrestler they were, I couldn't compete with their look because I wasn't on steroids. I didn't take it personally, though. I was happy for Davey. At least I had Toronto!

Two days later I was in the dressing room at Maple Leaf Gardens after a strong win over a guy named J.J. Dillon. Later in the card I charged out, saving the babyface in Leo's match, beating him back to the curtain to a huge pop. The plan was for me to come back in two weeks and wrestle Leo for their North American title.

And then I was in Regina, the only thing keeping me away from Julie and Jade a five-hundred-mile drive. I was watching the last match through a little hole in the dressing-room wall, waiting for my cue to hit the ring on my old friend Killer Khan, setting up our upcoming feud around the territory. What happened next will play forever in my head. The crowd roared when I hit the ring, nailing six-foot-five Khan until he fell out onto the floor.

"C'mon! C'mon!" he yelled.

I was grateful that he was doing his best to make me look good, so I jumped out after him. But I misjudged the distance to the floor and spiked my leg into the cement, hyperextending it like a stork! The crowd groaned and winced in empathy. In a second I knew the only big break I'd be getting was in my shattered right knee.

As I rolled on the floor groaning, Killer Khan backed right off, and the crowd closed quietly around me with stunned, sorry faces.

Hito crouched beside me, shaking his head sadly. "This one bad. Very bad." I rode right through the night, with nothing but a leaky bag of ice to stop the swelling.

I'd had to go on a waiting list for knee surgery. Shortly after I was injured, Tom moved back to Calgary to work for Stu again. Besides, Michelle was pregnant, and they could have the baby for free in Canada. Their baby girl, Bronwyne, was born in May.

I finally had my knee repaired on June 26, four months after I hurt it. To make full use of the recovery time, I'd had surgery to remove all four of my wisdom teeth the next day. Now it was Canada Day, the eve of my twenty-seventh birthday, and I was in no mood to celebrate. Julie was going home to Regina to visit her grandmother, leaving me to hobble around on crutches. Some birthday present. She actually hissed at me like a hellcat as she stomped down the front steps and loaded a smiling Jade into my grey Caddy. Honestly, I was glad to see her go. As they pulled away from the curb, I waved goodbye in silent sarcasm from the front steps, and it was no surprise to me that only Jade waved back.

The air in the house had been thick with anger for so long that the sudden silence jarred open my emotions. I plopped down on an old, half-stuffed chair and allowed myself an exercise in self-pity. I touched my swollen face, and then my sore knee with its fresh stitches. I felt like

Frankenstein's monster, or at least the King of Pain. But the physical pain was never as tough as the doubts and fears I carried deep in my heart. This was one of those times when I really needed Julie, and she just couldn't or wouldn't be there for me, for reasons I didn't understand, and still don't.

Tom and Davey were galloping ahead of me as Julie was pulling away too. I studied the cracks on the ceiling long enough that they began to form abstract pictures, but it was when I closed my eyes that the real picture came into focus. I had endured enough with Julie. If it wasn't for Jade, and the baby on the way, I'd have given up by now. Acceptance of that truth, sad as it was, helped me to collect myself.

I could never leave my babies, but I had no intention of being miserable, on some manic roller-coaster ride, for the rest of my life. I'd stayed true to myself, playing it smart and safe, refusing to take steroids, but it was obvious just by looking at Tom and Davey that using steroids had made all the difference to their careers. The knee doctor had said it was going to take me up to six months to recover! I couldn't afford not to work for that long a stretch. But I'd just heard that the Tunneys had suddenly broken off with the NWA and had climbed into bed with Vince McMahon and the WWF. If I wanted to get ahead in the world, that left me with only one card to play. Japan. Shimma had booked me for four weeks in October. I had to be ready!

A few days of being alone, but not lonely, at my house did me some good. At the end of the week I was in better spirits and went down to the big Stampede show to say hello to the boys. One of the main attractions was Abdullah, whom I found in the dressing room, happy as ever. "Hello, Gabe," he said. For some reason, Abbie called everyone Gabe.

I took a seat not far from the ring, forced to be a fan for the night. Abbie worked over Jerry Morrow, and when the ref disqualified him, he grabbed some steel folding chairs and threw them into the ring and then tipped over the timekeeper's table. Just like old times. Then Abbie came toward me and I gave him a look. I can't! My knee! As much as I tried not to, there I was bashing him over the head with a crutch. He whipped his bladed thumb across his forehead. Blood poured. "Hit me again!" So I did.

What a strange business, where bloodletting could be offered and appreciated as kindness.

That night Abbie went out of his way to make me look good, maybe as a favour to Stu, or maybe to me. The scared little boy wrestling fan in me who once dreamed about the terror of Abdullah The Butcher couldn't have been happier as he rolled his eyes at me, bleeding, while I shook my crutch at him. My dad would've smiled and playfully called him a black bastard. Me, I called him a cool cat. Thanks, Abbie.

15

SINK OR SWIM

I STARTED WRESTLING AGAIN ON AUGUST 10, which was way too soon. The plan was for me to do tag matches for a while, mostly standing on the apron. In the dressing room at the pavilion before my first match back, my dad introduced me to George Scott, one of the famous Scott Brothers who'd worked for him back in the 1960s. George (who, it later struck me, bears a striking resemblance to Donald Rumsfeld) was lured out of a long and prosperous run as NWA booker for the Crocketts to become the WWF's booker and one of Vince McMahon's top soldiers. He'd come to Calgary to make Stu an offer he couldn't refuse.

Vince wanted Stu's territory. If Stu didn't sell, McMahon would work his way into the territory anyway, and we'd be out of business and broke too. At least there was an offer of a buy-out.

George was standing beside Stu as my dad explained the WWF's proposition to me. Stampede Wrestling would shut down, the WWF's TV show would replace Stu's show, and my parents would get U.S.$250,000 up front and ten per cent of all house shows subsequently run in any of Stu's regular towns, including Vancouver. My reaction was instant relief, although I didn't reveal the extent of it to George. My parents had lost a fortune, and it seemed to me that selling the whole headache to McMahon would guarantee them a comfortable and well-deserved retirement.

Of course, I had practical concerns about my own future. Stu went on to explain that the WWF had offered to move Bruce into an office job as their representative promoting all the towns in Western Canada; Vince would also hire Dynamite, Davey, me and maybe eventually Big Jim (who was still working Louisiana) as full-time wrestlers. I was immediately envious of what they had in mind for Bruce because he'd be home every night.

I told George that I didn't have any aspirations to languish at the bottom of their cards. He smiled and shook his head, "You don't get it. You're gonna work with all the top guys in all the top angles. We're going to make you a big star, Bret." I thought, Yeah, right.

In a few days, he said, Dynamite and I would fly down to WWF television tapings so McMahon could take a look at us. I levelled with George, telling him that I could barely walk across the room — it wasn't exactly a good time to show off my skills. He told me the match would be short and I wouldn't have to do much. I didn't want to lose out on the opportunity, so I agreed. My dad asked me to keep everything under my hat for the time being

I met up with some of the boys after the show. When I got home at about 3 a.m., I was startled to find Wilk asleep on my bed. He explained that Julie was at the hospital and had called him to come babysit Jade until I got home. By late the next afternoon, Julie was still in labour, and I called Stu to try to get out of working in Edmonton that night. He calmly said, "You'll need the extra money."

That's how I found myself being told the news that Julie and I now had a son on a grimy gas station pay phone in Red Deer. Dallas Jeffrey Hart was born on August 11, 1984.

About a week later, Tom and I flew east and spent all day backstage at the Hamilton Civic Center watching WWF wrestlers go about their routine at a TV taping. We'd been required to be at the building by 11 a.m. and found out that TV tapings were an all-day affair. We weren't allowed to leave until after the matches were over, just before midnight. The WWF provided no food, there were no nearby restaurants, and we got hungry. Wrestlers wandered by: Superfly Jimmy Snuka, Roddy Piper, Greg Valentine, Adrian Adonis, Tito Santana.

Large sound-proof panels served to partition off an area where the wrestlers took turns churning out their TV promos, doing the same sixty-second spot for dozens of different markets, just changing the name of the local arena or town. Although I'd gotten better on the mic, I cringed when I heard how precise and intense the WWF wrestlers were with their promos. The New York territory was infamous for its walk 'n' talk, and these were some of the best mic men in the business. I knew I was in trouble. This would be sink or swim.

Jay Strongbow, better known as Chief, approached us with his hands behind his back and his lower lip jutting out to set up our TV tag match. Chief was a heavy-set Italian, now in his mid-fifties, who had got away with wrestling as an American Indian for years. These days Chief was an agent, a foreman, who carried out the boss's orders. I was relieved when he told me to lose the Buddy The Heartthrob gimmick; we'd be going with Bret Hart.

From the way Chief sized Tom up, it was clear that his reputation had preceded him. He told Tom to take the fall however he wanted, alerting us to make sure the tag match, including intros, was less than four minutes long.

Vince McMahon, whom Chief referred to as The Emperor, waved Tom and me over. Vince was six-foot-two, combed his hair straight back, and was wearing white running shoes and a red suit jacket with padded shoulders; to me, The Emperor looked more like Big Boy from the hamburger chain. Giant men, ripped and cut, tanned and oiled, passed by vying for his attention. I had no choice but to accept the undeniable truth that he had the power to change my life forever, for better or worse.

Tom, never much of a conversationalist, replied with a grunt when Vince complimented him on his muscled look. Then, glancing at me, Vince said dryly, "I like my wrestlers to spend a lot of time in the gym. I'm looking forward to your match." I hoped he understood that I had just come off knee surgery. Then Chief called him away.

My first WWF match turned out to be a disaster. I wasn't accustomed to guzzling a jobber, working such a short match. I'd been off for so long that I was rusty, and as I slammed the jobber, my knee gave out. Tom, who was perched on the top corner, groaned because I slammed him facing the wrong way. I had to go back and pull the jobber around by his legs. Tom rolled his eyes and frowned at me just before he launched into a perfect dive.

I was horrible. And I knew it.

Vince met us when we came back. He didn't even look at me as he said, "Nice work, Dynamite!"

The WWF tapings lasted two days, during which they got three weekends of TV in the can. In Poughkeepsie, New York, Hulk Hogan and David Schultz greeted Tom and me with big smiles. They appeared to be the best of pals, kidding each other and play wrestling. Tom and I sat watching as their friendly tussle escalated into a full-blown scrap, with Schultz cinched up in a front face lock. For forty-five minutes at least, they overturned furniture and got nasty rug burns on their knees and elbows, until Hogan won when a seething Schultz gave up. And that was the moment their friendship ended.

I was in another four-minute match, this time singles, and I had a much better outing, doing a perfect piledriver. But when I came through the curtain, Chief met me with a perturbed look and said, "That's Orndorff's finish! Don't use it again!"

At the end of the night, Tom and I each got paid U.S.$50. The day before we'd got Cdn.$75. Even the biggest stars were only paid this token sum for TV, since the WWF felt the wrestlers should be grateful for the exposure. Dynamite grumbled to me that he didn't fly all that way to get paid fifty bucks. He told Stu to tell the WWF to go fuck themselves. He didn't need it; he and Davey had Japan.

On the Sunday night of the August long weekend, I bent over the crib, gazing at Dallas. He had big beautiful eyes, not one hair on his head and his mom's mouth. Things were no better between Julie and me.

My right knee would never survive Japan. I realized that if I wanted to feed my family, I needed to heal and fast: I'd have to take steroids. This was one of the most difficult decisions I ever made. I called Tom, and within minutes he showed up at my house armed with two loaded needles, one for each butt cheek. Later on that night I lay shivering in a fever, running to the bathroom with diarrhea and vomiting. It turned out the steroids were from a veterinarian and were meant for horses. Tom got sick too.

Davey, who'd been charged for hip-tossing that Calgary cop, was panicking about the possibility that he'd be deported as a result, and rather suddenly announced that he and Di would be getting married in October. All this time, no one had any clue of the huge decision my father was in the process of making—to sell or not to sell. On Friday, September 6, Stu finally let it slip that he had sold to Vince, and that this would be the final taping of the Stampede Wrestling TV show.

Bruce was beyond livid: Stu and Helen had kept him out of the loop. His grief and fear came out as fury, and he refused to work. He even tried to rally the boys to boycott the show. It's been said that Stu sold Stampede Wrestling because he felt he owed it to my mom to get out of the business with a retirement nest egg, but what he told me, more than once over the years, is that the biggest reason he sold was because he just couldn't tolerate the way Bruce ran things.

After the last TV taping, we went on the road for a week, winding up at the Edmonton Fieldhouse on September 15, 1984, for a final cage match. Most of the boys spent the week drowning their fears of uncertain futures in beer.

There I was, climbing the steel mesh of the cage with a ghastly long gash in my forehead. I was mad, glad and sad that it was all over. I was teamed, with an equally inebriated Dynamite, against Rotten Ron Starr and Bad News. Everyone bled except News.

Rotten Ron, with his red Afro and Southern drawl, was as creepy a wrestler as there ever was. Fans would spit on him, and he'd catch it in his own mouth, swallow and smile. I happily planted a boot into Rotten Ron's face. Dynamite had fought free from Bad News, and together we made our escape up the sides of the cage, climbing over the top, barely out of the clawing grasp of the heels. We could see the faces of fans, who had seen us through so much. Halfway down the outside of the cage, we dropped to the floor to an explosion of joy drenched in sadness.

I wobbled back to the dressing room, numb. I said my final goodbyes to Karl Moffat, the Japs and, in particular, The Cuban. So many of Stu's crew were good hands, but with Vince McMahon in the ascendant, it was the dawn of the age of steroid freaks.

Although I was under no illusions about my chances of success in the WWF, at least I had a new job. And I was concerned about what would become of them all.

Hito. For him it was over, and he knew it. But he smiled like an old cat, and I couldn't help but feel that he still had a few lives left; he'd land on his feet somewhere.

Ross. Wayne. Nothing.

But aside from Bruce, nobody was angry. How could they be? Stu had been losing a lot of money for a long time but still paying their wages, and they all knew it.

When fans who had been with us since 1948, through all the highs and lows of the Calgary territory, tuned in the next week to see the show, it had simply vanished, and Vince's show was on instead.

Something uniquely vaudevillian was lost forever.

For me, it was a thin line between love and hate. I wouldn't miss the endless white lines, the bad weather, the physical pain and the loneliness, but I'd miss the boys, the fans and the towns. As the van rocked and rolled down the highway back to Calgary, J.R. and the boys harmonized through one last rendition of "Hang down your head, Tom Dooley, hang down your head and cry. Hang down your head, Tom Dooley, poor boy you're bound to die."

I was unsure whether it was the beginning of the end, or the end of my beginning.

PART TWO

THE FOUNDATION

16

PAYING MY DUES IN THE WWF

JUST BEFORE I STARTED full-time with the WWF, I did a quick tour in Japan: I was skeptical about all the promises George Scott had made about what the WWF had in store for me and wanted to have some kind of safety net. I worked hard on the tour and earned another six weeks in Japan to start in February 1985.

On October 22, I wrote Julie a letter from Nagita about how I was feeling about my present and my future:

> . . . these past months have been hard on me and I'm quite confused—physically, mentally and emotionally drained. I feel like a wounded animal stuck with spears, staggering around aimlessly . . . I keep going on like there is nothing wrong. Sooner or later I will break. I want to break, to let it go in an agonizing wail—but I just can't seem to let it out. I knew that my dad's business could end. I actually used to look forward to it. Yet twenty-seven years of my life just went out like a match. Suddenly, I find myself poisoning myself with steroids just to maintain a foothold and it doesn't mean a damn thing.
>
> I'm proud of myself. I believe I am (I was) a great wrestler, but . . . was I really any good? My career is nowhere. It makes me sad to see Tom and Davey so huge over here while after five tours here I'm still a nobody. What hurts the most is that if it wasn't for my dad the promoter I wouldn't have made it at all.
>
> I know you've heard all this before but you need to understand, it hurts me, maybe a little, maybe a lot. It just hasn't hit me yet. I keep thinking that there must be more to life than pro wrestling and someday I might need to prove that to myself.

I flew into Calgary from Tokyo on a Thursday afternoon, just in time for my WWF debut on its first ever swing through Western Canada. Julie brought Jade and Dallas to meet me at the airport, but the joy was short-lived. The next day I hid my travel bag on the porch and slipped out of Jade's sight so she wouldn't see me leave. Gone again.

The WWF show was an eye opener. I was instantly relegated to opening-match status—I was no longer a big fish in a little pond. The crowd at the Saddledome was small and unenthusiastic. It was as disheartening to them as it was to the Stampede wrestlers they'd passionately supported to see us now reduced to fodder for the WWF crew. After years of fast-paced, realistic wrestling, the fans didn't immediately warm to the WWF's slower, showier style. Even at the first show, it was apparent that the WWF was going to have a tough time becoming accepted in Calgary.

For the next four days I travelled through familiar territory with an unfamiliar crew. No more vans. Now I was flying on commercial jets with a band of vagabonds who often behaved like children. They thought they were really bad, but they didn't have nothin' on the boys in the van—except for Adrian Adonis that is! He'd have fit right in. Food fights, spitballs and pranks. (I suspected right away that he'd get along great with Jim Neidhart.)

I knew a few of the guys from Japan and Toronto: S.D. Jones, Quick Draw McGraw, Greg Valentine. I was happy to see Dave Schultz. André was lacing up his size-twenty-two boots when I went to shake his hand, but he still wouldn't look at me.

On my last day on the Western Canada leg, I straddled a chair in the dressing room in Winnipeg to talk with Dr. D (Dave Schultz). For some reason, Angelo Mosca decided to get on me about Bruce killing Stu's territory with a heel ref. I was surprised and more than a little grateful when Schultz told him to shut his mouth. Later, Schultz pulled me aside and said, "You don't ever need to take any shit from these guys, Brit. You're as good a worker as anyone they got! Work on your mic skills, but as a worker, there's not anyone 'round here can tell you a thing."

After the matches I ate at the hotel restaurant, where I found Quick Draw, my roommate for the night, face down in a plate of food. He'd overdone it with the Placidyl again. I helped him to our room and kept an eye on him during the night.

The first road trip I took in the United States for the WWF began in Columbus, Ohio, on November 14, 1984. I'd long ago lost my driver's license because of the speed limits I'd had to break to get the Stampede crew to my father's towns on time, and I still had no credit card, so there I was at the airport hanging around hoping I'd run into some of the boys.

Eventually I caught a cab to the Ohio Centre, where I, once again, had to persuade a security guard to let me into the building.

I was very early, but I didn't know where else to go. I crashed out on a wooden table in the empty dressing room, with a baseball cap pulled down over my face and my bag as a pillow. I was startled awake by some guy who looked like Barney Rubble pulling on my toe, asking who I was and what I was doing there.

I sat up and told him I was Stu Hart's kid.

"You don't have a match, but we can throw you in the battle royal. I'm Pat Patterson, the agent."

I'd certainly heard of Pat Patterson and his tag partner, Ray Stevens, considered by many to be the best tag team of the 1970s. Pat was famous for his bumps and his ring psychology, and he'd only recently retired. Behind the scenes, he was also famous for being gay and not caring whether the wrestlers knew.

The WWF was simultaneously running three towns a night with different crews. Pat was a road agent now, like Chief Jay Strongbow. He ran the dressing room, posted the lineup and, after getting his orders from Vince and George, he often had the unenviable task of giving the wrestlers their finishes. At that time, the assigned finishes were based largely on seniority, of which I had none, so I didn't expect anything great. It was all part of paying my dues in the WWF.

As I got dressed for my match, I was self-conscious about the way my pale white skin stood out against the tanned and overly muscular physiques that filled the dressing room. From here on, I'd have to hit the tanning bed and the gym religiously.

My second WWF show was in Dayton and was like the first.

On the third night, in Cincinnati, Pat told me I'd be the opening bout with a really green kid from Brooklyn named Steve Lombardi and just to do the best I could. I tried hard, and, all in all, that little match wasn't bad. Pat was so thrilled with it that I soon realized that Steve was Pat's boy. That had nothing to do with me, though. I found Pat to be friendly, good-humoured and easy to deal with.

I was grateful to be working, mostly putting guys over or doing twenty-minute broadways. Clearly, at this point they had no plans for me. On the bright side, things were a little better with Julie, but it was often hard to talk to her at night. I roomed with another wrestler whenever I could to save money, and there's things you're just not going to say to your wife with a half-naked wrestler lying in the other bed watching CNN.

As the plane climbed over Atlanta headed for California, I reclined in my seat. Compared to rolling down the Trans-Canada Highway packed shoulder to shoulder with fourteen full-sized wrestlers and a couple of midgets, with no heat and the oil light on, even my coach seat felt roomy. The plane was oddly empty. Then the stewardess served me a delicious turkey dinner. "Happy Thanksgiving," she said. My first American Thanksgiving.

When Pat handed me my cheque at the end of the tour, I thought my eyes were playing tricks on me. For only four days in Canada at poorly attended shows and five cities in the United States, they paid me US$2,400. I was blown away. When I called Julie to tell her, all she said was, "So I guess this means you'll be gone forever now?"

"Julie, I'm not sure how long this is going to last, but I'm prepared to hang on here as long as I can. Think of the babies."

Silence. Then, "I think Dallas is crying, so I'd better go." Click.

As my dad had predicted, the WWF was quickly becoming a well-oiled tank running over any and all competition, fuelled mostly by the organization's ingenious mass marketing of Hulk Hogan. My thinking was that it was better to be in the tank than under it.

Unbeknownst to me, there were big things brewing. In the summer of 1984, Vince McMahon had pitched a plan to his staff that was so ambitious no one thought it could be done. Vince wanted to make wrestling mainstream, to make it cool to like it. He wanted to manipulate the demographic of the WWF's audience, targeting the niche created by the fledgling MTV network. He outlined a brilliant marketing strategy to marry rock and wrestling in a kitsch entertainment extravaganza oozing with glam, headlined by a bizarre mix of celebrities, with wrestling as the backdrop. He had a date and a venue in mind: March 31, 1985, Madison Square Garden. Tickets would go for an unheard of US$100. Vince planned to put his spectacular out over closed-circuit TV, where it could be viewed in bars and theatres all across North America. It would be called WrestleMania. He believed in it so strongly that despite the doubts of some of his own staff, he was ready to roll the dice, and while I was on the road for those first months, plans were being made that would change the face of wrestling once and for all.

The buildings were nearly full or sold out wherever we went in the United States. The Kiel Auditorium in St. Louis turned out to be no different. Historically, St. Louis was the NWA's key city, and the Kiel had been the home of pro wrestling's greatest workers, including Pat O'Connor, Lou Thesz and Harley Race. I had a so-so match in a big ring as hard as cement.

After the show, a lot of the wrestlers were eating at the JoJo's near the hotel. Chief sat down next to me — he'd been a respected worker in his day, but it was obvious that he hadn't missed many meals lately. He asked me what the office had in mind for me, and when I explained what George Scott had promised, he seemed incredulous. "You believe that, do ya?"

I didn't know how he wanted me to answer that, so I told him my only choice was to believe it.

Chief took a bite out of his sandwich and after considerable chewing and thinking he asked what I wanted Vince to do with me. I'd seen what they'd done for the Tonga Kid, an eighteen-year-old Samoan who got lucky when they teamed him up with a Polynesian Tarzan by the name of Superfly Jimmy Snuka. If they wanted, they could make a star out of anyone.

"It'd be nice if they gave me some kind of a push," I said. "If I ever got the same push as Hulk Hogan, they'd be chantin' my name next week. It's all about who they want to make and break."

Chief barked out, loud enough for the other wrestlers to hear, "So you think you're Hulk Hogan, do ya? I can't believe you! Hey, did you hear this? Young Hart here thinks he's better than Hogan." I tried to explain, but Chief wasn't interested in listening.

Late one night that November, I walked into a café near the Holiday Inn in Oklahoma City and saw Sergeant Slaughter sitting quietly by himself. Sarge was a huge draw, almost as big as Hulk Hogan at the time. His storyline grew out of the Iranian hostage crisis: With The Iron Sheik as his archrival, the once despised drill sergeant was now a great American hero. He even had his own G.I. Joe action figure. Wrestling storylines have always exploited wartime animosities: first the American good guy versus the Germans and the Japanese, and now it was the Russians and the Iranians.

Sarge invited me to join him; we talked about his family, his time in the business, his career as a real soldier—he left the army for wrestling. He was kind enough to listen to me too, and he had some advice: "One thing I do know is, watch your back. Vince is a ruthless guy. He'll tell you whatever you want to hear, so what he says doesn't mean much if you ask me, but good luck, kid." He left a tip on the table and walked across the street to the Holiday Inn.

He was a thoughtful, decent guy who, it seemed to me, would be far happier doing something else. But after Hogan, he was the biggest star in the company, and nobody walked away from the kind of money he was making.

After I finished eating, I plopped myself down in the hotel lounge, where a stunning blonde came to sit next to me. I took a sip of my beer and said hi and she said hi back. The Tonga Kid's tongue slid out over his lips like a Komodo dragon, and he didn't waste any time coming over to make a move on her. Jimmy Snuka stopped him, "Young Stu Hart here is doing just fine, brudda."

I kept telling myself that I wasn't trying to pick her up, yet all I was doing was trying to pick her up. Soon she was telling me that she was involved with a married Oklahoma state trooper who promised he'd leave his wife but never did. That night she'd got tired of his bullshit, got mad, and ended up at the bar. She had a tight, hard, athletic figure, so I asked her whether she worked out.

"Sure do, with my boyfriend. He's as big as a truck, all 'roided-up 'n' all. Sometimes I even load up his needle and give him his shot."

"Do you, ah, think maybe you could give me a shot?" I asked shyly, immediately embarrassed at the absurdity of the come-on.

A little while later, she sat on the edge of my bed carefully draining the serum into a syringe, snapping the needle with her fingers like a pro. She asked me to drop my pants, jabbed the needle deep into my butt and then rubbed me with alcohol. I made a half-hearted attempt to hike up my pants, but she pushed me slowly down onto the bed. I thought, It's not like anybody's ever going to know. I half expected a big, angry Oklahoma state trooper to kick in the door with his gun blazing, but then that thought vanished, replaced by a much better one.

Less than two weeks later, in Toronto on December 9, 1984, George Scott gave Sergeant Slaughter his walking papers. I couldn't believe the WWF let him go, but soon they were grooming an unskilled jobber named Corporal Kirchner to do his gimmick. The message was clear: We were all expendable.

It turned out that Sarge's action figure got him fired. The WWF had launched its own line of merchandise, including action figures, offering their wrestlers 5 per cent royalties. Sarge had got an unprecedented deal for himself, and Vince wouldn't stand for it.

As a little fish I found myself swimming as hard as I could. In thirty-seven days straight I'd covered ten states and four provinces. If I was honest, I was riddled with awe and amazement, mesmerized, reeling, unable to comprehend the enormous scope of all I'd seen. The whole time I was away my heart longed for home: If the money had been no good, or if they'd fired me, I would have been gone in a flash. Instead, America pulled me into her embrace and wrapped her arms and legs around me. I was confused and I stayed confused, because as much as I wished that it would all end, with every short break, I couldn't wait to start back again.

Word of Vince's grand vision *WrestleMania* had finally trickled down to the dressing room. A lot of the boys were nervous because so much was being gambled on one big show: If it was a failure, it could mean the premature demise of the WWF.

But the masterfully orchestrated media hype in the months leading up to *WrestleMania* was already resulting in sold-out shows every night, whether Hogan was on them or not. Wrestling was becoming huge. Vince's timing couldn't have been more perfect. While seizing power was a ruthless move, it was also a bold and brilliant one. He barged into any city or town regardless of who the promoter was. In particular, he stuck it to Verne Gagne in Minneapolis by staging well-run shows in Verne's backyard with his own former stars. He did the same to Ole Anderson in Atlanta. Decent promoters were powerless to stop Vince as he looted their talent rosters. While it was bad for the promoters, it was good for the boys: It looked like the old nickel-and-dime mentality was giving way to the future—pro wrestling was going national under the direction of a guy who seemed to have what it took to make everybody into bigger stars than they'd ever dreamed they could be.

I was grateful to be aligned with the conquering army and was especially glad that McMahon had chosen to broker a deal with Stu rather than forcibly taking his territory. To the best of my knowledge, offers were extended only to my dad, to the LaBelles out of Los Angeles and to the Tunneys in Toronto, because Vince liked and respected them. McMahon intimidated me, yet at the same time I respected how he had treated my dad.

George Scott had talked to me in Toronto, right after he had fired Sarge, telling me to keep up the good work, and also asking me to sound Tom and Davey out—Vince wanted to bring them in. Then he threw me a curve: "What's this I hear about your brother Bruce trying to get a wrestling licence to run against us in Calgary?"

What are you doing, Bruce? I thought. Then, What are you doing to me? I said, "I don't know anything about that, George, and I certainly don't have anything to do with it." But I was going to find out.

When I arrived at Hart house on Christmas Day 1984, the entire family was there except for Ellie, Jim and their three baby girls. Jim was working the Memphis territory, managed by a guy named Jimmy Hart. Stu was eager to hear about my trip, and I was just as eager to tell him.

After I'd brought Stu up to date, we talked about what to do with Bruce. When Stu had questioned him on whether he'd applied for a promoter's licence, Bruce had vehemently denied it. Stu didn't believe him and was worried that Bruce would queer his deal with Vince, and that I'd be a casualty too.

Later that day I found a moment to ask Bruce for myself, and he swore up and down that there was nothing to the rumour. But he also said that he thought that the WWF wouldn't be around long and that he didn't think it was any crime to be ready when it folded. I told Bruce I'd seen Vince in action, and that he was wrong: The WWF was only getting bigger and stronger. I pleaded with him not to do anything that would appear to Vince to be underhanded because it would jeopardize Stu's deal and my entire future. Just then Bruce's young wife, Andrea, called him away from our conversation, and he seemed relieved for the excuse.

She was sitting in the living room talking with Michelle and Julie, all of them with babies in their arms. Julie was in a sulk again, though she always apologized for her bad behaviour after the fact. I'd built up a nest egg and, with bountiful cheques coming from the WWF, I made the decision to sell the dilapidated house in Ramsay and move to a neighbourhood better suited to raising a family. Guilt over my unfaithfulness was like a flashing light in a dark corner of my conscience: I just wished that something I did could help make Julie happy.

There were more undercurrents that Christmas. Tom and Davey were huddled by the picture window in the living room, a snowscape of the city in the background. Davey had recently been found guilty of assaulting that Calgary cop, but much to everyone's relief, he hadn't been thrown out of the country or sent to jail. Instead he was fined and put on probation.

I let Tom and Davey know that Vince was drooling over the idea of hiring both of them, but Tom said if the way the WWF was using me was any measure, he wasn't interested. But both of them were acting strange. When I asked whether something was up, they said no.

A few minutes later, Ben pulled me aside to tell me that Tom and Davey had just double-crossed New Japan, who were partnered with the WWF, and jumped over to All Japan. Each got a signing bonus of US$20,000 and a $10,000-a-week guarantee. (I later found out it was really $6,500 a week.)

That evening, I asked Tom again whether anything was going on. He said, "Gabe, fer fook's sakes, nothin's up." It was the first time in years that he completely kayfabed me. It hurt that I was trying to watch their backs as best as I could, with no consideration from them for mine. Because of the strong relationship between the WWF and New Japan, I'd been allowed to work both companies, but now New Japan would surely fire me—as a direct consequence of what Tom and Davey had done.

I watched them tossing back beers as they chatted with Stu, who was clueless about all the machinations. Across the room Bruce was talking with Ross, Owen and Owen's girlfriend, Martha, and I knew something was up with Bruce too. We were all out for ourselves.

My mom was busy shooing five cats away from spraying on her Christmas tree. She loved putting every strand of real silver tinsel in its perfect place. She was happier than I ever remembered her that Christmas. She was surrounded by ten grandchildren, most of them under two. Eleven, if you count Tom and Michelle's Bronwyne, which my mom always did. Even more grandkids would soon be on the way, with Alison, Georgia and Diana all pregnant. Maria was pregnant too, and Smith had his hands full: His Puerto Rican beauty was on the edge of a breakdown, possibly because being married to Smith hadn't been all she'd hoped for. Through the window, I could see Dean chipping ice off the front porch steps. He was living at home too and also got a little bit crazier every year.

Then Georgia and Alison came through the swinging doors from the kitchen, each carrying a huge roast turkey. I picked Jade up and let her pull the chain on the dinner bell, and Keith rounded up all the stragglers to come eat. He and Leslie had been smiling all day because they'd just won $100,000 in the lottery. Wayne said grace and thanked God for Keith's good fortune.

I looked over at my mom. For her, the greatest Christmas present was that she and Stu were finally out of the business, but in my dad's eyes I saw an emptiness that told a different story.

When Julie saw my booking sheets that New Year's Eve, her face drained of colour. I wanted to make as much money as I could while I could, and I'd asked George Scott to book me steady. As of the next morning, I would be gone for fifty-five days, although I'd pass through Calgary twice on the tour. She barely spoke to me for the rest of the night. That was our pattern: What little time I had at home was ruined by her dread of when I'd be gone again. I finished packing my bags and rolled into our crowded bed, where Jade sweetly slept, sprawled out next to Julie like a tiny star. Baby Dallas was asleep in the crib.

As I lay there I couldn't help but think, If you won't hold me, I'll find someone else who will. Just then, Julie wrapped her arms around me and whispered softly in my ear, "I'm sorry."

"I know. Me too."

What else was there to say?

17

"TURN US HEEL AND CALL US THE HART FOUNDATION"

AN EIGHTEEN-YEAR-OLD RED-HEADED ITALIAN KID named Carlo gave me a ride from the airport in Toronto to Hamilton, Ontario, on my first day of the new tour. He was the last and only fan of Buddy The Heartthrob Hart.

As soon as I arrived at the Hamilton Civic Centre an irate George Scott confronted me. "Your two buddies are going to be damn sorry they did that!" New Japan had called Vince, who'd called Stu, expecting him to order Tom and Davey to renege on their new arrangement. But they weren't about to give up their lucrative deal for Stu, which made him look like a toothless old hound. "Well, *your* February tour to Japan is cancelled!" George barked. "And I'm hearing a lot of crap about your brother Bruce too. What's he going to do, run against your dad?"

I told George once again that I knew nothing.

A few minutes later in the dressing room, I stood with Don The Spoiler Jardin, his lips pursed and arms crossed, as we set up our angle with George and Chief. That night on TV, as the referee backed me away, The Spoiler pretended to load a chunk of steel into his mask. I came at him, he head-butted me, then pinned me, one . . . two . . . three. There was hardly any reaction from the crowd, who'd already sat through three hours of similarly one-sided matches, waiting for Hulk Hogan to appear. I cringed knowing that my Stampede fans, pretty much the only fans I had, would now see me as a jobber. It is so important not to be labelled a jobber in the eyes of the fans. It can easily become a stink that is almost impossible to wash off. I just hoped that 1985 would turn out better than it was beginning.

When I got to the building in Hershey, Pennsylvania, on January 10, the boys were already lined up all the way down a long backstage corridor waiting their turn to see Dr. George Zahorian, a urological surgeon and osteopath from Harrisburg who relished his $35-a-night gig as commission doctor because he enjoyed being around the wrestlers. Zahorian was a tall, nerdy professor type, sporting suspenders, a dapper suit, polka-dot bow tie and black-rimmed spectacles. I joined the line and found that the conversation was still buzzing over the latest scandal: On December 28, ABC had sent a film crew over to Madison Square Garden with investigative reporter John Stossel and had run into some literal obstructionism.

In the buildup to that first *WrestleMania,* the hype soared to the point where it wasn't unusual to see mainstream media around; their big probing question invariably was, Is it fake? The commentary in these stories was almost always done with sarcasm, in an attempt to portray wrestling as buffoonish melodrama. Maybe it was, but it was also great fun to watch and hard to do, and the media never gave anyone credit for that, preferring to point out that if the outcomes of the matches were predetermined, then somehow we were duping the fans.

When the WWF granted John Stossel backstage access after Christmas, it was to get more hype for *WrestleMania.* The wrestlers were preparing for their matches and didn't welcome the intrusion. The more Stossel pushed his microphone in everyone's faces, the more tense the boys got. Finally, Stossel challenged Dave Schultz, with the cameras rolling. In a nasal whine, he said, "I think this is fake." Schultz wound up and cuffed him hard, knocking him to the ground, and then chased Stossel down the hall threatening to smack him again. I can't say it was the right thing for Schultz to do, but I think wrestlers everywhere have always respected Dave for protecting the business. And Stossel found out that wrestling is as real as it is fake.

The story hadn't aired yet. Perhaps what Stossel should have been uncovering was the lineup to see Dr. Zahorian. Quick Draw came out of Zahorian's room carrying his own personal pharmacy: vials of steroids and an assortment of small boxes containing Valium, Percocet, Halcion, speed and his much loved Placidyls. He could have used a grocery cart.

When it was my turn, the doctor took my blood pressure and pulse. Then, like everyone else in the line, I handed him some crisp hundred-dollar bills and stocked up on twenty vials of testosterone, twenty Deca-Durabolin and four bottles of gonadotropin—to keep my balls from shrinking—along with several boxes of Halcion so I could sleep and a cache of needles.

We all knew Zahorian was a gouger, but at least he was a real doctor and his drugs were legit, which was better than buying gas from pushers at local gyms.

On January 21, 1985, I set my bag down in the dressing room at Madison Square Garden. I was still being billed as "plus one other match," but I'd finally made it to the greatest hall of them all! Then out of nowhere, there he was, grinning like an evil spirit—that big rhino, Jim Neidhart. We had one of those backslapping embraces. Reinforcements, finally! It felt as though I'd been all alone in prison and a thug from the old gang had just been sent up. Jim looked the part too, sporting a chiselled flat top and a long, pointy goatee that gave him an odd resemblance to a mountain goat. He was now going by The Anvil, playing off his world-record anvil toss at the Stampede. That first night, he had a ten-minute squash match and went over strong. It looked as though they had plans for Jim, and I was happy for him. Meanwhile, they thought they were doing me a favour by letting me do a twenty-minute broadway with Rene Goulet. Since Rene was basically a jobber, it was a clear sign that I wasn't going anywhere.

After the show, the boys drank and caroused at the Ramada on 48th and 8th, and I sat at the bar with Cowboy Bob taking it all in. Jim and Adrian Adonis hit it off like two bad dogs that like the same mischief. The place was packed with fans. One of them was Angel, an over-the-hill strip-per who, I was told, had been quite striking in the Sammartino days. Her witchy-black hair fell loosely over melon-sized tits that oozed out over clothes that once fit. Adorned with cheap costume jewellery and a star tattoo under one eye, she'd talk dirty, but that's all she did.

At Poughkeepsie TV the next day, I felt like a puppy in a pet store put-ting on my best face: pick me, pick me. They didn't even have me work, which meant I wouldn't get any exposure on TV for another three weeks.

At least with Jim around, I wasn't alone anymore.

On my first brief stop in Calgary, on January 25, Chief glared at Bruce, whose face kept twisting into a silly smirk. It got to the point where I thought Chief would wipe that smirk right off my brother's face. "You think this is funny? I don't get what's to laugh about, Bruce. Look at that house out there. There's nobody here."

Bruce flushed, and his smile vanished. "It's not my fault you guys can't draw up here."

Chief shook his head and walked away. In truth, the poor attendance was nobody's fault. It was going to take a while for the WWF to get established in Stampede Wrestling's old turf.

Near the end of the show that night, Chief approached me with a lady from the wrestling commission. "Tell him what you just told me."

She said that Bruce and a guy named Peter Rasmussen, the front man with all the money, had got a promoter's licence back in early December and would be running their first Stampede show in February.

Chief shook his head and left me standing there. I was steaming mad, wondering how Bruce could do this to me and especially how he could do it to Stu.

Bruce was nowhere to be found.

I sat next to Jim at a bar in Grand Rapids, Michigan, as he conversed happily with André the Giant about American football. I was drinking my beer, contemplating the six months that had gone by since I'd started with the WWF, amazed that I was somehow still hanging in there.

Just then Jim asked me, "Hey, Bret, who do you think are better conditioned athletes, football players or soccer players?"

I remembered that as a teenager André had been on the French national soccer team. With him staring at me intently, I answered, "All I know is that you won't see a soccer player sitting on the sidelines with an oxygen mask over his face."

André slammed his huge hand on the counter. "Another round here, and get him a beer too." He pointed his huge finger at me. Jim grinned and pulled his goatee while I sighed with relief. The temperamental giant had finally forgiven me.

We celebrated Jim's thirtieth birthday in Phoenix in the Rodeway Inn lounge. He and André both wore loose-fitting flowered shirts. Quick Draw was out cold, with his forehead flat on the table and his hands hanging limp at his sides.

Princess Tomah, a genuine Chippewa lady wrestler now in her seventies, had worked every territory in her day, including Stu's. She showed up at the Veterans Memorial Arena offering to help out, and Chief was kind enough to let her hang around and do the odd errand. Tonight she was drunk and happy to be back with the boys, behaving (and looking) like that white-haired, sex-starved granny in the *Playboy* magazine cartoons. She kept offering to turn us all into real men, but there weren't any takers.

André, Jim and I were still laughing about the cartoon I'd drawn earlier that night. For the last month or two I'd been secretly drawing on the blackboards in all the dressing rooms. No one knew who was doing it, but everyone was amused, especially André, who would laugh with a King Kong roar. My cartoons were usually of a buck-naked Chief doing something obscene: On this night he was banging Princess Tomah, arms proudly crossed, two feathers in his headband. Chief was such a straight guy that he never ran around carousing, which is what made it so funny.

Two days later, at the Los Angeles Sports Arena, Mr. T was sitting in the front row. This short, thick-set black actor, with his mohawk and pounds of gold chains, had been launched to iconic heights by his role in the brand-new TV show *The A-Team*. Three years earlier, he'd appeared in *Rocky III*, as did Hulk Hogan, and Vince wisely planned to capitalize on their prior association by teaming them up at *WrestleMania*.

Dave Schultz was in a really foul mood. He pulled Jim and me aside to say that he was furious that Roddy Piper had been given the main event spot at *WrestleMania*; he was determined to hijack the angle for himself. He wanted Jim and me to watch his back so he could drill Mr. T. "By the time it hits the papers, they'll have to stick me in the main event. I won't hurt 'im bad, just enough to get a story." Jim and I tried to sound supportive, but when Schultz moved off, I pulled Jim aside and told him not to do anything that might get us fired.

Schultz had been in hot water ever since he slapped out Stossel. Chief was well aware that he was a ticking time bomb, so he hired extra police and told them that if a guy fitting Schultz's description came anywhere near the ring, they were to cuff him and drag him back to the dressing room. Then he told Schultz he was off the card. The fuse was lit.

A few minutes later I heard a commotion. Jim and I tore out of the dressing room, and there was Schultz with his hands cuffed behind his back, spitting mad, on the cement floor outside the dressing room. The police had apprehended him before he got to Mr. T., and he was about to be escorted to the airport in handcuffs and put on a plane out of town.

At the TV taping in Brantford, Ontario, near the end of February, George Scott pulled me aside with some big news. They had a gimmick for me—a huge one.

"After *WrestleMania*, yer gonna ride out on a horse. A different one every night, just like the Rhinestone Cowboy. You can ride a horse, right? Cowboy Bret Hart! Can you imagine that? We'll sell the action figure with the horse in the same box! It'll be great!"

I found myself agreeing, even thanking him, but I hated it. That night on the drive back to the hotel, Jim couldn't stop laughing at how funny it was, but then, every few minutes, he'd tell me how lucky I was.

At 1 a.m., I knocked on George's hotel door. He was just about to crash after another long day of TV; his tie was loosened, and he was shielding his eyes from the light in the hall.

"George, I don't want to be a cowboy."

"Are you kiddin' me? It'll be great!"

I told him I was sorry, but I couldn't even ride a horse and, where I come from, if you called yourself a cowboy, you'd better be one. I was surprised to hear myself suggest to him that since Jimmy Hart, The Mouth of the South, was already managing Neidhart, they could turn me heel, put us all together and call us The Hart Foundation.

I sometimes forget how patient George was with me. He patted me on the shoulder and told me that with my face I could never be a heel, but not to worry, they'd come up with something. Being the booker, George had to feel like a butcher constantly carrying a tray of mouth-watering steaks past a pack of big, hungry dogs.

There was dread in the dressing room in Detroit. The 20/20 report had aired the night before, February 21, and it was clearly an attempt to hurt the business. But it didn't turn out that way. The prime-time network exposure only made the business hotter, and Vince McMahon realized, perhaps for the first time, what would become a cardinal rule of his: Any publicity is good publicity.

Meanwhile, back in Calgary, at the very moment that John Stossel was on the air trashing the business, Bruce's partner, Peter Rasmussen—the guy with all the money and with his name on the Calgary promoter's licence—told Bruce he didn't need him any more. Bruce had hooked him up with a TV slot opposite the WWF and helped him to trademark the Stampede Wrestling name. They had rings made and had hired the talent. What Bruce hadn't taken into account was that he was unpopular with the wrestlers: Shortly after Bad News was hired, News told Rasmussen that the only thing wrong with the new endeavour was that he needed to get rid of Bruce. So, on February 22, 1985, Rasmussen ran the first Stampede Wrestling show in Calgary with no Harts involved.

Five days later, the WWF show came through town, and Bruce showed up hoping to pick up without missing a beat. Chief bluntly told Bruce the WWF didn't need him anymore either.

After being left off the TV schedule one more time in early March, I decided it was time to stand or fall. If down was the only place for me to go in the WWF, I should get out and try my luck in Japan, where maybe I could earn enough of a name to come back some day.

So I worked up my nerve and phoned George first thing the following morning—and was completely caught off guard when he told me they were going to do exactly what I'd suggested. At TVs (our slang for TV tapings) on March 25, I'd walk out as a heel, they'd tag me up with Neidhart and call us The Hart Foundation.

Three days later, at the HoJo's in Toronto, Tom and Davey were at the bar. Despite the fact that they'd kayfabed me about their Japan deal, I was more than happy to see them. More reinforcements! They'd just signed with Vince up in his hotel room. He'd told them they could make big money as his tag champs and keep their Japan deal too. "Goin' to call us the fooking British Bulldogs, Gabe," Tom chuckled. "We start on March 25." Davey said that right after they signed with him, Vince climbed up on a small table and danced!

Much to my relief, Jim thought that tagging up with me was a great idea, especially if they put us against the British Bulldogs. For the next several days we tried to come up with a finishing move in time for TVs. I recalled watching two humungous mohawked wrestlers called The Road Warriors on AWA wrestling one night. For their finishing move, one of them scooped up their opponent, planting him on his shoulders, while the other one clotheslined him off the top turnbuckle. I groaned at how perilous it was: the helpless victim landed right on top of his head. I remembered thinking it would be easier and safer just to bear-hug the guy and do a running clothesline off the ropes. When I ran the idea by Jim, he loved it. We now had a finishing move, which we named The Hart Attack.

The third part of the team was Jimmy Hart, our manager. In the early 1960s, Jimmy was a rock 'n' roll singer-songwriter with a group called The Gentrys, who had a number-one hit called "Keep on Dancin.'" He was small, wiry and bearded, wore dark shades and a white blazer with huge black musical notes all over it; as a prop he carried a white megaphone with a siren on it. He was friendly but extremely jumpy, and he snapped his gum while talking a hundred words a minute in a high, shrill voice. We liked him.

Our first ever tag match took place at Brantford TV, to be aired after WrestleMania. With the much despised Jimmy leading the way, we walked out to boos and a shower of garbage. Like Jim, I wore mirrored sunglasses and did my best to act cocky as I strutted across the ring with my arms flung wide. We made quick work of the jobbers until the ref gave us the cue to go home. Jim tagged me in, then hoisted the jobber into a bear hug while I tore off into the ropes and came off with a vicious flying clothesline. It looked stiff, but it was as easy to take as a simple back bump. I covered him for the pin as Jimmy hit the siren. We sneered as we walked past the angry fans, loving every second of it.

Minutes later, Tom and Davey marched out to "Rule, Britannia," wearing matching red tights with the word BULLDOGS up the legs in white lettering, red and white boots and Union Jacks sewn on the backs of their trunks. Davey was chest out, chin up, grinning, while Tom looked quite serious as they proceeded to tear the house down with some great high-flying and powerhouse moves. The crowd went crazy! The wrestlers, the agents and especially George and Vince all popped as they watched the TV monitors in the back.

The next day we all flew into Newark, jumped into a rental car and drove up to Poughkeepsie for the March 25 TV taping. None of us were on the bill for *WrestleMania*, which would take place six days later. We'd miss out on the big payday, but there was nothing we could do about it. At least I was headed for seventeen days at home.

Afterwards, the bar was packed with fans, ring rats and cocaine dealers. Don Muraco, a big, rugged Hawaiian who truly resembled the Incredible Hulk, with thick veins like earthworms up and down his massive arms and shoulders the size of bowling balls, chatted away with Ken Patera. Patera won four gold medals in weightlifting at the PanAmerican Games in 1971 and represented the United States at the 1972 Olympics and was perhaps legitimately the strongest pro wrestler of all time. Jim suspiciously disappeared with Adrian Adonis, a Cuban coke dealer named Robert and Robert's thick, bull-faced bodyguard, Tarzan. Tom was chatting up the big-breasted Angel, who was talking dirty in his ear. Davey shook his head and laughed at how Tom was drooling all over her.

I went back to my room to call Julie, who was happy that I was finally coming home. When I headed back to the bar, I ran right into Davey coming down the hall with a big grin on his face. Behind him, Tom had Angel over his shoulder. As the three of them marched past, Don Muraco poked his head out of a room and broke up laughing. He called out, "I knew you Bulldogs were tough, but I didn't know you were that tough!"

Home to bliss. I gave Julie a gold ring for her birthday. I presented a big white Gund teddy bear to Jade, soon to be two, and a smaller one to Dallas, to chew on with his two big teeth. When we headed in the door at Hart house, Stu's big paw reached out to me as he called to my mom, "Dear, there's someone here to see you!" The flip-flop of her slippers approached and there were more hugs.

Stu wasn't happy that I turned heel. I told him it was my idea, but he still thought I was being punished on account of what Bruce did. As for Peter Rasmussen, his version of Stampede Wrestling folded in three weeks. On the home front, Alison, who was pregnant with her second child, was having marital problems with Ben. Cats, dogs and little Hart babies crawled everywhere.

During that time at home, I finally got my driver's licence reinstated. I also got an American Express card.

I never even bothered watching *WrestleMania*. It was the furthest thing from my mind.

18

THE PUSH BROTHERS

For weeks Jimmy and I had been trying to come up with a nickname for me. One morning—April 27, 1985, to be exact—on a layover in Philadelphia, I read in the newspaper that Thomas Hitman Hearns was retiring from boxing after being KO'd by Marvelous Marvin Hagler. Hitman Hart. I liked the sound of it.

That night was going to be the first ever match between The Hart Foundation and The British Bulldogs, four brothers-in-law in the city of brotherly love. A certain pride began to take over: It was time to show America what Stu's crew could do! George Scott was making a two-and-a-half-hour drive from Greenwich, Connecticut, just to see the match. I mentioned to Tom that if we did well George might give me and Jim a push, and so he started calling us The Push Brothers.

At the sound of "Rule, Britannia," The Bulldogs marched out to face us. Fifteen minutes later, at the halfway mark, a lot of the fans were standing. I came across as a decent wrestler who was all too easily influenced by Anvil, his mean bully brother-in-law, and led astray by his shady manager. I made a point of showing the fans the occasional drop kick just to impress them. The crowd hated the fact that this one-time jobber could actually wrestle. It was a guilt trip; if these fans had only loved me, I wouldn't be behaving this way.

Ah, the joy of being a heel! Anvil and I built heat masterfully. We were vicious, merciless and sneaky.

"Let's go!" I called out to Jim and Davey.

I pulled Davey up off the mat and Anvil hooked him by the arms. I came off the ropes with a high knee, and at the last second Davey moved, and Anvil and I collided. Davey tagged, dramatically. I fed into Dynamite, bumping everywhere. Into Jim. Into turnbuckles. Snap suplexes. A clothesline that looked like it tore my head off. Anvil was hoisted up on Davey's shoulders as I was flat on my back looking at the lights. I remember thinking, I love this heel bit. Dynamite gingerly stepped onto Jim's back and dove, crashing head-to-head with me. When Jimmy Hart tried to come through the ropes to interfere, Davey added to the already huge pop by tossing Anvil over the ropes right on top of him! Dynamite hooked my leg for the one . . . two . . . three. "Thanks, Gabe," he said.

I travelled all over the United States and Canada, but I was spending more time at the HoJo's in Newark than anywhere else. All the wrestlers who worked the nearby towns would eventually find themselves planted on stools in the lounge, where they had a cheesy house band that played until 2 a.m. The boys on the B and C teams were talking about how the gates had dropped off after *WrestleMania*, despite a highly rated *Saturday Night's Main Event* special on NBC that aired on May 12, 1985, and marked the return of wrestling to prime-time network TV in the United States after an absence of thirty years. The only guys still getting the big cheques were the ones on Hogan's undercard. Hulk was still as hot as ever.

Tom and Davey were lucky to be booked in all the big cities with Hogan right off the bat, but Jim and I more often worked small towns. Everyone got paid a percentage of the gate, and Tom and Dave were taking home cheques between $5,000 and $10,000 a week, which was considerably more than Jim and I made. We were glad for them, and there were no sour grapes; better them than anybody else. We became a gang of four, looking out for one another as friends and brothers.

Of course none of us was perfect. Jim loved his beer and his recreational drugs, and he would party until all hours of the night. Tom and Davey loved their beer, their pills, their steroids and their workouts. My release, my amnesia or maybe my anaesthesia, was women. Sex seemed like the lesser of all the sins that lay in wait for us.

One night I went looking for Jim in Adrian's room. When I knocked on the door, asking if Jim was in there, I could hear Adrian's hushed voice saying "Don't open it!" Then I clearly heard Jim say, "It's just Bret, he's okay." They unlatched the chain. What a crew! It was a clubhouse for bad boys: Jim, Adrian, Roddy, Muraco, The Iron Sheik, even Mr. Fuji, the old Japanese-Hawaiian wrestler with the bowlegged Charlie Chan gimmick. They'd filled the bathtub with ice and bottles of beer. On the table was a mound of coke. There was an awkwardness, a distrust of the promoter's kid. Roddy offered me a rolled-up dollar bill. I hesitated more at the idea that I might have to pay for it rather than what it might do to me.

"How much does it cost?"

Muraco smiled, "It's on us."

I snorted two short lines.

A joint was rolled and passed around. Before long all of us were talking and laughing about everything from our childhoods to the territories we'd worked. Adrian loved to talk about workers and angles. At first I was reluctant to say much, but soon I opened up and told them about my life as a Hart. They seemed surprised that I had an interesting take on the business, finishes and workers. While we were talking, Sheik stared at himself in the mirror while doing hundreds of free squats. Then he'd twist his long handlebar moustache, the sweat dripping from his bald head down his huge traps and his rock-hard gut.

There were knocks at the door all night, but Adrian manned the peephole. Not just anybody was let in, in fact, nobody was. I think Roddy was starting to realize that I wasn't a bad kid, just a young Canadian wrestler trying to find my way in the business, like he'd done not that long ago. Roddy said if Jim and I were going to make any money, we'd have to get them to let us do promos. He made me promise to practise doing promos in the mirror, on planes, in my room, anywhere.

The sun started to peek around the edges of the closed curtains. We ran out of beer, out of coke, but never out of stories. It was funny how we all did this as a way of keeping *out* of trouble.

Every few nights from there on in, it was the same scene: a group of wrestlers getting through the night, with camaraderie and other crutches. In the background the late-night TV news was my thread to the real world. There were wars in Iran and Iraq, the Philippines and El Salvador. A state of emergency had been declared in South Africa, where the iron-fisted whites were losing their grip. The endless conflicts in the Middle East and Northern Ireland continued to flare. Meanwhile, in the world of wrestling, the tanks had rolled. Vince was like a triumphant Napoleon, his rivals broken and defeated.

One morning in late May, I left Jim snoring away like a hibernating bear and went down to the Newark HoJo's restaurant. By now I'd tried just about everything on the greasy menu and had concluded that it had to be worse than prison food. The only ones who enjoyed it were the roaches darting everywhere.

While eating breakfast I noticed a new waitress with a great body, golden-brown skin, full red lips, eyes like a doe and dark hair. I was surprised when she said, with a Jersey accent, "You're Bret Hitman Hart." I was disappointed when she told me she'd be quitting at the end of the day. Rosemary was a twenty-one-year-old Puerto Rican bombshell.

I told her I had to go to Poughkeepsie that day for the TV show but that with some luck I could be back early enough to give her a ride home if she liked. She said okay.

The Hart Foundation worked a TV match, but Jim and I were disappointed, yet again, to not have any interview time. The Bulldogs sure did though, and they were horrible. When Vince saw Tom and Davey stumble and trip through their interviews, he immediately put them with old Lou Albano, a hard-drinking blabbermouth manager. Lou was roly-poly, with a mop of curly black hair and a grey beard. Real diaper pins poked through and dangled from his cheek. Without Captain Lou, The Bulldogs would have been lost.

When we got back to Newark that evening, Jim went to the bar, and I went looking for Rosemary. We sat parked in my car behind the hotel just talking. It was a little after two in the morning when I drove her home through rundown neighbourhoods marked with graffiti. A rat as big as a cat scurried across a deserted crosswalk.

She lived above a bodega. When I parked in front, she leaned into me and we kissed. It gave me butterflies. She slipped me her phone number as she got out of the car, smiling, "Call me, okay?" I saw her mom in the window.

Back at the hotel I found Jim and André still in the bar. I felt like celebrating, but I'd missed last call. I left Jim to settle his tab and went up to the room, tying a T-shirt over my eyes so Jim wouldn't wake me up when he got in. Soon I was in a deep sleep but thought I heard the distant sound of running water. Nah, on second thought, it sounded more like . . . someone pissing on the rug! I pushed my blindfold up. The room was still dark, but I could see Jim's silhouette, casually leaning on the TV stand, a hand on his hip, swaying as he emptied his bladder for what seemed like an eternity. I was not amused.

That morning, as we packed our bags in a hurry to catch the airport shuttle, Jim seemed to sense I was a bit uptight. Maybe it was the way I banged my suitcase on the bed. He innocently asked, "Something wrong?" The happy look on his face made me hesitate, but then it just came out. "As a matter of fact, Jim, I woke up this morning and saw you standing at the foot of my bed pissing on the rug. I walk around in my socks and . . ."

Jim cut me off. "What are you talking about? Show me!" He dropped to his knees and ran his hands through the carpet. "You dreamed it!" He laughed, "I think you owe me an apology."

I looked closer, even running my foot over the rug. Damned if it wasn't completely dry. Maybe I did dream it. "I guess I do owe you an apology, Jim."

"Accepted!" he declared as he pulled his suitcase up off the floor and a flood of piss poured out of the corner of it.

I broke up laughing!

"I'll be goddamned," Jim muttered over and over, while I laughed all the way onto the plane.

I slept all the way to Kansas City. The rumour had gone round that Harley Race was threatening to show up with a shotgun when the WWF came to town, because the Missouri territory was his, and everyone, especially Hogan, was anxious about it. Harley simply walked into the dressing room and held his finger up to his lips, signalling everyone to be quiet as he snuck up behind Hogan and then slapped him as hard as he could on the short ribs. Hogan turned around wincing, and seeing Harley, he turned white as a ghost. Hogan had to be thinking, Oh my God, now what the heck do I do? Then Harley smirked, extending his hand in friendship, and Hogan seemed more than a little relieved.

After he peed in his own suitcase, Jim and I had decided not to room together any more. But when I tried to go to sleep simply staring at the ceiling, I knew for certain that this was going to be a long road ahead. I was twenty-seven, and I was never going to survive it if I didn't find some female company or human touch along the way. Sometimes when I called home I wouldn't get an answer. That night in Kansas City I broke down and called Rosemary instead. I knew it was wrong, but it was either that or night after night of booze and drugs with various wrestlers, or climbing the walls in my hotel prison cell.

I was parked behind the HoJo's in Newark in early June, after fifty-four days on the road. I was relieved to be going home in the morning. Rosemary was pressed in close, her lipstick smudged, and I finally had to come clean with her. "I have to tell you the truth. Rosie, I'm married."

She stiffened and moved away from me.

"I've got a little girl and a little boy, under two years old, at home. I understand why you're angry with me, but I'm just very lonely down here. I guess you won't want much of anything to do with me, but then again if you did . . . I like you a lot."

"Take me home!" she said, her eyes hurt, wet and angry. But when she got out in front of her parents' place, our eyes met, and she seemed to soften. Maybe she needed me as badly as I needed her. "Call me when you come back."

I was home for three days and then I was on the road again, and it wasn't Julie I was dreaming about.

At the Los Angeles Sports Arena, Jimmy Hart grabbed me and Jim. "C'mon, hurry up! We got interviews!"

Suddenly it was The Hart Foundation standing with Mean Gene Okerlund, and my frozen stare was fixed on the camera. Jimmy rattled off most of the interview, with Gene playing a great straight man. Anvil gruffly barked a few lines, and then it was my turn. I said a couple of words into the mic and passed it back to Anvil. The cameraman played the promo back on a tiny monitor to see if it was a keeper. I watched as my eyes darted every which way—clearly I was terrified! If Vince were to see that, it would be our last interview! I tore off down the hallway to the dressing room and returned in a flash with my mirrored shades.

We cranked out our promo again. Not bad. Not great. I vowed to get better. From that day on I wore sunglasses—to hide the nerves that showed in my eyes.

During June and early July 1985 we mostly worked with the Bulldogs, who were the talk of the territory, stealing the show every night. The Foundation was getting some recognition, mostly from the boys and sometimes the agents, but never from Vince or George.

After a singles match between me and Dynamite in Denver, Chief came up to me, beaming. "You're really startin' to get it, Stu!" Chief had started calling me Stu, after my dad, which I took as a huge compliment. "You keep this up," he said, "and they'll have to do something with you."

Chief had taken a shine to all of us by now, especially Tom and me. He had a genuine love for the business, and he knew better than most who was doing the work night after night. It also didn't hurt that Chief secretly loved my blackboard drawings. By now he'd discovered that I was the artist. Like a political cartoonist, I drew depictions of sordid stories involving the boys and whomever, enhanced solely by my imagination. Whenever I drew anybody with clothes on, the cartoon didn't seem funny, but the orgies, usually with Princess Tomah at the centre of it all, were hilarious. The wrestlers would fall over laughing, André the loudest. Chief would stand staring at them with his hands on his hips trying not to laugh, "That damn Stu," he'd say.

More and more it seemed that the Stampede boys were beginning to pick up the pace of the territory. There's no argument that big men, such as Hogan and André, were over with the fans because of who they were. They drew the house, but the truth is that they never worked the kinds of fast-paced, beautiful masterpieces we did.

After a match at the Rosemont Horizon in Chicago, Terry Funk pulled me aside to tell me, "I've been watchin' you guys every night. That match between the four of ya'll is the best damn tag match I've ever seen anywhere since I been in the business! Nobody can touch it!" But the one comment from this time that made the longest-lasting impression on me came from the legendary Pedro Morales. The former WWWF champ was a kind, almost shy, Puerto Rican wrestler who rose to equal the fame and legend of

Bruno Sammartino. "I'm a goin' tell ya somethin', Hitman. You always hear 'bout guys in the business who tell you they never got a break, or the promoter screwed them, or they got hurt, all kind of excuses, good or bad. But you remember this, remember it was me who told you: You cannot stop talent! No matter what, sooner or later, it proves itself. You, my friend, have talent! Someday you're gonna be a big star in this business."

And then there was Jesse Ventura, Adrian's former long-time tag partner. Jesse had been a bodybuilder and, in the Vietnam War, was a decorated Navy Seal who came home with more than his share of demons. To forget them he lost himself in the surreal world of wrestling. Jesse was an extremely sharp guy who spoke privately, and in an articulate way, about why wrestlers should unionize. He knew any attempt would be a waste of time unless Hogan and the key guys got behind it, which they didn't.

When a blood clot in his lung retired him as a wrestler, Jesse became a colour commentator, providing analysis that added realism to the matches, but tinged with sardonic wit. He had respect for Jim's college background as a shot-putter and mine as an amateur wrestler. He always managed to take the heel's side, finding sometimes far-fetched rationalizations to justify our deplorable behaviour. Sitting alongside the straight-faced Gorilla Monsoon, or Vince himself, Jesse wore fluorescent feathered boas, huge sunglasses and a tie-dyed bandanna to hide his balding blond head.

What Jesse Ventura did for The Hart Foundation in our early days shouldn't go unremarked. He was arguably our first real fan, the one lone voice singing our praises. He raved about The Hart Foundation in his TV commentary, calling us his favourite team and predicting greatness to come.

By July the paycheques for the first WrestleMania finally came. Word in the dressing room was that Vince had locked up the money in a high-interest account for ninety days so he could collect a little premium before paying the boys. Nobody was complaining, because the lucky few who were on the big card came into huge windfalls that left those who weren't on it green with envy.

When I called home late that month, I was concerned by the disheartened tone in my mom's voice. She'd heard rumblings that Bruce was doing all he could to persuade Stu to start up Stampede Wrestling again. It'd been almost a year since Stu shut down, and he seemed aimless and restless. My mom handed him the phone and I could instantly hear that the lion was back in his voice again. Stu told me that he didn't know what Vince would think if he opened back up, but being as Vince hadn't run anything in Calgary in five months, and hadn't paid Stu a nickel of their supposed deal, it might be worth finding out where he and Vince stood.

September 8, 1985. I was lined up waiting for Dr. Zahorian again. Seven days earlier, Ricky Romero Jr., who was working for the NWA as Jay Youngblood, died in his sleep. He was my age, twenty-seven, and he'd taken too many downers. Five months before Ricky Jr. died, Mike Von Erich, the second youngest of Fritz Von Erich's five-son wrestling dynasty out of Dallas, committed suicide by overdosing on Placidyl. He left a note that read, "Mom and Dad, I'm in a better place. I'll be watching."

These deaths didn't stop anyone from lining up to buy more.

The last I'd seen Ricky Jr. was when we teamed up back in Toronto when I was Buddy The Heartthrob and he was already on his way to becoming a star in the Carolinas. Mike had lost his older brother, David Von Erich, to an accidental overdose a year and a half earlier, in February, 1984. David was slated to be the next NWA world champion but instead he died, only twenty-six years old.

One by one I watched damn near everybody come out of Zahorian's room with grocery bags full of drugs, even Vince. It often happened that wrestlers bought so many drugs that they couldn't carry them in their suitcases and had to ship them home.

No one heeded the warning signs, though I tried really hard to be moderate. But the touring life forced you to alternate between running on empty, which wasn't so bad because you were exhausted enough that you could fall asleep anywhere, to running on adrenalin, in which case you were too wired to sleep no matter how worn out you were. Wrestlers used drugs and alcohol to mediate the highs and lows.

On September 28, Jim and I appeared on Vince's *Tuesday Night Titans* show, a campy takeoff of *The Tonight Show*, which was supposed to afford the fans a rare glimpse of the wrestlers out of character. I had rarely ever talked to Vince McMahon at the time, and when he turned to me, I blurted out a line from Robert Redford's movie *The Natural*: "We're the best there is, best there was, and the best there ever will be!" Little did I know it would soon become my trademark line.

Ellie and Jim moved back to Calgary from Memphis in October. Ellie was quick to pick out a house on the Bow River, which she figured was perfect for Jim, as he fancied himself a fishing enthusiast. He could wade out knee-deep and pull in trout any time he liked. Jim was more than sold on it when

Stu co-signed the mortgage. Stu's kindness stemmed from his joy at having Ellie and their three girls nearby, but also because Stu liked to keep Jim pointed in the right direction. He'd long been the peacemaker in their marriage.

Vince had encouraged Stu to start back up again because he had no intention of bringing the WWF back to Western Canada. Vince basically cancelled their deal, but he did promise Stu that if the WWF ever did return, Stu would get not the ten per cent to which they'd originally agreed, but five per cent. Vince had decided he wasn't going to pay, and there was little Stu could do except sue, which would have cost me, Davey, Jim, and maybe even Tom our jobs. But the light was back in Stu's eyes. When I called he gave me a sound argument that the business, if run properly, with minimal cost, could turn a profit. And Bruce wouldn't be in charge — Cuban would be his right-hand man, and that was final. But after the debacle with Rasmussen and Vince, Bruce had lost his house and was forced into bankruptcy. No doubt providing jobs for Bruce and his other children was a factor in Stu's decision to get back into business.

Stu got himself a TV slot right before the WWF show and asked me whether Jim and I would do him a favour and work Friday, November 1, for him. So there we were, back at the old Pavilion, doing a four-way double disqualification, with me and Jim trying to out-heel Rotten Ron Starr and a Tennessee Elvis impersonator known as the Honky Tonk Man. The Pavilion was barely half full and my heart went out to my mom.

The next day, in Omaha, when I walked into the dressing room, a tight-lipped and serious Pat Patterson came up to me. "Jim missed his flight. He won't be here tonight. Did you hear about Rick McGraw? He died last night — overdosed in his sleep."

The dressing room was silent. Quick Draw wasn't even thirty years old, and he left behind a wife and a baby daughter. The cause of his death was labelled a heart attack, but we all knew that his heart had given out under deadly dosages of downers. That night all the boys drank, celebrating the life of a departed friend. Just over the border at Fat Jack's, in Council Bluffs, Iowa, I sang "Born to Be Wild" at the top of my lungs, along with Steppenwolf and Cowboy Bob's younger brother, Barry O.

During the fall of 1985, Jim and I often rode with Chris Pallies, otherwise known as King Kong Bundy, a bald, six-foot-four, 450-pound monster of a wrestler who was built like an egg on two sturdy legs. Julie and I even nicknamed Dallas Little Bundy because he was husky and still didn't have a single hair on his head. Bundy wasn't your typical fat guy. Nothing jiggled when he stomped around. He had a sharp wit, was never short of a putdown or a comeback and often broke me up laughing when he jokingly made fun of . . . well, everybody.

Every few weeks I somehow managed to get Bundy and Big Jim worked up enough to have sumo fights in the dressing room. In Phoenix one night, Jim was just out of the shower and made the mistake of taking Bundy on when he was barefoot, sopping wet and naked. Bundy had just worked and charged Jim, slamming his back flat against the wall! Jim was flabbergasted and Bundy rubbed it in for the rest of the night . . . the week . . . the year. . . The memory of a naked Jim in this struggle is still instantly amusing to me. I was constantly pressing both of them for a rematch, but Bundy was immune to my prodding. Like a proud elephant that would never again let a measly rhino push him around, Bundy would laugh and say, "Let me tell you, little man, that dumb Neidhart doesn't stand a chance!" I got a kick out of how he always referred to both me and Jim as little man.

On November 26, I was riding with Bundy in Jacksonville, Florida, and he eased the car to the side of the road because the space shuttle was about to take off. We got out and leaned on the hood of the rental car. Low and behold a bright flashing light rocketed through the sky, and we watched it until it disappeared. Most wrestlers forget there's a real world out there, and it was really cool that Bundy found this way to remind me. When I called home to tell Julie about it, she told me that someone had finally bought our crappy house in Ramsay, a miracle only slightly less incredible.

By Christmas Eve, as everybody milled about at Hart house, my mom wore the look of someone who had miraculously survived the wreck of the *Titanic* only to find herself being hauled up the ramp of the *Lusitania*. Bruce had already manoeuvred the Cuban out of his job as Stu's booker by constantly going over his head till the Cuban gave up and let Bruce book. The air in the room was full of jealousy that somehow Tom, Davey, Jim and I had been spared the ghastly fate of the others: we were working for the WWF and no one else was.

I sat and talked with Owen, now twenty, who'd found himself a reluctant warrior in the monk-like world of amateur wrestling at the University of Calgary, and who planned on becoming a physical education teacher. I suggested that he give the pro wrestling thing a shot while it was hot. It might be perfect timing to get in, make some money and then go back to school. As a teenager, Owen, like me, never wanted anything to do with the wrestling business; he'd worked once in a while at small rodeos to earn some cash, always under a mask, so it wouldn't affect his amateur status.

The more I talked about the cities I'd been to and the money I was making, the more his eyes lit up, until he turned to Martha, who mocked the whole idea. Martha clearly wore the pants in their relationship. She did little to hide the fact that she didn't particularly like our family or the business, even though I could have pointed out that it hadn't been that long since she was a kid pounding her hands on the mat after my matches at the Victoria Pavilion.

Michelle, Andrea and Diana all looked stunning: a silent competition. Diana held five-month-old Harry on her lap and sat talking with Alison, who was cradling eight-month-old Lindsay. For a reason known only to themselves, Smith and Maria had seen fit to name their baby girl Satanic Ecstasy. My mother called her Tanya, whether Smith and Maria liked it or not. Smith buzzed around me like a giant fly, trying to interest me in an assortment of mostly illegal get-rich-quick schemes.

I soon found Jim, who made it clear that he hated the house on the Bow that Ellie had picked out for them. He carried on forever about the long, bellowing whistles from passing trains, the horrid winter weather, the icy river and the damp, chilly house. I saw it for what it really was; Stu was becoming too frequent a referee in their yelling matches. Jim wanted out of their new house and to be as far away from Stu and Calgary as possible.

He'd get his wish: Tom, Dave, Jim and I had to fly out to work first thing on Christmas morning.

I truly felt terrible about being unfaithful. It was so weird: I was on top of the world and ashamed of myself at the same time. I wrote a note to myself that read, *Dear God, I don't know what to say, I don't know what to do. I'll leave it up to you.*

I was in my room at the Five Seasons Hotel in Amarillo on January 5, 1986, when Julie called to tell me that she knew all about my affair and was leaving me. As I drove to the matches that night, I could still hear the reverberation of the busy signal I got when I tried to call her back. My heart rattled with fear.

Julie had gone through my old hotel receipts and found a recurring 201 area code phone number. I remembered the first rule of the wrestlers' handbook when it came to these kinds of problems: deny till you die. Julie called Rosemary, who conceded nothing despite Julie's persistence. Whatever information Julie did manage to glean drove her to her own wild conclusions, which were probably pretty accurate. I professed only friendship with Rosemary, but who was I kidding? There wasn't much I could do to defend my actions any more.

After hours of long-distance conversation, we'd finally find some basis of forgiveness, but by the next morning she'd be leaving me all over again. Every time I got off the phone with Julie I'd call Rosemary, who felt terrible. But this was all my fault. I put in a distress call to my mom and dad, who were more than understanding. My mom went so far as to say that this kind of thing was inevitable and kidded that maybe Stu might have been happier if he'd done the same thing. Stu drove right over to the house and spent a couple of hours talking to Julie. It took three days, but after pleading from all three of us Julie decided to come down and see me. Rosemary could easily have stirred everything up, leaving nothing but a huge crater for herself to move into. Instead, she took one in the heart for me and helped me fight to save my marriage.

Julie was with me through Milwaukee, Pittsburgh, Philly and then right into the eye of the hurricane, Newark. She was like an angry lioness, and I had a new swipe across my nose daily. I'd heard how she was leaving so often that I'd finally resigned myself to accept it. By the time Julie got home everything was off, again.

I finished that tour on January 21 in Billings, Montana. Michelle had driven down from Calgary to pick up Tom and drive him home. I begged a ride. For the whole snowy, eight hours home, Michelle enjoyed telling me how I'd blown it with Julie. I sat quietly through the drive fearing that I really had.

After they'd dropped me off, I found Julie sleeping, the babies nestled beside her. I rolled in next to her and wrapped my arms around her. She sighed and held on.

Two days later I went to see a twenty-three-room luxury house that had both mountain and city views and a forty-eight-foot indoor pool. The local economy had bottomed out, and the builder was desperate to sell. "Oh, Bret," Julie gushed on seeing the spacious kitchen. My heart so wanted to find a way, but my head knew better. We went home to the reality of the small apartment we'd temporarily rented.

The next morning I made the call. By the time I was back on the road we were set to move in—on April Fool's Day.

Within days, Julie was back on the warpath again, and I was actually relying on Rosemary to keep my spirits up. That was really unfair. Smack in the middle of an agonizing phone conversation, Rosemary and I decided we had to stop this. We both had our TVs on in the background, and just at the moment we made our decision, the space shuttle *Challenger* blew up. We sat in silence, both of us watching at opposite ends of our phone connection. That was the end of us too.

Over the next few weeks it was hard to get my mind off how miserable I was. Every time Julie issued the ultimatum that she was leaving, I pictured my kids growing up in Regina: How would I ever see them?

There was growing tension in the dressing room about the upcoming NBC *Saturday Night's Main Event* special where all the angles for *WrestleMania II* would be set up, determining who would be on the big show. It was like Vince and George were walking by with that tray of big steaks again, and every dog in the kennel was snapping and jumping pretty high.

At the Holiday Inn in Fresno, California, on February 12, Cowboy Bob had overdone it again, but had made it safely back to his room. Then he made the mistake of getting up for a piss call, accidentally opening the door onto the hall, which overlooked a central atrium. He heard a commotion six floors down in the main lobby, so he leaned over the railing, naked, with one leg stuck behind him to hold his door open. But his toe slipped, and the door clicked shut.

In the lobby, Piper and Muraco were in the process of being arrested by a bunch of pissed-off Fresno cops after a high-speed car chase that ended in a rolled-over rental car! That's when Cowboy Bob decided to march out of the elevator buck-naked, hollerin' drunken epithets in his deep nasal whine.

The cops couldn't believe their eyes.

Don and Roddy stood frozen.

Soon Bob was throwing wild punches. The cops shot him with tranquilizer darts that he looked at, pulled out and then laughed at, saying, "Is that all you got?" This little scene made the newspapers.

Two days later, in Phoenix for the *SNME* show, Roddy went off on George Scott in the hotel lobby. George made the mistake of wagging his finger in Piper's face, and Piper damn near bit it off.

At the taping, Bundy shot his angle with Hogan, pretending to break his ribs, and Piper set up his upcoming angle with Mr. T, whipping him with a belt. The rest of us anxiously waited to see what scraps of meat our masters would drop for us on the *WrestleMania II* card.

19

THROWN BONES

I NEVER HAD ANY IDEA how long any of this would last, so in mid-February that year, I brought my parents down to watch me work Madison Square Garden. My mom hadn't been to a wrestling match since she and Stu had met when he was working New York in the 1940s. She'd watched some heel beat up on Stu and ran out of the building in tears.

Now, all these years later, she and Stu sat watching me and their son-in-law, the heels, take on The Killer Bees, who were B. Brian Blair and Jumping Jim Brunzell. The Bees were fast and light babyfaces who wore black-and-yellow-striped trunks. They had great psychology and were excellent workers. My dad still hadn't warmed to the idea of me being a heel. I'll never forget the stunned look on Stu's face as I viciously jackhammer-stomped a quivering Jim Brunzell lying out on the floor by the ring.

We built our heat up like wolves on a wounded calf, at one point doing a move we called the sandwich. I threw Anvil into Brunzell, shoulder-tackling him into the turnbuckles. Moments later, we went for the same move again, but this time with Jim throwing me. Brunzell moved, and I hit the turnbuckle so hard I nearly broke my collar bone. Brunzell slithered through Anvil's legs and tagged a fired up Blair. The Garden exploded as the Bees made an awesome comeback, with me barely holding on for dear life as the bell clanged again and again over the noise of the roaring crowd. This one was a draw.

As I passed by my mom and dad in the crowd on the way back to the dressing room, my mom's eyes were as huge as the smile on Stu's face. He didn't look like he minded my being a heel any more.

Vince greeted us at the curtain with "Great match, guys!" Wow, he finally noticed us. He actually spoke to us.

Jim and I had to wait around all night, since we'd given Bundy a ride to the Garden and he was on last. In the dressing room, George Scott pulled me aside to tell me I'd be working with Ricky The Dragon Steamboat at *WrestleMania II*. Anybody who ever climbed into the ring with Ricky

Steamboat would tell you that he was one of the best workers of all time. This was the chance I had been waiting for!

I was in great spirits by the end of the night. As we rode down in the backstage elevator, I challenged Jim and Bundy to one final be-all and end-all sumo match in the dressing room. Bundy dismissed the idea with a laugh, saying, "I don't waste time with midgets." We came out of the elevator laughing, and without thinking about it I walked straight outside. I usually left during the show, when the street was all but deserted, but the show was over. I walked into a frenzied mob of about a hundred fans. Bundy and Jim tried to pull me back inside, but Bundy had a ton of heat for breaking Hogan's ribs on *SNME*. As soon as the fans caught sight of him, he and Jim were slapped, kicked and spat on, while teenage girls hung all over me, leaving lipstick kisses on my face and shirt.

When we finally made it into the car, Bundy and Jim chewed me out for almost getting us killed! They were right. I was new at being a heel in America.

Then we drove up the ramp of the parkade onto West 33rd Street, where the same unruly mob immediately descended on our car like a bunch of wild baboons. We locked the doors just in time! They were beating on the windows and rocking the car up and down, their growling faces pressed up against the windows. Bundy, squashed in the back seat, put on an angry scowl: It was the only thing we had to scare them back! I could barely see to manoeuvre through traffic, so I went right over the curb and down the sidewalk. The fans followed, pounding on the car until I escaped down a maze of Manhattan side streets. We let out a collective sigh and had a good laugh, then Jim sternly lectured me to never do that again. But I was lost, and before we knew it, I was driving right back down West 33rd Street!

"Hart! Ya dumb fuck!" Bundy yelled in utter disbelief.

We tried to hunch down so as to remain undetected by the mob, but it was impossible for the fans not to notice Bundy's giant head, shining like a light bulb. "It's them!" the mob cried, and they pounced in one long angry carwash of beating hands and fiery-eyed faces!

And so we went through the whole thing one more time—laughing and shouting our fool heads off. Ah, the life of a heel!

For the next nineteen days, all I could think about was wrestling Steamboat at *WrestleMania II*. Ricky was a perfect opponent for me, with the way he sold, writhing in pain, making the crowd cry with him. And I was the perfect hot-tempered heel for him, needing to be taught a lesson for my own good. I was looking forward to our match in Boston, where we'd feel each other out for the big show.

As soon as I walked into the dressing room at the Boston Garden on March 8, I could tell something was up by the droop in Chief's face. He pulled me out into the hallway to tell me that my match at *Mania* had been scratched. I'd been demoted to the twenty-two-man battle royal instead.

I sulked as I dressed, unable to shake off my disappointment. Ricky seemed to notice how badly I was taking this. Since we weren't going to work together at *Mania*, our match in Boston meant nothing special any more; still, Ricky gave me a generous finish. "Let's go out and show them what they'll be missing at *WrestleMania*," Ricky said. He was right. I walked out to have what would turn out to be one of the milestone matches of my career.

As I made my way to the ring behind Jimmy, I glared, cold with anger, like I had no intention of losing.

The Dragon came out looking as dashing and fit as a suave Bruce Lee, wearing black tights and a confident smile. The crowd rose to greet him.

From the moment I jumped him from behind, we understood each other, and we danced a match filled with intense passion. Throughout, The Dragon died beautifully in an awesome display of wrestling as art— the great work, rarely attainable, built layer upon layer—until he cradled me for a one . . . two . . . three. While The Dragon stood weary but victorious, I lay on the mat pounding my fists. I felt in my heart that it actually was real, that somehow this loss cost me my chance to dance at *WrestleMania*.

The match aired live on NESN. That was the first time Gorilla Monsoon ever referred to me as The Excellence of Execution.

At Poughkeepsie TVs on March 11, I ran into Jake The Snake Roberts. He wore a big smile, and it was no wonder, given the way George fussed around him and his twenty-foot python. Being a good worker and one of the best talkers in the business, Jake was just what Vince was looking for.

I approached George with the idea that it might make for a good end to the battle royal to have André press me over his head and throw me over the top rope onto Anvil on the floor. At the end of the night George told me that André loved my finish for the battle royal, so that's what we'd be doing at *Mania*. It could never compare to a match with Steamboat, but it was something.

The first *WrestleMania* had been such a big success that the question was how to make *WrestleMania II*, on April 7, 1986, even bigger. Vince came up with the idea to hold three simultaneous events, in different time zones, and beam them via satellite to more than two hundred closed-circuit locations throughout the United States and Canada: a three-ring circus for the media age. These were still the days of rudimentary cable and satellite TV, so nothing like it had ever been done. People in each local arena could watch what was going on in the other two venues on big screens, which would have to be specially installed.

Hogan and Bundy would be the main event at the Los Angeles Sports Arena, in a steel cage. In these glory days of Hulkamania, it was common to see wrestlers walk up to him and shake his hand, thanking him for putting food on their tables. I was one of them. Hulk had a star on his own private dressing room door, a company limo and a Lear jet, but no one thought he didn't deserve it.

In Long Island, New York, the main event would be a boxing match between Roddy Piper and Mr. T.

On the big day, I was in the dressing room in Chicago as André explained to me how he wanted to go into the finish. He was wearing bright yellow trunks as he leaned over to tie the laces on his massive boots. His teeth looked like rows of corn in the mouth of a gigantic piranha. I ran his idea through my mind before innocently suggesting to him that if Jim and I doubled up on him, we could go for our sandwich move and he could give me the big boot from there. André thought about it while his huge fingers worked the laces tight. The dressing room was suddenly quiet. I saw a frozen stare on Tom's face, and I wondered what I'd said wrong. Then André smiled and said, "Yeah, boss, I like that better." A few minutes later, Tom told me that it was unheard of for anyone to suggest the slightest change to André. But I knew better. André was a great worker and appreciated that my suggestion made the finish better.

When all but eight combatants had been eliminated from the battle royal, Jim and I beat on William Refrigerator Perry of the Chicago Bears. Together we tossed him across the ring, but he rolled to his feet and came right back at us like a bowling ball, hitting two pins for a big strike and the pop of the night. Finally it was down to just me, Anvil, and André, and I found myself running into André's boot. It wasn't long before the giant was lifting me up over his head. He tossed me out of the ring and dumped me thirteen feet to the floor, where I landed in Anvil's waiting arms. It was a long way down!

By the time Hogan beat Bundy in the cage match in L.A., I was sitting in the Chicago Hyatt bar with Julie, Ellie and Jim. Most wrestlers didn't kayfabe any more, but The Hart Foundation and The Bulldogs did. We were old school. So across the room, Tom and Davey were celebrating their world tag-title victory. The road had brought us a long way from riding five hundred miles a day in Stu's van. I raised my beer in salute. Tom acknowledged it with a nod from across the smoky bar that only I could see. Good luck, brother, have a good run. I was proud of all of us.

After *WrestleMania II*, I found myself humming the "Movin' on up" theme from the sitcom *The Jeffersons*. Jim took his family as far away from Stu as he could get, buying a big monstrosity of a house in Tampa, Florida. Tom, Michelle and the baby moved in with me until Tom could find a house out in the country. Even Davey purchased an acreage on the outskirts of Calgary. We all bought into the dream, on credit.

With the ten days I had off, I did my best to spend time with my kids, while exploring my big new house, swimming in my own indoor pool—though I still couldn't swim very well—and soaking my aching muscles in my Jacuzzi. I'd look out at the city skyline and picture the kids someday walking out the back door and up the grassy hill to the schoolyard. I was relieved that I was able to get my family away from Ramsay. All I had to do was work hard and long enough to pay for this dream—and come home at the end of my run safe and sound.

I spent considerable time visiting my mom and dad too. Stampede Wrestling, like a leaky ship, listed dangerously with Bruce at the helm. I'd hold my mom, her head against my chest as she cried. "We're losing everything, dawling." Then she'd wipe her nose with a Kleenex and I'd sit with her and Stu in the kitchen and tell them stories about my travels. Stu would sigh, relieved to see my mom smile for a change.

One afternoon, Owen walked into Stu's kitchen looking great, like he'd been spending time in the gym. He asked me whether I still thought he should get into the business, and I told him, "I've heard that in the few shows you've done, you were really good. The sooner you get into the business, the sooner I can get you down to New York, where you can make some big money before it runs out."

Within a few weeks, Owen was wrestling full-time for Stu.

On the road, Jim and I might as well have been chained together at the ankles, convicts in a moving prison. We spent more time with each other than we did with our wives, and we never had an argument. Other tag teams weren't so lucky, usually ending up with deep-rooted animosities and bitter falling-outs. But we had a custom of cracking each other's backs before every match. Sometimes, just before we went through the curtain, I'd reach over and gently hold Jim's hand. Sometimes I'd start to skip. Soon he'd join in, and we'd burst out laughing. Then we'd march through the curtain all serious, as heel as ever.

He preferred to leave the handling of the specifics of our matches up to me. I used reverse psychology on him, and it worked every time. If I told Jim he couldn't do something in the ring, he'd go ahead and do it just to show me he could. Like war buddies, Jim and I kept each other's hopes alive.

My pay for *WrestleMania II* was a disappointing $2,000, the same amount I got for my match with Ricky The Dragon Steamboat in Boston. That was generous for a house show, but not for the biggest show of the year. When I heard that other guys in the same battle royal were paid four and five times as much as I was, and that The Bulldogs got $20,000 each for their tag-title match, I wrote a note and handed it to George, along with my cheque. The note read, "I'm sorry but I feel slighted and would rather not accept it at all. This does not reflect my partner's view or my feelings toward you and the promotion. I'm grateful to be here and will continue to give you everything to the best of my ability."

George handed me back my cheque and told me he'd see what he could do. In the end I received double the amount and so did Jim, but in hindsight I can see that the real favour George did me was in not showing my note to Vince. I probably would have been fired.

As it turned out, it was George who was fired, on June 20 that year. The word in the dressing room was that Hogan and Roddy had taken against him. They didn't like his booking, perhaps because he was always pushing his Carolina boys, and had said to Vince, "He goes or we go." Just like that, George was gone. I will always be grateful for the crack in the door he opened for me.

After Rosemary, I had sworn to change my ways, but it didn't take me long to realize that Julie could never truly forgive me. And I still couldn't take being alone. I became even closer to my wrestling family, but unfortunately too many of them were in love with cocaine, and I wanted to stay away from that.

There was plenty of truth to the adage that bad girls make good company. So I played a game with myself. After the shows, I'd walk into a bar trying to stay under the radar. I'd sit in the gunfighter's seat and scan the room looking for a girl into whose arms I'd like to fall at the end of the night. I would zero in on the prettiest one, challenging myself to see whether I could win her over in the few short hours I was in town. If I struck out, it really didn't matter to me.

I'd swoop down, friendly and yet at the same time elusive, and often ended up surprising myself, waking up with some beautiful girl curled up beside me. I have never forgotten the blue-eyed mulatto with ringlets in her hair. Or the model who could play classical piano. Or the beautiful French dancer who pranced around my room like a cat. It's hard for me to hate the memory of her panting phrases in my ear and me not understanding a word of it.

I was proud and guilty all at once; in this dichotomy of conscience the guilt never diluted the pride. I suppose some may judge me harshly; if only they could walk a mile in my shoes, they might be surprised to find that they couldn't lace them up fast enough. When all was said and done, my fondness for women kept me out of trouble. It may have even saved my life, when you consider how many wrestlers died from their drug and alcohol addictions.

Early in September, Chief mentioned to me that they were short one wrestler for a west coast swing and asked whether I knew anyone who could work on short notice. I suggested Owen, who was getting raves as a new high-flying sensation for Stampede Wrestling and had been named rookie of the year by wrestling magazines and the marks who wrote newsletters. Chief gave me the go-ahead. Owen was stunned that I delivered him the chance to impress the WWF and maybe to get hired full-time.

But the future looked tenuous for me and Jim. There was a buzz in the dressing room that The Bulldogs were going to lose the belts, and it was doubtful that The Foundation would get them. This was despite the fact that we'd had the best bouts by far with all the tag teams, including The Rougeaus, one of whom was the same Jimmy Rougeau I started out with so long ago, who was now called Jacques. The Hart Foundation had yet to have a single photo in the WWF's monthly magazine or program, and we never won a match on any of the house shows.

Jim referred to us as "pseudo superstars," an expression that I thought was an astute description of our situation. We were on TV just enough to be recognized everywhere we went, but we didn't make the money that most TV stars made. We had bought big houses that we were rarely able to enjoy and that were actually owned by the bank. I was sick of the whole routine, but I had too much at stake now. The only way I knew how to provide for my family was what was keeping me away from them.

I could sense an excited nervousness in Owen as he introduced himself around the dressing room in Denver. He'd come a long way fast from doing backflips off the top turnbuckles in the ring that was always set up in Stu's yard. He wore turquoise tights with silver lightning bolts up the legs. He looked thick and muscular, and his long blond hair hung in his face as he laced up his boots. He would work under the name Owen James, and team up with S.D. Jones against me and Jim.

Owen was a high-flyer, which meant that in order for him to have a great match, I needed to catch him on everything, to be his net. I'd never really seen him work, but I was determined not to fail him. He explained to me how to be there for all his high spots, which were complex and high-risk, but I had no problems with any of them, and soon we were in the ring.

The crowd at the McNichols Sports Arena cheered loudly from the opening bell as Owen launched into some great moves. As soon as we locked hands I supported him as he ran up the middle of the ropes like steps, standing on the top one. From there he jumped up, landed with the seat of his ass on the top rope and bounced off into a backward somersault, landing smartly on his feet. He hip-tossed me across the ring, and in seconds he tore the roof off the building as I threw him into the corner and he jumped effortlessly to the top of the turnbuckle and did a standing backflip. I caught him perfectly, rolling back for a near fall. Finally, Jim and I cut him off and worked him over like a couple of thugs, building some great heat until he hit us with a double drop kick. After Jim staggered to his feet, Owen scrambled through Jim's legs and tagged S.D., who made a New York–style comeback before tagging Owen back in.

When we cut Owen off again I could hear disappointment in the crowd, which was totally behind him and excitedly wondering who this blond-haired phenomenon was. Jim held him in the bear hug as I pulled him to the mat with our running clothesline for the one . . . two . . . three.

"Thanks, Bret," Owen whispered as I rolled off. He was all smiles. Not one flub. That was our first match together. He was far better than many of the top babyfaces working the WWF. I told him I'd work on getting him a tryout soon where Vince could see him. But Chief was reluctant to put Owen over too strong, even though all the boys raved about him.

Chief had been in a miserable mood since Pat Patterson was chosen over him to replace George Scott as the new booker. It was Roddy who told me that I had to start dealing directly with Vince. I figured I would: There was Owen's future and mine to discuss, and I'd also heard from my family that he had decided the WWF would return to Calgary.

The following day at the TV tapings I knocked on Vince's door, and he invited me in. I asked whether he was happy with my performance, and he said he was, so I asked what I needed to do to get more of a push. He said who got pushed was his call, and that I needed to work on my interviews more. I suggested that he might consider letting me and Jim do more of them, and possibly a SNME spot. He said he'd think about it. I raised the issue of the WWF going back to Calgary, and he immediately volunteered that he'd never run Calgary, or any of Stu's towns, without giving Stu his arranged percentage. I asked him whether there was any way that he could move the upcoming WWF show in Calgary ahead one week, because Stampede Wrestling was doing a big blow-off angle—the climax of a long storyline—at the same time his show was scheduled to run. He said he wasn't involved with scheduling and that the dates were set months in advance. Vince's WWF show would kill Stu's struggling Stampede show, and we both knew that. After an absence of almost two years, the WWF, with Hogan, The Bulldogs and even The Hart Foundation, was sure to sell out in Calgary now on any night of the week.

As I stood up to leave, I mentioned Owen to Vince, telling him that he was really good, better than me. Vince said that Owen was too small, that he could only be a babyface and that he had no room for another babyface. I suggested that as there were no masked wrestlers in the business anywhere, Owen could be the WWF's version of Tiger Mask, and Vince could get big merchandising out of a masked hero. Vince liked the idea and told me to have Owen come to Rochester TVs for a tryout. As I left I asked him whether I could come see him now and then and get a report card on how I was doing and what it would take for me to climb up the ladder to the bigger matches. He said he was always available at TVs. I was more than pleased with myself as I stepped out the door past the lineup of wrestlers all looking to make their pitch, hopeful that Vince would throw them a bone.

That night, I called Stu and told him what Vince had said about their deal and that I got Owen booked. Losing Owen to Vince would practically put Stu out of business, since Owen was clearly Stu's best hand. But Stu understood that Owen deserved a break like anyone else. He also asked me to tell Vince about his latest pet project, a kid he wanted him to look at named Tom McGhee, who was one of the world's strongest men. It was just like my dad to try to ensure that McGhee would have a bright future with Vince even though he knew what losing a top star would do to his own business.

As a favour to Stu, Davey and I made another brief appearance for Stampede Wrestling on September 29. I stood in the bathroom of the Victoria Pavilion thinking that Owen reminded me a lot of how I used to be not so long ago. While he soon would be briefly stepping into my WWF wrestling world, on this night I was briefly stepping back into his—to find Bruce doing all the same shit to Owen that he'd done to me. That night Owen looked as mad as I used to get.

After Davey had come back from doing his interview with Ed Whalen, Ross asked me to go out and do mine. WWF TV was over strong now, and both Davey and I were considered larger-than-life superstars. As I climbed through the ropes my old Calgary fans chanted, "Bret! Bret! Bret!"—

which was not the reaction I wanted, seeing as I was now a total heel. So as Ed interviewed me I overplayed an obnoxious cocky attitude, wearing my mirrored shades and ranting about how The Hart Foundation was the greatest tag team ever to come out of Calgary, not The Bulldogs, that the WWF tag championship should rightfully be ours and it was only a matter of time before we'd prove that. I ripped into an astonished Whalen and my old fans for not having enough respect for me. By the time I left the ring the fans were booing. It felt weird.

As I left the dressing room that night I turned to Owen and said, "See ya next week in Rochester." I couldn't help but notice the handsome, muscle-headed rookie, Tom McGhee. He couldn't walk across the ring without tripping.

I flew Julie into Sacramento for a four-day run in California. After a two-hour drive we checked into the San Francisco airport Amfac hotel just after midnight. We'd barely got into the room when Roddy called to invite me down for a beer, not knowing that Julie was there. I hated to miss the opportunity to talk with Roddy, because I learned so much from him every time I did. Julie was tired and said she didn't want to get in the way, so I told her I was going down for one beer and I'd be right back. What a mistake.

It was 3 a.m. by the time Roddy and I staggered out of the lounge and into the elevator, headed up to his room. The bartender let us each take one beer with us. When we got to Roddy's room he tackled me from behind and we had a full-scale brawl, knocking over anything that wasn't nailed down. Just when I thought I had Roddy pinned, he'd manage to put a thumb in my eye and go on the offensive again, sending us crash-ing into the walls. It was while we were struggling on the rug that we noticed a pair of feet and looked up to see a skinny hotel security guard looking down at us. This polite little man pleaded with us to call it a night. Roddy promised him that we would if he would only go and get us one more beer apiece. I was thinking that's exactly what we *didn't* need. The security guard took off and returned with the beer only to find that we were at it again and had tipped the bed over! He pleaded with us to stop because we were going to get him fired. I stood up to leave, but Roddy tackled me again, this time taking the guard crashing into the wall with us! When another guard showed up, I managed to escape and head four doors down the hall to my room. Julie hadn't gone to sleep after all, and had been waiting for me all this time. The fury that awaited me when I opened the door to my room was far worse than anything I'd left behind back in Roddy's room!

The next morning, when Roddy saw Julie in the lobby, he was quick to apologize to her, taking all the responsibility like a perfect gentleman. I never heard a thing about it again.

As soon as I set my bag down in the dressing room in Rochester, I spied both Owen and Tom McGhee anxiously getting dressed. Chief approached me, sullenly. "Ah, Stu, you're working with McGhee and we need him to catch one on ya."

"What?" I asked in disbelief.

He shrugged. "Vince wants him over."

I went straight to Vince's room, walked right in, and asked why he wanted me to put over an unproven guy in one of my regular towns when he had a whole backstage full of jobbers. It was a wrestler's right to consider who he lost to. If bookers sensed he didn't care, he might find himself losing all the time.

"You're the only one I can trust to get him over and show me if this guy can draw me money," Vince replied.

What was I supposed to say to that? "Vince, if he's any good, you'll see it after I'm done; if anyone can get him over, I can."

He promised me that the match would never air on TV anywhere.

I found McGhee with Owen, and told him that if he trusted me, I'd get him over, "Give me your three absolute best moves. If you have a good match, Vince will have big plans for you." I designed a match that was really simple, inserting his big moves at just the right times. While I worked out my match with McGhee, Owen did his best to design a match with a chubby jobber who clearly didn't have the skills he needed. I knew that Owen, coming from a Stampede background, would struggle with the concept of eating up a jobber in four minutes.

Owen went into his first spot, where he ran up the ropes like steps, but the jobber didn't support him and he slipped and fell flat on his ass. It went downhill from there. Finally, Owen came off the top with a beautiful dive for the pin fall. As he came back into the dressing room I saw the disappointment in his eyes.

Minutes later I walked out with Jimmy Hart to a chorus of boos. Then McGhee came out looking like a handsome, well-muscled statue with curly golden locks. The crowd cheered as he jumped straight up to the ring apron and skipped right over the top rope. Once the bell sounded he did everything exactly as I'd told him. As good as he looked, he was horrible, pathetically phony. I struggled to manoeuvre him into place without the fans realizing his shortcomings, putting on an absolute clinic for anyone who ever wanted to know how to make a big green guy look great.

When I came back through the curtain, Vince and Pat had swarmed all over McGhee. Afterwards it was Tom who told me that Vince nearly wet his pants while watching the TV monitor, as he exclaimed loud enough for all to hear, "That's my next champion!" I felt bad that Owen had been completely ignored while McGhee not only got hired, but it appeared like he was going to be elevated to superstar status! Not only that, Vince seemed to think McGhee did it on his own.

Back at the hotel, Roddy told me I should have made McGhee look bad, but I just couldn't do that. The next morning Owen went home totally dejected.

In late October, after an arduous sixteen-day run, I was stretched out on the carpet in front of the fireplace playing with Dallas and his growing set of WWF action figures when Tom called from somewhere on the road to tell me that Jim and I were getting the Tag Team belts in January. "Vince wanted Davey and me to drop them to Sheik and Volkoff, and I told him fuck that, we'd only drop 'em to the hardest working team in the territory, so there ya go, Gabe! The Push Brothers are getting the belts!"

I thanked him. I had no doubt that it was only because of Tom that The Hart Foundation would finally get a serious push.

Little did anyone know—least of all Jim, Tom, Davey and me—that The Hart Foundation and The British Bulldogs would have one of our last great matches on November 1, 1986, at the old Boston Garden.

We huddled together in the damp, sweaty dressing room going over the finish that Pat had given us. As usual, Davey and Jim sat with blank, empty stares as Tom and I envisioned it all for them. The Bulldogs were going over, as always. I had a couple of new spots I wanted to experiment with, and I laid them out to Davey while Tom threw down a couple of Percocets with a gulp of coffee. Pat gave us the nod and out we went, wearing our new black gear with a pink stripe down the side of each leg.

The Bulldogs marched out with their new mascot, an actual, ancient Bulldog named Matilda, who was only slightly cheaper and caused only slightly fewer headaches than their now ex-manager, Lou Albano. Lou was always getting drunk backstage and at Tom's urging, more as a joke, Lou told Vince to go fuck himself—as it turned out, one time too many.

As we went into the finish, Anvil hoisted Dynamite up and slammed him hard to the mat. Tom grimaced as he moaned, "Ooh me fooking back!"

Afterwards, in the dressing room, when I asked him whether he was okay, he told me it was just a spasm. He would turn out to be very wrong.

Back at the Ramada bar Tom seemed to be fine as he chatted it up with a couple of the regular ring rats, Grizelda and Slippers. The ten Percocets he took throughout the night made the sharp pain go away long enough for him to pretend it was nothing to worry about.

Judy, the seamstress who made our wrestling gear for us, had mentioned to me that she had a nice new colour she wanted Jim and me to try: neon bubblegum pink. After careful consideration we realized wearing pink would get us instant heat and give us a new look for our *SNME* debut. Still, in the dressing room in San Diego where we were doing pre-tapes for *SNME*, Jim and I felt funny pulling on those pink tights.

I was dressed and picking up my tray in the cafeteria when Vince, who was sitting with Dick Ebersol, head of NBC sports, yelled at me, "Stop! Don't move!" Heads turned. It got suddenly quiet. I thought we were in some sort of trouble, and I couldn't imagine why. Vince stood up and circled around Jim and me grinning, "Don't ever change that colour! That colour is you! It's what you guys have been missing all along! From now on I don't want you to wear anything but pink!"

The following night in L.A., Jim and I had an excellent match with The Bees, building great heat on Jim Brunzell. For the finish The Bees put on yellow and black masks, and Brunzell switched places with Blair underneath the ring apron while I provided a distraction for the referee. Tagging back in, I confidently dusted my hands off and dragged the guy I thought was Brunzell to his feet for a bodyslam when Blair small-packaged me for an easy one . . . two . . . three. The L.A. Sports Arena exploded. In my opinion we'd had the best match on the whole network special. As we came back through the curtain, a beaming Dick Ebersol jumped up and gave us a high-five.

When I phoned home in mid-December, Julie told me that Tom had seriously hurt his back during a match in Hamilton and that he'd been taken away in an ambulance.

As soon as I got off the road, I went to see Tom at Holy Cross Hospital. It turned out that he had two ruptured discs and was set to have emergency surgery. He was livid because Davey and Diana had shown up with a photographer from the *Calgary Sun* with the intention of taking a picture of him in his hospital bed. Then I told him that Vince had asked me to bring the Tag belts back with me after the break. Tom defiantly told me to tell Vince to go fuck himself, so I left it for the two of them to sort out. I understood that belt was a badge of honour: It was Tom's belt until he lost it.

Michelle blew my mind when she confided that she'd had absolutely no idea that Tom's back was bad. She knew he had drugstore-sized jars of Placidyl and Percocet, and also told me that it was routine for him to drink forty ounces of vodka every night before bed. Now the doctors were insisting that his career was over, and she had no idea how he would support the family. I had no idea how Tom's injury would affect my career either, or what would happen with the belts.

On Christmas Eve, Michelle, her brother Mark and Duke Myers picked Tom up when he was discharged from the hospital. They drove home at a snail's pace because every little turn or bump caused him to scream in blinding pain.

While Tom was on his way home, I was on my way to the airport in a taxi to work Washington and Richmond on Christmas Day. At my house, we had celebrated as best we could a day early. Thankfully Jade and Dallas were too young to know the difference.

20

"CUTS IN OUR HEADS LIKE PIGGYBANKS"

I SAT IN A TINY BAR across the street from the Amfac hotel in Los Angeles listening to Koko B. Ware banging the keys on a piano and singing "When the Saints Go Marching in." He was a short, squat black wrestler from Memphis who had a great voice. As I sipped my beer with Anvil, looking out over the bar, I could see numerous faces from my past.

Harley Race had given up fighting Vince and had joined him instead. He was throwing back beers with Bill Eadie, the one-time masked super-star, who'd sworn to me in Japan that he'd never work for McMahon again. Here they both were. Sitting with Davey Boy was Billy Jack Haynes, the big wrestler from Portland I had last seen twisting his own ears with pliers in Stu's van because he wanted to have cauliflower ears like the pros.

I spotted the smiling face of The Mississippi Mauler, Big Jim Harris, now wrestling as Kamala. I'd last seen Jim painting white circles on his black face in Croydon, England, when we were working for Max Crabtree. The Honky Tonk Man, Wayne Farris, was sitting with Jimmy Hart, his black hair in an Elvis Presley pompadour. Terry Gibbs, who once com-plained about working with me, was there too, bowed under the impossible task of trying to have a good match with Tom McGhee every night. No mat-ter how hard Gibbs tried, they stunk the building out.

The lure of big money in the WWF was enticing wrestlers from everywhere.

It was easy to see that Koko loved entertaining the boys. "Oh Lord I want to be in that number, when the saints go marchin' in." Well, there were few saints among us. A snowstorm was about to hit Los Angeles, and once I caught a whiff that coke was on the way, I latched onto a girl I'd been chatting up and said, "Get me outta here!"

A few days later, at TVs in New Jersey, I found out that Jim and I would still be getting the Tag belts at the end of the month in Tampa. Tom was going to make the show just to drop the belts to us, a really big gesture for him considering the severity of his back injury. But he also wouldn't want to miss out on his involvement in an angle that would lead to a big payday at *WrestleMania III* in Pontiac, Michigan. Vince was confident that the third edition of his extravaganza would pull more than 90,000 fans to the Silverdome, but not everyone was so sure.

When I asked Vince how my future was looking, he advised me to buy the biggest house I could find. I looked at him blankly and said, "I already did."

For the next few weeks Davey had special tag partners to take Tom's place. I was thrilled to be in the ring with Mad Dog Vachon, The Crusher and Bruno Sammartino. We'd started to use the heel referee, Danny Davis, to do the same thing that Alexander Scott had done back in the old Stampede territory. Unfortunately, Danny wasn't very good, though he was a nice enough guy.

I went home in mid-January and saw Tom again. He was in so much pain it seemed impossible to imagine him wrestling in less than two weeks. He'd lost fifty pounds and looked pale and weak. The doctors couldn't have more strongly advised him to never wrestle again, but he refused to listen.

Three days later, I left home early in the morning. The plan was for me to get a rental car after I landed at the Pittsburgh airport and pick Jim up when his plane got in from Tampa. There I was waiting at the curb when I saw Jim, in handcuffs, being escorted from the terminal by a squad of Pennsylvania state troopers. He didn't make the matches that night in Struthers, Ohio. I finally met up with him in the bar at the Quality Inn, where he told me he'd been charged with punching a U.S. Air stewardess, which was a federal offence. Jim assured me he'd never laid a hand on her, and I believed him. We both feared this would cost us the tag title. But Vince said he thought this was a clear-cut case of a wrestler being targeted for harassment, and he hired the sharpest lawyer he could find to make U.S. Air sorry that they ever picked on one of his wrestlers.

On Super Bowl Sunday, we were stuck at the Holiday Inn in Tampa because Vince needed us a day early for TVs. Vince threw a Super Bowl party, which was a nice gesture, and especially enjoyed by Stu and Georgia, whom I'd brought down for a visit. Stu was putting holds on any wrestler who didn't know enough to run the other way!

Super Bowl XXI turned out to be another lopsided contest. The New York Giants thrashed the Denver Broncos, and I considered that maybe wrestling had become so popular because our orchestrated finishes were often more exciting than the outcomes in pure sports.

The next afternoon, at the Tampa Sun Dome, some of the boys had to blink back tears as Davey helped the frail shell of The Dynamite Kid through the backstage area. When Tom painfully pulled on his gear it hung on him, and even I felt tears come to my eyes at seeing this broken machine that once ran like no other. Pat explained that *all* Tom had to do was walk out to the ring. So that's how it was an hour later, with Matilda leading the way. Dynamite hadn't even got to the ring yet when I came from behind and delicately knocked him to the ground with Jimmy's megaphone. After a few minutes of making Davey look good, Jim and I double-teamed him, as Dynamite stayed curled up in a ball outside on the floor with Danny Davis looming over him and ordering him to get in the ring. Then Jim hoisted Davey up, and I tore into the ropes delivering the Hart Attack for the finish. The whole match was only four minutes long.

Jimmy jumped into our arms, and the three of us, along with Davis, headed back to the dressing room. As Davey helped Dynamite back through the curtain, each and every wrestler and agent respectfully stood up from his chair and applauded Tom, even Vince.

I looked down at my new belt, realizing what being a champion had cost Tom. I wondered what it would cost me. In that moment I vowed never to forget that wrestling is a work, and I also vowed to pace myself for the long haul. I wanted to come out the other end in one piece.

At the *WrestleMania III* press conference, Vince revealed how he planned to fill the Pontiac Silverdome. They'd turn André heel and pit him against Hogan for a huge main event, a match that had been talked about for years. Piper would take on Adrian Adonis in what was billed as Roddy's retirement match. One of the best wrestlers at that time was Macho Man Randy Savage, a flamboyant, second-generation wrestler. He was set to face Ricky Steamboat in what was sure to be a classic, anticipated as the best match on the card. Jim and I were satisfied to have secured a main event spot: a six-man tag match in which Danny Davis would team up with The Hart Foundation versus The British Bulldogs and Tito Santana. The thought was a six-man tag would take some of the load off Tom's back.

The Foundation finally made the cover of the program, and the WWF came out with new action figures of us. For me, the dolls were the first clear indication that we might actually hold on to the belts for a while, even though there was a lot of talk that because of Jim's assault charge we'd be short-term champions.

As I waited for my match at *WrestleMania III* on March 29, 1987, I watched on a backstage monitor as Bundy slammed Little Beaver and then delivered a 450-pound elbow drop on the ninety-pound midget. I couldn't help but laugh when the three remaining midgets turned on Bundy and backed him off! Too bad Bundy didn't see the hilarity of it—he prided himself on being a serious monster heel.

The building was so huge they drove everyone out to the ring in a motorized cart, complete with wrestling ropes. I looked out at the crowd, and I'd never seen or heard anything like it. People have never stopped asking me what it was like to wrestle in front of a crowd of ninety-three thousand. The truth is, I really don't know. At the start of the match The Bulldogs bumped me and Jim out of the ring, and then they picked up a terrified Danny Davis, hoisted him over their heads and threw him over the top rope. While I was trying to break his fall, Danny poked me in my right eye; after that, what should have been one of my greatest memories is nothing but a painful blur. For the finish, Danny clobbered Davey Boy with Jimmy's megaphone in the midst of a four-way brawl for the cheap win.

Roddy defeated Adrian and rode off into the sunset.

Randy Savage and Ricky Steamboat delivered what many in the business would say was the best match of all time—at least to that point.

When it came time for the main event the fans were electric. I never saw André work harder until Hogan finally clotheslined him to the canvas. Hogan was able to pick André up and slam him like no one had ever done before. Then came Hogan's finish, the running leg drop. All I can say is that I never heard a sound like that of ninety-three thousand people counting André out along with referee Joey Morella.

I had twenty-three days off, and my eye was so sore that it teared the whole time. Stu wore the stoic face of a man doing his best to appear upbeat, but Bruce's booking—ball shots, heel refs and fuck finishes—was driving him crazy. The business wasn't so bad in the small towns, but in the big cities of Calgary and Edmonton it was awful. Stu's only real joy was Owen, who was not only an exceptional worker, but honest and committed to his cause. If Owen was willing to give it his all, Stu felt he couldn't give up.

Tom was scaring us. He now kept three huge Bullmastiffs and had amassed an arsenal of shotguns and pistols. When we took the kids to visit him and Michelle, he sat on his back porch shooting at anything that moved, even though the kids were playing nearby in the sandbox. He seemed to take some sick pleasure in blowing the back legs off jackrabbits while he washed down pain pills with vodka and orange juice. Julie and I were happy to get the hell out of there, and after that we made a point of not bringing the kids around when Tom was home.

Davey and I helped Stu out by working a couple of weekends (which would ultimately benefit Vince, since our matches would build heat for an upcoming steel cage match between The Foundation and The Bulldogs when the WWF returned to the Saddledome in May). At the Stampede Corral, on April 17, I was lashed at the wrist with Davey in a four-corner chain match in front of a good crowd of nearly 4,000 people. The winner was the first one to touch all four corners, one after the other. Fans behaved like yelping hounds hot on my trail. Beaten senseless, I limply put up my hands trying to fend off Davey, both of us bloody messes, but he dragged me up from the mat by the strap of my singlet and tossed me over his shoulder. As Davey staggered from one post to the next, slapping his bloody hand on each turnbuckle pad, he pretended not to notice me touching each one with my own bloody hand. Then, as he drew close to the final corner, I jerked the top rope, spinning him around the other way. I dropped behind him and tagged the pad before he did, crumbling victoriously to the mat, too weak to stand. The crowd frothed at the mouth as I stumbled down the aisle toward the dressing room, past fierce angry glares, F-words and middle fingers.

Like in a bad dream, all too soon my suitcase was packed and ready to go again. As I trudged down the steps of my house, my aches and pains were only just beginning to subside, and I was just starting to get used to being a dad again.

The Foundation and The Bulldogs were now pitted against each other in steel cage matches for the belts. It was a kindness to Tom, a lot easier on him than a regular match, though nobody watching would have guessed. Cage matches are exciting because of the suspense of the teams trying to climb out and, of course, because of the blood, but in truth they are simple to perform. We were on last almost every night, and we gave it our all, in intense, physical, suspenseful Stampede Wrestling–style. Gory too—we were determined to make these the greatest cage matches in WWF history, and so each night we took turns blading. After only seven shows we all had deep cuts in our heads like the slots in piggy banks. The finish every night was Tom's, and it soon became the standard ending of cage matches everywhere. If it was Tom and me still in the cage at the end, I'd be trying to make my escape over the top, standing on the turnbuckle, when Dynamite, covered in blood, would grab my ankle and pull me down, crotching me on the top rope. Then he'd begin to slowly crawl toward the wide open cage door, with me crawling and bleeding behind him, unable to catch up. The suspense was incredible! Anvil would try to interfere from the floor, Davey would grab him and a vicious fight would ensue between them. Just as Tom stuck his head through the open door, out of nowhere Jimmy Hart would slam it as hard as he could on Tom's head, knocking him back inside. Then I'd slither over the unconscious Dynamite and out through the open door.

Victorious, The Hart Foundation would stumble past the fans, dripping blood. These matches made skeptics into believers.

I was finally expecting some big payoffs for all the blood and hard work. But I found out from Tom that since Junkyard Dog and Paul Orndorff were the main event each night, the big money went to them.

At the TV tapings in Buffalo on June 2, an angry Vince summoned all the wrestlers to a meeting to discuss the latest embarrassing incident.

Hacksaw Jim Duggan, a bearded goliath with the personality of a big, friendly St. Bernard, had made the simple mistake of giving his storyline archrival, The Iron Sheik, a ride to Asbury Park, New Jersey, where they'd be working against each other. The Sheik brought along a few cans of beer and lit up a joint, even though Duggan asked him not to smoke in the car. New Jersey state troopers pulled them over, and the odour of marijuana was all the probable cause they needed to search the car. They discovered coke in the Sheik's shaving kit, so he and Duggan were both arrested.

It was hard to tell what made it a national news story—the rival wrestlers riding together in the midst of their huge America-versus-Iran feud or the fact that they'd allegedly been caught doing drugs together. Duggan's hometown of Glens Falls, New York, a sleepy suburb of Albany, had been busily preparing for a WWF-sponsored Hacksaw Jim Duggan Day, with Jim's father, the much respected local police chief, presiding. Needless to say, the moment was lost.

Vince had immediately fired them, and now he was giving us a long lecture on the absolute necessity to kayfabe. "The days of a six-pack and a blow job are over!" he shouted. All the wrestlers had this say-it-isn't-so expression on their faces. And then he told everyone that he was instituting a mandatory drug test for cocaine and that anyone who failed would be suspended for six weeks without pay. The second time you'd get mandatory rehab, paid for out of your cheque. Third strike, you're fired!

Anvil had just been acquitted of assaulting that stewardess and then got himself bankrolled by Vince to counter-sue U.S. Air. He had thought that the world was looking pretty rosy!

I was actually relieved that cocaine testing would soon be in effect, and hoped that it would force more wrestlers to clean up before someone else died.

So Hacksaw and The Iron Sheik were gone. Scanning the room as Vince talked, I realized that a lot of the old faces were now missing. One new arrival was Dingo Warrior, a six-foot-two 'roided-up bodybuilder named

Jim Hellwig. Like Tom McGhee, he looked fantastic, but he didn't know a headlock from a headlight!

In pro wrestling in the late 1980s, all you really needed was a good gimmick or the right look to be a big star; wrestling ability took a back seat. (Although McGhee was let go before the year was out, a hopeless case.) At that time, a number of great workers came into the WWF, plucked from the last remnants of the dying regional territories. One of them was George Gray, called One Man Gang, a four-hundred-pound wrestler with a black mohawk and a scruffy beard who wore small black sunglasses and a frayed blue jean vest emblazoned on the back with a skull and crossbones. On TV One Man Gang was quite the angry character, but in real life George was a gentle guy who liked to read a lot.

Killer Khan was another monster heel lining up behind Kamala to cash in on Hulkamania. Then there was Scott Bam Bam Bigelow from New Jersey, who was possibly the best working big man in the business. Bam Bam could dive off the top rope with the agility of a cat. He had a sculpted red beard that emphasized a squared-off jaw, anchoring his big, round face and framing a missing front tooth. His bald head was covered with tattoos of flames. He was still green and soon had a lot of heat from all the wrestlers for bragging about his big payoffs. One night, in the ring at Madison Square Garden, André got his hands on Bigelow and practically killed him—for real. That was all the attitude adjustment Bigelow needed, and he changed his ways.

Another new arrival was Ravishing Rick Rude, a guy around my age from Minneapolis, with a dry wit and an easygoing manner. He was tall and thin, with long, curly dark hair, a thick moustache, meaty forearms and washboard abs. He was considered a legit tough guy and serious pro arm wrestler.

As we all knew, Vince had grown up fantasizing about becoming a wrestler. As a boy he dreamed up a gimmick for himself, a filthy rich heel who would throw money out to the crowd and buy his way out of everything. When Ted Dibiase, a second-generation wrestler out of Amarillo, joined the WWF, he became The Million Dollar Man, the embodiment of Vince's dream. Ted was brawny with chiselled features and was always immaculately groomed. He'd been taught by the Funks and was being positioned to become the next NWA world champion when Vince changed all that. Now Ted was going straight to the top as the WWF's hottest heel. He had his own personal valet named Virgil, worked by Mike Jones, which was intended to be a dig at NWA booker Dusty Rhodes, whose real name was Virgil Runnels. (Vince never missed an opportunity to take a jab at anyone he believed had crossed him.) Ted also lived his gimmick outside the ring. The Million Dollar Man was driven everywhere by stretch limo, stayed in four-star hotels and flew first class, all paid for by Vince, which set the boys to grumbling because most of the larger wrestlers had to cram into coach seats.

Sitting across from me in the meeting were two new pretty boys from the nearly defunct AWA: Shawn Michaels and Marty Jannetty, a high-flying tag team known as The Midnight Rockers. It was their first day in the WWF, and I was scoping them out like a lion staring at two antelopes. The Hart Foundation desperately needed a new team to work with, having pretty much run our course with The Bulldogs, The Bees and The Rougeaus. Jim muttered to me that they were too small and skinny, but I knew that once The Hart Foundation got some serious heat on them, the young girls would get behind them and we could last a lot longer as champions. Back then, Michaels was a lean blond with nary a muscle on him. Marty Jannetty was shorter and more compact with shaggy brown hair. Neither was as innocent as he looked: they came in with a notorious reputation for rocking after midnight, which might prove interesting for them considering Vince's new hard line.

As it turned out, that night at the Hilton Playboy Club in Buffalo, the Rockers got rowdy, breaking bottles and glasses, and causing a drunken disturbance. Vince felt they had missed the whole point of his lecture and fired them. The Rockers lasted only one day in the WWF: So much for our hopes of a new tag team to work with.

Six weeks later, the dressing room at the Houston Summit was abuzz with the results of the WWF's first ever drug tests for cocaine use, which had taken place on June 23 in Indianapolis. The first to go was Jake The Snake Roberts, who was hit with a six-week suspension. He'd gone straight to Vince to ask why Brian Blair hadn't been caught too, so Vince suspended Blair. That sure didn't help us, since Jim and I had been working with The Bees almost every other night.

The news from home kept getting weirder. One late night in mid-July, when Jim and I were driving around Glens Falls looking for somewhere to eat, he told me an incredible tale featuring his mother and Smith's wife, Maria, who had been on the edge of a breakdown for years. When he was home last time, Jim's mom, Katie, and my sister Alison volunteered to babysit their three kids so that Jim and Ellie could have a romantic couple of days in the mountains at Banff. As Katie and Alison crossed the driveway to Hart house with Jim and Ellie's kids and Alison's baby girl, they were startled to see Maria balancing on the railing of the second-floor balcony, just above them. She was naked but for a heavy winter parka that hung open in

My mother in 1947, the year after she met and fell in love with my dad.

My favourite photo of me with my parents.

The portrait of me that hung with photos of the rest of the clan on the living room wall at Hart house.

I loved cowboys, and I loved my Roy Rogers holster and six-guns.

The whole family posing with Rocky Marciano after the 1964 Calgary Stampede parade. Stu had just cracked Dean on the ear for acting up.

Hart house front and back, and
Stu's "dungeon."

The 1967 Hart family Christmas. Back row, from left: Smith, Wayne, Stu, Helen, Owen, Keith, Bruce. Front row, from left: Dean, me, Ellie, Diana, Georgia, Allison, Ross.

My Grade 9 school photo.

Me on the left, wrestling in the Calgary city high-school championships in 1974. Like Dean before me, I won. As a reward, Stu gave me the use of his old gold Brougham.

At 17.

My late brother Dean, when he was my hero.

My mom with André The Giant in Calgary, July 1977.

The 1977 Stampede parade. In the back seat are Bruce, Owen, me and Georgia, with Stu up front.

My Puerto Rican adventure with Smith in 1978 put us both on the front cover of *Body Press*.

From the left, Bruce, me and Keith, in shirts promoting the Puerto Rican territory.

Bob Leonard

Defying the law of gravity
with Tom Billington,
the Dynamite Kid.

Bob Leonard

Tom and I with the British Commonwealth title belt, 1979.

Left, Julie at the arena in Regina in 1979, and in 1980 at my place.

Stu and I backstage at
the Victoria Pavilion.

Stampede Wrestling with
Leo Burke in 1980.

With Wayne.

Bob Leonard

My first ladder match,
with Dynamite,
in Regina in 1981.

Bret Hart Archive

VOL. 21
NO. 39
50c

OFFICIAL
WRESTLING
PROGRAM
FOOTHILLS
ATHLETIC
CLUB

Body
Press

The tolls of the mat sport are evident in this photo of Davey Boy Smith
after suffering a severe head gash in a Regina bout with the Dynamite Kid
is assisted by Bret Hart (r) and bystander. The wound required eighteen
stitches.

Davey Boy Smith, covered in blood, makes
the cover of *Body Press* after he let Dynamite
do the cutting.

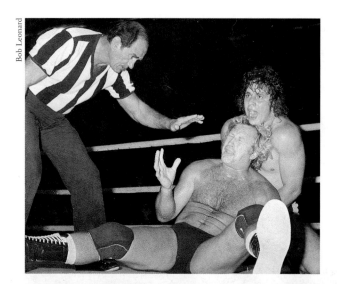

On the Stampede super-card in 1981, with Nick Bockwinkle, the AWA World champ. Lou Thesz, the six-time NWA World Champion, is our special referee.

Working with Dave Schultz in the summer of 1981, with Hito and Cuban getting involved.

In Sapporo, Japan, with Tiger Mask. February 1982.

North American
Champion, 1982.

An elbow smash on Archie
The Stomper Gouldie, 1983.

Tom and I in Dubai in February 1983. Tom had come back too early from knee surgery.

Julie and Jade, our first-born, 1983.

The young stallions. Tom, Davey with his bullet head, and me.

With Hulk Hogan in Japan in 1984.

the summer heat. She seemed to be imagining herself to be an Indian scout on the lookout, one hand to her forehead: "I think rain come."

Katie had a zesty, upbeat California attitude. She calmly waved, smiling, and said, "Yes dear, that's great!" And then went up the stairs to lure Maria in off the railing.

Later, Maria came down to the kitchen where Katie, in an attempt at normalcy, offered her a Snickers bar. For no reason anyone else could understand, Maria grabbed it and hurled it, as hard as she could, at Alison, who had one-year-old Brooke in her arms. Maria then attacked Alison and started dragging her around the kitchen by the hair, with Katie valiantly try-ing to intervene. In the fierce struggle Alison focused on a finger and, fear-ing for not only her own safety but that of her baby girl, bit that finger as hard as she could! Maria never even flinched but continued to pull on Alison's hair, so Alison just kept on biting that finger. Then she made eye contact with Katie, who had tears running down her cheeks. Katie said, "Sweetie, that's *my* finger."

Stu finally heard the commotion and came to the rescue. Jim's poor mom ended up with six cracked ribs and a nearly severed finger. Alison had a bad case of whiplash. A few days later, Stu bought Maria a one-way ticket home to Puerto Rico. Smith had no choice but to let her go; he may have actually been relieved. When Maria was led out of the house, she turned to Alison with a glimmer of lucidity in her eyes and told her how sorry she was.

When Jim and I walked into the Glens Falls Ground Round that night, the hostess asked whether we were with the wrestling party in the back. We assumed it was a fan party, and decided to avoid it: I was just too tired. We sat ourselves down at the bar, ordered food and wet our whistles with a few frosty pitchers of beer. Every so often Jim would shake his head in dis-belief about what happened to his mom.

For some reason a grumpy, old, bulldog-faced waitress instantly took a dislike to us. As the night drew to a close, she offered last call to everyone but us. We had words, and in our heated exchange I called her an old bitch. Her jaw dropped and she stomped off to the kitchen. This was normally Jim's role when we were out in public, but on that night he sat on his stool, amused. He actually clapped and said, "Well done!"

With no more beer for us, I had a sudden change of heart and suggested to Jim that we crash that wrestling party. And we literally did: A partition was blocking off the back of the restaurant, and when we blindly gave it a push, we accidentally knocked some people down on the other side. Then we pried it open with our fingers and fell into the room.

This was no fan party! Vince was having a private office party with a long table full of brown-nosers, not to mention Hogan and the recently suspended Brian Blair. I was in no shape to be talking with Vince, who still intimidated me. Jim and I couldn't get out of there fast enough. We backed up on rewind, but when I looked behind me I saw six policemen in riot gear, led by the grumpy old waitress, who was pointing right at me! I pushed Jim back into the room, saying, "You deal with Vince and I'll deal with them!" As I tried to finagle myself out of it, Jim Troy, one of Vince's top soldiers and closest friends, was suddenly at my side. He explained to the cops that I was with Vince's party, and just like that they dropped the whole thing, and Jim Troy was leading me by the arm back to the party. I could only imagine how all of this might look to Vince, on his clean-up crusade, but when I nervously sat down it became apparent that Vince was totally bombed. A few minutes later he had to be helped out to his limo.

The following morning Jim and I, both hungover, drove up to Lake Placid for the second day of TVs. Later that afternoon at the arena an equally hungover Vince called me over and said he needed to talk to me. He led me down a long corridor into a room and closed the door but became embarrassed when he couldn't remember what the heck he'd wanted to tell me. He finally said, "Don't worry about it; it couldn't have been very important if I can't remember what it was." After how quickly The Rockers had been fired, I was grateful for his forgetfulness.

In the dressing room in Cedar Rapids, Iowa, on September 7, I was approached by Jack Lanza, another one-time wrestler now turned agent for the WWF. Stooped like a black-moustached buzzard, with a personality to match, Lanza liked to make up the rules as he went along, but this time he was passing along a new rule straight from Vince: no more blading in the WWF. I thought it was typical that we'd find this out just as we were preparing for another gory cage match, this time with the virgin-headed Killer Bees. Banning blood would take a lot out of the big gimmick matches, but too many fans were now smart to the blade.

Though I'd bladed when I thought it would increase the artistry of the match, the practice was clearly stupid, and stopping it was a step in the right direction to protecting wrestlers. What bothered me was that Vince banned blading four months too late. My forehead had so many deep cuts in it from our recent run of cage matches that I could easily pull the slices apart with my fingers. Pat Patterson later explained that the real concern was that AIDS could be spread by all that self-inflicted bleeding in the ring. I was relieved, and at the same time I felt bad for ever having done it.

By the end of September 1987, it finally felt like The Hart Foundation was picking up steam. Our first major angle since getting the belts was about to air on NBC's *SNME*. In the dressing room before the taping, Pat laid it out: Jim and I would interfere in Honky Tonk's match with Macho Man Randy Savage. Just as Macho was about to win, we'd charge in and put the boots to him, and while we held Macho down, Honky would threaten to break his guitar over Macho's head. The lovely Miss Elizabeth, Randy's real-life wife and attractive ring valet, would get in Honky's way and plead with us all to stop. Honky would then shove her to the mat and unload his gimmicked guitar over Randy's head, shattering it to pieces. To touch a girl on TV was unheard of, and all of us would get big-time heat as a result. It all went as planned, and the crowd was totally incensed as the three of us heels came back through the curtain.

Later that night I also learned that I'd be working a singles match with Macho on the next *SNME*. Macho now was the hottest babyface in the territory, next to Hogan; it was a great opportunity to be able to showcase my talent with a top worker who respected me too. The show averaged sixty million viewers, much larger than any pay-per-view, even *WrestleMania*. When I called home that night I got the bigger news that Julie was pregnant again, due in May. Maybe if my career turned around our love would too.

21

"MORE MAIL THAN HOGAN"

JUST WHEN I THOUGHT THINGS WERE GETTING GOOD for The Hart Foundation, I was completely caught off guard when Dino Bravo, a big, bleached-blond wrestler from Montreal who was chummy with Pat Patterson, let slip to me and Jim that Vince and Pat were taking the belts off us at the next TV taping, which was only seven days away. Dino seemed to enjoy the crushed look on our faces, even laughing at us because we didn't know.

When I called Pat, he confirmed we'd be dropping the belts to a newly formed team called Strike Force, Rick Martel and Tito Santana. I told Pat that we'd be more than happy to put them over, but I didn't think it was right that I had heard about it second-hand from Dino Bravo and with so little notice. Losing the belts meant we'd be making considerably less money.

And so it went: We gave up the Tag belts on October 27, 1987, in a short but feisty TV match with Martel and Santana taped in Syracuse. In those days, if you lost a belt in a match that hadn't aired yet, you continued to wrestle as champion at house shows until the title change was broadcast. So, for the next few weeks, that's what Jim and I did.

Life on the road gets to you. This one night in Phoenix I was actually the last to leave the Rodeway Inn lounge, which is saying something, given the rough old wrestlers and heavyweight boozers, such as André, Harley and Jim, who were my competition. As I was heading to my room a plastered Princess Tomah threw her arm around me in the lobby and offered her services. When I told her I had to get up early, she looked at me with pitying eyes and said, "I remember when the boys used to have fun!"

Fun?

I picked up the house phone and called Tom. "I've got a real babe here, and I'm not kidding. What's your room number?"

A few minutes later I knocked at his door, covering the peep hole with my finger. The chain rattled and the door swung open. Tomah was standing next to me, stark naked, wrapped in a sheet from my bed, which she threw off, exposing droopy tits that hung down to her belly button, as she let out a war cry. She then threw herself into the room on all fours saying, "Give it to me the hard way!"

"Oh fookin' hell!" Tom groaned.

I closed the door on them, laughing all the way back to my room. I kept waiting for Tom to kick her out, but when she didn't come back to get her clothes I tucked them into a pillowcase and left them outside his room. Tom remarked to me the next morning that it didn't matter to him that Tomah had spiderwebs on her fanny, and just like that I had my next blackboard drawing and caption!

I still had my *SNME* match with Randy Savage to look forward to, not that we got to do it our way. On the afternoon of November 11, we met and worked out a great match, but less than an hour before showtime, Vince summoned us to his office. He wanted a completely different match, tied to a TV storyline around me working Randy's ankle. When I explained that working Randy's ankle would limit his mobility and take the speed out of the match, Vince cut me off: "You're the great worker, figure it out."

Randy and I lit into each other right off the bell and, even with the changes, it went great. At one point he catapulted me off the apron onto the floor and I spiked my heel into the cement, cracking the bone. I painfully worked around it. For visual effect I pulled his boot off and stomped and kicked his ankle, which hurt my foot more than it did his. Then I whacked Randy's leg on the ring post and heard it go bong. I didn't mean to, but I ended up giving him the same heel injury that I'd just sustained myself, one of my rare accidents. Randy never said a word about it, just kept working like the pro he was. Both of us in excruciating pain, Randy finally small-packaged me when I tried to slam him from the ring apron for the victory. Vince congratulated us as we came through the curtain, and Randy gave me a pained hug before limping off with his arm over Liz.

Vince kept coming up with new ideas to feed his wrestlers to the media and fan maw. On American Thanksgiving weekend 1987, he launched a new pay-per-view event called the *Survivor Series*.

The taping of the first *Survivor Series* turned out to be Bundy's last day. He'd saved up enough money to go home. As a parting laugh I carefully drew Bundy on the blackboard, on all fours, violently gagging and puking up a pile of various shapes, sizes and colours of bitten-off penises. I wasn't sure what I was implying, but it broke up the locker room, with Bundy laughing the hardest. Never to be outdone, he labelled the penises with the names of all my brothers. Amazingly, he got them all right.

Another friend gone.

I worked hard in the *Survivor Series* and surprised myself by being pleased that I got raves in the *Wrestling Observer Newsletter* for being the best performer. (Dave Meltzer wrote, "Hart was fantastic.") This was long before the Internet, and the sheets were the way fans, and even promoters, got their info about the business. But I had a problem with anyone who wasn't in the business writing about it as if they knew what they were talking about. I've always maintained that the only way to really know who is a great worker and who isn't is to have wrestled him. My usual attitude was that Meltzer, and others, were making a living off other people's sweat and broken bones by exposing a business they really had no part of. But then I'd come home to find my mom reading the sheets with Stu. Promoters were so tight-lipped that the only way anyone in the business could learn anything about what was going on in other territories—and sometimes even in their own territory—was from someone outside the business. That was the ultimate irony: most wrestlers hated the sheets, but they were the first to flock around if someone brought one into the dressing room.

I was looking forward to getting home for Christmas, but my last stop was another command performance for Vince in Atlantic City: The Slammy Awards, Vince's high camp version of the Grammys. Worn out and weary I dragged my suitcases through the lobby of the Caesar's Palace hotel, laden with toys I couldn't wait to take home to my kids.

The night before the show there was a rehearsal. Under the guidance of a choreographer who'd been with the now defunct 1980s troupe the Solid Gold Dancers, all of us had to sing and dance, which clearly wasn't our forte. She wanted Jim and me to dance across the stage during Honky's performance of his theme song, but I offered that it might look better if Jim went to throw me and I reversed, sending him sliding across the stage on his knees. From there I could run and jump neatly over top of him, and together we'd come up snapping our fingers and coolly dance off stage. She loved it.

From nine to noon the next day, we did a rehearsal. Then we did the whole show without an audience in the afternoon, so if there were any screw-ups in front of the crowd they could edit them out. As a rib, during the actual performance that evening, when I sent Jim sliding across the stage on his knees, I threw him as hard as I could, launching him like a giant, out-of-control pink tumbleweed. Jim ended up rocketing across the stage on his ass, trying as hard as he could to put the brakes on so he wouldn't crash on the tables down front. He came to a stop on the very edge of the stage, and then I realized I somehow had to jump over top of him with less than a foot to land on! Feeling a bit like an Olympic long jumper, I ran and jumped, my boot barely grazing the top of Jim's head. We came up smooth, snapping and dancing, and exited the stage. Dick Ebersol loved it.

Then we changed into pale pink tuxedos and took our seats in the audience to watch The Emperor perform. Vince gave his all to a WWF-created rock song called "Stand Back," confidently gyrating his hips like Tom Jones. But the message of the lyrics he belted out—all about how no-one could stop him as he headed for the top—wasn't lost on wrestlers who had rehearsed and then performed a show for him three times in the space of twenty-four hours, with no food or drink provided by the management. Was he singing about all the promoters he'd wiped out or the wrestlers he was wearing out?

The topper was the last number of the night, also written especially for Vince and the *Piledriver* album that the Slammys were designed to promote. Vince had all the wrestlers assemble on the stage to sing "If You Only Knew" in unison, and there we were, actually singing about how our destiny belonged to Vince.

To the best of my knowledge, no wrestler was ever paid one cent for anything having to do with the Slammys or the *Piledriver* album.

"You'll be rich and famous in a far out profession." That's what the fortune cookie said when I cracked it open at the end of a Chinese meal at Christmas. On January 1, 1988, I lay in a cold, lonely room at the Knights Inn in Lansing, Michigan, listening to Mikhail Gorbachev on TV talking about perestroika and an end to the nuclear arms race and taking stock of 1987.

I'd had a good showing at *WrestleMania III*, with a payoff of US$15,000 (only a disappointment when I thought about the fact that Vince had drawn that record crowd of 93,000 to the Silverdome). Jim and I had won and lost the world tag titles. Julie and I were still holding on to a fragile dream with the big house, and our third child on the way. I guess I had no right to complain, because not everyone in my family was doing so well. Smith, without Maria, was more bitter and miserable than ever. Dean's life now consisted of getting high and simply existing. He made it look like he earned his keep at Stu's by tinkering around on old Cadillacs and moving piles of bricks and debris from one end of the yard to the other for no apparent reason. Bruce and Ross lived and breathed for Stampede Wrestling, Ross taking no pay and living on what he earned as a schoolteacher. Wayne still refereed and served as a driver; I could never figure out why my parents never gave Wayne, who was so reliable, a larger role. I guess it was a case of the squeaky wheels getting all the grease. Not that any of their sacrifices and obsession made that much difference: even the local Calgary fans now regarded the dying embers of Stampede Wrestling as small-time compared to the WWF.

Owen was carrying the territory, having incredible matches with a round, heavyset wrestler named Mike Shaw and that big old biker, Karl Moffat, who was now Jason The Terrible, wearing white coveralls and a hockey mask and wielding a chain saw. Karl had actually turned out to be a decent worker but had become a juice freak, addicted to cutting himself every night. Stu had also attracted Chris Benoit, out of Edmonton, who was like a carbon copy of Dynamite, but without the meanness; an ex-CFL linebacker named Flyin' Brian Pillman; and some great, but small, Japanese wrestlers, Hiroshi Hase and Fumihiro Niikura, who went as The Viet Cong Express. Owen had also become a star in Japan and won the IWGP Junior Heavyweight Championship, the top singles title of New Japan—no small feat.

My mom was constantly miserable because the so-called family fortune was still being blown on Stampede Wrestling and all their hangers-on. Whenever I showed up at the house with Julie, Jade and Dallas, she kind of clung to me like I was a level-headed bastion of sanity. She and my dad would pull up chairs in the kitchen, lower the volume on the TV and, as Stu put on the kettle for tea, they'd eagerly listen to my latest stories and news about the business.

I'll never forget Stu watching a video of the Slammys at Christmas, laughing so hard at Vince's singing that he had tears in his eyes. He asked me over and over with a huge smirk on his face, "So Vince is actually out of the closet, is he?" Vince wasn't gay, but in Stu's world, only a gay man would have camped it up like Vince did.

The schedule had become merciless, with double shots every weekend, a show in two different towns on Saturday and then again on Sunday. My life was a whirlwind of airports, second-rate hotels, gyms and dressing rooms. It was slightly more tolerable because Hulk was back from his vacation and the pay was better; between him and Macho, we now had two top babyfaces for the buildup to *WrestleMania IV*.

Every morning I'd feel all those head-snapping turnbuckles I'd now become famous for, and my knees were permanently stiff from jumping off the middle rope. Every day it took me fifteen minutes in a hot shower to be able to make myself stand upright. I was always in pain; one day a shoulder, the next a knee, an ankle, a split lip, a real cut, a shiner and always my aching back and what seemed to be a permanently hyper-extended left elbow from being whipped into the ropes by incredibly strong men. Tom and so many others tossed a couple of Percocets into their mouths before every match, and all too frequently I'd begun to do the same. I hurt.

After my matches the agents would happily give me a swat on the ass with a clipboard, saying, "Helluva match!" I'd return to the dressing room with the fans' spit all over me, to the point where Tom would get violently ill at the sight of the goobers and throw up in the sink. Still, I loved the energy, the feeling of being totally spent, undressing in a puddle of my own sweat.

The Bulldogs were suffering. Davey was the star now, and he was getting tired of doing everything Tom demanded of him in the ring and then babysitting Tom every night. It also got back to Davey that Tom openly complained that it was Davey's fault he'd injured his back in the first place.

Perhaps as a distraction from their mutual discontent, Tom and Davey hit the gyms as hard as ever, but with two new workout partners, The Warlord and The Ultimate Warrior (formerly The Dingo Warrior). Some of the WWF wrestlers now looked so freakish from steroids it appeared they might explode. The self-injected load of testosterone or God knows what in my butt cheeks made me think, long and hard, about why I stayed in the business. No one seems to know if Hunter S. Thompson actually wrote these lines often attributed to him: "The TV business is a cruel and shallow money trench. A long plastic hallway where thieves and pimps run free and good men die like dogs. There's also a negative side." But in my opinion, the world of TV wrestling was in a dark closet at the end of that hallway.

Survivor Series had been an overwhelming success, so Vince decided to go for a third pay-per-view a year, dreaming up the *Royal Rumble*, to take place every January. It would be like a battle royal except that it would start with two wrestlers in the ring, and then someone else would come out to join them every two minutes. The winner would be the last man standing. The first one was timed to air the Sunday before the Super Bowl, when the NFL was off. I was chosen to be the first guy into the ring, and I wrestled for thirty-six minutes in an all-out effort to get Vince's attention, with the hope of landing a decent spot for *WrestleMania IV*. It didn't work: All I was offered was a spot in the thirty-man battle royal.

Early one morning in February, I was awakened by a call from Vince. He was interested in Bad News and asked me whether I thought he could do any business with him. He also said he wanted to try Owen out again, with the mask gimmick I'd suggested.

As I cleared the sleep from my head, my immediate thought was to denounce Bad News, my old nemesis. But Ross had recently asked me whether there was any way that I could get News booked in the WWF because Owen was having the exact same problems with him that I used to have, being eaten alive and cut short on his comebacks. Also, News was overpriced, and they couldn't afford him anymore. So I praised him to Vince. As for Owen, Vince laid out some big plans, telling me he'd spare no expense: His art department would design Owen a costume with a cape, and he himself wanted to come up with some kind of high-flying name for Owen, featuring a bird or a rocket.

I called Stu and cleared the way for Owen to come to the WWF. Then I called Bad News. He was shocked that it was me, of all people, calling to tell him that they wanted him in the WWF.

Topeka TV on February 17 was Bad News's first day. They had big plans for him to be a top heel working against Hogan. I thought, Good for him, just as long as he doesn't work with me!

Coincidentally, that same day, the Cuban Assassin was finally set to have his long-awaited WWF try out. It would be the biggest break of his long career—God knows, he'd earned it. They wanted to pair him up with Nikolai Volkoff, billed from Moscow, because he was a legit Cuban and his hard work would carry the team.

When we passed Bad News out back by the ring trucks, Jim gleefully remarked to him, "It's great to have the old gang here! You, and now the Cuban!"

Bad News picked up a lead pipe and shouted, "If that mother fucker's here, I'll kill him!" It turned out that despite the fact that Cuban had been the best man at News's wedding, their wives had a falling out. Somehow News and Cuban, once the closest of friends, had now sworn to kill each other on sight. News took off and, seconds later, chased Cuban out of the building, swinging the lead pipe while Cuban slashed away at the air with his knife. Chief and a bunch of the agents broke it up, and then Vince summoned them both to his office: He fired Cuban before he'd even had a chance to step foot in the ring. He had bigger plans for News. So much for Cuban's break of a lifetime.

I went home to celebrate Julie's birthday in March. Afterwards I was planning to take three-year-old Dallas on his first big trip with dad to *WrestleMania IV.* As I stood in the kitchen, watching Julie pack Dallas's small suitcase, the phone rang.

"Hitman, it's Vince. I wanted you to hear it from me first," he said.

"Damned if I can figure it out, but we receive more mail here at the office for you than for any other wrestler in the company—I don't know if it's that greasy hair or what. So I'm turning you babyface."

I was totally caught off guard.

"You get even more mail than Hogan," Vince continued. "I'm going to split The Foundation up! I'm going to give you that big push that you've deserved for so long." At *WrestleMania IV*, he explained, Bad News and I would team up at the end of the battle royal to eliminate Junkyard Dog, but News would double-cross me and throw me out. When he was presented with a giant trophy, I'd attack him and smash the trophy to pieces.

I asked how this would affect Jim.

Vince chuckled and said, "One angle per person. Jim will have to wait."

He had said that I got more mail than Hogan. I just kept repeating that to myself in disbelief. I got garbage bags full of mail addressed to me at every TV taping, but I never imagined it was more than what Hulk got.

The next day I carried a mesmerized Dallas off the plane in Philadelphia, rented a car and strapped him into his child seat for the drive to Atlantic City. For the next two days, Dallas had the time of his life, playing with all his favourite wrestlers up close. All his action figures had come to life; he recognized everybody instantly. Hogan was especially nice to him, as was André, who called him over with his booming voice. Dallas was awestruck as he approached the giant, who hoisted him up onto his knee.

As the pay-per-view was about to start, I couldn't find Dallas anywhere: My heart jumped when I saw him, fifteen feet up, leaning over the edge of a scaffold! He had a big grin on his face as I took the steps two at a time, stretching to catch him by an ankle as he tried to scamper off on me! Thank God!

Macho and Liz were nice enough to babysit while I dressed and went over the battle royal with Pat and the newly renamed Bad News Brown, who was now acting like my best friend. The battle royal went as planned, and when I broke the sturdy trophy into pieces, I got a rousing cheer and, just like that, became a babyface.

In the main event, with a little help from Hogan, Macho Man won the world heavyweight title.

After the show I did my first solo interviews backstage, until nearly 3 a.m. I was getting better at talking, and for the first time I made reference to having survived Stu's dungeon. Eventually I carried a conked-out Dallas in my arms, through the fans in the lobby and up to my room.

On the way home my bag was bulging with *Ghostbuster* toys. On the stopover in Denver, I put Dallas on the phone with his mom, and he happily told her all about his big trip. After a few minutes he handed me back the phone. I didn't want to alarm Julie, so I never mentioned how he'd locked himself in the bathroom, let alone how he'd climbed the scaffold. When I hung up and turned around, Dallas was gone! I frantically searched everywhere for him. What if he'd gone into the ladies room? Or got on a plane? I soon had gate agents searching too. Finally, way down in the distance on the moving walkway, I spotted him gliding toward me with a mischievous grin on his face, holding the hand of a smiling security guard. I was so relieved to see him I just smiled back. I don't know what wore me out more, Dallas or *WrestleMania IV*!

As a babyface I found myself doing jobs for Bad News at the house shows almost every night. They were building him for Hogan. I wasn't happy being a babyface, especially a losing one. Some push!

Bad News still had no psychology or charisma. One night after a long, boring brawl at Madison Square Garden, Vince remarked to me, "Bret, you could have a great match with a broomstick!" I replied, "It's hard when the broomstick is mopping the floor with you." He laughed, but I didn't.

I just happened to be home on May 17, when Julie delivered a beautiful, seven-pound, fifteen-ounce baby girl. We named her Alexandra Sabina. With my heart full and empty at the same time, I boarded a plane the next morning. Back to work.

On June 22 at the TV tapings in Binghamton, New York, my solo career was suddenly over. Vince decided to reform The Hart Foundation as babyfaces, he said, because we were too good to keep apart. Yet we immediately started doing jobs for The Rougeaus, who'd just turned heel. They even had Jimmy Hart as their manager now. All in all, I was just glad to be back with Jim.

Noticeably missing after *WrestleMania IV* was Harley Race, who'd ended up in emergency surgery having a foot and a half of his intestine removed. And then he got served with divorce papers. Honky made a big mistake when he joked in the dressing room that Harley didn't have any guts any more. Honky was one of those wrestlers who never had an ounce of real hardness in him. When one of the least tough disrespected a legendary tough guy like Harley, several of us took exception, and Dynamite got up and backhanded Honky right off his chair. Honky wept like a baby after that, pleading for forgiveness.

With Harley gone, Tom needed a new drinking partner. He latched onto Joe LeDuc, the French-Canadian lumberjack whom Vince renamed

The Maniac. The moniker suited Joe perfectly. Every night for over a week, Tom and Joe drank and took dangerous amounts of pills. Joe was no stranger to pills, but Tom was also spiking his drinks. Still, it was Joe who carried Tom back to his room every night. When it came to taking pills, Joe wasn't human.

Then Tom vowed that this would be the night that Joe went down. I sat and watched them drink. At one point Joe was slumped in his chair, halfway to la-la land, when Tom flattened his lit cigarette with his fingers and carefully set it atop Joe's big, bald head. When it started to burn, Joe sat up, and the cigarette fell down the back of his shirt. Without saying a word, Joe flexed his back and squeezed the cigarette out on his chair, then staggered off to his room. This was all amusing to Tom, but the next day Joe was fired. The pills didn't bring him down. Tom did, in less than a week!

On my thirty-first birthday, my mom and Georgia threw a surprise party for me up at Hart house. I looked around at the herd of grandkids. Tom, sporting a nice dress shirt, jokingly rolled his eyes at me as he joined in singing "Happy Birthday." Numerous young wrestlers who worked for Stu were there, including Brian Pillman. He sang with a smirk, and a rasp in his voice, a reminder of the esophageal cancer he'd overcome as a child. Dallas and Jade's eyes were big and bright, lit by the flickering candles on my cake. My mom was the only one who noticed that my eyes were wet when Dallas helped me blow out the candles.

There was clapping and the tune of forks clinking on glasses. All eyes were on me. I think it was that night when I realized that some members of my family were waiting for me to trip and fall. I also had to face the fact that chances were that I would: the world was littered with wrestling tragedies.

Bruce was despondent because Stu had finally sacked him as booker; Stu could no longer afford to tolerate Bruce's way of running the show. He replaced him with Keith, which meant Leslie was in charge too.

I glanced over at Jim, who was his own worst enemy and a bad gambler in life. Money burned a hole in his pocket; the more money, the bigger the hole. He lived as if tomorrow was never going to come, spending lavishly on himself, buying custom-made jewellery, jet skis, fishing boats and motorcycles. Ellie rarely saw a penny of it because, for reasons known only to him, he kept her and their kids on a strict allowance.

Of all of us, when it came to finances, it was Tom who seemed to be in the best shape. He was the only one who'd paid off his house. Both he and Davey were beyond cheap on the road, but at home they lavished their wives with cars, fur coats, jewellery and cash. It seemed like nobody worried about tomorrow except for me.

The person I wanted to talk to at my party was Owen, because he'd be starting with the WWF in a few days, but Martha dragged him out of there early. Owen was about to join the rest of us young stallions, ever racing. The adventure was in not knowing where we were going. The danger was in not seeing that our destinies were not ours to control, no matter how hard and strong we ran.

More deaths added to my sense of foreboding. On July 4, while driving to a match in Gander, Newfoundland, Mike Kelly swerved to miss a moose and lost control of the van. It rolled, killing his brother Pat Kelly, Dave McKigney—and Adrian Adonis. Pat's brother Mike survived, though the crash badly injured his leg. I flew down to Bakersfield, California, for Adrian's funeral. His wife said to me, "He was so big, nothing could ever hurt him. Now he's dead."

Then Bruiser Brody was stabbed to death. I had always been grateful to Brody for bucking me up with some kind words during my first months on the road with the WWF, when Chief was riding me. The last time I'd seen him was during a chance meeting at the airport in Detroit. André rode on those airport trolley carts that zip around inside the terminals, so Jim and I hopped on. Coming around a corner, we ran into Brody, who laughed at the sight of us. My last memory of him was his wave and his smile. On July 17, Brody had been called into a dressing room in Puerto Rico by the booker, Jose Gonzales, who also wrestled under a mask as The Invader. Gonzales, whom I remembered from my time in Puerto Rico as an easy-going guy, stabbed Brody with a butcher knife and left him to die on the dirty bathroom floor. Supposedly, Brody had been a bully to Gonzales in the ring one time too many, and Gonzales snapped. All the wrestlers were too scared to help Brody, so they sat there for over an hour while he died. No wrestlers would testify against Gonzales because they were afraid that if they did they wouldn't live long enough to get off the island! Gonzales used self-defence as an argument and was acquitted. This was one of the most horrible things that ever happened in the wrestling business.

It's strange, but wrestlers often die in threes. On July 24, I heard that J.R. Foley passed away. Lung cancer came and took him quickly, too quickly for me to even visit him one last time. "Swing low, sweet chariot, coming for to carry me home." J.R. was an indelible character who, despite his shortcomings, made the world a better place. At his funeral in Calgary, they played all his favourite songs from the van. I know he'd have been proud of the nice turnout at his service.

22

EVERY DOG HAS HIS DAY

VINCE ADDED A FOURTH PAY-PER-VIEW to the annual rotation, *SummerSlam*, the first one scheduled for August 29, 1988, at Madison Square Garden. Despite losing every single night in singles and tags for the past ten months, oddly enough The Hart Foundation landed a title shot against Demolition. Bill Eadie was now known as Axe, Barry Darsow was Smash, and together as Demolition, they'd trounced every team in the WWF. Clearly The Foundation wouldn't be going over at *SummerSlam*, but once more I saw a golden opportunity to have a great match and maybe even steal the show.

After I'd been brutalized by Demolition, both of them big, strong, realistic workers, I tagged Jim, who cleaned house, smashing into them with flying football tackles and high drop kicks. Suddenly we had the whole building standing. There was a deafening roar as I pulled back on the top rope as if it was a giant bow and launched the 280-pound Anvil right on top of Axe and Smash, who were standing out on the floor. For the finish, Axe whacked me across the back of the head with Jimmy Hart's megaphone. We lost the match but stole the show.

Later that day, Ultimate Warrior dethroned Honky Tonk Man for the Intercontinental belt in fifteen seconds. Hogan shared some of his glow with Macho Man when they teamed up against The Million Dollar Man and André. For a cartoonlike finish, Miss Elizabeth stripped down to her bathing suit as a distraction so that Randy and Hulk could regroup and win the day. There was nothing sleazy about Miss Elizabeth's move — it was tasteful and funny. At that time, the WWF was all about family entertainment and marketing to kids.

After the show, Owen, Jim and I chowed down on corned beef and cabbage at a Manhattan pub called The Blarney Stone. The place was filled with cats, which reminded us of Stu's kitchen. Owen, who really hated that there were so many cats at Stu's house, winced in disgust.

"C'mon, Owen," I said. "This many cats means there aren't gonna be any rats, are there?"

Since starting in July, Owen had gone by different names: The Blue Angel, The Blue Demon and The Blue Laser. Vince hadn't delivered on the costume or the name he promised, and Owen wore gear cheaply made by a friend of Martha's. I urged him to spend a few bucks on a better outfit, but he confided that if he did it would hurt Martha's feelings. The topic of conversation moved to The Bulldogs, who'd stunned us all by giving their notice. They were going to quit the WWF as of the *Survivor Series* in November. Tom had decided that they'd go back to Japan and Calgary, even though Stu's territory was on its last legs. I wondered what the two of them would think, being back in the van in forty below zero weather, driving past that giant green statue of Stu on their way to Saskatoon. I did envy the fact that they'd finally be home.

Jimmy Hart had worked on some entrance music for The Hart Foundation, a repetitive guitar riff that sounded like a powerful locomotive going down the track. And a marketing suit had handed me a pair of silver Mylar wraparound shades that I would wear every night and that they would sell in the arenas. I was asked to give a pair to one lucky kid at the start of each match. At first the kids would back away: They still remembered me as a heel. After a couple of months of TV, though, it was like feeding squirrels in a park: There were more than enough kids hoping they'd be the lucky one. This little ritual would become a big factor in my identity as a babyface.

Despite these signs of life, business wasn't what it used to be, and payoffs were down unless you were on Macho's cards. Vince decided that he could no longer afford to pay the wrestlers' air fares home; he'd only pay for a one-way ticket, and then we'd have to pay our own way back. The majority of the wrestlers lived in Florida, a cheaper flight than heading back to Calgary. As a result, on my three days off between tours, I often couldn't afford to go home. Instead, I stayed in a hotel and saved up my flights for the next break. There I was caught between a financial rock and an emotional hard place: Julie knew in her head why I wasn't coming home as much, but neither she nor the kids liked it. Then again, neither did I.

Curt Hennig, whose moniker was Mr. Perfect, was a second-generation wrestler with curly blond hair who was new to the WWF. Inadvertently, he set off the chain of events that turned out to be Tom's undoing. Hennig, a great worker, was an equally great ribber. He put several heavy steel locks on the handle of Jacques Rougeau's suitcase to make it heavier than it already was. Jacques wrongly assumed The Bulldogs had done it, and told Hennig that if they did it one more time he would take it up with Vince. Curt, still ribbing, went directly to Tom and told him what Jacques had said. Tom was furious that Jacques was going to rat him out for something he didn't even do, and barged into a dressing room where Jacques was playing cards and slapped Jacques across the head from behind, knocking him off his bench.

Jacques never pretended to be a tough guy, but he had enough balls to stand up for himself. He lunged at Tom, who snatched him in a front face lock, choking him down to the carpet. He let him up, only to have Jacques charge him again. Tom cracked him in the mouth before taking him to the floor again; this time Tom cinched up on him until Jacques tapped his hand on the floor in surrender. Brother Ray arrived on the scene just then and politely asked Tom to let Jacques up. Tom did, and told Jacques not to be stooging to the office and blaming him for stuff he didn't do.

Ray Rougeau was a former Golden Gloves boxing champ and despite his less-than-threatening appearance he was respected for being legitimately tough. He'd injured his knee a week earlier working against me and Jim, and he'd been icing and wrapping it every night. Tom, forever the bully, had an audience of wrestlers around and couldn't resist taunting Ray.

Ray meekly offered, "I've hurt my knee." Tom replied, "Yeah right, Ray. You come and see me when yer knee's better. I'll be waitin' for ya."

Since The Foundation was working nightly with The Rougeaus, it was hard not to notice that they were simmering over these insults. And every night Tom made a point of asking Ray how his knee was. I warned Tom to ease up. Then at the TV tapings in Toledo, Tom was wrapping up a conversation with Pat Patterson. They were the last two in the lunchroom. As they got up and walked out the door, Jacques sucker-punched Tom, knocking all his front teeth out. As Tom was bent over, dazed and stunned, with blood pouring out of his mouth, Jacques drilled him until Bad News intervened to save him. Meanwhile, Pat jumped around like a hysterical woman. The Rougeaus had their bags waiting by the back door and bolted before Tom even realized what was going on.

At first I was upset, and contemplated getting involved. But the more I thought about it the more I realized that Tom had been asking for this for years and that everyone who'd been bullied by him would rejoice at the news. I decided this wasn't my fight.

The Bulldogs had to leave the next day for a WWF tour of France. Vince called Tom in France and offered to pay for his dental work, but he insisted that when they came home he wanted both Tom and Davey to meet him in his hotel room at the San Francisco TV tapings. He'd have The Rougeaus there along with Pat and he wanted them all to make peace. He told Tom that if he and The Rougeaus carried on feuding, he'd hold back his royalty cheques, his pay-per-view cheques and his pay for the French tour. Tom grudgingly accepted Vince's orders. It was a sad surprise to most of the wrestlers when Tom, our legendary pit bull, basically had his balls cut. Those of us who really knew him realized that getting his teeth punched out was the beginning of the end for him.

Dynamite was good for his word when he shook hands with The Rougeaus in front of Vince. On November 24, he even sold for both of them at The Bulldogs' last WWF match at *Survivor Series* and worked a couple of high spots with Jacques. He simply couldn't afford not to. But he brooded terribly.

I played no serious role at *Survivor Series*. Vince had his cast of superstars, and I wasn't one of them. In fact I was lucky to still be in the WWF, considering the way they were lopping heads off: They'd just fired Muraco; J.Y.D.; the released jailbird, Ken Patera; and The Killer Bees. I don't know about the others, but I suspect The Bees were let go because they'd been talking union with Jesse Ventura.

During the show, Owen mistimed a leapfrog on Greg The Hammer Valentine, who drove his head straight into Owen's groin as he tried to run underneath him. Owen somehow managed to not only finish the match, but even dove off the top rope onto Valentine for the finish, only to have him move. I didn't find out until the next day that one of Owen's testicles had swollen to the size of a softball and he'd gone home in horrific agony fearing they might have to remove it!

On December 6, I had a TV match with that old warhorse Valentine, and we worked an angle where Honky came out and interfered by smashing me over the head with his gimmicked guitar. Jim got a big pop coming out to save me. Despite all the praise, all I had to look forward to every night was doing the honours for Honky. And little did Honky realize that by being matched with me, he'd been demoted to the undercard. With his skinny arms and bandy legs, Honky's punches and kicks looked like they couldn't break an egg: he was just so damn phony. The old-school boys, who prided themselves on realistic matches, had all but been eradicated. I was beginning to feel like one of Stalin's generals waiting for my turn to be executed as the ranks swelled with even more ripped and muscled freaks, most of whom had no real talent to work. The Ultimate Warrior was going to be Vince's new superstar. Characters such as Ravishing Rick Rude, Big Boss Man and Hacksaw Jim Duggan (back from being fired) had replaced the Steamboats, Muracos and Pipers.

Back in Calgary, Owen was recovering from his injury, which luckily did not need surgery. Not surprisingly, The Bulldogs, now back in the Stampede Wrestling fold, sold out the Pavilion. But then Stu and Keith gave the book to Tom because he'd always been good at coming up with finishes. Unfortunately, he was incapable of writing a legible format every week and couldn't handle the task of booking. Pain and painkillers and vodka had already played havoc with him, and the Rougeau situation sent him further down the path of the bitter, abusive drunk. He blamed Davey for whatever displeased him rather than acknowledging to himself the now unavoidable failings of his worn-out body.

Davey lamented to me that it was a big mistake to have left the WWF and that he was sorry that he had. Meanwhile, Tom, all 'roided-up and on painkillers, hot-shotted the territory with gimmick matches filled with blood. It worked initially, but after a few weeks it completely killed Stu's business.

I called home a lot, longing for love and support, confiding my fears and doubts to Julie. But she was again talking about leaving me. I knew it was hard for her, but I also knew I was working hard to do the best that I could for her and the babies. Alexandra Sabina, whom we all called Beans, was already walking and had four teeth.

It was time to build for *WrestleMania V*. Hogan and Macho had paired up as The Megapowers, but they were now split up so they could build to compete against each other for the world heavyweight title. I was anything but optimistic about being given any kind of spot, and my doubts were confirmed when they put The Foundation with Honky and Valentine, now known as Rhythm and Blues, at the house shows leading up to *WrestleMania*. The four of us tried to pretend that it might mean something on the big show, but we all knew that it didn't.

We all got a good laugh out of the March 1989 issue of *Mad Magazine*, which inserted WWF superstars into the lead roles of current big movies. Jim and I found ourselves starring in the *Mad* version of *The Untouchables*, in which Honky Tonk did me in with a guitar. Funnier than the cartoon was how mad Jim got because the artists had drawn him with a meek face and small shoulders. It really bugged him a lot.

I brought Jade and Stu to Atlantic City for *WrestleMania V*, since both Owen and I were on the card. Stu roomed with me and Jade and told me with perfect recall of the times he'd been to Atlantic City in the 1940s, when it was a swinging seaside resort town.

On the morning of *WrestleMania V*, a call came for Stu, who stood in his long, striped nightshirt talking with a big smile on his face.

"Yeah, Reg . . . how the hell are you?"

Reg Park had been a respected bodybuilder once upon a time. He was an easygoing guy and the conversation started out friendly, but Stu couldn't believe his ears when Reg suddenly said, "Stu, you were always afraid of me. You never had the balls to try me, or I would have shoved your head up your ass!"

Stu was pacing the room with the receiver pressed hard against his cauliflower ear, his jaw set like granite. "Reg, if you wanted to try me, why didn't you try me?" Even the veins in his sturdy white legs seemed to swell with rage—I was sure Stu was about to head downstairs and face off with Reg right there in the lobby! Jade was wide-eyed, wondering why Grampy was getting so upset.

Then Stu abruptly sat on the bed and slammed the phone down. A shy, almost embarrassed smile broke over my dad's face. One I'll never forget.

"That was Owen. The little bastard got me!"

Owen, now under a mask and cape as The Blue Blazer, worked with Curt Hennig, who was fast becoming the best wrestler in the company. Owen had recovered from his injury; he anticipated an action-packed match with Curt, but they were only allotted eight minutes. Curt was good enough to give Owen more than his fair share; he respected both me and Owen for our workmanship.

I managed to get Randy and Liz to watch Jade, who totally idolized Liz. A couple of female fans I knew from the area had taken Jade to a beauty salon and had her hair all done up and got her a fancy dress so that she looked just like her idol. My match went fine. Afterwards I stood with Jade in the back watching Hogan win the World Heavyweight belt back from Randy. When it was over I knocked on Randy's door and told him and Liz that I thought he'd been a great champion. He and Liz had worked hard for all of us.

I had so much more respect for Randy than for The Ultimate Warrior, who was getting over more every day just because of his look. His matches, however, consisted of him quivering and shaking as he gripped the ropes with his twenty-inch, tasselled arms. He never really sold anything for anybody as he tripped around waiting for the gods to energize him. Eventually he'd explode into running clotheslines and, as a finisher, pick his opponent up over his head, drop him hard to the mat and then race across the ring three or four times as if it somehow added to his momentum before he dove on top of the downed wrestler for the one . . . two . . . three.

What Warrior never appreciated was that it took a dressing room full of people to make up for his shallow performances night after night; workers such as me, DiBiase, Hennig and Rude, who made bums like Warrior look like gold. Vince had to be pushing Warrior because he was thinking that Hogan was losing some of his shine.

I arrived in Milan on my first WWF tour to Italy on April 8, 1989. I was exhausted from the long flight when I walked into the dressing room and ran my finger down the lineup posted on the wall. I was startled to see that

I'd be wrestling André! Being a technical wrestler, I didn't have a clue how to wrestle a giant. I think André must have smelled my fear. He laughed and said, "Don't worry, boss, I'll call it out there."

I walked out to a nice round of applause and tore right into André. I was as surprised as the crowd was when he fell back and tied himself up in the ropes. I hit him with punches until he told me to take off into the ropes, where I promptly ran into his huge foot. I was thrilled to hear the crowd behind me. At one point as I lay under the bottom rope, André put one foot on my chest and then the other on my stomach. I took a deep breath thinking I could support him, but all the air left my body. It felt like I'd been jacking up a truck and the jack fell. This was André's way of reminding his opponents that if he wanted to, he could kill you as easily as fall on top of you. A wrestler found out fast if André didn't like him. He stepped off, and I could breathe again, but it wasn't long before I saw him lean like a house, then collapse on top of me with an elbow drop. If he'd been off by an inch or two . . .

My feet stuck out from underneath him, kicking like when the house fell on the witch in the *Wizard of Oz*. In truth, André was a great worker—I never felt a thing.

After the match he told me that he'd specifically requested to work with me at least one time because he considered me to be a great wrestler. It meant more to me than he would ever know.

When I boarded the tour bus at the backstage door, I saw two young girls crying uncontrollably as they held a sign that said "We love you Hitman." Jimmy Hart couldn't get over it. "That's something really special, someone ought to film that. That's not something you see anywhere else for anybody else in this business."

I went out drinking with Italian girls and talked about American politics and music. Owen stayed mostly in his room; after a few days he seemed on the verge of cracking, as did many of the wrestlers. Warlord and Warrior said they thought they were shrinking because there were no gyms and the food was too un-American. By the time we arrived in Cagliari, on Sardinia, the wrestlers were almost ready for an uprising.

I spent my last days in Italy at a strange hotel in Sassari that had some sort of a cruel zoo out back. Locked in cages and looking to be barely alive were exotic birds, a bunch of mangy baboons and a miserable wart-hog. I felt a kinship with these poor creatures and fed them apples that I mooched from the hotel. On the final night of the tour Warlord slept on a couch in the lobby because he was terrified that he would miss his wake-up call for the flight back to America.

When I got back I had a disappointing match at the Spectrum Arena in Philadelphia, a twenty-minute draw with Curt Hennig. We'd worked out what we thought was a great match before we got into the ring, and it wasn't as though we didn't try hard, in fact we tried too hard. But it turned into a sloppy struggle that left both of us wondering whose fault it was. The following night, in Toronto, we had the exact same match except this time everything clicked and we had the entire building on its feet.

With Curt, I was able to do moves that I could never dream of doing with Bad News or Honky. We adjusted to each other's timing in an epic back and forth battle where we constantly gave back to each other. I had Curt beat after I came off the second rope, spiking his chest with the point of my elbow, hooking his leg for a one . . . two . . . when the bell clanged. Curt made his escape while I grabbed the house mic and pleaded for five more minutes. Curt turned to leave, signalling me to turn my back on him. In a flash he was back in the ring, viciously beating me down to the mat. Curt climbed to the top turnbuckle, but I popped up to my feet and greeted him with a fist to the gut, causing him to lose his balance and crotch himself on the corner strut. The crowd was going crazy as I dragged him off by the hair and clobbered him from one corner to the next until he bounced out of the ring and slithered away in full retreat. The fans thundered their approval. It was one of the best matches I'd had in years, and I owed it to Curt, a great worker.

The WWF was finally doing some Hitman merchandising, and a tank top and my trademark shades were on sale and doing well. The WWF devoted a special issue of their *Spotlight* magazine to me that spring, with a seductive head shot on the cover. I'll never forget Greg Valentine joking that just looking at it made him want to fuck me. It was the biggest selling wrestling magazine to that date. In a Japanese wrestling magazine being passed around in the dressing room about the same time, there was a gruesome, full-length picture of Dynamite with his head shaved and scarred and all his teeth knocked out. He looked awful, and I was embarrassed for him. The Rougeau incident haunted him, and he seemed to be self-destructing. Michelle and her kids had temporarily moved into my house because Tom had thrown them out in a fit of rage.

My shirts sold out, but that didn't seem to mean anything to Vince. Despite the push he'd promised me, he had me putting Perfect over to get him ready for Warrior and Hogan. The chemistry between us only got better, and we easily had the best match on the card. Despite the fact that I felt betrayed yet again by Vince, it didn't show in my matches. I was the guy he counted on to get guys over so that they could make the big money.

23

WAGES OF SIN

I SPENT HOURS AND HOURS OF 1989 rolling across America with Owen. We'd always been close, but it was on those long, lonely trips that we really bonded. I loved his mischievous sense of humour, his directness, his good nature and his integrity. He had a deep respect for both our parents, and he was aware of the sad truth that so many of our siblings seemed more and more helpless and hopeless, always relying on Stu to bail them out. Like me, he never wanted to become one of them. It meant a lot to me when Owen told me that he had faith in me, and that I was well regarded by the other wrestlers for being truthful and dedicated.

His hopes and dreams, doubts and fears, were much the same as mine. He was going to marry Martha on July 1; he knew that few in the family really appreciated her, and he couldn't have cared less. I told him how I'd gone through similar experiences with Julie not being accepted and that he should just follow his heart. Owen liked that Martha was smart and controlling: He had no doubt that she'd keep him on the straight and narrow. He also liked how he was treated by her family.

Owen hated being a jobber and asked me what I thought he should do about his situation. It was obvious that Vince had no plans for him, no matter what he'd said, so I suggested that it might be time to leave the WWF and try Japan—if he stayed much longer, a jobber was all he'd ever be. Then he could come back when the WWF was hungry for fresh talent again. I passed on to him what Pedro Morales had told me: "You can't stop talent." He confessed that he planned to give his notice at the next TV tapings. Quitting the WWF was a bold decision, but he was young and talented in a business where so few were. He'd be back someday.

Just before he quit, I remember Owen and me driving through Eugene, Oregon. I couldn't help but read the glaring words radiating from a huge billboard: "The wages of sin are death!" I thought about Julie back home. Lately she'd become paranoid about being "alone" in the house, even though the place was full of people, including a live-in nanny and handyman. Julie's moods were up and down, and she had recently checked herself into a hospital with severe chest pains. The doctors told her it was all in her head and released her. I was worried about her, but I had my own chest pains—of a different sort: that petite, redheaded hairdresser from Boston; that melt-in-your-mouth blonde corporal from the Wisconsin National Guard; the knockout Budweiser girl from Baltimore. I was such a bad dog that I wondered whether I'd end up in heaven or in hell. I smiled at the vision of a place where a guy like Owen would be dressed in white, playing checkers, while another guy gently plucked a harp. This was a sharp contrast to another vision, where a devil with a face oddly similar to Jim's, wearing red tights, sets aside a pitch fork, pulls on his beard, and pounds nails into my head like in that *Hellraiser* movie.

Owen's wedding was another overcrowded and plastic affair at Stu's house. Surprisingly, the Hart clan showed considerably more class than some of the Patterson clan, one of whom put his cigarette out on one of Stu's oriental rugs, leaving a deep, black hole. Tensions were such that he was lucky he didn't get beat up. Bruce was Owen's best man. Just days before the wedding, Tom had broken Bruce's jaw in an overreaction to some petty slight, so it was more than awkward to have them both there.

Stu sat passively in the kitchen, stoic and tight-lipped. Stone cold sober and unable to relax, he was on display like a regal silverback gorilla at a zoo. Looking at my father, I thought about how the toughness in truly tough men never really dies out. The night before, Dynamite and Davey had turned on each other in the biggest angle that Stampede Wrestling had seen since Stu started up again. But my father saw it for what it was: The last gasp of his dying business.

Two days after the wedding, things got bleaker. Wayne had quit in disgust over the disorganization, and Ross had stepped in to drive the van on a long, rainy, miserable trip through northern Alberta. The crew was late as usual, and Ross put the pedal to the metal despite desperate pleas from the boys to slow down. The van hydroplaned; he lost control and veered head on into an oncoming car, sending Davey crashing through the windshield. Davey needed eighty stitches in his head. I think the only reason he didn't die was because of his thick, powerful neck. He was left with permanent vision problems and neck pain. Karl Moffat injured his knee, which ultimately cut short his budding career. I really think if Moffat hadn't got hurt, he would have gone a long way in the business. Also injured was Chris Benoit, but he managed to recover fully. Ross was devastated.

Since Owen had by now quit the WWF, he was called back into action after a brief honeymoon to fill in for Davey. Owen and Dynamite ended up selling out the Pavilion for the next three weeks in what would ultimately be the last great matches for both Dynamite and Stampede Wrestling.

For me the highlight of the summer of 1989 came when Curt and I wrestled in Anchorage, tearing the house down. In my opinion it was one of the top five matches of my entire career, and it wasn't even caught on film. People who were there have never forgotten it, and they still bring it up to me to this day.

At one point I climbed up from outside the ring and Curt rushed the ropes, sending me flying off the apron, sailing fifteen feet in the air. I cleared the timekeeper's head by a hair and crashed chest-first into the steel barricade behind him. I wasn't hurt, but nobody knew it, not even Curt. As I lay on the floor writhing in agony, I smiled to myself, content that I was dancing with a real artist. I eventually climbed back in, turned the tide and we proceeded to give the Alaskan fans a whale of a match. I absolutely loved working with Curt!

A disgruntled André wasn't happy about being left off the *SummerSlam* card in favour of a black bodybuilder and actor called Tiny Lister, who had played Hogan's nemesis in a B movie Vince had co-produced, called *No Holds Barred*. For most of the summer André had been main-eventing the house shows with Warrior, and he was disgusted at having to lose every night to an arrogant and unskilled nobody who hadn't paid his dues; André insisted on jobbing out in less than fifteen seconds, taking a series of, you guessed it, clotheslines. Grim-faced, André would roll out of the ring and lumber back to the dressing room as sell out crowds chanted, "Bullshit," with some fans even demanding refunds.

But Warrior was Vince's new superstar. Knowing Vince, he probably found it onerous to keep paying André his contracted percentage of every card he appeared on, plus picking up the costs of a valet and the two first-class seats the giant needed every time he flew. André's deal was a promise written in stone by Vince's dad, and André was just starting to realize that Junior might not feel compelled to honour it in perpetuity. In Anchorage, André told me with a sour look on his face, "Vince is nothing like his father. When his father gave me his word that was all I needed." André was like an old circus elephant, and I sensed that if Vince had his way, this circus was moving on without him.

The Hart Foundation had been re-formed again, and we were more than deserving of a break. But just hours before our match at *SummerSlam* on August 28, Vince told us that we'd be losing, in an ill-conceived non-title match, to his newly crowned tag champs, The Brain Busters, Arn Anderson and Tully Blanchard.

There was history here. At the height of our tag title reign for the WWF, Tully and Arn had been the hottest team in the rival NWA. The NWA had been recently bought by Ted Turner, who had renamed it World Championship Wrestling (WCW). Turner, the broadcasting mogul behind CNN, was now coming after Vince. With the intense rivalry between the two companies, diehard fans had long awaited this match up. But now Vince had poached these two from the opposition — and wanted us to lose to them: it was an immense blow to our pride. If we couldn't beat them in a non-title match, then when could we beat them? We stood our ground in a long, tense discussion with Vince, but then we grudgingly complied, knowing we held no cards. I was worried we'd crossed the line with Vince.

We left before the show was over, zipping up the New Jersey turnpike disappointed and pissed off. I looked forward to drowning my misery with our new favourite friend, Jack Daniels. When we got to the hotel bar, SummerSlam was still on the big screen, and I tossed down a few shots. I was sitting there lamenting that I didn't see how things were going to get better when some guy at the end of the bar got physically pushy with a pretty strawberry blonde. Before I knew it I had intervened, telling him to scram. She stayed. She was perfect.

I awoke early the next morning with a slight hangover and leaned across my bed to find a note: "Thanks for saving me. Love Connie." I rolled back over thinking that it was she who had saved me.

Like Julie, in my own feeble way, I was afraid to be alone.

Vince had promised The Brain Busters that they'd make more money in the WWF than they ever had before, but it didn't happen, so they gave their notice in favour of going back to work for Ted Turner. So our sacrifice to put The Brain Busters over at SummerSlam ended up serving no purpose whatsoever.

The Rockers had resurfaced in the WWF when the AWA finally went under. The day after SummerSlam '89, Vince put us together in a taped-for-home-video babyface match at TVs in Springfield, Massachusetts. Like I'd predicted, the four of us tore the house down with a twenty-minute broadway. Shawn and Marty were both energetic, and Shawn in particular displayed an agility and coordination I'd never seen before in pro wrestling. Unfortunately for them, at that time the fans would never buy guys their size beating the huge 'roided-up monsters that roamed the WWF tag team division.

When The Hart Foundation and The Rockers came back to the dressing room, everyone congratulated us, even Vince, who smiled like a lizard and called it " . . . a terrific, one-of-a-kind match!" As I headed off to the showers, I thought to myself, He still needs us. We're safe.

Three weeks later I went to talk to Vince at the Cincinnati TVs. The lineups at his door had been getting longer at every taping. When my turn came I began to address my financial problems, explaining to him that I wasn't making enough money to cover my expenses and pay my own way home. Vince bluntly said that if I wasn't happy I should go somewhere else.

"As hard as I've worked for you, all you can tell me is that if I don't like it, I should go somewhere else?"

His expression was cold, and all he said was, "Yes."

By coincidence, that night Flyin' Brian Pillman was in Cincinnati for a visit home. Dynamite had taken a huge dislike to him, and with Stampede Wrestling floundering, Pillman had decided that the time was right to look for another spot. He'd just been hired by WCW. He came to the WWF show with me that night, and when he heard what was going on, he gave me Ric Flair's number and urged me to call.

Ric Flair was NWA world champion and was their booker too. I knew Flair liked me, because Bobby Heenan had brought him into the WWF dressing room earlier in the year just to meet me, which was more than unusual because the competition was just not allowed backstage. Flair was immaculately groomed in a flashy designer suit and had long, platinum-blond hair. He strolled right up to me with a piercing smile.

"Sir," he said as he shook my hand. "What a pleasure it is to finally meet you. I've waited a really long time to tell you that you're one of my heroes and a great worker. It's truly an honour, and I've waited a long time to say it to you!"

The *Observer* often raved about Flair being the best in the business. I'd never seen him work because it was impossible to follow the rival TV show on my schedule. Steamboat, Piper and Harley, among others, all had great regard for Flair as a worker. We chatted for a time, and he left me saying that if I ever needed a place to go, to call him. Now seemed like the right time.

The very next morning I put in a call to WCW. I spoke with a wrestler named Kevin Sullivan, who was their assistant booker, and at first he didn't believe it was really me. He told me to call back in an hour, and when I did, he told me that Ric Flair fell off his chair when he heard that I'd called. Sullivan declared, "He's a real mark for you!" Then he put me through to

Flair, who immediately offered me a contract for $200,000 a year, all expenses paid, and with plenty of time off.

WCW's offer was appealing, especially considering that with Vince we were supposed to get an unspecified percentage of the house, and Vince paid whatever he felt like. That was his game. That's how he kept all the heat in the dressing room: expertly feeding that competitive fire called jealousy. I told Flair that I'd think about it. At that moment the Carolina coast was being pounded by Hurricane Hugo, so Flair and I agreed to talk again in few days, literally after the storm passed, to see if we could make the deal.

Four days later in Spokane, rumour of my possible departure, which could only have been leaked by the WCW office, had spread throughout the wrestling media and the dressing room. I didn't confirm or deny, I didn't talk about it at all, but still Jimmy Hart shook my hand with tears in his eyes. "I can't believe they're gonna lose a talent like you. You're the greatest, and I'm not just saying that. I don't understand why they treat you the way they do. God bless you!"

Hugo had ripped up the Carolinas, leaving ten people dead and doing millions of dollars in damage. When I was finally able to get through to WCW to accept their offer, a somewhat embarrassed Ric Flair dutifully explained that he wasn't authorized to make any money offers and that I'd have to discuss terms with the boss, Jim Herd. I was put through to Herd, who gruffly gave me a story about meeting his budget, then passed me off to Jim Barnett, who used to work for Vince. Barnett offered me a contract for $156,000, which was barely more than I was already making. The impression I got was that Barnett viewed this as a chance for him to show his worth and save the fifty grand. I felt they were reneging and turned them down flat. It was like I'd just done an eight-day broadway in which I didn't win and I didn't lose. But deep down I was relieved. The WCW had not yet had a chance to prove that they would be serious competition to the WWF, and they were still widely regarded as second-rate. I never said one word about my discussions to any of the boys. Eventually it was dismissed as just a rumour and forgotten.

When I arrived home on October 4, Julie seemed nearly as pensive as I was. She suggested we walk over the hill to meet the kids when school let out; Jade was now in Grade 1 and Dallas in kindergarten. We left the nanny to watch baby Beans, and as we walked Julie told me that she was pregnant again, due in June. When we first got together, we had always dreamed of a family of four children, so I was overjoyed. I wrapped my arms around her and told her how happy I was. Julie was reluctant to have another baby, but I deeply wanted our fourth child, hoping maybe that this one would be the glue that kept us stuck together. As we walked home, Julie had her arms crossed in front of her chest and a scared look on her face. I held Jade and Dallas's tiny hands, and it was tough to say which of the three of us was the happiest about the news of another baby coming.

In the five years since I'd started with the WWF I'd become accustomed to flying more miles each year than most pilots. I'd acquired a knowledge of which airlines and airports were good and bad and compiled maps in my head of almost every town, big and small, in North America. With a decline in house show gates in the United States, Vince decided that the WWF would seriously invade Europe, so my mental compass was about to broaden even more.

On October 20, 1989, in André's hometown of Grenoble, France, I sat staring into my espresso at the Park Hôtel, my mind reeling with an overload of images. Vince's circus had tripped together from New York to London to Brussels and now all over France, and after a week straight we were all sick and tired of one another. Because of the unfamiliar surroundings and the language barrier, the wrestlers clustered together more than ever, like a chain gang. Italy had been bad, but the mood amongst the wrestlers on this European swing was combustible. Payoffs were down and we were far from home. On the bus between towns I couldn't help but joke, "Which one of you crazy bastards is going to crack first?" I called the waiter over and paid the cheque and decided that the thing I needed most was to go for a walk, away from all of them.

As I walked past the marble and bronze statues of Le Jardin des Fontaines Pétrifiantes, I was remembering our first night, in London. The televised special went well enough. After all, England had its wrestling fans, and it was a rarity for them to see the likes of Hulk and André: We were just beginning to get over big in the U.K. I couldn't help but see a glimpse of the future and the past when Rollerball Rocco and a bunch of the English boys dropped their bags in the dressing room. Pat had hired them to work the opening dark match. Rollerball's Black Tiger gimmick had long since died in Japan, and now he and the other lads toiled endlessly for a few quid, crisscrossing the UK riding four to a car. In the WWF dressing room they wore envious expressions that reminded me of pack horses who suddenly found themselves corralled with groomed Clydesdales. The Brits were awestruck as André lumbered past. To them he might as well have been a brontosaurus.

Roller's face lit up when Hulk came into the dressing room. They'd been good buddies in Japan and Roller had no doubt bragged to everybody that he and Hulk were friends. But that was millions of dollars ago; sadly,

Hulk barely remembered him. The dejection on Roller's face was pitiful, and at the same time, I felt empathy for Hogan. So much had changed for all of us.

I'd by lying if I said that it hadn't bothered me that after I made my entrance at the London Arena to a rousing ovation, second only to Hogan's, I then had to dutifully, and in short order, put over that lethargic boulder, Dino Bravo.

After a couple of hours I'd walked quite a distance from the hotel, and decided to stop and relax on a bench. I leaned back, remembering how all hell broke lose on the third day of the tour, in Brussels. After the show most of the boys surfaced at a rock 'n' roll bar near the hotel. The proprietress, a stunning Mulatto woman with a sexy French accent, made the kind mistake of giving all the wrestlers drinks on the house. Jack Daniels appeared before me; the price and the timing were perfect. I proceeded to get smashed.

A while later Jim Duggan and I found ourselves alongside the train tracks in front of the bar toking a hash pipe with a bunch of college kids, one of whom said he was the son of the Australian ambassador. Duggan and I had become close friends. Sometime later, I was high and drunk and reeling in the arms of a comely French college girl, then I somehow ended up engrossed in conversation with a very drunk Jim Troy, who was now Vince's vice-president of operations, the second highest position in the company after Vince's wife, Linda. My ear began to bend when he started to talk about Stu, Vince and loyalty. I remember him poking Shawn Michaels in the chest hard and snorting, "You don't know shit, kid! This guy," he continued, pointing at me, "his family *is* the business."

At maybe 3:30 a.m., André lurched toward me, leering with a grey-toothed grin. He took a huge bite out of a big pear soaked in high-test grain alcohol and handed it to me. I took a bite, as did Shawn, Koko, Duggan, even Jim Troy. If you think you can get into a lot of trouble biting an apple in Eden, you wouldn't believe what happened after biting that pear in Brussels! There are few times in my life when I actually got insanely drunk. This was one of them. I ended up enlisting the French girl to literally carry me back to the hotel, where I crashed into bed with the whole room spinning. She curled up next to me and promised to wake me up so I could make the nine-thirty bus. At around 5 a.m. I was jarred from my sleep by the sound of breaking glass and what had to be a wrestler, obviously one who had cracked, yelling profanities. I wanted no part of it.

In the morning I had a massive hangover. On the way to the elevator I couldn't help but notice that dozens of the tiny, elegant crystal chandeliers that hung outside each door lay on the carpet smashed to pieces. When the elevator door slid open in the lobby I was startled to see an army of police in riot gear, with billy clubs and shields, glaring at me with eyes that said, Try your bullshit now, wrestler man.

The whole lobby was pretty well demolished.

On the bus I found out that a huge fight had broken out between Koko B. Ware and Troy, seconds after I'd stumbled away from them at the bar. Troy, a former hockey player who once gooned for the New York Rangers, held his own before fleeing in a taxi with Koko in hot pursuit. Koko somehow got to the hotel first and decided to wait in the lobby for Troy. When Troy came through the doors, an enraged Koko tackled him, crashing through the plate glass walls of the gift shop.

Around the same time, The Rockers were in the hallway on my floor, drunk and angry, destroying chandeliers because the hotel operator couldn't connect a long distance call for Marty, who was concerned about his dad's recovery from heart surgery.

That morning Koko boarded the bus looking scared that he was going to get fired. The whites of his eyes were blood red and his hands were covered with glass cuts. And he was fired—that night. The Rockers were spared, I think mostly because Pat had a bit of a crush on both of them. They only had to pay the cost of the damage they'd done.

We took a plane to Paris. I remember the coach driver zooming by the Arc de Triomphe and the Eiffel Tower. No time to even stop. It was how I often saw the landmarks of the world, with my forehead pressed up against a bus window. The most striking image I'd ever seen of the tower was of Hitler's army marching victoriously past, and it came back to me vividly now.

The show in Paris went out live on TV across France. There was heat between Hogan and Macho over how Hogan had carried a supposedly wounded Liz back to the dressing room at the conclusion of their match in Brussels. Hogan professed innocence, honestly having no idea how he could have done it any differently. Randy became insanely jealous if any man even looked at Liz, which happened a lot because she definitely wasn't hard on the eyes. He never let Liz out of his sight, and she lived her life like a bird in a cage.

In the dressing room in Paris we learned that Troy had been fired too. None of the boys had believed that Vince would can Troy, as the office usually was held to a different standard than the rest of us.

After the show I ran into Koko in the hotel lobby, surrounded by sympathetic wrestlers. Fighting to hold back tears, Koko implored me to understand that Troy instigated the fight by hurling racial slurs at him. "What was I supposed to do? He kept telling me to eat fried chicken, watermelon, and I couldn't let him talk to me like that!"

"Koko," I said, "you can't beat up the second-highest suit in the company and not know you're gonna get fired!" Koko started to sob uncontrollably. Everybody looked at me like, you big meanie, why'd you have to go and say that for? Well, because it was the truth!

Having walked about ten miles from the hotel to get away from all the other wrestlers, I was stunned to see none other than Hacksaw Duggan stroll by, his trademark two-by-four replaced by a newspaper under his arm. He was as surprised to see me as I was to see him. Many years later we'd still laugh about the coincidence.

When I called home Julie was in an exceptionally foul mood. She'd acted this way the whole time she'd been pregnant with Dallas, and I calmly decided that if I had to go through this kind of hell for nine months, I'd endure it without complaint because it was probably a sign that our last child would be another son: We'd have a matched set, two girls and two boys.

At Maple Leaf Gardens in Toronto on October 29, after we'd got back from the crazy European tour, Chief pulled me aside to tell me that Vince wanted him to personally thank me for everything I was doing lately. Tonight, for the first time, I'd be going over on Dino Bravo. Chief added, "I told Vince to tell you himself. You're working so hard, your stuff is selling, you're over with the fans, and they're not doing anything with you."

A troubled and bewildered look came over Bravo's face when he was told that he was losing to me, and I tried hard not to look too happy, though I was. I hated losing to inferior workers, especially in Canada, and in Toronto, which was such a hot market.

It's not as though Dino Bravo was that bad, but he sure wasn't great. I have my own theory on the three qualities it takes to be a great pro wrestler. The first one is look or physical presence. On a scale of one to ten, Hogan, being such an awesome specimen, might rate a ten, for example. Although it always helped, it wasn't as important to be tough as it was to look tough, especially if you were a heel. The second quality is the ability to talk, to sell yourself; Hogan might score another easy ten, whereas a guy like Dynamite would have to work to earn a two. The third is wrestling talent, the ability to work. Here it would be just the opposite: Hogan would rate the two and Dynamite would get the ten. A score in the high twenties adds up to a great wrestler.

To me, Dino Bravo had low numbers. He looked sluggish, had no personality and was a so-so worker at best. If I had to rate myself at that time, I'd say I had a good, muscular frame warranting about a seven. On mic skills I'd be lucky if I was a four. But on actual wrestling ability, I'd give myself a ten.

While the earlier matches were on, Dino came to me wondering if I'd do the high spot he'd seen me do with Curt Hennig, where Hennig catapulted me off the apron and into the steel railing on the floor. I hesitated, remembering how only a few years before, I was working with the Hillbillies in Toronto and crashed into the fence doing the same spot, cutting my mouth up. "I'm not really up for that, Dino," I said, then, seeing the disappointment in his face, I allowed myself to be talked into it. I'd regret not following my gut instinct.

Dino and I did our usual dance where I eventually wound up on the floor outside the ring. Lying on the mat next to a heavy microphone stand, with a WWF cameraman peering down at me, I was directly in the line of fire of this one female fan from Toronto who always hated me, and now spewed angry curse words in my direction: Didn't she know I was a good guy now? I gallantly pulled myself up onto the apron, only to be met by a barrage of Dino's forearm smashes across my back. The referee, John Bonello, stepped between us, pushing him back, and it was while I was standing on the apron with my back to the crowd, knowing the spot was coming, that I realized it was quite some distance to the steel fence, that it was bolted to the floor and that it wasn't going to budge when I hit it. But it was too late! Dino, right on cue, rushed the ropes and launched me backwards into the air. As if in slow motion I twisted and braced myself, but my foot was tangled in the cord from the mic stand, and I feared that it would catch and pull me downwards, head first into the fence. Somehow, in a millisecond, I was able to shake my foot free then—*wham!*—my chest hit the top of the fence, and I crumpled to the arena floor. In very real agony, I was unable to catch my breath. My first thought was, Don't die, don't die. It felt like I'd crushed my rib cage or maybe even punctured a lung. As I twisted around on the floor, nobody seemed to realize this wasn't part of the show! I thought, Just hold on . . . somebody will know I'm seriously hurt. Oh no they won't . . . my selling is realistic, so nobody realizes I can't breathe. . . . I might die here on the floor of the Maple Leaf Gardens. God, what an awful way to go.

Over a full minute went by before Dino came out to get me and bent over to ask if I was okay. I was unable to speak. For some reason he took that to mean that I was fine and began stomping me on the back! With no alternative I pushed myself up, and Dino happily rolled me under the bottom rope and covered me for the pin. To give you an idea how much it meant to me not to lose to Dino any more, instead of just lying there so help would come, I actually kicked out. I rolled back out to the floor, where I lay flat on my back. Now it was apparent to most everyone in the arena except Dino and the ref that I was seriously injured. I could feel my sternum jutting to a point in my chest, and I was still only able to make short, rapid gasps for breath. But Bonello hadn't caught on, and he stalled, intentionally breaking the count for the second time. It seemed to take forever until, but at last I heard eight . . . nine . . . ten, and the bell sounded to a chorus of boos. While I struggled to breathe through clenched teeth, Dino had his hand raised in the ring. Finally some ushers were kneeling beside me and Bonello waved for help. Bonello's eyes offered reassurance that I wasn't going to die on a sticky blue mat.

I was rushed by ambulance to the hospital where, hours later, I was diagnosed with a fractured sternum, five cracked ribs and a bruised heart. Doctors advised me that I'd be out of action for at least three months.

The next day I flew home, desperately wondering how I'd make ends meet. No work: no pay. Pat called to tell me not to worry, saying that Vince would look after me financially while I was recuperating because they had big plans for me. That night I literally breathed a little easier with Julie nestled next to me. I winced as I rolled over on my side, and I couldn't help thinking that the man who never gets hurt just did.

24

BROKE AND BROKEN

VINCE'S GENEROSITY EXTENDED TO $200 A WEEK while I healed. Luckily my $10,000 *SummerSlam* 1989 cheque arrived to cover me. Still, I found myself going back to work after only eighteen days. My ribs would bother me for years, and I had to be careful taking hard falls and turn-buckles. There's a certain art to being able to work hurt and not disappoint your fans. I'm proud to say that nobody noticed a thing.

But my health issues were nothing compared to what was going on with my brother Dean. He had been urinating blood for years, we found out later, but had been too afraid to get it checked. Instead he chose to ignore it, persuading himself that it would go away. But then he began to have fainting spells and, by the time he was diagnosed with Bright's disease that fall, his kidneys had lost ninety-five per cent of their function. In December 1989, he had a dialysis tube inserted in his arm and had to undergo treatments almost every day. The family talked incessantly about who could be a kidney donor for Dean; the doctors told us that anyone who needed to be physically active to make a living shouldn't even con-sider it. Those who were left gave it some thought, but each waited to see whether the others would step up.

The truth was that for years the whole family had been keeping a cordial distance from Dean. He had ripped off a lot of people with various schemes, more often than not his own siblings, friends and even Stu and Helen. It sounds harsh to say, but whenever I went to visit Hart house, where Dean still lived, I made sure to lock my car, otherwise who knew what Dean would be tempted to do. I resisted the urge to have him over to my house, as did everyone else; he couldn't seem to stop himself from ripping people off. We all felt sorry for him, but he was no longer the charming, handsome, funny guy we all knew as kids. Like Smith, Dean had burned every one of his bridges. On one of his trips to Hawaii, he'd got beaten up—we never got the real story as to why—and after that he'd become spaced out, gaunt and uneasy. In recent years he'd also become a bitter opponent of both Bruce and Ross, envious of their roles in Stampede Wrestling.

When I saw him, Dean would always tell me that he loved my work, was a big fan of mine and was proud to tell people he was my brother. He also made a point of introducing me to his new girlfriend, Tammy, a woman from the Morley reserve. Then Dean got Tammy pregnant. Although this was another worrisome arrow in my mom's heart, her bigger concern was his health.

Roddy Piper had recently resurfaced in the WWF. He was one of the few people I trusted enough to confide my deepest personal affairs. I told Roddy about how Dean was withering away and about how cowardly I felt not offering to donate a kidney to my own brother, hoping that perhaps Smith, or one of my other non-wrestling siblings might step up to the plate instead. It was a relief to have someone who would listen to me compassionately. Roddy told me that he had come out of retirement because home had proved to be a hard adjustment for him; he was miserably glad to be back with his brothers on the road. It wasn't as though Roddy had problems back home, it was more like he was beginning to fear that *he* was the problem back home. While trying to fit in he was upsetting the balance. I could easily relate.

On December 15, 1989, Stu finally gave in and pulled the plug on Stampede Wrestling for the last time. He'd blown most of his fortune over the last four years. He and my mom finally told me that Vince had not fulfilled the terms of their deal, and Stu hadn't wanted to confront him on it. He and my mom were worried that if he got into a conflict with Vince it would cost me my job. Like an old king, Stu was drummed out of the business with no fanfare, a heart filled with memories and an empty till.

That Christmas, Hart house was covered in deep snow as my mom did her best to carry on the traditions of the season. I limped up Stu's back steps, my ribs still sore and having injured my knee in a match with The Rockers. I'd iced it and wrapped it and kept on going, finishing all my bookings because I couldn't afford to be off. My mom's face lit up as I came through the kitchen door with Julie and the kids. And she sat with me in the kitchen as Bertie, a giant, white King Kong Bundy of a cat, hobbled into the kitchen with his front leg in a cast. He was a recent adoptee who had belonged to an elderly wrestling fan from Manitoba who had passed away: He'd been dropped off with a broken front leg and in need of a home. Bertie would knock on my mom's bedroom door with the cast and she'd call out, "Who is it?" She'd get a big smile on her face when she opened the door to find him patiently waiting there.

Looking around to make sure that no one else could hear, my mom confided that Dean and Ross had recently got into a scuffle on the back porch.

Dean had welcomed about a dozen of his friends from Tammy's reserve to flop at Stu's house, sleeping on couches and all over the place. Finally Ross and Alison confronted Dean about it, on behalf of my mom and dad, and he and Ross ended up going at it. When it was over there was no real damage to either of them, but that didn't stop Dean from phoning the police and having Ross charged with assault. The local media made a news story out of it, which, with Dean's kidney problems and the end of the business, hadn't made Stu and Helen too happy.

My knee throbbed as my mom took me into the living room to show me her Christmas tree. I adjusted a stray strand of tinsel thinking that with all the chaos around here at least let my mom have her perfectly decorated tree. Then Owen walked in with Martha, who might as well have been holding her nose it crinkled so much at the odour of cat pee that permeated parts of the house. She and Owen had recently paid cash for a brand-new house, which was something the rest of us only dreamed of. Both of them had worked very hard, saving every penny.

Owen shook my hand with a big smile that brought about even bigger smiles from my mom and dad. He scooped Beans up in his arms laughing, "She's sure getting big!" We all had tea with gobs of honey in it as Stu turned up the volume on the TV so we could watch flickering images of Germans hacking down the Berlin Wall. Owen announced that he was going to work in Germany, just after the New Year. We couldn't help but compare the political situation in Europe to the crumbling wrestling territories over there. The European promotions were still in business, pushing feeble old stiffies such as Axel Dieter and his cronies, but with the flash and glitter of the WWF wrestlers seen on TV everywhere, Vince would be taking over soon enough.

By Christmas Day I still couldn't walk, so I called up Terry Garvin, Vince's talent coordinator, and told him I was in too much pain to make the Christmas Day show. For the first time ever, I got to spend Christmas with my kids.

But I was always job scared, waiting for the axe and trying to avoid it, and from the tone of Garvin's voice I figured he hadn't believed me. On Boxing Day I climbed on a plane. I hobbled from California to Nebraska to Ohio, wrestling in such pain that by New Year's Eve I finally gave up and came home again. I limped silently through the front door and snuck upstairs shortly before midnight. Julie was curled up in bed dozing, waiting for me to call home. A kiss was all it took to make her year: we celebrated out first New Year Eve's together since 1985. Beans woke up thirty-four seconds before midnight causing Julie and me to miss the count down. But as Beans danced around the room in her pyjamas, I couldn't think of a better way to kick off 1990. This was my year to bounce back and change my fate.

I took time off to heal. My knee doctor told me that I'd worn the cartilage down to the bone, that I had the knees of a sixty-five-year-old man, and that I'd need to have plastic joints put in within ten years. The very thought put a deep scare into me, but by January 8, I was back in the ring jumping off the second rope and landing on my knee the same as always.

By Valentine's Day that year, signs of strain between Emperor Vince and The Hulkster, those former soulmates, had begun to show. It looked like Hulk's incomparable star power was starting to drive Vince crazy because it gave Hulk power over him. Vince, being Vince, prepared a first-strike policy, though the war was still in the head-game stage and Vince was fairly subtle about it. He let Hulk have control of his own bookings while he devoted all his time to Warrior; he had always been a mark for bodybuilders, and Warrior was a prime specimen. Vince would send little zingers Hulk's way, joking that he was too old, too slow, always with a needle in it under the laughs. Since he had given Hulk control of his own schedule, it was hard for Hulk to complain.

Then Vince told Hulk to put Warrior over in their championship match right in the middle of the ring at *WrestleMania VI*. This was him practically daring Hogan into proving he could actually do a job straight up. Hogan agreed to do it but showed up in the dressing room with a long face and a distrustful look in his eye, clearly afraid that this was a sign that he was on the way down. It was the first time I saw Hulk Hogan second-guess himself. He was still the WWF's biggest draw and worked whenever he felt like it. He still flew on a Lear jet and had his own limo, and a man servant named Brutus Beefcake who carried his bags. Basically he was in, out, and gone. Although Hogan was still deeply respected, to the boys he had become a guy we used to know.

On the other hand, most of us couldn't stand Warrior, who had blossomed into a grunting prima donna. He flew first class with a paid valet, travelled to the arenas by limo and had his own private I'm-the-star dressing room. He never sat with us in the locker room bullshitting or playing cards. In the war Vince was launching, we were still rooting for Hulk.

I lasted through another hectic winter in the WWF, frustrated at doing jobs in both tags and singles. I tried to convince myself I was climbing the ranks whether The Emperor liked it or not. My matches were often quite dramatic, especially when I worked against such muscled monsters as The Powers of Pain, who were Warlord and Barbarian. Despite their savage appearance, they were two of the friendliest guys in the business. Sione Vailahi, billed as Barbarian, was a Samoan from the island of Tonga who reminded me of a muscled-up Grover from *Sesame Street*, complete with the lovable animated accent. Terry Szopinski was The Warlord. He was six-foot-five and over 320 pounds of nothing but muscle, but he had the disarming facial features of a cute, bald-headed baby. He'd squeeze me like a bag of groceries as I'd violently try to fight my way out, lashing my forearms across his giant back and shoulders. I'd have a good sweat going and I could make it look like I was crying. Kids in the audience would chant, "Go Bret Go!" All the heels loved working with me, and all I needed was a break.

The Hart Foundation was also busy putting over the new tag champions, André and Haku. Haku was from Tonga, thickly built and quick, and most of the time easygoing. When provoked he could get mad enough to bite your nose off, like some drunken idiot found out one night in Baltimore. André loved Haku.

These matches with us would turn out to be some of André's last great moments in the ring. André seemed pained, sad and longing for the good old days. He was pale and sickly, and many of us wondered whether he was trying to drink himself to death. Haku carried the load for him, but he still loved going out and working. He made a point of making Jim and me look strong: selling, tying himself in the ropes, even letting me do a sunset flip on him. Afterwards, I'd draw our matches on the blackboard for André. His ass, as big as a piano, teetering above me, was a funny but scary vision that few people ever got to see! It was strongly rumoured he'd be done after the big Japan tour that was coming up right after *WrestleMania VI*, on which I was also booked.

Any hopes The Foundation allowed ourselves about winning the belts from André and Haku were dashed when we learned that The Demolition would be getting them back at *WrestleMania VI*, which was going to be held at SkyDome in Toronto on April 1.

In March, after working in Auburn Hills, Michigan, I was whisked away by Lear jet to South Bend, Indiana, to wrestle again that same night, taking The American Dream Dusty Rhodes's place against Macho Man in a main event with a packed crowd. Since the last time we had worked together, Randy and I had wanted another match, but with no time for preparation, this one would hardly count. I'd kept my gear on and literally jumped out of the limo and ran straight down the aisle into the ring, through a frenzied crowd that had waited nearly an hour to see the main event. Randy and I clicked like we'd worked a million times together—and saved the show. It was proof that I was over enough to work a main event singles match and not disappoint the crowd. The office surely had to be realizing that I had the versatility to have great matches, playing babyface heel one night, pure babyface the next, in tags or singles. I tried hard to keep the faith that my day would come.

Julie was far too pregnant to come to *WrestleMania*, so I invited Stu and Helen. The afternoon before the extravaganza, The Hart Foundation did an autograph session at a shopping mall. I only say it because it's true, but we had the longest line of all the wrestlers. Helen and Stu had a great time with the fans, and with each other. My mom's wit and Stu's old-fashioned boyish innocence made them a gifted comic team, and they'd had years to perfect their act. Many of the local fans knew Stu because Stampede Wrestling aired across Canada. Others had become acquainted with him through Jesse Ventura, who never missed an opportunity to say I'd come from Stu's dreaded dungeon, the toughest wrestling pit of 'em all. I could see it meant the world to my parents that the fans regarded them kindly.

That evening in the lobby lounge, Stu and Barry Darsow took to rolling around on the carpet, even knocking chairs over. The wrestlers were cheering, and Barry had the look on his face of a guy who didn't know what he'd gotten himself into. He was grateful when my mom broke it up.

In the bar that night the big buzz amongst the wrestlers was about Dr. Zahorian, who had been busted by the FBI three days earlier. Some felt bad for him, but I thought he got what he had coming.

Pat had told me that our *WrestleMania VI* match with The Bolsheviks would only be about fifteen seconds long; it seemed a shame to me to be such a non-factor in a big show in Canada. But with the pressure off, I could relax that night, lying in bed leafing through the *Toronto Sun*. It made me smile when I read sportswriter Frank Zicarelli's comment, "The Hitman is the best wrestler in the world today." Buddy The Heartthrob had come a long way. But then a strange thought crossed my mind: Were the two giant stone gargoyles perched outside my window, with their tongues hanging out and their thumbs in their ears, laughing at me?

I'd had a four-day break at home before the big show, during which I spent many hours working on a special cartoon for André, a montage of every name wrestler who had worked in the WWF since I'd been there. In the dressing room before my *WrestleMania VI* match, I passed around the framed drawing for all the wrestlers to sign. Finally I brought it over to André, who grasped it in his big hands and turned it over in order to sign it too. I stopped him and said, "It's for you, boss. That's you there, right in the middle, carrying everyone on your back."

Suddenly I realized that André was fighting back tears and frantically looking for an escape: He had way too much pride to break down in front of the boys. I quickly pointed out to him, and everyone else who was staring, my caricature of Adrian Adonis with angel's wings atop a cloud plucking a harp. André gave me a big smile and said, "Thank you, boss."

Minutes later The Hart Foundation got a huge pop when we beat The Bolsheviks with our finish in less than nineteen seconds in front of a record crowd of 67,678.

Later that night Hogan went out and put over Warrior right in the middle of the ring, just as Vince had dared him to do, leading him through the whole match. The torch had been passed and only time would tell whether Warrior could carry the WWF as its new champion. After the match, Hogan said to me, "You watch. Warrior will fail. And Vince'll be calling me, begging me to come back." I liked Hogan, and I hoped he was right.

How very strange. That's what I thought to myself as I took in the spectacular sight of 53,742 much louder than usual Japanese wrestling fans inside the cavernous Egg Dome on April 11, 1990. I rested on one knee trying to catch my breath, while keeping a headlock clamped tightly on the furry, catlike head of the new Tiger Mask. This young boy, Misawa, was nothing close to the original but, in all fairness to him, those were a mighty big pair of shoes to fill. For me it was like being in a time machine.

The flight over to Japan had been packed with a crew of huge wrestlers taking up all the seats in business class. After clearing our way through customs and immigration, we were herded onto a little bus for the hour-and-a-half ride to Tokyo. By the time Curt Hennig and I climbed on the bus, there were only two seats left, one at the very front and one at the very back. Just then, the sliding doors of the airport parted and out lumbered an extremely inebriated André the Giant! Curt and I locked eyes realizing that the front seat was always André's, and we simultaneously raced for that last seat in the back, scrambling, laughing and fighting, the other wrestlers cheering us on. I guess that's why they called him Mr. Perfect, because he got there first! The only spot left for me was the six-inch space next to André, who was just coming up the steps of the bus. There was a big grin on Curt's face when I finally wedged myself in beside the giant. By the time I got off the bus I was carsick and soaked in sweat. In the hotel lobby, Japanese fans thrust old photos at me: "Please sign, Breto Harto." I shuddered, remembering my early days there.

That night, after the show, high up in my hotel suite, I peered out at the now familiar skyline of Tokyo. I took a sip of Kirin beer that I'd brought back from the dressing room, appreciating the thought of Inoki's old general, Sakaguchi, who approached me and offered me a job with New Japan when I finished up in New York. One of the Japanese fans had handed me an old photo of Dynamite, Davey and me: There was Tom looking mean, Davey with a big naive grin and me looking envious and desperate. I had finally passed Tom and Davey, the dark horse of the three of us.

Superimposed on the flickering neon of a Tokyo night was the shimmering reflection of a violent kids cartoon from the TV. I clicked the remote just in time to catch my favourite sumo wrestler, Chino Fuji, tossing some opponent on his ass. When I was first in Japan, Fuji was a nobody, but now he was Grand Champion. Good things come to those who wait.

While I was away in Japan, Dean's girlfriend Tammy had given birth to a little girl, named Farrah. After I got home I went for my usual visit with my parents to find my mom very worried for Dean. His doctor had called to say that he had not been following his rigid diet and had missed numerous dialysis appointments. Mom hoped his baby daughter might help him stay focused on what he needed to do to stay alive.

Stu put on the usual pot of tea, and then asked if there was anything I could do for Davey. I told him I'd already mentioned Davey to Pat, who seemed more than a little interested. My mom also asked whether I could please put in a word for Bruce, saying he'd take anything. All three of us knew that Bruce was a much harder sell: Chief and the others had little regard for Bruce because of the way he'd screwed up for the WWF the first time round and undermined Stu's business with his horrible booking. But Bruce had two kids to support, and another one on the way, all on what he could earn as a substitute teacher. So I promised that I'd try.

My last day at home found me looking out my picture window watching Jade and Dallas flying down the driveway on their new bikes past a For Sale sign. Sometimes I felt a lot like my dad, who used to pull the For Sale sign down and then put it up again, depending on how his finances were doing.

As I packed for the next trip, I looked at the dozens of pairs of pink and black tights hanging in my closet and wondered whether Superman's closet looked like mine. I smiled at the three hearts embroidered on the right leg of my tights, one for each kid, thinking about how I'd soon have to add a fourth. When I signed autographs, I made one dot for each of them, trailing off above the word *Hitman*. Most fans probably thought they were bullet holes, but commemorating my kids with every signature was my way of reminding myself why I was doing all this.

As I folded my gear into my suitcase, my distress built because the moment was fast approaching when I'd have to say my big goodbye again. Dallas stood tall and handsome. "This makes you the man of the house till I get home." Jade with her long legs, long brown hair and big brown eyes fought to hold back tears as she gave me a tight squeeze. Little Beans, unable to meet my gaze, tried not to crack, then blurted out, "Bye bye, Daddy," before falling apart, tears trickling down her chubby cheeks. I hugged her gently. Then, like a sliver, I pulled myself out, kissing a very pregnant Julie goodbye.

On June 2, Bill Eadie—Axe of Demolition—was diagnosed with an erratic heartbeat. If he took his medication, he was at no risk at all, but his fate had already been decided. Vince didn't want the complications of Bill dying in the ring in front of the fans. He brought in Brian Adams, an ex–air force amateur boxer from Hawaii with long, black hair and a six-foot-five frame, to become Crush, the third member of Demolition. Bill was led to believe that they'd be a three-man team from here on. Like André, Bill was being put out to pasture, but Vince didn't bother to tell him.

On June 5, Julie's water broke, and I was on a plane home, determined to be there for the birth this time.

As I raced down the hospital hallway a nurse directed me to Julie's room, but when I arrived the door was closed and I was not sure I had the right place. As I waited just outside the door, I heard a slap and a good strong cry. When I walked in, Julie's sister Sandy handed me my son. I gazed down into the eyes of a dark-haired, serious little baby who looked like he'd come out swinging. I called home and told the kids. Jade laughed excitedly, "Dallas is so happy that he's dancing on the kitchen table!" Then I called my mom and announced she had a new grandson, "an eight-pound baby boy, named Blade Colton Hart, just like I ordered."

That night a perfect day was capped off when I answered my phone and Jim said, "Congratulations, daddy. I just finished talking with Vinnie Mac. We're getting those belts back at *SummerSlam*."

I spent my thirty-third birthday wrestling Curt Hennig in Amarillo. Chief had orders for Curt to beat me, but Curt went to him on his own and insisted that we do our usual draw instead. Curt liked our match just the way it was, especially the bit at the end where he jumped me after the bell. He thought it got him far more heat than if he simply beat me. Few wrestlers but Curt would have done that for me.

Rude was carrying Warrior through every match. That night he found himself wrestling him to the mat, whispering in his ear that if Warrior potatoed him one more time he'd rip his head off and shove it up his ass. Warrior, who never showed much regard for his fellow wrestlers, melted like putty. Maybe that was why, in an unexpected moment of generosity,

Warrior allowed the boys the use of his limo after the show so we could go out and celebrate my birthday.

In the wee hours of the night Jim, Curt, Rude, Beefcake, Superfly Snuka, Mike McGuirk and I were guided to a hotel room by our old friend Jack Daniels. Mike, a petite blue-eyed blond, was our on-road ring announcer and the daughter of legendary wrestler and promoter LeRoy McGuirk out of Oklahoma. He'd wanted a boy so badly that he always called his little girl Michelle Mike. Soon a joint was lit and passed around, the beds were moved out of the way and we all took to wrestling on the rug. Both Curt and I were decent amateurs in our day, but we couldn't budge Rick from his all fours position; he was incredibly strong. I couldn't have spent a birthday with better friends. Even Jim good-heartedly got on all fours, only to be pinned in seconds by Curt. Beefcake, who admitted to having no wrestling skill, wanted no part of it, even when we encouraged Mike McGuirk to take him on. Being the daughter of a legit shooter and an Oklahoma girl at that, there was more than a good chance that Beefcake would have had his hands full, and he knew it!

I flew home the following day, worn out and weary. On July 4, Jim called to tell me that Beefcake had been critically injured in Tampa. An out of control, bikini-clad parasailer had fallen out of the sky and smashed full force into his face with her knees. When they dragged Beefcake out of the water, his eyeballs dangled out of their smashed sockets.

Adrian had died on July 4 two years previously; Davey was nearly killed a year ago, and now Beefcake had been seriously injured. Many of us wondered whether July 4 was cursed for wrestlers.

One night I was home, the next I was at the notorious Stay Out Club in Chicago. Jim and I followed the boss, known only as Mr. Bill, to his cramped office, where a bleached-blonde silicone princess wearing only panties amazed us with her flexibility by doing several backward handstands. Her huge white breasts hid her face as she arched back—and lost her balance, knocking some of Bill's prized framed photos off the wall. Lying face up on the carpet among cracked and broken glass was an old black-and-white publicity photo of The Hart Foundation, the very first one ever taken of us. I remembered that we celebrated here the night before we won the belts the first time. As I looked down at our young faces I realized just how far we'd come.

Back on my bar stool, I looked over at Jim, remembering a scene earlier that year in New Orleans. I'd abandoned Jim in a bar on Bourbon Street and gone next door to a strange voodoo shop. Amidst chicken feet hanging everywhere and jars of mysterious ancient potions lining weathered shelves, I'd had my palm read by a portly old black woman in a black linen dress. I was silent, not wanting to give her anything to go on, as she traced her long red fingernail along my palm lines. "You have a red-haired companion, a friend; he's trouble, not so much for you, but trouble to himself. Definitely a bad influence." Holy cow, I thought, she hit that one right on the head. She went on to tell me that when I reached middle age I was going to have a bad accident, but I'd survive. Her eyes burned deeply into mine as she told me about a strong source of power coming from Connecticut, and how at the end of the summer, my life would change financially. She told me I was an entertainer of some kind and that I would eventually become a bigger star than I ever imagined. In life, there are a lot of strange signs on the road that go unnoticed. When I told Jim what she'd said he howled with laughter, calling it a foolish waste of ten bucks, which was far less than he'd spent drinking in the time I'd been gone.

Then Curt Hennig appeared before me with two more shots of Jack Daniels, insisting that I gargle it, which had become a ritual of his. I complied. I pulled a picture out of my wallet, which I'd torn out of a magazine, of a scruffy baby chimp wearing a cute double-breasted army jacket with epaulets. I handed it to Jim: "That's going to be our new look, pink and black ring jackets for *SummerSlam*." We all laughed, but I was serious. That's when Curt told us that The Road Warriors were set to join us all around the end of August. Jim and I looked at each other concerned: The Demos and The Road Warriors would be a natural match up.

I really wanted to believe the voodoo lady.

Most of us wished that Hogan would come back and reclaim his crown.

I got to see exactly what kind of champion Warrior was during a show in Omaha. Propped up on a stretcher a few feet outside the dressing room was a Make a Wish kid who looked to be down to his last few hours. There was not a hair left on his head, and not even his Warrior face paint could mask his sad eyes. Sickly pale and barely breathing through a ventilator tube, the boy wore a purple Warrior T-shirt and green and orange tassels tied around his biceps to honour his hero. His mother and father and an older brother and sister were with him, patiently waiting for the promised encounter with The Ultimate Warrior.

I bent over to say hello, as did all the other wrestlers on the way into the dressing room. It was odd, but there was Warrior actually sitting with us: he usually kept to himself in his private dressing room. By the time the third match started, a WWF public relations rep poked his head in and politely asked Warrior if he was ready to meet the dying boy. Warrior grunted, "In a fuckin' minute. I'm busy." I thought to myself, Busy doing what, talking to a bunch of guys you can't stand anyway?

As the night wore on the family waited just outside the dressing room door, the boy hanging on to his dying wish to meet his hero. As I was returning to the dressing room after my match, I was relieved to see that they weren't there any more; I assumed that the kid's wish had come true.

Warrior's entrance music played while Jim and I quickly showered in hopes of beating the crowd out of the building. We'd have to hurry since Warrior never went over ten minutes. We dressed, grabbed our bags and took off. As we rounded a corner down a backstage ramp, we came upon the boy and his weary family, who had been moved there so as not to get in the way of Warrior's entrance. I thought, That lousy piece of shit. He'd made them wait all night, unable to summon the compassion to see this real little warrior. Hogan, Randy and countless others, including André, never hesitated to take the time to meet a sick, dying kid. My disgust for Warrior magnified a thousand times. To me he was a coward, a weakling and a phony hero.

Philadelphia had always been a WCW stronghold, so the fans were delighted when the legendary Road Warriors, who'd just defected to the WWF, appeared out of nowhere during our match with Demolition at *SummerSlam* that August. The Road Warriors were largely responsible for The Hart Foundation winning back the World Tag Team title; we didn't care that they helped us and basically stole our thunder, we just wanted the belts.

As Axe and Smash brawled back to the dressing room with The Road Warriors, who'd be known in the WWF as The Legion of Doom, I crawled behind Crush just as Anvil launched himself over the top rope like a torpedo, knocking Crush toppling backward over me for the one . . . two . . . three. I'd been in the ring for most of the match, and with the temperature outside soaring to over a scorching one hundred degrees, the Philly Spectrum was an oven. As the crowd cheered I was too spent to even get up, so I lay on my back staring at the lights, taking in the moment. Jim grinned as he dropped the belt across my chest. He pulled me to my feet and we hugged each other, knowing we'd worked damn hard to regain the belts. The pink and black attack was back!

Being the pros that they were, all three of The Demolition were waiting to greet us with hugs and congratulations in the dressing room. When we walked in, Hulk called out, "New champions! Let's give 'em a hand!" It meant so much to us to hear all the boys give us a standing ovation with The Hulkster leading the way. It felt like The Foundation's defeats were erased in that one moment.

At TVs I had a good chat with Vince. I suggested to him that when my run with the Tag belts was over, it might be time to give my face a rest, and asked him if he'd help me get booked in Japan. He chuckled as he assured me that I had nothing to worry about: He was far from done with me. He also added that he was trying to find room for Davey, and that he'd received a refreshing letter from Bruce in which Bruce had expressed his thoughts on the wrestling business. Vince said that he not only found the letter interesting, but he also asked me to pass on to Bruce that he might consider implementing some of his suggestions in the future, and that perhaps Bruce could play an active role.

When I called home to tell Stu and Helen the news, my mom told me they didn't have enough money to pay their phone bill and that Stu was thinking of selling Hart house. Someday when they were gone, they figured their children might go to war over the house: Selling it now seemed to them the smartest thing. They were relieved that there might be some breaks in the offing for Davey and Bruce.

My mother was upset about the way the WWF was playing off the impending war in the Persian Gulf. Vince had brought back the exiled Sergeant Slaughter, who was older, heavier and humbler than when I'd last seen him. Once the symbol of American patriotism, Sarge was now slated to be Vince's top heel. Wartime hostilities also brought back the humbled and hobbled Iron Sheik and an ancient but real Iraqi wrestler named James Mustafa who would now be called Colonel and wear a military uniform. Wrestling had a rich history of playing up wartime animosities — but always after the war. This one hadn't even happened yet

I'd waited a long time to be able to ask for some days off, and I was happy to be safe, secure and free to rejoice for one full week at home. Unfortunately, as soon as I walked in the front door, I found that Michelle had left Tom the day before and she and the kids were now holed up at my house again.

Tom was knackered. His entire body was broken; his shoulders, his knees, his neck, his back and worst of all his heart. I tried to defend him, even offering to talk to Vince for him. Michelle tearfully explained that Tom had neglected to pay any of his US taxes and was now unable to go back there until he paid — he owed a lot of money. The day before I got home she alleged that Tom had threatened her with a gun and actually said he was going to kill her, so she, Julie and all the kids had spent the night hiding out in a motel until I got home.

Julie was cold and distant and all the kids were terrified and ran for cover every time there was a knock at the door. Tom phoned constantly, but when Michelle tried to talk to him he threatened to come over with a bottle of vodka in one hand and a shotgun in the other. When I tried to reason with him, he hung up on me. By week's end he was threatening to kill Julie and our kids too.

On my last day at home Jade ran in the front door looking scared and grabbed her cousin Bronwyne's hand. "We gotta hide! I saw your dad parked in his car right down the street!" All the kids scurried off. I jammed on my running shoes and marched straight out to face Tom. Even though he couldn't miss me coming, he seemed startled when I pulled open his car door and got in.

"That twat send you down here?" he sneered, clutching the steering wheel. He was trembling and looked unkempt. He'd never bothered to fix his teeth, even though Vince had given him the money for it, and his hair was scruffy and dark sunglasses hid bloodshot eyes.

"What the hell are you doing, Tom?" I asked. As mad as I was I couldn't help but feel sorry for him. "What's this about you saying you're bringing your gun over to my house to kill everybody? Tom, your kids and my kids are all terrified of what you might do, and I gotta tell ya, just lookin' at you, you're starting to scare me too. You don't have a gun, do ya?"

"Nah, fook."

This legendary, nasty little rock of a man slumped over the steering wheel and began to cry. "Fookin' broke I am. I've thrown it all away. I'm done. I'm goin' back 'ome." Tears dripped off his chin, helplessly, and I could tell he hated himself for being weak. "I can't even wrestle any more." He was biting his top lip so as to angle the tears into his mouth. I'd never seen him cry. We'd both been blessed with innate ability and passion, but his life and his choices had caught up with Dynamite. Just when my career was starting to take off, his was ending. My heart went out to him even though he was a classic example of that old adage: what goes around comes around.

A few days after I left for the road again, Michelle handed him a one-way plane ticket to England and told him to never come back.

The Dynamite Kid, one of the greatest workers of all time, broke and broken, a bona fide wrestling tragedy. He had been an untameable stallion, but now this crippled pony was on his last ride, to the glue factory.

25

THE REAL PUSH

BECAUSE I ALMOST ALWAYS WRESTLED second from last each night, finding a decent dinner was usually a hit-and-miss affair. It was Denny's, if I was lucky. After eating (and usually drinking), when the wrestlers got to their rooms, they'd still be supercharged on adrenalin, almost euphoric. It was impossible to fall asleep in time to be able to get up to make that early-morning flight unless you took something to help. Then in the morning a lot of wrestlers would take something to help them wake up, like Ephedrine, commonly known as trucker pills; with a couple of those in them, they could rush off to the gym as soon as they got off the plane in the next town. The days of wrestlers chopping lines of coke were mostly gone, replaced by amino acid pills and protein shakes, but there were still syringes loaded with steroids—the WWF was a muscleman meat factory. Then there were the pain pills that were popped like candy. All too often I can remember washing them down with coffee. Looking at Dynamite that day in his car made me realize that if I was falling apart, I wanted to know it. So I stopped taking the pain pills.

On October 9, at TVs in Springfield, Illinois, Jim and I were finishing up a photo shoot when word came that Vince wanted to see us. We headed over to his backstage office, where there had been a revolving door of wrestlers coming in and out all morning. Vince opened his door and said, "I need to talk to both of you. Bret, I'll see you first. Jim, you wait outside."

The first thing he said was, "Bret, we're going with you in singles." With the Tag belt I thought I had a rock-solid position, but now everything was uncertain again.

"This is going to be the *big* push," he said. "The *real* push—the one I've always promised you. The one you've been waiting for. The one you deserve. You'll be involved in all the major angles with all the top men, and it's not going to be like all those other times where we didn't come through. The plans I have for you are bigger than anything you've ever imagined."

We studied each other. I asked, "What about Jim?"

Vince's face grew serious. "I'll be letting seventeen guys go today and Jim's not one of them. I'm thinking I'll try him at the announcing table for a while, putting him on salary with a pension and full company benefits. I can't let him go—he owes me a lot of money from all his legal fees."

Vince's plan was that The Foundation would drop the belts to The Rockers at the next TVs, at which they'd also be taping *SNME*.

When I left the room Jim looked like a prisoner preparing to see the warden. Afterwards, he did his best to appear upbeat, but it was easy to see he was devastated. At least he had his ongoing countersuit against U.S. Air and the hope of an eventual settlement.

One Man Gang, Haku, Honky Tonk, Tito Santana, Greg Valentine and Bill Eadie were let go. And then there was Bad News, who, upon being given notice, not surprisingly grabbed Vince by the scruff of the neck and told him he was lucky that he didn't kill him for all the lies he'd told him. Then Rick Rude quit after finding out how much Warrior was paid for *SummerSlam* compared to what he got for carrying their entire match.

It was going to be a whole new team, but it looked like I had a starting position.

On October 29, I drove to Fort Wayne, Indiana, with Kerry Von Erich, another of Fritz Von Erich's sons. Kerry was a big, handsome, well-built kid with a kind streak a mile wide who wouldn't think twice about giving you the shirt off his back. I loved how genuine and considerate he was, especially to the fans. To that point the highlight of his career was beating Ric Flair for the NWA World Heavyweight title in May 1984 in front of more than 40,000 of his fellow Texans at a tribute card to honour the memory of his oldest brother, David. Unfortunately, like his brothers, Kerry had a history of drug problems and was often mistaken for a dolt by wrestlers who didn't know him well.

That night I mentioned to Kerry that I'd decided to bring my brother Bruce down for *Survivor Series*. I'd become sympathetic to Bruce's struggle to support his family and how desperately he still wanted to be part of the business. Since Vince had raved about his letter, I took it upon myself to play matchmaker in hopes that Vince would meet with Bruce and maybe give him a job. In many ways Bruce had a great mind for the business, if only he could reign himself in from doing the really stupid things. Kerry and I talked on and on about our brothers and good times that we'd both had as famous families in such a strange business.

Just as we neared Fort Wayne, Kerry confided that he'd made up his mind to join his brothers in heaven. He was only waiting for God to tell him when. I said, "Kerry, your children will always need you, even more than your brothers do. You have to think of your children." He allowed me to think I'd made him change his mind, but I feared it was only lip service.

For our *SNME* match the next night, The Hart Foundation marched out wearing pink and black Civil War jackets to drop the belts to the Rockers. Jim and I were sombre, thinking this might be our last ever match together. Pat wanted it to be best of three falls, so the four of us had spent the afternoon creating a match that had a mixture of great moves and cute little rehearsed spots. We all dug deep to find ways to top our last *SNME* match, which many considered to be one of the best tag matches ever.

What started out as a terrific match snowballed into a colossal clusterfuck after Jim accidentally broke the top rope. The match was taped and could easily be edited, but the ref, Freddie Sparta, couldn't figure out that he needed to temporarily stop the bout and fix the rope, even though I explained it to him. Both teams needed the rope to do our best spots, and without it the whole match turned into an embarrassing night of miscues until finally The Rockers beat us. I was furious at Freddie. I hoped that before the match aired in a couple of weeks we could somehow do it over. I wanted it to be a great moment for both The Rockers, Shawn in particular, whom I respected and who had admitted to being a bit of a Hitman fan.

Five days later in Milwaukee, Jim lugged his bags into the dressing room with a huge grin on his face. He'd had a long telephone conversation with Vince earlier in the day and was absolutely stunned when Vince told him that he'd changed his mind. He wasn't going to air The Rockers winning the belts—The Hart Foundation would keep them, for now. To Jim it was a stay of execution, but my heart sank. What was to come of my push, the real push, the one that Vince just promised me? I never thought I'd see the day that I'd be disappointed to find out that I was keeping a belt. I'd made the mistake of getting my hopes up.

Calgary was quilted by an early winter. Under the blanket of white lurked a darkness that made its way up snowy steps and into Hart house.

My mom sat riveted to the TV in the kitchen, concerned about the tension in the Persian Gulf. Living for four decades in Canada hadn't muted her American patriotism any more than her New York accent. While America was preparing to kick the hell out of the mother of all evils, Alison's four-year-old daughter, Brooke, raced into the kitchen and came to a screeching halt in front of my mom. "Grammy! Dean's dead!"

"That's not funny, Brooke!"

But upstairs in the boys' bathroom Stu, Smith and Georgia knelt beside Dean's naked body. Smith cried as he ran his fingers through

Dean's hair, kissing him on the forehead and pleading in desperation, "No, Bizz, don't die!"

One look from Stu told my mom all she needed to know. Dean had ignored his doctors one time too many. Only the night before, the hospital called again, and Stu told Dean he would take him for a dialysis treatment first thing in the morning. Stu had woken him, but when Dean went to wash up he keeled over.

Dean Harry Hart, dead at thirty-four.

At that moment, I was with Bruce and Jim in Providence, Rhode Island; it was the day before the *Survivor Series*, and I'd arranged for Bruce to meet with Vince. All of us were called into a small office in the back of the Civic Center, where Chief handed me the phone. "It's your pop."

Stu came on the line. "I hate to have to tell you this, our Dean Harry has expired, he's no longer with us. He succumbed late this morning."

Some sour-faced old fart was yelling at me to get the hell out of his office and off his damn phone. I put my hand over the receiver to tell him that there was a family emergency, that my brother had died, but he wasn't listening. So I raised my voice and told him again, only this time I added that he better get out before I threw him out.

After the show in Providence, Bruce, Jim and I drove down to Hartford, Connecticut. Being the old-school wrestling promoter that he was, Stu told me to finish my bookings—there was nothing that could be done for Dean any more. I would have gone home anyway, but I could tell by the look in Bruce's eyes that he didn't want to face it yet, so I kept on, trying to keep a handle on my grief.

The following day was American Thanksgiving, and at the Hartford Civic Center wrestlers gorged on a catered turkey dinner. *Survivor Series* was only hours away. Bruce and I mostly kept to ourselves, telling each other stories about Dean. Word of our brother's passing spread among the wrestlers, and dozens of them paid their respects.

On our way to the lunchroom Bruce and I had run into Vince and Pat coming out of an elevator. They were in a great mood, and Pat gave me a crisp slap on the back, "Cheer up, you look like someone died, for Chrissakes." I managed to calmly say, "Yeah, Pat, our brother Dean passed away." Neither he nor Vince seemed to take the news on board and walked cheerily away, annoying yuk-yuk laughs reverberating down the hall in their wake.

Bruce had expected a warm welcome from Vince. Now doubt and rejection added to the sadness on his face. "Don't worry, Bruce," I tried to reassure him, "they're just busy, and it must be that they don't know."

In contrast, neither of us will ever forget the kindness of Kerry Von

Erich, who smiled and said, "Don't worry, he's up there right now with my three brothers. They'll look after him."

I didn't know whether I could even work, but the memories of how Dean loved my matches and of our good times together growing up inspired me. I wanted to dedicate the match to his memory.

It was bizarre to meet Vince's new gimmick: a towering red-haired kid from Houston named Mark Callaway, his Huck Finn features hidden by the dark circles painted under his eyes to give him the look of a cadaver. He was The Undertaker, dressed all in black, complete with a wide-brimmed hat. Pat explained to all of us that Vince wanted him over super strong, didn't want him even leaving his feet.

How odd that, today of all days, my job was to battle death in a strange kind of morality play.

Once The Undertaker was eliminated by disqualification, I was to be the last man standing against The Million Dollar Man.

As fate would have it I was the first WWF wrestler to ever lock up with The Undertaker. Little did I know that, much farther down the road, he would wind up being the last wrestler to work with me in the WWF.

Once Taker was eliminated the stage would be set for me and Ted DiBiase to steal the show. Losing can be a beautiful thing if it's done right. The Hitman character was generally seen as a wrestler who, try as he might, could never quite win. This made him more human than, say, Warrior or Hogan. His constant struggle to make it to the top was endearing to the fans because it was something they could identify with in their own lives.

In his live commentary Roddy told the world that I was dedicating this match to my brother Dean, who had died the day before, knowing it would sink into the hearts of wrestling fans everywhere. The only fans who didn't know were the ones in the building.

We had a beautiful up-and-down exchange full of near finishes. As I slid in behind Ted with a quick crotch roll, the crowd counted along with the referee, one . . . two . . . but Ted, the old pro, kicked out yet again. I could feel Dean's presence next to me, smiling. I pushed off Ted and headed over to the corner perching myself on the middle rope. Suddenly, in my mind, I was alone. No Ted, no crowd. I'm a kid back at the Pavilion, outside on the grass, standing over Dean. He has Curly Clark, a big, freckle-faced, red-haired program seller, clamped in a full nelson. They're both sweaty and panting with their shirts off, and then Curly finally taps out and Dean, the smallest of the Hart kids, springs to his feet with big eyes and a handsome smile. My hero!

Then I snapped back to the Hartford Civic Center and the sold-out *Survivor Series* and I was about to launch myself off the ropes at Ted, thinking, This is for you, Dean. I know it isn't much, but it's all I got. It was time for me to slip and fall on a banana peel, breaking the hearts of the fans, who wanted me to win this one for my brother. I dove across Ted, but as we fell to the mat he rolled through, cradling me, his fingers tightly locked. There was no escape. I kicked out just a hair too late. My eyes were cold, wet and hurt. I hoped Dean enjoyed it. For me, the emotion was always real, especially the heartbreak. The camera captured my sorrow for all the Harts watching on TV back home, where my intentions were understood.

When I returned to the dressing room, Ted embraced me, sweat and tears indistinguishable.

As expected the rest of the pay-per-view was centred on Warrior and Hogan. I hung around backstage taking in their silent competition for that elusive top spot, but I think wrestling fans were beginning to see them both for what they really were, two colossal steroid freaks who did little or no actual wrestling. If you watched either one of them wrestle once, you'd seen all that they had.

I was hoping that Vince would take a moment with Bruce, but the more we hung around, the more it bothered me that neither Vince nor Pat even offered their condolences. Once the show ended, Bruce, Jim and I simply went back to our hotel.

November 27, 1990. A miserable, viciously cold day in Calgary.

The Harts gathered around the dining-room table. It seemed only fitting that we tell some stories about Dean and all the characters he'd charmed and conned over the years, and it wasn't long before we were all smiling. Tammy put on a brave face holding her and Dean's daughter, hoping that with the help of Stu and Helen she'd survive all this. Finally the Hart clan, minus the grandkids, bundled up against the twenty-below weather and piled into various cars to drive to a small parcel of Stu's land two minutes down the hill from Hart house. In brutal wind and snow, we shivered through our last words before scattering Dean's ashes. The tears froze on our cheeks.

Back at Hart house we listened to a cassette tape Owen had sent from Germany on which he talked passionately about Dean and how much he wished he could be there with us.

There were those in the family who felt that my parents should have had a more elaborate funeral for Dean. Personally I loved the honest simplicity of it, and I think Dean would have liked it just the way it was.

On January 16, 1991, fighting began in the Persian Gulf. Three days later, at the *Royal Rumble*, Slaughter dethroned Warrior for the WWF World title. The angle felt eerie to most of us in the dressing room. Some of us debated whether wrestling was too much of a cartoon to make light of something as serious as war, especially one where the US was bracing for a high body count. Yet, most of the wrestlers had faith in Vince, since he'd always had an uncanny sense of giving the public just what they wanted and his gambles always seemed to pay off. And Vince had a vision of more than 100,000 fans coming out to *WrestleMania VII* at the Los Angeles Memorial Coliseum to watch the WWF's real American hero, Hulk Hogan, give that traitor Slaughter what he had coming. The WWF even asked Slaughter to burn the American flag, but he flat out refused: He had enough heat as it was. He had received death threats, and there were bomb scares at the buildings he worked in.

The *Royal Rumble* did nothing for me, Jim or Davey Boy, who was waiting in the wings for his own supposed big push. He was now calling himself The British Bulldog and really looked the part, being bigger than ever. He wore long, braided hair extensions beaded in the colours of the Union Jack that also adorned his impressive sequined cape.

At the TVs in Macon, Georgia, on January 28, Jim and I were once again summoned to see Vince. He told us we'd be dropping the tag straps at *WrestleMania VII* to The Nasty Boys, two school chums from Allentown, Pennsylvania. Brian Knobbs was a loud, lovable three-hundred-pound kid with a blond mohawk. Jerry Sags was also a slab of a man with a black mohawk and one tooth missing up front. They took the numerous complaints from the boys about their stiff, sloppy work good-naturedly, as a bit of harmless teasing. The truth was they were as wild as two Brahma bulls in a china shop, and most of the boys loved them because they were true to the spirit of wrestling's notorious wild men of the past. They reminded me a lot of Adrian Adonis.

Once we'd dropped the belts, I figured it was time for that singles push Vince owed me. Curt Hennig had taken the Intercontinental belt from Kerry Von Erich, whom Vince pulled the plug on pretty fast, and there was now a buzz about me and Curt working a program. Curt was the best heel in the company, maybe even in the business, at that time, and I knew he'd be keeping the belt for a while, especially since Hogan would obviously be winning the World title from Slaughter at *WrestleMania VII*. The IC belt would need to stay on a heel to balance out the cards. My instinct told me to wait: It was the guy who worked with Curt *after* his next opponent who was a more likely bet to get the belt. I'd have to outwork everyone, even Vince, and I knew I could.

On March 12 at Biloxi TVs, The Foundation was to take on The Legion of Doom for a home video. Even though we were still the champions, we were supposed to put them over, as the video would come out after *WrestleMania VII*. I didn't care. I'd come to like and respect the team who were once The Road Warriors, and this would be our one and only chance to work with them. Joe Laurinaitis, or Animal, had a wide mohawk and was a thick powerhouse. His partner, Mike Hegstrand, or Hawk, was a big, loud raspy-voiced character with a long, sinewy torso. I always thought the best actual wrestlers of our generation came out of Minneapolis: guys like L.O.D., Rude, Hennig, Warlord and Darsow had all grown up watching the AWA's greatest workers like Bockwinkel, Ray Stevens, Mad Dog Vachon, even the Brit tough guy and shooter Billy Robinson, all of whom had a more credible style than most American wrestlers.

About an hour before our match, Hawk tilted his head back and plopped three or four Placidyls in his mouth as if he was trying to impress me and Jim. By the time we made our way to the ring, Hawk was half asleep on rubber legs. Needless to say what should have been an all-time classic turned into a bore as Animal, Jim, and I did all we could not to expose to Vince or the agents that Hawk was nearly comatose. I liked Hawk, but I was disappointed that he ruined something that meant a lot to the rest of us.

After the Gulf War ended, Vince decided to move *WrestleMania VII* from the L.A. Coliseum to the L.A. Sports Memorial Arena. The rumour was that Slaughter had so much heat that there was fear of a bomb threat, but many of us in the dressing room thought it was because ticket sales were slow. With the war over, the Slaughter angle was quickly losing steam.

Kerry Von Erich opened the show by defeating Dino Bravo. Upon his victory Kerry came up grinning and shooting his fingers like six-guns in what would turn out to be an eerie prefiguring of events yet to come for both of them. Hogan looked tanned and muscled and was decked out in an American flag bandanna. Randy Savage looked more like a lime-green psychedelic space cowboy as he worked on his match with Warrior. Davey Boy beat his close friend Warlord in only four minutes. The look on Warlord's face told me he was just starting to realize that he'd been given a thumbs-down for a serious push.

Jim and I went on early in what was really a call to go out and kick the show into high gear. The Nasty Boys headed out with Jimmy Hart, who was wearing a spray-painted motorcycle helmet as protection from us. Our music played and off we went, the pink tassels on our epaulets swinging as we high-fived fans on our way to the ring. I pulled open my jacket to expose the shiny gold belt that had meant so much to me once upon a time. But now I was galloping beyond that. Beware the dark horse!

We ended a terrific match with some classic Foundation. With the ref pushing me back into my corner, we turned our backs long enough for Jimmy to toss the half-dead Sags his crash helmet, which Sags then smashed beautifully over Anvil's head. Then he pulled an equally blown-up Knobbs across Anvil's chest as he rolled under the bottom rope. By the time I stepped out on the apron the ref was diving down for the count, one . . . two . . . see ya, Jim!

Exhausted, I stood at the back curtain watching Warrior summon some mystical power to beat Macho Man, with the help of his new heel valet, Scary Sherri Martel. But up in the crowd tiny Miss Elizabeth left her seat, climbed into the ring and with superhuman strength hurled the robust Sherrie over the top rope. Then she made up with Randy in the middle of the ring to a huge pop. Miss Elizabeth was truly a flower among the weeds.

As for Hogan and Slaughter, from where I stood they looked like two elephants tussling over a water hole. Slaughter barely tapped Hogan on the head with a steel folding chair, and Hogan bladed himself, but even with the blood the match was a hokey affair, with Hogan wagging his finger in Slaughter's face before the big boot and the leg drop. Same old story. Vince knew he needed a new one and he wasn't going to find it in Warrior, or Hogan.

The day after *WrestleMania VII* was Julie's birthday. We sat parked in a rented convertible looking out over Red Rock Canyon, just outside Las Vegas, sipping wine coolers in the warm breeze. The thousands of giant red boulders reminded me of a *Roadrunner* cartoon. We were relieved to have found some peace and quiet after six days in L.A. running around with so many Harts and a teething Blade. The night before he'd slept between us as we quietly whispered back and forth so as not to wake him. Then Blade sat up looking cranky, slapped me on the hand and then brought his fat little hand down right on Julie's forehead, as if to say, You two, keep it down, I'm trying to sleep! He rolled over and fell back asleep instantly. I laughed so hard I had to get up and leave the room.

I told Julie I thought that if I could have a good run for three years I could make enough money to pay off the house and come home for good. I loved Julie, but somehow I had turned into this—wrestler. On good days, she still saw me as her hero, but she was long past tired of having to share me with the wrestling business.

The next day at Vegas TVs, Pat asked me if I knew how to put on a scorpion death lock. I told him no, but that I could figure it out. So I went in search of a wrestler who could show me. The only one who knew was a Mexican named Konan. As I lay on my back he held the heels of my boots in his hands, threaded his leg between mine, stepped over me while crossing my legs and jammed one of my feet under his armpit, all while twisting me over like a Boston crab. This move looked great but was a total work in that it was damn near impossible to put on somebody unless he let you, or he was out cold.

After my match, as I looked out at the crowd, there were pink and black signs everywhere. The Hart Foundation music, now mine alone, thumped loudly as I strutted past the Gorilla position, the long table where Gorilla Monsoon sat wearing a headset sending the matches out. I passed by Vince, who looked more than impressed by my crowd reaction. I took a chance and asked, "So are you gonna give it to me or not?" He grinned playfully and said, "Yeah, I'm gonna give it to you."

The next day, in Reno, Pat handed me an interview sheet requiring me to do interviews for upcoming matches with Curt. I told him I'd pass unless they were planning to put the IC belt on me. Minutes later, in Vince's office, I counted on my fingers how many times he'd failed to come through with his promises. By the time I got to the eighth finger, Vince cut me off, chuckling, "Forget all about it. It's ancient history. Think about the future, Bret." I looked him in the eye and told him that history repeats itself over and over.

We both laughed like I was kidding, but I wasn't. Pat came in and interrupted us to tell me I had to come up with a name for my new finishing move. Between the three of us we tossed around different ideas until finally I threw out, " . . . executioner, eliminator, sniper, sharpshooter . . ."

"That's it!" Vince cut me off smiling. "I like that! Sharpshooter!"

I saw a glimmer in his eyes that told me if his head were made of glass I'd see all kinds of gears whirring around in it.

The next day Julie came with me on a tour to Japan. I was happy to see a familiar, smiling face waiting for us in the lobby of the hotel in Tokyo. Hito, bowlegged as ever, had moved back to Japan a few years earlier, after finishing up his career in Calgary. He was now oddly content running a profitable noodle shop left to him by his late sister. He kindly took Julie and me out for dinner and drinks, and we talked about old times. Hito spoke well of Owen and regarded Stu like he would a father.

The next day the WWF had me booked to reunite with Jim for one more tag team match in The Tokyo Egg Dome. There was no pressure on me whatsoever because I knew it would be nothing but easy working with The Rockers. Unfortunately, once we got out there, the serious Japanese fans didn't buy the phony rehearsed high spots. Just because there were sixty-something-thousand of them didn't mean that they weren't the same dead-pan Japanese fans. We took it up a notch, and it felt good hearing both Snuka and Valentine say afterwards that it was the best tag match they'd ever seen.

The main event pitted Hogan and a Japanese star named Tenyru against The Legion of Doom in a blood-filled orgy of gore that made no real sense, but at last got a reaction out of the lifeless crowd.

Most of the wrestlers were set to fly home the next day except for me, Earthquake and Hogan; we would take an early train to Osaka for one more show in Kobe. So after the show that night, Julie and I hit the heart of the Rapungi district, eventually winding up at the Hardrock Cafe, where various wrestlers fraternized with Madonna's road crew and with chain-smoking ring rats, who'd only sprung up in Japan in recent years. Julie had formed so many thoughts about Japan from what I'd told her about my previous trips she was thrilled to finally see it for herself. L.A., Vegas and Japan all in one trip was a far cry from being at home in the kitchen with the kids.

After my match in Kobe, an anxious Earthquake asked my advice on what he should do about being openly challenged by the equally massive Koji Kitao, a sumo sensation now trying to make a name for himself as a pro wrestler. Quake was big John Tenta, a four-hundred-pound mountain of a man who shook the ground when he walked and hailed from Surrey, B.C. He had been the Canadian amateur super heavyweight champion, and had enjoyed short-lived notoriety in Japan in earlier days as a white sumo wrestler, where he was undefeated. I really didn't know what to tell him. Quake sat there simmering and aggravated, concerned about what he might do if Kitao got him mad enough; his only real worry was that someone might jump in on their match. When Hogan and I both assured him that we'd watch his back, it seemed to calm him considerably.

The two big men circled each other furiously, like Rhodan and Godzilla, huffing and puffing, sometimes drawing close enough to take swipes at each other. The spectator's faces wore perfectly frozen looks of horror like you'd see in those old Japanese monster movies—the only thing missing were the shrieking sound effects! Finally Kitao put his tail between his legs and backed down to catcalls from the crowd, then slunk back to his dressing room knocking and smashing things as he went. I felt like announcing over the PA, Rhodan is dead, you people can go back to your homes!

Quake came back grinning from ear to ear. Hogan and I patted him on the back. "You showed 'em!" I beamed. I always thought it was a funny little fight, especially since they never once touched each other!

While Hogan got ready for his match, he asked me what Vince was doing with me. I considered Terry a friend so I told him where I stood. I was surprised to hear him say, with a hurt look on his face, that Vince was trying to bring him down; his WWF deal was up soon and he told me that Ted Turner's WCW was interested in him. It was easy for me to see that Terry liked his ovation that night because it showed Vince that Hogan could always go back to

Japan, that maybe the WWF needed Hulk Hogan more than he needed them. But, as he confided to me, Terry really didn't want to go anywhere

Vince had one more jerk-around in store for me. In May he announced that he'd changed his mind and was putting me back with Jim. Three weeks later, after much worry on my part, I was summoned to see Vince at the Sacramento TVs, where he did another about-face: I'd be taking the Intercontinental belt from Curt at *SummerSlam* at Madison Square Garden, just like I'd figured out back in April. I remembered that day in 1979 when Hito told me Vince McMahon said I didn't have a big enough name to wrestle in Madison Square Garden. As I left Vince's office, I felt a deep sense of pride and accomplishment. The Intercontinental belt was the first step in my far-off dream of being the WWF world champion.

Steroids were about to give the WWF a different sort of jab in the ass. On June 27, Dr. George T. Zahorian III was convicted by a jury in Harrisburg, Pennsylvania, of four counts of distributing anabolic steroids to a body-builder who was working as an undercover informant for the FBI, four counts of distributing large quantities of schedule III and IV controlled sub-stances to the same informant, four counts of distributing anabolic steroids to four professional wrestlers between November 1988 and March 1990 and two counts of using his office condominium, valued at $3.7 million, to facil-itate the distribution of controlled substances. The condo was immediately seized by the U.S. government.

Zahorian maintained throughout his trial that as a physician to various wrestlers he'd done nothing wrong by providing steroids, which he said were necessary considering the physical demands inherent in pro wrestling. His lawyer argued that as a physician Zahorian should be allowed to pro-vide steroids for performance enhancement, and Zahorian testified that he was unaware of a law that had gone into effect in November, 1988, banning the sale of steroids for anything other than the treatment of disease. Zahorian was set to be sentenced in about two months: he faced a maxi-mum of forty-four years in prison and $3 million in fines.

During the Zahorian case, investigators found FedEx waybills that linked shipments from Zahorian directly to the homes of several wrestlers, including Hogan, as well as to Vince at his new monolithic office building in Stamford, Connecticut. During the trial, Zahorian described Hogan as already having a serious steroid abuse problem when the two first met in 1984, and he admitted to dispensing steroids to fifteen to twenty wrestlers at an average TV taping.

What had started the Feds looking at Zahorian in the first place and whether they'd been after Zahorian himself or had simply used him as a stepping stone to try to get to McMahon, no one knew. The fact is that prior to the Zahorian indictment, Superstar Billy Graham and Bruno Sammartino had made negative comments about the WWF to the media and the Feds, claiming that ninety-five per cent of WWF wrestlers were abusing steroids. Zahorian's testimony confirmed that. Graham had become severely crippled in recent years, and he blamed it on steroid abuse, painting himself as an unfortunate guinea pig from a time when the dangers of steroids were not known. He said he was speaking out to save a new generation of wrestlers from ending up in a wheelchair like he did. The media circled the scandal like sharks in a feeding frenzy.

As soon as Zahorian was found guilty, Vince called a meeting to let his wrestlers know that starting in a just a few weeks he would voluntarily implement a drug testing policy even stricter than the one used for Olympic athletes: Everyone had to get off the juice. He made it clear that this time it would be impossible to cheat because there would be *two* people watching you piss in a cup.

In June 1991, I had started writing a weekly column for the *Calgary Sun* about the wrestling life, and the first one also promoted the WWF card for the upcoming Stampede Week. TVs were going to be in Calgary and Edmonton during the 1991 Calgary Stampede. I expected Vince would figure that Calgary was the perfect place to start making me a star. I couldn't help but ask myself what I would do if Vince really did come through with my big push and I didn't make it. What if my self-perceptions were wrong and I didn't get over like I always believed I would? Although I thought I was over, I didn't really know, and I'd be heartbroken if I found out otherwise right there in my hometown of Calgary.

Pulling up to the Saddledome I could see the Pavilion and was flooded with memories; but Stampede Wrestling was no more. Foley was dead. Schultz and Dynamite were finished for good. Bad News, thank God, had been put out to pasture like a mean old bull. Bruce and Jim were still holding on to faint hope. The only two Stampede boys still really running were Davey and me. That night as I walked out to my music I was blown away by the thundering response. It touched me in a way that said, You hang in there, Bret Hart. You show 'em you're the best!

After the tapings, Stu and Helen invited Vince and all the boys to Hart house for homemade corned beef sandwiches and beer. Davey Boy asked The Nasty Boys to stay over at Stu's house, intentionally misleading Sags, who was severely allergic to cats, by telling him that Stu had got rid of them all. Sags soon started sneezing and broke into a rash and was forced to flee.

Vince arrived with Pat, Howard Finkel, Terry Garvin and a black ring announcer named Mel Phillips. Mel was something of a whipping boy for all of them, and before long Vince and Pat were doing everything they could to get Stu to stretch him in the dungeon. Stu thought they only wanted to make fun of Mel, and at first he wouldn't go for it.

A couple of months earlier, on a bus ride somewhere in Europe, Mike Tomay, a rookie referee, made the mistake of confiding to Jacques Rougeau that one night when he shared a room with Mel Phillips he was awakened by Mel straddling him buck naked at the foot of his bed and sucking hard on his big toe!

"Then what happened?" Jacques asked.

Mike said, "I told him I didn't like it and to stop, and he did."

Between fits of laughter Jacques told everybody on the bus. Of course none of us could stop laughing either. When we got back to the States I had little choice but to immortalize the incident on the blackboard, adding Mel to the long-standing, ever-changing orgy with Princess Tomah and Chief. Mic in hand and still wearing his announcing tuxedo, Mel Phillips hung by his lips from Chief's big toe! This was a big hit with the boys, so I drew it everywhere for a while.

After an hour of prodding from Vince and Pat, Stu was finally persuaded to get his hooks on Mel. From the kitchen, we could hear sharp screams followed by giddy laughter and grunting coming from downstairs. I hurried down to find Mel stripped down to his undershirt, slacks and socks, and inquired whether he wanted Stu to show him how to put on a flying toe hold. Neither Vince nor Pat wanted to get too close: Stu stretching either one of them would have been a beautiful thing to watch, and they knew it. Stu let Mel off easily enough, climbing off him like a forgiving spider. It turned out to be a wonderful evening for everyone, except maybe for Mel Phillips.

By mid-July the latest WWF crisis was an interview that Hogan did on *The Arsenio Hall Show* in which he flat-out lied and looked bad doing it. I was embarrassed hearing him say he'd never taken steroids, except once for an injury. If he'd been honest, it's likely we'd never have heard another word about it. But now the media was all over Hogan, calling him a hypocrite because he had always preached to kids that they could be like him by saying their prayers and taking their vitamins. Reminiscent of Tricky Dick Nixon, Hogan would find out that it's the lie that'll bring you down.

A few days after the interview, Hogan told me that Vince had given him direct orders that he was never to admit to taking steroids, so he had no choice but to lie. I never bought that: Nobody should be able to make you lie about something so obvious. If it's true that Vince told him to lie, it shows the extent of Vince's influence.

When I thought about myself and steroids, it occurred to me that all the commotion might actually benefit me. Compared to the rest of them I was relatively clean.

On August 10 in Des Moines, I posed for pictures with the Intercontinental belt, which I hadn't even won yet, for the cover of the November issue of the WWF's monthly magazine. I'd never known Vince to cancel a magazine cover yet, so it was a great sign that nothing was going wrong this time.

That same day, Vince called all the wrestlers to a meeting where he introduced Dr. Mauro Pasquale, a world-renowned expert on drug testing. Vince was caught off guard to find that most of the wrestlers were vehemently opposed to the drug testing; he didn't seem to realize that a lot of the guys were physically addicted to steroids.

When the angry wrestlers called him on whether the bodybuilders in his fledgling World Bodybuilding Federation would be tested—men who had guaranteed contracts and medical benefits that the wrestlers still didn't have, paid for with revenue generated by the wrestlers—Vince swore that in his bodybuilding federation no one would be on steroids. It seemed ridiculous to me that Vince thought clean bodybuilders could compete with steroid freaks.

At the meeting, the wrestlers were told that they would have six weeks to wean themselves, and that then Dr. Pasquale would ensure that every wrestler in the WWF had acceptable testosterone levels. If you failed a test, it would be three strikes and you're out. It was tough for many of the steroid freaks to decide what was more important, their jobs or their 'roids.

My matches with Curt Hennig remind me of those Spy vs. Spy cartoons in *Mad Magazine*. We were comparable in age, size and background, and we had a similar look, except that Curt's mane was long, blond and curly. Both of us were second-generation wrestlers whose fathers were respected men in a tough business; we shared an understanding of what it was like to fill their shoes. But until I saw Curt in the locker room before the show August 26, 1991, at Madison Square Garden, I'd been anxious: The rumour was that he wouldn't show because his back was too messed up. In fact his injury was bad enough that he'd been forced to do nothing all summer long but fish.

Aware that this match could end up being Curt's last one, I wanted to give him the best send off I could. He told me he'd been unable to do much to get ready and he trusted me to take care of him out there. It was a big night for me, with Stu, Helen, Bruce, Julie and my kids in the audience.

Curt had put on a little weight from not working for over two months and his back was tight. Often during the match he winced from jarring spasms. I made myself as humanly light as possible to help Curt, who gave all he had. I could actually see my mom and dad looking on from the front row of the first loge. If there was ever chemistry between two wrestlers, there was none better than that between me and Curt, who insisted that night that I kick out of his finish, the Perfectplex, something he had never done for anyone else. Going into the finish, when I was on the mat selling, Perfect pulled me to the middle of the ring, parted my legs and dropped his leg across my groin. Then he rolled backward smartly to his feet, parted my legs and went for it again, but as his leg dropped across my stomach I wrapped it with mine, hooking him into the sharpshooter from my back. I twisted to my stomach and pushed myself up to a standing position with the crowd right behind me thunderously chanting, "Let's go, Bret!" Before I could even hold the pose long enough for Perfect to submit properly, Hebner rang the bell. In the aftermath, it was Curt's idea that I should rip his blue singlet off and wear it over my shoulder like a battle trophy. I kissed the Intercontinental belt before I held it up over my head and paraded to all four corners, standing on the second rope bull-horning the crowd with my fingers, something I'd do for the rest of my career.

When I left the ring I took the short steps up to shake Stu's hand and hug my mom, with the cameras following me. I'd never seen my mom this happy. It was as though she'd finally made peace with the darn wrestling business, after all these years. Stu looked so proud: Here he was, forty-five years later, back at MSG, that good-looking kid from Edmonton with the virgin ears and his cute little girlfriend from Long Beach. He grinned and clapped, nudging my mom to join in, but she couldn't have been clapping any harder.

The only sour note for me was that Julie missed the match because she'd gone shopping. By the time I got to the hotel, she was inexplicably in a bad mood. As had become a pattern at every pay-per-view I ever brought her to, we launched into an ugly, heated quarrel, for reasons I've never understood. I ended up celebrating the biggest moment of my career so far at the Hardrock Cafe with Jade, Dallas and Bruce, who sat picking at his burger as though somebody had hit him over the head with a sledge hammer. He was deeply worried because back at home Andrea had been rushed to the hospital in premature labour. Every time I brought Bruce down, something went wrong, and I felt horrible for him.

I flew home from *SummerSlam* with Julie and the kids and found out when we arrived that Andrea had given birth to a baby boy who they named Rhett. He was so sickly that it didn't look like he was going to pull through. The whole Hart family became gravely consumed with little Rhett fighting for his life.

26

"YOU'RE OVER, BROTHER!"

As PART OF THE ONGOING WAR with Ted Turner, that November Vince pulled off a coup, wooing Ric Flair to his team, along with the actual WCW Champion belt, which Ric brought with him like a captured flag. I would face Flair for the first time at the New Haven TVs on November 13, and I was looking forward to finding out whether he was the best worker in the business, as all the marks and wrestling commentators generally declared. Flair was what my Dad called a "routine man," because he did the same match every night no matter who he worked with. He also liked to call every step of the match with little input from me.

For a guy nearing fifty he was in great shape. Ric took his usual bumps and cut a blistering pace. When we talked before the match, he had suggested a finish that called for me to do a flying tackle where he'd catch me and stagger backward with the two of us toppling over the top rope only to be counted out for the finish, which would be a double DQ. It was a simple move that I'd done countless times with less skilled wrestlers, but at the end of the match, when I dove into Flair, he stood too far from the ropes, mistimed it, and didn't have the strength to catch me, so we fell down in a heap! On the spot Ric came up with a makeshift finish that, not surprisingly, benefited him and not me. I wasn't going to make a big deal out of it, but back in the dressing room, I was annoyed to hear Flair crying to me about what happened on the finish, implying that I had screwed up. He showed me, right then and there, that he wasn't as great as he was supposed to be. I'd heard there were a lot of wrestlers who didn't trust or like Flair, and I was starting to see why.

On December 3, I was in San Antonio, which I loved because I got to visit the Alamo and I always stayed at the historic Crockett Hotel right next door. After having a decent match with a relatively new arrival named Skinner on a one-time-only pay-per-view called *Tuesday in Texas*, I zipped over to the airport in a rented Mustang convertible to pick up Owen, who'd flown in from Germany. I'd suggested to Vince that he could team Owen with Jim and call them The New Foundation, and Vince had gone for it. I was in a great mood as I pulled up to the terminal and spotted him waiting for me curbside with a big smile. I hadn't seen him for over a year.

Most of the wrestlers were meeting at a strip bar after the show, one of our regular hangouts in San Antonio, and as we drove over there Owen told me that things had gone well for him in Germany and that Martha was expecting their first child in March. He was happy to be back in the WWF and said he thought he could work well with Jim. I told him Jim was thrilled about it too. Jim was thrilled in general: he had finally won his settlement from U.S. Air, a whopping US$380,000. Owen asked me for advice on how to handle Jim, and I told him that I'd tried just about everything but that in the end it was reverse psychology that worked best.

He shook his head as he told me how unbelievably over I was in Germany. I could tell it also meant something to him that I had the Intercontinental belt. We talked about home, about losing and missing Dean and about Rhett's struggle in the hospital.

The previous day I'd been to El Paso, where some buddies I called Cheech and Chong had given me a giant baggie filled with Mexican dirt-weed. So, of course it figures that before the tapings in San Antonio, Vince called a meeting to inform all the wrestlers that in a few weeks drug testing would be expanded to cover any and all non-prescription drugs, including marijuana. Vince said that with the FBI and the media waiting to pounce on him, the WWF couldn't take a chance on another scandal. I believed, and still do, that Vince's decision was short-sighted. With weed taken off the menu, even more wrestlers wound up as alcoholics; instead of smoking a bit of weed holed up in their hotel rooms talking about the business, they roamed hotel bars drunk and on downers.

I handed a big, fat joint to Owen and explained that it was probably the last time we'd be able to smoke pot for a while. Owen, so strait-laced most of the time, let his hair down, and we both took a few hits. We pulled up to the strip bar feeling good.

Inside, a bunch of wrestlers crowded around Hulk at the far end of the room. Beefcake was there, having recovered enough from the parasailing accident to come back for limited duty. Unfortunately, with steel plates holding his face together, he could no longer wrestle in a serious capacity. Standing off to the side were Hawk, Animal, Curt, Bossman and Ray Hernandez, a muscle-bound Tampa powerhouse who worked a Hercules gimmick. I introduced Owen around, spotted Jim and Davey at a table, and ordered beers for us all.

Vince came in around midnight. That was unusual enough because Vince didn't make a habit of hanging out with the boys. But what really turned heads was that Vince was shit-faced, his tie hanging loosely around his neck. Pat Patterson tagged behind him trying to persuade him that it was a bad idea to be there in his condition, but Vince had decided that he was going to have one last party with the boys before the new drug policy went into effect. Sergeant Slaughter offered to keep an eye on him and act as his designated driver, so Pat fled through the front door, as though he'd been chased out by the sight of all those naked women.

Then I heard Hogan daring a wild-eyed Hawk into doing the L.O.D. finish on Vince right there in the bar. Suddenly Animal crouched behind Vince, stuck his head between Vince's legs and picked him up off the floor. Vince was laughing as Animal walked him over to all of us. Hawk had already climbed up on the bar, gripping a stripper pole, assuring Hulk that he was going to take Vince's head off. I thought, Wow, he's actually going to do it, but at the last second Hawk thought better of it and leapt off the table, gently hitting Vince with his arm. Hulk and Beefcake caught Vince and set him on his feet to a round of golf claps from an assortment of ass-kissers who seemed to materialize on cue. I rolled my eyes at Jim, who boldly declared, "The Hart Foundation would have had the balls to do it!"

"Damn right!" I had a beer in one hand and a shot of J.D. in the other, but was conscious enough to think, My God, what did I just say? Owen's eyes got big. I considered running out of the place as I watched a determined Jim nonchalantly pick up a grinning Vince like he was jokingly hugging him. The boys parted before me, and Hulk stared as if there was no way I had the balls to do it. I set my drinks down and before I could even think about it I leapt high in the air clotheslining Vince with a thud! His head bounced off the carpeted floor, his skinny neck stretched out like a turtle's. There we both were lying on our backs, and I thought, What have I done?

"You owe me a drink, Hitman!" Vince drunkenly slurred.

"Don't worry, I'm buying."

"Double Dewars on ice."

We tossed them down.

Last call came and went and the lights came up, but nobody was leaving. Davey had Vince over his shoulders and was running around looking for a place to powerslam him! The police were called to clear us all out. With Owen and an assortment of strippers in my car, we joined a train of about thirty cars about to head downtown for a party in Flair's penthouse suite at the Marriott. The procession couldn't get by a police cruiser, parked in front of the strip bar, so Slaughter, with his big chin sticking out, burned the rubber off his tires as he pushed the cop car to the side of the road.

At about 3 a.m., the drunken mob descended upon a young male desk clerk to call Flair's room. No answer, so Vince demanded a key. The flustered clerk said it was against hotel policy, but Vince cut him off. "I'm Vince McMahon. Give it to me right now!" He got the key.

We all packed into the elevators and headed up to the fortieth floor. We piled into Flair's room, waking Earl Hebner, the referee, who was asleep on a rollaway bed. Flair hadn't yet returned from his own night of misadventure, so we made ourselves at home. It was a beautiful suite with a full-sized bar, but the bar was stocked with only one full bottle of vodka. The party was about to die when a bag of dirt-weed mysteriously appeared and joints were rolled and lit. I saw first-hand what the boys thought of Flair when everybody used his king-sized bed as a urinal, even Vince, stripped down to his boxers, black shoes and socks, and his tie. I remember Hercules and Curt laughing as they hosed it down, and for some reason, I thought nobody would have done this to Harley Race!

Then Vince got it in his head to have some fun amateur wrestling with us. When he came for me I was careful and playful with him, as was Curt. Then Vince took Hawk down and pinned him to the floor. When he grabbed Herc, Herc hurled Vince upside down into the air, but Vince somehow bounced off Earl's rollaway and landed on his feet. Vince gave Herc a sober glance that said, In the morning, if I can remember any of this, I'll fire you! (In fact, only days later Herc was released.)

Then Vince sized up Jim: "Ya big rhino, you're the only guy I haven't tried yet!" Jim twisted the tip of his beard and asked Vince whether he'd ever seen that scene in Die Hard where Bruce Willis tackles some villain and they both fall forty floors down to the lobby. Vince nervously glanced at the window knowing that Jim was crazy and drunk enough to do something like that. He decided to leave Jim alone.

By sunrise Flair still hadn't made it to his own party, and I was drunk and leaning on a stripper as she helped me get my room key in the door at the Crockett Hotel.

That morning everybody had to drive up to Austin for the second day of TVs. Vince was red-eyed and red-faced, still clearly feeling the effects of his wild night. In his office I told him that he could hold his head up high for having the balls to hang with the boys for one last hurrah. And then I promptly went out and drew a big blackboard cartoon of Vince in his boxers pissing in Flair's bed. It broke everybody up, especially Vince!

A few days later, Owen and I boarded a plane at LAX to go home. I took my usual seat toward the back of the cabin, where I found myself surrounded by an all-girl basketball team out of Chino, California. I was trying to read but was pleasantly distracted by their loud chant: "Who rocks the house? The Hitman rocks the house!" I lowered my book and they gathered around, flirting and telling me they'd voted me the best-looking guy on the plane. I looked over at Owen and he just smiled and shook his head.

We had Sunday dinner up at Hart house three days before Christmas. My mom was still worried about Rhett, who was a long way from being out of the woods. Hart grandkids scurried about the old house, and I wondered whether Rhett would ever be able to race around like them. It warmed my heart to see both my mom and dad smile when they passed me the current issue of *Alberta Report* magazine, which called me the most famous Albertan in the world.

The following night I fell asleep next to Dallas in his bed, only to be woken by an angry little voice calling out in the dark, "Dad! Dad! Dad!" It was Blade. Julie and I reached him at the same time, at the top of the big stairs. He'd noticed I wasn't in my bed and thought I'd left like I always did. I felt a pang in my heart hearing him crying out for me. His tears stopped as soon as I scooped him up, and as I held him close I felt his heart beating fast. But on Christmas Day I was gone again.

On December 30, Roddy pulled me aside at the building in Bangor to tell me that he had some big news: Vince had told him that I'd be losing the IC belt to Jacques Rougeau, who now cartooned as The Mountie (the real RCMP had threatened to charge him with impersonating an officer, which grabbed a few headlines across Canada). My heart sank into the pit of my stomach as Roddy explained the angle: I'd supposedly come down with the flu, and despite gallantly trying to defend the IC belt against The Mountie, he'd beat me for it. Then Roddy would fill in for me two days later at the *Royal Rumble*, challenging The Mountie to an IC title match, and Roddy would win. After that, he'd drop the IC belt back to me at *WrestleMania VIII*. Roddy said he was giving me advance warning so I'd be prepared when Vince told me at the next TVs.

I hauled my stomach out of my boots: Yes, I was losing the belt, but if Roddy put me over at *WrestleMania VIII*, it would be the biggest thing to ever happen to me.

The big contest coming up at the *Royal Rumble* would be Ric Flair against Macho Man. Flair had been working around the United States against Hogan, still wearing WCW's World Title belt and calling himself the real world champion. To this day I don't know why Flair didn't have more consideration for his old colleagues still struggling in WCW. For Vince it was a chance to stick his thumb in the eye of Ted Turner, but Flair had to know how much the use of their belt would hurt his former wrestler colleagues at the WCW. Vince decided that the winner of *Royal Rumble* 1992 would automatically become WWF world champion, and the boys assumed it was Flair whom Vince had pinned his hopes on to carry the territory, at least until the WWF's legal woes cooled off. I thought that if Flair won our belt, it would give too much credibility to WCW. The wrestling talent in the two outfits was comparable, but Vince's camera crew and post-production work were light years ahead of WCW's—which is saying something, because WCW did have Turner Broadcasting behind it.

A week later, Vince finally told me about his plan for me to lose the IC belt and win it back. He also said that sometime in the fall I'd drop it to Shawn Michaels. He asked me whether I had any problem with that and I told him, no, that I had a lot of respect for Shawn. Thanks to Roddy's heads up, I was able to tell Vince that his plan for me sounded terrific. He seemed relieved.

So, on January 17, in Springfield, Massachusetts, I walked out to the ring looking as sick as I could and dropped the IC belt to The Mountie. Despite knowing where it was all leading, I flew home feeling dejected about missing *Royal Rumble* and the payoff that would have come with it. My only consolation was a rare weekend off.

As if all the bad press about steroids in the WWF wasn't enough, now allegations began to emerge about gay management preying on vulnerable teenaged boys in the ring crew. At one time or another most of us had seen Terry Garvin hanging around these young men, but none of us knew what, if anything, went on behind Garvin's closed door. Then a former member of the ring crew, Tom Cole, came forward in the *San Diego Union-Tribune* with the alleged details. Vince was doing all he could to contain the scandal.

On February 16, we worked at Long Island's Nassau Coliseum. Jim wasn't expecting that there'd be a drug test, but there was. All evening long he stalled Chief and the pecker checkers by saying he was simply unable to pee. He also refused to put over one of The Beverley Brothers, a new team, and left the building that night having never taken the test. Vince was already pissed off with Jim because he hadn't paid him back for footing the legal bill in the U.S. Air suit, despite winning a big settlement. The next day at Tampa TVs, Jim was summoned to see an irritable Vince, who curtly fired him. Jim slammed the door behind him and went looking for Chief. When he found him, he grabbed a TV monitor and hurled it at Chief's head like a shot put. When Chief ducked, it hit a WWF television director in the leg. Then Jim burned rubber out of the parking lot.

With Jim gone, they threw Owen together with Koko B. Ware (who had been hired back after his European misadventures) and renamed the team

High Energy. Despite it being a lame idea, Owen stayed upbeat and full of that supposed high energy as he and Koko tried to get over as best they could. On the bright side, Martha gave birth to a baby boy. They named him Oje, which was Owen's nickname when he was a baby.

On March 4, as a result of the allegations of sexual misconduct, Pat Patterson, Terry Garvin and Mel Phillips all resigned, though none of them admitted to having done anything wrong. Vince and Bruno Sammartino ended up debating the whole sorry mess on *Larry King Live*. It was too late to nail that closet door shut, and all sorts of people who'd ever had any kind of a falling out with Vince suddenly brought out their own stories of sexual improprieties.

If I was looking for a vote of confidence, I got it at the HoJo's in Boston—from Harley Race. The WCW was in town, and as both crews of wrestlers hung out in the bar that night, the WCW boys hovered around the WWF ring rats like they were in paradise.

Harley had found his footing again as a heel manager to a colossal, red-headed monster of a man named Vader, who wore a red leather mask that looked more like a jockstrap. Vader was now WCW world champion and one of the biggest names in Japan too. I admired Harley, having battled back from divorce, intestinal surgery, a bad boating accident and bankruptcy to land a good contract with WCW. I was grateful when he pulled me aside, ordered me a beer—he no longer drank—and asked me whether I had plans to leave Vince any time soon. I told him I'd be crazy to leave now, especially since WCW hadn't been very professional in their dealings with me thus far. Still I sat listening quietly as Harley told me of WCW's plans to make a serious run at Vince, using Turner's money. The timing was perfect, he said, for me to land a big fat contract: "Bret, you're the best damn worker in the business now." That was an amazing thing for a man as respected as Harley to say. I told him I'd keep his idea in mind, but the weird thing was that I was actually beginning to sympathize with Vince a little.

Vince had been as cold and ruthless as a man could be, and it was now as though his harsh treatment of his wrestlers had finally caught up with him. I'd been in the WWF for seven and a half years, and in all that time I'd never seen Vince have anything whatsoever to do with what Terry Garvin and Mel Phillips were now suspected of. And the crippling accusations that he "pushed" steroids on his wrestlers seemed opportunistic. Vince made it clear that he liked his wrestlers to have good physiques, but that how you went about achieving that was your own decision. It seemed to me that all Vince was guilty of was looking the other way, but in that regard he didn't seem any different than the owner of any major sports franchise, or the Olympic committee, for that matter.

And Vince was the man who had brought pro wrestling out of smoky halls and small arenas and made it into family entertainment that crossed age, economic, gender and national boundaries. We were now heroes, with our own action figures. Not only was it good for the fans but, even with the merciless schedule and being treated as a disposable commodity, the life I led now beat nickel-and-dime payoffs and travelling packed like a sardine in a frigid van with the sting of fresh gig marks carved into my forehead. If Vince went down, where would any of us be then? Sure, there were a lot of legitimate gripes, but I wished the energy that went into concocting far-fetched accusations could have gone into solving some real issues.

I spent my four days off drawing a poster-sized montage of every WWF wrestler I could think of as a special send-off gift for Hulk. By all indications he'd be riding into the sunset after *WrestleMania VIII*, heading for Hollywood. With his reputation as a hero to kids severely damaged and a ton of money in the bank, I didn't think he'd be back. Hogan off steroids would leave him looking much too mortal. To me Hulk, like Vince, had taken the business to its highest peaks, and seeing Hulk fading out without any glory seemed wrong.

Stu, Helen, Georgia, Julie and all the kids came to Indianapolis for *WrestleMania VIII*. Julie bitched constantly once she arrived, trying her hardest to ruin the entire experience for me. The higher my career went the more my marriage bottomed out: Julie acted as if she resented my popularity. The night before *WrestleMania VIII* we wound up in a bar near the hotel with my red-headed Italian fan-turned-friend Carlo, who'd come down from Toronto. Vince's son Shane walked in—he was on the road doing various jobs, setting up the ring and refereeing, learning the business so that someday he could take over the reins from his dad. I'd always done my best to watch out for him, and he liked me for it. As he approached, a startled Julie jolted toward me. When he greeted me with a handshake, I smiled and said, "Let me introduce you to my wife." Shane turned beet red. There was an awkward silence. Julie seemed furious—and I had no idea why. Carlo whispered, "He just goosed Julie big time!" Obviously Shane hadn't had a clue who she was. Shane quickly took a stool at the other end of the bar. I was inclined to forget it, but when I looked over at him, I noticed he was studying me with puzzled defiance. I thought, Okay, he knows I know what he did and thinks that since his daddy owns me, I won't do anything. He was wrong.

Because it was the night before a big match, I wasn't drinking. And Julie's foul mood had made me even more testy. I slammed my boss's kid against the wall, telling him through clenched teeth that if he ever touched my wife again, I'd rip his head off. I never would have hurt him, but I had to let him know I wasn't afraid of who he was. Then Carlo pried me away, Shane still protesting his innocence.

The next day all the Harts crammed into a black stretch limo to go to my big match with Roddy. Stu was up front with my mom, and all of the rest of us were squeezed in back as fans screamed and surrounded the car. Blade, who was wearing a black miniature version of my ring jacket, looked like a tiny replica of me and was laughing hard as he slapped his little hands on the window. Beans told me she didn't want "Rolly Pepper" to hurt me. She never liked watching me get beat up. Jade was nine now and still riding herd on Dallas, who was at that age where he was starting to suspect that wrestling might not be real. I hoped they could forgive me, someday, for being gone so much. As the limo pulled away everybody was as excited as I was about my big match with Roddy—except for Julie.

Backstage at the Hoosier Dome, I passed around the drawing I'd done for Hulk and made sure every wrestler signed it before I gave it to him. Hulk loved it. I wondered whether he'd ever be back.

As I put on my gear, it dawned on me that I didn't get nervous for matches any more. Even this one, where Roddy and I had planned that we were going to go against Vince's policy just this once. I was going to get a little juice: our babyface match desperately needed it if we were going to steal the show. In a toilet stall I carefully snipped and taped up my blade. With 68,000 fans in attendance and hundreds of thousands more watching at home on pay-per-view with VCRs going, four WWF cameras, not to mention all the wrestlers, I'd have to be a real pro to make the blood look accidental.

When Roddy and I came nose to nose in the ring for the opening stare down, I had to look away or else I'd have cracked up. We'd worked a shoot, and the fans believed this match would be like no other, especially since The Hitman and Roddy Piper had never really worked before.

The story built slowly, the wily veteran and the hungry kid giving no quarter. When the time was right the ref stopped me and told me to fix my loose shoelace. While I leaned over to tuck it into my boot, Roddy blindsided me with a fist to the face, and I crumpled to the mat, covering up to spit the blade out of my mouth. Roddy kicked me several times in the face, never touching me. I cut a one-inch slice right over my right eyebrow, deep enough to convince all the boys afterwards that it was the real deal or risk being exposed. At first the blood was barely noticeable, but soon my face was a mess.

Soon enough, a crazed Piper had knocked the referee down and stood over me holding the ring bell high over his head as he prepared to brain me like a seal hunter delivering the final blow. He hesitated while I groped and clawed my way to my knees. With my head covered in blood, I gave Roddy my baby-seal eyes. Roddy expertly milked it. Feigning a change of heart, he seemed to come to his senses just long enough to toss the bell out to the timekeeper in disgust. Pulling me to my feet, he blasted me with a punch. I leaned and swung back at him with a desperate, wild blow that he easily ducked under as he clamped me in his finishing move, the sleeper. The captivated crowd was hanging on every move. I spun toward the corner flailing for the top rope, but my escape was just out of grasp and I began to sink. Supported by Roddy I jumped up and kicked off the top corner pad, knocking us both backwards with all my weight, crashing on top of Roddy, who couldn't use his arms to break his fall. It had to hurt, the way we landed with a thud!

I rolled backward holding his elbows tight. Piper was pinned beautifully. The ref came back to life on cue for the one . . . two . . . three! With the crowd cheering loudly, Roddy gave me a hug, and I told him, "Thanks, cuz, I'll never forget what you did for me today!" Roddy said, "I love ya, brother," and buckled the IC belt around my waist.

Now for the real work.

I came through the curtain pretending to be concerned that I was going to need stitches. Chief, Lanza and a bunch of the boys gathered around me to see how bad it was. Chief brushed my hair away, "Maybe a stitch, Stu, but you'll be all right." Roddy was there, concerned, apologizing, and we both knew we'd fooled them all.

Little did we know that Flair and Randy, who went on right after us, had secretly planned to get juice too. Flair was so obvious as he cut himself repeatedly that when he came back with several long, bloody cat scratches on his forehead, an angry Vince fined them each $500 for blading. He never said a word to me because he thought that mine was legit.

After *WrestleMania VIII* came three long days of TVs. My match with Piper not only stole the show, but many felt it saved the pay-per-view altogether. And so began my second reign as IC champion.

Four days later I was in Munich. I loved being back in Germany! As I rode on the bus down cobbled streets I listened to my Walkman thinking about how in 1936 Hitler watched in disgust as the black American runner Jesse Owens sprinted to win the gold medal at the Berlin Olympics. I thought back to 1981 and my old Hanover days, with Jim, when I was the biggest loser of the tournament. Well, Axel Dieter, you old pimp, take a look at me now!

Fans were pounding on the sides of the bus for blocks before we finally pulled up to the back of the arena, where an even bigger crowd excitedly waited for us. Owen had told me I was really big in Germany, and judging by all the signs being held up, it appeared to be true. When I stepped off the bus girls screamed and cried uncontrollably, some even fainting.

In the dressing room Chief told me I was the opening match. I argued that I was the Intercontinental champion and that as I understood it I was very popular in Germany so it was therefore crazy for me to be first match. But Chief had his orders, so I did go out first. I think I made my point though. As soon as I came out, my music blaring, the sellout crowd exploded. Teenaged girls overran barricades and leaped past security guards, who were helpless to stop them; they literally knocked me down, hugging and kissing me. I'd never seen or heard anything like it, not even for Hogan at the height of all his glory. Hulkamania was a phenomenon, but the reaction I got was more like Beatlemania! It wasn't just teenaged girls, there were older women too, and even men and boys reached out to me. Flowers flew at me from everywhere, and boxes of chocolates, wrapped gifts, and lots and lots of teddy bears! I gently pulled myself up, smeared with lipstick, and made my way through the crowd to the ring. I did my strut to all four sides, and the crowd exploded each time. When I dropped down to give my shades to a little girl, thousands of people sighed, ahhh.

As I got set to take on Dino Bravo, he said, "You're over, brother." They cheered for every move. As I sold, they chanted my name so loudly that I could barely hear myself think. When I beat Bravo, the place came totally unglued.

Leaving the building was another frenetic scene. An astounded Chief met me at the top of the ramp, "You were right, Stu. They love you! I've never seen anything like that—ever!" That night the hotel was overrun with Hitman fans, many of whom had camped out in the lobby.

In Dortmund it was worse, if that's any way to say it. I loved it!

The only other wrestler to get a huge response was The Undertaker, who was greeted everywhere we went by hundreds of kids dressed in black with rings under their eyes.

Then we stormed the U.K. In London, Birmingham, Sheffield and Glasgow the reception was as incredible as in Germany. As I'd predicted, Vince had stumbled onto a gold mine. American wrestling was huge in Europe, and all the WWF wrestlers were household names.

27

"LISTEN TO ME, AND I'LL CARRY YOU."

MAYBE IT WAS HAVING had a steady diet of adulation that caused me to stick my head up a little higher than I normally would when Vince called a meeting at TVs at the end of April. If anyone had anything they wanted to say, Vince offered, we should feel free to speak up. After a number of minor questions were posed, I put up my hand. Steroids had aided a lot of wrestlers in recuperating from injuries, I said, and now that we were all clean, maybe Vince could consider giving us a lighter schedule. Many of us were on the road three hundred days a year, and, in the dressing room, complaints about the gruelling pace were constant. Vince got annoyed at me and said, "If you can't handle it, then maybe you should consider doing something else."

"You told us to speak our minds, so that's what I'm doing."

Vince scowled across the room. "You're the only one complaining," he said. The unspoken reality in the room was that we were all working so hard for a lot less; Vince's beloved World Bodybuilding Federation was fast becoming a financial disaster, kept alive only by the proceeds from the WWF.

I looked around and asked, "Okay, everybody, who has a complaint about the schedule?" and raised my hand. Only Hawk and Knobbs raised theirs in support. The rest of the boys stared at their feet. I lowered my hand. All we ever did was complain, but it seems only to one another.

Typically, after the meeting, various wrestlers thanked me for speaking up, explaining that they hadn't joined in because they were scared to lose their jobs, as they had good reason to be. A lot of the steroid freaks were now missing from the roster, the latest casualty being Davey Boy, who had just that day got a six-week suspension for testing positive for steroids.

That night, while being interviewed by Mean Gene Okerlund, I did one of my first shoot interviews, in which the real Bret Hart talked through the Hitman character. "For all the times my father's been in my corner and for all the times that he's backed me up," I said, "I want to dedicate my IC title win to my dad. Happy seventy-seventh birthday!

This is for you!" Bending reality into my storylines was becoming a trade-mark of mine.

The birthday party was held a few days late, on May 5, so that Owen and I could make it. Ellie was up from Florida to surprise Stu, and they hadn't seen each other in a while. There was such joy in Stu's eyes when Ellie walked in.

If the stories were right, back in Tampa, Jim had a serious cocaine problem and was blowing all the money he'd won from his lawsuit, riding around on his brand-new Ninja motorcycle with what was left of his riches stuffed into his fanny pack. An exasperated Ellie had finally left him to his own undoing.

Rumour had it that Vince had big plans for *SummerSlam* 1992. J.J. Dillon, Vince's talent coordinator, whose job was basically doing Vince's dirty work when it came to fining, firing and delivering other bad news, let slip that the pay-per-view was possibly going to be in either Washington, D.C., or London, England. I went to see Vince. If he still wanted me to drop the belt to Shawn Michaels, I had an idea for that match that I wouldn't even tell him until he promised me that he'd never use it for anyone else. Vince agreed, so I told him about the concept of a ladder match. The more I told him the more he liked it.

Also, if *SummerSlam* was held in England, I suggested, why didn't I drop the IC belt to Davey there, and Davey could, in turn, drop it to Shawn shortly thereafter. The pop in the U.K. would be huge because Davey was a homeboy. Vince told me he liked both ideas. At the next TVs, he asked me to show him a ladder match. I could do it with Shawn, I said.

I rang Davey as soon as I left Vince's office to tell him, but he was so down about his suspension that he showed little enthusiasm. Even though it was three months away, the match with Davey soon became almost all I thought about, piecing it together move by move in my head. I'd kept an old but terrific finish of Leo Burke's tucked away in my head for just the right moment, and this would be it.

The bigger news hitting the dressing room was about Liz flying the coop on Randy. She'd apparently become fed up with Randy's controlling nature, and had gone into hiding. Randy was fluttering around like a broken-hearted peacock. He really loved her, maybe too much, and we all felt for him. To the best of my knowledge, he'd been true to her all these years. I remember envying Randy for being able to bring his pretty wife on the road, but in hindsight it seems to me that never being out of each other's sight contributed to the demise of their fairy-tale romance.

By the time I got to TVs in Hamilton, on June 1, it was official: *SummerSlam* would be at Wembley Stadium in London. Davey was back on the road, and Vince was going ahead with my idea to drop the IC belt to him.

A big black wrestler by the name of Charles Wright had just joined the WWF. He was bald and covered with tattoos; management gave him a voodoo gimmick and called him Papa Shango. That night in Hamilton, Vince started an angle between Shango and Warrior that was so cartoonish that it would have been funny except that it was evidence of one of the few times that Vince was embarrassingly off the mark. The fake blood and flash-paper fire were so phony that the fans laughed when it wasn't intended to be funny. Meanwhile Warrior was selling it to death. Clearly Vince was missing the balance that had come from Pat Patterson's contribution of wrestling smarts. Another perfect example of that loss of balance was Vince's idea to reunite The Legion of Doom with a ventriloquist's dummy named Rocco, which was supposed to be a long-lost childhood toy that had some kind of power to lead them on. The gimmick drove Hawk, in particular, crazy.

And there was Owen, making the very best of being tagged up with Koko, who clapped and sang like he was in a gospel revival tent. Owen danced and clapped along, smiling through clenched teeth, wearing ridiculous, baggy, fluorescent-green pants held up by suspenders, because it was better being a funky white boy than taking hip-tosses from old Germans.

Macho Man was the WWF world champion, and he was still working with Flair. Randy had been stuck with the big belt with the hope that he could carry a company that was sinking fast. At least he and Flair were having reasonable, credible matches, in contrast to Warrior and Shango. But nobody was over anything like Hulk, who was now doing TV commercials for Right Guard deodorant. It infuriated Vince that Hulk had cut him out of the deal. Hogan still remained the biggest name in wrestling, even when he was gone!

I managed to get back home for my thirty-fifth birthday. While I was home, Vince sent up a camera crew to shoot vignettes revolving around fictitious tension in the Hart family, which was part of the storyline to build heat for my match with Davey at *SummerSlam*. (Wembley Stadium was completely sold out—more than eighty thousand tickets went in less than ten hours!) In some of the vignettes my mom was portrayed as being so emotionally distraught by the family friction that she couldn't finish the interview; in others, Bruce was told to knock me for having a big ego, which he did a little too persuasively!

On July 20, I shot an angle with Papa Shango, and it wasn't anywhere near as phony as the voodoo angle he did with Warrior. Charles Wright was a tad green, but he was big, strong and eager to improve, and I was happy to help him any way I could.

The following day I arrived early at the building in Portland, Maine, to make sure that the fifteen-foot ladder for my match with Shawn Michaels could be climbed up on both sides and that it was sturdy and safe to work with.

I was dog tired. I'd been working hard to build up my cardio, and the three matches I'd wrestled the night before could only help, as long as I didn't get too beat up. Early that morning, I'd worked out at a local gym and was amazed to see Ric Flair blazing a trail on the Stairmaster next to me, despite being hungover from his usual night of hard drinking. Flair was easily one of the fittest wrestlers I have ever seen. As he sweated out his poisons, he didn't show any sign of slowing down.

Later on Shawn came and found me in the dressing room, scratching his head as he tried to figure out what this crazy idea of a ladder match was all about. I knew how successful this type of match had been in my dad's territory, and I could just imagine its potential in the WWF.

That night, Shawn and I put on a decent trial run. Unfortunately, Vince missed it.

After the TV taping there was the usual party atmosphere at the hotel, but I was careful not to indulge. As part of my training regimen leading up to *SummerSlam*, I cut back on drinking and late nights. Davey, however, had no trouble throwing them back. So we were all surprised the next morning when he was suddenly in severe agony. He'd injured his knee during his match the night before but the handful of Demerol he'd taken afterwards had numbed him enough to convince him he was okay. Then, in the wee hours of the morning, the drug wore off. Davey was rushed home to where he and Diana were living in Florida and ended up being off for the rest of the summer, which made me worry about our upcoming match — and about him.

A few days later, Owen also injured his knee; he would be out of action for the next few months.

As the summer slipped away, I spent my time training and working on another big cartoon drawing of all the wrestlers, this time for Vince. I couldn't help but feel indebted to him. I constantly phoned Davey down in Florida, but all Diana could tell me was that he was out with Jim somewhere. I finally tracked Jim down just hours before I was leaving for England and was shocked when he told me that he'd just taken Davey and Diana to the airport. Davey was high as a kite when he caught his flight, Jim said, because he'd been up all night smoking crack with him! Jim told me that Davey had a gorilla on his back and he was worried about him. I wished Jim would take a good look at himself.

I couldn't have been more disappointed in Davey, and feared he would end up making us both look bad. I remembered Vince asking me, back in Binghamton, if I was sure I could go on last in the main event.

"I can promise you nobody will be able to follow us!" I'd said. And when I asked Vince whether he wanted me to run the finish past him, he told me, "I don't want to know; surprise me." I'd never, ever heard him say that to anyone else before—or after—but now I truly had no idea what surprises the match was likely to have in store.

When I arrived in London, hundreds of fans poured out of the hotel lobby to chant my name in the streets. I set out to find Davey, but he was off somewhere with Diana and his family. I didn't see him until the required entrance rehearsal at Wembley stadium the night before the show. When I asked him why he hadn't returned my calls all summer, he wasn't able to look me in the eye. He fessed up that he'd been smoking crack with Jim for weeks and was now terrified. He'd gone back to being that same helpless kid I'd rescued from Dynamite ten years earlier.

"Trust me, Davey, and I'll do all I can to get you through tomorrow, okay?"

He nodded, and I sat him down for a crash course, going over and over our match and making him recite the moves back to me. It was now completely up to me to save our match.

The following day we arrived at Wembley early. The sun hid high in an overcast sky, but there was a collective sigh of relief because it looked like it wasn't going to rain.

Shortly before the show was to start I was summoned to a meet and greet with a room full of fans, most of whom had been given British Bulldog T-shirts as part of a promotional contest. There was one little boy wearing a Hitman T-shirt confidently arguing to some of Davey's grown-up supporters that I was going to win. As he held his dad's hand, he politely asked me whether I could give him my glasses when I came out. I tussled his hair and said, "If I can find you, they're yours."

In the dressing room Hawk gave me a sour smile as he casually popped three Placidyls into his mouth and hung his tongue out where they stuck just long enough for him to wash them down with black coffee—I guess Rocco the talking dummy was getting to him even more than I'd thought. Why anybody would do that was beyond me. I liked Hawk and sensed in that instant that he was at some personal breaking point on his own road to self-destruction.

Once the show started I worried and waited, fearing that the other wrestlers would run too long, leaving me and Davey with not enough time to tell our story. If we ran out of time, it would be my tough luck, since if

Davey beat me in a short match, it could ruin me in England. One positive note was that the referee was Gorilla's boy, Joey Morella, who, in my opinion, was the best WWF ref. I knew he'd do his best to help me communicate with Davey once we got out there.

I was amazed to see Hawk, who was nearly out on his feet, climb onto a rented Harley Davidson and wobble all the way out to the ring, behind Animal and their manager, Paul Ellering, who were also on bikes. Not that this should be recognized as some kind of amazing feat in itself, but the truth is that it was. Considering that he was barely conscious from bell to bell, the fact that Hawk—with the help of his opponents, Mike Rotundo and Ted DiBiase, and of Animal—somehow had a match, is a testament to all of them. But it mattered little, since Hawk upped and quit the next day, leaving Animal to fend for himself.

Warrior and Randy had a decent World title match, but their ongoing angle never made much sense and only got more convoluted when Ric Flair, managed by Mr. Perfect, was the one to cost Warrior the belt.

The sky was a beautiful purple-blue by the time our match was called. Davey went out before me to a huge ovation.

I was banking on my sense that the British fans truly loved me, but would feel they had to support their fellow countryman. To all the fans watching via satellite I'd be a huge underdog. Today I'd break all their hearts and win their undying loyalty: I was betting my career on it.

The aisle was so long that my usual entrance music played twice as I made my way to the ring, the picture of confidence in my leather ring jacket. English football horns trumpeted through a crowd of all ages while Union Jacks fluttered in the soft breeze. I was eased by the sight of numerous pink and black signs, and I had the distinct sense that God was with me as I silently vowed to show Vince, Davey and the world how good I was.

As I stood nose to nose with Davey he appeared to be every bit as determined, both of us unflinching warriors refusing to give way before battle.

While a thunderous "Bulldog" chant reverberated through the stadium, I unbuckled the belt, held it up to my lips and kissed it. I handed it to Joey, who held it up to the crowd, while I dropped out to the floor to give my sunglasses away. To our mutual surprise I was able to place them on the little boy I'd promised them to earlier. His dad smiled, impressed that I was a man of my word.

Back in the ring, Joey gave Davey and me the rules, the three of us momentarily awestruck by the size of the crowd. We pushed off with Davey looking strong and serious. The crowd was ours and the bell sounded. At first Davey outmanoeuvred me with simple and realistic wrestling, but after only a few minutes, he was breathing hard.

"Bret, I'm fooked," Davey panted as I had him clamped in a side head-lock. "I can't remember *anything!*"

"Davey, just listen to me, I'll carry you."

Joey shot me a worried look. This would be the test of my career.

So, that's how it was, me calling out every single high spot for Davey, sometimes even the necessary facial expressions, helping him conserve what little stamina he had for a comeback that was still more than thirty minutes away. Every time Davey picked me up, I went up like a feather. He went up for me like a full refrigerator.

I made sure I didn't overdo it as a heel, knowing the fans would forgive me in the end when I lost. Twenty-five minutes into the match I locked Davey in a sleeper hold, and the crowd immediately got behind him, cheering him on to revive himself as he crawled to the ropes gasping for air. I snapped a beautiful boot straight into his face, grazing the tip of his nose like I'd snapped it hard with my finger to wake him up.

The drama built, layer upon layer, as every move that came followed a logic that never detracted from the story. I hit Davey with my whole arsenal, finally locking on the sleeper again. As he sank to his knees, I called the spots into his ear, and he rose up to his feet with me on his back. Staggering backward, he rammed me into the corner with all his weight, nearly snap-ping my neck in half on the top rope for real! But there was no time to sell as I slapped on the sleeper one more time. Again, Davey sank to his knees, as Joey muttered, "Do you guys hear that crowd? This is unbelievable!"

We went into a beautiful sequence of moves, ending up with an old Hart Foundation–Bulldogs spot where a groggy Davey went for a press slam but lost his balance and accidentally crotched me on the ropes, to the roar of the crowd.

I'd carried him as far as possible, and now Davey took over for his long-awaited comeback. I called out all his big moves for him, and after I'd taken them all, Davey dragged me to my feet by my singlet straps, revived enough to signal with his hands that it was time to finish me off with his running powerslam! Always incredibly strong, Davey easily twirled me over his shoulder and charged across the ring, flattening me to the mat for the one . . . two. . . but this time it was me who astounded the crowd by barely kicking out! Clutching his face, a tearful Davey only half feigned amazement as he finally realized that I'd put together a masterpiece.

I dragged myself to the ropes and fell out to the apron. Davey suplexed me back in, but I dropped behind him, gripped him tightly around the waist, and jerked him into a perfect German suplex. This time Davey kicked out!

As we got to our feet I attempted a front suplex, but Davey didn't budge. Instead, he blocked it, lifted me straight up, and dropped me painfully hard on the top corner strut, nearly castrating me. A half-inch over and the match would have ended right then and there!

Davey climbed up to the top corner and, before he had time to think about it, we did a standing vertical suplex off the top, crashing to the mat below. This was considered the most high-risk, breath-taking move in the business at that time.

As Davey draped an arm over me for the one . . . two . . . I kicked out again at the last possible second. The crowd was stunned, but they'd only seen the appetizers; the best was yet to come!

After a double clothesline, both Davey and I lay writhing in a heap as Joey started a ten-count. If the fans only knew that I had come up with this move one night at about three in the morning. I had woken Julie up and somehow managed to talk her into lying on the floor next to the bed to see whether it would work. Now I entwined my leg through Davey's, and before anybody quite knew what I was up to I twisted him over into my sharp-shooter with no escape . . . right in the middle of the ring!

The crowd went nuts as I fought with all my strength to stop Davey from crawling to the ropes, dragging me behind him. When he reached them, there was an explosion of relief. Nobody had ever escaped the sharpshooter before! As I dragged myself to my feet, exhausted, I could see my invisible banana peel lying in the middle of the ring. Joey kept muttering, "Unbelievable!"

The time had come to break the hearts of all my fans and forever change my destiny. "Let's go home!" I called as I slammed one last lifter into Davey's chest, rocking him hard enough to send sweat flying into the air. I squeezed his wrist as the cue to reverse me into the ropes, and I dove over him for a sunset flip, the simplest move in wrestling. But instead of falling backwards, we did the old Leo Burke finish: Davey fell forward, hooking my legs with his arms, collapsing on top of me and pinning me beautifully. One . . . two . . . three! We did it! I did it!

There was a deafening roar as "Rule Britannia" played and Joey gave Davey the IC belt. After thirty-seven gruelling minutes, I lay on the mat feigning being heart-broken, but in fact I was elated. I was also exhausted and in considerable pain, but I knew that the handshake at the end would top it all off, the last detail in this drama.

I made out that I was too pissed off to shake Davey's hand. I'd planned all of this with Davey, but it became painfully obvious to me that he'd forgotten all about it. I desperately tried to make eye contact, but he was oblivious as Diana climbed into the ring crying, I can only assume for real. I'm thinking, C'mon, Davey, look at me and we'll make them all cry, but Davey never caught on. Instead he was trying to milk the crowd. I was thinking,

The drama is with me, not them, for fuck's sake please look at me, Davey! After too many attempts I gave up and just walked over and shook his hand. He'd completely missed one of the tiny moments that can make it all more real. But what could I do? The torch had been passed.

Everything hurt, even my fingers were sore.

When I got back to the dressing room most of the boys had already left on the bus, but the ones who'd seen the match seemed blown away. I understood the art of losing and the power of sympathy. I knew that in the weeks to come, it would be me who was over; over more than Warrior, Savage, Flair, even Davey. All of them had been excellently executed!

I've always believed this was my greatest match, especially because I'd carried Davey all the way through it without anyone being the wiser. My dad would tell me later that it's one thing to have a great match, but it's another thing to have a great match in front of eighty thousand people.

Despite knowing it was all a work, and one that I had orchestrated, a deep sense of sadness came over me hours after the match. Losing the IC belt seemed all too real to me.

Later that night, I limped into the crowded hotel bar where most of the wrestlers, fans and office were celebrating after the show. Vince came up to me and told me I was the greatest athlete he'd ever seen and that he only wished he had one ounce of the athletic ability I had. Jack Lanza and Shane McMahon told me that I had the greatest match of all time and that they'd both had goose bumps up their arms watching it. I was surprised to see Pat Patterson back, but there he was gushing all over at what a masterpiece it was, especially as I'd pulled it off without any help from him. I told him that I was glad to see him back, and that I'd felt he was unfairly railroaded during the sexual misconduct allegations.

By the time I limped to my room and called home, the pain of the match was setting in. Julie barely spoke to me, handing the phone to Blade, whose voice lifted my spirits, but only until he said he missed me, which made me feel sadder. Dallas and Jade were both very emotional while Beans, probably the luckiest of my children because she cared the least about wrestling, consoled me for losing. Julie came back on the line and said she was sorry. I wondered whether she even knew what for. Sorry for the loss of income or for how she'd treated me for the last year or two . . . or three . . . or four. I loved her dearly, but as we talked I couldn't deny that my heart was broken and empty.

The next day I flew to America and ended up at the usual Holiday Inn in Baltimore watching the match on tape in my room. There was a knock at the door, and I was surprised to see Randy Savage and Ric Flair come strutting in. Randy grabbed my hand and told me, "Brother, that was the mother of all matches!" Flair said, "Hitman, let me shake your hand!" A couple of hours later, Shawn Michaels came by. He said he heard I had a tape of *the* match and he wanted to watch it, and so we did. He stared at the screen with a look of amazement, and when it was over he stood up, shook my hand, looked me in the eye and said, "*You* are the best, man. In-fucking-credible."

With the help of a local framing shop, I was able to give Vince his drawing at TVs the next day, along with a letter. Given all that was to happen later between us, I now have to remind myself that at the time I really did mean it.

> Dear Vince, It has often been difficult for me to express to you my sincere gratitude for everything you've done for me . . . I wanted to thank you for giving me a chance and I will forever appreciate all the faith and trust you've put in my ability. Over the past eight years, and in particular this last year, it has been an honor and a privilege to have played such an important role, to fulfill my wildest dreams, to create works of art on a ring canvas. I created this little masterpiece for you. I hope it makes you laugh and that it brings back fond memories of what has been an incredible eight years. I thank you, my family thanks you and I look forward to another eight more. It's been a blast. Bret.

I worried that it reeked of opportunistic suck-holing, but I still handed it to him, and he seemed quite moved. By the time I left Vince's office, I'd somehow managed to get Bruce sort of hired again. Unfortunately when Bruce called Vince he was conveniently unavailable and Bruce was handed off to J.J. Dillon. When I spoke with Vince afterwards, he no longer seemed interested in Bruce, who, he told me, had told J.J. that he was going to be some kind of saviour of the WWF and that all of Vince's current storylines were horrible. According to J.J., Bruce said he was going to single-handedly turn things around for the WWF. Of course Bruce blamed J.J. for the misinterpretation, but I doubted that I'd ever be able to get Bruce a chance again. If Bruce didn't have bad luck he had no luck at all.

On the last day of September, I sat on the balcony of a huge hotel suite looking out over the historic landscape of Berlin. Earlier, I'd posed for a

WWF photo shoot at the Brandenburg Gate. I stood where the Reichstag once was, buying tiny chunks of the Berlin Wall to take home as souvenirs.

That night I left them standing and cheering at the Deutschlandhalle after a terrific match against Papa Shango. Everything I hoped might happen after *SummerSlam* was happening, and I felt almost out of control as I rocketed ahead.

There wasn't a ticket to be had for Sheffield, Birmingham, Hamburg, Munich, Dortmund, Kiel or Berlin; in fact the entire tour was sold out months in advance. The European fans were watching American-style pro wrestling for the first time, and it was like another wall coming down. Germany loved me as I loved it, and I actually enjoyed the long scenic bus rides from city to city, usually sobering up from one wild night to the next. I had my headphones on listening to Pearl Jam's Eddie Vedder yelling about running away and seeing the world. Every day mobs of screaming fans, mostly teenaged girls, waited for me at the hotels. I was more over in Germany than any other wrestler I'd ever seen anywhere in all my years in the business. I wondered about a conversation I'd had with Chief at the Winnipeg TV tapings. Chief told me that Vince was looking for a new world champion and there was a list with six names on it, three of them circled, and mine was one of them. "You're on it, Stu, so don't fuck up! They're thinking of putting the big belt on you!" I was flattered, but I'd learned not to get my hopes up because nothing is ever for sure in wrestling.

If I wasn't wrestling Papa Shango I was working with Ric Flair, who had taken the title from Savage on September 1. Every night the crowd stood and cheered while Flair staggered past them dragging the World belt on the ground behind him. In the eyes of my fans he was lucky to still have it. Flair and I had our best matches over there, while I took such a good beating against Papa that when I heroically battled back and put him in the sharpshooter, German fans wept with joy, chanting "Hitman" over and over. Every night the barricades were stormed, and more than once I was knocked flat, sometimes with security lying next to me, smiling at the mass of tangled, sweaty arms pinning us down while I was flooded with kisses and hands squeezing my butt and crotch. I couldn't help but think, You wanted it, you got it!

I was Vince's brightest hope now, and I finally understood that he needed me as much as I needed him. Life was great.

When I got home from Germany, I found myself in a dressing room in Red Deer, Alberta, to work a sold-out show with Ric Flair. Chief pulled me aside to tell me that on Vince's direct orders I was to catch the very first flight the next morning to Saskatoon TVs and go straight to the building to see him. When I arrived in Saskatoon and saw the WWF's always immaculately clean ring trucks and the stagehands all wearing matching blue coveralls unloading state-of-the-art TV production equipment, I was struck by the contrast with the old days, when one of Stu's dilapidated vans and a rusty old ring trailer would have been parked out back.

I patiently sat in a chair at the end of a long backstage hallway waiting to see Vince, who was having a closed-door meeting. After a few minutes the door opened and out came Flair, who turned around and shook Vince's hand in the doorway. Neither of them saw me waiting at the end of the hall as Flair briskly walked away in the other direction. Then Vince turned and saw me and waved me over. He shut the door behind us. I could detect neither good nor bad as I tried to read his face. He took his seat, tenting his fingers as he looked at me.

"You've been with me now for how many years?"

"Eight years," I replied, realizing that I'd been with him longer than any other working wrestler left in the company, with the exception of Mr. Fuji, who was a manager now. Everyone from the early days was gone.

"And how many towns have you missed in that time?

"One."

Vince praised me for my dedication. Then he said, "I've done everything I could think of, put the Tag belts on you, and the Intercontinental belt, and I finally reached the point where I don't know what else to do with you."

I wondered if this cold-hearted son of a bitch was actually firing me the very same day that he was supposed to be flying my dad up to be in my corner! I envisioned trying to explain all this to Stu. The blood going to my heart began to churn thick as mud, when suddenly Vince broke into that goofy grin and said, "So that's why I've decided to put the World belt on you tonight!"

Dead silence. I simply did not grasp what he'd just said.

"Hell, aren't you going to smile or something?" He laughed that famous Vince McMahon yuk-yuk-yuk. I promised him I wouldn't let him down.

He said he wasn't worried about that. All I had to do was keep on being the best worker in the business, and he'd take care of the rest. "Nothing's ever written in stone, but my plans are to keep the belt on you for at least a year. Congratulations, Bret!"

We talked a little longer about what this would mean. "From now on you'll fly only first class," Vince said. When I asked him if that meant the customary limo every night in every town, like all the champions before me had had, he said no, and that he was also cutting out the private dressing room complete with fruit basket. I told him I didn't mind because I preferred to be one of the boys anyway.

I was in complete and total shock as I shook Vince's hand, promising him that I'd do the best I could every night for him and the company. I left the office like I was walking on air, called Julie to tell her what was going on and asked her to pull Jade and Dallas out of school so they could fly up to celebrate the big moment; it would be easier without the two little ones. Then I called Stu and Helen.

As the day went on word got around to all the boys, and I was congratulated by every one of them, even Warrior. Vince had also told me that Flair was fine with it, that he had great respect for me and was honoured to put me over. So on October 12, 1992, I came out to a sold-out crowd in Saskatoon, where I'd had my very first pro wrestling match fourteen years earlier. Saskatoon. Who'd have ever guessed!

As Flair made his way to the ring, with his manager, Mr. Perfect, I hoped this would be one of the last times that Flair called the match for me. I was going to be the king now.

We had the usual tight, repetitive match. Early on, when I had Flair locked in an arm bar, he told me to climb up to the second rope so it would appear to put more pressure on his arm. Somehow, when he jerked me down, I rolled my ankle, injuring it. I had no choice but to keep going.

Minutes later he called for a figure-four leg lock. I scooped his legs and limped around to lock it in when he unexpectedly kicked me off sideways. I fell backward and jammed the middle finger of my left hand on the taught ring rope, snapping it at the knuckle. I sat looking at it and realized that it was bent rather oddly: It felt like I couldn't uncross my fingers. I calmly reached up and grabbed it with my right hand and snapped it back, hearing Curt groan from the ring floor right behind me as he watched me do it. Nothing was going to ruin this moment!

Flair called every spot, even the outdated ones, including a barrage of his painful, stiff open-handed chops that left red handprints across my chest. Some guys liked it stiff, while some worked too light and phony. To me, chops were stupid and brainless and went against everything logical about the business. We're only supposed to pretend we're hurting each other; when you really are hurting and being hurt, you're the mark. The only guy more stupid than the guy chopping you is the guy taking them. I suffered through more than enough chops, out of respect, before exploding into a huge comeback. I suplexed him off the top corner into the ring and stepped into the sharpshooter. My mind flashed back to all those wrestling magazines I created as a kid; the times I made my own championship belts out of cardboard and broken bottle glass. Ric Flair pounded his hands on the mat screaming uncle, and my childhood dream became a reality. I was champion of the world!

The crowd was stunned, and so was I! No one figured I'd be the one to pull the sword out of the stone. I had to respect that Flair at least passed the torch to me. I came back through the curtain, limping and holding my finger, to an ovation of handshakes and backslaps, Owen clapping the hardest.

Before I was taken to the hospital, I did a live interview with Mean Gene Okerlund in which I said,

> "Since I was small I've been involved in wrestling, my whole family's been involved in wrestling and I've dedicated my whole life — to wrestling. My father taught me, took me on the mat and made me feel the pain and I've listened and learned technical wrestling. I've had my share of wins and losses and I've waited for my whole lifetime for one chance and I've got that chance. I want to thank every single wrestler that I've ever worked against. I've wrestled the greatest wrestlers in the world and learned so much. I want to thank each and every one of them, especially Ric Flair. I want to thank you for stepping into the ring with me tonight and giving me that chance. I also want to thank all my fans all over the world for supporting me all these years. And to all my friends that have backed me up. Most of all I want to thank God above. God almighty, thank you for the greatest moment in my life! I'm proud to be the WWF World Champion!"

Oddly enough, the title match never aired on TV and afterwards, Flair promptly gave notice that he'd be finishing up in a couple of months to go back to WCW.

I limped back to my room late that night after a visit to the hospital revealed that my finger had been dislocated. Julie and the kids were too exhausted to celebrate much. I fell asleep in my cramped hotel room, tired, sore and hungry.

The following night at Regina TVs it was announced that I was the new world champion, and I received a long ovation. After the show I celebrated with all the wrestlers at the hotel bar. Taker, Curt and Shawn Michaels grinned at me with the deepest respect. Owen, Bruce and Davey all slammed down empty glasses and even Stu honoured me by tossing down a shot of J.D. It burned his gums and eyes and really lit him up, like Dracula drinking holy water.

28

ONWARDS AND UPWARDS

I QUICKLY ADJUSTED to being the biggest star in the company, the guy with the heaviest load and the biggest pay. I got a $55,000 cheque for *SummerSlam* 1992, and my paycheques tripled to around $6,000-7,000 a week. I finally believed that I'd one day be able to pay my house off, and took down the For Sale sign for good.

One of the first wrestlers I called after I won was Roddy. I'd already said to Owen that I was relying on him to help me watch my back, because as much as the wrestlers all said they were happy for me, everybody wanted my spot. Roddy echoed those words, stressing how important it was for me to get close to Vince, to try to be his best friend. I'd already been told by Pat that Vince liked to hear from his champion every day, so I was calling Vince daily even though to me it just felt like brown-nosing.

On October 27, at TVs in Terre Haute, Indiana, Vince and Pat told Davey it was time for him to drop the IC belt to Shawn. Instead of reminding Davey that dropping the belt to Shawn was part of the plan all along, Pat explained that they could only push one babyface champion at a time, and I was it. This sowed seeds of discontent in Davey. Meanwhile, I did my best to be a friend to him, reminding him not to take it personally. But Davey grumbled long and loud about leaving to go back to Japan or WCW.

Over-the-top gimmicks had been the fad for some time in the WWF. Vince's newest creation was an evil clown he called Doink, to be played by Matt Bourne. In fairness to him, I have to admit that Matt had an uncanny ability to be a creepy clown; Doink had potential. But when Vince shot an angle having Davey lose to Doink, Davey misread the opportunity. Instead of realizing that working a program with a hot new heel would be good for him, he chose to listen to Diana, who was increasingly calling the shots and who convinced Davey that he was above jobbing out for a stupid clown.

As Vince's new champion, I was counted on to fill Hulk's shoes. Being a successful world champion requires more than just being the best worker, and in fact, sometimes the best world champions aren't the best workers—

Hogan and Warrior being the prime examples. Although I had a massive grassroots following, I didn't have the level of promo skills or charisma of Hogan. I wasn't six-foot-eight with twenty-four-inch arms. Strangely, it worked to my advantage. My athletic physique was as realistic as my wrestling, and Vince, in the midst of the steroid scandal, was doing his best to turn his business around based on my believability. If anything, I was the perfect contrast to Hogan, especially for fans who were sick of his all too familiar act. I was recognized for being an artist and a storyteller. If Hogan was the Elvis of wrestling, I was the Robert De Niro.

Vince needed me to steer clear of any and all trouble, and he was counting on the fact that I could work a four-star match with almost anyone. The days when the WWF was stocked with the best lineup of heels in the business to get Hogan and Warrior over were gone. Now almost all of the great heels that Vince had invested so much TV time in had disappeared from the WWF under the harsh light of the steroid scandal, and some were now riding high in WCW.

Soon enough, I was launched on return bouts with Flair, who seemed bent on sabotaging our matches. I wasn't sure whether he was doing it accidentally or on purpose, but he was never there for me on my comeback and seemed to bungle the finish every night. I began to refer to Ric's ring style as full blast, non-stop non-psychology. He made things up on the spot and did them whether they made sense or not. As a technician Flair was one of the best, but I was baffled by how little he really knew about building a great match. And I was even more baffled by how this went undetected by fans and sheet writers, who continued to worship him.

On November 18, Vince phoned to tell me he'd just fired Warrior and that, unfortunately, Davey was going to be next. He wanted to tell me first so I could prepare for any backlash that might happen as a result. He said that Warrior and Davey had been receiving shipments of growth hormone from a dealer in the UK who'd just been busted. Vince was so under the gun that he fired them both immediately. The fanciful vision I'd had of me twisting Warrior into the sharpshooter and him screaming uncle at *WrestleMania IX* vanished forever. After so many wrestlers had lain down to make him a star, Warrior would never return the favour. As for Davey, he was out of work and trying to get on with WCW.

Taker and I knew we were being heavily relied on to be the new leaders. Vince also pinned his hopes on Shawn, who was beginning to blossom into an obnoxious pretty boy heel who took great bumps, comparable only to

Perfect or Dynamite. He was a tag team wrestler finally finding his niche as a singles performer. I fondly remember Shawn praising me the night I won the belt and telling me how grateful he was that I had finally opened the door for the smaller yet better workers who never got a break. "Guys like us!" he smiled and slapped me on the back.

Vince was building six-foot-seven Scott Hall as a takeoff on Al Pacino's *Scarface* character. He cut promos with an obviously put-on Cuban accent and a toothpick dangling from his lip until he flicked it away. His neck was adorned with fake gold chains and a tacky razor medallion, his unshaven face was framed by long, greasy black hair and one casual curl carefully positioned to hang right down the middle of his forehead. Hall was well built but still green. On Curt's suggestion he was dubbed Razor Ramon. Since Vince was dangerously low on heels, Razor was mega-pushed to the top and set to work with me in January at *Royal Rumble* 1993. Another potential top heel was Yokozuna, a huge Samoan named Rodney Anoai, whom Vince billed as a legit sumo wrestler and passed off as Japanese. Mr. Fuji was his manager. Last but not least was The Beast from the East, Bam Bam Bigelow, with his tattooed head. He'd departed a while back only to reappear with a much-improved attitude. He couldn't have come at a better time.

I desperately hoped Vince could build some of these heels for me as soon as possible.

On November 25, after a long match at *Survivor Series* in Richfield, Ohio, I caught Shawn Michaels by the ankles as he was coming off the top rope with a flying drop kick and put him into the sharpshooter to retain the World title at my first pay-per-view as champion. Shawn confessed to me that he wasn't in working shape to go a long match, so I paced the match a lot slower than I would have liked, as a favour to him. Vince said the match was right on the money, which was all I needed to know.

In Montreal, in early December, Pat brought me and Ric together and diplomatically told Flair to start trying harder. Ric was as obliging as ever before we got into the ring, but the match turned out exactly the same — maybe this was just how he worked. Then Ric apologized to me for our matches not being better, explaining that he was simply burned out and was dealing with family problems. I wanted to believe him, so I did. He would be leaving soon, anyway.

On December 14, at Green Bay TVs, Vince pumped my hand and slapped me on the back as he closed his office door. Then he said, "I thought you should know Hogan's coming back, but he'll have nothing to do with my plans for you and the belt. He'll only be working tags with Beefcake for a short time as a favour, to help promote a movie he's got coming out."

I pictured Hulk shaking his head, with a big grin on his face, maybe a little relieved that the belt was on me instead of Warrior, or worse. I thought he'd be glad to see it on someone who'd at least worked hard for it, someone who respected and protected the business. I still had such respect for Hogan that if Vince had asked me to step back and hand him the belt, it would have been fine by me.

Vince had his problems to deal with in Green Bay. For the past six months, he had been building Kevin Wacholz as a psycho-killer ex-con named Nailz. Kevin cornered Vince in his office and screamed at him for fifteen minutes about all the lies he'd been told. His yelling got so loud I had goose bumps up my back as I listened from down the hall. Suddenly there was a loud crash—Nailz had knocked Vince over in his chair, choking him violently, until Lanza, Slaughter and a swarm of agents teamed up to pull him off. Nailz walked out and immediately called the police and accused Vince of making a sexual advance to him. Vince was charged with sexual assault (the charges were dropped shortly thereafter). Some of the boys actually admired Nailz for snatching Vince and then covering his tracks well enough not to get charged himself. The last thing Vince wanted was yet another scandal. The FBI was about to indict him for receiving steroids through the mail from the convicted doctor, the WBF was sinking fast and his wrestling empire was on shaky legs too. I wanted to come through for him: only days earlier he'd said to me that he hadn't always done right by his wrestlers but that starting with me he was going to change all that.

On my Christmas break, Julie and I celebrated what had to be the best year of my life. It appeared that we might actually succeed after all: the house, the kids, the dream. It all looked so nice through my rose-coloured glasses. But there I was leaving on Christmas Day again. When my bags were packed and set by the door later that night, Blade came down in his pyjamas and said, "Can I come to the 'port, Dad?"

Boy I'd sure miss him. He was already two and a half. I picked him up and said, "You can come if you promise me that you won't cry when I leave." He nodded and scampered away to put on his winter boots.

It was midnight when Julie and Blade dropped me off. We had a long hug and then a few short tight ones and a few good kisses. Blade said he wouldn't cry—and he didn't.

I took my seat up in first class next to Owen, who had been upgraded for the flight, and who wore the same heart-broken expression as I did. In a few hours we'd be sleeping on the airport floor in Toronto, with our bags for pillows, waiting to connect to another flight to work back-to-back double shots.

TVs were now every third Monday and Tuesday. On the other Mondays of the month, Vince added a show called *Monday Night Raw*, which would alternate between live and taped matches. The concept for *Monday Night Raw* was that it would be at the same venue each week, a historic 3,500-seat theatre within walking distance of Madison Square Garden called The Manhattan Center. In January 1993 alone, the WWF produced something like fourteen hours of TV and a major pay-per-view. For the shows that didn't air live, commentary was over-dubbed in a number of languages at the WWF's slick in-house production facility in Connecticut and beamed via satellite to networks worldwide. That's not to mention the forty-two towns run that month with two teams of wrestlers for the house shows. This schedule became normal. They published it for fans in the monthly WWF magazine under the banner "Killer Kalendar"—and that's what it was.

On January 9, 1993, I had to do another return match with Flair at the Boston Garden, billed as a one-hour marathon match; it was the first show of a weekend of back-to-back double shots. I'd come up with a good finish that I ran by Vince, but when I told Flair he began telling me what we were going to do instead. I finally cut him off and, with regret, dressed him down in front of several wrestlers. "Ric, I'm the champion and this is how it's going to go." He dropped his jaw, turned red and sat on a bench saying, "You're the champ."

Ric still managed to mess up the timing for every fall. I was furious when Dave Meltzer wrote in *The Wrestling Observer* that Flair had carried me for the whole match when it was, in fact, the other way around.

There were some interesting moments at *Royal Rumble* later that month in Sacramento. Lex Luger was a former WCW wrestler whom Vince brought into his World Bodybuilding Federation, and then lured to the WWF by promising him the moon. It wasn't working out so well. Luger was now called The Narcissist and, before every match, had to pose in front of a full-length mirror in the middle of the ring, tassels hanging from his white trunks. Although he was in fabulous shape and he was steroid-free, he looked small in the ring. To the fans, his new, conceited persona was as uninteresting as the faltering WBF. During Lex's routine streams of people headed to the concession stands.

That night Shawn was defending the IC belt against Marty Jannetty, who showed up drunk and unkempt from an all-nighter. Wasted, Marty fumbled and stumbled his way through the match, but, much to his credit, the fans never noticed. Vince fired him as soon as he got out of the ring.

A new arrival to WWF was Memphis promoter and wrestler Jerry The King Lawler. He was Honky Tonk's second cousin and had a similar build: soft and pudgy, with not a muscle on him. Lawler had a lot of heat with various wrestlers who'd worked for him over the years; to get even, several of them took the time to shit in his crown and left it for him to find in the showers.

I was glad to see former WWF World Champion Bob Backlund return for the battle royal. I'd never forgotten how, when I was in Japan in the early 1980s, he'd bought beer for all the boys on the bus. The mark in me got off watching Flair and Backlund, two very different legends from the old school, working in the Rumble. Bob was as clean cut as they came, whereas Flair loved to walk on the wild side—they were two of the longest-reigning champions of my era, from two different territories.

It was hard for anyone to complain about who they were working with after watching poor Undertaker carry Giant Gonzales, a seven-foot-six, very affable Argentinean who couldn't work at all. He was so skinny they couldn't put him in trunks; instead he had to wear a ridiculous looking flesh-coloured unitard with muscles airbrushed all over it.

As for my match with Razor Ramon, he was still so green I called everything. I was afraid that Scott could break my neck with his finish, The Razor's Edge, a move where he'd press you up by the arm pits and then fall forward, dropping you right on your neck. Instead I came up with a clever way to get out of it by dropping behind him and backsliding him for a pin fall. It turned out to be an up-and-down fight until I came up with the sharpshooter out of nowhere and he submitted. When I was handed the belt I saw Stu and Helen standing in the front row clapping.

And Yoko had won the rumble, so now he'd be the heel to face me at *WrestleMania IX* in Las Vegas in early April.

At the hotel, someone pointed out to me that Dave Meltzer was lurking about in the lobby, reluctant to come into the bar. Eventually, my mom introduced me to him. Meltzer was very polite and a bit nervous as I glared at him. I whispered to her afterwards, "He's no friend of mine, Mom."

On January 26, I flew out to Las Vegas with Vince, Pat and all the top boys to kick off the hype for *WrestleMania IX* with a huge press conference. Afterwards, Vince and Pat said that I had come across as humble and that was exactly what they were looking for to help project a wholesome image now that it was almost certain Vince would be indicted by the Feds.

I managed to get home for one day before dashing off to Madison Square Garden, and was saddened to hear that André had died. He'd flown to France for his father's funeral only to be found dead in his hotel room the morning after. I pictured him walking through the Pearly Gates with a big smile on his face, for once not having to duck, saying, "Hello, boss!" There would never be another giant like André.

The last time I'd been in Europe I wouldn't have believed it possible that I'd be returning as world champion. On February 1, I arrived in Manchester, and Knobbs rang my room to tell me that he'd tracked down Dynamite. He'd phoned him to say he was coming over and invited me and Chief to go along with him as a surprise. Tom and The Nasty Boys had toured together in Japan a few years back. Knobbs and Sags had been charmed enough by him to allow him to use the tops of their heads as ashtrays while they rode the bus.

We found Tom's flat in a miserable, graffiti-stained ghetto on the outskirts of the city. The windows were boarded up and the charred remains of a car were smouldering out front. He answered the door in a T-shirt and blue jeans looking James Dean normal, with a V-shaped physique. It was the first time I'd seen him steroid-free since I'd known him.

"Fookin' niggers did it," he said, pointing at the car as he invited us in.

Tom took a seat on a shredded old couch, moving slowly as he eased his way into it, smoking a cigarette. He rudely referred to his girlfriend, Joanne, as a daft stupid cunt enough times that it embarrassed everyone except him, and she looked shell-shocked by his behaviour. Chief's face gave away his disappointment and disgust. When Knobbs innocently blurted out that I was the champ, Tom nodded and replied, "Intercontinental, right?"

"No, Dyno, he's the world champion now. He's got the big belt."

When I won the world championship, I recall thinking, I'd love to see the look on Dynamite's face when he finds out. I got to see it now. His first expression was one of disbelief and shock. Then, for only a moment, he seemed happy, like it confirmed his own greatness in some way. No sooner had I begun to see that he was maybe even proud of me, and his face turned sour: his look said, This is what things could have been like for me if I hadn't become so broke and broken. Then, briefly, optimism seemed to wash over him: maybe somehow I could help him? But as the thought formed, he lifted his chin, indignant, his pride hurt—he didn't want anything from me or anyone else.

While we were there, people drove by and threw things at his house, which, he explained, is why the windows were all boarded up. Tom was finding out that there was a heavy price for his bigotry. He still had a real sore spot about Davey, and for that I couldn't totally blame him. Davey had trademarked The British Bulldog name before Tom or even Vince, and now he refused to let Tom—the original British Bulldog—use his own ring name to make a living.

In the car on the way back to the hotel, Chief said he regretted that we'd gone to see him. Dynamite was one of his favourites, and now his memories would be forever ruined.

Tom showed up at the hotel that night. He'd thought things over a bit and was now blown away by my position and desperate for any kind of a lifeline from me. I'd already been talking to Chief and Vince about trying to do something for him. But when I told Tom, he shook his head, "Nah, I'll never go back." I left him in the bar with Knobbs and Sags, where he was soon crying in his beer. All our hearts went out to him. Dynamite was hard to love, but we did, and it was heartbreaking to see the best worker I ever knew finally reveal his inner agony at the mistakes he'd made and how things had ended up for him.

After the show on February 6, we all drank at Cookies, a rock 'n' roll bar in Frankfurt that was always packed with Fräulein. I somehow ended up in Bammer's room with two large German girls, and by 5 a.m. I was suplexing and Russian leg-sweeping one of them on the giant bed. I liked to think of it as training for my *Mania* match with Yokozuna. Then Bam Bam elected to pick the bigger one up over his back and give her a Samoan drop onto the bed. There was a loud crack as the bed frame broke; all we could do was laugh as he sat on his ass with the bed collapsed all around him. Bammer had been through a lot of ups and downs, but he had a great attitude now. We'd been working almost every night having fantastic matches.

After the final show of the tour, we bussed it to Düsseldorf and would head home in the morning. That night Taker, Papa and I said farewell to Flair in the bar, it being his last day before he'd go back to WCW. After our last match, in Dortmund, Ric had clasped my hand and said, "My friend, you are truly a great worker." I'd decided that Vince was right when he said that Flair wasn't ruining our matches on purpose. He was just from a different era, when all the spots were called in the ring, and he was the one calling them.

Later that night, seeing that Flair's door was open, I knocked, and he invited me in, waving me to sit down while he finished a phone call with some bigwig from WCW. Ric spoke highly of me and my work and described my popularity in Europe as being like Elvis. He also said some kind words about Taker. The way Ric put us all over just might come in handy one day.

On February 18, I heard that Kerry Von Erich had committed suicide — shot himself in the heart. Left a note that said he was joining his brothers in heaven. Owen and I were deeply saddened, but who could be surprised. As the son of a wrestling promoter, Kerry never found it easy living up to the hopes and expectations put before him. I've always thought that despite the closeness of the Von Erich boys, they were still so competitive that they thought topping one another with this final exit was the ultimate act of bravado.

I remembered my mom telling me about the first Von Erich son who'd died. Little Jackie Jr. had played with Smith and Bruce back in the late 1950s when Fritz worked for Stu under his born name, Jack Adkisson. A few weeks later, the Adkissons were living in Buffalo, where Fritz was wrestling, and Jackie was electrocuted by a power line at a trailer park. I also couldn't forget that cold day in February 1984, when Dynamite, Davey and I were working over in Japan and heard that Kerry's older brother, David, who was in Japan working for Baba's promotion, had just died of a drug overdose. The same thing took Mike Von Erich on April 12, 1987. He was high when he zipped himself inside a sleeping bag that he filled with rocks and rolled himself out of a small boat and drowned. And the youngest brother, Chris, had shot himself on September 12, 1991.

I just wished there had been something I could have done to help Kerry. We all did.

On February 22, Owen and I flew to Texas for Kerry's funeral, held in the local Baptist church. Fritz and Doris had recently divorced, but they put on a unified front, stoic in their acceptance. Of their six sons, only Kevin remained. I could see that it meant a lot to Fritz that two of Stu's boys were there.

When they lowered Kerry's casket into the earth, I couldn't help but think, We'll see you at the gates, brother.

When I read my booking sheets, I realized I'd see Hulk at TVs in North Charleston, South Carolina, on March 8. Even though he'd been making the odd appearance on various shows since December, I hadn't laid eyes on him since *WrestleMania VIII*, when I'd given him his drawing. I really thought he'd be proud of me, so when I pulled up to the back of the arena, I went looking for him. I didn't have to look far. He was standing chatting with Beefcake, leaning against the wall on the ramp. His appearance had changed drastically: He looked like a lean old walrus. He was tanned and wore red spandex tights, big white boots and a bandana covering his balding head. I approached with a huge smile and my hand extended in friendship. Hogan gave me a dismissive nod and wouldn't shake my hand. I withdrew it and walked away. I figured that because I was champion now, he saw me as the competition. Hulkamania had run so wild that it had burned itself out like a grass fire, and here I was, one of the new, brightly coloured flowers popping up to haunt him.

The day only got worse. Owen was getting a push, working with Bam Bam. While springing up to the top rope for a back somersault, he slipped coming down and tore a ligament in his knee, injuring himself so badly that instead of being given a push, he was pulled out of the ring and taken to the hospital. He was expected to be out for a long time.

The only positive thing that happened was that I managed to talk Yoko into lying on the dressing-room floor where, much to his surprise, I crouched down atop his twisted thick calves and was actually able to put on the sharpshooter. I didn't picture beating him with it, but none of the fans would think it would be possible for me to turn him over; the move had the potential to be a great spot for *WrestleMania IX*. Vince was having him destroy all his opponents, and I was shaping up to be a huge underdog.

Wrestlers' deaths continued to come in threes. After André and Kerry, the boys openly wondered who'd be next. It was Dino Bravo, only forty-four years old.

On March 10, Dino was found dead in his home near Montreal. He'd been shot seventeen times, so that the precise shots formed a circle in the back of his skull. Rumour was that he had double-crossed the Mafia in the trafficking of contraband cigarettes. A nervous Dino had recently confided to close friends that his days were numbered.

On April 2, 1993, I brought Stu and Helen with me to Vegas for *WrestleMania IX*, where my mom was also going to have a family reunion with her four sisters. Stu beamed at once again finding himself the centre of the sisters' attentions, as he had been when he first fell in love with all of them in the 1940s in Long Beach, New York. I left them to reminisce and went to my room just in time to answer a call from Vince, who asked me to come to his suite to talk. I knocked on his door and he answered it with that goofy grin. We sat down, and Vince said, "This is what I want to do. I want you to drop the belt to Yoko tomorrow."

This was not what I had expected. I sat there dumbstruck as he went on to explain how Fuji would screw me by throwing salt in my face, blinding me. After Yoko was handed the belt, Hogan would rush to my aid and in some kind of roundabout way Hogan would end up winning the belt from Yoko right then and there!

Like I was handing Vince my sword, I told him I appreciated everything he did for me and I'd do whatever he wanted.

Vince said, "Don't get bitter. I still have big plans for you." Sound bites flashed through my mind of Vince assuring me that I was the long-term champion, and not to worry about Hogan, who still hadn't even spoken to me yet.

As I stood up to leave, I asked, "Did you take the belt from me because I didn't do a good enough job?"

"Of course not! I'm just going in a different direction. It's still onwards and upwards for you. Nothing is going to change too much for you."

I was totally crushed

As I lay in bed that night, the more I thought about what Vince had in mind for Hogan, the more I felt that it would completely backfire on both of them. The hokey finish would stink, maybe not immediately, but in the weeks to come my fans, who were the biggest contingent in Vince's paying audience at that time, would gag on it. There was something different about my fans. They really believed in me as a person.

By the time I got to the dressing room the following afternoon, word that I was losing the title had leaked out to the boys. Most of them were quiet and some were angry. The Nasty Boys, Shawn, Taker and several others expressed their utter disappointment. Knowing I was losing the belt didn't stop me from planning on having a great match. I went over everything with Yoko and designed the match so that all the best moves were left for the final minute.

Hulk arrived with his entourage: his wife, manager, Beefcake and Jimmy Hart. Clearly he'd been in the know all along, probably from the first day he came back. Now he was suddenly acting like my long-lost old pal and wearing a big smile that rightfully belonged to me.

During our match, it was hot and dry in the desert heat, but a cool breeze made it impossible to work up a healthy sweat. An exhausted Yoko stampeded like a runaway elephant, short-changing me on my comeback and editing out all my best spots. I was furious that he would take it upon himself to go home on his own. That's how I came to find myself crouched low, desperately hanging on to Yoko's two massive calves in the sharp-shooter, fighting with every ounce of strength not to let go. Fuji was caught off guard by the sudden ending, and it took him forever to find, unwrap, and throw a packet of what was actually baby powder into my eyes, supposedly blinding me. I fell back as Yoko hooked my leg and Hebner counted one . . . two . . . three. Right on cue, Hogan hit the ring protesting the injustice that had been done to me, and Earl put on that classic expression of utter stupidity that all pro wrestling refs wear when convenient. As I feigned blindness Hogan helped me out of the ring.

Fuji stayed in the ring, absurdly challenging Hogan to a title match with Yoko right then and there. Yoko was still teetering from exhaustion and looking for a second wind that wasn't there. Hogan blinked in astonishment at his sudden good fortune. As scripted, with my face buried in the crook of my arm, I waved him to avenge my loss. "Go get 'em, Hulk!"

I was really thinking, Go ahead, Hogan, take from me what I worked so hard to get. We'll see just how long you last! Hogan was champion again without even having a match—and before I'd even made it backstage. He simply ducked the powder Fuji threw in his face, clotheslined Fuji and dropped his big leg on Yoko. I could hear the one . . . two . . . three, the roar of the crowd and Hogan's music thumping. I couldn't help but stare at the TV monitor watching Hogan work the crowd with the same old posing routine, a hand behind the ear, shaking the world belt in the air as if to say it belonged to him all along.

A few minutes later, Hogan came up to me excited and happy and said, "Thank you, brother. I won't forget it. I'll be happy to return the favour."

I looked my old friend in the eye and said, "I'm going to remember that, Terry."

As for Yoko, I was always a little pissed off at him for going home on me and not letting me show Vince, Hogan and everyone else that we could tear the house down without their bullshit finish. Even so, it was the best match that Yoko ever had.

29

"BROTHER, YOU DON'T KNOW THE WHOLE STORY!"

BARCELONA, APRIL 24, 1993. One man's sunset is another man's dawn.

The past ten days touring Europe had been a boost to my pained, empty heart. I sat on a small balcony outside my hotel window seven floors up, listening to my Walkman and looking out over rooftops, church spires and steeples as a huge red sun drifted below the horizon. I'd come to know the distinctive smells of many cities and as I inhaled deeply, I decided that Barcelona's could be called Mediterranean melange. I'd been working hard with Bam Bam, and I was content knowing that our match that aired live across all of Spain that night had been excellent. The Barcelona twilight melted into night until the only glow in the sky was from a silver crescent moon and a few twinkling stars. My mind drifted to a hazy memory of Brussels, the first night of the tour, standing drunk on a corner with Bam Bam at four in the morning listening to some street musicians.

From Brussels we went to London, where I realized by the size of the crowd waiting for me at the airport that losing the belt hadn't swayed my faithful fans one bit. I was more over than before. I laughed to myself as I remembered doing a morning talk show in London where I was supposed to promote a new WWF album featuring a sappy song I'd recorded months earlier. As horrible as it was, with a little production magic, it miraculously reached number four on the U.K. music charts. Talk about a one-hit wonder.

A stuffy older man and woman hosted the talk show, and they had no clue who I was. They seemed skeptical when I told them that more than eighty thousand wrestling fans had filled Wembley Stadium to see us the previous summer. They droned on about whether or not wrestling was really a sport at all. I admit to being tired and cranky, and I was even less amused when some pear-shaped bloke in a red devil outfit joined us on the set and kept poking me in the stomach with a cheesy plastic pitchfork while I did my best to respond to their uninformed questions. During a short commercial break, I jerked his plastic pitchfork and told the startled devil that if he poked me one more time I'd shove the pitch fork up his ass!

The most interesting part of the tour had been Belfast, where the dreary streets looked tired and downtrodden, British soldiers with machine guns stationed on many corners. We'd stayed at the Europa, whose claim to fame is that it's the most bombed hotel in the world. As I checked in I was approached by a timid taxi driver who mentioned that his two boys were my biggest fans; he offered to give me a free tour of the real Belfast. Soon we were driving past political murals. As he showed me various bombed-out sites, we talked some. His name was Sean, he was thirty-four, but he looked ten years older. We passed the cemetery where only a few months before, at an IRA funeral, mourners attacked and brutally killed some spying Ulster loyalists who were in the wrong place at the wrong time. Sean gave me an Irish Catholic history of Belfast and drove me to killer triangle streets, which, he explained, were intersections where kills could be made from three different angles and where people were randomly murdered all the time in the crossfire. It gave me pause when he said, "It's not *so* bad. Nothing like America!"

When he was showing me the H-block, we got pulled over by an Ulster special police officer, and Sean broke into a sweat. He hurriedly filled me in that this officer, whom he'd seen many times before, was nicknamed Lurch by Catholics such as him, and had killed many of them. Lurch, who was about six-foot-five and dressed in an all-black uniform that reminded me of an SS storm trooper, approached the taxi suspiciously, machine gun in hand. It was a tense few minutes as Lurch questioned us. I handed over my passport while Sean explained. While Lurch ran a check on us, a terrified Sean confessed to me that he had a criminal record for gun-running and that he'd done two years in the H-block himself, where they'd worked him over pretty good. He was in at around the same time that Bobby Sands died while on a hunger strike. But after a very long ten minutes Lurch let us go.

Sean invited me for tea at his house. While we sipped from our cups, his wife told me that one of the hunger strikers lived two doors down, and she explained how the death of Bobby Sands eventually lead the way for some positive change in the Catholic cause. IRA prisoners were now to be treated as POWs rather than common criminals. Meanwhile, Sean pulled his young boys out of the school across the street. They were shaking with excitement to meet me. They showed me their room, where magazine pictures of me were plastered all over the walls. They also told me not to worry because I was better than Hulk Hogan and I'd win back the title in no time!

That night at the show in Belfast, a mixed audience of Catholics and Protestants were content to let out their aggressions watching wrestling.

Many hugged me and held tightly onto my hands as I walked around the ring after my match. Sean gave me a decorated and varnished hurling stick to take home with me to Canada. I thought it was nice of him to do something like that, since money didn't come easy for him.

On the drive to Dublin I found the emerald Ireland I'd hoped for dotted with quaint moss-covered cottages and farms with sheep grazing in rolling pastures. At the show, I was amazed to find an even more adoring crowd, who wrapped me in Irish flags after my match with Bam Bam. They seemed to regard me almost as a son who'd come home.

Few people could imagine the life I lived. I'd come to feel like an explorer who'd travelled to far and distant lands and was loved by the people he encountered. I would never forget this breathtaking, spectacular, surreal time in my life.

WCW was beginning to give Vince a run for his money on the pay-per-view side of things, although their house show attendance was horrible. Vince fought back by scheduling a new annual pay-per-view to bridge the gap between *WrestleMania* and *SummerSlam* called *King of the Ring*. The inaugural event would be held at the brand new Nutter Center in Dayton, Ohio, on June 13, 1993.

I stayed focused and carried myself with dignity, which was appreciated by the boys and, more importantly, by the fans. As soon as Hogan had taken the belt back, house show attendance nosedived. WWF wrestlers were paid a percentage of the gate, and it made me feel good when most of the boys told me they hoped I'd get the belt back. With paycheques shrinking and pink slips looming, the discontent in the dressing room was bad enough that many who feared they were about to be sacked took it as a mixed blessing. Tito, Darsow, The Beverley Brothers, Earthquake and even the pretty ring announcer, Mike McGuirk, suddenly vanished. Within a couple of weeks Duggan and The Nasty Boys were gone too.

WCW was waiting in the wings with huge guaranteed money contracts; they had made overtures to Hogan over the last year or so. I wondered whether Vince had put the belt back on Hogan with such a cheap win over Yoko just to lower his stock should he decide to go to WCW. Still, former WWF names such as Rick Rude, Jake The Snake and Sycho Sid, to name only a few, all landed WCW contracts at one time or another with lots of perks and time off. Davey was there now too, feuding with Vader.

Owen had come back to work because he couldn't survive on what Vince paid him while he was hurt. Martha was pushing him hard to pack it in, and he'd applied for a job with the Calgary fire department. Meanwhile he taped his knee and carried on despite the torn ligament. He took pride in the actual wrestling, but he had the same love-hate relationship with the business that I did. You can't stop talent, but, unfortunately, in Owen's case, he'd been stopped by one thing or another every time he was on the verge of a break.

King of the Ring was a one-night tournament concept, and it was a good sign that my stock was rising again when Vince told me that I'd be crowned the winner. My guess was that Vince was starting to build me for what I already knew was coming, a *SummerSlam* showdown with Hogan—in many ways, a showdown between my fans and his. On May 24, I was summoned to a secret photo shoot in Halifax to do promotional shots for *SummerSlam* 1993. Hogan and I posed doing a mock tug of war with the World belt, standing chin to forehead, sneering and gritting our teeth. If I faced Hogan at *SummerSlam*, win or lose, I knew he'd be booed and I'd be the underdog. What didn't occur to me is that Hogan knew it too.

On May 29, Vince called me at home to tell me the big news that I was getting the belt back. What I didn't expect to hear was that he was getting ready to call Hogan and hated the thought of telling him that he was too old and tired for a company whose marketing strategy was now based around a "new generation" concept. Vince wanted to make Hogan into the Babe Ruth of the WWF and use him as more of a special attraction. He asked me not to say anything until he had spoken to Hogan.

Ten days later, Vince called again. He warned me that he was about to tell me something that would make me really angry: Hogan was flat-out refusing to put me over, saying I wasn't in his league. Vince had decided that Yoko would be getting the belt instead. I couldn't believe that Hogan would do this to me. I remembered him shaking my hand at *WrestleMania IX*, and telling me he'd be happy to return the favour. Vince said he'd have one more meeting with Hogan to try to sell him on it, but if he didn't go for it, I'd work with Lawler at *SummerSlam* instead.

Hogan didn't go for it. I wanted to believe that Vince hadn't told me the whole story, and I made up my mind to confront Hogan as soon as he'd dropped the belt to Yoko. I'd wait till then, because it didn't seem right for me to change Yoko's destiny.

I showed up in the dressing room for *King of the Ring* in a dark mood and promptly drew a blackboard cartoon of Beefcake with his face buried in Hogan's ass cheeks with a caption that read, "Be careful, Brutus, you don't want to loosen the screws in your face . . . speaking of screws . . ." I was taking my frustration out on Beefcake, which wasn't right, but I was too pissed off to know it at the time.

What Hogan had done was perfectly clear to the boys, and they enjoyed the humour of my cartoon. Since Hogan rarely bothered to come into the dressing room, he didn't see it, but Beefcake sure did and went slinking back to Hulk. But it didn't matter to me: Hogan was no longer one of the boys, and he never would be again.

I was determined not only to have the three best matches on the pay-per-view, but three of the best matches of my career.

Razor and I opened the show. For some reason, Pat told me not to win any of my matches with the sharpshooter, so I worked a spot with Razor where he stomped and broke my fingers as an excuse as to why I couldn't use them for the rest of the night. His work had improved a lot since the *Royal Rumble*, and we pulled some clever spots going into the finish, with Razor falling backward off the top and me twisting to land on top of him for a pin fall.

My second bout was with Mr. Perfect. Vince hadn't done much with Curt since he'd returned to full-time wrestling after recovering from his back injury. Curt wanted to have a great match just to show Vince that he still could, and he did. In what many would come to rate as our greatest bout ever, Curt and I danced a tango that left them speechless backstage. Our impromptu pre-match interview was casual and hilarious as we kidded each other about whose dad was tougher.

With timing like Ginger Rogers and Fred Astaire, we worked a rugged babyface match with most of our old great spots. Just as I went for the sharpshooter, Curt bent back my taped and supposedly broken fingers, bringing me instantly to my knees. He went for his perfectplex, honouring me by letting me kick out of his finish again. I went for a standing suplex, and we jackknifed backward over the top rope where Curt slammed his bad back hard across the ring apron. With both of us lying on the padded floor, a grimacing Curt rolled in first and I crawled in right behind him. Hebner stepped between us long enough for Curt to slide in and fold me up in a small package, but I managed to flip us over, pinning Curt cleanly with a one . . . two . . . three. It was a classic. Curt beamed with pride when I shook his hand in the ring.

I went backstage and watched Hogan and Yoko on a monitor. They moved in slow motion like a walrus squaring off against a hippopotamus. I rolled my eyes at how lame the finish was. Hulk proceeded to knock Fuji off the ring apron only to turn around and see a Japanese photographer in an obviously fake beard on the apron with his camera. Hulk got close and the cameraman exploded flash paper, supposedly burning Hogan's eyes. It was a disgraceful way of doing the job. When Yoko pinned him, the crowd seemed relieved it was finally over.

Once Hogan got back to his dressing room, I knocked on the door and stepped in. Jimmy Hart, Dave Hebner and Beefcake were with him. I said, "Terry, I want to speak with you."

We stared at each other.

"You told me at *WrestleMania IX* that you'd be happy to return the favour, and as I understand it, now you don't want to even work with me, you won't put me over and I'm not in your league."

Hogan stood there speechless, so I carried on. "Well, you're right, You're not in my league. On behalf of myself, my family and most of the boys in the dressing room, you can go fuck yourself."

He stuttered, "Brother, you don't know the whole story."

"I got the story directly from Vince," I said. "Terry, you haven't said ten words to me since you got back almost four months ago. If you want to level with me, then go ahead. I'm right here!"

"I can't."

"Why not?"

"Because you just told me to go fuck myself."

"That's right, and I'll tell you again. Go fuck yourself."

I turned and walked out, heading straight for the ring to wrestle Bam Bam for the main event finale of the tournament. Bammer and I had our best match ever. After twenty long minutes of Bammer bouncing me around like a basketball, I jumped on his shoulders, dived down to grab his ankles and pinned him with a victory roll. There was no mistaking who the real champion was.

At the end of the show, I stood triumphantly on the podium, wearing a purple cape and crown and holding my sceptre, being interviewed by Mean Gene, when, as planned, Jerry Lawler came out to attack me. Lawler recklessly bashed me with a wooden stool and then picked up the heavy wooden throne and smashed it down hard on top of me—he really hurt me. I vowed to myself that I'd get even with him later.

When I finally got back to the dressing room, Vince pulled me aside to lecture me about how it was unprofessional of me to tell Hogan off. In fact, of the three of us, I felt that I was the only one who was being professional.

"Winning the *King of the Ring* is great," I said, "but it just doesn't pay the same as being the world champion, and you and I both know it!" It was one of those rare times when Vince had no comeback.

For perhaps the first time in my career I really did believe that I was the best worker in the business and that I would never take a back seat to another wrestler again.

The next day I was so sore that I could barely drive to the building in Columbus for TVs. As I hobbled in, Hogan came straight to me. He motioned with his big finger, "C'mere."

I stared at him, and he softened and asked me, "Can I have a word with you?"

I nodded and off we went for a walk.

Terry told me that, yes, I was supposed to win back the belt, but that when Vince changed our contest at *SummerSlam* to a non-title match, he no longer wanted to do the match with me. But I clearly remembered the photo shoot we'd done with the belt and that Vince had told me I'd beat Hulk with the sharpshooter. I knew what I'd been told—and I stood firm.

"Vince said that you said I wasn't good enough for you to even consider putting me over and that I wasn't in your league!"

"That's just not true, brother!" With a mad look in his eye Terry tugged me by the sleeve toward Vince's office and barged right in. I didn't mind. I wanted to know which one of my supposed friends was lying to me. Vince directed pleading eyes at me. And then when Hogan retold his version Vince coolly lied to my face. "I never, ever said it would be a title match."

I realized that there was some kind of head game going on between Vince and Hogan, and I was merely a pawn to be played with and discarded.

When Hogan left the office, he had tears in his eyes. It would be a long time before I'd see him again. He finished up a few days later, and most of the boys suspected he'd be back just in time to score the main event spot with Yoko at *SummerSlam*. Either way, it wouldn't be me. I had Lawler whether I liked it or not.

When I made my rounds through the dressing room, several of the boys patted me on the back and praised me for telling Hogan off. Kevin Nash laughed hard as he described the look on Beefcake's face when he saw my blackboard drawing. Nash hailed from Michigan, played basketball in Europe and was now called Diesel; he was playing the role of Shawn's bodyguard. At just under seven feet, Kevin had an imposing presence that was offset by his good-natured sense of humour.

I was so physically wrecked from the three matches the day before that the promotion gave me the day off to recover: a first. I left to clear my head. Five hours later I got back to the hotel from a bar with a pretty girl with long black hair. In the wee hours of the morning she slept with her breasts pressed against my back. I thought of Julie, how she'd sleep with her breasts against my back just like this girl. I forgave myself as always. I wasn't so bad, I was just very stressed and lonely.

As for Vince and Hogan, their actions spoke louder than their words— and even their words contradicted each other. I kept thinking, I will show them that I really am the best there is, the best there was and the best there ever will be.

PART THREE

STEAL MY CROWN

30

LONE WOLF

To be a great wrestler, you have to be a real athlete and a great actor. To be a great champion, you need to be the best storyteller of them all, because your job is to work with the top hands, whoever they are. Whatever his opponent's age, size, skill or style, whether he is a heel, babyface, Olympic-style shooter, showman, big brute or clumsy oaf, the champ has to have the versatility to bring the best out of each contender. A champion needs to be a champion first to his fellow wrestlers, and to protect and honour the profession for their sake. Or at least that's the way it used to be when I was involved in pro wrestling. Even without the belt, I wanted to play this role and leave my mark on the business for years to come. My formula was simply to outwork and outwrestle my competition. And I would never stab backs.

On the other hand, champion wrestlers tend to hold on to their power like despots, and I shouldn't have been so bitter toward Hogan. He was only guilty of being as greedy as he felt he'd earned the right to be. When I realized that my *WrestleMania IX* cheque was ten times bigger than the biggest cheque I'd ever got before, I wanted to dip my cup in too and never stop. Vince McMahon's previous torchbearers—Hogan, Macho and Warrior—had made so much more than the rest of us all those years.

Throughout that summer of 1993, Yokozuna was the man. He sat in his first-class seat stuffing his face like Henry VIII. Lex Luger was in first class too, a perk left over from his old World Bodybuilding Federation contract. Back in coach, I tried not to let it bother me, but it did. I put Lex over without complaint. Although he was a mechanical worker who stuck to the basics and stayed there, he was a pro—safe, agreeable and easy to work with. I hoped maybe Vince would change his mind and put the belt back on me, but Lex was the one who got the *SummerSlam* match with Yoko.

Hogan was playing hardball in negotiating his contract, and I found out later that Hogan was being pressured by the Feds to roll over on Vince. Subpoenas were being served right and left, and I was sure to get one too.

Vince went to work repackaging and building Lex to be his next superstar. First he erased The Narcissist, then dressed him in skimpy red, white and blue trunks and turned him into his new all-American hero. The face turn was accomplished by having Lex slam Yoko on the deck of the USS *Intrepid* in New York Harbor on Independence Day. No one had ever been able to slam Yoko, not even Hogan. Vince loaded Lex into a red, white and blue bus christened The Lex Express and with much flag waving and hoopla sent him off on a heavily hyped promotional tour, all summer long, across America. Vince couldn't have done more to get Lex over.

I continued to be called upon to put Lex and Yoko over at house shows. I found myself toying with the notion of going to WCW, which was still throwing buckets of money around to all-too-eager former WWF stars. They'd been turning up the heat with improved TV production too, but they still didn't have the hang of it, and their stuff came across, as Vince liked to say, like a "rasslin' show." Their house shows were improving, but they didn't draw despite having some exceptional talent—Sting, Vader, Pillman and a muscled-up Chris Benoit, who looked like Dynamite and was working like him too. There was also a guy from Texas with long, blond hair by the name of Stunning Steve Austin, who impressed me a lot. WCW never did much with him, and I thought if he ever became available Vince should snatch him fast because I'd really work well with him.

The biggest war the wrestling world would ever see was heating up, but this time Vince wasn't steamrolling over small-time promoters such as my dad. He was taking on Ted Turner, with all of his arrogance, business savvy and billions of dollars. McMahon and Turner poked each other in the eye every chance they got, upstaging each other's pay-per-views, screwing each other out of arena bookings and raiding each other's rosters. The WWF's house show business had been down, but the return matches between Yoko and me were drawing Vince some of the biggest houses he'd had in years. Meanwhile, wrestlers who came over, such as Kevin Nash, joked that back in the WCW they were still only working in front of empty chairs.

Yoko was no longer that humble kid who'd shuffled his feet and blushed when he told me that he'd be honoured just to be in the same ring with me. Now he was King Shit. I understood all too well that the belt can do that to you, and I knew it wasn't his fault. Yoko was agile for his size, and like every Samoan wrestler I ever knew, he was a hard worker. When he ran out of gas, I took the action to him so he wouldn't need to move around too much. I bounced my fists off his sweaty head while he rolled his eyes, panting and giggling like a little kid. He'd come off the ropes for his big leg drop, and my head would disappear under his fat thigh with the crowd gasping out of fear. The truth was he never, ever hurt me with it, but afterwards the imprint of his red nylon tights would stay tattooed on my face for days.

Then Vince had me job out to Mr. Hughes, a rookie who was as big and black as he was stiff and green, and I felt I had no choice but to take a good look at my contract. I found out that it rolled over on December 31 and that, if I wanted to jump to WCW, I'd have to give my notice by September 30.

In pure sports you win or lose based on ability, but in pro wrestling, even if you're the best, your credibility can be won and lost in no time at all with the stroke of a promoter's pen — if you don't stand up for yourself. I was still Vince's biggest star, especially in Europe, so I had a good hand in this poker game. As Vince pushed Lex and Yoko past me, I kept my cards close to my vest and my head down through what would be one of the most gruelling and difficult WWF summer schedules ever.

Each time I got home I'd train, tan and play touch football with Dallas and his friends over at the schoolyard. Then, just two and a half days later, I'd find myself plopped down next to Owen as the wheels of the plane tucked themselves underneath us and we headed out on the road again, and we'd compare notes on the goings-on at Hart house. One time that summer I'd stopped by to find my mom upset and crying in her office. Stu sat across from her, with his glasses pushed up on his forehead, his lips pursed and the tip of his tongue sticking out, as he fidgeted with his hearing aid. My mom hesitated to tell me what was wrong until I insisted. As a result of the last few years of Stampede Wrestling, and a few bad investments, they were nearly broke. Although Stu couldn't hear us, I had the feeling he knew what we were talking about. When he left the room for a moment, my mom told me, "We've done a few things with our savings that we shouldn't have." Stu came back and she lowered her voice, adding, "It would break his heart to tell you." I told her not to worry, I would always be there for them. Owen was angry that Bruce, Ellie and Smith were ceaselessly burdening our parents with their money problems, and I figured that this is what my parents had been doing with their life savings: bailing them out.

Owen had given up all hope of ever making it as a top wrestler and was anxiously awaiting news about getting on with the fire department. I reminded him that being a firefighter carried certain risks and that maybe if he hung on a little longer things would improve; I'd nearly thrown in the towel back in 1984, when my fate suddenly changed and the wrestling business saved me. He gave me his little-kid grin and said, "Nah, I'm ready to go home." I told him to hang on until after *SummerSlam'93*, when I thought I'd be in a better position to speak up for him. That was when I expected to play my hand with Vince and press him to re-evaluate and renew my contract. I was going to gamble that he couldn't afford to lose me, especially since WCW was the last place I really wanted to be.

I often spoke to Roddy Piper on the phone. He told me that, although it was clearly a long shot, making action films in Hollywood was the next plateau for me to hit. He stressed to me that I should pressure Vince for control of my Hitman name while I could. I was one of the few wrestlers who actually performed using my birth name, and nobody could ever take that away from me, but Vince could afford to fight for years over my ring name if I split from the WWF.

With the long buildup for me and Jerry Lawler at *SummerSlam '93*, I was disappointed to hear that Stu and Helen would be unable to attend the pay-per-view. Stu had finally relented to undergo long-overdue knee surgery. He'd never had bad knees, but in a bizarre mishap, while receiving a lifetime achievement award from WCW in Atlanta, he tripped getting into the ring, blew out his right knee and had to be carried back to the dressing room!

After a show in North Tonawanda, New York, near the end of July, I walked into a trendy bar with Carlo and stumbled right into Shawn Michaels, who was busy insulting a young woman. When she answered him back, he grabbed her face and gave her a good shove, which triggered a bunch of guys to surround him, jostling for the right position to kick the hell out of him. Diesel, his pretend bodyguard, stepped in for real. One guy held a broken glass and another inched in closer, hiding brass knuckles behind his back. Neither Shawn nor Diesel had seen the brass knucks. I stepped in right behind the guy with the knucks and calmly said, "What do ya think yer gonna do with those?" Eventually, Diesel, Carlo and I backed the unruly mob away from Shawn. He had clearly been way out of line. Shawn's lip had sparked numerous dust-ups over the years. I remember him telling me how once he had been in a drunk tank down south mouthing off to a bunch of cops, who then proceeded to open the door of his cell and beat the hell out of him.

These days, things were wearing on Shawn. He'd gone through a divorce, and on top of that he was worrying about an upcoming court case, resulting from when a TV jobber named Chad Austin was paralyzed in a match with The Rockers in December 1990. Unlike his cocky, boy-toy persona, the real Shawn was often insecure and emotionally fragile. I could tell by the bloody tips of his fingernails, which he nervously chewed on, that he was heading for a breakdown. Shawn's problem (as with so many other wrestlers) came when he mixed downers with alcohol and either forgot who he was or thought he was somebody else. Luckily for him, Diesel, Razor, a host of fellow wrestlers and I were never far away.

I was never sure whether the routine mixing of downers and alcohol was a case of wrestlers trying to kill their pain with drugs or kill their drugs with pain so they'd have an excuse or justification. Shawn and Razor were among the worst, but in those years they also lured into their fold Sean Waltman, a young up-and-comer known as The 1-2-3 Kid. Seeing them wasted and passed out in bars and restaurants after the shows made me fear one of them would be the next Rick McGraw. Razor noticed that more and more I preferred to go off on my own and nicknamed me The Lone Wolf. I didn't want to travel the road they were on.

On August 12 in Calgary, I ran into Davey at B.J.'s Gym and I was taken aback at how huge he was. Obviously WCW wasn't drug testing at all. He happily told me that there was a good chance WCW might put the World belt on him soon.

Later that night, Davey and Diana were at a Calgary rock bar, where an obnoxious drunk was going around goosing women. He'd been told twice by the bouncers to stop. When he groped Diana, she warned him that her husband was The British Bulldog, but it only seemed to egg him on. It wasn't long before a rocket-fuelled Davey had snatched him in a front face lock and choked him out by leaning back and lifting him right off the ground. When Davey released the hold, the drunk fell backward, smashing his skull like a glass jar of pickles on the cement floor. There was a flood of blood. The bouncers, who knew the guy had been asking for it, ushered Davey and Diana out the back door, and they fled the scene. The guy from the bar was in a coma for thirty-two days and was never the same after that. And Davey found himself embroiled in a costly legal battle just when things were starting to look up for him.

The following day, I had a long meeting with Vince at Madison Square Garden. While I thanked him for my *WrestleMania IX* payout, I told him I felt frustrated with the direction I was going in. Lex was never going to get over, especially with *The Wrestling Observer* ripping him apart for his mechanical work rate. In Vince's usual evasive way, he switched trains on me, telling me that he needed both Owen and me to work a couple of shots down in Memphis for Jerry Lawler's struggling Mid-South promotion. I pointed out that Vince had refused to allow me to help my father when Stu was in the same situation, saying he couldn't afford for me to get hurt. Vince assured me that if Owen or I were injured in any way he'd take care of us as though we were working for him. I only agreed because I needed Lawler to work with me at *SummerSlam*.

On August 16, Owen and I arrived in Memphis. As our plane landed, I thought back to the day that Elvis Presley died, when I had a dream that the world was ending. In my dream, I sat on the back steps of Hart house with Owen, Ross and Georgia, all of us serene as we waited for the end. The western sky, in front of us, was lit with a deep red mushroom cloud that drifted toward us. Behind us, framed by a pale blue sky, lay the quiet innocence of Calgary.

Owen and I headed down to the Mid-South Coliseum, where we were to work a tag match against Lawler and Jeff Jarrett, the son of wrestler Jerry Jarrett. Jeff was about Owen's age and size, with long blond hair and thick legs; he was working a gimmick for Vince as a rhinestone cowboy country singer called Double J. Despite all the dirty deeds the fans had seen Lawler do on WWF TV, in Memphis he was still a beloved babyface. Memphis had always been the most insane outpost of the goofiest and phoniest types of wrestling and wrestlers, going back to the 1960s, when promoter Nick Gulas and his son, George, ran the territory. (George was the all-time worst example of a promoter's kid going over all the time, beating everybody when he couldn't beat his own pillow at night. He'd cry out, "Daddy says go down!")

Jackie Fargo, Mr. Pogo, Lawler and Honky Tonk were all born from this hillbilly territory. Jeff Jarrett was one of the rare exceptions from Memphis who could work. Lawler had the biggest crowd in years, more than five thousand rasslin' fans hollerin' and hurlin' garbage at us. Owen and I saw a whole new relevance to the old joke: "What has a hundred legs, three teeth and an IQ of thirty? The front row of the Mid-South Coliseum." The ring made the worst rings I'd ever been in seem like featherbeds. It had wired garden hoses for ropes, and sharp bolts jutted out beneath the pad-less, cloth-covered turnbuckles. The patchy old ring canvas had little or no padding underneath.

As heels, Owen and I snatched the house mic and borrowed from a combination of *Cool Hand Luke* and *Deliverance*—"What we have here is a failure to communicate"—followed by me twisting Owen's ear while he squealed like a little ole pig, spoofing the hillbillyness of it all. We had a great time working the fans up and went on to have a fabulously phony match with Lawler bleeding, pleading and crying in desperation, reminding me a lot of the televangelist Jimmy Swaggart. Owen and I made faces, cussed and wiggled our asses as we wound up our punches like Dusty Rhodes. By the end the fans were fixing to fetch ropes to string us up.

Lawler was more than grateful. Owen and I actually looked forward to going back two weeks later for a return cage match. The day after that cage match, I'd work with Lawler at *SummerSlam* '93—if I didn't trip and kill myself in his pathetic ring or get lynched by hillbillies in the parking lot.

Those two Memphis shows would end up being some of the most fun that Owen and I ever had in the ring together

I had a bad flu when I worked *SummerSlam* '93, but there's no such thing as too sick for a pay-per-view. Everything was centred around Lex and Yoko's American hero angle. Undertaker was expected to carry Giant Gonzales again, and like with so many horrible workers he'd been saddled with, he made a silk purse out of a sow's ear. As for me, the Hart family had now been written into my storyline. My mom and dad had been in the audience at *Monday Night Raw*, and Lawler took to ridiculing them with a series of one-liners: "Hey, Stu, I heard you wrestled when the Dead Sea was only sick!" By the end of it, my mom pretended to be in tears. Even Stu's legit knee surgery was said to be the result of Lawler having shoved Stu in the stairwell as he was leaving the building.

Owen and Bruce sat in the front row, representing the Hart family, dressed in their finest Western wear. Owen was bummed out because he'd just learned he'd been rejected by the fire department. His dream of a happy home life was put on hold, and again wrestling was all he had.

My match had a great storyline that Pat put together, only he didn't tell Bruce about a rib they had planned for him. As I stood in the middle of the ring, Lawler hobbled out on crutches, grimacing with each step. Bruce and Owen did an interview from the front row, blaming Lawler for Stu's knee injury. Lawler explained that he was on crutches because he'd hurt his own knee in a car accident, and as badly as he wanted to whip me, Doink the Clown (Matt Bourne) would wrestle for him. Of course, The Hitman went ballistic when Doink came out. He was carrying two pails and made out to the fans that they were filled with water, but when he hurled one at the crowd, they were relieved to find it was filled with confetti instead. As Doink got closer to where Owen and Bruce were sitting, it looked like he was going to dump confetti on them too. Totally caught off guard, Bruce took a pail of water right in the face while Pat and Vince rolled with laughter backstage.

Owen had caught wind of the rib before the match and had warned Matt that if he got a drop on him he'd rib him back for the rest of his days. This was a serious threat because Owen was a serious ribber! Matt managed to soak only Bruce.

Matt could work when he wanted to and built up terrific heat. Soon enough I had him twisted into the sharpshooter, with my back to Lawler, who crept up behind me, revealing to the fans that he really wasn't hurt at all. He hit me across my face so hard with his crutch that I was worried he'd split me open! I was furious that, once again, he seemed to enjoy being dangerous. Writhing on the mat in real pain, I decided to make him pay for every bit of it. Lawler knew he'd hurt me and gave me some working kicks before fleeing the ring. Jack Tunney, who was still playing the role of figurehead president of the WWF, appeared in the aisle to tell him that the people had paid to see him wrestle me and that since he wasn't really hurt he had to turn around and have a match or face permanent suspension.

The crowd was on fire as I busted my way past a half-dozen refs to get my hands on Lawler. It was payback time and he was in trouble! It'd been two and a half months since he'd jumped me with the sceptre at *King of the Ring*, and it still hurt me to take a breath. I unloaded on him, potatoing him with every punch, and soon he was jabbing me in the throat with a piece of broken crutch, working, building his heat better than any heel in the business at that time. He punched and kicked me, pulling every dirty trick he could think of, until I rallied with another stiff, full-force comeback. When I stepped into the sharpshooter I almost bent him in half—for real. He begged and pleaded for me to ease up, but it was payback time.

The ring filled with referees and agents who pretended not to be able to pull me off Lawler; many of them had trouble keeping straight faces as they actually leaned their weight on me—they didn't like him either! After subjecting him to four minutes of excruciating agony I released Lawler, who was so pained he couldn't move. Keeping to the storyline, the ref announced that because I wouldn't release the hold, I'd been disqualified. Of course I became incensed and attacked a groaning Lawler as they carried him off on a stretcher.

When I came back through the curtain I smiled as I watched Lawler crawling like an alligator to his dressing room. Singer Aaron Neville, who was there to perform the national anthem before Lex's match, laughed, shook his head and said to me, "You did a job on him, man!"

As I drove up to Grand Rapids TV with Owen and Bruce, I was in a good position to negotiate. I'd been subpoenaed and I knew it wouldn't sit well with Vince to have me testify while there was animosity between us. The first thing I asked him was why he couldn't do more with Owen. I pointed out that he'd never come through on his promises to Owen and that with the shortage of talent, it would be a damn shame to see him quit the business. Vince feigned surprise at the directness of my remarks, but after a few minutes he promised me he'd come up with something for my brother in the next few weeks.

Then I told him I didn't like anything he was doing with me. I pointed out that as hard as he tried to paint over me with Hogan's and Luger's colours, the pink and black kept coming through: The fans weren't going to let me fade away. It wasn't fair that he still expected me to carry the shows and do the brunt of the work, while Lex got the belt and the top pay. If he didn't have anything big in store for me, I said, I was thinking of taking a year off. The colour drained from Vince's face, and when I closed the door behind me, I knew I had him.

Just before I flew to New York to testify at the grand jury on September 22, Vince's lawyers carefully prepped me. One even wrote me a note that read, "If asked about the indictment, [say] it's absurd, that after nearly two years of investigating, the Federal Government would indict Vince on an alleged $530 steroid purchase from 1989 when steroids were legal." Vince's lawyers encouraged me to be honest, yet they counselled me on what was safe to say. I went in to the hearing unafraid to tell the truth and braced for almost anything, but what went on in that room still falls under the legal cone of silence.

Meanwhile, my lawyer, Gord Kirke, crafted a tactful letter to Vince, listing my demands for a better deal, including the rights to my Hitman name. He also reminded me that, should I wish to opt out of my contract, I needed to submit a letter of resignation to Vince by the end of September. If I decided to stay, I could rescind it. Even though I knew it was just legal manoeuvring, that awareness didn't shrink the lump I had in my throat when I signed it. When Vince received it, the whole WWF office erupted into chaos.

After the next TVs, in Glens Falls on October 19, I talked with Vince and Pat at a Holiday Inn bar until 3 a.m. I explained that I'd prefer not to go anywhere, and that all I wanted was a fair deal. I said I'd quit over it, and at last they believed me.

The next day, Vince surprised me with a crazy idea for a storyline. He wanted me to have a falling out with one of my brothers, possibly Bruce. He'd grown jealous of me, so he'd challenge me to a match. I'd take the high road, refusing to fight my own brother out of respect for my parents. Then maybe it would be Owen who would step in and offer to face Bruce instead. Bruce would work against Owen and wipe the floor with him so badly that I'd have to come to Owen's rescue. The idea was that I'd eventually end up taking Bruce on at *WrestleMania X*. Then, after all that, Vince would put me with Lex at *King of the Ring* in June 1994, but he hadn't made up his mind who'd go over. I felt confident enough that if it came down to a popularity contest between me and Lex, which it likely would, I'd win.

I could imagine how devastated Owen would be to have Bruce beat him so handily. As badly as Bruce needed a shot in the arm, Owen was a better worker, and he really deserved this chance. I suggested that if I had a pretend falling out with any of my brothers, it should be with Owen.

Pat argued that Owen couldn't handle it, and I suddenly realized that for all these years it was probably Pat who had kept Owen down. I had no idea why, but maybe Pat thought he wasn't big enough to make a huge impact with the fans. I insisted that Owen could do it, assuming I agreed to any of this. Vince raised his index finger as he ran it through his mind. "Hold on a second, Pat. Maybe he's right, Owen would be just fine." I said I'd think about everything and get back to them in a few days.

Afterwards, I told Owen what Vince and Pat had proposed. He actually loved the idea. He reminded me that it was a work, and that this could be the break of his career. Why shouldn't he be able to make main event money working with me like anybody else? I told him there'd be no turning back: We'd have to do this old school: no more riding together, hanging out together. Never insult the fans' intelligence: make them believe it's real. And, I reminded him, I'd have final say on everything.

On November 7, I flew to WWF headquarters to meet with Vince and Pat. I was happy to see the cartoon I'd given Vince hanging behind his desk. Vince joked that he was worried that I was turning into an Ultimate Warrior. I laughed and said. "No, I'm worried about turning into Tito Santana." Tito was a hard worker who'd been used up and pushed aside.

Before I signed my contract, I wanted to make sure I had the rights to my Hitman name and the freedom to pursue acting, as Roddy had suggested. I'd recently agreed to let Carlo represent me, and he was bursting at the opportunity to get me into Hollywood. Vince agreed, which was a huge victory for any wrestler at that time. We shook on it, with Vince telling me that he and I had been friends for so long that we didn't need a contract. Our word was our bond. But days later, Vince sent me a twenty-page agreement. It was even more controlling than the old one, and my lawyer told me I'd be crazy to sign it.

On November 12, J.J. Dillon called to say that Vince had signed off on my revised contract. The thought crossed my mind that a victory over Vince probably meant he'd fuck me somewhere down the road.

31

KANE AND ABEL

IN THE DRESSING ROOM in Niagara Falls in mid-November, I heard that Vince finally had been indicted by the Feds. Then the WWF took another hit when Jerry Lawler was charged with having sex with an under-aged girl. My entire *Survivor Series* match was centred around Lawler and his constant jabs at my family; without him, the match would mean nothing. Lawler was hastily edited out of the weekend TV show, with no explanation given to the fans, and Shawn was thrown in to replace him at *Survivor Series*.

On November 23, Smith, Bruce, Keith, Wayne, Ross, Georgia and my parents all flew into LaGuardia. Vince had invited my brothers to have a brawl at the *Survivor Series* against three masked wrestlers and Lawler—now Shawn would be standing in his place—with Stu managing from the floor, and he thought it best that we have a rehearsal at the WWF's TV studio in Stamford the day before the pay-per-view. I got the Harts, Shawn and The Knights (the one-time-only name they picked for the masked wrestlers) in the ring to explain how the match would go. Owen gave me a nudge to alert me that Bruce had pulled the biggest and greenest of the Knights aside and was giving him a script the size of *Gone With the Wind*, with Bruce presum-ably playing Rhett Butler. I told Bruce the spotlight needed to be on Owen because *Survivor Series* would be the beginning of Owen's heel turn on me. After I explained what everybody's role would be, Bruce went right back to designing the match around himself, and I had to reprimand him in front of everyone. Shawn muttered at him, "If *my* brother was world champion and the best in the business, I think I'd quit fucking arguing with him and start listening to him!" There was nothing Bruce could say in response to that. He shut up, but I could tell the reprimand stuck in his craw.

That night at the Boston Garden I had a strange sense of melancholy as Keith, Bruce and Owen got dressed, while Stu sat with Killer Kowalski reminiscing about the old days. We wore Olympic-style singlets with no leggings, my brothers all in black and me, The Captain, in pink. Martha sat in the front row with the rest of the Hart family, holding Oje. Shawn did a superb job carrying the match, though in fairness everyone worked hard. The biggest pop of the night came when Shawn staggered past Stu on the floor and Stu drilled him with one of his big elbow smashes, which Shawn later told me he was honoured to take.

Owen was highlighted throughout the match and eliminated two of The Knights, but midway through the match, as planned, he "inadvertently" collided with me on the apron and ended up being the only Hart brother eliminated. After throwing a tantrum he left the ring, only to come out afterwards when we were all celebrating the victory to yank me down off the second rope and give me a hard push. I tried to reason with him that it didn't matter because we'd won anyway, but he still acted furious.

Walking back to the dressing room with my brothers after that match was a magical moment. We all knew going in that we weren't expected to have the best match on the card, we were just expected not to have the worst one either. The Hart boys had more than risen to the occasion, and I was proud of my brothers. Stu had a twinkle in his eye.

A week later Owen and I cut promos saying we'd patched everything up and were teaming up at the *Royal Rumble* to defeat the current WWF tag champs, The Quebecers, who were Jacques Rougeau and Pierre Ouellette. My fans would see this as conciliatory gesture to keep the peace in my family, one that would put my shot at regaining the World title on hold. Pursuing the tag strap was seen as a voluntary step down.

There was a shot in Honolulu on December 8. Owen and I landed early that morning. There was no sense in getting a hotel room because we were flying out after the show. In a few more weeks we'd be bitter enemies on TV again, so I said, "C'mon, hang out with your big brother and live a bit!"

That day I introduced Owen to my two surfer-dude buddies, Christian and Tate, who offered to show us around. We hiked through a dense tropical forest, clearing a path as we went, until we came upon a gorgeous fresh-water pond. Hanging from a thick, heavy branch was a long rope, and soon we were swinging from it and dropping off into the water, all except for Owen. Bobbing in the water I yelled up to him, "It's okay, Owen, it's safe." Grinning, he shook his head. "Nah, I don't wanna take a chance on getting hurt."

An hour or so later we hiked up to the salt-water pool in Diamond Head, Christian and Tate lugging a cooler of beer and a bucket of KFC. I took three strides and jumped into the pool. I kept calling Owen to come in, but he was so cautious that he wouldn't. I finally coaxed him out and we straddled the pool wall like a horse, while big, warm, salty waves washed over us. Hanging by our arms we looked out at the blue Pacific as little crabs scurried over the rocks. A pensive Owen said, "There are some at home who don't understand how hard you've worked to get this far. They think Vince just hands you everything on a silver platter. They're so envious of you and me!" I knew full well that the business had saved us and that if we were back home with the rest of them, we'd likely be sinking fast. I told Owen I'd do what I could to get Jim and Davey hired back. Davey quit WCW after he had been extradited back to Canada to deal with the assault charge stemming from his bar fight. And Jim had already blown the $380,000 from U.S. Air.

"Someday we'll come back here with our kids and hang off this spot and remember this moment," I said as I leaned against the rocks with a beautiful red ball of sun blazing above the blue ocean. "To hell with the diet, Owen, you only live once!" The beer from the cooler was ice cold, and we devoured the last pieces of fried chicken.

Blade, Beans and I managed to track down several invisible monsters who were holed up in my bedroom. Kicking open the door to an explosion of giggles and imaginary bullets, I crashed onto the king-sized bed but, like always, I wasn't going to make it. As Beans put bandages on me, Blade dribbled some water into my mouth from a make-believe canteen, tongue stuck out in concentration. My dying scene was interrupted when Julie called out that we were going to be late.

For the first time since becoming a wrestler, I got to celebrate an uninterrupted Christmas Day at home. As we walked into the kitchen at Hart house for another Christmas dinner, Stu and Helen were quietly watching TV as barking dogs and hissing cats wove their way through a maze of legs — people and chairs. An excited stampede of nieces and nephews raced in to greet us. Our three eldest disappeared upstairs to play dolls or down to the dungeon to play wrestle. Life at Hart house hadn't changed much.

Stu lit the stove and put on the tea kettle. "How's tough guy?" he gruffly asked Blade, who was struggling to hold on to Bertie the cat. Then we sat sipping tea while the various lean novice wrestlers that Stu was schooling hung around doing chores and marking out at the same time. "Karl, dawling, would you let the dog out?" my mom said as she smiled at me. Karl was one of the famous LeDuc clan out of Montreal, and Stu and Helen had just let him move in. They always had a meal and a place to sleep for any lost, out-of-luck wrestler wannabe.

It wasn't long before we gravitated to talking about wrestling, my mom pretending to make her usual fuss: not that again. Stu immediately barreled into a story about how, way back in the 1930s, this old shooter, Reb Russell, of similar size and personality as Dynamite, had been in a hotel room in Newark one night when a couple of "black fellas" climbed up the fire escape, came through his window and held him up with a straight razor. Old Reb tore into both of them, with one of them slashing his back as he choked the other one out. Stu said that Reb had prevailed in the end, tossing both thieves off the fire escape to the pavement below.

Stu loved to talk about the tough guys of the business. In his opinion, Haku, Earthquake and The Steiners were the toughest guys around right now. He told me he liked the promos Owen and I were doing, and I could see that the fan in him was eager to see his sons take centre stage at *WrestleMania X*. The talk eventually turned to whether Vince would go to jail. My parents were concerned about what would happen to him and how it would affect me and Owen. I told them that Vince was too clever to wind up behind bars, and that when I had called him about his indictment, he had sounded in good spirits, optimistic even.

That Christmas I received the best presents in the world: Memories of the holidays to keep forever. I played road hockey with Dallas. Dallas also dressed Blade up to look like Razor Ramon. In his fake toy gold neck chains, with a greasy curl on his forehead, Blade announced, "Say hello to the bad guy!" Sometimes I'd push the living-room couches against the wall and wrestle Dallas and Blade, and before long Jade and Beans would join in, and it would go until I let all four of them pin me. Then there was seeing Beans through losing her front tooth, and a much appreciated one-on-one conversation with Jade, now almost eleven, who looked so tall and slender that my eyes welled up as I asked her not to grow up too fast.

At least this time when I packed my bags my heart was full. I'd had a great Christmas and things seemed to be back in alignment between me and Julie.

Every week Vince held on to the belief that Lex would still get over, even though my popularity only seemed to climb higher. It didn't help Lex's cause when the fans voted me the most popular superstar in the WWF. These were my last great days as a babyface hero working in America.

In the days leading up to *Royal Rumble '94*, Owen and I enjoyed our last rides together. On January 12, 1994, at TVs in Florence, South Carolina, Owen and I were paired up against The Steiners for a special home video match. The Steiners were generally happy gorillas, but they'd left a successful career in WCW for Vince's promise of even bigger money, which hadn't materialized. Rick and Scott were impressively built, both outstanding NCAA wrestlers out of Michigan. Rick, the older of the two, was generally more easygoing. He wore amateur wrestling headgear over his short black hair and kept a stubbled beard. Scotty had a mean streak a mile wide, but only if you gave him reason. Sometimes he'd be sprawled out on the carpet in the dressing room, and if either Owen or I made the mistake of walking past him, he'd hook an ankle and pull us to the floor, doing his best to stretch us while we did everything in our power to stop him. Luckily, Scotty was always pretty playful with us. One time in Johnstown, Pennsylvania, Scotty had Curt Hennig tied up like a pretzel after Curt had ribbed him. For over an hour Scotty threatened to shove his thumb up Curt's ass, and the scary thing about it was there wasn't a damn thing Curt could do to stop him, until finally Scotty let him go.

I brought Dallas and Blade to *Royal Rumble '94*. Owen and I decided that we didn't want our kids thinking there was any real problem between us, so we pulled the boys aside in the dressing room to smarten them up. I felt like I was explaining the birds and the bees. Dallas was both relieved and surprised to be in on the secret; I made them both promise not to tell anyone. It was important that they understood that Owen and I didn't really hate each other, because the business was never more important than family.

When Owen and I went out against The Quebecers, Dallas and Blade were in the front row, and I was soon placing my shades over Blade's head. He accepted them like he should have been the kid to get them all along. The storyline called for The Quebecers to badly injure my knee, and then the referee, Earl Hebner, would abruptly stop the match, declaring The Quebecers the winners. Owen acted like he was furious because I hadn't tagged him in. As I struggled to my feet, Owen booted me hard in my injured knee, sending me crashing to the mat. The incensed crowd booed him out of the building because it looked to them like I wouldn't be able to take part in the rumble.

I limped out second to last, to a huge pop, and Lex and I eliminated the last two heels before facing off in a buildup that the fans had been waiting to see. After a flurry of punches, Lex picked me up with his back to the ropes and attempted to dump me out. I fought to free myself, but the two of us toppled backward over the top rope. It was critical to the storyline leading into *WrestleMania X* that our feet touched the ground at the exact same second, even when watched on instant replay and in slow motion by fans around the world. Lex controlled how we went over, and it was a testament to his skill and professionalism that it came off so well.

For the next several minutes WWF officials debated who was the real winner of the rumble. Vince's popularity contest culminated in this moment. Pumping my fist in the air it was obvious to me the crowd was mine—though the refs declared it a draw.

When we left the Providence Civic Center afterwards, Dallas and Blade hid Owen under some jackets on the back seat so the fans on the back ramp couldn't see him.

We drove to Stamford that night so we could shoot promos first thing Sunday morning. That's when Vince gave me the news: "I'm putting the belt on you at *WrestleMania X*. Because of the tie finish last night, we'll have a three-way tournament. Earlier in the show you'll have to wrestle Owen first, and Owen will go over. But then Yoko gets past Lex, and you'll take the strap from Yoko at the end of the night with Piper guest refereeing." It'd been fifteen years since Vince had said I didn't have a big enough name to wrestle at Madison Square Garden. I'd already won the Intercontinental belt there, and now it was sweet vindication to hear this very same man tell me that I was going to regain the world heavyweight championship there too.

Over the next few weeks Owen and I did intense, realistic interviews in which I did my best to sound like a big brother who was sorry it had all come to this, while Owen came across as a jealous hothead trying to knock his older brother off his perch. With Taker off (the storyline was that he'd died in a much-hyped coffin match, but in fact Vince had given Mark time off because his wife was pregnant) and Yoko spent, our angle took the forefront of Vince's booking. The card for *WrestleMania X* was shaping up to have fewer celebrities than previous years; with the negative press about Vince's steroid trial, the WWF had become a dirty word. Vince lost significant sponsors and TV slots in major markets, and WCW, with financial backing from Turner Broadcasting, could afford to gobble them up—and did.

February began with a tour to Austria, Germany and Israel. I knew from the mood on the flight over that somebody was going to screw up and lose their job. The Steiners had been trying to get out of their contract so they could go back to WCW, where a better paying deal with a much lighter schedule was on the table. Vince wouldn't release them, so they began intentionally roughing up some of the TV job boys, forcing him to change his mind. It looked like this European tour would be the last hurrah for The Steiners in the WWF.

On the first day of the tour, Marty Jannetty locked the driver out of the bus and was about to drive off with all of us. Many of the boys cheered him on, but when Marty looked at me for encouragement, all I could say was, "Not one of those guys will help you when they fire you *again*, Marty!" He immediately put on the brakes. He shook my hand and thanked me, then opened the door for the driver and took his seat.

Everywhere we went hysterical fans beat on the windows and ran alongside the bus, chanting, "Hitman! Hitman!" I saw what it meant to these fans for me to be their hero, which caused it to mean even more to me. I couldn't believe that somehow I was bigger than ever in Germany. That year I was paid the tremendous compliment of receiving my third Bravo award in as many years for being their number-one sports hero. I was grateful for the special amenities from the European promoters and tour managers, who made sure I had the best hotel suites. There was often a complimentary bottle of red wine or chilled champagne waiting for me when I walked in. In Dortmund I had a marble whirlpool, antique brass bed, a splendid balcony view of the city, and temptation knocking at my door. One of my regular Fräulein was standing there looking sexy as hell in high-heeled black boots, tight blue jeans and a black leather biker jacket. But the bus was leaving the hotel really early the next morning; I was simply too tired. I went to bed alone and then lay there staring at the ceiling. I knew Julie would have a hard time appreciating that I had just said no to a stunning, black-haired twenty-two-year-old vixen with pouty lips and long legs.

While checking out of the hotel at 4:30 a.m., I saw the tour manager, an efficient, serious little Scotsman named Jake, doing his best to sort out the wrestlers' unpaid bills. Marty Jannetty, drunken and red eyed, was barely able to stay standing as Jake tried to go over his bill with him. Scotty Steiner steamed across the lobby, ripped the bill out of Jake's hand and slapped it on the front desk, pinning it with one finger of his right hand while with his left hand he put a finger to his nostril and blew a nasty green snot across it. By the time we landed in Rome to make our connection to Israel, Marty had been fired again and was already on a plane home.

After clearing the heavily secured airport in Tel Aviv, I spent most of the day sleeping in my room at the Holiday Inn on Hayarkon Street. That night I had a cold bottle of Goldstar beer in my hand at a cool disco built in the ruins of a building that had been hit by a Scud missile during the Gulf War. It had no roof, and I felt like I was back at the Alamo. A moon-lit sky and a balmy Mediterranean breeze made for a perfect night. I downed a long gulp. It was impossible not to notice how bold, beautiful and direct the Israeli women were. I hung out for a while but left early so I could be rested for an early-morning guided tour of Jerusalem that the promoter had set up for me.

Dorit, my guide, quickly figured out that I have a fascination with history. I was amazed that she'd never even heard of pro wrestling: We came from two completely different worlds. Accompanying us on the hour-long ride to Jerusalem were a driver and two security guards who wore several pistols each, strapped to various parts of their bodies. Dorit was an expert on the history of the region based on historical facts, not religious teachings. She told me that Jerusalem means "city of peace" in Hebrew and described it as the centre of the civilized world, the promised land, with a history going back four thousand years.

As we got closer to Jerusalem I studied the rounded gold dome I could see off in the distance, against a pale blue sky dotted with white clouds. The

Dome of the Rock is the holiest place for Muslims after Mecca. As I entered I was abruptly snatched by the wrists by a long, tall gangly Arab version of Abe Lincoln with bushy black eyebrows, thick, muscled forearms and huge, strong hands. He bared his white teeth: "Come, you, wrestle me now!" I had a tough time getting free and suspected that this wiry old fellow had milked a lot of camels in his day. I had an unsettling image of the two of us rolling around, a tangle of arms and legs, Arab Abe putting me in a camel clutch. This was his home turf, surely Allah would side with him. It was a serious standoff, and I didn't take it lightly, because wrestlers were expected to be as tough as they were on TV at all times. I was relieved when a stunned Dorit snapped at him to leave me alone and shooed him off. So much for his dream of beating The Hitman!

Soon I was looking up at the high white stone of the Wailing Wall. I scribbled a small prayer on a slip of paper, "Please God, get me home." I stuck it up high, next to thousands of others, in the cracks between the huge stone blocks. Then we made our way across an open plaza, and I looked up to see a group of Israeli soldiers with machine guns slung over their shoulders casually leaning against a couple of parked Jeeps. Dorit and my security guards froze with fear upon hearing what sounded like a small stampede behind us, and the soldiers jumped to attention, cocking their guns. A sigh broke out across the plaza as I was suddenly mobbed by forty or fifty Israeli schoolchildren who couldn't believe it was me. Some were on their knees kissing my hands as the rest chanted, "Hitman! Hitman!" The soldiers recognized me too. I signed autographs and posed for photos with the soldiers next to their Jeeps. It made me uncomfortable to be idolized in such a holy place, and Dorit simply couldn't believe what was happening.

At our next stop, we retraced the path along the Via Dolorosa that Jesus took as he carried his cross to the place of execution. Dorit said that when astronaut Neil Armstrong visited the city and was told that these were the very steps that Jesus climbed on his way to Golgotha, Armstrong said that it was harder for him to climb these steps than it was for him to walk on the moon. I was particularly amazed by the imprint of a human hand in a white stone wall. Dorit told me it was said that Jesus leaned there while carrying the cross. My hand fit inside that imprint.

We went on to the Dead Sea. We all stripped down to our underwear—even the security guards—and waded in, with Dorit cautioning me not to get the salty water in my eyes. I floated like a cork, awkwardly at first, but then I realized it really was impossible to sink in the waist-high water—it felt like I was floating in an invisible chair. The water burned and tingled my little scratches and mat burns, and especially my skinned-up shins, which had been scabbed up for years from all the front turnbuckles I'd taken. Smearing the mud from the sea bottom on my cuts healed them almost instantly.

We then went for a drive high into the rocky cliffs that overlook the Dead Sea, with the desert of Jordan visible on the other side. I took a position along a ledge of rock where below me three beautiful brown eagles criss-crossed the sky. As I sat there I remembered the time Julie's sister, Sandy, asked me what animal I would be if I could choose. After much delibera-tion, I told her a lion, because they were certainly the toughest, being the king of the jungle. They're agile and they love their cubs. She asked me for a second choice, and I told her an eagle, for much the same reasons. The third choice? After much thought I said a polar bear, because of their perse-verance in surviving the fiercest cold, and doing it all alone. Sandy explained that my first choice, the lion, was how I wanted people to see me. The second choice was how they did actually see me. The third choice, however, was what I really was inside. Thinking on that, I stared down into the cavernous rocky cliffs with the soaring eagles, and I prayed to God to help me hold on for just a little longer. With his help I would not end up as a polar bear, cold and lonely, or as a wrestling tragedy, bitter and broken.

That night as I took on Yoko, Jewish and Arab kids sat together cheering me on. Yoko accidentally came down too hard on me and my nose spawned a river of blood that I defiantly wiped away. I made my comeback with poor old Mr. Fuji taking forever to climb up on the apron with his bad knees, clinging to his Japanese flag on a pole. I grabbed Fuji by the collar of his kimono and waited for him to say "Now," so I could magically move out of the way of the charging Yokozuna, who was coming at me from behind. One . . . two . . . three. Jerusalem. My heart was full as I looked out at all the happy faces.

I arranged for all the wrestlers to take a similar bus tour the next morn-ing while Dorit took me back to Jerusalem. After another inspiring day spent exploring the city, I arrived at the building in Tel Aviv to wrestle Yoko again. When I saw Randy and Owen, they looked like someone had turned a light on in the back of their heads. Randy shook my hand, thanking me over and over for telling him to go on the tour. And Owen told me he wrote a prayer about getting home safely to Martha and Oje and put it in the Wailing Wall. I told him I'd done the exact same thing.

After the show I went to a hotel bar right on the beach, where I struck it rich with an enchanting beauty. To her I was a welcome distraction from the never-ending violence. We strolled along the beach, lit by a full moon; the beach still bore the scars of being pounded with Iraqi missiles. It was a warm night. Salty green waves rolled up to our feet. She walked me to my hotel room and eagerly pinned me to my door with sweet kisses. I thought, I could fall in love with this girl. *Thou shalt lead us not into temptation* was floating around in my head. I settled for one last kiss. As she walked slowly away down the beach, my heart pounded with regret. "I'll be back," I called out. She turned for a moment and smiled at me.

Within a couple of days, I was back in Frankfurt, Germany, one of my all-time best towns in terms of fan reaction. After the match I climbed onto the babyface bus and flopped down into a plush seat. The driver answered calls from the back to turn on a porno movie for the short ride back to the hotel. Scotty Steiner was picking on Tiger Jackson again. The Steiners wouldn't be gone soon enough for poor Tiger, who meekly pulled his cap off and tucked his chin in, like a sad little ghoul, so that Scotty could slobber on two of his fingers and slap Tiger hard on the top of his bald head. Tiger had learned from too much experience: if he didn't cooperate by taking his hat off, Scotty would hit him in the head ten times. Tiger was thirty-five years old, proud, with a lovely wife at home. He took his punishment without saying a word. I had told Scotty he was a better man than to pick on a midget. He always agreed, but that never stopped him. The wrestling business was and always will be filled with bullies, who stripped down and dressed right beside the backstabber, who was next to the clumsy oaf who didn't mean to hurt you, next to the worker you could trust with your body and your life.

Someone interrupted the porno movie and popped in an Ultimate Fighting tape. Most of the boys got to comparing Ultimate Fighters to pro wrestlers. The UFC guys pounded each other's faces and snapped limbs for real, all for a measly $50,000 grand prize. I was proud that wrestling was a work.

I got to thinking what a strange life I led. I'd said I'd get out of wrestling after five years to go home and be normal, but that was twenty years ago now, and this vagabond odyssey had long since become the only normal I knew. My house was bought and paid for, and there were two new cars in my garage. The thought of my kids growing up so fast made me promise myself I'd get home in three more years. By then I'd be forty.

It was hard to believe that in a few days I'd be back in Calgary. I envisioned myself pacing around the pool with the stereo blasting and a tape of my matches on with the sound turned down. I didn't need to hear the hype, I just needed to think. About everything.

WrestleMania X was less than a month away.

32

REL WORL SIMPION

OVER THE NEXT WEEKS, as I drove seemingly endless miles of highway between smaller venues from New York State to Wisconsin, I occupied my mind by studying all the angles to my upcoming match with Owen at *WrestleMania X*. Being Vince's top seller in merchandise was rewarding me with an extra $200,000 per year in royalties, so whatever I did, I had to be careful not to jeopardize that. I thought that Owen's prospects as a cute, bad-tempered underdog, much like the original Hitman character, were really looking up. I couldn't go too soft or too hard on him; I'd need to devise spots that would highlight his high flying while still keeping him heel. I'd have to cleverly outwrestle him, with a tinge of reluctance and regret.

On any given night my view from a bar stool was much the same. Taker was never far off, tipping back a shot of Jack Daniels, his big arms blue with tattoos of skulls and crosses in the dim bar light. Referee Joey Morella would be off in a corner doing his imitation of Freddie, the gay ref from Boston, bugging his eyes out, arching his back and sticking out his butt, much to the amusement of the ring crew, refs and agents. Yoko usually sat at the bar puffing on a cigarette and stirring a vodka and Diet Coke. Never far away were his two fellow Samoans, The Headshrinkers, Samu and Fatu. They were said to be related to Yoko, but the joke was that all the Samoan wrestlers claimed to be bruddas. They were worried about Yoko's weight. Since winning the belt, he'd gone from 450 to 600 pounds. He'd stuff his face with hot dogs and candy bars in the dressing room, but then, like a hot-tempered hippopotamus, he'd kick over tubs of iced sodas because there was no Diet Coke left.

Shawn, Razor, 1-2-3 Kid and Diesel often asked me for advice, on anything from their matches to life on the road. I guess they thought I was a good guy to talk to because I never had any axes to grind. But I was more than a little pissed off when Shawn went to Vince and stole my idea for a ladder match, proposing that he try it on at *WrestleMania X* with Razor. It was hard to complain since I was getting the belt back, but that didn't make it right.

With house show business down across North America, Vince was setting up more foreign tours than ever before to many countries we'd never visited. The wrestling phenomenon was reborn in places such as Hong Kong, Singapore, Philippines, the Middle East and India. The future was calling for me to be a real world champion, the first one actually to wrestle all over the world, even in Japan, where the WWF would soon go head-to-head for the first time with the deep-rooted empires of New Japan and All Japan. I held no allegiance to either and welcomed the chance to return to Japan as the WWF champion.

On March 12, Hogan showed up, sitting in the front row of WCW's Saturday-night TV show. Vince was hurt but told me that he was going to let Terry go: The real war between the WWF and WCW started right then and there. He also told me he'd rather have ten Bret Harts than one Hulk Hogan: I didn't know how to take that, coming from Vince.

Three days before *WrestleMania X*, Owen and I met in Stu's dungeon to construct an entirely different match from the one we had planned. We sat on the old, frayed medicine balls and cleared our heads. I looked at Owen and said, "We're changing everything. This is what we're gonna do . . ."

When I set my bag down in the dressing room at Madison Square Garden on March 20, *The Wrestling Observer* was being passed around. Even before I got the belt back, Dave Meltzer was predicting that my days as champion were numbered. I'd been in New York for a few days already doing media and appearances, and with two big matches, it was going to be a long day. I had the heavy responsibility of opening and closing the pay-per-view in what was expected to be the biggest grossing show of the year.

Julie, Carlo and Gord Kirke had all come to New York to celebrate the big moment, along with New York film agent Michael Frankfurt, whom Carlo was wining and dining. My parents couldn't be there because my mom was having problems with her heart and had been in the hospital. Lawler was back, the heat from his statutory rape charge being judged to have cooled off enough (the charge was eventually dropped), and he used my mom's illness as part of the storyline, saying that the stress of her two sons doing battle was too much for her to bear. I have to say that of all the celebrities Vince hired over the years for *WrestleMania*, none was more co-operative and happy to be there than Burt Reynolds, who was our guest announcer that night.

My music played, and as I made my way to the ring the noise of the New York fans was like fuel in my veins. I kept repeating to myself, Keep Owen heel. He and I clicked perfectly. He played the nasty little brother, cheating viciously at every turn, and I kept outsmarting him, but never in a way that made me look overconfident or cocky. It was a real back-and-forth struggle, and led into working the match around me injuring my knee. Owen went at my leg like a cat attacking a crippled bird. We had the greatest hall of them all coming apart at the seams, twenty-three thousand fans locked into every move. I slammed Owen's thick chest with some hard lifters. He swung for my head with a fist, but I slipped under it. Sleeper! Owen desperately fought his way to the ropes, forcing me to break the hold. He kicked his leg back for a vicious ball shot that left me writhing on the mat. This really got the crowd hot. I was so happy for him that they hated him. He dragged me to the middle of the ring, twisting *me* into the sharpshooter. The fans suddenly realized that Stu must have taught it to both of us! Nobody had ever got out of the sharpshooter, there was no known escape! I twisted, reaching around to hook Owen's ankle, and pulled his leg out from under him, sending him toppling chest-first to the mat. The fans were standing as I rose from the ashes like a Phoenix, having somehow manoeuvred Owen into the sharpshooter instead!

But Owen clawed his way to the ropes again. With the crowd hanging on every move, he charged me in the corner, and I caught him square on the chin with a boot, spinning him completely around. I climbed up on his shoulders and dove forward for a victory roll, but in a split second, Owen collapsed in a squat, on top of me, pinning my shoulders to the mat for the one . . . two . . . three! We came back to the dressing room to back-slaps and congratulations from all.

Yoko was walking around like he was on death row. It was just dawning on him that he was about to lose the top money spot. I knew how it felt; like all ex-champions, he was immediately uncertain of his future. He went on to have a horrible match with Lex, who was unable to garner much sympathy. In a lame finish, the guest referee, Mr. Perfect, disqualified Lex for touching him, and the fans seemed glad when it was over

Not surprisingly, the ladder match between Shawn and Razor stole the show, and why wouldn't it? Even though I'd asked Shawn not to use my original finish, where the heel falls off the ladder and crotches himself on the top rope, he went ahead and crotched himself and tied his foot up in the ropes, while Razor climbed up and took the Intercontinental belt. I watched it on the monitor in the back thinking, You thieving bastard.

Finally, Yoko and I enacted our usual David and Goliath story. Soon I was dragged to a corner so Yoko could squash me like a grape for his finish. He climbed up on the second rope, then slipped and toppled backward. I was quick to move out of the way, because if he landed on me for real he'd most certainly kill me! I was on him like a monkey on a beach ball, hooking his big leg to reclaim the WWF World Heavyweight title!

The rafters shook when guest referee Roddy Piper proudly raised my arm in victory. The ring filled up with wrestlers—Lex, Tatanka, Razor, Kid—and then I saw Gorilla, Pat, Vince and even Burt Reynolds in the ring! Macho Man charged out and gave me a hug. He had tears in his eyes when he said, "I'm proud of you, brother! You deserve it!" Then Roddy and Randy, two legends, told all the boys to pick me up. Like in a dream, suddenly I was back in Grade 8 on my friends' shoulders after I had punched out that bully Brett McFarlane. It's curious that at *WrestleMania* X, a total work, I felt a similar kind of triumph.

I saw Julie, Carlo and Gord in the audience clapping. Owen stood in the aisle glaring at me with burning blue eyes. Despite how he pretended to seethe, he was so happy, he could have kissed me.

This was one of the greatest nights of my life, arguably the highlight of my career, and I was grateful that a beaming Vince had given us this moment. I was exhausted and dripping in Yoko's sweat in the hallway when suddenly Julie was beside me. She was wearing a nice new outfit, and when I didn't give her a sopping wet hug, she misinterpreted it. By three in the morning, the celebration cancelled, Julie was gripping her suitcase with her eyes ablaze. "Bret, I want a divorce. We're done! And I mean it this time!" She slammed the door behind her. I expected her to come back, but she didn't.

When I showed up for TV in Poughkeepsie the next day, I was as deflated as I'd ever been. My heart felt abandoned and scorched, with bits of ash blowing around in it—and yet I was champion of the world.

For the next several days I toured England feeling so despondent about Julie that even being mobbed by fans didn't make me feel better. I called home on her birthday, but the phone bleeped and bleeped. I could only assume that she was out with her friends. When I dropped my bags on the dressing-room floor at the Royal Albert Hall, I remembered the last time I wrestled there thirteen years earlier. It occurred to me that Julie was leaving me then too. Things hadn't changed.

Every night Owen and I worked an even better match than the night before. It was always the pop of the night when I reversed Owen's sharp-shooter and came up with mine, with a remorseless Owen tapping out. We'd perfected the story of what a mean little brother he was.

Between matches Owen occupied himself with orchestrating ribs in the dressing room. One of his latest victims was Oscar, the fat rapper manager of a new black tag team called Men on a Mission, or M.O.M. Three-hundred-pound Mo was cool and mellow with a dyed-white buzz cut and carried the team. Mabel was a 450-pound mass with a white mohawk, who didn't do much but stand there in hideous, baggy purple silk pants. But their gimmick capitalized on the new rap sound, and when Oscar came out shouting on the live mic, "Get your hands up in the air!" he really pumped up the crowd. Owen egged on The 1-2-3 Kid until he tried to seize the heavy, out-of-shape Oscar in close quarters. Kid expected to manhandle Oscar and jumped right on his back, but Oscar panicked, charging back and forth into the walls and knocking Kid silly!

Back in Israel, I was touched to see a street kid about eight years old waiting to greet me at my hotel. He was wearing a crudely sewn pink and black replica of my ring outfit and holding a cardboard sign that read, HITMAN NEW REL WORL SIMPION. I put my arm around him and asked who helped him make his outfit. In broken English he proudly explained that he had made it all by himself and added, "I don't want to bother you. I just want to look at you. You are my hero."

When the bus pulled away for double shots in Haifa and Halon, the boy rode his bike alongside, popping wheelies and giving me the bullhorn sign. At every traffic light he'd catch up and wait below my window so he could pull his Hitman shades down and pop another wheelie just for me. He kept up with us for miles. Soon the boys on the bus were cheering him on. Just when we thought he couldn't keep up any more, he'd come around a corner and give me the bullhorn sign, until he finally faded into the distance. I never saw him again. I loved that little boy.

I finished off the tour in Tel Aviv with Owen, on last in the main event, pro wrestling's version of Cain versus Abel. Later that evening I strolled down the soft, brown-sugar sand behind the Holiday Inn in Tel Aviv. Another beautiful night, the black sky filled with stars and the red blinking lights of Israeli military jets fading in and out between clouds. The shore was still lined with barricades that looked like giant steel jacks glistening in the moonlight. The girl from last time gave me a long kiss goodnight and walked out of my life forever. The scent of her perfume lingered as I lay in bed tasting her on my lips. What started out as a slow tremor of guilt soon thumped in my chest, and like something had suddenly taken over my controls, I grabbed for the phone to call Julie.

It was a long call, but we patched up our battered warship and sailed on—again. I told her if things went right for me as champ I really could be home in only three more years and asked if she could last. She said she could, but I heard the sob in her voice and felt like a real bastard as I smelled the Israeli girl on my fingers. The world was my cage, and home was a dream that I wet my lips on.

At the end of April, I called my mom to tell her some good news: Because of the success of the angle with Owen, Jim and Davey were going to be hired back, that is if Davey could get out from under his assault charge.

From the lilt in her voice, I could tell that the jolt of joy was as good for her as the electrical one the doctors had given her heart. I told her I'd come up to see her and Stu that Tuesday to wish Stu a happy seventy-ninth birthday before I left for a tour of Japan.

I arrived at Hart house around four-thirty with Julie and the kids in tow and parked beside Owen's new van. I couldn't help but smile at seeing one of my mom's crayoned signs taped to the outside of the kitchen door. "Happy 79th birthday Grampy!" She'd hang a perfectly lettered sign with the relevant details for birthdays and other occasions because with such a big family, it helped everyone to keep track. We barged into the kitchen, and I could see Stu's tattered ostrich-skin cowboy boots sticking out of the stairwell where he was sitting talking on the phone. He put his huge hand over the receiver and bellowed upstairs to my mom, "Tiger, there's someone here to see you." Jade clamped a large toy tiger in her arms, and Beans carried a small gift box in tiger-striped wrapping as I heard the flip-flop of my mom's slippers coming down the stairs. Stu wasn't so big on receiving presents but loved it when we brought something with us for my mom.

Over the years, Stu affectionately modified my mom's nickname from Tiger Belle to Tiger Balls. She let out her gorgeous laugh when she saw that the box was filled with tiger-striped ping-pong balls. Soon a pot of coffee was brewing. Stu was still trapped on the phone. My mom explained, "It's Diana. She and Ellie call him every single day about Jim and Davey." She cupped her hand over her mouth to whisper, "They're losing everything now."

I wanted to wish my dad a happy birthday. My mom pleaded with him to get off the phone, but Stu had a hard time saying no to his daughters, and the conversation stretched on. Stu finally told Diana that he just wanted to say goodbye to me before I left, and she took offence. With a pained look, he sighed, "She hung up on me!" I shook his hand, but the phone rang again. This time it was Ellie. Stu put his hand up, signalling me that he didn't want me to go, so I chatted with my mom a while longer. After a few minutes he set the phone down to tell me Ellie wanted to thank me herself for the new break for Jim. But Ellie was cold and distant as she went on a bitter rant about how Vince McMahon owed her and Jim a living, conveniently overlooking the fact that it'd been Jim who'd got himself fired in the first place and that he was lucky to be hired back at all after throwing that TV monitor at Chief. As far as I knew, Jim hadn't paid Vince back for the lawyers who'd won him the settlement, which was all gone now anyway. When I hung up, I realized that she hadn't thanked me for anything.

There was a lot of doom and gloom at WWF headquarters. Vince had to pay out two huge settlements: one to Jesse Ventura for $810,000 in back royalties and a staggering $26.7 million to Chad Austin, the jobber paralyzed by The Rockers. Not to mention that Vince's trial was fast approaching. Bam Bam and Yoko, who kept up with the business in Japan, warned me that the WWF tour was going to bomb big-time.

That first day, the Japanese press was mostly interested in the impact of Hogan going to WCW and Vince's legal woes rather than the tour itself. Nonetheless, when I peeked through the curtain at the crowd in Yokohama, it wasn't such a bad house after all. I was working a title match with Macho Man. Although he'd never worked Japan, his exposure on Vince's TV had made him a legend over there. He saw me as the ideal opponent to, in a sense, restore him to his proper place: Vince hadn't done anything with him for so long that it was beginning to eat at him. All Randy wanted was a little respect. When Jack Lanza came to us and flatly said to me, "Catch something quick on 'im," it wasn't hard to read the dejected look on Randy's face. It showed Randy how little the office cared. Not so long ago, Lanza would never have spoken to Randy like he was a jobber. So I told Randy, "Let's just do it for us." We went out that night and had a beautiful match, although I did give him a small spud when he caught a boot in the face, opening a gash in his eyebrow. The blood only added to the drama, and the usually sombre Japanese fans came to their feet when I slapped on the sharpshooter and Randy tapped out.

"Sorry 'bout your eye," I said back in the dressing room. It was a deep cut, but he smiled and said, "That's okay, it's good for the business."

Lanza came up to us, his bad eye looking like a burned-out headlight, and swatted us on our asses with his clipboard, "Great, guys!"

Randy shot back, "Save it, Lanza!"

I thought the Japanese media would appreciate how I worked completely different matches with Macho, Yoko and Bam Bam, but it didn't seem to mean anything to them. I thought back to Puerto Rico and couldn't believe it'd been sixteen years since I was a naive kid sitting out on the rocks in the ocean promising myself that I'd make my mark in this crazy wrestling business. I owed so much to my old teacher, mentor and friend Mr. Hito. Upon arriving in Osaka, Owen and I went to visit him at his restaurant. He looked thin and beat up and I could see every dent and scar, but he was just as sharp as ever.

He cooked us up a Korean barbecue and while we talked I thought back to when he taught me the *art* of wrestling; how to fall, how to protect myself and how to protect the guy I worked with. When I thought about The Rockers breaking Chad Austin's neck, it dawned on me that thanks to Hito, I'd never seriously injured a single wrestler. From what he said, it seemed

Hito was wise enough to be content being an old dog chained to the porch, yet I sensed he really missed the way things used to be.

The night before the final show of the tour, I sat with a dog-faced 1-2-3 Kid in Sapporo. By the end of our one day off, we had grown tired of samurai soap operas. Restless at the hotel, we had ended up at a sleazy fuck show. Only a little while back I was bobbing around in the Dead Sea—how did I end up here?

Pretty Russian girls were lying on the stage rolling condoms over tiny thumblike dicks, getting fucked and giving blow jobs, while Japanese businessmen fingered them and laughed. It's strange where people end up in life. A voice in my head reminded me that once upon a time I cut my head with a razor for $50 a night and thought nothing of it.

After the last show, we were bussed straight from the arena to a chartered plane for an eight-hour flight to Guam. We all slept on the plane and ate only dry cucumber sandwiches that we washed down with beer. When we landed we were sent straight to the building like cattle. In the dressing room, wrestlers were flopped out on dirty floors, too tired to chow down on pizza. Owen and I spotted a fully stocked gym out back, and as wiped out as we were, we squeezed in an intense workout—we hadn't seen a gym in two weeks.

More than once that night, I felt my legs buckle and go out from under me, but the crowd was so pumped up we couldn't help but work hard for them.

After the show, we went straight back to the airport. All I remember of Guam is a few palm trees. Back on the chartered plane, the only thing to eat was more pizza, with plenty of beer to wash it down. Like hungry animals we obliged. We crossed the international Date Line, and when we landed in Honolulu we lived the entire day of May 12, 1994, all over again—like Guam was just a dream.

Owen had turned twenty-nine a few days earlier, so I suggested to him that he stay over with me to celebrate in Hawaii. My two surfer dudes were waiting at baggage claim, only now there were three of them. Tate's younger brother, Todd, had come along. While Owen and I always made a point of kayfabing, today would be a rare exception because the surfer dudes couldn't care less about our storyline. We went straight to the beach, where we strapped on some life jackets and took off in a six-man rubber dinghy. The sun was high and bright, and waves splashed my hand as it hung over the side. Owen and I each held a beer, and he was as purely happy as I'd ever seen him, and then maybe so was I. After about a half-hour we coasted close to the shore, ready to get back on land, when Chris decided he wanted to show us the barrier reef, where the ocean floor drops off a couple of miles off shore. A few minutes later he idled the dingy and pointed to where the blue water fades to black and said, "That's hundreds of feet deep." Then the motor cut out. From the worried looks on the surfer dudes' faces, I realized we were out of gas.

Tate kept asking Chris whether he thought he could swim ashore. Chris stood on his tiptoes and peered out at Waikiki, a couple of miles away. No sooner did Chris decide that he could do it than he changed his mind. He explained that there had been shark attacks in the area recently. We had no flares, no food, no drink, and we were drifting farther and farther out to sea.

Owen thought it was all a rib and just smiled at me.

"Owen, I'm not kidding."

"Good try, Bret."

After a half hour, when we really started to cook in the hot sun, it dawned on Owen that this was no joke. All we could do was hope that someone would rescue us, maybe the coast guard. Finally, Christian decided that waiting wasn't going to get the job done and dove into the water. I feared for him, but he was a terrific swimmer. I reminded Owen of the episode of *The Simpsons* where Homer gets lost at sea, but Owen was in no mood for humour. Then I joked about what would happen if Owen and I were lost for several weeks. Perhaps we could even upstage the negative headlines about Vince and be seen as a welcome diversion! The whole wrestling world, along with our friends and families, would search everywhere for us and finally when we were rescued, when we would meet the onrush of reporters, Owen and I would kayfabe like the pros we were and persuade them that despite being lost at sea in a dinghy we still weren't talking to each other! A smile started to break on Owen's face, and we were both grinning as we caught sight of a motorboat speeding toward us carrying Chris waving a gas can. In no time we were safe on Waikiki beach.

Afterwards, Owen and I went back to the saltwater pool and gorged on fried chicken and cold beer. That night, Taker was back on the card. He'd been home for a few months, and it was great to see him. After the show, Owen and I went back to kayfabing because there were too many fans around, but later on, like two colliding marching bands, the babyfaces and the heels ran into one another on a Honolulu street corner. Lost wrestlers. Ones like Owen, who were out long past their bedtimes. Ones so cheap they wouldn't blow their dough on beer or girls or expensive hotel rooms. And, of course, wild ones, who lived just for moments like this. Nobody had slept yet and delirium was setting in.

Taker had a grin on his face like Jack Nicholson when he got returned to the ward in *One Flew Over the Cuckoo's Nest*. We soon sat at a crowded strip bar with beautiful, naked girls prancing around us. Everyone was doing shots in honour of Owen's birthday and Taker's return.

I hugged Owen on a street corner just before he left for the airport. It was one of the few times I ever saw him celebrate; he was drunker than I could ever remember him being, smiling his face off, sunburned and swaying. I slapped him on the shoulder, "I'm happy for ya. Oje! 'Bout time you let your hair down."

"I had such a great day," he said. "I'll never forget it." And neither would I.

Hours later I lay in bed, the room spinning just a bit. I wasn't expecting anything as the China doll I'd brought back to my room stared at the ocean from my balcony. She turned around casually unbuttoning her white blouse. I was captivated by her shy smile. As she worked my jeans off I looked deep into her catlike eyes. My lust was always stronger than my guilt.

I felt like I was being carried by a strong current in a fast river. With Owen and me headlining, Anaheim, San Jose, Chicago and New York did the best house show business since the glory days of Hulkamania. We were each making $7,000 to $10,000 a week. Even Martha stopped hating wrestling for a while.

We headed back to Europe at the end of May, landing in Nuremberg on May 29.

After the show that night, I asked one of the locals where there was a good rock 'n' roll bar and he suggested a place called Lizard Lounge. I told Oscar, the manager from Men on a Mission, to meet me there, but when I showed up with Kid, my faithful sidekick of late, it turned out to be a heavy metal hangout with neo-Nazi skinheads guarding the door.

Then Oscar strolled through the front doors, oblivious to the slack jaws and scowls of the doormen. When he said, "Wassup Bret?" I told him to stay real close. Only then did he check out the place and realize he might as well have come to a Klan rally. But Oscar was a man, and he wasn't going anywhere. So we had a few beers, and Oscar confided that he was afraid that something was going to go off between him and Shawn, Razor and Diesel, who'd made it clear that they didn't like M.O.M. I told Oscar if it got serious to tell me and I'd keep an eye on things. Then Oscar shuffled out, nodding politely to the skinheads at the door, who nodded back dumbfounded, no doubt wondering whether he had brass balls or no brains!

By four in the morning, Kid and I were at The Green Goose, which was packed with American GIs and drunken WWF fans who spent every mark they had travelling from town to town partying every night with the touring wrestlers. Kamala's former ring manager, Harvey Wippleman, had met an

English fan in Germany and married her like she was a mail-order bride. Yoko, a big, fat bullfrog with a ponytail, sat perched on his lily pad, a cigarette hanging from his lips next to Mabel, black as coal and as big as a mountain. Which lucky girl would win their hearts? Diesel weaved his way toward me way through the sweaty mob. Vince had just put the IC belt on him so he could work with me at *King of the Ring*. Since he'd come to the WWF, he had only been Shawn's bodyguard, and he was worried about how he would handle our match. I liked Kevin and said I would do all that I could to make him look good. He told me that earlier that evening, Shawn and Razor got so wasted on pills and booze that some fans helped them back to the hotel and tucked them into their beds. The pill problem was getting dangerously out of control.

Berlin was the crown of the tour. When I did an autograph session they had to shut down major downtown streets. I signed for more than four hours to keep the peace.

Then it was on to Italy. In Milan, after a barn burner with Owen, I stood on the middle rope in the corner watching him storm down the aisle, turning back to flip me the bird. I nearly burst out laughing as he jammed his thumbs under his armpits and flapped his elbows, shouting, "You're a chicken!" My music blared as young kids pressed in around the barricades and I high-fived hundreds of eager hands as I made my way down the aisle. I couldn't help but feel as though my hand had been touched by angels.

The next day the bus drove by the ruins of the Colosseum in Rome, where gladiators had once fought starved and tormented lions, tigers and bears to the death as a form of entertainment. Near the Colosseum hung colour posters trumpeting the rivalry between Owen and me. Whatever it was that we were doing certainly made more sense than what they did back then. Who'd have ever thought that two Hart brothers would battle it out in Rome right across from the Colosseum? Sometimes it was too much for both of us.

33

BIGGER THAN I EVER IMAGINED

In Baltimore for *King of the Ring* on June 20, the talk in the dressing room was all about Hogan signing with WCW. Turner's operation had begun taping all its shows from Universal Studios theme park in Orlando. It made for a strange TV audience. The wrestling show was looked at as a free attraction by vacationers who were herded in and out and had to be prompted to cheer and boo because they didn't have a clue what the story-lines were. But Hogan had already had some positive impact on WCW's ratings, and there was concern for the financial stability of the WWF. It had settled the big lawsuits and was now staggering from two failed ventures: the WBF and the disastrous launch of a bodybuilding supplement line called ICOPRO. I kept thinking that if only Vince'd find some new talent for me to work with, I could do so much more for him. I was facing Diesel, with Shawn in his corner, so Jim walked out with me, and it was just like old times. I retained the World belt when The Anvil attacked Diesel because Shawn kept on interfering during the match.

Minutes later, The Anvil slammed Razor into a post to help Owen win the *King of the Ring* tournament—and the fans suddenly realized that The Anvil had only helped me keep the belt so that Owen would have a chance to take it from me later. Just like that, The Anvil was a heel, aligned with Owen. Owen never looked happier than when the huge, purple *King of the Ring* crown was placed on his head. I just hoped for Jim's sake, not to mention Ellie's and their kids,' that his troubles with drugs and booze were over, which he insisted they were.

I had been on the road for twenty-three days straight, and I couldn't remember ever feeling this tapped out. It wasn't just me—everyone was wiped. The last three days of the tour were TV tapings in small towns hundreds of miles apart: Bushkill and then Bethlehem, Pennsylvania and finally Ocean City, Maryland. I had to arrive each day by eleven to do promos, media and photo shoots, and then I was expected to work at least twice each night. I almost always finished up well after midnight, when there was no hot water left in the showers. On the night before I was supposed to be in Bushkill, I drove two hundred miles on only a few hours sleep, then caught a morning flight from Toronto to Newark. There to meet me at the airport was the smiling face of Marcy Engelstein, a Bette Midler–like blonde two years younger than me. We'd met after a match back in the 1980s, when I was limping along with a badly sprained ankle and she asked me if I needed help. We fast became close friends and she'd been helping me ever since. When we met she didn't know anything about wrestling or me, but she quickly took to, and was taken in by, the strange mix of humanity in the wrestling business. I rode with her to countless towns, which was always a much-appreciated respite as I was often dead tired. Marcy developed an uncanny ability to accurately analyse my career in ways nobody else could. My trust in her judgment became vital to me and when I wasn't riding with her, I always called her right after my matches to see how I came across. She'd been flying under Vince's radar for years, leading a team of diehards who rallied my fan support in every nook and cranny of the world, growing a vast international network of contacts and connections and doing it all before the age of the Internet. Marcy saved my ass lots of times in lots of ways, but on this particular trip I really think she saved my life.

With Vince's trial only days away, we weren't expecting him to be at the Bushkill taping, so we were surprised when he walked in, his neck in a soft brace following recent surgery. I was about to take on The 1–2–3-Kid, who was pacing around nervously. It was a big match for him, but I also knew it was important to someone else, a ten-year-old named Jason, pale and thin, clutching a Hitman teddy bear under his arm. Even cancer couldn't take away his smile as I draped the belt over his narrow shoulders. When I told him I'd dedicate my match to him, he excitedly coached me to beat Kid but not to beat him too bad. We posed for pictures, and I signed his shades. I'd been told that Jason wasn't expected to see next week. When I said goodbye to him, he hugged me tight. Later I showed a Polaroid photo of him to The Kid, as an exercise in keeping our perspective.

The enthusiastic, small-town crowd knew there was little chance that The 1-2-3 Kid could take the belt from me. I rocked Kid with some of the best lifters I'd ever thrown, and he took them beautifully. After only a few minutes the crowd was in awe and kept cheering like crazy—right up until Kid climbed to the top turnbuckle and went for a drop kick. I caught his feet in mid-air and stepped into the sharpshooter. He tapped out instantly and I was crouched down beside him, helping him, as the crowd applauded both of us. This was the true art of wrestling: no cheer and boo signs needed here. When the match was over, Vince smiled and thanked me for being the hardest working wrestler in the business, and Jim was stunned to hear him. Jim was only just starting to realize that I wasn't just one of the top guys, I was *the* top guy.

It struck me as odd when Pat told me that my next big angle would be with Bob Backlund, who'd first won the WWWF World title back in 1978. The new marketing angle of the WWF was that we were the new generation, whereas WCW was the retirement league. I did my job, heading off to Ocean City, where I scored a clean win over Backlund in a classic old-school match. But when I went to shake his hand, the normally good-natured Bob flipped out and cracked me across the face with a stiff slap. Then he pounced on me and locked me into his cross-faced chicken wing, a serious shoot hold that was every bit as painful as it looked. After several long minutes a hysterical Bob had to be pried off me by agents and referees. As I lay writhing in the ring like a twisted-up old coat hanger, Backlund stared at his hands as if even he couldn't believe he'd just gone nuts: He played his role perfectly.

I still had one last match to do with Owen, at the end of the night. And I was not looking forward to the five-hour drive in the dark that'd get me back to Newark in time to catch an early flight home. As Joey Morella checked my hands and gave me instructions at the beginning of the match, he suddenly said, "I don't know how you do it. You're the best worker I've ever seen, brother, I mean it!" Afterwards, when he was leaving with Harvey Whippleman, I called out to him to be careful driving home. I was so burned out I could barely keep my eyes open, so Marcy took the wheel and got me to the airport on time.

I slept all the way home on the plane. The phone was ringing as I walked into my house. It was Marcy, who could barely get out the words to tell me that on the same road we'd travelled, Joey had fallen asleep at the wheel and veered into a ditch. He was killed instantly and Harvey Whippleman was badly injured (he eventually recovered). People would accuse Vince of causing the deaths of many wrestlers over the years in various ways, but I can say that Joey was most certainly a victim of the WWF's Killer Kalendar. It could just as easily have been any one of us.

Julie was coming with me for a tour of the Far East, including The Phillipines, Hong Kong and Singapore. After a wild all-night flight on July 14—after which the wrestlers were banned from flying Cathay Pacific Airlines—Julie was amazed by the frenzied reception that greeted the wrestlers when we cleared customs. It was the first time she became aware of the magnitude of my crazy day-to-day life on the road.

The bus ride to the hotel was an eye-opening series of contrasts that neither of us was prepared for. Gardeners manicured lush green lawns of palatial

André finally forgave
me for that crazy drive
to the airport.

The early Hart Foundation.

Julie and I in 1986.

King Kong Bundy with Dallas, Julie and Jade at our house.

Our Christmas photo in 1990, everyone dressed in Hart Foundation jackets. Jade and Dallas are in the back row, Sabina— Beans—is on my lap and Julie is holding Blade in the Hitman shades.

Animal and Hawk
backstage with
Beans, Jade and
Dallas; and Beans
with the Hulkster.

Hart-throb, or at least that's
what even the guys told me.

Owen in his favourite blue shirt; and Stu and I at Owen's wedding at Hart house.

My four children, Christmas 1990.

Mugging for the camera with Dallas, and with Blade (below)

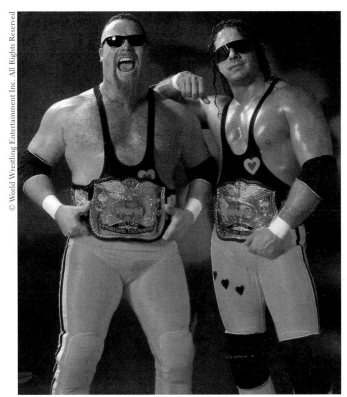

The Hart Foundation with our Tag Team belts.
Below, backstage at *WrestleMania VII* with Willie Nelson.

My friend Roddy Piper.

In action with Curt Hennig at *SummerSlam* in 1991.

Intercontinental Champion, 1991.

Jade with Rick Rude.

Davey and Tom with Dallas.

Dallas with Miss Elizabeth and Randy Savage.

With Roddy at *WrestleManiaVIII*.

Stu and me posing in his kitchen with the WWF World Heavyweight belt in 1993.

I've got Owen in a side headlock.

Stu and me with Shawn Michaels at the *Survivor Series* in November 1993.

Playing to the crowd from the heart

With Davey at *SummerSlam* 1992.

With Shawn at
WrestleMania XII.

Stone Cold at *WrestleMania XIII.*

Brothers and champions.

Brothers in the ring. Owen, *WrestleMania* X.

The New Foundation. Left to right, Owen, Pillman, me, Jim and Davey.

Me and Taker at the Berlin Wall in 1996.

In Kuwait with the U.S. 7th Cavalry Garryowen Tank Division. That's me, Owen and Davey in the middle.

With Earl (on the left) and Dave Hebner.

My parents' fiftieth wedding anniversary, on New Year's Eve 1997.

With the Great One.

Goldberg with Blade.

Stu in the office he shared with my mom. Her chair is empty.

Allen Turowetz

With Ali after my
stroke in 2002.

Jim Allen

Cinzia.

Marcy Engelstein

In the summer of
2005, with Vince.

homes that seemed to flash by in an instant, only to be replaced by countless cardboard shacks in which poverty-stricken families barely existed.

At the hotel, we were ushered to a huge suite that had a balcony with an oceanfront view, revealing a rundown plaza over which hung a pall of thick smog that stuck to everything in the hot, humid air.

The following day, Julie and I went for a stroll along the beach, but we were taken aback by the numbers of beggars and drug addicts, many of whom sniffed glue from plastic baggies while they pleaded with us for spare change. A murky-green tide washed slime and garbage up at our feet, and one desperate Filipino woman tried to sell me what appeared to be her ten-year-old daughter for some quick sex. To escape the beggars and drug addicts, I paid $80 for a horse-and-buggy ride so we could see the sights, but the road was lined with street people and prostitutes. The driver whipped a small, emaciated black pony until I finally insisted he let us off. I figured the poor horse was about to drop dead as it panted and wheezed, with white froth and snot hanging from its nose.

On the walk back to the hotel we stepped over discarded syringes and manoeuvred our way past street people who were shooting up, or sitting naked, or fornicating, as sad-eyed kids sniffed glue to make it all go away. A warm sprinkle of polluted rain pissed down on the whole wretched mess, but even a downpour of biblical proportions couldn't have begun to wash this place clean. Back at the hotel I looked out the window and saw rising up from this cesspool an inordinately large number of Catholic church spires that, despite the grime that was everywhere, were immaculately kept.

That night we all bussed to the other end of Manila for the first of two shows in as many days. It was pouring rain as the bus made its way through bustling streets. We were paralyzed by the sight of such widespread human degradation: It actually made what we'd seen around the hotel seem tame. Expensive cars zoomed by the poor. No matter what direction I looked, I could see people hiking up their dresses and pulling down their pants to urinate and defecate wherever they pleased. Manila reminded me of a backstage toilet in Poughkeepsie after three days of TV tapings. It seemed to me that there were police everywhere who were just as helpless as anyone else to do anything about it.

Both shows were completely sold out and the enthusiastic fans seemed to love every bit of them. I had a tremendous fan base in the Philippines, and the letters they'd written to me over the years told me that there were good and decent people there, but I don't know how they managed to keep their heads above the squalor. I felt a renewed gratitude to people who devote their lives to environmental and humanitarian causes in an effort to keep the whole planet from turning into a living hell.

Hong Kong was a different story. We stayed at an Omni hotel located right next door to a Planet Hollywood, where we were given free drinks all night, every night, because celebrities rarely got out that way. Hong Kong was the land of Rolexes, silk suits and knockoffs. Julie and I went shopping and visited pagodas, Buddhist temples and markets where the stink of fresh fish hung in the air and ducks hung from hooks, which didn't seem so bad after Manila.

Backstage, the agents announced that Vince was acquitted of all charges. Now he could turn his attention to fighting off the onslaught from Ted Turner and WCW. I had no doubt that Vince would set things right, and I was eager to help him.

When I looked at Vince's roster, I didn't see anyone who could unseat me as champion, unless he had a new star somewhere under wraps. Also, it would take a couple of months to build someone up. Still I had a strong hunch Vince would head into winter with a new champion. Vince was growing desperate for fresh talent, but there were few wrestlers left to bring in or bring back. I mentioned that Chris Benoit and Stunning Steve Austin might be available, both of whom were working for a brash, upstart outfit called Extreme Championship Wrestling.

ECW was based out of a bingo hall in Philly and was fast becoming the number-three player in the business. Their TV shows aired in only a few markets, but they were starting to have an impact and, in my view, not a good one. They prided themselves on what they called hard-core wrestling, the bloodier the better, with wrestlers who purposely hurt each other to get a pop. Alternative music was big at the time, so ECW billed itself as alternative wrestling. For wrestlers who couldn't get into WWF or WCW, they were another option.

At TVs in Cincinnati in early August, I learned what I already suspected. Vince was indeed thinking of a new champion and was toying with the idea of putting the belt on Bob Backlund. I argued that this was not something Vince should do. I liked and respected Bob, but he wouldn't be able to carry the house shows. The idea also didn't mesh well with Vince's slick, humorous new generation promotional campaign. Backlund was older than Hulk Hogan and just a little younger than Ric Flair.

But that night I went to sleep happy because a friend of mine named Mitch Ackerman, who was with Disney studios, had come up with a line on an acting gig for me that I was really looking forward to. On August 23, I met with Steven North, the producer of a TV series filming near Calgary called *Lonesome Dove*, based on the critically acclaimed book and miniseries by Larry McMurtry. They were going to start on a script for me right away.

August 29 in Chicago. *SummerSlam '94* was the inaugural event for the brand-new United Center, and twenty-three thousand tickets sold out in hours. The entire Hart family was there except for Keith and Alison, and all of them were going to be involved in the storyline of the cage match between Owen and me, which the WWF had told us was going to be our last match together. We knew the match itself was going to be easy, despite the fact that we couldn't chance any blood because the latest ticks on Vince's hide were citizen groups lobbying to censor TV violence. Vince was forced to remove anything even remotely violent or he risked losing his time slots. Besides, neither Owen nor I wanted to put my poor mother through a match where two of her sons were covered with blood. Our only option was to make as many dramatic near-escapes as we could.

Owen came through the cage door looking cut in his black singlet and tore straight into me. For the next thirty minutes we brawled up and down, back and forth, until finally Owen made a last escape over the cage. I climbed up to the top and managed to catch him by the hair and pull him back inside. I suplexed him standing off the top corner; falling backward, I held him safe and secure. Then I tried to escape, but Owen caught me by one foot, dragged me back and twisted me into the sharpshooter. I'll never forget the pride I felt when I heard the crowd pop even without the blood. I slowly reversed the sharpshooter as Owen frantically fought his way to the ropes.

Below us, sitting behind Bruce, was Jim, who was doing a great job looking like a school bully slouched at his desk. Owen and I climbed over the top to the outside. Owen discreetly braced a leg through the bars as I gave him one last bash into the cage, and he fell back, hanging upside-down, as I dropped to the floor. The crowd exploded. Right on cue Jim jumped over the railing and took Davey out from behind with a clothesline, while Davey purposely flipped Diana over the railing to get her involved. They thought this was clever, but it infuriated me and Owen. Jim and Owen worked me over inside the cage until Davey peeled off his shirt and led my brothers in a charge over the top to rescue me. Jim and Owen made a quick getaway, and while I was being helped out I looked up to see an amused Smith straddling the top of the cage, posing and flexing his muscles. When it was all over, it was hailed as the greatest cage match of all time, which it certainly wasn't, but it was surely the best one without blood.

I arrived home on September 3 for five days' rest before heading over to Europe again. I had one important thing to do. I saw Owen enough on the road that I rarely visited with him at home, but this time I drove over to his perfect house. We both loved our coffee, so I'd bought him a cappuccino machine, which I left on his front steps along with a note.

It has truly been a pleasure working with you and I'm
sure going to miss all the fun and high energy you
brought with you to each and every match we had. I
always knew you were a great and gifted worker and I'm
very proud of you. I'm happy to have helped in any way to
bring your talent to the forefront where it always
belonged. Owen, you're all pro! Good luck in the future,
call on me when you need me, and come home in one
piece. Love, Bret

Back on the bus in Europe. Davey and I worked tags all over Germany and
the U.K. with Owen and Jim. The thing I remember most about that tour
was Shawn, Razor and Nash talking to me in Hamburg about the idea of
forming a clique of top guys who strictly took care of their own. This was
what Buddy Rogers did in the 1950s, working only with his selected clique
to get him over, so they could monopolize the cash flow. These boys
wanted me to be the leader, to voice concerns pertaining to the group as a
whole. Even though they were my friends, I couldn't see it, and with the
exception of Nash, their degree of pill popping was something I didn't want
to be around. I told them, "Ultimately everybody has to work their way to
the top all by themselves. If someone can outperform me, every night in
every part of the world, then go ahead, step up and do it!"

September 27, 1994. Poughkeepsie. I gingerly took a seat in Vince's office,
sensing the decision had been made about me dropping the belt. Backlund
had slammed me as hard as he could ass-first into the mat in a dark match
the night before at TVs in Utica. I wouldn't find out for another two weeks
that he'd actually cracked my pelvis.

This new Crazy Bob was beginning to get over. The Howdy Doody heel
with his red brush cut was a character disappointed with the crowd for booing him, since he'd always been so true and good; he was angry at them for
having lowered their moral values. In the dressing room, Bob continued to
be the picture of class. He often had his face buried in huge books about
politics, or he'd be working out, in push-up position, relentlessly pushing a
little metal wheel with handles on each side, back and forth, back and
forth, on the dressing-room floor.

Vince began to lay out the finish for our *Survivor Series* match. Owen
would be in Bob's corner and Davey in mine in a submission match where
only they could end it by throwing in a towel. At some point Owen would
incapacitate Davey, and in an emotional twist he'd persuade my poor
mother, who would be seated in the front row with Stu, to throw in my

towel out of fear for my safety, costing me the title. Even though I was losing the belt, I liked the drama of it. My feelings about Bob getting the belt had completely changed. He was trying so hard, and besides, how would I feel if a young buck had misgivings about putting me over some day?

I felt kind of bad for Bob when Vince told me that he'd only be champion for three days and then drop the belt to Diesel. By then I'd be at home, supposedly injured, and Diesel would take my place wrestling Bob at Madison Square Garden. Diesel was six-foot-nine: maybe Vince felt he needed a champion physically as big as Hogan. I suggested to him that he keep the belt on Bob—there was plenty of time for Diesel to make it to the top—but his mind was made up.

Vince was full of surprises that day. He went on to say that he was thinking of moving me up to being more of a spokesperson, the Babe Ruth of the WWF, as he originally had in mind for Hogan. He told me he wasn't putting me out to pasture and, more importantly, he said my salary wouldn't change; in fact, he insisted, it would go up. He caught me further off guard when he presented me with a handsome custom-made pink and black leather jacket with my name sewn onto it. But the more he talked, the more I wondered whether this was, in fact, the end of the line, just as it had come for Macho Man and even Lex, who, as of late, knew nothing but the sound of their own tires spinning. But for the time being, I was still his champion.

At the end of September a match between Owen and me, once again billed by the WWF as the last we would ever do together, was supposed to be the highlight of the debut of yet another of Vince's TV shows. But my broken pelvis clicked with each step. I confided to Owen that I was hurt and that not only could I not take any bumps, I wasn't sure I could work at all. Owen told me not to worry, that he'd do all the work. The match turned out to be a ballet of two brothers who really loved each other. After we pushed off, Owen slapped me, spinning my head: sweat flew, but he barely even touched me. The slap sound came from Owen slapping his own thigh. We worked like this until we eventually wound up in some kind of a leg lock, which looked painful, but was as comfortable as crossing our feet watching TV. I sold it like crazy while Owen pretended to press against my knee with his boot. We took the match higher and higher, totally faking every move, while the crowd, Vince and all the boys in the back marvelled at how intense it was. Finally Owen appeared to have me beat as he climbed the top rope. Then Davey tripped him up, causing Owen to lose his footing and crotch himself on the top rope. Owen writhed in mock agony as I slid over him, hooking his leg gently. "Thank you, brother," I said. It was the most pain-free match I ever had.

That October I was back in Calgary with time off to work on *Lonesome Dove*. Despite early-morning set calls and the freezing cold, I was having more fun doing the show than I could ever remember. Being picked up before dawn for sunrise drives out to the set was a peaceful way to wake up; there was wildlife everywhere, even a huge, antler-less moose who loped alongside the van, framed by a backdrop of snow-covered Rockies rising out of early-morning mist. The days were long, but I was happy with my scenes, especially one where I brawled in a saloon, slamming a cowboy across a table, when, bang, I got shot, or squibbed, and fake blood oozed out of my shoulder. No retakes in wrestling, I thought, before going absolutely nuts on everybody in the saloon—and they loved it. In fact, they wrote me in for the season finale to be shot in early December.

By the time I got to TVs in Bushkill, Pennsylvania, on November 8, the news was only just hitting, and hitting hard: Randy had jumped to WCW. Jack Lanza told me how Randy called Vince at four in the morning, drunk, to tell him he'd signed: "Randy never even gave Vince a chance to make him a counter offer." I found Vince in his office, and I could see he was shaken. I told him, "I've only really worked for two people in my life, you and my father. I want you to know that no matter what happens, I'm loyal to you." Vince had tears in his eyes and so did Lanza when he came up to me later to thank me for being so supportive.

That same day I found out it was going to be Shawn and Diesel in the main event at *WrestleMania XI*, which I had no problem with. I just worried that it would be awfully hard on my body to keep this thing with Bob red-hot for another four months to be able to carry off an "I quit" submission match at the big show.

The Freeman coliseum in San Antonio was always a good building for me. Bob and I were going to be on early in *Survivor Series '94*, leaving the spotlight for Shawn and Diesel to have their falling out, which would start the buildup to their match at *WrestleMania XI*.

After thirty-five minutes, I finally wrestled Bob into the sharpshooter. Owen tried to interfere, but Davey cut him off at the pass and chased him full-sprint out of and around the ring. Owen rolled under the ropes, and Hebner intercepted Davey, giving Owen time to hit me with a bulldog, saving Bob. I pulled myself up by the ropes, shaking my fist at Owen, just as Bob pounced on me and slapped on his painful cross-faced chicken wing. Davey again tore after Owen but, just as he was about to catch him,

Owen dropped flat and Davey tripped and collided head-first with the steel ring steps, pretending to knock himself out. Owen did a beautiful job of acting sorry as he tearfully tried to revive Davey. Meanwhile, I fought helplessly to escape Bob's chicken wing. Owen begged our mom to throw in the towel, and after much pained deliberation my parents nonchalantly stepped over their unconscious son-in-law, with Owen begging them to end my suffering. Stu angrily refused, but Helen, in a great, teary performance, couldn't take it any more and tossed in the towel. To their dismay, Owen was so happy he'd cost me the title that he jumped up and down with glee and raced back to the dressing room. I could hear the furious crowd as Stu and Helen helped me to the back, as Bob strapped on the World title belt. In the end, I was honoured to pass the torch to Bob.

After the match, one wrestler after another paid me their respects. What touched me the most was when Earl Hebner said to me, blinking back tears, "If anybody ever says you're not a total pro, I'll punch them in the mouth."

I'd been overthrown. According to the storyline, I'd suffered a shoulder injury in Backlund's cross-face chicken wing and had to be sent home until early January to recover, the longest off-time I'd had in ten years.

On November 29, in Calgary, there was a press conference announcing the debut of the Calgary Hitmen. Earlier in the year, legendary NHLers Theo Fleury and Joe Sakic had invited me to co-found a junior hockey team in Calgary whose coach and general manager would be their one-time mentor Graham James. Theo thought it would be a good idea to name the team after me, and I thought the media exposure would more than offset the investment they wanted from me. That day, the logo was unveiled along with the team colours, which were my ring colours of pink, black and white. The logo featured a phantom-like hockey player in a goalie mask bursting out of a triangle. Our celebration that night was diminished by a couple of local sportscasters who hated wrestling, plain and simple, because they thought it promoted violence. Overlooking all the accomplishments of a local boy, they declared that I was a horrible role model for a junior hockey team. With the NHL on strike at the time, I couldn't help but wonder whether the only reason they ripped on me was because they needed something to talk about. The story got national exposure, and Don Cherry defended me on *Hockey Night in Canada*. Hitmen merchandise flew off the shelves. As Vince so often proved, sometimes a little controversy can be a good thing.

On Christmas Day at Hart house, I was seated next to my mom at her end of the long dining-room table. She always had me sit to her right, and then she'd hold my hand. How could I not feel tranquility about how my life was turning out? I was thrilled to have a hockey team named after me, and I was on TV in *Lonesome Dove*, getting paid to play cowboys and Indians, while still flying around the world playing the role of a hero to millions of kids. Maybe that palm reader in New Orleans was actually right, and I would become bigger than I ever imagined. As the plates were being cleared, my mom gazed at me with love and pride.

My father also smiled at me from the head of the table. The former Canadian amateur champion stooped a bit when he walked now, more because of his bad knees than his back. He was happy that Ellie had made it up from Tampa for the holidays. The downside was that she'd left Jim behind, free to indulge in his vices and roll around with his demons. Stu was happy as long as Ellie was happy, but he was disappointed at how Jim had turned out.

Both my parents looked tired, no doubt from worrying about everybody all the time. Maybe they'd never done the math to realize that twelve kids would produce fifty or sixty grandkids, an almost infinite circle of concern. They were just plum tuckered out.

34

THE CLIQUE

By New Year's Eve, I was packing to leave again. I couldn't help but feel like a tired horse being hitched to the wagon one more time. I had a feeling that 1995 was going to be a tell-tale year for me. I told myself that it was out of my hands and just to do my best.

After having been off for six weeks, it was downright weird to be in the dressing room at The Houston Summit; I rubbed my weary eyes at the sight of Captain Kirk standing right in front of me. William Shatner was there to do a bit spot on *Raw* to promote his new sci-fi series, *Tech Wars*. He was an agreeable sort of guy, but all business. At the end of my match with Jeff Jarrett, whose manager was The Roadie, I have a vague memory of telling Captain Kirk, "Go ahead, give The Roadie one more!" I was more than amused to watch Shatner drop The Roadie with an elbow smash and fire him over the top rope.

Meanwhile, Jim missed several shots after Christmas and got himself fired again. It was too bad, because Vince had been going to put the Tag belts on him and Owen, and Owen would have been the perfect babysitter. It didn't help when Ellie dug him a deeper hole by calling J.J. Dillon and Vince's secretaries to plead for Jim's job; when it was to no avail, she cursed them all out.

Davey was also faltering in the face of serious drug problem. One minute he'd be talking to me and the next minute he'd completely zone out. He was also distraught because his mother was dying of stomach cancer back in England; while riding with me he took so many Somas, a potent and popular muscle relaxant and pain reliever, that he turned into a trembling zombie, slurring over and over, "I've got problems."

Since taking the belt, Diesel had proven he didn't have enough experience to have a good match with Backlund. To the serious fans he'd had a short climb to the top and it was damn near impossible for him to get anything close to sympathy, being a giant bad-ass trucker. But after I got back in January, Kevin seemed less interested in advice from me and I began to notice how Shawn, Razor and Kid cozied up to him as if he were a prized

Great Dane. They were all trying to sniff his ass; I'd had mine sniffed enough to know. Kevin was soon resented by some of the other wrestlers because he wasn't a champion for all of us, but only for his little band of buddies.

On January 22, 1995, we had a title match at the *Royal Rumble*. Vince was worried that his new superstar could end up a total heel, which would be bad for business. My fans wanted me to get the belt back, and I assured Kevin that the only way to go was to let me be the aggressor, yet keep him strong. After a solid back-and-forth battle, with all kinds of outside interference from Owen, Shawn, Backlund, Jarrett and The Roadie, the match finally ended in a disqualification. Afterwards, Kevin shook my hand and thanked me for giving him his first decent match as champion. He didn't seem to understand that all I would have had to do to turn him heel was to have started selling dramatically; but I didn't operate like that.

Shawn won the battle royal, which set up his main event spot facing Diesel at *WrestleMania XI*. But NFL all-star defensive tackle Lawrence Taylor was sitting in the front row and ended up stealing the show right out from under Shawn and Diesel when he got pie-faced by an irate Bam Bam Bigelow.

Just like with Yoko, Diesel's head got very big, very fast on the promises Vince fed him to make him feel important and the big cheques, the perks and the almighty spotlight. But Kevin was also finding out that being champion was a lot of hard work. Just like me, he'd believed Vince when he was told that he'd be champion for a long time. But Diesel wasn't drawing, and it agitated him that the hype leading up to *WrestleMania XI* was focused not on him but on a match between Bam Bam and Lawrence Taylor.

At a press conference in San Francisco, Shawn and Diesel openly sat together in front of the fans and the media: a complete and utter disrespect for kayfabe from the champion and his opponent. Even though by then some fans—the so-called "smart marks"—were starting to understand pro wrestling was a work, not to kayfabe was an intentional affront to old-school ways and an insult to the other wrestlers. It was bad for the business and I couldn't have been more disappointed in them both.

A tenacious WCW was adding more pay-per-views. Vince had exclusivity deals with many of the cable conglomerates that aired the WWF, similar to the deals that kept anyone else from running wrestling in "his" buildings. To maintain control of the cable outlets and hold on to the pay-per-view industry that he, in large part, helped create in the first place, Vince soon promised to deliver a pay-per-view every month. What started out as the annual *WrestleMania* extravaganza each spring had already grown to five major shows a year with the addition of *King of the Ring* in June,

SummerSlam in August, *Survivor Series* in November and *Royal Rumble* in January. Now, for every month that there wasn't an already established pay-per-view, we were going to do a new series called *In Your House*. *WrestleMania* would still be the biggest show of the year, with the original big four feeding it and the *In Your House* pay-per-views keeping the story-lines going. The danger was that with so many pay-per-views between the two promotions, the market would become saturated and the big shows would become nothing special. Not to mention that it was getting too expensive for the casual fan, who, as a result, would be forced to choose between WWF or WCW.

In Your House was scheduled to debut in May, and Vince would need his depleted, burned-out crew of wrestlers to dig a little deeper to help him turn the tide against WCW. Colour announcer Jim Ross had just become Vince's right-hand man in the booking department, with Pat staying close to Florida now. For the first one, they booked Hakushi to work with me, but Vince also wanted me to work on the same show against Lawler and put him over in order to build for a huge rematch at *King of the Ring*.

On April 2 I flew down to Hartford for *WrestleMania XI* with Dallas and Blade. I was dreading my match with Bob because I knew Vince's idea that the two of us would use only submission holds in the match was guaranteed to stink the building out.

When I marched out to face Bob I got a huge pop, but from the moment the bell rang the match went downhill. Roddy Piper was the guest referee and kept sticking a live mic in our faces, asking, "What do ya say?" which only sounded comical and made the crowd laugh. I cringed, thinking nobody laughs during my matches unless I want them to! As hard as Bob and I tried, the match deteriorated into a farce. Finally Bob went for his chicken wing, and I slipped under and reversed it, hooking his hold on him, falling backward to the mat. Bob was finding out, as I had, that the hold hurt like hell, so bad that as Roddy stuck the mic in Bob's face and asked, "Do you give?" Bob could only manage to scream, "Yes!" Bob was specifically supposed to say "I quit," but with the painful hold cutting off his air, Roddy finally had no choice but to ring the bell and declare me the winner. This was, without a doubt, my worst pay-per-view match ever.

Diesel had a good match with Shawn, in which they both worked hard, but Shawn went out of his way to outshine the champion, reminding me of a *Bugs Bunny* cartoon in which Bugs outsmarted a ferocious, but clueless, bull. When Shawn gave Diesel his superkick finish and covered him, Earl Hebner twisted his ankle as planned, and after an eternity he finally crawled over to make the count. When Diesel kicked out to boos, I immediately knew that Shawn had played him. Diesel would, in fact, beat Shawn moments later, but it wouldn't be enough to build Diesel up for their return match at the *In Your House* pay-per-view coming up in June. All anyone would remember about Diesel's championship match at *WrestleMania* was Shawn Michaels, which was, clearly, what Shawn intended all along. In the ensuing panic in the dressing room, all plans were scrubbed, and Shawn was turned babyface the following night on *Raw*.

As for the main event, Lawrence Taylor put in a damn good effort, considering how inexperienced he was. Bam Bam worked his ass off carrying L.T. through the match and put him over with an elbow smash off the second rope, the saving grace in what was the worst WWF pay-per-view I could remember.

Shawn's sudden face change threw a monkey wrench into everything. I saw right away that he was my direct competition now. I had been around for eleven years, five straight as a babyface; some of the fans were looking for a new star, and clearly it was going to be Shawn. He wasn't tough enough to pretend to be Bret Hart. There's no denying that he was a great talent, but a great worker has to be able to wrestle everyone, and Shawn was only capable of carrying the opponents that suited him. He had the girls screaming for him when he did silly Flair spots, like having his opponent pull his trunks down to his ankles during a sunset flip, but most of the men in the audience hated him for being too much of a cutie boy.

After TVs on April 5th I stood off on the side of the road with Dallas and Blade on a dark star-lit night arcing our piss in three varied heights. As the moon peaked out between clouds I felt proud as I wondered how many other wrestling dads over the years had enjoyed this same kind of moment with their sons.

Bang. On April 21, I was in Germany again. There was a lot of negative talk among the boys about Diesel, Shawn, Razor and their rather obvious clique. Most of the wrestlers were finding Shawn's attitude hard to take and were relieved that he wasn't on the tour. The boys were always the first to feel a slide in business, and many of them let me know that they were much happier with their payoffs when I was champion. It reminded me of how I felt when Warrior took the belt from Hogan.

I sat with Davey, Lex and Jeff Jarrett at The Sugar Shack in Munich. I may have been a toppled king, but I was still tearing the house down every night, especially in Europe.

Davey had cut his hair and now sported a flat-top that gave him a fresh, chiselled look, and he was enthusiastic about the possibility of forming a new tag team with Lex. I enjoyed reminiscing with him about our old Stampede days and soon had him laughing about the time Jim stuck fish eyes in the pockets of Davey's pants. I was happy to see him laugh, and I kept giving him little jabs in the ribs every time he tried to order. He'd been laughing so hard, with those big dimples showing, that he was never able to get his order in. He told me he hoped to work with me again and that he was thinking of turning heel just so he could challenge me. "Fookin' clique's trying to take over now," he said. "Fookin' Shawn is barely two hundred pounds sopping wet."

"Shawn's a decent guy, but he's got his little hang-ups," I replied. "Unfortunately, one of them is being an asshole."

I celebrated the safe end of another tour at Cookies in Frankfurt and thought about how I could blow them away at *In Your House* by working two totally different matches with Hakushi and Lawler. Diesel was wrestling Sycho Sid as a carry over from *WrestleMania XI*, and I doubted they could top me. What Sid Eudy lacked as a worker he made up for as a great-looking specimen; he was well muscled at six-foot-nine, with a big square jaw and curly blond hair. Owen and Yoko were going to win the Tag belts at *In Your House*, which would help now that Owen and Martha were expecting their second child in October. Owen and I had no idea if or when we would ever work together again, and I kidded him, "Don't worry, we'll do the dance of death somewhere down the line."

Our match wasn't expected to mean much as Hakushi and I opened that first *In Your House*, on May 14, 1995 in Syracuse, but we completely blew them away with unexpected aerial moves that'd only been seen in Japan. Then I rolled him up tighter than a sushi roll for the pinfall.

Diesel and Sid delivered the kind of sub-par match that was to be expected.

My second match, with Lawler, had a ton of heat, especially when Hakushi interfered by helping Lawler steal a pinfall on me. At the end of the night, Vince told me that my matches saved the show. Kevin was irritable and gave me a look as though he wanted to kick that gold belt across the dressing-room floor to me.

Over the next few weeks I watched Sid and Diesel struggle to carry the main event while I cruised through matches with Hakushi. Meanwhile, Lawler and I were building heat for a rematch at *King of the Ring*, for which I'd obliged Lawler by letting him come up with any kind of match he wanted.

I got Chris Benoit a try-out at TV in Johnstown, Pennsylvania, on June 7, working with Owen. They put on a wrestling clinic that would have

impressed any wrestler anywhere. There was another new arrival from
WCW, Paul Levesque, a hook-nosed bodybuilder who came out of Killer
Kowalski's wrestling school. He was a decent worker who was quick to cozy
up to his old pal Kevin Nash.

That night, I drove to Pittsburgh with Owen and Benoit. I could tell by
the way Owen talked about the baby coming that he relished having a second child. Benoit looked really happy for him, and I realized then that
these two were close. Like Owen, Chris was a notorious ribber, and I
enjoyed hearing of their old antics when they were in Calgary and Japan
together. I thought for sure Benoit would be hired, but both Pat and Jim
Ross passed on him for reasons that nobody in their right mind could ever
understand, especially considering that Vince was so low on talent.

There was the usual fired-up Philly crowd for King of the Ring on June 25,
a growing number of whom were becoming hard-core ECW supporters,
largely because the promotion was based there. The match of Lawler's
choosing turned out to be a "kiss my foot" match. The silliness of it ended
up being just what this crowd was looking to sink their teeth into. Lawler
and I delivered another intense brawl, which ultimately ended with me
propped up on the top corner, plucking my laces, pulling off my boot, and
cramming my toes into Jerry's mouth. I even crunched Jerry up like an
accordion and stuck his own toes into his mouth.

Diesel injured his elbow, which was a real no-no for the champion,
because everything was built around him and now he couldn't work.
Payoffs were down, morale too.

On that flight home I finally found time to study my lines for my first
episode of the new season of *Lonesome Dove*. I'd done two shows as mountain
man Luther Root and was now written in as a semi-regular character. I saw
Lonesome Dove as a sabbatical from wrestling. I'd still wrestle weekends, but
I'd finally have more time at home, where I celebrated my thirty-eighth birthday and my thirteenth wedding anniversary. I spent time with my kids riding
hard around the bike paths of Calgary to keep up my cardio conditioning and
the elasticity in my knees. My world was spinning as fast as the blurred spokes
of my wheels. Blade rode in front of me, and I had to admire him when he
said, "Don't worry about me, man. I'm a happy little kid!" So was I.

Shawn was now the Intercontinental champ. While I'd been home, the
clique had managed to manoeuvre themselves into all the top spots, and it
wasn't sitting well with the boys in the dressing room.

I showed up for *Raw* in Louisville, Kentucky, on July 24, where I was
booked against Hakushi again. I liked him enough to have established him

as a serious heel, but, unfortunately, because of his kindly nature, everyone who had worked with him since had made a point of eating him up. He seemed relieved to see me and got real serious when I explained that we'd just have to go out and show them all over again. I put together a match filled with all the aerial moves we thought were too risky to do at our *In Your House* match. Midway through it, I was on the floor when Hakushi hit the far ropes and did a cartwheel, a handspring and the back-somersaulted over the top rope, spinning right on top of me in what Dave Meltzer aptly described as the first space flying tiger drop ever seen in the United States. With one kick out after another, we tore the house down until I suplexed him standing off the top and twisted him in the sharpshooter. The Louisville Gardens came unglued.

Back in the dressing room, Owen stood with a bunch of the other wrestlers clapping as he said, staccato, "The best there is! The best there was! The best there ever will be!"

Davey Boy double-crossed Lex and turned heel. Undertaker was, once again, called upon to work a miracle, this time with Mabel, who had won the *King of the Ring* crown. And Bob Backlund was running for president of the United States. Not really, but they had a lot of people actually believing that he was a candidate!

As an offshoot to my on-and-off feud with Lawler, the storyline continued that his mouth had become infected from my toes so I was now to wrestle his dentist, Dr. Isaac Yankem, at *SummerSlam* in August. Yankem was actually a curly haired, broad-shouldered six-foot-eight rookie named Glen Jacobs, who'd only just started working Lawler's Memphis territory. He later became known as Kane. I found it hard to get excited about working the cartoon storylines that Vince had for me, especially a September *In Your House* match I was supposed to have with Pierre LaFitte because he stole my ring jacket. I did my best to make these lame duck angles fly.

The night after Evansville TVs, at Mattingly's, a sports bar owned by the New York Yankees, Taker sat with me and confided that he didn't trust Shawn. While I'd been away, the clique had been prancing around acting like their shit didn't stink.

Our attention turned to a disturbance at the far end of the bar. Shawn had made some kind of a racial slur, and the situation was escalating because Razor stepped in and head-butted a black guy. Diesel was there standing guard over Shawn, who'd taken a handful of Somas and was in no shape to back up his own words. Lurking in the shadows was Paul Levesque, who was now working as a snooty, rich aristocrat named Hunter Hearst Helmsley, eventually to be known as Triple H. With him was his girlfriend, Joanie Laurer, a fellow graduate from Kowalski's school, who was now working as his valet, Chyna. She was a female bodybuilder who resembled the *Incredible Hulk* cartoon character with a black wig on, but spoke with a little, squeaky high voice. Chyna was built better than most of the boys, but as far as I know Vince didn't steroid test the girls.

Earlier that day Vince had told me Diesel wasn't cutting it as champion, making the excuse that it was because of his elbow. But I'd always thought that Diesel was as good as dead after he worked with Shawn back at *WrestleMania XI*. I suggested to Vince that Kevin needed sympathy, and I knew how to get it for him. I could beat him for the belt by using an idea that came to me while watching Sabu in ECW crashing through tables. It was a new finish designed around dropping the belt back to Kevin at *WrestleMania XII*. As I explained it to Vince, he frantically scribbled it in his big black book.

Three days later, wrestling was all a strange, faraway dream. I sat on the *Lonesome Dove* set in a saloon called The Ambrosia Club waiting for my next scene. I was thrilled to hear that it was all but certain that I'd be a full-time cast member next season, playing the sheriff in all sixteen episodes.

On August 6, Vince called to tell me that he wanted me to win the belt, at *Survivor Series*, by crashing through a table. I listened to Vince tell me my finish as if I'd never heard it before. The only thing I could come up with was that he'd read what he'd written down in his black book and somehow actually thought it was his idea. All I could do was hope that he'd write down all my ideas from now on!

But it was Shawn he wanted me to drop the belt to at *WrestleMania*, not Kevin. "Do you have any problems with that?"

I thought about it. Despite how the boys felt about him, Shawn was a hard worker and had paid his dues as far as I could see. Of course I had no problem with it. The timing was perfect. I could go right into my sheriff role, filming all summer long, and reappear just in time for *SummerSlam '96*.

By mid-August, Pat stepped down to take a break, voluntarily making room for Vince to hire Jim Ross's mentor, the one-time Louisiana promoter (and more recently WCW booker) Bill Watts. I took this as a positive, especially since Watts was a hard-nosed, in-your-face, tough guy who liked his wrestling to look real.

I had a better match that anyone expected with Dr. Isaac Yankem at *SummerSlam*. I was pleased to find that despite being green, Glen Jacobs had a willingness to listen and learn. I told him to be proud of himself, and he was.

On September 4, WCW launched a Monday-night show called *Monday Nitro* to go head to head with *Monday Night Raw*. The centrepiece of their debut show was a surprise appearance by Lex Luger, who, like Randy, had read the writing on the wall and left the WWF before it was too late.

Owen and Yoko lost the belts to a young cowboy team called The Smokin' Gunns. Owen was now the proud father of a brand-new baby girl, Athena. For all those times he'd pulled pranks on me, I'd told everyone, straight faced, that he named her after Stu! It was kind of funny how mad he got when everybody kept congratulating him on the birth of his daughter Stuella. I enjoyed finally paying him back.

I didn't mind putting Shawn over at *WrestleMania XII*, but I knew that Shawn wasn't the guy to fill my shoes, and I was damn sure he wouldn't draw any better than I did. One big difference between me and Shawn, which would cost him, was that I appreciated my undercard. I always took the time to shake the hands of even the lowest jobber. A relatively small babyface always needs the heels to make him, but Shawn treated a lot of the wrestlers like they weren't good enough to work with him. The clique had managed to alienate themselves from nearly everyone, even the ring crew. Ron Harris, one of the big, bald-headed twins called The Blues Brothers, didn't take kindly to Shawn's remarks about his match. He grabbed a terrified Shawn by the neck in the shower at Madison Square Garden and told him if he wise-assed him again he'd shove his head up his ass! Shawn had even berated Chief, in what was the beginning of the end for one of Vince's most loyal generals.

Bill Watts lasted only a few weeks, resigning on October 13 when he realized that Vince just wasn't listening to him. It got back to me that Watts quit over Vince putting the belt on Shawn. He thought Shawn was too damn scrawny and that the belt should stay with me. Vince brought Pat back to work with him on booking, but lessened his load by putting Jerry Brisco in charge of all the wrestlers. Brisco cozied up to me, pretending to be an old friend, one of the boys, and as there didn't seem to be any choice, I tried to trust him.

The day after Watts resigned, Shawn yapped off one too many times, this time to a bunch of Marines in a Syracuse bar. According to Davey, who was there with Kid, Shawn hit on a soldier's girl, who was waitressing. By the end of the night the three wrestlers were loaded up on Somas, and the willing waitress offered to drive them back to their hotel. They staggered out to their car, only to be met by—depending on what version of the story you believe—four to nine angry Marines. The three of them were helpless. The soldiers jerked Shawn out of the front seat, and Davey and Kid fumbled in slow motion to get out of the back. Kid made a pathetic attempt to throw some karate kicks, but he was so out of it they pushed him over like a scarecrow. Davey was so pilled up that he was barely able to stand, but as hard as they tried, they couldn't take him down. He winced when he told me how they slammed Shawn's head in the car door and pummelled him with fists and boots, with Shawn too drugged up to even put his hands up to shield his face.

At *In Your House* in Winnipeg on October 22, Shawn made a brief appearance, explaining that he'd been jumped by nine Marines and would be out of action for a while. He conveniently forfeited the Intercontinental belt to Razor that same day, via an ECW import called Shane Douglas, so he could go home while his face healed up. Because the IC belt was still a big money spot, the attitude in the dressing room was that it was the clique looking out for their own again.

I was a guest announcer for Diesel's match with Davey, and we got into a pie-face pushing kind of thing while I was at the announcers' table. Diesel got no help from the Canadian audience, and the match bombed badly enough that Vince hurled his headset down in disgust and hissed, "Horrible!" It was around this time that WCW accomplished the unthinkable by beating Vince in the ratings, which only made things seem that much worse.

My match with Diesel at *Survivor Series* was brutally physical; we complemented each other, working and building the match for more than twenty-five minutes until I dove over the top onto Diesel; he moved out of the way and I bounced hard off the padded floor. Diesel pulled himself up the ropes and back into the ring while I slowly got to my feet. Walking past the announcers' table I began to climb up on the apron when Diesel charged past Earl Hebner, using the top rope to catapult me crashing backward into the table, which was nowhere near gimmicked enough. It didn't break the way it was supposed to and it was a loud, bruising crash.

As I lay hurt and helpless atop the shattered table, Diesel came out and tossed me into the ring like a rag doll, all the while taking his time appearing to be upset about it. He raised his black-gloved fist and pulled me up for his jackknife finish when I dropped and folded him up in a quick small package for the one . . . two . . . three. The crowd exploded! On what was my forty-first pay-per-view, I won the WWF World title for the third time. Diesel furiously bumped down the ref and gave me not one, but two, very sloppy and painful jackknife power bombs that knocked all the wind out of me. Referees hit the ring like Keystone Kops, and Diesel left them laying on the mat. In an unscripted moment, he stood over top of me, dropped the World belt across my chest, glared down and snarled, "Don't forget who did you the fuckin' favour." This was the same guy who, two years earlier, did nothing but suck up to me.

I thought Vince would play up the fact that I was now a three-time WWF World Champion, but I was wrong. The day after I regained the title, *Raw* was live from Richmond, Virginia, but the announcers only mentioned in passing that I was champ again, showing a brief clip of the match. It was Shawn's first day back since getting beat up, and he and Diesel took centre stage. Diesel made out like it was a tainted win for me. Not all the fans bought the pay-per-views, but everyone watched *Raw*, and for a while Diesel's side was all a lot of them had to go on.

Later in the show, Owen worked a dandy little match where he jumped up and delivered an Inoki-style spin kick to the back of Shawn's head. According to plan, Shawn carried on briefly, but then collapsed to one knee and fell unconscious. Soon paramedics frantically worked on him and Vince was in the ring, his headset off, looking visibly distressed. Owen played confused and left Shawn alone. And that was how they went off the air. It was done so realistically that almost everyone watching on live TV thought Shawn was really hurt. There were tearful girls everywhere, overshadowing the fact that the World title had changed hands.

Two days after I won the belt, they finally had me do an interview, but it was on the taped *Raw*, which wouldn't even air until a week later. Such tactics certainly weren't designed to make the champ look strong. In fact, before I'd even said a word, Backlund came out of nowhere and chicken-winged me until I was rescued by referees and agents and helped to the back.

I'd given Vince a five-star match with Diesel, but it was so quickly passed over that it was soon forgotten. Even the buildup to my *In Your House* match against Davey on December 17 was non-existent, with all the attention being lavished on the ex-champion and the apparently seriously injured Shawn.

Diesel continued to imply, during his live TV interviews, that I only got the belt back because I sucked up to Vince. I now had the belt, but I didn't have the power that usually came with it. Clearly Diesel and Shawn were in control, and I was only carrying the belt until Shawn could dispose of me at *WrestleMania XII*. What with Hogan, Lex and Diesel having failed at taking my position, Vince seemed determined to put me in a holding pattern and make certain that Shawn became the new king.

Vince must have realized that he had to do something with my match with Davey, so he flew Diana to Richmond TVs with the idea that maybe Diana could turn heel on me too. I didn't like it one bit. First of all, I thought it took away from Owen being the black sheep, but also with so many relatives turning on me—Owen, Jim, Davey, Bruce and now Diana, along with Diesel saying that I was a suck-up—a lot of fans would have to conclude that I must be hard to like.

Vince suggested that Owen, Davey, Diana and I talk over what we should do. Diana said matter-of-factly, "I'll just tell Vince that I'll do whatever he wants me to do." I gasped and warned her, "Never, ever say you'll do anything they want! They'll make you shave your head and walk backward out there!"

A few minutes later, Owen and I stood talking privately in the hall outside Vince's office. Owen had real concerns that Diana would come off looking bad as a mother and a parent and make the whole family look bad. Then we noticed Diana eavesdropping from around the corner. When we all went to Vince's office to talk about it, Diana ignored our warnings. Her very first words to Vince were, "I'll do whatever you tell me to do, Vince." She so infuriated me and Owen that we shot the whole idea down in front of Vince, who decided it would be best to leave her out of things until Davey's upcoming assault trial was finished.

I racked my brain for weeks trying to think of a way to make the match mean anything at all. Davey offered nothing, relying on me to figure it all out. My mind was a big blank. It was while driving to the Hersheypark Arena on the day of the match that I saw a pharmacy sign and it dawned on me that a little accidental blood would change everything. I bought razor blades and scissors. As I headed out to the ring I was determined to break Vince's holding pattern and blow them away one more time.

Davey and I spent fifteen minutes building a two-part story. As I'd anticipated, in the early going the crowd was less than captivated by our storyline. After giving them an unsurprising part one, I straddled Davey atop a turnbuckle and climbed up to attempt a standing suplex off the top rope. But when I went to suplex him, he blocked it, and with his amazing strength he lifted me and threw me crotch-first onto the top rope. The crowd gasped as I collapsed to the floor, where I discreetly coughed the blade out of my mouth. When I got up Davey charged me from behind, levelling me head-first into the steel steps. I cut high in the hairline and blood poured hot. As Davey worked me over, my head looked like a bloody pulp and even the simplest moves popped now. People praised Robert De Niro for his dedication when he gained 150 pounds to become Jake La Motta for *Raging Bull.* How come the same compliment isn't paid to pro wrestlers who bleed in the name of realism?

After a desperate climax of false finishes, I wrapped Davey up in an old-school Oklahoma roll for the pin.

When I got back to the dressing room, the commission doctor declared, "It's a cut from the stairs!" as he put five stitches in my head. Dave Meltzer described it as "yet another five-star performance." Slowly, I was earning Meltzer's respect. And I was proud of the fact that Meltzer and all the other wrestling fans could never say for sure that I bladed intentionally.

After the TVs the next day, a bunch of us were up in Curt's room drinking beers. Razor had taken a handful of Somas and wilted in a slow-motion sit-up; soon he was floating off to dreamland while the rest of us sat around telling war stories. Mabel was really bummed out, having taken some heat for collapsing on Taker while delivering an elbow drop, shattering Taker's eye socket. Luckily, Taker would be able to work around it as long as he wore a protective purple mask, resembling something out of *Phantom of the Opera*. Curt sang my praises while denouncing the clique to The 1-2-3 Kid. Staring at Razor, Curt rummaged through his toilet bag, hit the switch on an electric shaver and casually buzzed off Razor's right eyebrow. Kid took up for Scott as Curt menaced the other eyebrow: "Don't do it, Curt, c'mon!" At first Curt heeded Kid, but when we all thought he'd forgotten, he suddenly blurted out, "Fuck you, Kid." He hit the switch and shaved off Razor's left eyebrow. Razor never budged, only managing a dreamy smile.

35

THE SNAKES ARE DOCILE

BY JANUARY 1996, Vince was looking high and low for talent. Just in time for the *Royal Rumble* he brought in four-hundred-pound Vader, who had quit WCW after being thumped good by Paul Orndorff in a dressing room argument. Even Jake The Snake slithered back. He'd left the business to find God, vowing never to return, and when he reappeared in the dressing room, he seemed weathered and humbled. He was broke and divorced and still appeared on Sunday-morning evangelical shows to tell everyone who would listen how Jesus helped him beat his cocaine addiction. I was happy to see the arrival of Steve Austin, now called The Ringmaster, with Ted DiBiase as his manager.

Royal Rumble marked Shawn's first appearance since his face was mashed, and he won for the second year in a row, dancing and twirling around the ring and pulling his tights right down past the pubic line. Things like this made me and a lot of the boys wonder about Shawn.

That night Taker and I also worked our first major pay-per-view. He was wearing his protective mask from when Mabel had fallen on his face. For the finish, Taker tombstoned me in the middle of the ring and pinned me with my arms folded across my chest, just as Diesel lumbered down the aisle and pulled Earl out of the ring, stopping him from making the three-count. The pay-per-view ended with me bent over in the ring having injured my knee for real, lucky to still have the belt, and Taker stalking Diesel all the way back to the dressing room. I have to say it did little to build me for *WrestleMania XII*.

The following day, at Stockton TVs for *Raw*, I taped my sprained knee and managed to work a reasonably good match with Dustin Runnels, son of Dusty Rhodes, who did more than look after me. He was working a gimmick as a transgendered freak named Goldust, who wore a gold latex jumpsuit, gold face paint and a long, blond wig that he took off just before he wrestled to reveal a white buzz cut. Goldust was one of the better characters the WWF had come up with in some time, and Dustin was doing a great over-the-top job of portraying an androgynous weirdo. Vince got bombarded with hate mail and phone calls from gays and parent groups because kids were chanting "Faggot," and he ate up all the controversy with a confident smirk. If fans loved it or hated it, they were watching; it's when they didn't care that he had something to worry about.

Vince's latest project was "Billionaire Ted" skits, which mocked Ted Turner as a redneck and mocked his acquisitions from WWF as over-the-hill has-beens. He had two old men spoofing Randy and Hogan as Nacho Man and The Huckster. Vince had built them up, and now he was knocking them down. When I went out to do a live promo with Vince, he told me just to shoot about everything. But when I sarcastically asked him whether I should say the WWF was the Shawn and Diesel show now, he stammered nervously and stopped me.

On January 27 I arrived at the brand-new Bryce Jordan Center in University Park, Pennsylvania, to find a huge story breaking in the dressing room. The Road Warriors and Miss Elizabeth had shown up in WCW, and word was that Diesel and Razor were considering jumping too. This was a shock to everybody, especially Shawn, who looked anxious at the thought of being left behind. Despite the overall tension between the boys and the clique, Shawn and I had never let on to each other that there were any problems between us. He told me that he hoped Diesel and Razor would stay because after he became champion at *WrestleMania XII* he figured on working with them. I suggested he had fresh guys to work with, such as Vader and Austin. He nervously chewed on his nail, spit out a piece and shook his head. "I think I'd rather work with Hunter and do another little program with The Kid." I had spoken up for Owen, Jim and Davey over the years, but I never pushed them to the exclusion of everybody else, as Shawn fully intended to do with his clique. I realized then that The Heartbreak Kid didn't have the heart to be champion.

Shawn was only working a few select bookings so he could train hard to prepare for *WrestleMania XII*. I thought it was odd that without even consulting me, Shawn and Pat had already decided that we would meet in a one-hour marathon match that would go into overtime, during which Shawn would somehow beat me with his finishing move, the big superkick. Shawn was trying to read my face when he told me about it, and I could tell he was fully expecting me to balk at putting him over. He perked right up when I told him that I'd put him over clean in the middle, and he thanked me profusely.

I told Vince that after *Wrestlemania XII* I'd be taking six months off to do a full season of *Lonesome Dove*. I felt I was due to give my face a rest in North

America after twelve straight years, but Vince said he really needed me to work the foreign tours. I told him no problem. Working the foreign tours would keep me from getting too much ring rust, and besides, I liked seeing the world.

On January 31, 1996, I took Julie along on a tour of India. On the plane, Razor shaving-creamed Savio Vega, a Puerto Rican black belt, then drew all over his face with hot pink lipstick. He should have known better than to mess with a fiery Latino. Soon enough, Razor was stumbling up and down the aisle holding his detached ponytail in his hand, asking passengers in his phony Cuban accent, "You see who cut my hair, man?"

Owen sat talking with Louie Spicolli, a good kid who was one of very few TV jobbers to find his way to working as a preliminary boy appearing in the opening matches for the WWF. Sadly, Louie had developed the worst case of slow suicide since Rick McGraw, much worse than Razor, Shawn, Kid or Davey. The day before the India tour, Louie suffered a drug-related seizure, but there he was on the plane. I heard Owen warn Louie that the pills would kill him if he didn't smarten up. Louie said he'd seen the light, and I wished I could believe it was true.

The Leela Hotel in Mumbai was a fortress that locked out the poor. A hotel guide offered to arrange a tour and, after sleeping off the long flight, Tatanka came along with me and Julie to see the sights. The prison-like gates of the hotel parted, and we drove down Mahatma Gandhi Boulevard past pristine temples, shrines, churches and mosques. I found it hard to appreciate their beauty or even their spiritual significance when they were surrounded by slums. It was Manila all over again.

Those more fortunate buzzed around in taxis and small motorized buggies called Jeepneys. They honked and churned past the destitute, who struggled to navigate oxcarts and scooters through a fast-moving maze of buses and trucks that billowed black exhaust into a hazy sky.

In this exotic land filled with penury, I suddenly looked up to see a giant billboard that announced Hitman jeans. Some creep was posing as me, with long hair, a big nose and a fat gut, shirtless, wearing the knock-off name-brand item. At first we got a chuckle out of it, but the more I thought about it the more it pissed me off that on the other side of the world someone had stolen my name and was making money from my sweat.

I always thought it would be quite something to be able to say I'd touched every ocean, if only because there aren't many people who can say they have. When the guide stopped our taxi at a beach, it was plain that he was uncomfortable just being close to the water. The Indian Ocean at Mumbai was a scummy-green soup littered with garbage. In the air were incense, spices and cooking oil combined with sweat, piss and shit. As we made our way to the shoreline, watching people casually defecate in the sand, we were besieged by friendly beggars, most of whom were small kids. Hundreds of poor walked alongside us in happy anticipation, tapping us frantically on the arms. There was a tiny girl of about four carrying a naked baby who couldn't have been a year old. With bright smiles and big eyes they somehow managed to be polite and respectful in their poverty.

I dipped the toe of my hiking boot into the slimy water just as a young boy stepped into a pile of human shit that squished through his toes.

The guide made it very clear that we shouldn't give the beggars any handouts, but Julie broke down and pressed American dollar bills into their grubby hands. One after another the lucky children were brutally pounced on by older kids, who were pounced on by even older kids until only God knows where the money ended up.

There was a young boy with a spider monkey tied to a tattered rope. He shook a small electronic toy drum that rat-at-tat-tat-ed Michael's Jackson's song "Beat It" for about twenty seconds, during which the monkey did somersault after somersault. Not to be outdone, a desperate snake charmer of about the same age was trying to play a flute with one hand and arouse a cobra with the other. The snake was docile, likely because the boy kept whacking it hard on the back of the head. It would rise up swaying only to receive another crisp crack.

In India they spared the cows and the rats. We stopped at a Jain temple where thousands of rats roamed everywhere, well-fed and cared for like pets. In the department stores, I saw sacred cows strolling down the aisles, bulls in a china shop, only they were so accustomed to roaming among the wares that they didn't damage anything. Clerks hurried to clean up their droppings.

When our taxi pulled up inside the gates of the hotel compound, I was accosted by five angry Indians shouting and waving pairs of Hitman jeans. I explained rather curtly that the bum pictured on the back pocket wasn't me. They fiercely contested this as they surrounded me shouting excitedly, pleased with themselves for actually having found me. Finally, I pointed at the red heart-shaped tattoo on the impostor's biceps. I rolled up my sleeve to show them I bore no such mark. They were rendered speechless for just a moment and then took to arguing fiercely among themselves. I left the bellhops to shoo them off.

That night I defended the title against Yoko, who, along with several others, was ailing from Bombay belly. We'd all be warned not to drink the water or even get it in our eyes or noses. It was, to say the least, a shitty night, with most of the wrestlers soiling their trunks. Yoko looked sickly pale as he did his bonsai drop. I made extra sure to get out of his way in plenty of time.

Yoko weighed more than seven hundred pounds now and could barely get in and out of the ring. I figured that soon Vince would see him as a liability.

The following day I was asked if I'd mind going to visit some school kids. The girls, in their blue and white uniforms with their hair neatly tied up, were the picture of courtesy, kneeling on the floor with their hands folded. In contrast, the boys were so delirious with excitement the teachers lost control of them and they stormed the stage. Julie was touched to see how happy they all were to see me. When we were whisked away by a limo, I looked out the back window and made the bullhorn sign to the boys, who chased after us with huge smiles. I wonder if those children ever had any idea that it meant more for me to meet them that day than it did for them to meet me.

On February 3, we left for Bangalore, the computer capital of India. Bangalore was hot and dusty, and seemed less poverty-stricken than Mumbai, yet there were still numerous people sleeping on sidewalks.

At Martha's urging, Owen decided he had to see the Taj Mahal, but the promoters in Delhi explained that it was simply too far. I thought it was something that Julie would appreciate too, so I joined in on the request. Reluctantly the promoters hired a big bus for the four-hour drive to Agra. Upon boarding I wondered why the driver sat in a compartment encased in bulletproof glass that he locked from the inside. Owen had talked many of the boys into coming, some of whom were still sick with the runs; he told them they'd never forgive themselves if they missed seeing one of the eight great wonders of the world.

The bus jerked and shifted gears, weaving through the bustling streets of Delhi. The sky was curry-brown from pollution. Barefoot kids played soccer. Skinny, mangy dogs wished they were sacred cows instead. Elephants working at construction sites like living bulldozers reminded me of the woolly mammoths on *The Flintstones*. Workers balanced huge bricks on top of their heads three at a time. Whenever we made a rest stop, young girls begged, with cheerful smiles.

A little way out of Delhi I noticed what I was sure was a dead body, neatly covered by a white sheet, laid out next to the trash. After seeing three or four more such bundles I asked the guide about it and was told that I was right: a caretaker's wagon came around to retrieve the dead for cremation.

As we got farther into the countryside, the highway thinned to a dusty, two-lane road barely wide enough for one vehicle. The driver shifted gears, swerving side to side to miss the worst potholes and avoid traffic; by the time we got to Agra we all had motion sickness. It was hard for me to appreciate the sparkling, diamond-encrusted marble of the Taj Mahal after having seen such human suffering on the way.

Two hours later we hesitantly boarded the bus for the death ride back. The kamikaze driver explained that after 10 p.m. there was a curfew in Delhi; if we weren't back in time we'd have to wait till morning before we could enter the city. The traffic got heavier as it grew darker, and our driver played chicken with tankers and oxcarts, passing numerous smouldering, burnt-out wrecks that hadn't been there on the way to Agra. Those Stampede Wrestling black-ice hell rides, even the time Smith drove André to the airport, they were a merry-go-round ride compared to this. God, don't let Julie and me die here, I prayed as Tatanka crossed himself.

The drive back took seven hours. I found myself pounding on the bullet-proof glass screaming at the driver, but he gave me a confident thumbs up, grinning at me with teeth stained red from betel nut. He thought I was cheering him on for doing such a good job! A dog was crushed under the wheels of the careening bus and nobody batted an eye. When we pulled into a truck stop for gas, another bus, packed with Indians, pulled up alongside us, and they began spilling out. Three or four of them commenced to throw up violently. Owen shouted, "Hey look!"—as though this was a sight to see. Jerry Brisco raced to the window, camera in hand, to get a closer look. It probably made my trip and everyone else's on that lousy bus to watch the ripple effect on Brisco, who scrambled down the steps and upchucked his curried rice.

We finally made it to Delhi, only minutes before curfew. I called home from our room to check on the kids, and Stu told me that Davey had been acquitted of his assault charge. Apparently that dumbass Karl Moffat testified that Davey was every bit strong enough to suplex someone on his head, which the man who had been injured accused Davey of doing to him. It was just like Karl to take the stand to swear that wrestling was the whole truth and nothing but. The prosecutor seemed to be gambling that Davey would never confess that the pro matches were choreographed, but luckily for Davey, he had no problem saying so.

Although he had won the war, the legal battle depleted him financially to the point that his only coping mechanism was to take more downers. This is the point when things really started to get out of hand for Davey.

On day six of the India tour, Diesel told me that he and Razor were really going to WCW, for $750,000 a year, which was more than I was making. They had given Vince notice and were down to their last ninety days in the WWF.

By the time I set my bag down in Louisville, Kentucky, on February 18 for an *In Your House* cage match with Diesel, I was beyond tired. The ring had been gimmicked in such a way that when Diesel had me beat and was making his escape, Undertaker suddenly exhumed himself from under the ring floor and snatched Diesel's leg, pulling him beneath the boards to avenge his interference in our match at *Royal Rumble '96*. Smoke effects were billowing while I climbed over the cage and out of the ring to retain the belt. Once again, the pay-per-view ended with Undertaker and Diesel backing each other down while I slunk back to the dressing room with the belt. Being saved by interference at two pay-per-views in a row did nothing to keep a babyface champion like me strong.

I was completely caught off guard when I called the *Lonesome Dove* offices later that day and producer Steve North calmly told me that the series had been cancelled. He said that ratings were great, but production costs were too high. Hearing this broke my heart. Now the new dawn I was riding into was only a dimly lit path, and I was uncertain whether the path even went anywhere.

I decided to stick by my original plan and take at least six months off anyway. Carlo and I had come to a parting of the ways; in fact, I was only too happy to put in a good word for him, and he ended up with Jack Tunney's job as president of the WWF's Canadian arm. My new acting agent, Barry Bloom, could use the six-month hiatus from wrestling to get me established. Barry and I agreed that he'd have nothing to do with my wrestling career, even though he represented a bunch of WCW talent. I never lost sight of the fact that wrestling buttered my bread. In the dressing rooms I kept the news that *Lonesome Dove* had been cancelled to myself.

The next day, I was happily surprised to see Roddy at the Cincinnati Gardens for *Raw*. He'd recently been appointed the new figurehead interim president of the WWF, replacing Jack Tunney's character role. That afternoon Vince got me, Shawn and Roddy together and carefully rehearsed the live interview we were to have that night, building heat for our title match. Shawn was scripted to outwit me all the way through it.

When I went out to do the interview, he was already in the ring with Vince. Every word out of Shawn's mouth had so much more impact than what I had been told to say. And Vince was right there to make sure that Shawn was humble, lovable and not too Shawn-ish. On mic, he bragged about how well conditioned he was as he lifted his red and white candy-striped leather vest exposing a rock-hard six-pack. When Vince asked me about my conditioning, I coolly described myself as being a lot like the little pink rabbit in the Energizer battery commercials that just keeps going and going and going.

At just the right moment Roddy stormed out in his role as the president and explained the rules for our upcoming one-hour marathon match. I knew right then that I'd better get ready for the hardest fight of my career.

While I was over in India sick with the shits, Shawn had been home training like a lunatic. Damned if he wasn't in incredible shape.

In late February, Jim Ross and a WWF camera crew flew up to Calgary to get some footage of me training for the big match. They had filmed Shawn in sunny San Antonio, where he ran the steps at a football stadium, did upside down sit-ups and pretended to spar with his mentor, Jose Lotharo. Vince was selling Shawn as a guy trying to realize his boyhood dream of winning the gold. I was portrayed as the wily veteran from the dungeon who had every intention of being the champion for a long time.

February in Calgary is the coldest time of the year, but they had me jog along Scotsman's Hill so they could get panoramic views of the city with the Rockies in the background. I don't think J.R. and the camera crew were trying to be funny, but I couldn't help but see the humour in the footage they shot. It was so icy that I had to run carefully, so it came across on film like I was running about a mile an hour. Another magic moment taped for the world to see was when they asked me to swim laps in my pool. But the topper was when they filmed Stu stretching me in the dungeon, an eighty-year-old man tying me up in knots with me eagerly tapping out!

I trained for that match as hard as I ever had for anything. Shawn was eight years younger than me, and I wasn't going to let him outshine me. Like me and Davey at Wembley, I wanted the fans to remember the loser in this one. I would break their hearts and disappear until Shawn had nobody to work with except me. I saw a rematch up ahead with me taking back the title, which would build up for yet one more match where I'd be more than happy to put Shawn over—to once and for all thrust the torch into his hand. Done right, Shawn and I could draw money for years with a big rivalry, taking turns putting each other over.

I found Shawn at lunch-time on the day of *WrestleMania XII*, and we sat down to compose our match much like musicians composing a song. I let him piece much of the first twenty-five minutes together while I figured out the rest. We sat for over three hours, tweaking each spot until we could sing them in our heads. I told him I expected we'd be working a rematch when I came back in six months. In order to feed the supposed heat between us, I wouldn't be shaking his hand after he won. Instead, I'd simply walk out, leaving the crowd to assume that I was really pissed off at the ref's decision. Shawn nodded and said, "No problem." He'd spent much of the morning practising a special entrance, being lowered to the ring by a steel cable. I was impressed with how focused he was.

Warrior was back, looking very jacked-up on steroids. During his match with Hunter he blew up badly, even though it consisted of three clotheslines and lasted a mere 1:38. As the show went on, many of the boys, tears in their eyes, sought me out to thank me, as was the custom on a day when the belt was to change hands—if you'd carried the belt with dignity and worked hard.

On account of Diesel and Razor's defection to WCW, every wrestler was being leveraged to sign a new long-term contract. There was guaranteed money, which had never been offered in the WWF before, but the contracts were one-sided, with little protection for the talent. I was glad I was leaving for a while. My contract would expire while I was off, leaving me in a great bargaining position if I wanted to play the WCW card. I didn't ever want to end up there, but if I could show Vince my loyalty by *not* going, I thought I could ride out my career in the WWF in grand style.

Shawn did make a spectacular entrance, sliding down to the ring from a steel cable strung from the rafters while his ring music thumped "I'm just a sexy boy . . ." He seemed to explode from the ceiling as fireworks went off around the arena. His waist-length blond hair was neatly pulled back, and the words Heartbreak Kid were emblazoned on the ass of his white, silver-trimmed tights. The Boy Toy had come to fulfill his lifelong dream.

In stark contrast, I marched out with little pomp and circumstance, wearing a new ring coat and a black outfit. I looked every bit the tough ring general, serious and confident, the dutiful torchbearer. I could see Dallas and Blade sitting in the front row, next to Georgia's middle son, Matthew, whom I'd brought along on the trip because he was such a good kid. Matt's friend T.J. Wilson, who was like an adopted Hart kid, was also with them, along with Georgia and my mom. Stu was seated somewhere else with Freddie Blassie.

The crowd was intense, anticipating the passing of the torch. From the start, Shawn made it clear that this wasn't going to be so much a great work as a great contest. It was rather obvious to me that he'd been coached to lean on me as much as he could. He did sneaky tricks, such as dragging his heavy, steel-toed motorcycle boots across my face, scraping my lips up, which led to a subtle hour-long potato harvest. At one point while I was on the floor, Shawn climbed up to the top corner and dove out on me. He overshot and was flying head-first toward the railing, if not the front row. If I didn't catch him, he might seriously hurt himself. I put my own body on the line and quite literally pulled him out of the air, right on top of me, saving him and his lifelong dream of being champion.

We were both able to remember every spot we'd mapped out only hours before, two great wrestlers in their prime trying to outdo each other under the guise of working together. I've always believed that the intention was for Shawn to drag me off the mat for the last twenty minutes. But it made for a beautiful story—the lion and the gazelle, or perhaps the wolf and the fox. If fans go back and study this one closely, they'll see that at times I was stiff, but I was never slow or heavy.

Our match seemed to unravel in slow motion as my heart beat strong in my chest. Shawn took some fantastic bumps. From the way he went dead weight on me, I assumed he was getting tired, and I was somewhat surprised that I had to keep dragging him off the mat. At the fifty-minute mark I dove out through the ropes like a spear, flattening Shawn in the aisle. Once back in the ring I took in the sold-out crowd and it reminded me of when Muhammad Ali stood in his corner and looked over at George Foreman in Zaire. Unlike his, my fate was decided, but I was determined to keep my dignity.

Shawn was up on the apron; as I went to suplex him in, he dropped behind me. I was quick to reverse and German suplex him straight back. When I did, he bit his tongue, which had nothing to do with me, but he decided to slam me in the gut with a stiff punch anyway. One potato, two potato, three . . . until I had no recourse but to snap a stiff boot square into his face, letting him know the next one would be serious. With cocky arrogance Shawn waved me on to keep it coming.

With five minutes remaining I hoisted him up like a sack of cement and snapped him in half across my knee. I smiled at the time clock. I had told Shawn the last five minutes were all his, and we were right on schedule.

I leaped off the second rope only to be jolted by a vicious stiff boot to the jaw from Shawn, and then one potato after another. He took every liberty he could, stiffing me on drop kicks and elbow smashes. Even so, we both knew the match was a masterpiece. When Shawn nailed me with a high flying elbow, I crashed hard to the mat, and Shawn proved to have been playing a bit of possum. Suddenly he nipped up to his feet with all the energy in the world.

I was there to catch Shawn on all of his daredevil pinning combinations. Following the script to the letter, I delivered as promised. Howard Finkel finally announced, "One minute remaining!" as Shawn slammed me and made his way to the top turnbuckle. I could see thirty-eight seconds remaining on the clock when Shawn came off at me with a drop kick. Catching the world by surprise, I grabbed the heels of his boots and he crashed to the mat. I stepped through and twisted him into the sharpshooter, and the crowd roared its approval at the surprising twist that I might actually win. But it was all part of the final swerve.

As I arched back, careful not to put too much weight on his back, I heard the crowd counting down ten . . . nine . . . eight . . . until Shawn, hanging on for dear life, was saved by the sound of the bell.

I'd won! At least in my eyes—and those of my fans! Earl handed me the belt, and I dropped to the floor to leave, passing newly reinstated WWF figurehead president Gorilla Monsoon in the aisle. I was totally exhausted, gulping some much needed air, as I heard Monsoon on the house mic ordering me back into the ring to go into sudden-death overtime. I willed myself to turn around and contest Gorilla's decision. While I argued with him, the bell clanged and the match resumed.

I pounced right on the wounded Boy Toy, pounding him mercilessly. Three minutes into overtime, it was time to go home. This had been a beautiful movie to watch, especially since the crowd loved us both by the end of it. It was probably the greatest match I ever had, or close anyway. I squeezed Shawn's wrist to give him the cue that we were going home. In this ending, the better man would lose.

I fired Shawn into the corner, following closely, and he sprang up and dropped neatly behind me. The relentless pink soldier turned around as Shawn, in utter desperation, delivered a superkick and caught me square on the jaw. I went down hard and the crowd roared with excitement as we both struggled to get up from the mat. The big kick was coming. I fought to stand but couldn't. Shawn waited for me in the corner, stomping a foot in anticipation. I staggered upright and walked right into it, blindly, the superkick connecting like a shotgun blast. I crumpled to the mat. A drained Shawn collapsed on top of me hooking my leg as Earl slowly counted one . . . two . . . three!

The crowd exploded as Shawn's music played. I couldn't believe my ears when I heard Shawn angrily tell Earl, "Tell him to get the fuck out of the ring! This is *my* moment!" I dropped out to the ring floor and left him there on his knees, crying with the belt in his arms. I had firmly placed the torch in that little monster's hands. But I also knew that no one was going to forget about me. With my head held high, I walked to my waiting Lincoln and burned rubber up the ramp as the credits rolled.

That night after the show, the hotel bar was packed with celebrating fans. I chose to hole up in my room with the kids and enjoy the cold bottles of beer that I had chilling in the sink. I let out a long, silent sigh, knowing that I could leave on a good note. As a character I couldn't be torn down and used up. I was a free agent in a strong position. Go ahead and see if you can carry the company, Shawn.

A third generation of Hart wrestlers—the adolescent Dallas, Matt, T.J. and Harry, along with five-year-old Blade—pulled the mattresses in my hotel room onto the floor to turn them into wrestling mats. The sight of them with their shirts off getting all sweaty meant the world to me. They stayed up until 4 a.m. eating pizza and wrestling. It made me think of my brother Dean and me as kids.

The next day Owen called me from *Raw* to tell me that the buzz in the dressing room was that I had real heat with Shawn because I didn't shake his hand at the end of the match. It didn't hurt to let some of the boys believe that. I watched the live *Raw* feeling uneasy in my easy chair as Shawn stood before Vince in the ring saying it was the toughest match he'd ever had. He praised me, closing the page on my chapter, trying to sweep me out of the minds of the fans.

It took a couple of days for Vince and Shawn to phone me. Vince told me how grateful he was, as did Shawn, but I had the feeling that Shawn probably only called because Vince told him it was the right thing to do. In those days Vince was still old school that way.

36

"I'LL NEVER GIVE YOU A REASON
TO EVER WANT TO LEAVE"

AFTER MILLIONS OF MILES, I was finally going to be home for a while—
except there was little time to settle in. Just five days after *WrestleMania XII*,
I packed my bags again for a seventeen-day tour of Germany: I'd promised
Vince I'd work the foreign markets while my face was having a rest in North
America, and personally I was regarding it as a grand farewell tour. The big
question on everyone's mind was whether I was going to hang up my boots.

On April 11, Vince hired a camera crew to shoot a heart-felt interview with
me on the banks of the Rhine in Bonn. One of Vince's suits tried to script it,
but I ignored him. With a weary, almost fed-up glare, I spoke passionately
about how, after all the years on the road, family had become strangers and
strangers had become family. It was time for me to change that. The interview
was overnighted back to WWF headquarters, and I wondered if they'd even
use it, since I hadn't said what they wanted.

I would have liked to have given Shawn some guidance, but he thought
he already knew everything. The one thing that Shawn had in common
with Warrior as the champion was that they both liked to ring Vince up with
all their complaints, like two nagging wives. But, unlike Warrior, there was
no denying that Shawn had charisma and ability: The only thing stopping
him from becoming the phenomenon of his dreams was some patience,
maturity and judgment. I know he was waiting for me to put him over to the
boys, to say, You're the man. I would have liked nothing more than to be
able to do that, but with his attitude, how could I? I decided that though I
wouldn't stab him in the back, I couldn't endorse him either. Deep down
we both knew there was going to be a showdown between us someday.

In Berlin on April 17, the little war between Shawn's clique and the rest of
the talent escalated. They had clearly singled out Chris Candido and his
wife, Tammy Fytch, who now played the role of a pretty blond vamp named
Sunny. She was the first of the women now known as the WWE Divas, and
had become a bigger star than anyone expected when her sexy posters
became the hottest-selling WWF merchandise, which didn't sit well with
the clique. The caterers left Sunny a boxed dinner after every show to take

with her back to the hotel. One night when she opened it up, she found a pile of human excrement. She was horrified and went home the next morning in tears. I thought, the Mafia leaves its calling card by wrapping a fish up in newspaper, but the clique shits in your dinner.

On this tour, I worked my first matches with Steve Austin. He took a lot of pride in his work, and it meant a lot to me when he told me that he'd like to work with me for the next six months because he'd do nothing but learn from me.

On the flight home I studied my reflection in the lavatory mirror. I sure looked weary and beaten up. I thought back to the days when I'd watched tired old Paddy Ryan lacing up his boots and had sworn to myself that I'd never stay too long. That wasn't me. Not yet.

By May 8, I was at The Kuwait Hotel, which was nothing short of a luxury prison, with no entertainment, no nightlife, no women, no rock 'n' roll and no booze. The highlights of my day were working out in a well-equipped gym at the hotel and watching *Larry King*.

The sponsors of the five-show tour were wealthy Arabs. One afternoon they took me, Owen and Davey out on a fishing boat, and Davey hooked a three-foot yellow shark. An epic tug of war went on for about an hour, like something out of Hemingway, with Davey holding on, drenched in sweat, the veins popping in his arms. When he finally reeled it in, it still had a lot of fight left as it flipped all over the deck. Davey was so impressed with its inexhaustible will to live he insisted it be set free.

Back at the hotel restaurant, I was stirring my coffee and chatting with Razor The Moan, as a lot of the boys now called him. It was the final foreign tour for him and Diesel. Diesel had just put Shawn over clean at *In Your House*, a match during which Shawn went crashing through a table. How original. Razor told me an interesting tale: The clique had cooked up a plan where he and Diesel were going to take over the top spots in WCW, Shawn would take over the WWF and the clique would rule the entire wrestling business!

A boy of about eleven came over to our table wearing a handmade replica of Razor's gear, complete with a "gold" chain of cardboard and greased-back hair with a curl on his forehead. I immediately thought of the Israeli kid who'd pedalled his bicycle as hard as he could to keep up with the bus. This boy had been patiently waiting around all morning for Razor's autograph, and Razor seemed to enjoy making him wait. When Razor got up to leave, he stopped beside the boy as if to finally sign, then hesitated, looking back and forth between me and the boy. Finally he said to me, "I don't need to sign autographs any more." He left that little boy with the saddest look on his face. That was the moment when I lost the little respect I still had for Scott Hall. By day five the boys were getting bored and fidgety. "We know what athletes need!" our Arab hosts told me. "Everything will be there tonight!" With a nod and a wink, they promised us the world: hashish, alcohol and naughty women.

Davey, Austin and I arrived for the party that night with Duke The Dumpster Drose, a raw rookie out of Florida who reminded me of a friendly boxer dog and who had given up work on a law degree to become a wrestler. Of course, there was no hashish, but there was apple-scented tobacco in a big bong. As for alcohol, there was a lone bottle of vodka and some orange juice. And the women? There was a bevy of beautiful Kuwaitis, but their idea of naughty was that they were dressed American-style in jeans and tops that revealed their shoulders. Middle Eastern music was playing, and the girls did everything they could to get us up dancing, but it wasn't rock 'n' roll. Duke finally caved and not long after he got up, I allowed a young woman to entice me to dance, though I actually had my eye on a black-haired beauty with slender curves. Soon enough, Davey and Steve were dancing, too, though we couldn't stop laughing at what bad dancers we all were. Steve had to be worse than me, and that's saying something.

Then the woman I'd been hankering after pinched my back when she walked by, teasing me that she was angry that I was dancing with the other girl. I ended up talking with her on the balcony, away from the security chief, who was attempting to keep a close eye on both of us. With the Kuwaiti skyline in the background, she gave me her phone number and agreed to secretly meet me the next day before we went back to the party. A few minutes later one of our Arab hosts pulled out an issue of the WWF magazine in which there appeared a family Christmas portrait of me with Julie and the kids, which he passed around to all the girls. The young woman who had just said she would meet me glanced at the picture, then gave me a dirty look, and rattled off some guttural Arabic that was easy to understand without a translator. Davey, Steve and Duke looked at me as we all burst out laughing.In the end, the tour was a success, drawing close to thirty thousand fans every night. Beyond the boy whom Razor Ramon brushed off, what I remember most about the trip was when our hosts showed us burned, gutted homes and buildings where handfuls of Kuwaitis stood up to Saddam Hussein's army.

I did manage to get Julie a couple of white-gold rings encrusted with diamonds, more promise rings, but the only promise I was trying hard to keep any more was to come home in one piece.

Carlo called me to tell me about the clique's last WWF show together at Madison Square Garden on May 19. After Shawn beat Diesel in a cage match, the two sworn enemies embraced in the ring, much to the confusion of the crowd. They were soon joined by Razor and Hunter, and then all four stood on the turnbuckles giving the fans the clique hand sign in what they thought was a glorious send off.

Vince had already left the Garden; when he found out what they had pulled, he was livid. Backstage, the agents and the boys were up in arms, and rightfully so: They thought Vince should have nipped such behaviour in the bud. Vince reprimanded all four of them, levying $2,500 fines, and he ordered Shawn and Hunter to apologize to their fellow wrestlers. The other three had no excuse, but Shawn should have known this wasn't something the champion should do.

There were other things I thought a champion should never do. Young boys were now dressing up like Shawn, the same as they did for me, Razor, Taker and others. The problem was that someone decided it would be cute to invite them into the ring every night to do Shawn's Chippendale dance with him. It rankled many of us, not to mention a lot of the fans, to see impressionable boys imitating Shawn's strip-tease. I'd known him as a person who respected the business, and the wrestlers and fans, upon whose shoulders we stood. But that person seemed to be gone.

Also, with the gruelling schedule of the champion, Shawn's drug problems escalated to the point where referee Tim White, André the Giant's long-time babysitter, was now given the responsibility of driving Shawn around and carrying his bags. Shawn was finding out that it was harder than he may have thought to go out there and blow them away every night, and do it without getting hurt. The physical and emotional weight brought out the worst in him, and he became increasingly bad tempered. No champion since Hogan had his own dressing room, but now Shawn reverted back to the days when the champion felt the need to elevate himself above the rest of the boys.

And at no time in the past had the need for a strong and cagey champion been so urgent. When Hall and Nash appeared on WCW's *Nitro* as The Outsiders, it caused quite a sensation for the fans. Vince's way of retaliating was to turn Dr. Isaac Yankem into the new Diesel and an unskilled Rick Bogner, from Calgary, into Razor Ramon. It was Vince's way of saying that he created them and he still owned them. WCW's brash new boss, Eric Bischoff, countered with the best and conceivably the only great idea he would ever come up with: Every week former WWF wrestlers joined the new World order, or nWo, pretending to be an invading faction set on taking over WCW. The storyline implied that maybe the nWo wrestlers had been sent by Vince to subvert the opposition. The angle was done with an edge just real enough that a lot of the fans were open to the possibility that the nWo would somehow bring WCW crashing down. It kept them tuning in. On June 10, 1996, *Nitro* toppled *Raw* from the number-one spot, and stayed on top, week after week, for the next two years.

That same day, the WWF fired Louie Spicolli because of his drug problems and hired Brian Pillman, who was recovering from a Humvee accident in which he nearly lost a foot. He was in a lot of pain, and that pain would soon lead to his own drug problems. The one bright spot was that Yoko had finally been ordered to the fat farm at Duke University, which I really hoped would save his life.

Meanwhile I tried to figure out a routine that included more than just wrestling and all the psychodramas playing out in Vince's world. So far, the acting had been slow going. And, in truth, my heart just wasn't in it. I was finally home, and was consumed with the idea of making up for lost time with Julie, but she went out most nights and didn't return until long after I'd gone to sleep. Most of the time, I didn't know what to do with myself. I remembered when my dad first got out of the business: My mom seemed to forget all about him. I wondered whether Julie and I had grown apart, but then had to admit that we'd never really even had the chance to be together in the first place. I'd been gone since I met her.

Then I got a call from a documentary filmmaker by the name of Paul Jay, who'd seen my interview from Bonn and was so intrigued by the sincerity of it that he wanted to make a film about me and my life. I drove to Banff to meet him at the Banff Film Festival and immediately felt comfortable with him. I was interested in doing the project because, in wrestling, history is too often forgotten or rewritten. The only history pro wrestling sells you is what works for the business.

Vince had finally realized that I was a free agent. He was threatening to fire the other wrestlers who had doubts about signing their new contracts, but with me, he tried to gently coax me back. In New York for a couple of days taping on a WWF-approved video game, I went by limo to a meeting at Vince's house in Greenwich, Connecticut. I sat with Vince and Jim Ross on Vince's back deck, ducking their offers by telling them that things were looking good on the acting front. Of course I was lying. I told them I saw myself coming back to the WWF eventually and that I'd behave like I still had a chip on my shoulder over losing to Shawn. We'd work a rematch where I'd narrowly regain the title in another epic babyface contest. This could set up a third match, where I'd put Shawn over clean, but this time I'd shake his hand at the end of it and endorse him. Vince and J.R. told me they liked it. When Vince walked me out to my limo he said, "You're much smarter than people give you credit for." Having worked for the man for twelve years, I didn't know what to make of that, but I left him with the firm conviction that I was, as always, a team player.

On the first leg of my trip home I was surprised to find myself sitting next to Shawn on the plane. We smiled at each other and passed around the bullshit, and then I thought I should be up front with him about how we could work our eventual rematch. It was to our advantage that everyone thought we hated each other, including the boys, and best of all, nobody would know we'd even spoken. I told him I'd start building heat by making some remarks about his ring character, but it would all be a work. When I came back I'd beat him in a return match, probably around the time of *WrestleMania XIII*.

I saw the colour drain from his face. He clearly didn't like the sound of any of this.

I went on to explain that he'd win the belt back in a third return match, and then I'd endorse him, but I got the impression they'd promised him a really long run, like they always did, and he wasn't expecting any interruptions. I told him that our rematch didn't have to be right away—we could wait a while. I wanted him to know that I understood, better than anyone, that Vince needed him to be WWF's next big star and that he could trust me. In the end, nobody could make him like I could.

On my thirty-ninth birthday I went to visit my mom and dad. Out the kitchen window I could see Ted, Matt and T.J. wrestling in the ring that was always set up on the grass. I was amazed to see Matt doing standing backflips off the top corner and landing perfectly in the middle of the ring, which at that time was something few wrestlers in the business could do. Ever since *WrestleMania X*, Ted, Matt and T.J. had done everything they could to emulate Owen and me, practising their moves all day long. Davey's son, Harry, would be up from Florida soon to team up with T.J. against Ted and Matt for their big rematch at the Rockyford Rodeo. For a year they'd talked about how they would top last year's outing. To my knowledge, the Hart grandkids were the youngest pro wrestlers ever to perform in front of a crowd.

But just two days later, Matt lay dying at the children's hospital in Calgary. It was July 4, wrestling's cursed day. A barely pronounceable infection, necrotizing fasciitis—caused by a flesh-eating strain of streptococcal bacteria—may have entered Matt's body through a small cut on his thumb. He might have picked it up from the unwashed ring canvas. Georgia and B.J. were bleary-eyed, shocked and exhausted, yet they carried themselves with a dignified calm that amazed me.

Matt was spread out on a bed, tethered by a tangle of tubes and wires to life support. He looked really angry lying there, as though he was pissed off at God for putting him through this hell. His handsome face was puffy, his toes were a brownish purple-black and his vital signs were getting weaker. Julie and Georgia left me alone with him, and when I kissed his moist forehead, he was literally burning up. I rubbed his cold, blackened fingers, brushed back his damp hair and had a long conversation with God.

For almost two weeks Matt bravely clung to life while his body was ravaged and cooked from the inside. It became a national news story as Matt was given the dubious distinction of being the sickest boy in all of Canada. He fought on, but the only hope was to amputate all his limbs—and, if he survived, he'd surely have brain damage. Of course I wanted him to live, but I couldn't help but think what a tormented and frustrated life that would be for such a bright, athletic boy.

Matt died on July 13, 1996. And the grim reaper of wrestling wasn't finished yet. Not by a long shot.

On July 22, Vince was in Yakima, Washington, for a TV taping and decided to charter a plane to come to see me in Calgary. At a WCW pay-per-view two weeks earlier, the unthinkable had happened: Hulk Hogan had turned heel. Eric Bischoff had completely stunned the wrestling world, and Vince was getting his ass kicked, which was forcing him to rethink everything.

He put a contract in front of me and told me to name my price: "Whatever you want!" He told me Taker and Shawn were making around $700,000 a year. But I was in no hurry to sign. He left my house with nothing but my vague assurance that I'd come back in the fall.

Barry Bloom got me a role as a Viking on an episode of a kid's show called *The Adventures of Sinbad*, being filmed in South Africa, which would coincide with a WWF tour there that I had promised to make. In fact, the South African promoter threatened to cancel the tour if I wasn't on it. During the thirty-six-hour journey to Cape Town, with connections in London and Johannesburg, I all but made up my mind to go back to Vince. I wanted to help him turn the tide against Ted Turner. As an artist I still appreciated Vince's canvas, literally—his rings were the best, even his ring trucks were immaculate. I had to believe that his marketing savvy would, sooner or later, rear up and overtake Turner and WCW. But for now, Vince could do little but hang on. The WWF had become a cartoon with its hokey clown and pirate gimmicks; my intense rivalry with Shawn could bring back realism and turn the tide.

Cape Town has to be the most beautiful city I've ever seen. Everywhere I looked, whichever way I turned, there was another stunning view: black mountains, endless shoreline, spectacular foliage. The houses had a quaint charm, a legacy of the Dutch who'd settled there some three hundred years ago. Every afternoon in summer a cloudy mist, like thin white cotton, bubbles over Table Mountain, pours over the edge and hangs over the city until it vanishes again. It's some quirky manifestation of the weather and the lay of the land, but I was far more interested in its ethereal beauty than where it came from. And I was struck, of course, by the contrasts of the poor black townships that circled the city like the rings in Dante's hell, where nothing much had changed despite the end of apartheid.

I flew to Johannesburg for two huge outdoor shows. Of the whole lineup I got the best reactions from the crowd every night, and in a big TV special being filmed in Sun City, I'd headline against Steve Austin, who was now going by the name Stone Cold. Johannesburg was a sprawling place where black-on-white crime was rampant. Most whites I knew there carried pistols. I learned this while following them through the necessary metal detectors at local nightclubs.

After the first show in Johannesburg, I stopped to have a beer with Davey and Owen in the hotel lobby bar, and they told me they were getting the Tag belts. Just after midnight, Jake Roberts stumbled through the front doors whacked out on something with three black prostitutes leading the way. The Preacher Man had finally cracked, his Christian values tossed out the window. He gave me that old, sinister smile—a look part reptile, part devil. I could have sworn a forked tongue darted out between his lips. I couldn't help but come as close to feeling sorry for him as I ever would. Davey snickered and said, "Those are the same prostitutes 'e 'ad with 'im last night. So much for 'im being born again!"

I spent the last two days of the tour at the Sun City resort in a hotel bar packed with wrestlers, fans and beautiful women. I was overdue for a good time, and had numerous phone numbers crammed into the pockets of my jeans. I had to smile when I saw long-divorced Yoko with his tongue down the throat of a comely white South African lady who was helping with the PR work. She was very drunk. So was he. She'd be in for a *big* surprise when she woke up in the morning.

On the long flight home I had a lot to think about, not only about my future but about betrayal of trust in other areas I was involved in. While I was away, criminal charges had been laid against Graham James, coach of the Calgary Hitmen, for the sexual abuse of young hockey players under his charge in earlier jobs. He was later convicted.

On September 25, I headed to Los Angeles, where I'd been asked to do a guest spot on *The Simpsons*. Barry Bloom knew Eric Bischoff, of course, and he called before I left to tell me that Bischoff was eager for a meeting. I said we'd talk about whether that was a good idea once I had landed in L.A., but when I got to my hotel, Bischoff was already on his way up to my room.

He was a small, middle-aged guy with shaggy black hair and dimples. We talked for nearly an hour about, of all things, our mutual love of Western gunfighters, such as Wyatt Earp, Jesse James and Butch Cassidy (who hung around the streets of Calgary in the 1890s before going to South America, where he was killed). We got on so well I almost forgot why he had come to see me. Then he asked, "So, what's it gonna take to bring you to WCW?"

"I would want the exact same contract as Hulk Hogan, plus one penny," I calmly replied.

That flabbergasted him. "I can't do a deal anything like that, not right now."

"That's fine, I'm not really looking to go anywhere. I'm happy where I'm at."

"C'mon," he said. "At least give me something that I can go back to my people with. Anything."

I thought about it for a minute. "I'd think about coming to work for you guys for $3 million a year and a lighter schedule."

He said he'd take that home to the Turner folks in Atlanta, and we went right back to talking about gunfighters.

The next day I was picked up by limo and taken to a sound studio where it took me all of five minutes to do my voice on *The Simpsons*. The idea was that The Hitman had bought the evil Mr. Burns's mansion after Mr. Burns went bankrupt, and was now living in Springfield. I'd long felt that there were many similarities between Montgomery Burns and Vince McMahon.

On September 27, Bischoff offered me $2.8 million a year for three years if I came over to WCW. I told him I'd think about it, but now it was me who was flabbergasted!

Soon Vince was hearing rumours that I'd already signed with the competition. I called him on October 3 and alleviated his worries, telling him I wouldn't do anything until I had a long talk with him. We left it that he'd call me over the weekend. When he did, he asked me directly what the WCW offer was.

"Three million dollars for a lighter schedule, 180 days a year . . ."

He cut in: "I can't match it."

I told him I wasn't asking him to match it, just to make me the best offer he possibly could. We both knew that I didn't want to end up in WCW. I hated the thought of being used as an assassin against him and a company that I'd devoted my life to. "But, Vince," I said, "I'm in a position to make $9 million in just three years. I don't want to leave, but I don't want to be stupid. I have to think about my family. What would you do? Saying no to this is like tearing up a lottery ticket."

He seemed to understand my predicament but said, "WCW would never know what to do with a Bret Hart." He told me he needed a couple of days to think about it and then, just like Don Corleone, he said he'd get back to me with an offer I couldn't refuse.

After we hung up, I turned the world off and took off on my mountain bike, pedalling anxiously up and down the bike paths of Calgary. Bischoff was offering so much more money than I could have ever dreamed of that I couldn't help but think what accepting his terms would mean to my family. I was in a perfect position to set myself and my family up for life. I thought of the old, big-name wrestlers, legends from the past, who would show up in the dressing room from time to time having fallen on hard times, broke, crippled or close to it. Nobody in the dressing room cared about how many belts a guy had won, where he'd worked or how tough he was. In the end all that mattered was what he'd saved. Very few wrestlers ever made it outside the business, not in a big way, anyway. Now I was in a position where if I wanted to, I could pound out three more years and go home with no worries, at least not financial ones. But could I kiss my entire legacy goodbye in order to end up in WCW?

On October 9, Vince flew to Calgary to present his offer in person. We settled down for a talk in my dining room. As an opening act to the main topic, I brought up the Paul Jay documentary. He said he liked the idea and had no problem giving Paul access to the matches and the backstage area. Then we got down to it: Vince said he had a better deal for me than WCW. He wanted to sign me for twenty years, for a total of $10.5 million. The breakdown was $1.5 million a year for three years as a wrestler; $500,000 a year for the next seven years as one of his senior advisers; and then $250,000 a year for ten years thereafter, to be on standby as that Babe Ruth of the company Vince was always looking for. It was a satisfying feeling hearing him say, "I'll never give you a reason to ever want to leave."

WCW was offering almost as much for only three years, but when it got down to it I couldn't leave Vince, or our history together. I accepted the deal and we shook on it. His eyes glistened and he gave me that yuk-yuk smile as we agreed that all we had left to do was iron out some minor details. At *Raw* in Fort Wayne, Indiana, on October 21, I'd announce I was coming back to face Stone Cold Steve Austin at *Survivor Series*.

I felt badly, but I had to keep Eric hanging until my deal with Vince was done. Eric was making every concession he could think of, including offering to have both Flair and Hogan call me to tell me themselves that they had no hard feelings about some less than complimentary things I'd said about them in past interviews, and that I'd be welcomed aboard. Even Hall and Nash agreed to waive their favoured-nations clause, which had guaranteed that no one in a similar position could be paid more than they were making, just so I could come to WCW.

Vince was already advertising that I'd be doing a live interview on *Raw* to announce whether I was staying or going. I assumed the whole contract thing would be sorted out in plenty of time, but it wasn't until the Friday before I was to make my appearance at *Raw* that I received a very controlling draft contract, which, once again, my lawyer said only an idiot would sign. Since the draft bore no resemblance to the deal Vince and I had shook on, I called him. I could only reach his wife, Linda, who was now president of operations, so I had no choice but to tell her that all bets were off and that I would not appear unless my contract was worked out. Before I could tear up Bischoff's lottery ticket, I simply had to have my deal with Vince inked and dry. Carlo believed that Bret Hart going to WCW at that precise moment could devastate the WWF and pressed Vince to finalize my deal. Then Vince's office called to tell me that his legal department had accidentally sent me the wrong contract: This was the third time over the years that I'd been given this same lame excuse.

When I flew into Fort Wayne for *Raw* I had the WCW contract folded up in the back pocket of my jeans. I still didn't have a signed WWF contract, but my appearance on the live show had been heavily hyped in an all-out effort to finally beat *Nitro* in the ratings. One lesson I had learned in my twelve years in the WWF was that Vince stripped you bare when he was through with you, using up all or most of what you had left, including your name and persona. Carlo, believing my departure would be a disaster for the organization he worked for, helped me put together a contract that wrested more control away from Vince and gave me more protection than any wrestler had ever had before, though officially it was my lawyer, Gord, and my accountant, John Gibson, who handled the whole thing. The contract provided me with all the usual perks and also two ground-breaking concessions. The first was that if I was injured on my way to a show or in a match so that I couldn't wrestle, I'd be fully compensated for all my wages. The second allowed me creative control for my last thirty days if for any reason I was ever to leave the WWF. In short, this meant that my character didn't have to do anything I didn't want him to do, which would keep Vince from devaluing my stock on my way out. I liked hearing Carlo repeat over and over, "They can never, ever fuck you now."

I stayed in my hotel room until one hour before the show. Backstage I was whisked away to a room where copies of my contract were laid out on a long table. Carlo even had fancy pens on hand to commemorate the occasion. Vince seemed anxious as he signed, and when it was all done Carlo clapped and suggested we uncork some champagne after the show.

Within seconds of signing, I ran into Shawn. We spoke briefly as I waited for my cue to go through the curtain. He'd just done a nude spread for *Playgirl* magazine, which I thought was a dumb move for someone posing as a role model for young boys. I asked him, "Do you mind if I say something about your *Playgirl* magazine spread?" I wanted to start building our heat right away. He said, "Say whatever you want."

I marched out to my music wearing jeans, shades and a tight grey T-shirt and was interviewed by Jim Ross in the ring. The first thing I did in this completely unscripted live interview was thank Eric Bischoff for treating me with respect and making me such a great offer. I regretted that I hadn't had a chance to call him and that Eric was about to find out that I had just resigned with Vince along with the rest of the world. Mind you, I referred to Eric only as an unnamed rival because, to that point, neither organization had uttered the name of the other on their TV shows—but the fans knew exactly who and what I was talking about. (Dave Meltzer had put out such an accurate account of my contract negotiations in the October 14, 1996, *Wrestling Observer* that I was sure it was all coming from an insider from one or both organizations.) I spoke about not being greedy for money, but being greedy for respect and about how much soul searching I'd done. But when it came right down to it, I owed everything I'd ever done and everything I planned on doing to my WWF fans. "I'll be in the WWF forever!" I proclaimed. I said I wanted wrestling fans all over the world to have somebody they could look up to, somebody who didn't dance and pose for girlie books: "Shawn Michaels will never be as tough as me. He'll never be as smart as me. And that is why I've accepted the challenge to face the best wrestler in the WWF, Stone Cold Steve Austin!" For the first time in months, while I was on the air, Vince got the ratings he was looking for.

37

EVERYONE AROUND THE WORLD HATES AMERICANS

WHILE I'D BEEN GONE, Steve Austin had really flourished as a heel. By *Survivor Series '96* on November 17, he'd become such a good heel he was starting to turn babyface—the fans loved him! This was something he wanted to avoid because his heel run still had plenty of steam. He had such a great look for a heel, with a bald head and menacing eyes that burned a hole through you. He wore simple black trunks with black boots and came across like a real bad-ass son of a bitch. His promos were intense: His Texas talk and ornery look gave him a unique magnetism.

This was a big night for Steve. The week before *Survivor Series* he flew to Calgary to work out the entire match with me. He was a friend of Shawn's, and they had been having some great matches together, but standing next to the ring in my pool room Steve confided in me that Shawn wasn't the right guy to lead the company. I took this as the endorsement it was. In a surprising turn of events, Shawn was going to drop the belt to Sycho Sid at *Survivor Series*, so he could win it back in his hometown of San Antonio at the *Royal Rumble* in January. In the middle of all that, I'd be thrown into the main event to work a title match with Sid at the December *In Your House*. I wasn't sure how Shawn's losing the belt and then winning it back again would effect the big rematch that Vince led me to believe we were having at *WrestleMania XIII*. For now, all I could do was focus on my match with Stone Cold.

At *Survivor Series*, Steve and I worked fast and hard, and I only got tired near the end. I had no idea that Vince and J.R. were going to great lengths in their live commentary to subtly tear me down. When I heard it later, I got the first hint of what lay ahead for me. J.R. described me as being slow getting up and attributed it to ring rust. "Bret Hart, with a huge move, can't execute the cover . . ." Vince was quick to add, "He just didn't have it, J.R. He couldn't capitalize on it!" I felt that they were going out of their way to portray me as old and beat up, while I was only doing my best to make Steve look strong while still putting me over. The bout was filled with believable moves in one long, continuous fist fight. We brawled on the floor, levelled the Spanish announcers' table, broke down a metal barricade and duked it out in the front row! As Stone Cold closed in for the kill, he stalked me from behind, clamping on a cobra clutch. Much like I'd done with Piper at *WrestleMania VIII*, I jumped up and kicked off using the corner to topple backward, pinning Steve for the one . . . two . . . three.

When I walked around the ring high-fiving my fans, I was happy when Vince reached out to shake my hand. Still wearing his headset he smiled and with what I took to be the loving eyes of a father, he said, "Unbelievable!"

Later on that night Sid took the title from Shawn using a gimmicked TV camera to bash him while Shawn was distracted when his mentor, Jose Lothario, was supposedly stricken by a heart attack at ringside.

On November 20, Taker, Shawn, Sid and I appeared at a huge press conference in San Antonio. My *In Your House* title match with Sid was totally downplayed so they could hype Sid's match with Shawn at *Royal Rumble*.

The following week, the WWF headed over to England for shows in London and Birmingham, though Vince kept Shawn in the United States as he'd done with Hogan. If anyone wondered whether I was still over, the question was answered when hordes of chanting Hitman fans were there to meet us at Heathrow. Sold-out shows had become a rarity in the United States since I'd been away, but there wasn't a ticket to be had for the shows in the U.K. A fan explained it this way in a letter to *The Wrestling Observer*: "No adult male is going to support an obnoxious, blonde, ponytail wearing self-professed sexy boy. No matter how well he does in the ring."

I was grateful when a lot of the boys came up to me and thanked me for coming back; most of them still called me champ. In London, I worked a good, solid match with Vader. He was considered tough, quick and nearly as agile as Bam Bam Bigelow, but he was also one of the stiffest guys to ever lace up a pair of boots. He'd recently potatoed Shawn so badly that Shawn dressed him down in front of the boys, threatening that if it happened again he'd have his fat ass fired. But you had to be careful with the monsters of the business. They could mop the floor with you any time they wanted, and they were doing a guy my size or Shawn's a favour when they let us look good by pinning their shoulders to the mat.

Yoko, Fuji, Backlund and M.O.M. were all missing from the dressing room. The 1-2-3 Kid, Roddy Piper and the recently fired J.J. Dillon were all in WCW (no-one was sure why Vince had dumped Dillon). A lot of fresh faces had come in the few months I'd been gone; some I'd only met once or twice. The one who immediately stood out was Dwayne Johnson, pro wrestling's first third-generation worker. His grandfather, Peter, a tough Samoan powerhouse, had been a very close friend of Stu's. I told Dwayne that I remembered him as a little kid running around the dressing room when I worked in Hawaii back in the 1980s. He was shy around me, a nice, bright kid who was still innocent as far as wrestlers went. He was a handsome blend of black and Polynesian, well built and a real athlete; he'd played some CFL with the Calgary Stampeders just a couple of years earlier. Like me, he'd resigned himself to trying his hand in the family business and was anxious to learn. I wanted to see this kid make it, and I told him I'd help him all I could. I watched him in the ring that night, wrestling under the ring name of Rocky Maivia, and I remember coming back to the dressing room and saying to everyone, "Mark my words, three or four years down the road that kid will be the franchise." He already had the look and the skill. If he learned to talk, he could be great.

Another new face trudging around the dressing room was a frumpy curiosity called Cactus Jack. Everyone called him Jack, but his name was actually Mick Foley. Vince had just reinvented him as Mankind. He was a big kid from Long Island, New York, with a scruffy beard and bushy, long black hair. He was already a hard-core legend famous for his crazy, violent matches in ECW, WCW and Japan. But I found him to be a friendly guy, well read and intelligent, a far cry from the lunatic character he played so persuasively, complete with straitjacket and Hannibal Lecter mask!

In the dressing room in Birmingham, Mankind stalked me eagerly, waiting to work with me. I hoped he'd tone down all the crazy shit because the last thing I needed at that point was to get hurt. The more we talked, the more I could see that he had the gift of seeing a match unfold in his head like a movie, just like I did. And I was blown away by our match. Mankind took all the risks and bumps, yet he was exceptionally skilful and tight. Most amazingly, he was never stiff. He became not only one of my favourite characters in the business, but one of my favourite people too. Foley was one of only a handful of guys who I thought had a similar imagination for the business as I do. While I'd been off, his pay-per-view matches with Shawn were the ones that finally gave Shawn his opportunity to get over. Mick Foley was a great wrestler, and I was amazed that WCW had lost him.

In West Palm Beach, the night of December 14, 1996, I slid under the sheets hurting so badly that I had no choice but to wash down a couple of pain pills, plug in my heating pad and smear Icy Hot over my knees and back. I was supposed to wrestle Sid in our title bout the next day on *In Your House*. Wrestling with Jim in the Hart Foundation in the early days, I used to feel like the zippy Porsche to Jim's armoured tank. Now I felt like an old race car with my dings hidden before every match under a coat of fresh paint.

Our match turned out to be surprisingly good. Sid had come to respect me because I helped him when I could. During our match, Shawn sat with Jim Ross at the announcers' table ranting about his God-given right to live his life as he chose. Apparently the remark I'd made a month earlier about him posing for *Playgirl* had been eating away at him the whole time. Shawn got involved in the finish by climbing on the ring apron, where we collided, allowing Sid to jackknife powerbomb me to the mat for the win. I furiously jumped out and pulled Shawn's shirt over his head like we were in a hockey fight and pretended to beat him senseless. It looked fantastic. Sid came back to the dressing room thrilled with how it went, and Shawn seemed nothing but upbeat. But over the next two days of TVs in Florida he was noticeably distant with me. When I told Vince that I was concerned that I was pissing Shawn off, he downplayed it. Still, I asked him to clarify things for both me and Shawn, so we could do this thing right. He wouldn't listen. Instead of us sorting things out, Shawn went out and did an angry in-ring interview, with me as the target of his rage. I was disappointed to see him lose his babyface composure. I was thinking, Oh, Shawn, don't do this . . . stay humble . . . I'm only workin' . . . let me be the heel. I shook my head in utter dismay trying to figure out what was happening between us.

I spent my Christmas holiday aching all over, yet I worked with Leo Burke and a bunch of green local wrestlers he was training at my house in the WWF ring Vince had given me. Over time those young men became Christian, Edge, Glen Kulka, Teddy Hart (Georgia's son, Ted Annis), Mark Henry, the fake Razor Ramon, Kurrgan, Don Callis, Test and Ken Shamrock, who was the Ultimate Fighting Champion at the time, just to name a few. Despite the tension with Shawn, I was on top of the world, set to regain the title, while being the highest paid WWF wrestler of all time. That Christmas, Julie and the kids had everything, including me.

The WWF had been blitzing San Antonio for weeks in an all-out effort to fill up the Alamo Dome for the *Royal Rumble* on January 19, 1997. In the end, it was one of the most papered shows in the history of the WWF, but they did pack the Dome to the rafters.

Stone Cold was one of the first combatants in the battle royal, and the story was that he was unstoppable. He whooped ass on nearly everyone, tossing out a record eleven wrestlers, one after another—until I came out. We worked with each other, back and forth, until it was down to seven men left. Then I happened to catch Austin off guard and tossed him over the top rope, eliminating him, but the referees were conveniently distracted by Terry Funk and Mankind, who were brawling on the floor. Austin shot back under the ropes and into the ring and flipped Taker and Sid out, just as I dumped out the fake Diesel. Technically, I had just won the coveted title shot at *WrestleMania XIII*, but Steve came from behind, threw me out and was awarded the win instead. As per the plan, he hightailed it back to the dressing room as I went absolutely nuts in the ring, manhandling the referees.

I followed the storyline, once again complaining on mic that I'd been screwed. This was all great heat for Steve, and I went along, though I was wondering where the payoff was for me. Where was my character going?

But nobody came close to the terrific job that Shawn did in the main event with Sid, not even me. Afterwards I went to Shawn's dressing room to tell him that I was proud of him. He thanked me, and I thought everything was fine between us.

Terry Funk was only there for the one night, to be in the battle royal. It pained me to see him hobble across the dressing room afterwards. He was barely able to walk after taking so many hard bumps throughout his storied career, yet he had still given it his all, part machine, part masochist. This great worker and former NWA world champion pulled me aside in the showers that night and told me that he respected me for all I had given to the business all these years and in his opinion I was the best worker around. I left the building after the show feeling pretty damn proud of myself.

The only thing still keeping me babyface was Stone Cold, who kept coming out of nowhere like a villain in a good Western, jumping me and leaving me for dead every week. He reminded me a lot of Dave Schultz, in a different package but with the same intense meanness. Steve was a great chicken-shit heel, which I mean as a compliment. I loved working with him because it came across like we really hated each other; our interviews and brawls looked like even more of a shoot than the stuff I was doing with Shawn.

Much to my surprise, Beaumont TV on January 20 was the Bret Hart show. Although I was happy to play a major role on *Raw*, Vince had me do a carefully scripted in-ring interview that called for more complaining, which I thought was beginning to kill me off with the fans. "I was screwed out of my title match with Sid by Shawn Michaels. I got screwed at the Rumble by Stone Cold. I got screwed by the WWF," I said and glared down at Vince. I then pointed accusingly at him and said, "And I got screwed by *you!*" On live international TV, I quit, climbing over the guard rail and walking out through the crowd. It all seemed quite real, too real, but I did as Vince told me. In an intense promo, Austin ripped into me about whining and complaining all the way back to Canada. "The only person you could possibly beat up is your wrinkled-up old man in his little old basement!" (Stu always took it as a sign of respect when a heel wrestler mentioned his name on TV.)

The marks groomed by the ECW had grown in number: By the winter of 1997, they regularly bought up the tickets for the first few rows of seats at all of Vince's TV shows on the east coast just so that they could be heard on TV around the world booing the babyfaces and cheering the heels. They made life really hard for Rocky Maivia, just because they knew they could get under his skin. The general TV audience had no idea that it was the same group of ECW fans showing up everywhere. Instead they thought a trend was developing, and as a result hating the good guys and loving the heels actually started to catch on. At Beaumont, though, the fans were still cheering for the good guys. After I quit on live TV, Gorilla Monsoon announced that what happened to me at the *Rumble* was a travesty and he wanted to make up for it by inviting me, Taker, Vader and Stone Cold to participate in a final-four match at the *In Your House* pay-per-view on February 16, with the winner to face Shawn for the title at *WrestleMania XIII*. So back I came through the crowd, accepted the match and then brawled up and down the aisle with Stone Cold until we went off the air.

Afterwards, in his office, Vince introduced me to a bigwig from the USA cable network that carried *Raw*. They were both very pleased with that night's show, and the USA rep said it was the most exciting *Raw* they'd ever done. Vince gave me a proud slap on the back and said, "It's all on account of him."

On February 2, I was on dead last for the matinee of a double shot in Montreal, and the agents told me not to worry if, as a result, I was late getting to Ottawa that night. I got there as the opening match began, which was more than two hours before I needed to be in the ring for the main event. As I entered the back door of the arena, Austin caught me by the arm to tell me that Shawn and Hunter had been making a big stink about me being late. He also told me that Shawn was trying to drive a wedge between us: He'd actually told Steve a few days earlier that I'd been asked to put Steve over in Toronto and had refused. I told Steve there was no truth to that at all. There was no avoiding the fact that Shawn and Hunter were stirring things up behind my back: They wanted war rather than peace. That night Pat came to me and sheepishly explained, "Vince would like you to put Hunter over, just to show the boys."

"I don't mind one bit, Pat," I said, "but when the boys you are talking about happen to be only Shawn and Hunter, it does bother me."

I did the honours that night as I'd been asked, but I was steamed over the insult. I called Vince the next day only to hear him side with them, telling me that Shawn and Hunter also said that on top of my tardiness I was lackadaisical in the ring. I figured after all this time Vince knew me better than that.

"Where are you going with me?" I countered. "I thought you said I was going to play a major role in all the booking."

Vince gave me that yuk-yuk laugh. "Well, you probably think this is crazy, but you'll screw Shawn this Thursday at Lowell TV so Sid wins the belt. Then in the final four, at *In Your House,* Shawn will screw you out of winning, and from there Taker will work with Sid at *Mania* for the belt, and Shawn will put his hair up in a ladder match, and you'll cut it all off."

I was a bit stunned at how casual he was. "So, it's not me and Shawn at *WrestleMania XIII* for the belt?"

"It's too predictable now. I'm changing it."

But I could see this for what it really was. Shawn had refused to work with me or put me over, and it changed everything.

On February 7, I was sitting with Davey in the dressing room in Pittsburgh listening to Shawn bitch about Steve. I was slightly relieved to know that I wasn't the only one he feared. Poor Rocky Maivia was also being buried by Shawn and Hunter for supposedly not wanting to job, for not selling and for stealing their spots. Rocky was a good kid, and he tried to be polite and respectful, but he couldn't get them to like him at all.

Just then Vince, with his lawyer, Jerry McDivitt, waved me into his office. I handed him a clipping from a Quebec City newspaper. "As far as me being lackadaisical, believe what you want."

Vince put on his glasses to read: "there were only four thousand wrestling fans at the Coliseum last night in attendance at the WWF show and this is the reason the actors did not give their all. All the hoopla we have been accustomed to was absent. Only the match-up between Bret Hart and Steve Austin and the fight between newcomer Phil LePhon and Owen Hart drew fans to their feet. The finale between Farouq and Shawn Michaels did not produce the desired result."

I told Vince that I knew he wasn't being straight with me: everything he'd promised me was being changed because Shawn didn't want to put me over. If he was trying to ruin me, I said, I wanted him to know that I was aware of it. With this kind of treachery and deception, I might as well be in WCW. "I don't know if you realize it but I've only won three matches since I came back." Vince stammered that everything I said just wasn't true—he now had too much invested in me not to get everything out of me that he could.

On February 13, in Lowell, Massachusetts, the big news was that Shawn was forfeiting the World belt because he'd suddenly somehow sustained a career-ending knee injury and needed surgery. Taker looked at me like this was all bullshit and said, "I'll believe it when I see the scar. The little fucker doesn't want to drop the belt." Taker, Sid and I headed down the hallway to Vince's office. Shawn and Hunter, Pat, J.R. and Brisco were already there when we arrived. Vince seemed really upset that Shawn was hurt and was near to tears as he explained how I'd win the belt in the final four for my fourth title reign.

The catch? Sid would work with me in a title match on *Raw* the night after and Austin would cost me the belt, setting up a new makeshift lineup for *WrestleMania XIII* with Taker and Sid headlining in the main event while Stone Cold and I worked the semi-main event. I actually liked the new storyline, accepting that Taker and Sid had every right to be the main event. But as Vince went on explaining how everything was going to change, I looked over at Taker, who tugged on the corner of his eye and made a skeptical face. Sid was tight-lipped, and Steve wore an intense glare as we had our futures rewritten, probably fearful that he was going to be turned babyface just when things were finally taking off for him. He knew that Shawn was better to have as a friend than as an enemy. Back in the dressing room, Steve told me again that he supported me, but he added that he didn't want to get involved in dressing-room tensions. Steve was going to ride the fence.

Shawn did an in-ring interview that night that I watched on a TV monitor backstage along with the other wrestlers. He walked out without so much as a limp and with the heart-breaking trickle of the occasional tear, he talked of having lived his dream. Fans jeered him, so the cameras cut to close-ups of girls crying. He said he simply had to listen to his doctors. He'd not only hurt his knee, he had "lost his smile" over the last few months and was going home to find it. Every wrestler standing with me rolled his eyes as Shawn forfeited the title, handing the belt to Vince, who was caked in make-up and looked peculiarly Dracula-like as he, too, appeared to be fighting back tears. I'd worked a tag team match with Shawn at the Meadowlands only three days before, and there was nothing wrong with his knee. He hadn't wrestled since. I found myself agreeing with Taker—I'll believe this bullshit when I see the scar.

Three days later, I drove up to the back of the arena in Chattanooga for *In Your House*. A bad flu had hit the dressing room. Stone Cold was there, even though he was green in the gills. He barely spoke as we worked out the finish with Vader and Taker.

When the four of us hit the ring, Shawn's teary-eyed retirement interview played on the giant screen. Shawn was there, watching it all on a monitor in the back, while word trickled down to the dressing room that he miraculously wouldn't need surgery after all. Then Shawn pranced out swatting hands as he made his way to the announcers' table to guest commentate.

It was a great four-way match with battle-royal rules and the belt on the line. Vader potatoed himself this time, taking a boot while coming at Taker with a steel chair. He split his eyebrow open and bled everywhere, getting eliminated, and the blood kicked the match into high gear. The referee gave us the cue, and I delicately dumped a sick Steve over the ropes to the floor, eliminating him. In a climactic series of false finishes, as the referees were trying to drag Austin off the apron, I ducked a clothesline from Taker and tipped him out as Steve was hauled back to the dressing room. Then Earl Hebner handed me the belt to begin my fourth title reign. Despite the cheers from the crowd, I didn't have a single moment to appreciate it because Sid's theme music was pumping so loud to build up our title match on *Raw* the next night.

At *Raw*, which was in Nashville, I strode to the ring looking like a confident champion, even though Sid was the babyface and Nashville was his home-town. He was a good friend, but he scared me every time we worked because he was awkward and injury prone. I had a new idea, one never done before, where I would drag Sid over to the post and put on a figure four-leg lock around the post. It looked extremely painful and Sid writhed in agony while I hung upside-down from the outside corner. As I wrenched on his knee I smiled, because it was totally painless, looking so real but feel-ing so light.

After several commercial breaks and one more airing of Shawn's teary retirement speech, right in the middle of our match, we went into the fin-ish. At the end I'd somehow managed to bait Sid into sunset flipping me, then cleverly rolled through and twisted the six-foot-nine powerhouse into the sharpshooter. Sid desperately tried to power out of it, but he was done for. Then Stone Cold fought his way to the ring apron and cracked me with a chair. I sold it just long enough to be caught bent over so that Sid could step over me and powerbomb me to the mat, pinning me for the title win.

The WWF had just created a European Championship belt, and the first tournament to crown the new champion would take place on a sold-out nine-day tour of Germany that February. I was happy to get away from Shawn and all the other goings-on. This time I had decided to drive instead of riding on the bus with the boys. Getting to the venues was a chal-lenge, but I loved the fleeting freedom of the road, and somehow luck landed me at the buildings safely every night. The European fans were sympathetic over how my character had been screwed recently and cheered me on louder than ever. On February 25, I had a wonderful match with Owen in Hamburg.

I left for the venue in Berlin with time to spare, but I got incredibly lost in pouring rain. It was still early in the afternoon when I got to the building, but Vince was angry that I was late. It turned out they were doing the first live *Raw* in Europe that night to air on a tape delay in the United States and Canada, but I hadn't known this. I had been under the impression that Vince was just hiring a local camera crew to film a house show.

In the dressing room, Jerry Brisco told me that Hunter was going to go over on me: This wasn't so surprising since Shawn and Hunter had worked themselves onto the booking committee. I calmly said that I didn't see any sense in Hunter beating the most over guy they had in Europe less than a month before *WrestleMania XIII*, when Stone Cold and I were being relied upon to carry the pay-per-view. Hunter gritted his teeth while Brisco nervously repeated himself. I said coolly, "I'll take it up with Vince" and set off to find him. Vince was cool toward me but saw my point and changed the match to a disqualification, with Chyna interfering.

That night Owen and Davey had a rare gem of a match for the European Championship. Owen carried a super-charged Davey, who won when he flipped over and reversed Owen's small package for a beautiful finish, which tore the house down. Vince had made promises to Davey when he signed him, but he hadn't lived up to them and was trying to appease Davey by putting the European title on him.

By the time I got home on March 1, there were only three weeks to go until *WrestleMania XIII*, and I was nearly back to top form.

Before the start of the show in Springfield on March 9, I sat with Vince in an empty dressing room as he outlined a year-and-a-half-long program that would revolve around Stone Cold turning babyface at *WrestleMania XIII*. He pulled out a sheet of paper with two lists of names on it and handed it to me. The lists compared whom I could work with as a face as opposed to whom I could work with as a heel. I had to admit to myself that the heel list appealed to me more, especially from the standpoint of safety. Most of the guys I'd work with if I was a face were reckless and stiff, whereas the babyfaces were workers such as Shawn, Stone Cold and Taker. But actually turning heel? I wasn't sold on the idea by any means.

I fully expected to put Steve over at *WrestleMania XIII*, so I was taken aback to hear Vince tell me that he wanted me to beat Steve instead. He enthusiastically went on to explain that he'd come up with a concept that had never been done before and he was counting on me to pull it off. I would become the hottest heel in the WWF, but only in the United States: the twist was that he wanted me to slag the American fans as rotten to the core. To them I'd become a heel, but to the rest of the fans around the world, I'd still be a babyface. I said I had no idea how anyone could make this work with the worldwide television audience all watching the same shows.

"Everyone around the world loves to hate Americans," Vince said. "We come across like we're better than everyone else. This won't affect your merchandise sales because you'll be loved abroad for standing up to us Americans."

Once upon a time I enjoyed being a heel, at least in the ring, but I had no desire to alienate my audience. I admit I'd become accustomed to the adulation. Having a lot of young kids cheering their hearts out for me eased my loneliness, stroked my ego and made it tolerable to get up every morning and go to the next town. I told Vince I'd think it over.

As the evening wore on, I wandered the backstage hallways of the Springfield Civic Center tossing it all around in my head. If I turned heel, I'd have more control in the ring because I'd be driving the car. Not to mention that I wouldn't have to worry any more about my babyface character coming across as a whiner. If the reaction I'd just got in Germany was any measure, I could see where my foreign fans might actually buy into me bashing Americans. Best of all, Shawn wouldn't see me as a threat any more—in fact, he would need me more than ever.

But what about my mom? She was a patriot, and she'd hate every bit of this! I'd travelled Canada and the United States from one end to the other, to every big city and countless small towns, and I loved both countries. I had always seen myself as a North American, equally proud of my American blood and my Canadian heritage. As an America basher, I would be a heel the American fans would truly hate. And the American wrestling audience had already changed, booing the babyfaces and cheering the heels. In a very real sense it was the American fans who were turning heel, not me.

Before the night was over, I had sold myself on the idea. After ten strong years as a babyface I definitely needed to do something to pump some kind of new blood into my character. I talked myself into it, even though I couldn't shake the feeling there was something not quite right about Vince's plan.

I called him early the next morning. "As long as it's done smartly and I have my hands on the controls of what I say and do, I'm in."

"You won't regret it."

Vince told me to keep my upcoming heel turn to myself, so I did.

38

THE LION AND THE HYENA

ON MARCH 23, I arrived at the Rosemont Horizon in Chicago at about 10 a.m. for *WrestleMania XIII*. Vince had just let Stone Cold in on my heel turn and our role reversal, and he and I sat on the ring apron blankly staring at each other. Steve appeared anxious about how we'd go about telling our respective stories. I started tossing out ideas, and together we began piecing our match together. I told him if my new heel turn was going to seem for real, we had to go toe-to-toe right off the bell, onto the floor, over the barricade and up into the stands. Such an approach would make it all feel like a shoot. The fans would be close, so we'd have to keep our work tight. I looked him in the eye and said, "What would really make this a great match would be for you to get a little juice." Steve uneasily admitted that he'd never done that before, but he offered to try.

There was too much at stake for him to start practising at *WrestleMania*. "Steve, I'd be the first guy to tell you never to let anyone cut you, but in this situation you're going to have to trust me. I'll do it right." Steve quickly conceded that if we were going to get away with it, I'd better be the one to do it.

The plan was that he was going to pass out in the sharpshooter but never submit, and we both needed to figure out the best way to do that. I smiled at Steve and said, "Have you ever seen the scene in that movie *One Flew Over the Cuckoo's Nest* where Jack Nicholson's character tries to pull that heavy, bolted-down sink out of the floor and throw it out the widow so he can escape the nut house and go watch the World Series? You want him to succeed so badly, but as hard as he tries, he simply can't. That was the scene that made him, and that's what we're going to do with you." Steve was relying on me because he knew he could trust me. Vince had finally hired Ken Shamrock, a move I had suggested, and he was going to referee our match, lending the credibility he brought with him as champion of the brutal world of Ultimate Fighting.

As I came out like a lion, Steve was pacing the ring like a pissed-off hyena. I really felt like I was going out to have a fight after school with a kid I hated. I got a strong cheer, but there were enough angry signs and boos for me to see that my days as a babyface were truly over. Steve tackled me full force when I came through the ropes and the bell clanged.

As we brawled up the stands, I took a hard smack into the hockey boards, and Steve took a back drop from an attempted piledriver right onto the cement steps. I remember this part of the fight in slow motion. Shocked, amused and angry fans leaped and yelled all around us. The cheering was so loud I couldn't hear a thing. My fists bounced perfectly off Steve's head, and he never stopped fighting back. Ken Shamrock, wearing a sleeveless zebra-striped referee shirt, looked amazed at how close our work was, and how totally believable.

I eventually derailed Steve and started to work his leg. I dragged him over to the corner, dropped out to the floor and slapped on my figure four around the post. Steve sold it like I was breaking his legs! I let go and nonchalantly grabbed the ring bell, then left it on the apron as if it was a weapon abandoned while I sought a better one. Like a cool killer I grabbed a chair, but it was padded, so I put it down and picked up a metal one. I could see Julie and the kids in the front row. Beans was covering her eyes, sitting next to a grim Stu and a startled Helen. I prepared to break Stone Cold's ankle, as the fans remembered he'd done to Pillman a few months earlier, by methodically threading his shin bone through the back of the chair and stomping on it. I climbed up to the top corner to jump off and cripple him, but Steve was up to greet me and smacked me across the back with the chair, knocking me to the mat. While I was on all fours he cracked the chair across my back again, leaving me writhing and twitching in the ring. My heel turn was in motion.

Vince, commentating with Lawler, announced to the masses watching on live pay-per-view, "What excuse will Bret Hart come up with this time?"

Then Stone Cold attempted to put the sharpshooter on me as Lawler said, "Wouldn't that be the greatest thing of all time? For Bret Hart to submit to his very own hold?"

Steve had put the sharpshooter on wrong, and I raked his eyes breaking the hold, fighting back with a hard gut punch. I took off into the ropes, but he sidestepped me and threw me out to the floor. I spat out the blade from where it was tucked between my upper lip and gum. As we slugged it out on the floor, I said, "It's time!"

I faintly heard him say, "Maybe we shouldn't."

I reversed his throw and told him, "It's too late!" I hurled him crashing hard into the timekeeper, and he barrelled into the steel barricade. I calmly stepped over Steve, with Vince looking right at me and screaming fans only inches away. I grabbed his head and beat him with my fists like rubber hammers. Then I cut him perfectly, less than a half-inch long and as deep as a dime slot. No one saw a thing. The blood spurted out of his head as I gave him a serious thrashing. Despite all the vicious attacks he'd put me through, the crowd was now cheering for him as he fought to hang on. I retrieved the chair I'd discarded earlier and repeatedly smashed him in the knee, like I was bent on destroying him. I was actually doing the best I could to hit his knee brace every time.

I managed to beat the bloody but defiant Austin back to a corner, but like a school bully with his back against the wall, he kicked me full force in the balls. A total work. I clutched my crotch and sank backward. The tide had just turned.

Now a furious Stone Cold did all he could to put The Hitman away. The crowd seemed torn between us at times, but when he suplexed me off the top corner into the ring, Steve had the fans totally behind him.

After twenty minutes we went into the finish, but Steve threw me out on the wrong side of the ring—I needed to be near the bell I'd left on the apron. Steve went for the mic cord, while I subtly manoeuvred to where I needed to be. He quietly sighed with relief that I'd fixed the mistake, and as I leaned against the ropes from outside on the ring apron, he came from behind me and wrapped the mic cord around my neck several times, pretending to choke the life out of me. I sank to my knees, gasping and struggling, then grabbed the ring bell, desperately smashing the top of Steve's bald, bloody head. I untangled the cord from around my neck to find Steve flat on his back. It was time for this son of a bitch to pay! Twisting him into my sharpshooter, I wrenched backward with all I had. Blood gushed out of his forehead, but Stone Cold refused to give in and somehow found the will to resist me. The crowd joined with him in one long, groaning gasp! He slowly forced me to topple to the mat, but could he kick out of the hold that had never failed me? No! The Hitman held on with unyielding determination!

The fans cheered him on, but like Jack Nicholson in *Cuckoo's Nest* he just could not lift that sink. When I steadied myself on my feet and clamped the sharpshooter on even tighter, I broke every heart that Stone Cold had just won.

In the end, Austin didn't submit but was rendered unconscious. Shamrock stopped the match and raised my hand. The bell sounded. I coldly began to attack his knees, then stepped into the sharpshooter to give him some more, but before I could, Shamrock gripped me around the waist and threw me down hard to the mat. I was right back up and furious, with the taste of blood on my lips, and Ken and I squared off with fists clenched. He challenged me to bring it on, and the Chicago crowd came unglued. For him, a seed was sown for some other day. As for me, I stood alone but defiant, proud and unbowed, that remorseless pink soldier on his dark bloody battlefield.

As I dropped to the floor, signs danced in my face: "Bret who?" and "Go back to Canada!" But kids still pulled out the front of their Hitman shirts as they high-fived me to show me that they were with me. I touched hands of support that reached out, but one frothing-at-the-mouth, irate fan gave me the middle finger. I thrust one right back and mouthed, "Fuck you too!"

I loved it. The match. Everything. If I ever wanted my fans to remember just one picture of me, it would be that moment, as I was walking back to the dressing room.

As I headed past Taker, he smiled and said, "Helluva match, man, not a chance in hell me and Sid are ever gonna top that!" He said this respectfully, from one worker to another. I was numb with pride as I waded into my fellow wrestlers to handshakes and praise. When Steve came in, we shook hands as he beamed, all the while pretending to be upset about his cut head.

In *The Wrestling Observer*, Dave Meltzer wrote, "It was expected to be a one-man show. And fortunately for the name *WrestleMania*, the one man delivered to match of the year caliber. . . Hart and Steve Austin more than saved the show with a match phenomenal in work rate, intensity and telling the story."

The next day Vince pulled me into his office as soon as I got to the Rockford Civic Center and asked me whether Steve and I had taken it upon ourselves to get juice. Steve had denied it. So did I. Vince never said another word to me about it.

Then he asked me whether I was ready to give the interview of my life, and told me the points he wanted me to cover. The set up had begun the week before *WrestleMania*, when Vince had encouraged me to go berserk on camera and curse him out over the injustices I'd suffered, then shove him violently to the mat. He promised that they'd use the three-second delay to edit out my curse words, but they didn't bleep out a thing, and my crazed bout of rage had gone out everywhere except Canada, where the show didn't air live.

The interview I was to do that night would turn out to be the longest in the history of the business to that time, a twenty-two-minute live rant that I think was the best of my career. I wore black gear with a new black leather jacket that signalled my intentions: it had a menacing skull framed with a pink triangle on the back. (None of the fans would have ever guessed that the illustration was originally drawn by Jerry Lawler as a possible logo for the Hitmen hockey team.)

I started by apologizing to my fans all over the world for the foul-mouthed outburst they'd witnessed. And then I took a deep breath thinking, Here we go, this is it:

" . . . to my fans across the United States of America, to you I apologize for nothing. No matter how much I try to win, when I walk back to the dressing room, you treat me like I've lost. Even though Stone Cold lost, you cheer him as though he won. . . . You cheer on a pretty boy like Shawn Michaels. You let him screw me out of the World Wrestling Federation belt, but the WWF needed a hero, a role model, not somebody with earrings and tattoos posing for a girlie magazine, which is actually a gay magazine. . . . I thought I had a calling to come back and set the record straight and clean up the WWF—so I did. I came back and beat Steve Austin at *Survivor Series*. When I had my first chance to win the belt back, against Sycho Sid, Shawn Michaels interfered and cost me the belt. Nobody cared. . . . But then I was told, don't worry, you can fight twenty-nine other guys in the *Royal Rumble* and if you win that you'll get a title shot at *WrestleMania*. Twenty-nine guys later I won. I was the last legal man standing, but somehow it's justified that Steve Austin won. . . Gorilla Monsoon and Vince McMahon begged me not to quit. To think of my fans. So I did. I was told if I won the final four I'd get a title shot at *WrestleMania*. Sounds good to me. I accept. I come back. All of a sudden, your champion, your hero, Shawn Michaels, comes up with this life-ending, career-ending injury and forfeits the title so he can go back and find his smile. . . You talk about me crying, I saw everybody crying in the audience for that one. . .

"I've got one thing on my mind after being screwed over by everybody in the WWF—and being abandoned by all you good fans across the United States—I decide I'm going to go into this submission match and give Steve Austin exactly what he deserves. A good old-fashioned ass whipping. So when I do it, when I take that dirty, rotten, stinking hyena, Steve Austin, and beat him to a bloody pulp, you find it in your hearts to abandon me and cheer for him."

Most of the fans in the arena stood in stunned silence, not quite able to absorb what was happening. But there were those Hitman fans so loyal to me they believed that I had every right to feel the way I did because the WWF had, in fact, screwed me, and they were just as sick of it as I was. In their minds, I was addressing the segment of the American wrestling audience that had changed, and they hadn't, so they actually supported my heel turn. Lawler defended me too. So to stress to the TV audience that I was now, in fact, a bad guy, Vince proclaimed, "The poison is spewing from Bret Hart," as they cut to a sign that read, "Bret get a life!"

Hatred seemed to burn from my eyes as I ranted on along the lines Vince had suggested:

> "I've proven myself so many times here in the WWF. I've tried to be everything you wanted me to be, but it seems to me you don't seem to understand what it means to have dignity, poise, to bring prestige . . . to be a man that brings a little class . . . because you'd rather cheer for heroes like Charles Manson and O.J. Simpson. Nobody glorifies criminal conduct like the Americans do. All the other countries I go to around the world still respect what's right and what's wrong."

Contemptuously, I sneered, "Respect" and took a deep breath, diving in past the point of no return.

> "Now that we've made everything really clear with ourselves here tonight, it's obvious to me that all you American wrestling fans from coast to coast, you don't respect me. Well, the fact is, I don't respect you. You don't deserve it. So from here on in the American wrestling fans can kiss my ass!"

And then Shawn appeared at the top of the ramp and made his way to the ring so we'd be face to face as he had his turn.

> "Yo, Hitman! Nobody knows better than me, you have to have a handwritten note from the Lord Almighty to get the belt from you. I've tried and tried to take the high road. Now, Bret, I'm in no shape to wrestle. I know you're tougher than me. Blah blah blah. I admit that. That's fine. I don't have to be number one. I don't obsess like you do. I

do this cuz I like it. You do it because in your mind, Mark Man, you really think all of this is yours. What you need to understand, every time these fans reach into their pockets to watch you, me, or anybody else, they have the right to cheer or boo anybody they want. Now, you don't have to tell me, they're cheering me now, but they booed me before. But you didn't see me get all bent out of shape."

At that moment, one lone disgusted fan shouted out to Shawn, "You are a liar!"

Shawn went on to tell me all about the first amendment. "I don't want to get on my high-and-mighty roller coaster. Bret, my friend, you want to go? Let's go! We've got a saying in the United States of America. It's called, America, love it or leave it."

"Boy Toy," I said, "go back to the dressing room. Just get the hell out of my face."

"How'd you know I was in that gay magazine? You just had to flip through the pages, didn'tcha?"

The crowd popped. Shawn turned his back on me to play up to the fans. Quick as a cat I came from behind and went straight for his supposedly injured knee. I dragged him to the nearest corner, dropped out and slapped on my figure four on the post. As realistic as both our interviews were, we were both still working: he protected me by holding my foot so I could ease myself to the floor without whacking my head, which was the only dangerous part about putting that hold on.

Shawn's response was as carefully scripted by Vince as my rant was. He was a master puppeteer playing with a couple of marionettes.

On March 25, we taped *Raw* in Peoria, to air the following Monday. That night Owen and I concluded our three-year war, fulfilling the promise we made to each other when we started our brother-against-brother angle. Davey and Owen had a rematch for the European title, even though they were still the reigning WWF Tag Team champs. In the heat of their battle, I suddenly hit the ring and broke up the fight, like a big brother dealing with a couple of unruly younger siblings. I restored order long enough to get to a mic, and then launched into a monologue about family values. Angry fans booed me, but I appealed directly to Owen and Davey: "What are you fighting for? Americans don't understand family, they've based their entire history on brother against brother."

When they tore into each other again, I got between them and broke it up, pleading with Davey, "We fought each other at Wembley Stadium. We fought like two men and we hugged each other when it was over." He appeared to be moved by my words, especially as I pointed out how Diana had been used to drive a wedge between us. I turned at long last toward Owen, my embittered little brother. "Who was there for you more times than I was?" I pleaded with Owen, whose eyes glistened bright as his lower lip quivered in an Academy Award–winning performance. Despite the boos, I could see fans in the front row beginning to tear up too.

"Americans don't understand family! Davey, Owen — I'm asking for your help. Owen, look me in the eye. Hear me loud and clear, I don't care about these people. Owen, I love ya."

Tears streamed down Owen's face as he fell into my arms. The three of us embraced in the middle of the ring as the arena rained boos down on us. As Owen tousled Davey's flat-top, I nearly cracked up, but I was able to glare coldly into the camera with chilling hate for all those who opposed us. The new Hart Foundation was born!

Later in the show, Stone Cold did an in-ring interview with a white bandage covering the tiny cut on his forehead, seething about how he never said, "I quit!" I appeared on the giant screen telling him he just got his butt kicked by the real king of the jungle, and that I was finished with him. He hotly fired back, "No you're not. You'll have to kill me to be finished with me."

That night had one more wrinkle: I was slated by the booking committee to challenge Rocky Maivia for the Intercontinental title, and Hunter was insisting I beat him. I didn't see any need for me to beat Rocky; it wouldn't build heat for my new heel turn, and would only undermine a real talent. I insisted on a DQ instead, which infuriated Hunter. He and Shawn disliked Rocky intensely and were too myopic to see that Rocky was destined to become one of the all-time greatest megastars in the history of the business, The Rock. Looking back, I'm glad I got to work with him at least once.

Our match was nice, quick, simple. In the end, I pulled his legs out from under him in the corner, slid out under the bottom rope and locked him into the figure four around the post. Several referees later I still hadn't released the hold and was disqualified. Stone Cold charged out to save Rocky, but he was bushwhacked by Owen and Davey, and I joined in by pulling Stone Cold's shirt over his head, like I'd done to Shawn, and then pretended to beat him senseless. The Legion of Doom came to the rescue, squaring off with Owen and Davey, just as Steve battled back. In a rare act of cowardice, the Hart Foundation fled over the barricades and into the crowd to a chorus of boos.

It was working. Every night now, hostile fans waited outside the buildings for my arrival. I was finding out that the one thing that pissed off wrestling fans more than anything else was to attack their patriotism. By the time I got to the ring, I was covered in gobs of spit; coins, drinks and garbage dangerously bounced off my head as fans cursed and pelted me. It reminded me of the kind of heat Sergeant Slaughter had when he wore Saddam Hussein's boots during the Gulf War. After the shows I needed a police escort to get out of town. Even then, I often found myself speeding to outrun fans who chased me, hanging out their car windows, shaking shotguns and half-empty beer bottles while trying to run me off the road.

After six days at home at the beginning of April, I took off on two foreign tours, to South Africa and then to Kuwait. Promoters in both places demanded that Undertaker and I headline their shows or they'd cancel the sold-out tours, and though the dates overlapped, we both agreed to do double duty as a sign of our commitment to Vince during his time of financial struggle. Before I left I got an unexpected call from Eric Bischoff to say that he'd been blown away by my match with Steve. He wanted me to know that if things didn't work out with Vince, the door was always open for me at WCW.

My flight from Calgary to South Africa was the most luxurious trip I ever took, and that's saying something. I could truly say to myself that this is what it felt like to be a superstar. I made my connection in Heathrow, where I checked into a room at the Hilton right at the airport, which was included as part of my ticket. I enjoyed a comfy eight-hour sleep before boarding a British Airways flight direct to Cape Town. I dined on roast shoulder of lamb and slept flat in an egg-like seat that curled out like a bed. I felt so rested when I landed that I rented an Aston Martin and took off from the airport to find the hotel where I'd hook up with the rest of the WWF crew. Driving through Cape Town, the rolling clouds tumbled over Table Mountain and my heart beat contentedly in my chest. How could I know this would be my final world tour as a wrestling hero? How could anyone know, but for a handful of conspirators who met behind closed hotel room doors in the wee hours, long after the fans had gone home, long even after the boys had gone to sleep.

I spent the following day on a sightseeing drive around the Cape, thinking about how desperately I wanted to get home for good. Taking inventory, I had to admit that the aches and pains never went away anymore. There was increasing stiffness in my joints, and I could barely bend my right wrist at all, as much from working out on the weights as from wrestling. But I told myself I could still deliver that one beautiful story, of a character who always stayed true to himself and fought hard for what he believed in, and who had a fierce loyalty to those who, in turn, believed in him.

That night I drove to the building unsure whether my loyal Cape Town following was up to speed on the new storyline. I strode out to a huge pop, waving a South African flag: the Cape Town fans ate it up. (Of course, the sight of me flaunting the South African flag on *Raw* was intended to heat up the American audience even more.)

That night, and for the rest of that blur of beautiful little towns, Taker and I had some great matches. It was important for him to always be the monster, which allowed me the opportunity to stay face and stride out to the ring every night as a good and steady hero. Those few days in Africa have endured for me as lasting memories of a vanishing time in a business that was drastically changing.

I was tanned and refreshed when Taker and I arrived in Kuwait on April 8 to hook up with a completely different crew. Owen and Davey had just come from a live *Raw* in Muncie, Indiana, and they told me about an in-ring shoot interview Shawn had done that was so over the line they were both livid on my behalf. I didn't realize the full impact of it until I called my friend Marcy, who was so pissed off about the interview and disappointed in Shawn that she played the whole eighteen-minute rant to me over the phone. Shawn started off level enough, working, talking about how I'd put him in the figure four around the post a couple of weeks before and he wasn't going to say when he'd be back in action. After that, I couldn't believe what I was hearing: Remember, this was a time when pro wrestlers didn't go on TV to speak openly about the business or what happened behind the curtain. You spoke only about a guy's wrestling character, not his character as a person.

Here's Shawn:

> "Everyone is asking, Why is Bret Hart all of a sudden a 'bad' guy? Well, ladies and gentlemen, boys and girls, I'm not gonna lie to ya. Bret Hart and Shawn Michaels loathe one another. Whether it be out here or back there, make no mistake about it, Bret Hart hates my guts. And to be perfectly honest, I hate his. Now, we're gonna take the gloves off here. Bret Hart has not just recently turned into a bad guy; he has always been a bad guy. He comes out here and he talks about how . . . the World Wrestling Federation exploited his family. Well, I've got news for ya, ladies and gentlemen, Bret Hart is the one that asked his mother and his father to be on

TV. Bret Hart is the one that drags his sister and his children out on TV. The World Wrestling Federation exploits Bret Hart's family because he allows it . . . and the reason he allows it is very simple . . . for Bret Hart's own financial gain. If Bret can make a buck he'd sell his mother. That's the truth!"

Shawn was only just getting warmed up.

"Bret Hart has an obsession with Shawn Michaels and the World Wrestling Federation championship. Last year I won the World Wrestling Federation championship fair and square. But I want to digress to six years ago. When Shawn Michaels first started his singles career and became the Intercontinental champion, that's when Bret Hart also became the World Wrestling Federation champion. I ran support to him. I told everybody, including himself and his family, that I supported him. And I was second fiddle to Bret Hart for years here, and I did it with a smile on my face, because that's what a man does when it comes to business. But then, when it came for Bret Hart to return the favour, oh yeah he did it, but he did it kickin' and screamin' every inch of the way. And then, Bret Hart takes time off . . . he says, 'Cause he needs rest. What he did was take time off to see if Shawn Michaels and the World Wrestling Federation would fall flat on their face without him. Well, guess what, we didn't fall face flat anywhere! As a matter of fact the World Wrestling Federation did the best business it has done in six years."

Then Shawn turned to Vince, who'd been standing silently beside him all this time. "You're the boss, am I right or wrong?"

Vince smirked as he replied, "You're right."

What else could Vince say at that moment, with Shawn on a roll on live TV? But the fact is that when I began my first title reign, the WWF was in the midst of the steroid and sex scandals, and business dropped off because of negative press—not because I was champion. In fact, I carried the championship during the darkest days in WWF history, and any wrestler who was there at that time knows that. Vince knows that, I told myself.

Shawn carried on:

> "Bret Hart, he sat in Calgary and passed judgment on
> Shawn Michaels and he told everybody about my faults.
> And believe me, folks, I have got a truck-load of faults.
> But I have never, ever lied about that to any one of ya.
> He talked about my dancing. How could the fans of the
> World Wrestling Federation cheer a wrestler who dances?
> Who has long hair? Who pierces his navel? Who has
> tattoos? How could the fans of the World Wrestling
> Federation support something like that? Well, it's real sim-
> ple, they like it, you idiot!"

But every one of those comments I made was about his ring character,
not about him as a person. If I'd been taking personal jabs at Shawn
Michaels, I'd have talked about how he was a drug addict and how insecure
and neurotic he was—and I never did. As for the fans? Male WWF fans left
for WCW in droves when Shawn got the belt.

> "And Bret Hart . . . talks about his loyalty to his WWF
> fans. And that's ultimately what made him return to the
> World Wrestling Federation. Well, that is a load of horse
> shit. The reason Bret Hart returned to the World
> Wrestling Federation, after using a rival organization
> against this man and the company that made him what
> he was, he stabbed the World Wrestling Federation in the
> back! Why? For his financial gain! Bret Hart did not
> come back to the World Wrestling Federation for his
> fans, he came back for the almighty dollar!"

Hogan, Roddy, Razor, Diesel, Kid and even Curt Hennig had all abandoned Vince's sinking ship. I stayed loyal to him and to the WWF and
walked away from $2.8 million a year to take Vince's proposed $1.5 million.
But did Vince say that?

> "Now we're all wondering, why are you obsessed with
> the World Wrestling Federation championship? I'll tell
> ya, I wanted to be the World Wrestling Federation cham-
> pion since I was a little kid. It was a dream. Bret Hart is
> obsessed with the World Wrestling Federation champion-
> ship because he was born into it. If Bret Hart wasn't a

world champion he would feel like he had fallen short. When he goes home to Calgary he is still Bret The Hitman Hart, former World Wrestling Federation champion. Shawn Michaels, when he goes home, he's not The Heartbreak Kid, he's not Shawn Michaels, he's just plain old Shawn. Bret, you're The Hitman twenty-four hours a day. And the reason for that is Bret Hart cannot separate all of this from his real life. That's why he brings his family in it, and that's why he brings his friends in it. Bret Hart is obsessed with being in the limelight more than I could ever possibly imagine! Bret Hart, your obsession with me and the World Wrestling Federation championship will ultimately be, and I want you to read my lips, it will ultimately be your de-struct-ion."

Marcy told me that when Shawn was done, he took his suit jacket off to do his Chippendale dance and humped Vince's leg.

I called Carlo, and he said he didn't like the interview either. Carlo was in such a full panic, fearing for his job and not trusting a soul, that I had to shout into the phone to calm him down.

Next I called Vince. Without a moment's hesitation he told me that Shawn's behaviour was inexcusable and that Shawn would be dealt with. Thinking back on it now, I am astonished that I believed him: no one just went off like Shawn had done on a TV rant without Vince orchestrating every bit of it. I guess I just wanted to believe him. I asked him, again, whether he had any problem with our contract, and he reiterated that he didn't. I reminded him that I turned down a hell of a lot of money to stay loyal to the company, and that this was something Shawn should know. He agreed.

How could Shawn have forgotten that I put that torch right in his hand?

The Kuwait tour offered some relief and distraction. Owen and I had the privilege of spending a day and a half with the 7th Cavalry Regiment "Garry Owen" tank division. The soldiers took us for a helicopter flight out to Camp Doha on the Kuwait Iraq border, where we sat down to a hardy meal with all the soldiers in the mess tent, including the general. The chaplain, Corporal Ken Sorensen, who was a dead ringer for Father Mulcahey on M.A.S.H., told me the men loved to watch wrestling; many of the soldiers said they couldn't believe we'd come all the way out there to visit them.

They drove us in a Bradley tank to remote outposts where sentries stood guard. What impressed me most about these soldiers was their guts and their fear; they had the guts to take on anyone and they lived with the fear of knowing they might have to at any moment. I found the camaraderie of these men not very different from the camaraderie between the wrestlers. In the army they need to trust and respect one another and support each other, whether they like each other or not, which was no different than the bond between wrestlers working in the ring. As we were leaving, the general told us our visit had been great for moral and I told him, "Ours as well as yours."

On the ride back to the base Owen, Davey and I found ourselves flying through an azure blue sky over golden desert sands in an open military helicopter, happy to be alive and bound by our optimism that the new Hart Foundation would really get over!

As a parting gift the chaplain handed me a coin with an inscription that read "The angel of the Lord encamps around those who fear him and he delivers them. Psalm 3:4:7." The men of the 7th Cavalry gave me a Garry Owen pin. From that day on, even as I bashed American wrestling fans, I proudly wore the pin on my ring jacket as a way of letting them know how I really felt about Americans.

On April 11 Vader made the mistake of going bonkers on *Good Morning Kuwait*. He and Taker were appearing together on the show and had been warned in advance that the host was going to ask them the predictable question about pro wrestling: Is it fake? Taker diplomatically answered that wrestling is entertainment with athleticism thrown in. But Vader had worked a lot in Japan, where pro wrestling was still taken very seriously as a shoot, and where wrestlers put a scare into talk-show hosts all the time. So Vader grabbed the host by his tie and threw him down backwards over some chairs and a table, swearing that such questions were "bullshit!" He was immediately hauled off to jail, and threatened with three months' incarceration, mostly because it was illegal in Kuwait to swear on TV. Despite Vince's efforts to get Vader out, for a time the authorities wouldn't budge. They finally settled on house arrest at the hotel. When I finally saw Vader again, he looked like a big, bad dog who tore up the fence. As much as the business had changed in the twelve years since the David Schultz and John Stossel fiasco, some things never change.

On my second-to-last night of the tour, I carried a Kuwait national flag out to my match with Taker, which was being taped to air on TV back home. I ducked under him, like I'd done so many times before, but caught my boot in the canvas and felt something snap in my right knee, like a small fan belt breaking. I limped slightly for the rest of the match and right through to the following night, when the vocal crowd popped as I defeated Stone Cold in the final to win the Kuwaiti cup.

When I got back home, I was gratified to read in *The Wrestling Observer* on April 21:

> "Reality break, folks. It goes without saying that in the ring Michaels did a super job in 1996 . . . however, let's not rewrite history to say Shawn's reign was Hogan-like from a business standpoint, because nothing could be further from the truth. TV ratings collapsed in June of 1996 on Shawn's watch, not Bret's, and reached company all time lows for the rest of the year. Not just Monday night ratings due to *Nitro*—ratings across the board. Syndication died. Shawn's work in the ring can't be denied . . . but the buy rates fell through his reign and it was during Shawn's reign, for the first time in a decade that WWF in both ppv and TV ratings fell to no. 2 in the U.S. And when it came to house shows, while WWF had a strong year in 1996, its best months were February and March and who was champion at that point? The summer was good but there was a serious decline in the fall, at which point Vince threw everything he could to get Bret back, including promising him the belt. Let's not forget that there were numerous cases of Michaels throwing unprofessional hissy fits throughout his title reign in the ring."

I was still deeply hurt and pissed off though—and had no idea what to do about it.

39

"NO MATTER WHAT HAPPENS, I'M LOYAL TO YOU"

When I got home to Calgary, my doctor told me that my sore knee was serious: I needed surgery. They would have to do a scope and then shave the bone down in my knee, which could keep me out of action for up to six months. Even though I was protected by my contract in case of injury, I called Vince to let him know I'd do my best to be back as soon as possible. The week the surgery was scheduled I was supposed to do an *In Your House* match with Sid, but Vince told me Sid was injured too. He desperately needed me to do the match with Stone Cold instead, or the pay-per-view was in danger of bombing. Looking back now, I wonder about myself and my desire to please him at significant cost to myself: it couldn't have been all about being worried about my livelihood.

Without hesitating I told him I'd schedule the surgery for after the show. In less than a minute we formulated a new storyline in which Steve and I would carry our war through *In Your House* and onto *Raw* the next night, where we'd square off in a street fight. Steve would "injure" my knee, putting me out of commission. I'd have the surgery and do my best to get back for *King of the Ring* in June. As an incentive, Vince promised that if I came back in time, Shawn would put me over at *King of the Ring*. It was quite a thing to throw out to me, considering that Shawn and I hadn't sorted things out yet.

Vince told me he was grateful for my dedication and that he, too, was fed up with Shawn. But he was reluctant to discipline him, maybe out of fear that Shawn would end up in WCW with his old pals in the clique. For my part I offered to sit down with Shawn man to man and bury the hatchet, for the good of the company. I hung up the phone relieved that everything seemed salvageable and that my position was still solid.

During my match with Stone Cold on the April 20 *In Your House* pay-per-view from Rochester, New York, no fan could tell that my knee was blown. In a nice irony I viciously worked Steve's knee, even ripping off his knee brace and bashing his unprotected joint with a chair. When I finally softened him up enough to go for the sharpshooter, I intentionally stepped through backward so he could reverse it. Steve managed to reach back and find his knee brace and crack me over the head with it, gouging a deep, two-inch cut in the top of my head. I fell back and my momentum flipped Steve perfectly up to his feet so he could step right into the sharpshooter. Feeling my scalp with my fingers I knew I'd need stitches, and the last thing Steve and I needed right now was another bloody match. Luckily the blood caked in my thick hair and was unnoticeable. By the end of it, Owen and Davey hit the ring to make the save, and I limped back to the dressing room leaning on their shoulders, which set the stage for a big blow-off the next night on *Raw* in Binghamton.

The first thing I did when I got to the Broome County Veterans Memorial Arena on April 21 was ask Shawn to talk with me in private out by the ring, as a handful of technicians did sound checks. I told him I wanted peace. I didn't lay everything on him as being his fault, and listened without protest as he told me that morale among the boys was better when he was champion than when I was. I almost felt sad for him: he didn't seem to have a clue how wrong he was. Shawn said that his recent animosity toward me stemmed from my remarks about his knee, which he maintained was really hurt. What was I to make of that? Everybody in the dressing room was skeptical about his injury. So I referred to my own hurt knee, and conceded that it was hard to tell from the outside just how damaged a knee was.

Once again, we agreed that going forward, we would clear any negative comments with each other before putting them out there for the public to hear, and we'd work together as professionally as we always had, aiming for *King of the Ring* in June, if I could make it back by then. We shook hands and I felt good that we were back in sync.

The street fight with Stone Cold on *Raw* built up like a showdown at the O.K. Corral. That night I sacrificed all I had for Vince and his company, determined to turn my knee injury into a positive. Even though Steve and I had fought it out numerous times before, I'd never been the despised one before: the crowd was as bad-tempered as a pack of vicious dogs. Coins bounced off my sore, stitched-up head as I headed out to the ring in blue jeans, a blue T-shirt and Doc Marten boots. It was impossible to wear a knee wrap under the jeans, so I went out without knee protection.

Now the reluctant hero, Stone Cold paced the ring in his black AUSTIN 3:16 T-shirt and jeans, only to be pounced on by Owen and Davey at the sound of the bell. Shawn came to Steve's rescue, cleaning house all the way back to the dressing room, leaving me to deliver an intense shit-kicking to Steve, during which I methodically placed his ankle through the back of a steel chair and climbed up to the top turnbuckle. When I jumped off, Steve moved and I made out that I injured my knee when I landed. Of course, Steve promptly slammed my unprotected knees with the chair. We'd forgotten to calculate for no knee wrap: the damage and the pain were very real. It has given me pause to think that the knee problems I've suffered ever since were severely aggravated by this one angle on this one night. Then Steve twisted me into a sharpshooter and cinched it in until The New Hart Foundation, now including Brian Pillman, barged past several referees and agents to make the save. I was delicately placed on a gurney and stretchered out to a waiting ambulance with Owen and Davey shouting and pleading for the attendants to be careful as the camera crew followed us. I could hear Owen yell, "Watch his knee! Get 'im to a hospital!" with such emotion that I almost cracked up.

They lifted me into the ambulance, but just as it was about to pull away the audience realized that Stone Cold was sitting in the driver's seat—it was an ambush! Steve scrambled back and put a vicious beating on me before he was jumped by Owen and Davey and the whole ruckus was broken up by a gaggle of refs and agents.

When the ambulance finally pulled away, a steaming Owen huffed to Davey, "He's not gonna get away with this. We'll kill 'im. We'll kill 'im."

I had knee surgery on Wednesday, April 23, spending one night in the hospital. I barely got in the door of my house the next day when Vince called and said he needed me to be at *Raw* in Omaha, Nebraska, on Monday. I told him that the doctor had warned me not to do anything, but Vince assured me that if I showed up, I could come out in a wheelchair and nobody would touch me. In real life, the other members of The Hart Foundation—Owen, Davey and Pillman—were chomping at the bit to keep the momentum going, and I felt I would be letting them and the business down if I didn't show. The last turn of the screw? Jim would be there too. Vince explained that he wanted Anvil to come out in the final seconds of the show just as Stone Cold was about to get his hands on me in my wheelchair. Owen, Davey and Pillman would all be preoccupied at ringside, and I'd be trying to fend Steve off with my crutches. Out of nowhere, Anvil would blindside him, and I'd whack him with my crutch, knocking him off the ten-foot-high stage! Steve would land on a giant stunt mattress, in the dark, which would quickly be removed before the cameras found him sprawled out on the cement.

Although I didn't relish making the trip just four days after major reconstructive surgery, I told Vince I'd be there: I had a strong feeling that Jim being hired back depended on it. So that's what I did.

Over the next few weeks I came out in a wheelchair and then on crutches, for real. My heel turn, and the angles it spawned, were a huge success. We really had great heat, Vince's ratings were rebounding and the house show business was good, with Davey subbing for me in main events against Taker. There were all kinds of spinoffs involving The Hart Foundation that benefited not only Austin, but Taker, Mankind, Legion of Doom and, of course, Shawn. It was great to see the whole dressing room working as a team to beat WCW.

I worked TVs every week, ripping into America. Being a heel was fun, but I really feared where this was leading. The fans were so pissed off that I couldn't even hear myself talk when I did my in-ring interviews (though I couldn't have been more pleased when Meltzer wrote that my interviews were the best in the business all year).

The Hart Foundation wore black leather jackets like mine, except for Pillman, who wore a black leather vest—the jackets served as protection from the constant barrage of dangerous objects! We were having such a successful and creative run that I even went to Vince one more time to see about bringing Bruce in as a heel world junior heavyweight champion, the chance that Bruce had been waiting for all his life. Vince seemed to like the idea of revealing yet another secret member of The Foundation, which was really just the WWF's version of what Bischoff was doing with the nWo.

Vince told me he was still hoping that I'd be able to work with Shawn at *King of the Ring*. My knee was sore and swollen, and my recovery slow. If I was working with somebody I could trust, I thought I might be able to pull it off. The question was, Could I trust Shawn? What I should have been asking myself was, Could I trust Vince?

Raw, from Newark, Delaware, on May 12, opened with The Hart Foundation at the top of the ramp, with me in my wheelchair praising them as the best that the WWF had to offer. They all seemed legitimately touched when I borrowed a couple of lines from the Sebastian Faulks war novel, *Birdsong*, to introduce them: "'I would take these men into the mouth of hell to fight the devil. I would trust these men to breathe for me and to pump my blood with their hearts.' Jim The Anvil Neidhart, Davey Boy Smith, my lovable brother Owen and Brian Pillman. We are The Hart Foundation!"

At the end of the show, with the idea that I'd soon be working with Shawn at *King of the Ring*, I called Shawn out to the ring. The last thirty seconds were supposed to be mine, and then Shawn would give me his superkick, toppling me backward, out of my wheelchair, as the show went off the air. But the fan noise was so loud I couldn't hear my cue. Instead of the show ending with Shawn nailing me, we went off the air with me dressing him down. I felt bad about it, but Shawn thought I did it on purpose and was furious. I told him that they had the footage of him superkicking me out of my wheelchair, which they could replay all week on Vince's other shows. And they did—over and over.

On May 19, at *Raw* in Mobile, Alabama, Shawn and I built more heat for our *King of the Ring* match, but because my knee still wasn't ready and I couldn't go long, Vince's idea was that I'd promise that if I didn't beat Shawn in less than ten minutes I'd never wrestle in America again! A Hart Foundation member would be handcuffed to each ring post, and of course one of them would free himself to ensure that I won, just in the nick of time. During an in-ring interview in the first half of the night, Shawn was groggy and slurring his words. As I climbed into the ring with The Hart Foundation to open the second half, Shawn appeared on the big screen, wasted, and suggested on live TV that I couldn't get it up for ten minutes and that I'd been having some "Sunny days," a blatant suggestion that I'd been sleeping with Sunny. I couldn't hear him well because it was so noisy in the ring, so the remark sailed right over my head. When the interview was over, most of the boys were seething at how unprofessional it was. Any hopes we had of working together went out the window. Shawn was so out of it that night, Hunter and Chyna had to help him out of the building.

When I got home, Julie and Stu were upset about the Sunny comment, but it wasn't until Dallas and all his school pals asked me whether I was doing stuff with Sunny that I realized that Shawn had hurt my family. At that time, the pro wrestling code of honour was still clear: no man hurts another man's family. Jim Ross phoned me at home to apologize on behalf of the office and to promise that Shawn's unprofessional behaviour would be dealt with. I'd heard that line before. This time I felt I had to do something to settle the score.

Throughout that week I brooded about what to do. I wondered about beating the hell out of Shawn for real at the pay-per-view, but that could be costly to the company if he got badly hurt, and I also had to be careful of my knee. I decided to tell Vince that I had to pull out of the pay-per-view because my knee wasn't ready. Vince had a plan: Stone Cold would finally catch me alone, flatten me and bash the hell of my knee, taking me out of the pay-per-view storyline and what would have been a clean win over Shawn.

At the *Raw* in Huntington, West Virginia, on June 2, I had an in-depth talk with Vince. He told me that the company was in financial peril and that he was only just hanging on: The next six months would either make him or break him. He said Ted Turner was hell-bent on putting him out of business, and he told me he might have no other choice but to restructure my contract. Of course, I'd still get every dime he owed me, but I'd get it on the back end, years down the road. He added that he appreciated how hard I was working for him and told me not to worry about anything.

I sure didn't want to receive the money owing to me now at the back end of my contract, so I did call my lawyer to see what my options were if Vince tried to do that kind of a move, but when it came right down to it, I didn't believe that he ever would.

King of the Ring went down on June 8, according to the new plan. The next day we were all supposed to be at *Raw* in Hartford. Shawn was nowhere to be found. I happened to mention to Jim that as soon as I saw Shawn I was going to straighten him out once and for all. I never thought Jim The Anvil Neidhart could be a voice of reason, but he got a worried look on his face and pleaded with me: "Please, I just got back here! Don't do anything now! God, Bret, I need this job! Just forget about it." What could I say? I resigned myself to not beating the shit out of Shawn.

At about 6 p.m., I went into the bathroom to gel my hair before going across the hall to tape interviews. I was surprised to see Shawn's reflection go by me in the mirror. I could see he was uptight, so I smiled and casually said, "Hey, Shawn . . ."

He cut me off. "Fuck you! You haven't talked to me in over a fucking month, what makes you think I'm gonna talk to you now?"

Even though I had hair gel all over my hands, I was primed to go back to my original plan, but Shawn vanished through the doorway, past Crush, who was lacing his boots up and heard the whole thing.

I set out to find Shawn, but he was gone. I paced around the backstage area until Owen, Davey, Jim and Pillman came to find me.

"I know Shawn's watching from somewhere, waiting for me to leave this room," I said. "I'll bet you the second I walk out of here, he'll walk in. All his stuff is in here. Watch." I crossed the hall, walked into the interview room and cracked open the door to peek back out into the hall. Shawn strode past me into the dressing room. He was bent over fixing his boots when I marched straight up to him.

I pushed him to his feet. "You got something to say to me?"

He flicked a weak punch at me and missed. Balancing awkwardly on my good leg, I popped him on the chin, rocking him on his heels. He came for me, so I grabbed him by his long mane and pretended I was doing a hammer throw at the Olympics. I was dragging him around the room when a hysterical Pat and a frantic Lawler ran in and jumped on top of me. Unable to pry me off, Pat shouted for the other wrestlers to help, but Davey and Crush had no intention of saving Shawn. It was nothing but a scritch-fight really, but when we were finally separated, clumps of Shawn's precious hair fell from my hands. I blasted him: "Don't fuck with me or my family, you little fucker."

Shawn looked ready to burst into tears as he stomped across the hall to Vince's office. Shouting loud enough for everyone to hear, Shawn quit, saying it was an unsafe working environment. Then he stormed off, slamming doors behind him.

Vince looked like a jilted lover whose boy toy had up and left him. But he told me that this had not only been inevitable, but was long overdue, and that it was his fault for not dealing with Shawn sooner. He told me to take the night off. I felt silly to have come to blows over something so stupid, but while everything in wrestling was supposed to be bullshit, that bullshit was everything to me.

Before *Raw* was off the air, Vince was hyping the inside story of a backstage brawl between me and Shawn for sale to fans on his 900 number.

My scuffle with Shawn was the talk of the business. Meltzer wrote that I'd always been professional, and questioned the reasoning behind Shawn's claim that he couldn't trust or work with The Hart Foundation. Jack Lanza told me that Vince had known a real physical confrontation was coming before I did, because Shawn had told him he was going to punch me out as far back as May, at the Evansville *Raw*, but I couldn't tell if Jack was just trying to stir me up. I tried to put it all out of my mind, including Vince's talk about reneging on the financial terms of our contract, and did my best to heal up for the July *In Your House*, which was going to be in Calgary. I had two good distractions: Paul Jay and his High Road Productions crew arrived and began shooting the documentary on me. And the Calgary Flames wanted to buy The Hitmen. I knew a hockey organization such as the Flames were best suited to manage the team, and so I agreed to sell it

On July 3, Shawn agreed to come back: it's not like he had any choice — Vince had threatened to stop his $15,000-a-week paycheques. I hoped the little bastard would finally straighten up, but I was thrown for a loop when Vince told me that Shawn was going to guest referee my *SummerSlam* match with Taker at The Meadowlands on August 3. Shawn would turn heel on Taker, costing him the belt. Though I'd finally get another stint as champion, a sour feeling ran through me: as heels we'd be in direct competition with each other again.

One warm, beautiful night, Blade got upset while I was putting him to bed and started stomping around slamming doors. I finally picked him up and put him in his bed and told him to go to sleep. I was downstairs again chatting with Julie when Blade wandered defiantly past me wearing a Shawn Michaels T-shirt, hat and heart-shaped glasses, opening and closing his red leather-gloved fist. Julie and I struggled not to laugh. I coolly said to Blade, "What are you supposed to be?" He put on his most serious face and said, "I'm with the clique." Then he broke into a big grin and said, "Nah, I'm just buggin' ya, Dad!"

On July 6, the day of the Calgary show, I headed down to the Saddledome early with Julie, our kids and their friends, with the High Road crew following us. Austin and Taker insisted that they not be filmed out of character, and I only had Paul Jay's word that I could ask him to edit anything out that I felt could hurt the business in any way. Paul's crew was so good at what they did that most of the time I forgot they were even there.

I went over everything with Pat, putting the storyline and all the spots together. He wanted to involve my parents, Bruce and the rest of the Hart clan, who would be seated down front, right behind the rail. Owen would appear to be hurt and would be taken out of the match, only to return as the big hero and catch the fall on Steve after he had an altercation with Stu and some of the Hart brothers. This would be a huge night for Owen, setting up a big match between him and Austin at *SummerSlam*.

My anti-American rants had been going down big time with the Canadian fans. The Calgary crowd had shed its usual polite shyness and was ready to explode: Canadian flags waved everywhere. Owen, Davey, Jim and Pillman were pumped up and chomping at the bit, Brian reminding me of a happy jackal who'd befriended a pride of lions. We did a live promo from the dressing room that played on the big screen in the arena, and the crowd response was so loud that the brick walls shook. Leo and I had worked hard at polishing up Shamrock, who was really coming along now and was pacing the dressing room anxiously. Goldust had a hot feud going with Pillman, and the Legion of Doom couldn't have been more pumped. Hawk came to me knowing that it was me and Taker who'd got L.O.D. hired back. He awkwardly fumbled for the words to tell me that this time he'd give us everything he had, adding, "This match is for your dad." Beside Stu and Helen in the front row was Alberta premier Ralph Klein. I was worn out; my knee wasn't healed enough to wrestle safely, and I knew it. My doctor warned me that it needed at least three more months, but I had to be there for Vince, not to mention that I'd waited my entire life for this night, wrestling at the top of my game in a really hot angle in front of fans who had been there for me from the very beginning.

I was home and this was real.

"Oh Canada!" echoed majestically through the Saddledome, and then each member of The Hart Foundation made a separate entrance; first Pillman, then Anvil, then Davey, with Diana on his arm. After Owen proudly strode out, I stepped through the curtain and stood at the top of the ramp savouring the moment. There was no doubt that this was the loudest pop I'd *ever* heard.

We'd touched a nerve across Canada, but for the fans in Calgary it went much deeper than that. They'd grown up with and stood by Stu's old Stampede crew through decades of highs and lows, and now we were squarely on top of the business, all of us like brothers. These fans were here to thank all of us, especially Stu.

When I made my way to the ring, the explosion from the crowd gave me chills. The sight of the entire Hart family cheering in the front row, with a sea of fluttering Canadian flags behind them, made my chest thump like a war drum. I dropped down to the floor and carefully placed my sunglasses on my mother's head as she blushed. Stu smiled and winked at me.

Stone Cold and I squared off in the centre of the ring, nose to nose. From the second the bell rang, we set the pace for one incredible knock-down, drag-out fight that delighted fans on both sides of the border. Austin was loving being the hated heel again, every bit as much as I loved playing the hero. After Owen made an amazing Stampede Wrestling–style come-back, Austin cut him off and clotheslined him out onto the floor. Then Stone Cold jumped out and put the boots to Owen, in front of Stu and Bruce. When he rolled Owen back into the ring, Bruce threw a drink at Stone Cold's back. Austin turned around and jerked Stu to his feet by his lapels! The Hart brothers swarmed Stone Cold just in time: nineteen thousand screaming fans were about to do the same thing! Bruce was so mad about a couple of stiff shots Austin gave him that when I arrived to tip the balance and roll Stone Cold back into the ring, Bruce slammed a fist as hard as he could into Stone Cold's kidneys. Austin managed to pull himself up, only to be schoolboyed from behind by Owen. Bruce erupted like a tornado on the floor, taking on every heel in sight. When the referee made the all important three-count, nobody was paying attention to Owen because everyone was riveted to Bruce's unscripted comeback! Owen was furious at Bruce for stealing his big pop.

Still, the Saddledome came unglued as the pay-per-view closed with Austin being wrestled down by various Hart brothers, agents, referees and Keystone Kop–like security guards, who handcuffed him and took him away.

Hart kids swarmed the ring while Pillman and I went out and got Stu, whose knees were now so bad that we had to help him up the stairs. Jim Ross commented, "The family that has fought together survives together," as the entire Hart clan celebrated in one last glorious whoop-up.

Davey high-fived twelve-year-old Harry, and Blade stood next to me, bouncing on the bottom rope. Ellie and her girls rejoiced next to Martha while Owen stood proudly in the corner holding Oje, who twirled a tiny Canadian flag.

I spotted some smiling kid in the ring and asked, "Who are you?"

He excitedly said, "I just told them I was a Hart."

"Wave at the crowd and enjoy yourself!"

After the show, Bruce fell into a deep sulk because both Owen and I rebuked him for overdoing it on the finish. Sore as hell, I made the three-hour drive to Edmonton alone, dreaming up my interview for *Raw* that night. I walked out wearing an Edmonton Oilers jersey just in case I needed to offset the longstanding rivalry between Calgary and Edmonton. It wasn't so much that I was anti-American, I said, I was just very pro-Canadian. I was soon shooting about sensitive issues such as gun control, health care and racial hatred, Canada coming out on the plus side of the ledger on all counts. I promised the fans that I'd defeat The Undertaker at *SummerSlam* and become the World Wrestling Federation champion for a fifth time. The only other five-time champion was Hulk Hogan, and I wanted to tie his record before I ended my career.

Steve could hardly work the Edmonton *Raw* because of his bruised kidneys. As a result, Vince put on hold any plans to go forward with Bruce joining The Hart Foundation.

Over the next few weeks I switched gears from visiting sick kids at the Children's Hospital in Calgary with Owen to being spat on and pelted with garbage during a four-day loop through Texas.

We were extremely worried about Davey and Pillman, whose drug problems were getting worse. Owen told me that Davey was injecting liquid morphine; a few weeks earlier he'd tripped in his hotel bathroom and smashed his face on the bathtub, needing sixteen stitches. Pillman did his best to hide the pain from his fused ankle, but anyone who took the time to notice realized that it was a brave and excruciating struggle for him to get in the ring every night, and the painkillers, washed down with alcohol every night, were getting the upper hand.

I was doing my best to gingerly coax my own knee back, forcing myself to cut corners but still go all out, using more facial expressions and short-heat spots. Every night Owen and I worked exciting but easy matches against Stone Cold and Mick Foley, who was doing an amazing job of handling two gimmicks at the same time—Mankind and Dude Love, a tie-dyed, whacked-out hippie.

When Owen and I arrived in San Antonio for *Raw* on July 14, we made our usual visit to The Alamo. Owen had become my most reliable friend and supporter, and we ended up having an interesting talk about things worth dying for. We agreed that the wrestling business wasn't one of them.

That night Shawn and I saw each other for the first time since our cat fight. We were surprisingly cordial, yet neither of us offered any apologies. Once again we agreed to refrain from saying personal things about each other in our interviews and to leave each other alone, especially in light of the fact that we were both set to leave for a WWF-sponsored promotional cruise with a shipload of fans the following day. I tried to break the ice with Shawn by telling him about Blade dressing up like him, and he laughed.

In contrast to the week before in Alberta, Owen, Davey, Brian and I walked out to a blizzard of spit and a hail of boos. (Jim was briefly off, sorting out some contract problems arising from having signed with a small-time promotion before coming back to WWF.) As I stood with a Canadian flag draped over my shoulders, each of The Hart Foundation members spelled out the conditions of our various *SummerSlam* matches. If Davey lost to Shamrock he'd be forced to eat a can of dog food; if Owen lost he'd pucker up and kiss Stone Cold's ass; and if Pillman couldn't beat Goldust he'd wear his valet Marlena's dress. My vow? If I lost to Taker I'd never wrestle in America again.

I took some playful potshots about how the WWF should go back to Canada for the next *Raw*, where the girls were prettier and the beer was better, and I challenged any three Americans to a flag match. Though on the surface things looked pretty good, I was feeling more and more in the dark about where all this was going, unable to shake the uneasy feeling that something just wasn't right.

40

THINK WITH YOUR HEAD, NOT YOUR HEART

SummerSlam CAME EARLIER THAN USUAL that August of 1997. I brought
Blade with me to New York. He liked to carry my bag and massage my big
hands with his tiny fingers. It had been overwhelming to be Stu Hart's kid,
but I could see that being Bret Hart's kid could be just as challenging. Blade
drew pictures of himself wrestling as Blade Sidekick Hart. When he saw how
casual I was with the other wrestlers in the dressing room, he seemed completely at ease with all of them, including Shawn, who play-wrestled with
him in and around the ring while Taker and I worked out our match.
Watching Blade with Shawn made me lower my guard a degree.

This would be the biggest match Taker and I had ever had, and we
wanted to have a classic that would blow away his fans and mine, who had
been waiting for this fantasy title match for seven years. Taker really dug
the whole American versus Canadian angle, especially after The Hart
Foundation sent Vince's ratings right through the roof a month earlier at
the Halifax *Raw* and then again at the Pittsburgh *Raw*.

That night it seemed like the entire dressing room was lit up, plugged
into The Hart Foundation power source. Everyone came back after their
matches happy after having worked so hard, and it was building into a great
show. Then Owen, in the middle of a super match with Stone Cold, accidentally piledrived Steve hard, nearly breaking his neck. When Steve
moaned to him, "I hurt my neck. Don't touch me! I can't feel my feet,"
Owen was beside himself with guilt and dread. But he stayed calm despite
the jeering of twenty thousand fans until it came to him what to do. Like an
old pro, Owen played to the crowd, hoping that it would give Steve enough
time to recover. Steve somehow managed to crawl over and schoolboy
Owen like a weak breeze knocking over a cardboard cut-out for a horrible
but doable one . . . two . . . three. Steve was helped to his feet by the refs and
managed to wobble his way into the dressing room, where he was taken
right to the hospital. Owen wandered past me crushed and in a daze.

In an in-ring interview, Shawn, who was about to ref my match with
Taker, declared that if he didn't call it down the line he'd never wrestle in

America again either: another interesting twist. While going over the finish in the dressing room, Shawn had suggested that in order for him to get mad enough to swing a chair, I should spit on him. He'd swing, I'd duck and he'd crack Undertaker smack on the head! I asked Shawn whether he was sure, and he nodded. I told him I'd aim for his shirt.

Mostly boos greeted me when I went out, but I still had a lot of fans who believed that I had never deserted them. Shawn came out to an elaborate fireworks display, dancing like the stripper he must have been in a past life. Then Taker made his entrance, in pitch darkness, to funeral music and deafening pyrotechnics. At the sound of the bell we tore into each other, raging on in a beautiful dance of death like archrival superheroes, making and breaking each other. Shawn refereed right down the middle, with me grudgingly obeying him. Then I twisted Taker's long legs into the sharp-shooter; I let him kick out from respect for him, the only time anyone ever kicked out of the sharpshooter. He sent me bouncing right out of the ring and onto the floor. I dusted myself off, marched back in and went for it again. Taker rose up and made his comeback and nearly finished me off, while Shawn was diving to and fro to make every count. I dragged Taker by his stomach to the corner, where I attempted some kind of a half-assed sharpshooter on the ring apron, wrapping Taker's legs around the ring post, barely holding on. When at last he kicked out, he tossed me out right on top of Shawn, who was trying to get me to break the hold.

While Shawn collected himself I grabbed a chair, coolly slid back into the ring and busted Taker over the head. When Shawn finally got there to make the count, Taker kicked out. Shawn noticed the steel chair on the apron, but before he could spin me around and demand to know how the chair got there, I delivered one last kick to Taker's knee. We had words, with me finally shouting, "Fuck you!" Our finish needed perfect timing— I had to spit right on cue—but I was exhausted, my throat coated from working so hard. I hacked out an extremely large, milky-white slobber-knocker. It flew out of my mouth and hit Shawn on the chest, where it flew up to splatter him right between the eyes. He came at me furiously with the chair. I ducked at the last second and heard a smash and a huge pop from the crowd as Taker crashed to the mat. I waved Shawn over to do the count, which he did with spit dangling from his nose. Then he stormed back to the dressing room. I was sure he'd thought I did it on purpose.

Draped in a Canadian flag, with my music playing, I kissed the gold buckle of the belt, then dropped to my knees clutching the belt to my chest. I was aching all over, like one giant, throbbing bruise. When I came through the curtain I apologized to Shawn, explaining that I couldn't help the size of the gob and that it was an accident. He just thanked me for the match, and before either of us realized it we shook hands, for the first time in a long time.

I hunched over like someone had beaten me with a stick to untie my boots. I'd pulled my groin badly and I felt like I'd been impaled. Blade, in a long Hitman T-shirt, helped peel my pink wrist tape off and followed me everywhere with the WWF World Heavyweight belt draped over his shoulder and his ball cap on backward. I loved those moments.

That night I crawled into my bed with a bag of ice on my knee, a heating pad under my back and Blade sprawled out sleeping beside me. The next day, he and I caught a lift to *Raw* in Bethlehem, Pennsylvania, with Paul Jay in his production van. After all the angles that came out of *SummerSlam* '97, The Hart Foundation stood in the ring together licking our respective wounds.

We should have been triumphant, but instead it seemed like everybody's past was catching up with them. Michelle had just passed on the news that the nerves in Dynamite's back were damaged beyond repair after years of him deadening the warning signs with pain pills so he could go out there and have another great match. He was now paralyzed from the waist down and would be stuck in a wheelchair for the rest of his life.

Vince had just phased out the costly drug testing he'd instituted at the start of the steroid scandal. Of course the real danger was not steroids or coke but prescription painkillers. Every night deadly lines were crossed by too many of the boys, and at that time the most vulnerable was Pillman, trying to deaden his ankle pain just like Dynamite had deadened the pain from his back. Shawn, Davey, and Hawk were all serious abusers too. We all knew it—the wrestlers openly popped pills in the dressing room—but the agents seemed powerless to do anything about prescription drug use.

Chief, once some kind of voice of reason in the dressing room, had been put out to pasture without anyone even seeming to notice, though Vince would never have gone anywhere if it hadn't been for Chief and Pat Patterson. (After he retired Chief became a different kind of wrestling tragedy. He was left to babysit his young grandson one day and fell asleep. When he woke up, he found the child floating dead in his pool. I believed that Chief would never get over it, and my heart went out to him.)

As I started my fifth run as world champion, Shawn was being friendly enough, but I was unhappy with a sexually explicit new storyline centred around him, Hunter, Chyna and Shawn's newly arrived bodyguard, Ravishing Rick Rude, who was working as a manager while he was involved in an injury lawsuit. I was happy that Rude was back because he was a good friend, but Shawn was now on the booking committee with Brisco and

Hunter. The simple truth was that there was no trust between us anymore. Looking back now, I can see that this wasn't Shawn's fault any more than it was mine. Vince was the one who planted and cultivated the seeds of that doubt. Vince was playing with me and Shawn like a kid with his wrestling dolls, bashing his old favourite and his new favourite together like he was God himself.

On September 7, I worked at *In Your House* in Louisville with Del Wilkes, whose gimmick was The Patriot. It was hard to do anything extraordinary because Wilkes had worked only in Japan and wasn't over by any stretch of the imagination in the United States. What had been a red-hot American versus Canadian angle for the WWF lost its heat when the champion had to fight a cartoon—a hokey, masked marvel in red, white and blue that fans couldn't relate to because, with a mask on, he couldn't express pain or anything. When I asked Pat about the match up, he quipped, "The whole business is a fucking cartoon." I had nothing but respect for Del; we did all we could, but it was a tough haul.

Next came two days of TV and four hard matches, and then I flew up to Toronto for a charity dinner. Dory Funk Jr. had asked me a couple of months earlier if I'd mind working with Terry for his retirement match in Amarillo on a big card billed as *Fifty Years of Funk*. Mind? I had said that I'd be honoured. And Dory said that Terry, who like so many of the old-school boys had retired only to return again and again, actually meant it this time. So after Toronto, I connected through Dallas, where I caught a charter to Amarillo that was packed with the remnants of ECW. I looked at the heads of the young wrestlers, bandages hiding their gig marks, and they reminded me of my old Stampede days.

I had a bad flu but couldn't miss such a significant night. I crawled out of bed and drove to the fairgrounds, where I met up with Stu and Bruce, and was saddened to hear from them that Fritz Von Erich had died of cancer.

In many ways the Funk show was like travelling back in a time machine. Dory and Terry were old-school pros who kindly conducted business the way it had always been done. Japanese reporters swarmed all over as Dory led me down back hallways to a room where he gave me and Terry our finish in great detail. I was happy to put the title up against Terry, but at his insistence, he wanted to put me over, even though it was his retirement match. The Amarillo fans were so fired up about my anti-American heel status that I feared for Stu, who was sitting at ringside. The special referee was Dennis Stamp, that big, lanky wrestler who'd given me one of my first matches back in Amarillo so long ago. When it was over I was so sick I had to crawl back to bed before Terry could even thank me.

On September 20, I arrived in Birmingham, England, for the *One Night Only* pay-per-view. I got there a day early and found the wrestlers, suits and road crew drinking merrily in the hotel lounge. Hunter had to help a trembling, pilled-up Shawn out of his chair and up to his room, in clear view of the fans.

On the bus ride to the National Exhibition Centre Arena the next day, Taker and I were disappointed to notice that we weren't even pictured on the pay-per-view posters plastered all over town. Shawn and Davey were the main event in a European title match. We were baffled as to why the World title match was being ignored, especially when Taker and I had been the biggest draws in Europe for years.

But Taker and I knew how much this match meant to our U.K. fans, so we put our heads together and came up with one that was different from all the others we'd ever had. Actually, this one was for us as much as it was for the fans. I figured I'd finally find out whether the Brits and the boatloads of my German fans who were coming actually supported me in my war with the Yanks.

Before the show I talked with a little boy who'd been burned in a fire— his ears were gone. Then I found time to say hello to Davey's family. Davey had made the huge mistake of promising in interviews with the British tabloids that he'd win his title match for his sister, Tracey, who was dying of cancer. He'd been told he was going over, but on the day of the show Vince and Shawn changed the outcome. Davey was devastated. Shawn had openly bragged about how he was not doing jobs for anyone, but nobody wanted to believe he had such nerve. This went against the code of all wrestlers. Usually Vince or Pat would give me my finishes, but now Shawn, Hunter and Brisco were there to oversee. Something was going very wrong.

I've always felt that Taker was one of the most unselfish and best workers in the business. We told a great story that night in Birmingham that ended in a DQ, living up to the expectations of our legions of fans. I had no way of knowing it at the time, but Vince in his live commentary was doing all he could to paint me as the bad guy here in Europe, which was contrary to his own plan, or at least to the plan he had described to me. I also had no way of knowing that this would turn out to be the last truly great match I'd ever have in the WWF.

Shawn worked the main event with Davey, using every gimmick and prop possible to ultimately end up injuring Davey's knee and take the European belt. Vince, Brisco, Shawn and Hunter took great delight in intentionally designing a finish that made me and Owen look like total idiots. For the entire match, we were nowhere in sight as Hunter, Chyna and Rude worked Davey over while the British fans waited for The Hart

Foundation to rescue him. After Shawn won, he took the house mic and said, "Hart Foundation, this is for you! Diana Smith, sweetheart, this is especially for you, baby!" Diana was looking pretty—with stars in her eyes at being mentioned by Shawn even though he had just defeated her husband—seated beside Davey's parents and sister. Surrounded by his clique, Shawn put the figure four on Davey, and Diana leaped from her front row seat and hit the ring! Chyna grabbed Diana from behind as Owen and I finally charged down the ramp with everybody wondering where the hell we'd been all this time! As I pretended to help the wounded Davey back to the dressing room, we passed the burned little boy and Davey's sister Tracey, who was terribly upset and crying. I thought, In wrestling, never make a promise you can't deliver. I saw the light die in Davey's eyes that day, darkness seeping into a heart that was giving out.

Two days later, on September 22 at *Raw* in Madison Square Garden, I was summoned to Vince's office for a private chat. He rocked me with the news that he wasn't just thinking of breaching the terms of my contract, but was actually going to do it: in the weeks ahead, he wasn't going to pay me my full salary because of problems he attributed to Ted Turner. He told me that I was the Cal Ripken of the WWF and that he fully intended to pay me what he owed me on the back end of my twenty-year deal instead. "You'll still get every penny," he declared.

In a fatherly tone, he then confided, "I have no problem if you want to see if WCW will make you that same deal as before. I hear that Hogan is finishing up there soon. Your timing couldn't be more perfect." He went on to say that if I left, I would actually be doing him a favour because he was about to downsize into a northeastern U.S. promotion. Because of my fourteen years of loyal service, he said, he wanted to give me the opportunity to be able to approach WCW before everyone else did, since he'd be letting a lot of wrestlers go. He described me as the first guy in the lifeboat. "You don't even have to drop the belt if you don't want to. You hold all the cards." He even said that he would secretly help me negotiate my deal, if I wanted. His final words to me were that he'd see whether he could find the money somewhere to pay me, but for now I shouldn't breathe a word to anybody. If the news leaked out that Vince was in trouble, it would hurt my chances with Bischoff. Hurt *my* chances? I was so stunned by how many promises he broke in one short conversation that I didn't know what to reply.

I worked *Raw* like a zombie. New York had always been my best American town, and my loyal following of fans couldn't bring themselves to hate me like I was hated everywhere else. I feared having to sue Vince over my contract and also feared that WCW wouldn't want to pay me so much since I'd turned them down the last time. My worries were only compounded by disgust as Hunter and Shawn told me that they wanted me to call them gay in my interview, like a true homophobe. On the mic that night, Hunter referred to the business as a cheap whore with her legs spread wide apart, and he was right, but this was still supposed to be a kids' show.

Pat Patterson, back from his break, had Steve Lombardi win a battle royal so Lombardi could face me for the title at the Garden on November 15. Steve was a veteran jobber, but Pat thought it would be different to let a real dark horse win and have a shot for once. I said, "It's your most important market, and if that's what you want to do, go ahead."

Davey wasn't working: he complained that he'd hurt his knee in the title match with Shawn, but I thought what was really hurt was his Bulldog pride. I had a dark match that night with Taker and Shawn. He was professional and pleasant, and I tried to relax and take all of this one step at a time.

On September 24, Owen and I drove up to Toledo together listening to the audio book of *The Killer Angels*, Michael Shaara's wonderful account of the battle of Gettysburg. We reminisced about the time we were in Kearney, Missouri, touring the outlaw Jesse James's house, where he was shot from behind by one of his own men. Two brothers who are in the same business all their lives live and learn a lot together. I confided to him everything Vince had said. "Owen, I'm going to end up getting screwed in the end, with bad feelings for the business and the people in it. Vince told me the business isn't just about the money. What a hypocrite!"

"You'll have to sue 'im," he said.

That night during my match with Taker I did my usual job of taking a severe beating. So severe, in fact, that an overwrought mentally challenged kid hit the ring to protect me. When I came back through the curtain still wearing my belt, he broke away from the police, in tears, to hug me and tell me that he loved me. For some reason this scene was too hard for Davey to bear, and he told Lanza he was going home, for how long no one knew.

October 5, 1997. I took my time getting to the building in St. Louis that Sunday afternoon and arrived well rested for *In Your House*. When the agents realized that Brian Pillman hadn't arrived with me, they started calling around looking for him. He was soon found dead of a suspected overdose in his room at the Budgetel in Bloomington, Minnesota. Brian was a good friend, a brother among brothers, and we shared a special bond. Just the night before, I remembered Brian leaning back in his chair in the dressing room in St. Paul, his arms crossed, beaming at me with a sparkle in his eye, even though we'd just been talking about how much he distrusted Shawn and the clique, and how he was worried about his future. I gave him a friendly pat on the chest, and told him, "Don't worry, Bri." And we both broke into big smiles. That's how I'll always remember Brian Pillman.

All too quickly after we heard the news, it was business as usual, with everyone hurriedly putting their matches together for the pay-per-view. Vader, who was only trying to make the best of it, said, "Let's not worry about it right now, let's concentrate on the match." I wanted to blast Leon and say, "No, let's worry about Brian instead of the fucking match!"

That night was a blur as I worked with Davey Boy against the ill-conceived team of Vader and The Patriot.

When the fans tuned in to see the live *Raw* from Kansas City the next day, before the opening sequence even ran, Vince was in the ring announcing Brian's death, as all the boys broke character to stand together at the top of the ramp, breaking kayfabe in solidarity for a fallen comrade for the duration of a stirring ten-bell salute. Rude, Owen, Davey, Jim and I sadly bowed our heads. There were only two wrestlers who didn't come out—Shawn and Hunter.

All that day I'd been uncomfortable: Shawn said he wanted me to denounce him and Hunter as "homos," but I worried it would only lead to more tension between us. Since both of them were part of the booking committee, I did as I was told. "But I don't want you to say this kind of crap about me," I warned Shawn. The night deteriorated into a lame storyline, with Shawn and Hunter taking shots at me while I stupidly led The Hart Foundation in search of them everywhere in the building, never finding them. Duh.

I watched on the monitor backstage as Vince posed probing questions to Melanie Pillman, Brian's pretty, young, clearly distraught wife, live via satellite from her living room. She said to the camera, "It's a wake-up call. Your husband could be next. . . He lived for this business and died for this business. I hope no one else has to die." Owen and I felt so sorry for her. The whole thing struck us as a ratings ploy, exploiting this poor girl's misery for all the world to see, as if suddenly the WWF had turned into *The Jerry Springer Show.*

Things only got worse the next day. The camera came into the dressing room in Topeka to allow the fans to see Shawn pulling down his trunks and mooning them on the big screen and then kissing Hunter on the lips. Shawn, Hunter and even Chyna pointed at one another's crotches and told everyone, "Suck it!" Hunter called out to me, in the first glimpse I'd had of his obsession with his own penis, "I'm bigger than you, and I'm better than you, in more ways than one." Shawn then looked in amazement at Hunter's fly and winced as he exclaimed, "Good God! You could put an eye out with that thing!" The dressing room full of grieving, confused wrestlers, all wondering where the business was going.

As I drove back to Kansas City after the show, I looked up at a stunning autumn sunset and wondered what any of these antics had to do with wrestling. I also wondered why Shawn seemed to have such a hold on Vince. More and more air time was devoted to sleazy soap opera as the artistry of great work faded from the collective consciousness of the fans. Vince used to be the biggest fan of all: he had a passion for technicians, a love for characters and a deep appreciation for storytellers. I couldn't fathom how he could be the one encouraging the sabotage of what he and the old-school boys, and even the long-time fans, held so dear.

I felt like I'd been tossed in the air and hadn't landed yet, out of control and totally blind to what lay ahead. Because I was an independent contractor, my living depended not just on talent but on reputation. Remembering what Vince had done with Hulk and others, I felt a sense of foreboding: Vince was about to tear me down, destroying my credibility and marketability. I never understood how he could be so disloyal whenever he parted ways with those who'd sacrificed so much for him and his business. But for Vince, loyalty was almost always a one-way street.

My heart kept going back to Brian. Thirty-five years old with five kids. He went to sleep not knowing that his wife had just found out that she was pregnant again. Flyin' Brian was flyin' with the angels now. I recited the Lord's Prayer to an orange Kansas sky, adding a plea for myself: "God, I'll probably never be here again. Please get me home in one piece."

A couple of days later, I was in L.A. to do an appearance on *Mad TV* and was able to arrange a meeting with Eric Bischoff, who also happened to be in town. He was still interested in me, he said, but he couldn't negotiate until I had clearance to do so from the WWF. Eric told me that there were all kinds of ongoing legal battles between the WWF and WCW, going back as far as when Alundra Blaze, the champion of a short-lived women's division of the WWF, showed up on *Nitro* and dropped the WWF belt in a garbage can. Since Vince's logo was on the belt, Vince had WCW by the balls for trademark infringement. The latest court battle had Vince charging Eric with tortuous interference over the Hall and Nash deal, saying Eric had encouraged them to breach their contract with him.

I didn't tell Eric that Vince had said he *wanted* to help me make this deal, but I did tell him that Vince said I could leave any way I wanted, even as champion. Eric made it clear that it didn't matter to him at all whether I was still champion, advising me simply to leave on good terms.

I retained the title in a triple-threat match in San Jose on October 12 with Stone Cold, Hunter and my boy Shamrock. Shawn was the guest referee. After the match, with Jim Neidhart and Ken beside me in the dressing room, I made a short speech to Shawn, knowing that it was official that we would face each other in a title match at *Survivor Series '97*, which was going to be in Montreal this time. "I just want you to know that despite any differences we've had this past year, I have no problem working with you. You can trust me in every way to be a professional. What you need to know, Shawn, is that you're not in any danger." I added, "I also want you to know that I have no problem dropping the belt to you if that's what Vince wants."

He glared back at me. "I appreciate that, but I want you to know that I'm not willing to do the same thing for you." And then he left.

Jim snorted, "I can't believe that he just said that!"

There was no way I could ever drop the belt to him now: he'd just showed complete disrespect not only to me, but to the position of champion, which was an affront to old-school traditions and a betrayal of each and every wrestler who ever looked to me as a leader in the dressing room, or who had been a leader himself. What kind of arrogant little prick would say that to a champion offering to put him over? Since my deal with Vince was that I had creative control of my character for my last thirty days in the WWF, it was up to me whom I lost the championship to. I figured I'd drop the belt to Stone Cold instead.

Bischoff's offer from the WCW came through: $1.8 million a year for three years. I told Eric if he couldn't get me $2.8 to forget about it. He said he'd have an answer for me by the middle of the next week. If it turned out that I had to leave the WWF, I started to envision one last interview, thanking the fans, all the wrestlers and Vince, for everything he'd done for me. I still couldn't decide whether Vince was going to kill me off or if he was actually looking out for me, as he made out he was. Was it really so much to ask to be able to leave with my head up?

Oklahoma City *Raw* on October 20 was more of the same. Shawn pulled his pants down on camera while Hunter blocked the view with a cardboard D-Generation X sign. (*New York Post* columnist Phil Mushnick was the one who coined the phrase, in an article that was actually critical of the drift of the WWF into sex, sleaze and soap opera, and away from wrestling. Then Shawn and the clique took it proudly as their name, and DX came to life in the WWF as a rebel group of wrestlers out to defy authority and take over the business: the original members were Shawn, Hunter, Kevin Nash, Razor Ramon, 1-2-3 Kid and Chyna.) Even worse was the storyline where a gang of militant black bad-asses called The

Nation of Domination had their dressing room trashed and sprayed with graffiti and Canadian flags. By the end of the show I wasn't just portrayed as homophobic but as a racist too. These antics contrasted poorly with Vince's idea of honouring past NWA champions on this same show. I felt a little embarrassed when I shook the hands of Lou Thesz, Dory and Terry Funk and Danny Hodge, who was a champion boxer and also an Olympic silver medallist in wrestling.

The following day at a taped *Raw* in Tulsa I informed Vince where I was with WCW, stressing that the window he'd given me to negotiate with them closed on November 1.

"Well, whatever happens, we'll deal with it," he said. He told me that he was trying everything—even selling property—to be able to afford to keep me. Then he said, "I wanted to talk to you about *Survivor Series*. I want you to drop the belt to Shawn, but you'll win it back for a sixth time at the December 7 pay-per-view in Springfield, that is, if you're still with me."

"If I end up staying, it doesn't make any sense to me that you'd want to beat me in Canada and then have me win the belt back in the States," I replied. I told him word for word how Shawn had told me he wouldn't put me over. Vince's face got tense and red, and he asked me if I'd mind repeating everything I'd said in front of Shawn.

"I'd be happy to."

Later that night, Vince called us both to his office, and when we sat down he blurted out, "Shawn, I'm putting the belt back on you!"

Shawn began to cry, thanking me and telling me how much he respected me.

I said, "Shawn, you just told me four days ago, in San Jose, that you'd never put me over."

Shawn brushed away his tears, sniffling. "Sometimes I say the stupidest things. I always put my foot in my own mouth."

I had to get out of there. "I don't know what's going to happen at *Survivor Series*, and I'm not agreeing to anything yet," I said. "We'll see where all of this is going, and, Vince, you know what I'm talking about."

I called Eric, leaving him numerous messages over the next three days, but I never heard a peep. When I arrived at the Nassau Coliseum on October 24, Vince was there to greet me. He told me that he could pay me after all, that my money was no longer a problem. I told him I hadn't heard a thing from Bischoff and that if the money problem was solved I'd likely stay, but I also told him that until I heard back, I'd have to keep my options open. Then I left on a four-day tour of the Middle East, thinking that Bischoff was just jerking me around and that I'd likely have to stay on with Vince.

At the airport in Muscat, Oman, kids of all ages enthusiastically greeted me waving huge Canadian flags. I wondered where they'd got them and then realized that they were all hand sewn. There was a mosque right next to the hotel, and from the balcony of my room I could hear chants of prayer. I found myself praying to any God there was to help me make the right decision.

At the final show, in Bahrain, I retained the belt when Taker was disqualified. Despite being tombstoned, I was proudly clapped to my feet and presented with an Arab championship belt and a huge, bowl-like trophy. I *was* still a hero everywhere outside America.

October 31, 1997. As soon as I walked in the door of my house in Calgary, Bischoff called. He told me they were up to $2.5 million for 125 days a year. "What else is it going to take to get you down here?" he asked. I told him I'd talk to my people and get back to him right away. I called my lawyer, who kept saying over and over, "We have a sweetie of a deal." I decided to think everything through and call Vince first thing in the morning.

So on Saturday, I called Vince and told him what WCW had offered. "I want to stay with you, Vince, and my contract is fine just the way it is, but I need you to tell me where I'm going and what I'm doing. What's the rest of my story going to be?"

Vince told me that he'd think about it and call me back. But as the deadline crept closer, he still hadn't called. I finally tracked him down getting his hair cut in Manhattan. "Vince, I've only got until midnight." He told me not to worry about the deadline and to call him Sunday morning.

Minutes later I had my lawyer on the line telling me that Vince's word over the phone meant nothing in a court of law.

I had one last talk with Eric, who happily said, "What else? Whatever it is that you want, you better say it now!"

I hesitated, but then said, "I can be late sometimes. I've never missed a show in fourteen years or hurt another wrestler in my career. I'll always be on time for my match, but with Vince I'm allowed to get there at show time."

"What else?"

"Injury insurance. With Vince I'm totally covered for everything."

"We'll get you insurance. Anything else?"

After a long pause I said, "That's it."

"Done!"

"Done?"

"Done!"

I guess we had a deal. While I waited for the document to pop out of my fax machine, I called Vince. No answer.

It was nearly midnight on the east coast when Vince finally called back. His message to me, expressed with smug good humour, was that I should think with my head and not my heart. When I asked him what he had in mind for me, he gave me that stupid laugh of his and told me that first I'd put Shawn over at *Survivor Series*, then I'd put him over at a final four pay-per-view next month that would lead into a ladder match at the *Royal Rumble*, where I'd put him over again. Finally I'd challenge him to one last match on a *Raw*, where I'd promise that if I didn't win, I'd quit forever. Everybody would think I was going to lose but, Vince chuckled, "We'll fuck him and you'll get your hand raised."

"You've got to be kidding," I said. "I thought you'd come up with something to make me stay!"

Vince got irritated with me now. "I dunno, you tell me, what do you want to do?"

"Hell, Vince, you're the genius. You made me turn heel, made me say all kinds of things about Americans, and they all hate me now. You turned off my heat and gave it all to Shawn, and all I am any more is a lukewarm heel. *I* don't even know what to do with me."

Vince told me again to think with my head, not my heart, and take the WCW offer.

After we hung up, I checked my fax machine and saw the WCW contract coming in. I sat alone, in the dark, with tears in my eyes. I signed, put the contract back into the feeder, dialled the number and pushed send. I found myself reciting the Lord's Prayer as my fourteen-year career in the WWF passed before my eyes.

On Sunday morning, I called Vince at home. He was friendly and more than a little quick as far as I was concerned to advise me that I'd done the right thing. He still wanted Shawn to beat me at *Survivor Series* the following weekend. I cut him off. "I'm sorry, Vince. I've always done everything you've asked, but I can't do *that*. I'll put over anybody you want, but I will not, under any circumstances, put over Shawn Michaels."

"Where do you get this stuff?"

"Come on, Vince. I made myself clear to both you and Shawn in Tulsa. I'll drop it to Austin or Taker. Hell, I'll even drop it to Lombardi at The Garden. Vince, you told me I could leave any way I wanted! Remember?"

"I'll have to sue you."

"In my contract, I have creative control for my last thirty days."

"We could tie our assholes up in court for years over this."

I told him again that I wouldn't do it. "Everything has been geared toward the Canadian hero winning this match. It'll kill me off to lose to Shawn in Montreal after everything he's done. He's picked his nose on TV with the Canadian flag, and just last week he said that Stu is dead on international TV. I'd lose all my self-respect. If he puts me over, I'll be happy to put him over. We've got over a month until I go to WCW, Vince, surely we can come up with something."

For the rest of the week we went back and forth. He'd tell me I could win, then he'd tell me I couldn't. I stood my ground and refused to lose — for the first and only time in my career.

41

THE MONTREAL SCREWJOB

IT WAS NOVEMBER 8, the night before *Survivor Series* '97. I was in the dressing room at Cobo Hall in Detroit. Vince and I were still stalemated. I was worn out with conflicting emotions, grief vying with an adrenalin rush of clarity. I was convinced Vince would ruin me just for the sick pleasure of it. I kept reminding myself that if I'd stayed in the WWF, Shawn and Hunter would have done all they could to drive me out anyway. Jack Lanza pulled me aside to tell me that I was doing the right thing for the business: "I wouldn't drop the belt to that little motherfucker either!" I never knew whether Jack meant what he said or was trying to provoke a reaction out of me that would somehow play into his boss's hands.

I called Earl Hebner into a dingy dressing-room bathroom. I looked him right in the eyes and said, "Tomorrow, Earl, they're going to ask you to fuck me." His mouth twisted and his eyes filled with tears as he promised, "I swear on my kids' heads, I won't do it. I'll quit first! If they ask me to do that, I'll tell them to go fuck themselves, Bret, I swear!" I calmed him down, saying that all he had to do was tell me what the plan was, and I'd take care of it. I told him that I was going to insist that he be the ref because I trusted him to watch my back. The longer we talked the stronger his resolve became. I'll never forget the tears in his eyes as he shook my hand.

Word had leaked out that I was going to WCW, and all during the six-man tag that night I was tormented by a jeering mob chanting, "You sold out!" It bothered me that they didn't know I was pushed out, but at the end of the match, when I took my walk around the ring, *my* fans hugged me, and many broke down crying.

I kept feeling as though I was alive at my own funeral. My worries about what would happen the next day in Montreal tormented me all night long. Vince and I were eyeball to eyeball and nobody was blinking. I'll never understand why Shawn couldn't simply put me over, with me immediately dropping the belt to him on *Raw*, where a much bigger audience would see his win. I'd have my respect, and Shawn would have the belt.

I met Julie and the kids at the hotel in Montreal, and in no time at all, it seems, I was barging up the back ramp of the Molson Centre with them, Paul Jay's camera crew filming every step. Though Paul had wrapped up filming in September, I'd suggested he might want to film my last match for the WWF in Canada. Julie and the kids were swept up in emotional farewells. Blade and Beans were too young to understand completely what was going on, but they knew it wasn't good.

I went looking for Vince, and Paul suggested that I keep my hidden mic on. Vince said hello to Julie and the kids, smiling and kidding with them briefly, before we headed to his dressing room for a talk. He spotted the bright red poppy pinned to my shirt, and I explained how it was a Remembrance Day tradition. I brought up how this Canadian angle had really painted me into a corner: "It would be hard for me to come up short as a hero today." I bluntly asked, "So what is it that you want to do?"

Vince was grim-faced. "What do you want to do?"

Because word about me leaving had leaked out, I suggested some kind of run in. I told him I'd win tonight, and then I'd forfeit the belt on *Raw* in Ottawa the next day. This was a suggestion, not a demand. We talked about how we both felt betrayed. I brought up that nobody was supposed to know that I was leaving, but he was already smearing my reputation. Vince likened it to sticking me with a stick, which I took as his admission that he'd been poking at me intentionally to provoke me. Finally Vince said that he was determined to see this come out the right way. I sighed with relief, believing I now had the dignified exit I sought. Vince's tone softened as he said, "All we're talking about is Ted Turner. That's what's coming between you and me. That's all. I can't tell you how appreciative I will always be for everything you've done for this company. I'll be damned, even if it is Ted Turner's money and all that kind of shit, that's no reason for two people who've spent as much time as we have together, worked closely through the years, it's no reason to have any problems."

"I couldn't agree more," I said. "I didn't want to ever leave here. What matters to me is what happens to me right now. It might be all that I'm ever going to be remembered for. I don't have high hopes for down there. I loved my story here. My history will always be here, which is why I've been so stubborn. After fourteen years, to end it here on such a bad note wouldn't be right. I'm going to miss this place. So we'll leave it on that?"

"Uh huh. Okay."

"Feels better."

"Yeah."

I smiled then and said, "Ya never know, you might have me back someday."

Vince chuckled. "Love to!"

I pushed for clarity, "So, what is it you want to do today then?"

Vince then described in detail how DX would interfere when I had Shawn in the sharpshooter. The Hart Foundation would charge out to my rescue, and we'd end up in a big "schmazz," or brawl, where he wanted me to deck Hunter and even Chyna.

"The marks out there are thinking this is a shoot," he said. "I'm going to capitalize on that. I won't be out there commentating, and there'll be a slew of uniformed security at ringside. I'm open to anything."

"All right," I said and shook his hand. "I'll go find Shawn and go over all this."

"Whatever you want," said Vince. "I put you with Pat—he's the master—to work it through."

A few minutes later, Carlo took me around back of the Molson Centre, where I told him that Vince had decided to let me leave with my head up. Carlo broke down crying. In many ways, Carlo had brought me to this moment. He'd helped to structure the contract that gave me way too much power for it ever to rest easy with Vince or to allow to stand as a precedent. I trusted that contract to protect me. If it wasn't for me, Carlo wouldn't be where he was and neither would I.

After taking my mic off and changing into my gear, I found Shawn. One last time, I tried to be straight with him. He was visibly nervous and said he wanted no problems with me, that he had no problems doing anything. Pat told me that he thought it would be a helluva spot to let Shawn put me in the sharpshooter and then reverse it on him. It would be a great spot that would set the stage for a fantastic second half.

"Who's the ref?" I asked.

"Earl," Pat said.

I smiled to myself. "Okay."

I ran the whole scenario by Earl, Owen, Davey and Rude while Hunter and Chyna meekly nodded their heads in approval.

Vader pulled me aside to warn me. "Be careful out there, brother. Vince is known for fucking people in these kinds of situations."

"I've got it covered," I assured him, lowering my voice.

People still ask me, "Didn't you see it coming?" The truth was, I'd been reasonable in every way, and with Earl watching my back I thought I had nothing to worry about.

I paced around backstage and waited. When I heard Shawn's music drowned out by boos, I had no idea that he had just pretended to wipe his ass with the Canadian flag and then laid it out in the middle of the ring and pretended to fuck it hard. Back home in Calgary, Stu was watching in disgust. He took very real offence to Shawn's actions, as did everyone in the building and all across Canada. If I'd done that in the United States, I might have been lynched.

I grabbed my own flag, handed it to Blade and said, "Let's go, boy!" He marched all the way to the curtain with me, Jim, Davey and Owen, with Paul Jay's crew trailing right behind us. Hunter was not where he was supposed to be for the run in. An annoyed Rick Rude was suspicious. He pursed his lips and told me, "I'll watch your back in case they try to jump you or pull any-thing funny on you out there." Excitement and doubt pulsed through me as my music blared. I disappeared through the curtain to an explosion of noise.

I entered the ring tense but unafraid—and proud. If Shawn so much as tried anything, I'd take him out hard and fast. Shawn jumped me before the bell, but I battled right back, and we began working. We fought through the crowd, with me decking agents and referees one after another. Somewhere in the middle of it I locked eyes with Vince and shook my fist at him. Shawn was flopping and flying for me everywhere. Before long I had a blue and white Quebec flag wrapped around Shawn's neck, and The Molson Centre was coming apart at the seams. Only when I finally got him into the ring did the bell signal the start of the match.

Halfway through what was to be a thirty-minute match, I made my way to the top corner. When I leaped off, Shawn pulled Earl in front of me, and the collision left both me and Earl sprawled out on the mat. Shawn then stepped over me to put on the sharpshooter, but he crossed my legs wrong, so I called up to him, "The other way," and he switched them. As Shawn turned me onto my stomach, I saw Earl for a split second motioning with his fingers and Vince, strangely, standing at the ring apron wearing an angry scowl. Then he screamed at the bell ringer, Mark Yeaton, "Ring the bell! Ring the fucking bell!" Yeaton, in stunned disbelief, couldn't bring himself to do it. I frantically tried to reverse the sharpshooter on Shawn as Vince snapped hard at Yeaton—and the bell clanged, over and over.

I couldn't believe Earl fucked me.

It felt like all the blood in my veins had just evaporated.

Earl jumped out of the ring and ran away as fast as he could toward Jack Lanza and Dave Hebner, who were waiting at the top of the ramp with a car running.

My first thought was that I'd somehow let the whole country down.

Shawn put on a show, cussing and carrying on as if he wasn't in on the whole thing.

I saw Vince on the floor. The thought crossed my mind to jump out and go crazy on him. I looked over at Mark Yeaton, his mouth open and tears in his eyes. I leaned over the top rope, carefully aimed, and spit at Vince, hitting him right between the eyes. I saw Shawn hoisting the belt in the air in victory, and then being hustled away down the aisle by Hunter and Jerry Brisco. Vince kept trying to wipe my spit from his eyes.

The crowd totally got what had just happened and began angrily chanting, "Bullshit! Bullshit!" The Montreal fans were outraged: a spark was all it would take to have a full-scale riot—and that was a bad idea. I had to calm myself and think smart. What would my dad do?

Looking out at the stunned crowd, I fought the tears that were swimming in my eyes and thought, Don't you dare give these backstabbers the satisfaction of seeing you cry over any of this! Don't you dare cry! I worked so hard for him, fourteen years, all I wanted was my dignity.

They'd cut the ring mic, but the cameras were still rolling, so I painted WCW in giant letters in the air for all to see. Owen, Davey and Jim soon surrounded me. Owen said, "You don't look bad for this, they do! You were all class!" When I met their eyes, I could feel myself dying inside.

My lower lip start to quiver, so I bit it.

Owen stood beside me, and his strength helped me keep it together. He told me that he and Rick had been duped into looking everywhere for Hunter, when Hunter was at ringside all along. For what seemed like an eternity, I looked out at the sea of sad people who felt as betrayed as I did, knowing what disrespect had been paid to me, my family and millions of fans all around the world! I told myself to never forget this feeling, ever.

I jumped down from the ring and commenced smashing Vince's expensive TV monitors to the floor and tossing his headsets out into the crowd, surrounded by security guards who couldn't quite figure out whether this was part of the storyline. On my way backstage I passed by Blade, who looked equally sad and puzzled, then by Julie and the rest of the kids, all of them shocked to silence.

Surrounded by Paul's crew, I headed straight for Vince's office and tried to break the steel door down. I gave up and walked back toward the dressing room, hounded by Japanese reporters who thought I'd explain everything that had happened for them right then and there. I felt like The Terminator. I wasn't the only one. I saw the Harris twins kicking over barrels of garbage and punching the walls. The wrestlers were ready to riot too.

Nothing to do but go home now. Blade trailed after me as I headed to the dressing room, but when I got to there, I found my bag sitting out in the hallway. I picked it up and walked inside only to see Shawn sitting in the corner.

"Shawn, you weren't in on that?"

"I swear to fucking God, I had nothing to do with it!"

"You weren't in on it?"

"So help me God, I don't know anything about it!" He threw the belt on the floor and said he refused to wear it. Paul Jay's camera crew were right behind me filming everything they could. I wanted to rip Shawn to shreds—deep down I knew he was in on it all the way—but I didn't want to lose my cool in front of Blade. "Shawn," I said, "I'll judge you by what you do tomorrow on TV." I looked around at a roomful of stricken wrestlers and calmly said, "If they can do this to me, they can do this to anyone. Remember that."

Taker blew his stack and shouted, "Fuck! I'm gonna bring his ass down here. I want Vince to explain himself to me, you and everyone else!" He kicked the dressing-room door open. As he stomped off down the hall, I could hear angry wrestlers calling out to Taker where he could find Vince.

Paul's crew left so I could undress. I somehow found some humour in the fact that after his match Davey had borrowed my towel (as he often did), leaving me without one as I headed to the showers. My head was spinning and my heart had a giant hole in it as the water poured over me. Rick Rude and Davey appeared just out of range of the showers to tell me that, true to his word, Taker had made Vince open his door. Vince had rounded up a makeshift crew of bodyguards consisting of Slaughter, Brisco and his son Shane. I had my friends: Taker, Shamrock, Foley, Vader, Rude, Crush, Savio and especially Owen, Davey and Jim.

This whole thing could turn into a damn mutiny—or worse!

Finally Vince came down the hall with his posse and stepped into the dressing room.

"He says he wants to talk to you," Rick called to me in the shower.

"Tell Vince to get the hell out of here before he gets hurt."

Rick and Davey returned seconds later and told me in unison, "He says he's staying."

I told them to please warn him to leave. "If he stays, he's gonna get knocked out." But they came back with the same answer.

I came out of the shower sopping wet, with no towel, and calmly walked past Vince. I was actually thinking that if they ever did a movie about this, it wouldn't look very good if I beat Vince up naked. As I picked up a damp towel from the floor, Vince dryly offered, "It's the first time I ever had to lie to one of my talent."

"Who are you kidding, you lying piece of shit?" I shot back. Shawn now sat crying in the corner.

Brisco and Slaughter tried to clear everyone out of the dressing room. Owen was about to leave when Davey grabbed him by the arm. "Don't leave," he said. "Remember what happened to Bruiser Brody." None of my boys left.

With Davey, Rick, Owen and Jim on my left, I sat down and glared at Vince, surrounded by his henchmen, who all stood with their arms behind their backs. Taker was also there, offering me full support. Shawn was still blubbering like a baby, his head in his hands.

"You told me I could leave any way I wanted. That I was Cal Ripkin. That I was doing you a favour. That you appreciated everything I ever did. That for everything I've done there was no reason for any problems. You've told me nothin' but lies all week, all fucking year!" I said in a surprisingly calm voice. Then I added, "If you're still here when I'm finished getting dressed, I'll have no choice but to punch you out!"

Vince seemed unfazed, even tried to take credit for my deal with Turner, but I cut him off to remind him that I'd taken the lesser deal from Vince because I'd wanted to stay loyal to him. "After fourteen years, you just couldn't let me leave with my head up?"

I shot him down on every lie. I was calm and rational as I sized up the room and who was where, noticing too the look on Owen's face: I could see he was afraid of what it might be like to stay on with Vince after this, whatever this was, was over, but that he was backing me to the fullest. Like one of my best matches, I could see it all play out in my head. I knew a fight with Vince was likely to come down to a half-assed pull-apart, so I intentionally left my shirt off so no one could grab it. I'd be lucky if I got one good shot in before they all pounced on me. When I tied the laces of my hi-tops, I stood up and said, "Okay."

I picked up my knee brace, thinking to smash Vince over the head with it, but I tossed it down, declaring, "I won't need this!" and went straight for him. Cockily Vince came back at me and we actually tied up. Fourteen fuckin' years! I launched a rocket-launcher upper cut that connected with Vince's jaw. My right fist actually popped him like a cork off the ground, and he collapsed unconscious to the carpet. His cavalry jumped in, but they were too late. I found myself jostling with Jerry Brisco, who I would find out later was the one who had designed the whole screwjob for Vince. I told him if he so much as touched me again, I'd give him exactly the same as I'd given Vince, and the lying little coward backed away with his hands up. For the next forty seconds we all stared at Vince unconscious, splayed like an X on the floor. I calmly took my seat again and noticed that my hand was throbbing. I thought it might be broken. Shane pulled Vince into a sitting position and pleaded with me to let his father get his bearings.

I thought of my dad, who had been at home watching me get screwed on live TV, and my sons out in the hallway, and I remembered that Paul Jay was just outside the door. Vince was blowing like a horse, still out of it, and I couldn't help but think that maybe Paul should capture some of this. I angrily shouted, "Get him out!" Slaughter and Brisco dragged him backward by the armpits and plopped him on the bench across from me. I stood up and snatched my knee brace with a wild, mad look on my face, and I think I meant it when I shouted, "Get him the fuck out right now or I'll finish him with this!"

When I came toward him, Shane and his helpers propped Vince on his feet and walked him limping out the door. I would find out later that my punch lifted him high enough off the ground that when he came down he rolled his ankle and nearly broke it.

And as history would have it, Paul filmed a dazed Vince staggering down the hall.

The dressing room was now quiet, except for Shawn's sniffling. I walked toward him, thinking I should kick the shit out of him too, while I had the chance. Instead I held out my hand. "Thanks for the match, Shawn." He shook my broken hand and started crying even harder.

It all seemed so surreal. After a few more moments of silence, Jim said with a mischievous smile, "I guess they won't say anything to me any more about smashing TV monitors." Rude, Taker, Owen, Jim and Davey all burst out laughing.

When I got back to my hotel I asked Marcy, who was seething over how I'd been treated, to get the truth out to the media and the fans before Vince rewrote history—and with her vast network of contacts, I knew she could. It was an international news story before Vince's damage-control team had their morning coffee, and by then it was too late for Vince to smooth it over.

The next afternoon, while I was on the plane home, Vince had a talent meeting at *Raw* in Ottawa, during which more than a few of the boys nearly quit. After the match, wrestlers kept calling my hotel room saying that they wanted to boycott *Raw*. I deeply appreciated their support but told them to think of their families first. Ken Shamrock was one of those who nearly quit. Davey and Owen came home too; Davey pretended that he had reinjured his knee during the scuffle with Vince, but Owen didn't offer any excuse. Mick Foley actually quit.

I had no hard feelings about anyone staying on with Vince, including Jim, Davey and Owen. I left it up to them. If things got rough for all of them, I'd see if Eric was interested in any of them, but only if they wanted me to.

On the plane home, I'd been so dejected that my fist held up my chin the whole way, looking out the window with the occasional tear rolling down my cheek. I couldn't stop them and I didn't feel like hiding it. Jade just kept patting my hand.

Paul Jay's crew filmed me on the plane: I couldn't understand why Paul was so happy. He kept saying to me, "You're going to love what I got," but I wasn't getting it because I was literally in shock. Paul said the God of documentaries had shone down on him in Montreal and he had the whole conversation I'd had with Vince before the match on tape. But I wasn't processing what he said.

At home on Monday night I couldn't bring myself to watch *Raw*, so I called Marcy to find out what happened. When she told me that Shawn had walked out with the belt, said how he'd beaten me in my own country in my own finishing move and had run me out of the WWF, I finally knew for certain that Shawn had been full of shit when he swore to God that he wasn't in on it. Marcy was on a relentless campaign to get the truth out, and on a leap of faith she contacted Dave Meltzer. She'd never spoken to him before because she knew that I would have considered it a betrayal, despite the fact that it was clear that Meltzer had by this point become pro wrestling's most accurate chronicler. After a lengthy conversation with him, she pointed out to me that the one thing Vince seemed to be counting on to eventually save his ass on this is that I would never expose the business, and she suggested I talk to Dave. I had been considering it too, so on Tuesday, for the first time in my life, I gave Dave Meltzer a call. If Vince could do this to me, he could do it to any of the boys. I told Meltzer, "You don't have to take my word for this. You go ahead and try to disprove anything I'm telling you." He printed every word I said, at the risk of alienating the sources he needed to make his living. His meticulously detailed story about what has come to be called the Montreal screwjob has never been refuted and is now considered a historic document in the history of pro wrestling.

In the days after Montreal it was rumoured that Vince was going to lay assault charges against me. Apparently I broke his jaw and sprained his ankle. At first I thought, Great, bring it on. Vince would have to sue me in Canada, exposing the truth about what happened in a court of law. I'd be happy to swear to God and explain myself. But Carlo kept calling, building fear in me about what could happen in a long, costly legal battle filled with uncertainty. I paced my pool room and briefly found myself wishing I'd never hit Vince. Then I shook my head and laughed at how surreal this all was continuing to be. They could put me in jail, they could do whatever the hell they wanted, and I knew someday I'd be sorry for a lot of things, but I'd never, ever be sorry for knocking that son of a bitch out.

I didn't know at the time that Rick Rude had already called Eric Bischoff and told him everything that had happened. When I phoned Eric from my hotel room after the match, he howled with laughter over the fact that I had broken my hand on Vince's jaw. As far as he was concerned, the whole screwjob only made me hotter. On *Nitro* the day after Montreal, the nWo came out waving Canadian flags, and Bischoff called me "a knock-out kind of a guy." Hogan chimed in, "He passed the initiation!" Then Miss Elizabeth conducted as Bischoff, Hogan, Hennig, Macho, Nash, Razor, Kid, Konan, Virgil and the rest of the nWo sang the worst rendition of "O Canada!" I've ever heard! But in many ways it was the best too.

Stu and Helen were hurt by what Vince did to me. But Stu reiterated that, under the circumstances, I'd done the perfect thing. The love and support that my parents gave me was the only light I needed. If I'd beaten up Vince badly, I'd have looked pretty bad as well, but one punch was more than fair considering all the factors. What better way to say goodbye to a crooked boss than to deck him on my last day of work?

Davey was trying to get out of his contract and was already talking to Eric. Owen had asked to be released, but Vince refused to let him out of his contract, even when he told Vince that I vowed to never talk to him again if he stayed. This was only a work, of course, but we both thought Vince might feel bad enough to go for it. When I approached Eric about my brother, he was interested, but he didn't want to pay Owen the same money he was making with Vince.

As a favour to Owen, I spoke with Vince Russo on the phone—he'd gone from writing the WWF magazine to writing the shows, and we both thought of him as a friend. I told Russo angrily that McMahon wasn't good for his word and that it was impossible for Owen to trust anything he ever said again. My hostile tone wasn't directed at him, and Russo and I hung up on good terms. Seconds later, my phone rang, and to my startled amazement it was Vince McMahon. I concluded that he'd listened in on the entire call. He said, "I can't believe how truly selfish you are that you would want to hold back your brother Owen."

"How can you expect him to ever believe anything you say?"

"If you say another word to Owen, I'll sue you so fast that you won't know what hit you."

"Vince, if you had an ounce of decency you'd let him go, or at least let him make his own decision."

"Well, I'm not letting him go. And I'm never going to let him go! And you better get used to it. If you keep doing what you're doing, messing with Owen's head, I'll sue you with a smile on my face. And I'll sue Owen for breach of contract too!" He slammed the phone down.

I called Owen to tell him what happened. I said I couldn't do anything more or Vince would sue us both. For some reason, Owen apologized.

I told him not to worry; we would never let the wrestling business come between us. "I'll always be here for you, Owen. Do what ya gotta do and don't worry about me. Watch yourself. They'll be coming for you next, you watch. Watch your back, Owen, and I'll be waiting for you over at WCW. Just get home in one piece."

PART FOUR

PINK INTO BLACK

42

CASUALTIES OF WAR

I ALWAYS FELT THEY KILLED The Hitman character that day in Montreal. Every picture and mention of my career quickly vanished from the WWF's website. Vince McMahon was rewriting history to suit his own purpose, erasing me like I never existed.

Not surprisingly I'd become an overnight hero of a different sort for having the balls to KO Vince, but I knew he'd be coming after me. He openly challenged me on TV, but at the same time he was still talking about suing me for assault. Neither Shawn nor Hunter had the guts to admit their involvement, but it didn't matter: the boys had seen the yellow stripes on those two snakes long ago. Soon enough, Taker called to tell me, "I got it right from Vince. That little cunt Shawn, he was in on the whole thing."

One respected champion after another phoned me. Dory Funk laughed when I outlined what had happened, and said about me punching Vince: "You couldn't have done a more masterful job of doing the perfect thing." Pedro Morales was yet another former world champion who told me that Vince had a habit of doing this to every star he made, and said Vince had learned it from his dad: "Vince senior never gave me any warning about dropping the belt either. He gave me less than an hour's notice. I told him, you should prepare me for this." Pedro told me to watch my back, stand up for myself and never let them destroy me. Harley Race filled my heart when he said, "I'm proud of you, Bret." I felt like scrappy alley cat that had got in an ugly fight with a big, vicious dog; even though I was limping off, that dog was limping off too.

Vince was deep in damage-control mode. He gave a big talk to all the wrestlers at Cornwall TVs on November 11, 1997, saying that he did what he did to me for the sake of the boys and the business. Owen told me that nobody believed a word he said, but Vince's words seemed to do a number on Carlo, who did an about face, calling me to say that Vince's explanation made a lot of sense to him. I kept my disappointment with him to myself, but distanced myself a bit from him after that.

On November 24, Vince broke his promise that he would never tarnish my character after I was gone, the way he'd done to Hogan and Macho. First he teased the audience into thinking that I was going to appear on *Raw*, and then he had Shawn parade out a Mexican midget wrestler wearing a leather jacket and a Hitman Halloween mask. Hunter and Shawn quipped that they always knew The Hitman was short on talent, charisma and stature. I have to admit that I was hurt by such stunts. I was also worried about starting at WCW, though I kept a brave face for my family and the fans. Harley had warned me that WCW was a den of wolves too.

On my first visit to the WCW offices in Atlanta on December 14, I bumped into Hogan, Macho and Eric Bischoff, who smiled confidently at me as he said, "If you think you're a big star *now*, you're going to be an even bigger star when *I'm* done with you!" Hogan said what'd happened between him and me before he left the WWF was all Vince's fault. He said that Vince had bragged to him that he loved to ride the boys into the ground, "then cook and eat 'em." The truth was that Hogan didn't put me over when he had the chance for his own reasons. Because we needed to work together, however, I shook his hand when he offered it and told him I was sorry for anything I said about him after he left the WWF. He grinned back like I was an old friend. He also surprised me by giving me a compliment: he said he thought I was the best interview in the business now, even though I knew that honour really belonged to Stone Cold.

I made my WCW debut the next day on a sold-out live *Nitro* in Charlotte, North Carolina. I was a bit surprised that it didn't feel that much different to me than a WWF show. WCW was loaded with hard-working Mexican boys. I'd never been much of a Lucha Libre fan until I saw the dedication and effort those wrestlers put in every night. In particular, I loved the amazing work of young Rey Mysterio Jr., a masked lightweight Mexican who could spin through, up and over the ropes with backflips and beautiful dives and rolls. In my opinion, he is the most talented Mexican wrestler there has ever been. I felt mucho respect from all the Mexican boys as they came to me to shake my hand.

Paul Wight, the new Giant of wrestling at seven-foot-two and four hundred pounds, lumbered up to say hello. There were old-timers, such as Roddy Piper and Ric Flair, and great young talent, including powerhouse Booker T and, from the Stampede territory, Chris Benoit and Chris Jericho. Even Miss Elizabeth was there, now working as Lex Luger's valet. Curt Hennig gave me a big, warm smile and a slap on the back.

I felt honoured to shake Rick Rude's hand. He'd been at a taped *Raw* on November 17, which aired on November 24, just as he walked out live on *Nitro*. This was the first and only time a wrestler appeared for both organizations on TV at the same time. *Raw* was taped on alternate weeks from the live *Nitros*, and Bischoff liked to give out the results of *Raw* matches before they aired. Rude walked out there and delivered a well-spoken monologue about the rights and wrongs of professional wrestling. He said it was wrong for Shawn to claim he was the world champion when Vince had cheated me out of the title. A lot of wrestlers were disgusted by what Vince had done in Montreal, but Rick Rude was one of the few who actually quit the WWF for good over it.

Mick Foley had quit too and missed a *Raw* but then returned the next day. He was finally making a name for himself as Mankind. For him, going back to WCW would have been career suicide. Steve Austin called to tell me how sorry he was that it ended up this way for me but warned me that WCW was a black hole of bad booking and bad organization. Ken Shamrock had been so furious that he'd also wanted to quit, but I advised him to do what was best for his family and he finally elected to stay, though he said, "I'll always be one of your crew, Bret." Then he was quoted in a story in *Maclean's* magazine on the screwjob, saying, "I can't speak for what happened between Vince McMahon and Bret Hart, but I can say that Bret Hart was the kind of guy everyone looked up to."

Davey had to pay a $150,000 penalty to get out of his WWF contract in order to jump to WCW. For him, I was just the excuse: quitting was more about letting down his dying sister in Birmingham than it was about Vince betraying me over the way I got to leave. One week after Rude left the WWF, Jim was brought out to the ring to be humiliated and disgraced by Shawn and Hunter as part of a storyline, and then he was fired. Luckily, Eric liked Jim enough to sign him to a $150,000-a-year deal. I was glad to have Jim, Davey and Rude around.

That first night in the WCW dressing room in Charlotte, I also met Steve Borden, known as Sting. This hard-working pioneer of WCW was a well-built, born-again Christian with long, dark hair who worked a white-painted-face gimmick based on the movie *The Crow*; for his entrance, he was lowered from the rafters on a steel cable. He'd been famous for his scorpion death lock long before I ever came up with my own variation of it: the sharpshooter.

I was also impressed with the look of Bill Goldberg, a muscle-packed former NFLer who went simply by his last name. Bill was forced to retire from football after badly tearing an abdominal muscle. His former head coach, Bill Sleeman, later told me that if he had a whole team of Bill Goldbergs, he'd win the Super Bowl every year. Goldberg was bald headed, with an angry face punctuated by a goatee—all he needed to be intimidating was simple black trunks and low-cut black boots. He made his entrance to dramatic marching music, pausing just long enough to pound his chest in a haze of billowing smoke. He was destined to be WCW's new weapon in the battle of supremacy against Vince. Unfortunately, Bill was green and was injuring a lot of guys too.

I was bedazzled enough by that sold-out *Nitro* that for the first time I felt that WCW might actually work out for me. I had a great first interview and got a good pop when I said: "Nobody knows better than me what it's like to get screwed by a referee." That comment set me up to referee Hogan's World title match with Sting at the *Starrcade '97* pay-per-view in Washington, D.C., on December 28. Personally, I thought that appearing as a referee would be a lacklustre debut, but what did I know? What did I care? I wanted to comply, to do whatever they asked to the best of my ability—win, lose or draw—then pick up my cheque and come home safe. Nobody would accuse me of taking this business too seriously ever again.

The following morning at Charlotte airport, I ran right into none other than Earl and Dave Hebner. Earl came up to me with his hand out and an apologetic look on his face. I refused to shake his hand, warning him calmly, "Don't talk to me." He insisted that he didn't know what was up with Shawn and Vince until he was on his way out to the ring in Montreal.

"What d'ya mean you didn't know? I told you, Earl! You promised me, swore on your kids!" But in the end, I forgave him. I knew that Vince held Earl's livelihood in his hands, and the only thing Earl was guilty of was not having the guts to take a stand against the man who wrote the cheques. Then Dave asked me if I thought Bischoff would take either him or Earl on, and I told him I'd ask.

Vince's big news was that he was bringing in Mike Tyson to work an angle with Austin leading up to *WrestleMania XIV*, where Tyson would guest ref a main-event title match between Shawn and Stone Cold. At first, Bischoff laughed it off, saying he'd turned Tyson down. But then the WWF's ratings went through the roof and Bischoff wasn't laughing any more. All I could think about was how Vince told me he was in such financial peril he couldn't afford to live up to our contract, yet he was paying Tyson over $3 million for a few *hours* of work.

Tyson was part of a storyline with Stone Cold, who turned out to be the perfect anti-hero to go nose to nose with Vince's own new TV persona: Vince had become a dictatorial heel boss! To this point, Vince had been known to the majority of wrestling fans mainly as a ringside announcer.

With the truth out about what he'd done to me, he decided to capitalize on the intense heat by turning himself heel and making the betrayal all part of the "storyline." Owen was forced to confront Vince as part of the storyline, because the corrupt wicked promoter had screwed over his big brother. On *Raw*, Shawn and Hunter called Owen a nugget of shit that didn't quite get flushed down the toilet and, of course, I was the big, smelly turd. I admired how Owen refused to let Shawn or Hunter get to him, ignoring their swipes as if they didn't matter. Owen put Shawn over, and Shawn purposely potatoed him at one point, splitting his head open. Like me, Owen found himself making truces with Shawn while at the same time never trusting anything Shawn said or did.

Vince kept working angles based on what he'd done to me for real. It not only made the Montreal screwjob seem less significant, it made an increasing number of fans wonder if everything that happened between Vince and me was "only" the biggest work in the history of the business.

Meanwhile, Paul Jay and his crew were quietly holed up in their studio in Toronto, meticulously editing the documentary. Paul kept telling me it would be my vindication, and I wanted to believe him.

Back at home, things were not good. For eighteen years, I'd yearned to be home. Now that I was home more, Julie and I found that we were leading completely different lives. We had a lousy Christmas and barely even spoke to each other. She served a beautiful Christmas dinner on paper plates. The kids were too consumed with all their presents to notice her gesture, which only deepened her already dark mood. The truth was that none of us wanted to piss her off any further. I was dragging my heart around over what Vince had done to me, and Julie snapped at me to get over it. She was also threatening to divorce me again.

I surrounded myself with my sadness—I missed my old friends, the fans, all kinds of people from the WWF circuit, from hotels, gyms, restaurants, clubs, arenas and airports. I had also lost track of my old loves, some of whom I missed terribly, but the truth was I didn't want them to see me this way. I was hurt, vulnerable, changed: I had lost faith in the world. Bischoff wasn't going to ask me to wrestle until late January 1998, and I couldn't do any weight training because of my broken hand. I kept in shape through that unseasonably warm, brown Christmas in Calgary by riding my bike all over town.

I'd barely seen Owen or spoken with him since *Survivor Series*. On Boxing Day, up at Hart house, he seemed surprised when I greeted him warmly. He told me the WWF was only getting worse, with DX getting more vulgar every week, not to mention Sable, a sensuous valet, walking out topless for a *Fully Loaded* bikini match with painted-on black hand-prints to cover her breasts. When he asked me again whether I was mad at him, I told him again that we could never let the fucked-up crazy business get between us. With the money Vince was paying him, Owen said, he was thinking about building a big house on some land just across from Clearwater Beach. I told him just to do whatever it took to survive and to take care of his wife and kids.

"In three years when our contracts are up," I said, "we'll sit on each other's back decks and laugh about all this shit."

Stu and Helen celebrated their fiftieth wedding anniversary that New Year's Eve under the pall of the Montreal screwjob. Sipping tea in the kitchen, we reminisced about how happy and different everything was back at the Stampede show in July. What happened? I think 1997 was the weirdest year of my entire life.

My debut at *Starrcade '97* in December had been anything but brilliant. Eric told me my storyline was going to be about how I saved WCW by helping Sting win back the title from Hogan, which called for me to confront the referee after he made a fast count on Sting. In true WCW fashion, the referee forgot what he was supposed to do for real and made a normal count, but that didn't stop me from knocking him out cold and declaring myself the new referee. Sting resumed the match and beat Hogan seconds later. If I thought things were going to get better for me from there on in, I was sadly mistaken.

My fans tuned into WCW for a while, but according to the mail I received and the opinions of the fans I ran into in person, they had a hard time following the incoherent storylines—and so did I. In comparison, the WWF was well organized; usually Vince's storyboards were done months in advance. I also noticed a stark contrast between WCW's agents and Vince's. With the exception of Dusty Rhodes and Paul Orndorff, none of Eric's men had ever drawn a dime in the business. It was like having an NFL team run by a bunch of high-school coaches.

WCW took a fly-by-the-seat-of-your-pants approach to live TV. *Nitro* was three hours of high-flying matches mixed with live interviews starring Hollywood Hogan and the nWo, with Eric playing the part of a crooked promoter, just like Vince was doing. Many times, the ideas for the interviews were dreamed up just seconds before the befuddled wrestler had to walk out and deliver his lines, and they often contradicted whatever weak storylines were in place. Eric reminded me of a guy with a hundred birds pecking on his head all day long. Still, WCW was doing incredible business.

I tried my best to keep a low profile even though most of the boys wanted to pick my brain and hear all about what happened between me and Vince. After so many years of being at home in the dressing room and a leader, I was guarded and not so trusting. Hogan seemed to be the rock here, with waves constantly lapping up to him.

Hennig, Rude and Duggan looked out for me like big brothers. Scott Hall and Kevin Nash were plotting and scheming, trying to pull me to their side to help them get rid of Hogan. Everywhere, there were little factions of backstabbers. Many of the WCW boys despised Flair, especially Hall, Nash, Macho, the Steiners and Hogan. The only guys who didn't stir up shit were the Mexicans and some of the young talent—Chris Benoit was having some of the best matches in the business at that time with Booker T. Some of the best talent were the smaller wrestlers, such as Eddie Guerrero and Dean Malenko, both second generation, and young Billy Kidman, who reminded me a lot of myself when I was starting out. These were the unsung heroes of WCW, and they worked really hard at keeping everything going.

When I packed my bag to leave my house on January 23, 1998, for my first WCW pay-per-view match, against Ric Flair, Blade was the only one to wish me good luck.

I was worried about how Flair would work with me—with my still-injured hand, I needed to keep a close eye on him. Flair appeared to be trying to get along in this den of wolves and multiple wolf packs, but as hard as he tried, nobody liked him except his old cronies, such as Kevin Sullivan, Arn Anderson, J.J. Dillon and Mongo McMichael. Hogan took every opportunity to try to stir me up about Flair, but I said nothing. I let Ric do the match his way, even letting him chop me to his heart's content as he tried to show me how good he really was. I offered no resistance in what was, as usual with Flair, twenty minutes of nonstop non-psychology.

On January 25, Vince's stepmother, Juanita, passed away. She'd always been nice to me, and so, despite everything, I sent a card of condolence to Vince's house. I didn't expect a reply, and I never got one.

I couldn't find any way to be at peace with what I had. When a soul gets bigger than a mind can comprehend, it becomes easy to give up on trust and judgment. I heard two voices in my head, talking loud and fast, contradicting each other. Go left! Go right! Look out! I now measured time by how many more trips I'd have to take before I could say, "Fuck you, I'm going home" to the whole business—whatever "going home" meant. Would the day ever really come when I could walk away and not be another wrestling tragedy? I was forty-one now, and Harley Race was right about getting to the point where you were feeling every damn one of those bumps. My knees were running on borrowed time and so was the rest of me. I'd do whatever they asked, yet I'd be careful and work safe. Pedro Morales had told me, "There are only three things in this business—you, you and you." What he meant was that at this stage of the game it was imperative to protect myself, especially in the ring. So I did my job and waited for a much-anticipated storyline between me and Hogan to start. A Hitman-Hogan match clearly had the potential to be the biggest match of all time.

Meanwhile, back in the WWF, Vince converted Papa Shango from a gangsta into a pimp, whose line was "Pimpin' ain't easy!" *Raw* was becoming more about bra-and-panty Jello matches than about wrestling, with Jerry Lawler's commentaries going on about all the girls showing their puppies.

Still, the hype about Tyson refereeing the main event title match between Shawn and Austin at *Wrestlemania XIV* ignited the WWF into a roaring fire. The fire that Vince tried to put out, but couldn't, though, was the one raging in the hearts of my fans. At the *Wrestlemania XIV* press conference, a fan angrily shouted at Shawn, "You screwed Bret!" until he was dragged away. Shawn had to realize that screwing me would haunt him for the rest of his life; more than it would haunt me, which is saying a lot.

I was more than eager to see Shawn drop the belt to Stone Cold, whose character had become a gun-waving, beer-guzzling anti-hero perfectly suited to punishing the prima donna asshole who screwed over Bret Hart.

I often reflected on the five of us who had started out so long ago, galloping free like wild stallions: Dynamite, Davey, Jim, Owen and me. Dynamite was now stuck in his wheelchair, drunk and bitter, everything gone. It seemed to me that now Davey was falling lame like Dynamite, his drug problems getting worse, and Jim wasn't much better. Despite my broken heart, I was strong and free, and still at the front of the herd along with Owen. I fantasized that my brother and I were literally stallions, lathered with sweat, galloping up a Rocky Mountain foothill, steam coming out of our nostrils in snorts. We reach a ledge wide enough to stop, where two clear paths lead in two different directions, and we stare at one another with eagerness and apprehension, long tails swishing. Which way should we go? The dark horse shakes his head, then carefully picks his way south up the cliffside. The palomino prances to and fro, wanting to follow, but then takes the path to the north, and they part ways forever.

A lot of pro wrestling's old horses were falling away or dying off. Britain's Big Daddy Crabtree had died in 1997, Loch Ness was failing and then the legendary wrestler, BoBo Brazil, died at seventy-three. But the Grim Reaper of wrestling wanted more young bones too. On February 15, 1998, a drunken Louie Spicolli downed twenty-six Somas and died at the age of twenty-seven, drowning in his own vomit. The sad thing was that more guys were worried about drug testing being introduced as a result than about dying like Louie did, or like Brian Pillman had. Eric Bischoff was pissed off after the news hit the dressing room about Louie, and said to me: "Man, these guys are just getting dressed and nobody gives a shit."

Dave Meltzer wrote a scathing piece about how Louie's death should finally be the wake-up call for all wrestlers, but nobody was listening. The industry was too caught up with stunts such as Shawn Michaels jerking off a wiener on camera as Hunter wore a SUCK THE COOK T-shirt.

Vince appeared on *Off The Record*, a Canadian sports talk show, where he claimed that before I left, I'd become a real pain in the ass with a bad attitude; that I was disruptive in the dressing room; that I was breaking down physically; and that I was starting to miss dates. I guess that last one was my thanks for having shown up at Omaha *Raw* in a wheelchair only five days after surgery. But the determined interviewer, Michael Landsberg, finally got Vince to admit, after considerable squirming, that he had lied to me.

Owen had become the Intercontinental champion, and was working with Hunter and Rock, while I was working with Hennig and Rude. Then Shawn came down with another "career-ending" injury, four days before the lead-in pay-per-view for *Wrestlemania XIV*. Now he wouldn't have to put Steve over. I just shook my head. In the end, *Wrestlemania XIV* was a huge success, but it took Vince right up until match time to coax Shawn into dropping the belt to Austin. (On another note, Earl Hebner wasn't at WrestleMania at all, having been hospitalized with a brain aneurysm that could easily have been fatal. When I called to wish him a speedy recovery, he broke down on the phone.)

In the face of relentless competition from Vince, Eric Bischoff seemed to be burning out, and as a result, the disorganization at the WCW was getting worse. Though the house shows were still selling out, by March his TV ratings were beginning to slip. The WWF had figured out that the way to beat WCW was to get raunchier and sleazier every week. Vince's shock TV pushed the envelope of what the censors would allow, and Bischoff looked more lost and confused every day: he had to put out a product that fit within Ted Turner's squeaky-clean guidelines, and Vince knew it.

Maybe it's a good thing that Eric couldn't go that way, even if he'd wanted to. I liked Eric and often offered him ideas. I don't know if it was pride or politics that made him shoot them down one by one; his own angles rarely made sense. They'd fly me to TVs—paying for first-class air fare, hotel and a luxury car—only to leave me off the show. At the end of the day, in the WWF I got screwed for money, while in WCW I got paid well enough for so little output that I felt a bit too much like a whore.

I saw a rough cut of Paul's documentary, which was set to air in the fall, and now I understood what he'd been trying to tell me: The story of what had really happened to me in Montreal was going to be told, and it would be a vindication.

Eric had me turn heel by double-crossing Sting and revealing that, all along, I was part of the nWo. Vince's radical new direction was as brilliant in the ratings war as Eric's was weak. Aside from Stone Cold being one of the most popular TV characters in the world, Sable, Taker, Mankind and Rock were all coming into their own. On April 13, Austin wrestled McMahon to a DQ on *Raw* (because of interference from Mick Foley as Dude Love), the WWF shot out in front and never looked back. The ratings war was essentially over. I was the greatest weapon Eric had at that time, and why he never deployed me, I'll never know.

With my marriage and my career both falling apart, I felt darkness from all sides. I kept to myself more than ever, which wasn't a good thing. One day Julie summoned all the kids into the living room, against my protests, and told them we were divorcing. She then asked them to pick who they wanted to live with. The kids and I had been through this before, but when seven-year-old Blade broke into tears and cried, "I'm going with Dad!" it hit a powerful nerve in me. It had been six months since Vince had broken my heart, and neither Julie nor I knew how to fix it. This time I took Julie at her word. We officially separated on May 15, 1998.

Meanwhile, Stu and Helen had their own misery to deal with, being in a deep financial hole. I gave them $70,000 to get them through, making them promise me they'd use the money for themselves and not for those Harts who always had their hands out.

On May 17, I worked a good hard match with Macho at the *Slamboree* pay-per-view in Worcester, and that set up a tag match: me and Hogan versus Piper and Macho at the *Great American Bash* in Baltimore, which was a month away.

Death took yet another wrestler on June 2. The Junk Yard Dog, Sylvester Ritter, fell asleep at the wheel and rolled his car. He was forty-five.

I was worried about Davey, who told me that he and Diana were on the rocks too. He again confided to me that he needed help with his drug problem. I went to Eric on his behalf, and Eric said that if Davey got help, he didn't have to worry, his job would be secure. Sadly, even though Davey freely admitted he needed help, he wasn't yet ready to accept it.

At the *Great American Bash*, Macho and I cut a good pace, but Roddy and Hogan showed their age. Hogan was starting to remind me of Giant Baba, who was old, phony and uncoordinated, but whose fans loved him anyway. The whole storyline didn't make sense to me, or to the fans, but to Eric and Hogan it was all great work. My heel character had become a deranged, angry bad guy. My fans didn't like him, and neither did I. My original following was now outnumbered by a new breed of fans, who were like cartoon characters themselves. I couldn't remember the last time I saw younger kids or a family at ringside. Even *The New York Times* proclaimed that pro wrestling was no longer suitable for kids.

On July 20, I won the U.S. title in Salt Lake City when I beat up Diamond Dallas Page with a steel chair. Page was a close friend of Eric's, a scruffy, wiry older rookie who resembled a Scottie dog. He was playing the part of an old veteran, even though he'd only been wrestling a few years. He was a good hand who was always trying to improve. We had a kind of chemistry and got on well in and out of the ring.

I'd brought Blade with me to Salt Lake City, and he sat watching the monitor in the dressing room as Scott Hall took some kind of phony-looking bump into a TV production trailer while wrestling Kevin Nash. Minutes later, when Scott walked in, my eight-year-old son called out, "Hey, Razor, that was pathetic," cracking up the whole dressing room. During these sad and empty days, the only real joy in my life was Blade.

On August 4, I boarded a plane home after a *Nitro* in Denver and was happy to find Owen in the seat next to mine, smiling as if he'd been waiting for me. For the next couple of hours, we talked about the state of the business. He was disgusted by a recent angle on *Raw* that featured wrestler Val Venis and special guest John Wayne Bobbitt, where Venis put his penis out on a chopping block. Owen didn't like the guns, sleazy sex and female fans taking their tops off in the audience. He told me he wanted to resurrect his old Blue Blazer character just to change things up: perhaps becoming a masked superhero was a way to avoid involvement with the vulgar aspects of the show.

I had just moved, alone, into an old stone ranch house planted on the edge of a hill in the west end of Calgary, overlooking the Rocky Mountains;

because I had to travel so much, it made the most sense for the all the kids to live with Julie. I took the opportunity to invite Owen to come over to see my new place as well as watch a rough cut of Paul's documentary, now titled *Wrestling with Shadows*. I was worried that my dad came across as too harsh in the doc when I talked about him often stretching me hard enough to pop the blood vessels in my eyes and about my life passing before my eyes while he smothered me in various submission holds. I wanted Owen's honest advice because the last thing I wanted to do was hurt my dad, and I was relieved when he told me not to worry because it was all true. The thing that upset Owen was when, in the documentary, I compared losing to Shawn with blowing my brains out. My brother admonished me, reminding me, "We always said there's nothing in wrestling worth dying for."

The next day I got a script to do a Disney series called *Honey, I Shrunk the Kids*, in which I'd play myself. There was also a part for a Hart brother and I got Owen the job so we could spend some time together. Owen couldn't have been happier.

I lost the U.S. title to Lex Luger on August 10, only to win it back from him three days later. Titles didn't mean anything any more; they changed hands almost as many times as the WCW senselessly turned me from heel to babyface. At that time, Eric was pinning his ratings hopes on the return of The Ultimate Warrior. But within days, Warrior tore a biceps muscle and that was the beginning of the end for him, not that he could've been Eric's saviour anyway.

I'd given Eric and Hogan advance dubs of Paul's documentary, and they both called to tell me they loved it. I thought perhaps it would encourage Eric to keep me babyface, seeing as how wrestling fans would soon see me looking like a real hero in Paul's movie. I was baffled when Eric wasted Hart versus Hogan on a free match at *Nitro*, on September 28, throwing away a guaranteed moneymaker that the fans had been waiting years for. The plan, in my view, was insane. He wanted me to turn babyface during an in-ring interview, challenge Hogan, then get injured and have Sting take my place. When Sting twisted Hogan into his scorpion death lock, I would limp back out and doublecross Sting by DDTing him headfirst into the mat, turning heel again. To turn me heel at this point was so stupid it felt like sabotage.

Then I heard the news that my old pal Jim Duggan had kidney cancer, which only added to the weight I was carrying around. My divorce had also turned into a *War of the Roses*.

Julie and I had monumental fights, over money, over whose friends were on whose side, over . . . everything basically. And then we would make up.

We went through this cycle over and over again. I couldn't take the up-down, push-pull any more and sank into a deep depression. On October 11, while riding with The Giant from Milwaukee to Chicago, I found myself wishing I was dead. But then, when Paul Wight actually started to pull out to pass — in front of a speeding semi truck — I heard myself shouting, "Stop!" When both our heart rates had slowed again, the big guy looked over at me and said, "Thanks for saving my life tonight."

I worked *Halloween Havoc* with Sting in Las Vegas, retaining the U.S. title by beating him senseless with a baseball bat that was actually made of foam.

I could rarely bear to watch *Raw* any more but checked it out to see Owen's new turn as The Blue Blazer. I understood what Owen was talking about when I saw Vince McMahon appear to piss himself in the ring on live TV after Stone Cold pressed a .38 special to his head. With the WWF ratings going through the roof, Sable appeared in the highest-selling *Playboy* magazine of all time and Stone Cold was on the cover of *Rolling Stone*.

That November, Jesse The Body Ventura surprised political pundits when he was elected governor of Minnesota. Dave Meltzer wrote, "Pro wrestling is more real and more phony than people can imagine." The simple truth was that wrestling had never been more widely acceptable to the mainstream than it was that year. But it felt to me that I kept spiralling down, in my own estimation and in my fans' eyes too.

On November 9, a year after the Montreal screwjob, I thought I finally had my chance to show Eric what I was worth when I worked the Nassau Coliseum, wrestling in New York for the first time since coming to WCW. To my complete dismay, I had a meaningless match with Konan and did a run-in during the last few seconds of the show. But I refrained from complaining: Eric had just given Davey more time off to get his act together, though he'd had to let Jim go because he was clumsily missing shots — not showing up for work.

The high point of the whole year was the premiere of Paul's documentary at a gala in Toronto. After watching it with the audience, I got a standing ovation. A week later, I sat with Stu and the rest of the Hart family at the IMAX theatre in Calgary, where once again the audience got to its feet to cheer me. That felt especially good, because halfway through the screening, Bruce abruptly dragged his kids out because of how Stu was portrayed. But Stu told me he liked it, which was a great relief. Afterwards, I fielded questions from the audience, and I saw a warm smile on Owen's face when I said the only thing I missed about the WWF was him.

New Year's Eve, 1998. I had no idea when I bought my new house that the view would be like an ever-changing painting every day. I was alone and had my music cranked while looking out my kitchen window at a family of deer digging up fallen crab apples beneath a blanket of snow.

I eased myself into a more comfortable position on a huge round couch, where I could stare out at the distant lights of Calgary. I'd dropped the U.S. title again, to Dallas Page in Phoenix on November 22. The next day I worked a *Nitro* match in Grand Rapids, Michigan, against pint-sized Dean Malenko, a second-generation wrestler who was a good, capable worker, although his style reminded me of Cirque du Soleil—it was a little too rehearsed. When Malenko went for a standing suplex on me, I went up for him effortlessly in the air, straight as two dinner forks stuck together. Instead of taking me back for a simple back bump, Malenko decided to walk me the short distance to the corner, but he didn't have the size or strength and dropped me full-weight, crotching me and tearing my groin. I don't even know how I was able to bring myself to finish the match. I was in too much pain even to tell Dean how pissed off I was at him. Even worse, he dressed fast and left without acknowledging that he hurt me, or that he was sorry. As well regarded as little Malenko was, I lost respect for him as a professional that day. I could barely walk, let alone wrestle, yet Eric had me win back the U.S. title from Page in Chattanooga a week later, with a lame finish where The Giant helped me. As ridiculous as the storyline was, at least The Giant did do all the work.

I also managed to do another appearance on *Mad TV* in December, in a sketch about The Hitman becoming Jesse Ventura's lieutenant-governor and getting too physical at a press conference, where I'd rough up the cast before stomping off the set. The funniest bit came at the end of the show when I decked the heavy-set Will Sasso with a plastic chair, twisted him into a sharpshooter and fled. He followed me back to my dressing room, with a camera crew in tow, asking me what my problem was. I jumped him from behind, pulled his shirt over his head and appeared to beat him senseless. The show went off the air with cast members attending to Will, who actually got a bloody nose in all the excitement. As ole J.R. Foley used to say, "I never, erm, touched him."

Christmas had been especially bleak. Diana had got so fed up with Davey passing out like a zombie on the couch in front of the kids that she downed his entire bottle of Xanax right in front of him to prove a point. Sadly, it was young Harry who had to call 911 because Davey was too out of it to dial the number. Alison said that Diana had had her stomach pumped and that they'd read her the last rites. But Owen told me at dinner at his place on Boxing Day that, as far as he was concerned, the incident hadn't been life threatening and that Diana only acted like she was out of it when there were people around. I thought Owen was being a little too hard on Diana. She was having a tough time with Davey's out-of-control drug problem. Poor Davey. His sister, Tracey, had only just passed away in November and his mother, Joyce, was dying of cancer and was down to her last days in a hospital in England too.

No matter how hard I tried, I couldn't seem to escape the Montreal screwjob. With the release of the documentary, wherever I went people stopped me to shake my hand. A teary-eyed Marine came up to me at the St. Louis airport and told me he'd never watch the WWF again, and that he was proud of me. But I'd read in a *Forbes* magazine before Christmas that the WWF was now a $500 million-a-year company. In the last year alone, the company grossed $54.7 million, breaking all records. I had to shake my head at the irony of the fact that the whole thing started when Vince told me that the WWF was in financial peril! Vince had used what he did to me for real to turn his company around completely—and his words about WCW not knowing what to do with a Bret Hart echoed louder and louder in my head.

The heated negotiations over my divorce were basically done, and all I needed to do was sign the papers. Though I'd decided that marriage was not for me, I'd gone through some kind of strange metamorphosis: I now had no interest in the pretty girls at the hotels who threw themselves at the wrestlers after the shows. Oddly, now that everything Julie and I had owned had been divided up, we were getting along better than we had in a long time.

The constant pain in my groin was bad enough that I winced when I hoisted myself off the couch to pace around inside my big house, thinking and remembering. I promised Eric I'd delay my groin surgery until after WCW's Canadian debut, which was going to be in Toronto, on March 29, 1999. I thought I could make it because I could walk, run reasonably fast and take some bumps, but I'd have to go real easy. Eric had also apologized to me for how they'd dropped the ball with me from the start.

On February 1, Bill Goldberg and I were waiting on the runway in Los Angeles for Hogan and Bischoff to arrive for a chartered flight to San Francisco, both of us worried that we wouldn't get to *Nitro* on time. As we chatted I told Bill that I had an idea for WCW's debut in Toronto, which was coming up, a great angle that played on my popularity in Canada, especially after the documentary. Wearing my trademark skater shorts and a Hitmen jersey, I'd call him out and goad him into spear-tackling me like a freight train, only I'd hide a "steel" chest plate under my jersey, and he'd end up knocked out cold for the one . . . two . . . three. This of course would set us up to work together, with him coming after me to get even. "It's great television, Bill, and it doesn't hurt you one bit." Bill grinned and told me he was all for it.

Eric, Hogan, Bill and I missed all but the last three minutes of *Nitro* and hit the ring one after another in our street clothes. The next day I told Eric my idea about Goldberg and the steel plate and he told me he loved it too, but he thought Bill would never go for it. I explained that I had already run it past Bill and that he wanted to do it. Surprised, Eric told me we could do it. I suggested to him that with Toronto barely two months away, I'd need to be built up some, get a few wins and cut some good promos. We planned out my next few weeks leading into Toronto, and Eric asked me not to say a peep about our plans to anyone.

On February 7, I was flown down to Atlanta to sit in on a booking meeting that was supposed to determine finally where The Hitman was going at WCW. I wasn't surprised to find Hulk, Nash, Eric and the rest of the booking committee playing God with the careers of the wrestlers. First off, Hogan suddenly brought up rumours that I was going back to Vince, which would do big business. I downplayed the chance of it ever happening, while knowing this fear was really the only leverage I had any more. The only thing bigger than a Hart-Hogan match would be if I did an angle with Vince, but for all the money in the world, I would never let Vince make an angle out of something that hurt so deeply. I let them know I was happy to put over anybody they wanted, but it seemed to me that it didn't make much sense to beat me so often considering what they were paying me. Bischoff and Hogan stayed in the meeting just long enough to clear the way for me to work with Hogan in the fall. After they left, Nash, who was the new captain of the booking committee, told me there was no chance I'd be working with Hogan in the fall: he had Hogan with Goldberg.

"Eric was just here and we were all in agreement." I said. "Where were you?"

Nash walked off, bitching and shaking his head.

The next day, in Buffalo for *Nitro*, as part of an angle that was tied in with *Mad TV*, I was supposed to drop the belt to an unworthy and unreliable Razor, but at the last minute that was switched, and Roddy Piper was going to get the belt. I wanted to do all I could for Roddy, in return for all his years of being a true friend to me. I laid him out after the referee had also been knocked down. Then I attempted to drag the semi-conscious ref over to make the count, just as Will Sasso climbed over the railing. We got into a tug-o-war over the ref, with me pulling on his arm and Will pulling on his leg. When Roddy schoolboyed me from behind, with the ref just able to make the count, it got a huge pop.

Then Eric decided to go on a family vacation to France, leaving Nash in charge. Eric's last *Nitro* before his time off was February 22 in Sacramento; instead of building me up for Goldberg, he had me lose to Booker T. This made no sense to me at all, but Eric sheepishly told me that his booking committee insisted that it was time to see me do a job. I told him I'd done plenty of them and beating me was beyond stupid when they had so much invested in me. "Just put Booker over and we'll build everything after this," he said. I had nothing but respect for Booker T, so told Eric I'd do whatever he needed me to do. (I was pleased to see that despite my groin injury, Meltzer rated it a four-star match.)

Three days later, at *Thunder* in Salt Lake City, Eric was gone and Nash had the nerve to tell me that he'd taken my groin injury into account but he still wanted me to do a ridiculously long seventeen minutes with Disco Inferno. Disco was comic relief, and no way to build me for Goldberg, let alone Hogan. Next, at *Nitro* in Worcester on March 8, it was Malenko I would supposedly lose to. When I protested to Nash that I needed to stay strong for Goldberg, of course he didn't know what I was talking about. To me, it felt like Rome was burning yet again. Nash was doing all he could to kill me off, for reasons I'll never know. That time, I somehow managed to persuade him that Eric had something big planned for me, so, acting like he was doing me a huge favour, he threw me in with a big, clumsy rookie named Heavy Metal Van Hammer. I didn't lose, but it added nothing to my heat going into Toronto.

At home, my mom told me that Smith's on-and-off girlfriend Zoe — Chad's mother — had died of a drug overdose. I decided to go to her funeral to be there for Smith. A few days later Smith showed up at my place with Stu in tow, his excuse being that Stu wanted to see my house (clearly an excuse because Stu had just been over for a visit). I helped my dad into the kitchen where we soon got so engrossed in talking about Davey, and the pain he was in from a hurt back, that I didn't immediately notice that Smith had gone missing. I soon found him rummaging through my things in the living room, and I invited him back to the kitchen, telling him he had to stay where I could keep an eye on him. He sheepishly followed me. My dad told me he thought Eric Bischoff was the cause of Davey's problems and soon I was defending Eric to my dad: Davey's story was that he'd hurt his back on a malfunctioning trap door in a WCW ring. He and Diana were even talking about suing. I told Stu that as far as I was concerned, Davey was battling a morphine addiction more than any injury or infection, and he needed to get clean. Eric had given him lots of chances to do just that, but Davey was still procrastinating about going to rehab.

On March 22, I flew all the way to Panama City to find out I'd be off that night, but I managed to persuade Nash to give me an interview on *Nitro* to set things up for Toronto—because it looked like WCW was going to waste that opportunity too, even though I was over in Canada following the documentary release. In my brief interview with Gene Okerlund, I prepped my Canadian fans by challenging Hogan and Nash, and then subtly tossing Goldberg's name out for the very first time, planting a seed that I knew was sure to grow in the week remaining before the Toronto show.

At *Wrestlemania XV* in Philadelphia on March 28, Austin pinned Rocky Maivia, now known as The Rock, to win the World Heavyweight title, while Owen and Jeff Jarrett defeated D-Lo Brown and Test to retain the Tag Team belts. The WWF was red hot.

The next day at about noon, I walked into the Air Canada Centre in Toronto for *Nitro* and there were already a few thousand fans standing on the street in the frigid cold chanting my name. Eric had filled in the booking committee about my Goldberg angle, but, much to my disappointment, Nash and WCW road agent Kevin Sullivan had got to Bill and persuaded him that the angle would kill him off.

I tried to talk Goldberg back into it in the dressing room. "C'mon on, Bill. You're kidding me? We talked about this, remember? You loved it! Nothing's changed. You know this will set us up to work after my surgery."

When I left him, I ran into Nash, who'd now decided *he* would come down at the end and leave me laying, which made no sense at all.

I went and found Eric in his office. I knew that the ratings success of *Wrestlemania XV* had to be weighing heavily on his mind, but I still couldn't believe my ears when he said, "How 'bout this—you go out and tell the fans that you don't need them any more!"

In my first WCW refusal, I shook my head: no. "Eric, you hear that sound?" I said. "That's the sound of thousands of my fans, and *only* my fans, standing outside on the sidewalk, in the dead of winter, chanting my name. Why would I do that?"

He had another idea: we'd do everything the same, except that Hogan, not Nash, would come down at the end. He'd go to high-five me, but instead he'd double-cross me, jump me and leave me for dead. Dumbfounded, I asked Eric if I was going to work with Hogan instead of Goldberg. He said not until next fall. I asked if Hogan was going to be wrestling Goldberg. He said not anytime soon. I asked him, "Why in God's name would you fuck up such a great angle with something so stupid and pointless?"

Eric said nervously, "You'll have to convince Terry. If he says it's okay, then fine." Now I knew who was really in charge of WCW.

So I went and found Hulk and asked him. "So why would you come down?"

"I don't need to come down," he admitted.

When I relayed Hulk's response to Eric, he seemed surprised and relieved. Eric wanted me to feed the rumours that I was going back to the WWF, so he told me that after the bit with Goldberg, he wanted me to get on the mic and quit WCW. I had no idea what that would be about, but I agreed.

I felt like a cat in the dark, watching Hogan battling Nash in some kind of power play in which we were all caught in the middle; Eric was clearly in over his head, unable to cope with the warring wolf packs.

As I walked out to my music, there was a commotion going on in the entranceway. Kevin Sullivan was on the floor, frothing at the mouth in a seizure (in the dressing room the next day, he explained that he had miscalculated his GBH dosage). Who could make such stuff up? As I stepped over him, I couldn't help thinking, It's a good thing I don't follow the leaders around here.

I walked out wearing my friend Tie Domi's Maple Leafs jersey underneath my Hitmen jersey. I knew if Eric had seen it, he'd have made me take it off because he was already terrified that I was going to go over so strong with the Canadian crowd that it would turn Goldberg heel, which was going to happen anyway, no matter what we did. I received a thundering ovation from the crowd, and then on the mic, I accused Goldberg of hiding in his dressing room, biting his fingernails and trembling with fear. While I peeled off my Hitmen jersey to expose the Maple Leafs jersey, declaring Canada "hockey country," Eric was frantically running around backstage screaming at Goldberg to get out there before I killed him off. When Goldberg finally got in the ring, snorting like a Brahma bull, I taunted him, begging him to come and get me. When he spear-tackled me, the fans had no idea what was going to happen next. We both lay there without moving for what seemed like an eternity. Then I rolled him off me, counted him out, stood up, peeled my jersey off and threw it down on his unconscious body revealing the "steel" plate: the whole building came unglued. As Eric requested, I got on the mic and declared, "Hey, WCW, I quit!"

When I got home I actually contemplated quitting for real. It seemed to me that Eric just didn't have enough wrestling smarts to do his job: he had freaked out backstage because he thought I overshadowed Goldberg, but within hours the angle was being talked about as the best thing WCW had done in years. It even made the front page of *The Toronto Sun*, under the headline "HITMAN QUITS."

When I got home, I signed a two-year extension to my contract. I hoped it would dispel any fears that I was going back to WWF, which might give WCW the incentive to do better by me—not to mention that $2.5 million a year until 2003 was too good to turn down. Then I had my surgery. Davey was in hospital too, supposedly with a staph infection that had travelled to his spine. I believe he was actually going through withdrawal. I don't think it helped when WCW, not being able to reach him, FedExed termination papers to his house and Diana brought them right to him in the hospital. What did help was when Owen and Mankind visited him that same afternoon and put him on the phone with Vince, who told Davey that if he got clean, he'd have a job waiting for him. With Davey, though, that was a big *if.* The WWF was in Calgary for a sold-out non-televised show at the Saddledome on April 17. Owen asked me if I would come down and say hi to all the wrestlers. I decided I would, as a favour to him, but I also needed to do it for myself. I didn't want to carry around my bitterness any more.

I spoke to Eric the night before, and he told me to go down to the show, that it would really feed the rumours on the Internet. When I arrived at the back of the Saddledome, Carlo was there to meet me and seemed overly concerned about letting me come backstage. The closer we got to the dressing room, the more I realized that Carlo was the only one who had a problem with it. I was soon surrounded by the smiling faces of Owen, Mankind, Edge, Test and Papa Shango. Even Hunter came out to greet me, with Chyna, who clearly had had radical cosmetic surgery since the last time I'd seen her; she looked drastically altered, reconstructed and beautiful in a ghastly kind of way. I gave a hardy handshake to Ken Shamrock just as agent Jack Lanza waded in with a big smile, flashing a look of annoyance at Carlo, who was still standing around like a useless guard dog. "What the hell?" he said to Carlo. "Of course he can come down. Are you kidding?"

It felt good to see my old friends, and I could tell by the huge smile on Owen's face that it meant a lot to him that I was there. I was soon pulling my pants down just enough to show them the four-inch incision from my surgery. Then I went to watch Taker's match, and when the fans glimpsed me in the wings, they began chanting "We want Bret," over and over. After his match, Taker walked past me grinning and said, "You're next."

I noticed Stone Cold playing innocently enough with some black-haired girl's hand. I couldn't see her because she was all wrapped up in the curtain, but I assumed this might be a new girlfriend. Like so many of us, Austin had just gone through a divorce. Then Steve noticed me and I noticed that the girl he was playing around with was Diana. She'd dyed her hair. I'd seen Davey do a lot more than flirt, but still, this seemed a bit callous with Davey in the hospital, for whatever reason he was there. Steve left her to come over and chat with me; we parked ourselves on some equipment boxes, and soon we were talking about our divorces. Then Owen asked me to say hi to Earl, and I had no problem doing that.

Moments later, I stood with The Rock, who told me, "I'll never forget what you did for me." He also said that I should come back, that WCW was screwing me over worse than Vince had. Shawn wasn't wrestling any more, just playing the role of a commissioner, so he, Taker and Austin were the ones in charge. I shrugged and said, "I don't think so."

After the show, I sat with Taker at a bar and we laughed like the long-lost friends that we were. I went home that night feeling better than I had in months, because finally, at least in some sad, small way, I got to say a proper goodbye.

Three days later, on the same day as the Columbine high-school massacre, the Grim Reaper came calling for Rick Rude, who was found dead of a heart attack from an overdose of painkillers. He was forty. I'll never forget how Rick stood by me after Montreal. Rick was one of those guys who never took his wedding ring off; he'd wrap a piece of white tape around it when he went into the ring. He was the kind of guy who, when you needed someone to back you up, wouldn't flinch at all. Not for money. Not for anything.

And then, in early May, that crazy lumberjack, Joe The Maniac LeDuc, died. I can't express how much the constant string of wrestlers' deaths affected me. They developed drug habits and took such risks with their health, all for what? Just to make the next town? To entertain people? This sort of funeral march happens to most people when they hit their seventies. To me it felt like the casualties of war.

On May 17, I did a bit where I came out of the crowd on *The Tonight Show* to accept a challenge from Kevin Nash that I come back to WCW in one week to wrestle him. Jay Leno had been part of WCW's *Hog Wild* pay-per-view back in July 1998, and he laughed when I pulled out a WCW wrestling card with his picture on it and asked him to sign it.

Meanwhile, the Hitmen had won the WHL championship and were set to meet the Ottawa 67s in the Memorial Cup. Things had improved so much between Julie and me that I invited her, along with Blade and Dallas, to fly east with me to watch the game. On Sunday afternoon, May 23, 1999, the Ottawa 67s defeated the Hitmen in a heartbreaking overtime. Julie and I, along with the boys, stopped in the locker room to congratulate the team on a great season. Even though the team had lost, that visit was a sweet moment of competitive purity that one only finds in real sports.

I had to rush to make my flight to L.A. for my second live appearance on *The Tonight Show* the next day. While I was saying goodbye to Julie and the kids at the airport, we bumped into some of the mothers of the Hitmen players who were catching a flight back to Calgary. They were still tearful, and then one of them cracked a tentative smile and said, "Why are we crying? It's not like somebody died."

I connected to my L.A. flight through Toronto, but had no time at the airport to call home. I pictured the whole Hart clan sitting in Stu's kitchen watching the nationally televised Memorial Cup final and feeling the same passion and heartache as me. A couple of hours later, in the air, something ominous nagged at my heart. It couldn't be the game. I knew all about the game. Then the cockpit door opened and the pilot came out, and I just knew that he was looking for me. He handed me a note that read, "Bret Hart, please call home. Family emergency!"

I tried every phone in the first-class cabin, but as luck would have it, the only one that worked was next to the only other passenger in the compartment. At first I got nothing but busy signals. So I checked my voice mail to find a frantic message from Carlo asking me to call him right away. I knew at that moment that someone had died.

When I reached him, Carlo kept asking, "Are you sitting down?"

"I'm on a plane, of course I'm sitting. What happened?"

"Don't be alarmed. Don't get mad. I don't know how to tell you this. Are you sitting down?"

I was getting annoyed. "Just spit it out."

"Owen's dead. He got killed doing some kind of stunt in the ring."

I felt like my chest caved in. Carlo didn't have the facts yet, but all he knew for sure was that Owen was gone.

43

IF I GAVE YOU MY LIFE, WOULD YOU DROP IT?

THE NEXT DAYS ARE ALL IMAGES smeared together. I couldn't get back to Calgary until about five a.m. the next morning, and when I got home I went to bed. I hadn't slept at all since hearing the news, and I didn't want to show up at Hart house until I'd had a little rest—I wanted my parents to be able to lean on me. I couldn't shake the thought from my mind: What happened to you, my little Oje?

The night before, a sombre Jim Ross sat at the announcers' table at the *Over The Edge* pay-per-view in Kansas City with the cameras on the crowd, not daring to reveal what was happening in the ring to the live audience watching around the world. "This is as real as real can get," he said. "The Blue Blazer, known as Owen Hart, was going to make a very spectacular superhero-like entrance. Something went terribly wrong . . . this is not a wrestling angle . . . this is not part of the story . . ."

Hanging from a cable off a catwalk up in the rafters of the arena, Owen suddenly fell seventy-eight feet to the ring, smashing chest-first across the ropes, about a foot from a turnbuckle, bouncing hard onto his back toward the middle of the ring. He lay there for several minutes turning blue while paramedics worked feverishly on him, to no avail.

I pulled into Stu's yard at around eleven that morning. Hart house never looked so sad. Dean's old, crippled pit bull, Lana, was the first to greet me, her tail whacking my car door. I thought to myself that Owen would have laughed at the notion that the old dog outlived both Dean and him.

A swarm of reporters surrounded me as I made my way up the back porch steps. Stu was sitting at the head of the dining-room table going through pictures of Owen. I reached out for his big hand, and put my other hand on his shoulder. In the living room, grandkids were huddled together in little groups softly crying while various members of the family were giving interviews. My mom politely excused herself from a group of reporters to give me a big hug, crying as she held me tight. The story of Owen's fatal fall was covered by news outlets worldwide, all of which were asking if pro wrestling had gone too far.

When Owen had been dying in Kansas City, Martha had been home packing for the big move into their new dream house, across the road from what used to be Clearwater Beach. Leaving the media circus at Hart house, I drove over to see her. I was amazed by her composure. She had already called a lawyer friend of hers by the name of Pam Fischer to seek legal advice. I watched the news with Martha and there, on camera, was Davey, looking much better than he had in a long while. I couldn't believe it when Davey said that Owen's death was just an accident, and that it was nobody's fault. Who was Davey to say whose fault it was, when the police were still investigating what had happened? Davey then vowed that he'd return to the WWF to win a title in Owen's honour.

I left Martha to go to see my own kids. Owen was their closest uncle and, like the rest of the Hart grandkids, they were taking it hard. Perhaps it was a blessing that Owen's own children, Oje and Athena, were still too young to really understand that their dad was never coming back. When Julie comforted me, I broke down crying hard, sitting on the front steps. It felt somehow like I was responsible.

Because of my experience dealing with the media, Martha asked me to be a spokesperson for herself and her family. In the days after Owen died, I asked Marcy to relocate permanently to Calgary to run my office and be my personal assistant; I got her a ticket on the next flight out of New York. I did *Good Morning America* at four a.m., Calgary time, in Stu's living room with Martha and my parents. I arrived unshaven and weary. Martha's lawyers were there to guard against anything being said that could jeopardize her legal standing with the WWF, so I focused on how the business had strayed too far from the premise of two athletes telling a story using only their bodies. Pro wrestling had become a can-you-top-this ratings war of increasingly more dangerous stunts and sleazy storylines. Owen was no stuntman and clearly someone didn't know what they were doing. A union for wrestlers was long overdue, I said. At least if we had one, there'd be guidelines to distinguish between wrestling and stunt work, and there would be protection when someone got hurt.

Meanwhile, Vince left me numerous phone messages pleading with me to call him back. I couldn't bring myself to do it until I had a better idea of his role in Owen's death.

On Thursday morning, May 27, Martha asked me to come with her to meet the plane that was bringing Owen home. We watched as the closed casket, draped with a big Canadian flag, was placed into a hearse. The next morning at the viewing, I stared down at Owen in his coffin laying there with his fingers laced across his chest. It didn't look like him. When I kissed his cold cheek, it struck me that my little brother felt like a porcelain doll. Smoothing his hair, I kept asking, "Ahh, Owen, what were you thinking?"

I finally relented enough on the Vince front to have Carlo arrange to have Vince meet me on a park bench overlooking the Bow River where I'd spent so much time thinking about what Vince had done to me. Soon, three limos pulled up at my old house, and I led them to the park. A Calgary policemen told me, some time later, that Vince had hired him and some undercover cops to stake out our meeting in case I got violent. Apparently Vince was wearing a wire: the cop said he heard every word of our meeting and had been impressed with my dignity.

That whole May was cold in Calgary, and the backdrop of our meeting was a watercolour sky of ashen grey and swollen, black, angry clouds that would be crying along with us before long. Vince wore a long, heavy coat. He slapped me hard on the shoulders, hugged me and told me how sorry he was. "This is the worst thing to ever happen in the business, to the nicest guy who was ever in the business."

He asked me if he should go to Stu's, and I suggested that he might want to wait until after the funeral. I'd left Hart house not an hour earlier and Bruce and Ellie were still screaming for his head, but I didn't see the need to tell Vince that. When I asked him what happened, he told me he didn't know all the details, he was in make-up at the time. I told him that, in all likelihood, Martha would be suing him. I gave him fair warning that if he had anything to tell me, he should go ahead, but that we didn't need to talk about it. He accepted that and seemed to relax a little.

I told Vince that I didn't appreciate that they went on with the show after Owen died. He replied that nobody knew what to do, they were so shocked; and they were afraid the fans might riot if he stopped the show. That struck me as ridiculous, and I said that if Shane had been dropped from the ceiling, Vince would have stopped it fast. He stared out at the river and simply said, "We didn't know what to do."

I also didn't appreciate them airing a replay for profit either, and I didn't like watching *Raw* the day after Owen's death, when wrestlers sick with grief were given no choice about pouring their hearts out on live TV for ratings. I said a more fitting tribute to Owen would have been to celebrate his career by showing his matches.

Then I sighed and told Vince that this never would have happened to Owen if I'd been there. Owen always came to me for advice, and I would have shot such a stupid idea down fast.

Vince finally admitted, though I didn't know whether I could believe him, that "There isn't a day that goes by that I don't regret what I did to you. You need to come back and finish your career with me. I could put the belt back on you. . . . I could have a storyline for you by tomorrow morning."

I couldn't imagine getting back in the ring ever again, I replied, and aside from that I'd just resigned with WCW for another two years.

Vince seemed to mean it when he asked if there was anything he could do for me. When I still worked for him, we talked about doing a *Best of Bret Hart* video collection, but that was more than unlikely after Montreal. I didn't have much of a history if Vince locked up everything I did in a warehouse somewhere. "Well, it would mean a lot to me if I could have access to my video history and photos whenever I need them . . ."

He cut me off, "Anything you want."

"I don't want to lose my legacy. I don't want to be forgotten . . ."

He waved me off. "You don't even need to ask. Anything you want."

I found myself thanking him and telling him how much this simple gesture meant to me, especially under the circumstances. If the police cleared Vince, then maybe I could forgive him.

After two hours on that park bench, exchanging stories about Owen and finally even managing to laugh a little—for better or worse, Vince and I had fourteen years of shared history—we shook hands and headed back to our cars.

The WWF wrestlers and a lot of the crew and office staff made the long flight to Calgary for Owen's funeral. The May 31 *Raw* was already in the can, but *Nitro* was live and Eric left a message for me apologizing for not being able to attend. To his credit Hulk arrived in town quietly, on his own with no fanfare.

On Monday morning, May 31, I got up from my dining-room table, where I'd been writing the finishing touches of a eulogy to my brother, and went out for a walk. The Calgary sky was as grey as my mood and it cried tears from heaven on and off all day. When I got back I donned my best suit and drove over to Stu's to meet the motorcade. A dozen perfectly polished white limousines were lined up in Stu's front driveway, into which climbed various Harts all dressed in black. I was annoyed when I saw Ellie and Diana guiding Vince by the arm into Stu's limo; as far as I was concerned, he was far from forgiven yet.

Tension was smouldering among the siblings. I'd heard various rumours that Diana was pissed off because I'd got so much more TV time all week than anyone else. Bruce was upset because Martha wouldn't let him speak at the service. And Smith, who'd written a poem for Owen, was crushed when Martha told him he couldn't read it. Martha did ask both Ross and I to speak, and she requested that I tell some lighthearted stories about Owen before she delivered her own eulogy. Unfortunately, all these little things that I did to oblige Martha were only getting me heat from the rest of the family. It wasn't as though I wanted to be on TV right after my brother died, and I dreaded having to be on *Larry King Live* immediately after the funeral. All I wanted was to be left alone to grieve like everybody else.

The line of cars grew longer with each passing mile of the procession, with media and police helicopters overhead. The WWF wrestlers followed in a bus that bore a banner proclaiming, "OWEN YOU WILL ALWAYS BE IN OUR HEARTS." All that banner really told me was that Vince was treating the funeral as much as an exercise in damage control as it was about laying my brother to rest.

This was one of the biggest funerals that Calgary had ever seen, and people lined the motorcade route, many in their finest clothes, some bowing their heads and others holding signs. The Calgary police, in dress uniforms, closed major highways and provided a motorcycle escort all the way to the McInnis & Holloway funeral chapel, which was surrounded by thousands of people of all ages and walks of life. The chapel only held three hundred, so a separate room with TV monitors was provided for the WWF personnel and a PA system was set up outside for the public.

I remember seeing a blur of old and young battered faces. Owen's close pal Chris Benoit stood with Killer Kowalski, The Funks, Mick Foley, Taker, Bad News, Jericho, Hunter, Chyna and a cavalcade of other wrestlers.

The next thing I remember clearly is the heart-felt vow with which Martha closed her eulogy: "There will be a day of reckoning. This is my final promise to Owen. I won't let him down!"

The six remaining Hart brothers carried Owen's casket out of the chapel. It was the heaviest weight any of us had ever carried.

The procession then wound its way to Queen's Park Cemetery, where I'd so long ago raked leaves from headstones and made the decision to give the wacky world of wrestling a try. Tears filled my eyes when I saw a military officer in full dress uniform standing on an overpass at attention, saluting.

After Owen was lowered into the ground, the motorcade headed to Hart house, where friends and family from around the world gathered. It wasn't long before Pat Patterson came to find me. He wanted to tell me that he wasn't in on what happened to me in Montreal, but he shut up when I asked coldly, "So, where were you when they brought the midget out all dressed up as me?"

Finally, after doing *Larry King Live* from Martha's living room, I went home totally spent. I found a FedEx package from Carlo sitting at my doorstep among a forest of floral deliveries. I opened it to find Owen's bloody Blue Blazer gear inside. I held up the bloodstained blue mask that'd been cut off my brother, remembering that it was originally my idea for

Owen to wear a mask. I grabbed my coat, got away from the smell of all those flowers, and went for a long, long walk.

> *Smith's Poem for Owen*
>
> *Once you were here*
> *What a difference you made, dearest of dear brothers.*
> *To the hell that was raised when a dozen then played*
> *   without any others.*
> *Only heaven knows why you got chosen,*
> *and that you'll await us is our belief.*
> *I smell lily and rose and read each and every heart-felt card,*
> *through flows of grief.*
> *What is spoken is tasted*
> *and what is heard of your greatness is felt deep within our*
> *   heavy hearts*
> *and certainly all around this solemn gathering.*
> *As I still try to write in this, the 13th hour, Owen*
> *And search for words of praise and worth,*
> *I sense your presence pure and sweet.*
> *Owen, don't think I don't know*
> *that you are haunting our house already.*

Sadly, I'd lose more family than Owen after his death.

That Wednesday morning, tears came to my eyes reading about my brother's funeral in the morning papers while listening to Tom Petty sing about having a room at the top of the world and not comin' down. I'd be leaving for Missouri the next day with Martha, Pam Fischer and Ed Pipella, Martha's other Calgary lawyer. I had no misgivings about supporting Martha, who was determined to see the WWF pay dearly for destroying her life and her husband. I also needed someone to tell me for sure that Owen had not been murdered in some way. So I swore to Martha that I would be there for her no matter what happened, but I was having a tough time trying to get some of the Harts to stop talking to the media about Owen's death.

Still, my kids were over for a visit, and the sound of them playing lifted my spirits. I remembered how, whenever we landed in Calgary, Owen would grab his two carry-on bags, ready to race down the ramp as soon as the plane doors opened because Martha and the kids were always there waiting. As I flipped through the *Calgary Herald*, I couldn't get over the smiling face of my sister Diana, looking way too happy for the occasion as she posed with a bunch of sad wrestlers flanking a deflated Stu. There was a quote from Diana in the paper that made my blood boil: "Dad is like a father figure to Vince and Vince felt like Owen was one of his sons." Why couldn't they just say "no comment," at least until the criminal investigation was over and we knew whether any charges would be laid against Vince or his organization? This was what Owen's widow had asked us all to do!

I phoned Diana and I wasn't surprised that she turned on me like a grass fire. She blistered my heart when she tore into me about how Owen was a better wrestler than me and that I was jealous and had always held him back. She defended Vince, saying that this was no different than if Owen had hit his head in a cage match—accidents happen!

"All you have to say is *no comment*," I said. "How hard is that, Diana? Vince hasn't even been cleared of criminal charges."

"You hold it against Vince for what he did to you at *Survivor Series* because you didn't want to do a job for Shawn Michaels. You've got a vendetta and you're the only one that wants to sue anybody."

"Diana, this is about Martha. It's her decision!"

Then Ellie was suddenly on the extension, and I shouldn't have been so hurt or surprised when she coldly fired back, "You know, Bret, I've hated your guts since the day you were born and I'm glad to tell you that." I listened to them both screaming and yelling and it felt as though someone was pouring scalding water down my back. I was trying so hard to stand up for the whole family, to make them proud, and what I was asking Ellie and Diana to do was only what Owen would have asked of them himself, if he could have. I rose, clutching the phone, and erupted in a loud, booming voice, "If you two think for one minute that you're going to use Owen's death to get your husbands jobs, if you don't support Martha and Owen's kids right now, I will never, ever talk to either of you ever again!"

I slammed the phone down hard, then sat with my hands trembling as my kids all gathered around to comfort me. Then I actually called my mom to tell her the vicious, biting words that Ellie and Diana had said to me, as though I was a little kid again. She told me that she and Stu were firm in their decision to support Martha; it was the only thing to do; it was *their* decision; and it had nothing to do with me at all.

"Why do they all hate me so much?" I asked, and she broke down, "Dawling, they're all just so damn jealous of you. Jealousy is an ugly thing, and some of your brothers and sisters are infected with it. They don't mean it, they just wish that they could all be like you and have what you have." And then she comforted me as best she could.

In Kansas City the next day, Martha and I and her Calgary lawyers met Garry and Anita Robb, highly respected Missouri counsel who hoped to be hired to handle Martha's case. At noon we all went to a Kansas City police station where they showed us the flimsy sailboat clip the riggers used to attach Owen's harness to a single cable. The chief of police and a room full of detectives explained what they thought happened. Some of the cops in that meeting had been in the ring with Owen less than forty seconds after he hit the mat and they did everything they could to try to save his life.

I had heard that he was supposed to do the stunt with the same Mexican midget they paraded out as me after Montreal scissored between his legs, and was shocked when the cops confirmed it. The midget had only been nixed that afternoon. The officers calmly explained that Owen had been alive after he hit the ring and that he lay there for eight minutes with a severed aorta, his lungs filling with blood until he drowned. He had tried to sit up, to reassure the fans, but he couldn't. The impact when he hit the ring smashed almost all the heavy wooden ring planks and loosened all the ropes like they were rubber bands.

We were also told that criminal charges weren't likely to be laid but hadn't been ruled out.

Afterwards, the Robbs took us to Kemper Arena. As we headed up to the catwalk, Ed Pipella noticed a creepy insurance adjuster tagging along with us. When Ed quizzed him about who he was and what he was doing there, it turned into an ugly scuffle until security dragged the adjuster off.

It was a long climb to the top of the building. I wanted to get to the exact spot where Owen had fallen and started up a steep ladder to the catwalk. My stomach was queasy as I thought of a line from *The English Patient*, "If I gave you my life would you drop it?" Then it was a long, nerve-wracking walk along the catwalk to the score clock—and this was with the lights on. I could just imagine Owen having to race all the way up here as fast as he could in the dark, dressed in bulky coveralls, with a baseball cap pulled down to hide his face from the fans. Climbing over the railing of the catwalk must have been a terrifying moment. Standing next to the score clock, I looked out to where he would have hung. I pictured him fidgeting with his cape, breathing hard from the sprint up and then—ping—the sailboat clip holding his full weight released prematurely: the deep breaths he was taking would have provided more than the eight pounds of pressure the clip was designed to take. The riggers happened to be looking away at that moment, and when they turned back they were aghast to see that he was already falling, clawing at the air with his hands. I looked down and a chill went up my back wondering how in hell he let himself get talked into this.

If Montreal never happened, I thought, and I had still been in the WWF, I would've stopped this from ever happening to Owen!

By the time I got home, I was even more distraught and wildly confused. Owen had been so straight and so good, whereas I had always broken the rules, always been a bad boy, drinking, doing drugs and cheating on my wife. Why would God take the best one? Owen once said, "You can be a good person and do everything right and it doesn't guarantee you anything." Since his death, the Harts were forming into backstabbing cliques of their own, with Ellie and Diana fiercely demanding that Martha and my parents settle with Vince immediately, extolling the head of the WWF as some kind of saint who loved all the Harts.

Not surprisingly, a desperate Bruce, with his wrestling school and the broken-down vestiges of the Stampede Wrestling promotion, was looking for Vince to fund him in some way. Smith was talking about suing Vince because, he claimed, he and Owen were going to open a wrestling school together. Owen wouldn't have opened up a lemonade stand with Smith! Every time I encountered them at Hart house, Ellie and Diana demanded that I fill them in on the details of the lawsuit, yet every time I tried to make Martha's case, it turned into a shouting match, which only upset my parents and the grandkids. If Martha could've been a little kinder to them, instead of propping me up to take the heat, she might have avoided a lot of heartache, for herself and everyone else. But really, this whole thing should have had nothing to do with the other Hart siblings, or me.

In one of her many curt phone messages, Ellie implored me: "I've got the right to feed my family, and my dealings with Vince McMahon don't have anything to do with you, and nothing to do with Owen's death. Not everyone wants you to be their spokesperson." Ellie and Diana soon had Vince convinced that I was the driving force behind Martha's lawsuit. After Owen died, we had reached a delicate détente about my archive of matches for the WWF, which Vince totally controlled, and he had been on the verge of agreeing that I could have access to them. Now the WWF's in-house lawyer told my lawyer, Gord Kirke, that Vince simply had no recollection of any conversation with me on the subject. Vince now saw *me* as the enemy and seemed determined to make me suffer, as if I hadn't suffered enough.

Eric asked me to fly down and meet him in Chicago on June 25 to talk about where I was at. It was still nearly impossible for me even to think about getting back into the ring, but as the days passed, I realized that it wasn't right for me or my fans to let Owen's tragic death be the end of my career. Eric had been incredibly kind after Owen's death, telling me to take all the time I needed, and I didn't want to leave him in the lurch either.

At our meeting, Hulk was friendly and told me that he was anxious to finally work with me in the fall that year. Eric talked about putting the World title on me, but he understood that I wasn't ready to commit to anything yet and that I still needed time to heal physically and emotionally. Both of them listened empathetically as I told them about the problems in the Hart family since Owen's death and that Vince had offered jobs to both Jim and Davey, in effect bribing Ellie and Diana to be on his side against Owen's widow. Eric kindly said if it would help the situation, he'd hire Jim back and told me to have Jim give him a call. I left, shaking both their hands, content to show up at the Georgia Dome on July 5 for an in-ring interview on *Nitro*. Eric told me I could say anything I wanted wrestling fans around the world to hear. For the next ten days I thought about it almost all the time. I really didn't know what I'd say. Maybe it would be goodbye.

44

"WATCH THE KICK!"

WHEN I WALKED INTO THE DRESSING ROOM at the Georgia Dome, the boys rose from their chairs, one after another, to offer heartfelt condolences. In that moment, as in too many others, I felt more support and unity from my wrestling brothers than from my blood siblings. It meant so much to me when Randy Savage gave me a hug, with tears in his eyes. "Brother, I'm so sorry." Jim Duggan put his hand on my shoulder. "Sorry man!" (Hacksaw had beaten the cancer and was now back at work, minus his right kidney.)

Before I knew it, I was caught up trading Owen stories with Randy, Hacksaw, Crush and Brian Knobbs. I felt safe being back with the men who truly understood this life. These were my brothers from other mothers.

Suddenly, I was called out to do my interview. My terrible WCW entrance music rumbled and the crowd cheered as I made my way up the aisle, still having no idea what I was going to say! This was going to be a shot from the heart. Without even thinking about it, that day I left The Hitman behind and for the first time came out to the ring as Bret Hart, as real as real can be. No Hitman shades, leather jacket, ring gear, hair gel— not even the strut and the attitude. I did all I could not to break down as twenty-five thousand fans grew still for me, and for Owen.

And so, I learned at the same time as the fans did what was in my heart and on my mind. I told them what Owen meant to me and that I was at a crossroads in my life and I just didn't know if I'd ever be back. "I'm gonna take some time, put things in perspective, but if I never get the chance to ever say it again, I just want to thank all my fans everywhere that I ever had and still have. You've been with me from the very start and if this is the last chance I ever get to talk to all my fans all over the world, thank you very, very much. I wanna thank all the wrestlers in dressing rooms all over the world, it was a pleasure to work with each and every one of you. I hope I wasn't too stiff!"

I returned home to find another phone message from Ellie: "I want to know what's going on with the lawsuit. I want to find out what options mom and dad have. If you want to go through with this five or six years down the road, even two years, it's taking its toll on dad and we need to discuss this. It's not the only way to go. Enlighten me a bit. Di and me haven't done anything yet. We've got a bad rap. No more stress on dad."

What was I to make of that?

When I called my mom, she said, "I just wake up every day and try to live with it all day long all over again." Stu was never the same after Owen died. My mom wept, a few weeks later, when I confided to her that I'd been talking to Senator Harry Hayes's office in Ottawa and that they were in the process of nominating Stu for the Order of Canada, the highest civilian medal of honour in the country in recognition of the lifetime of charity work my dad had done.

My mom said that I needed to remember that she and Stu were with me 100 per cent, and that they were suing the WWF along with Martha. In an attempt to ease the family tension, Martha's lawyers were trying to work out an agreement that would allocate a portion of my parents' settlement to each of the remaining siblings if Stu and Helen died before the suit was settled. But Ellie, Diana and Bruce refused to sign any such agreement. Before long, Ellie was calling Martha's lawyers names again. The idea was scrubbed and the potential truce was quickly forgotten.

On July 27, Vince cooly stated on *Off The Record*: "Out of respect for Owen, I met with Bret. Bret carried the entire conversation. I really thought he wanted to talk about Owen . . . It was like looking into the eyes of a skeleton, in some respects. It seemed like he wasn't human. It was a very weird experience." Vince went on to pretty much blame me for everything related to Martha's lawsuit. I was already mad that he'd reneged on his promise to give me access to my footage, but when he referred to me as a skeleton and to my not being human, my anger flared into real hatred. But as far as criminal responsibility for Owen's death went, four days later he was in the clear. After two months, on July 31, then and only then did the Kansas City Police determine that there wasn't enough evidence for criminal charges against Vince.

WCW called me out of the blue to come work some house shows with Hogan; I actually looked forward to going back on the road. At the Cow Palace in San Francisco, Hogan did all he could to show me he could work a realistic style. It's fair to say that nobody, especially Terry, wanted the boys to come back saying how bad it was, because almost nobody ever had a bad match with me. It seemed to loosen everybody up when I took to the blackboard again, drawing Knobbs with ten penises and a speech balloon that read, "Now you know why they call me Knobbs." A lot of the WCW boys had only heard about the cartoons I used to draw in the WWF dressing rooms, and it was nice to see Sting and the rest of the boys crack up laughing.

I wasn't the only Hart-affiliated wrestler to return to the ring. Flying the couple in to New York City so that Davey could do an interview with the WWF magazine, Vince put Davey and Diana up at the Waldorf Astoria. In the interview Davey again did what Martha asked him specifically not to do, declaring that Owen's death was nobody's fault. He also garnered headlines in the Calgary papers about his courageous comeback.

I did some Florida dates leading to *Nitro* in Miami on September 6. Eric said he wanted me to work a hero-versus-hero concept for a couple of months, leading into *Halloween Havoc*. The hope was that the good reaction at the house shows with Hogan might help turn WCW's sagging business around. When I walked into Eric's office at Miami *Nitro*, I hadn't been seen on TV since the interview in which I'd said I wasn't sure if I'd ever wrestle again. I waited around all day until Eric finally broke the news that I would be part of a heel run in. I said, "After all these months I've come here to do what?" Given all that had happened, having me do a run-in on someone else's match would have been an incredible waste, and really dumb booking.

At 7:59, one minute before the live show started, Eric decided that I should do an interview, and then walked alongside me to the TV entrance-way inventing what he wanted me to say. I walked out to a good pop from the crowds but went into the ring and cut a shitty promo, talking about how I was coming back soon but I didn't know when. What should've been a huge kickoff for my return was just terrible.

I think Eric knew his days were numbered. First his boss, Harvey Schiller, was gone, then on September 10, Eric was too. Bill Bush, who'd been WCW's head accountant, took over from Eric, and the first thing he did was hire Vince McMahon's now-former scriptwriter, Vince Russo. Russo, a thin New Yorker with a black beard and moustache, liked to dress only in black and had the air of a carny magician. It was Russo who'd come up with the idea for the Blue Blazer to descend from the rafters in Kansas City. As soon as Owen landed in the ring, he was supposed to trip and fall as a spoof on wrestling superheros. That's why there had been no safety line—Owen had to release himself quickly so he could deliver Russo's prat-fall. I'm not laying blame here. It's punishment enough that Russo has to live with the knowledge of his role in Owen's death.

I saw a long, empty road ahead. The business was more dead to me than it had ever been before, but I still cared enough about my career that I wanted to have one last great match. I knew the Kemper Arena was the best place to do it, and that Chris Benoit was the only guy to do it with: a tribute match for Owen right there in front of the fans who watched him die.

I knew the end of my career wasn't so far away any more. I could still put out, but I could feel the pain every night and I couldn't truthfully make the claim that I was the best in the business any more. Wrestlers seemed so much more reckless now, and the business had sunk even deeper into violence and sleaze. Often, there was no attempt at realism, which couldn't have been more clear than on September 14 when Vince himself defeated Hunter to become WWF World Champion. Wrestling belts were just props now.

I actually had to talk WCW into letting me work with Chris Benoit in honour of Owen. Like anything else that made sense, it took them a while even to get behind it, and it was Chris who got them to do it. Chris had never forgotten that Stu, and Bruce, had got him into the business. Wrestling, old style, was all about trust and respect, the business of very tough men who could set aside those prized reputations when they needed to do so in order to make each other and the business. Benoit, despite being a young man, was old school. I wanted the Benoit match to honour my dad, the workers of his generation, the boys in the dressing room, those old-time fans—and, most of all, Owen.

October 4, 1999. Kemper Arena. I could feel Owen's spirit there with me, and that he was really looking forward to watching this match. I didn't want to disappoint him, but I'd been off for so long that my conditioning and timing weren't the best. I said a prayer, asking for Owen to help me out. I'd also invited Harley to be the special guest announcer, and he'd driven for three hours with a bad back to be there.

The fans were respectful and quiet when Chris and I started. The fact was, they weren't used to babyface contests any more and it was a hard sell. Too bad, I told them in my head, you're getting an old-time match whether you like it or not!

Twenty minutes later, we had the crowd riveted to every move as we neared the finish. Mickey Jay, the ref, gave us the cue and after a hard-fought battle, Chris went for his crippler finish. I blocked it, tripping him backwards to the mat. I sprawled over Chris and somehow came up with the sharpshooter, and the Kemper Arena crowd rose as one and cheered for both of us as Chris tapped out. I could feel Owen's presence. I looked up, fighting off tears, and gave Owen one last wave. Then I hugged Chris, who broke down crying. "Chris, he's up there right now watching us." I somehow knew that this would be my last beautiful moment in the ring, ever.

Back home in the kitchen at Hart house, my mom and Stu, too frail to attend, watched with tears in their eyes.

The WWF's legal eagles countersued Martha for U.S.$75,000, plus costs, which could easily add up to millions if she lost. They asserted that Owen's contract stated any litigation against the WWF under its terms would be brought in its home state, Connecticut, where punitive damages weren't awarded. Martha's legal team argued that the contract was terminated when Owen died, that it did not cover negligence by the defendant outside the ring and that since Owen died in Missouri and the suit was filed in Missouri, it should be heard in Missouri.

On October 23, Yokozuna died of a massive heart attack in a sleazy London hotel. He was thirty-four years old and at the time of his death he topped seven hundred pounds. On that same day, Vince McMahon offered shares of the WWF to the public and became a billionaire. Within days, Linda McMahon told CNBC that the McMahons would love to settle with Martha in a way that would take care of her and the children for the rest of their lives. But no such settlement had been offered, and one of her lawyers, Ed Pipella, fired back, in the *Calgary Herald*, that the WWF's threatened countersuit could more than wipe her out financially, no matter what Linda's fine sentiments were.

At WCW, we were hanging on for dear life trying to put over Vince Russo's weird storylines. Russo thought his storylines had a lot to do with the WWF's rise in the ratings war, but he didn't get, and never would, that the best wrestling needed at least to pretend to be real. He had grand plans for me—as a heel. I told him the sympathy factor for me was too strong to pull off a heel turn, not to mention that I'd been turned so many times already. He still wanted to do this big angle on *Nitro* where I turned heel on Goldberg the day after *Starrcade '99* in Toronto. I hated it all, but I was so angry at McMahon that I hoped Russo could bring the company back to life with his radical soap-opera booking. At the *Halloween Havoc* pay-per-view on October 24, he had me pretend to injure my ankle and give up to Lex in a single-leg Boston crab as part of the buildup. After the match, Liz gave me a big hug and told me she was sorry things had got so dark for me. "Things will get better," she said, and she sweetly added that I had always been her favourite wrestler to watch. Her words meant a lot to me.

The following night, I pulled up to the back of the building in Phoenix for *Nitro*, popped my trunk and got out to get my bag. One worried little boy, wearing Hitman shades pushed up on his forehead, stood blinking at me. "How's your ankle, Hitman?" he said. I hardly pretended this stuff was real any more, but as I lifted my bag I hissed, "It's pretty sore." After signing his shades, I limped painfully off: I had too much respect for both of us not to. I didn't see enough real fans any more.

That night, Russo put together a storyline that had me face Goldberg with my "bad" ankle. I wasn't too keen on getting hurt by Goldberg for real; he'd already hurt three or four guys, including nearly breaking Haku's neck. I liked Goldberg, but I was going to use this opportunity in Phoenix to feel him out in the ring.

When I jumped on Goldberg's back, I felt like a cowboy riding a Brahma bull at the Stampede. Bill's neck was so thick it was hard for me to grip him in a sleeper. He reached up and yanked me down, taking out a referee. When I rolled out to the floor, Nash, Razor and Sid came charging out and after a tough stand Goldberg was laid out. I crawled back in to the ring just before going off the air and covered Bill for the one . . . two . . . three. This would give me my second big win over him.

As usual, there were messages from fans on my hotel phone that night, a lot of sincere good wishes and the usual number of women offering themselves up to me. Clearing my inbox, I hit the gentle voice of a woman who called herself "The Nasty Girl," telling me once again that she was going to make all my sexual dreams come true. She'd been leaving me messages after every *Nitro* for months. She called me again later that night and got me on the phone. I tried to be nice, but I finally had to be blunt with her and hung up. Some fans I'd limp for, others I had no time for at all.

On November 2, I jetted off to England to attend the U.K. premiere of *Wrestling with Shadows*. Meanwhile, a compelling documentary that Paul put together on Owen, which included interview footage of Owen that had not been used in *Shadows*, was shown on TV in Canada and the United States. While in England, I finally had a chance to catch up with Dynamite on the phone and told him I'd be more than happy to pay for any back surgery that might help him get out of his wheelchair, but he said there was nothing that could be done. He told me he'd written a book, and laughed about how he was going to include a story about Stu scooping up cat shit with a spatula while making eggs for him. Stu was such a wounded soul right now though that I worried that Dynamite telling a ridiculous story like that would be hard on his already broken heart. (Later, I read Dynamite's book, and the story was there, along with all kinds of other nasty and depressing stuff. I have not talked to him since.)

November 19, 1999. I stood talking with Ric Flair, who I was going to work with that night. As he knew, I loved to hear stories of wrestling history, and he was telling about what happened when he finally got his chance to work with the real "Nature Boy," Buddy Rogers. Rogers had walked away from the business after a falling out with the Crocketts, and was only coming back for this one match where he was about to put Flair over. Before they started, Rogers grabbed Flair by the wrists, looked him square in the eye and said, "Just remember, kid, there's only one Nature Boy!" I glanced at Flair, wondering how long it had been since anyone had called him a kid. There was only one Nature Boy and it wasn't Ric Flair. I respected Ric for hanging on, but I vowed that nobody would see me wrestle old.

Julie, my kids and my nephew Marek, Tom's son with Michelle, all flew in for the big night in Toronto, on November 21, where I was slated to win the WCW World title.

I won my match with Sting after all kinds of hokey interference, then took on Chris Benoit in the final. Chris and I worked a good solid match, with me finally fighting off his crippler and slapping on the sharpshooter. Chris tapped out, I rolled off and Mickey Jay handed me the World title. Twenty thousand Toronto fans stood in one long, rousing cheer, wanting to believe that this moment really did mean something. I held open the ropes as Julie, my kids, Marek and Wayne Gretzky's kids all climbed into the ring to celebrate my sixth World title win. (Wayne and his children had been invited to the show, and though Wayne couldn't make it, his kids had spent the day hanging around with mine, and I invited them to join in.) When I came back to the dressing room, Curt Hennig was there to greet me with a handshake. "You're the iron man, Hitman! I don't know how you keep doin' it!"

The next day Julie and the kids went home and I headed off to Detroit for *Nitro*. On the moving sidewalk at the airport, I noticed a heavy-set black woman glaring at me and studied her stare long enough to remember it.

At Cobo Hall, I kept my babyface storyline going even though Nash and Razor always arrived on the scene to interfere in my matches. The wrestling was silly, but I went along with it because that's all I could do. Over the next few weeks I somehow even won the WCW Tag belts with Goldberg as my partner. After *Nitro*, I listened to a phone message from that Nasty Girl. She said she'd seen me at Detroit airport and she was furious because apparently I'd stood her up again: the next time she saw me I'd be a dead man! I'd received a lot of weird threatening messages in my time, but I put together the look I'd got at the airport with that scary message and a chill went down my back.

I kept working as many house shows as I could because I wanted to whittle down the number of days I was required to work in order to have more time off in the summer. I worked some house shows with Goldberg down south in Alabama and Florida. Goldberg was no fun. Every night he mowed me down with his full-contact spear tackle, only to have Razor, Nash and Sid run in for the DQ to save the belt for me.

Starrcade '99 came on December 19, 1999, at the MCI Centre in Washington, D.C. I sat on my bench strapping on my knee brace, wrapping my battered wrists and knees. My ribs were sore from Goldberg spearing me; they'd been tender for at least ten years, ever since Dino Bravo knocked me into that steel fence back in 1989. I stretched and paced as I waited for my match with Goldberg. "Whatever you do out there, Bill, don't hurt me," I said. I really wanted this to be a great match.

The storyline called for the referee to get hurt and be replaced three times, with Roddy coming out at the end. After wiping out the first ref, Goldberg and I brawled out on the floor, but once the replacement ref showed up Goldberg tossed me back in the ring, like a suitcase. He reminded me of the gorilla on that old Samsonite luggage commercial. Then he had me backed into a corner and drilled me with an elbow smash that I can only compare to someone swinging a pillowcase full of bricks. It was a stiff blow that left me dazed. Goldberg knew it too and whispered in my ear, "Sorry, brother."

He grabbed me in a front face lock and wrenched me backward, wiping out the second referee. I was still groggy as I pulled myself up, and I barely moved out of the way in time as Goldberg charged me in the corner, nearly hitting his head on the post. The impact shook the whole ring, and he was lucky he didn't really hurt himself. I slid out to the floor and pulled his legs toward the post to do my figure four around the post. I threw one foot up on the apron and felt Goldberg grab it like I'd told him to, but when I fell backward he let go! My head thumped hard on the padded floor and all my weight buckled on top of me like an accordion. The crowd was chanting "Goldberg!" as I pulled myself up. I had to carry on. This was *my* heat.

To give myself time to recuperate, I rolled Goldberg in and began fiercely working his leg—neither the crowd nor Goldberg had any idea that I was hurt. He snatched me by the throat and gave me a couple of punches as the third referee tried to break us up. I snapped a boot into his knee, fired him into the ropes and as he reversed me, I heard him call, "Watch the kick!" I had no idea what kind of a kick he meant and there wasn't much room coming off the ropes. Goldberg was standing in the middle of the ring, standing sideways to me, and his right foot flew just under my right hand, which I'd thrown up in an attempt to shield my face.

WHAAAAM!

I felt like someone chopped me with a hockey stick, an agonizing blow that sent me crashing to the mat where I lay holding my neck just behind my right ear at the base of my skull.

I was thinking, I've got to get up for the finish . . . but I can't remember what it is!

I got up anyway, just in time for Goldberg to spear-tackle me like someone running me over with a car. The ref was still down and Goldberg played to the crowd. Right on cue, out came Roddy, doing his best John Wayne imitation, making his way down the aisle in a referee shirt. I have a foggy recollection of clipping Goldberg from behind and quickly twisting him into the sharpshooter. The crowd was confused when Roddy didn't even wait for Goldberg to give up to signal for the bell. When Roddy took the belt and headed back down the aisle, I was as confused as the booing fans. I jumped out after Roddy. I felt nauseous, and my head was throbbing and my vision blurred, but I managed to race up and grab him before he cleared the curtain, where he handed me the belt. On autopilot, I followed the script, but I was totally out of it as I stumbled through the curtain.

I was dazed and glassy eyed and my neck was killing me. The dressing room was almost empty because the boys had rushed to beat the crowd out of the building, except for Roddy and the WCW trainer, Danny Coach Young. I told Danny I had hurt my neck, and he apologized because all he could do was hand me a few packets of Advil. I was in such a fuzzy state of mind, I barely remember handing Marcy the car keys because I knew I wasn't capable of driving back to the hotel. As we made our way thought the dark, in an icy rain, I was slurring my speech and Marcy was very worried. She wanted me to see a doctor, but I thought—in the way you think when you've just suffered a severe concussion only you don't realize it yet—that I'd just take it slow and see how I felt in the morning.

When I staggered through the sliding doors of the Marriott, the fans, who usually stampede over top of one another to get pictures or autographs, stopped in their tracks. Clearly something wasn't right about me. The lobby was a blur, and the walls of my room were spinning when I dropped my bag and passed out on the bed.

I woke up around five the next morning still in my clothes, drenched in sweat, with a pounding headache and an aching throb in the back of my neck. I slept miserably for a couple more hours and when I checked out, the front desk gave me a message from that crazy Nasty Girl. Her note said that she'd caught a bus all the way up from Detroit after I supposedly stood her up the second time and included an even more disturbing death threat than the first one.

It was ingrained in my nature just to keep on going, so I showed up at the building in Baltimore, still too out of it to know how out of it I really was. I went over everything with Russo as he set the stage for my heel turn. After the horrible finish the night before, I forfeited the World title on *Nitro* and gave Goldberg an immediate rematch. It was a total farce, with Nash and Hall hitting the ring and me double-crossing Goldberg again for a flat ending.

The next day in Salisbury, Maryland, for *Thunder*, I told Russo that I was badly hurt from Goldberg's kick and that I thought I might have a concussion. He still wanted me to work a match with Benoit, with Jeff Jarrett coming out to double-team him. Goldberg would charge out and spear Jarrett while I fled the scene with cameras following and Goldberg coming after me in hot pursuit. I'd race to my rented Cadillac, which would be parked on the back ramp with the keys in the ignition, and just as Goldberg reached my car I'd zoom out of the building. We'd go off the air with a seething Goldberg punching out the windows of a limo, a sharp steel gimmick hidden in his fist.

While Russo went over everything, I reasoned (in the foggy way a concussed person reasons) that I could do all that easy enough. All I could think about was getting home for Christmas. That night I had a good solid match with Benoit, who did his best to take it easy. Jarrett came out and then the one-man tank, Goldberg. When Goldberg speared Jeff, I ran down the aisle, jumped in my car and floored it out the back ramp just as Goldberg caught up and pounded furiously on my car windows. What nobody noticed was that as I pulled out, my car hit the icy pavement and I skidded out of control, having had no time to put on a seat belt, so there I was with a concussion, barrelling head-on toward a huge TV production truck! I thought of Owen in that instant. What would the world think if I got killed ploughing my car into a TV truck for some stupid stunt? People would say, "You'd think Owen's stupid brother would know better than that!"

Luckily the tires hit a patch of dry pavement and I burned rubber past the truck to safety. Even with my head full of fuzz I was plenty pissed off and came steaming back to blast Russo, but I completely forgot about it when I saw a worried Goldberg holding his arm in the air with blood pouring everywhere. The gimmick he was using had failed to break the window, so Goldberg decided that he'd simply break it himself. He did, but he sliced a twelve-inch gash the length of his forearm all the way to the bone. Paramedics tried to staunch the flow of blood and raced him to a hospital. I felt terrible for him; for the first time this big brute of a man looked very afraid as he was loaded into the ambulance. I showered and then left, not even remembering what it was that I'd been so livid about only minutes earlier—that I'd nearly got *killed* doing some stupid shit from the same screwball who scripted the stunt that killed Owen.

I bought Julie a ring for Christmas, which she unfortunately took to mean more than I intended. When my mom called to congratulate me, I downplayed it. When it became clear that the ring was just a present, Julie's disappointment put a damper on everything.

Over Christmas at Stu's, Ellie and I had another shouting match with Stu in the middle again. Stu was far more deaf than he was blind and he felt obligated to defend her, as he always did. I'd about had enough of Ellie. The way I tore into her put a scare into Stu. I shouted, "Ellie, this has nothing to do with you or me! This is all about Martha's decision to sue Vince for killing her husband! Your brother! How in the hell can you work hand-in-hand with Vince against your dead brother's wife and kids and your very own parents? How can you sleep at night?"

"Real easy," Ellie shot back.

Stu, who couldn't hear anything, kept defending her. "I don't believe Ellie is doing that!"

"Dad, she'll tell you herself!"

My mom took up for me, telling Ellie that she and Stu chose to support Martha and it had nothing to do with me. Ellie lashed out, accusing her of always taking my side. I'd had a nonstop headache from hell ever since Goldberg's kick and by the end of this scene my head felt like it was going to explode.

In Houston for *Nitro* on December 27, I went looking for Bill Bush and Vince Russo. I could barely remember Christmas, despite how crappy it was. I still wasn't sleeping well, and my head was pounding with the constant pain in the back of my neck. I told Bush: "I'm not a stuntman, I'm a pro wrestler, and from now on everything I do needs to be done in the ring." They both apologized profusely for the circumstances that put me in the state I was in; yet not ten minutes later, Russo told me that he needed me to drive a giant monster truck over the top of Sycho Sid's rental car, with Sid in it! As out of it as I was, I looked at Russo and said, "Are you guys for real? I just told you that I don't do stunts. I'm a goddamn wrestler."

On top of everything else, Russo was putting me with Jerry Flynn, an ex-kickboxer with limited pro wrestling ability. That night, while brawling out on the floor, Flynn leaped up with a spin kick and hit me so hard in the guts that I crumpled to the mat. I struggled to recover because either I had to or take more of the same. I finished the match, but I wondered why WCW thought the best way for me to get through my concussion was to work with a stiff rookie. Then I watched a fully loaded Cadillac with eleven miles on the odometer get crushed by the monster truck—all for a thirty-second ending to *Nitro*. Stu would've cried if he'd been there.

The first night I was at home again, I had a fantastic dream. I was sitting with Owen at my kitchen table. He had on his favourite baggy blue sweatshirt, and we actually laughed and talked about all the problems in the family since he died. He shook his head as though we both knew this would happen and told me he never had any doubts that I'd be fending off various siblings. In the dream, I got to tell him how much I loved him and he seemed at peace, which did a lot for me and my shattered heart and battered brain.

As the dream began to fade, I could feel myself pleading for it to keep going—don't let me wake up, I have so much left to tell him—but it dissolved and Owen was gone. I woke up with the sense that we'd really talked. That morning I found a thank-you poem from Martha tucked in my front door.

Bret's Poem

*Let it be you
who comes to bring the light, who
guides me with his hand held tight
let it be you
who navigates through all the grey
to help me see a better day
let it be you
who listens endlessly of broken lives
and shattered dreams
let it be you
who sees the ugliness of people's
souls in times like this
let it be you
who's tall while others fall, whose
heart is purest of all
let it be you
whose love and tenderness will not
let me slip into this great abyss
let it be you
who stands by faithful friend
until the bitter end*
(written with love by Martha, December 29, 1999)

As the millennium came to a close, I was relieved that 1999 was over. What a horrible year for me and all the Harts. At least Bill Bush called me at home to thank me for all I was doing. He asked me how long I could keep going and I told him: "I still have a few good years left."

Then my old friend Wilk called and told me to turn on the TV. So there I sat, at first amused but then disgusted, watching the embarrassing conclusion to Bruce's Stampede Wrestling show. Diana did a run-in to save fourteen-year-old Harry, who'd been dragged into his first angle. Soon, even Ellie was in the ring taking a bump. I could only roll my eyes in disgust. A farce like this made all of us Harts look bad.

45

THE LAST DANCE

PEOPLE WITH CONCUSSIONS are the last ones to figure out how badly hurt they are. I was more responsible than anyone for downplaying my condition to myself and everyone else. Somewhere inside me, a fearful voice cried out that I was seriously hurt, but that same voice warned me to quit listening to my brain because it was my brain itself that was damaged. So I let myself go on believing that the problem was a sore neck.

I drifted through every day in a pale-faced, sweaty, head-pounding stupor, pacified to the point of numbness by the four Advils I took every three hours. The turn of the millennium floated right past me. By January 3, 2000, I was in Greensboro, South Carolina, for *Nitro*, and in too much of a haze to heed my own vow to Bush and Russo one week earlier: that I'd only do wrestling and in a ring. I rubbed the back of my head as Russo laid out the script to hype my upcoming pay-per-view title match on January 14 with Sycho Sid. That night, *Nitro* opened as cameras caught Sid attacking me as I came into the building. I was thrown into backstage walls and knocked into a stack of steel trusses that broke apart, spilling everywhere, nearly clipping my knees and ankles and coming close to crushing all my toes. Working a backstage brawl was far more dangerous than an actual wrestling match. I was soon battered to the concrete floor, over thick wire cables and equipment boxes, where Sid stood pummelling me with a barrage of punches.

Only a few hours earlier, road agent Terry Taylor had successfully begged me to fill in for Kevin Nash for the rest of the week because Nash was out with a concussion, of all things. With nobody else to replace Nash in the main events, I said I would, even as I reminded Terry that I thought I might have a concussion of my own. Guys such as Taylor and Russo were quick to tell me how much this all was appreciated, assuring me that I'd be protected in every way possible. Unfortunately, this was a promise that neither one of them could keep or even had a right to make, because they weren't the ones in the ring with me.

Every night I crawled into bed, my head pounding and my neck aching: my solution was more Advil and another fitful sleep. In Florence, South

Carolina, for *Thunder*, I opened up the show standing glassy-eyed in my nWo T-shirt, along with nWo members Jeff Jarrett, Scotty Steiner and Kevin Nash, who appeared not to be suffering from a concussion after all. Russo's new acting commissioner, Terry Funk, had just ordered me to face him in a hard-core match later in the show. Somewhere in the back of my mind I remembered having his retirement match with him back in Amarillo. With a scornful over-the-top sneer, I coldly cut a promo: "I think I just might have to kill you tonight, Terry Funk!" I laughed to myself at how ridiculous I sounded, but I gave Russo what he wanted because I'd all but given up. I also knew that I could trust Terry with my body a helluva lot more I could trust the other WCW wrestlers.

Terry did all he could to go easy on my head, even as we brawled around the ring and on the floor with chairs, rubber bats and garbage cans. I beat Terry hard, loud and mercilessly with a steel chair, right down to his knees, because he made me promise to lay it in. Terry was old school, the King of Hardcore for real. He spent most of the match selling for me, flopping around like a fish. When he finally charged me with a steel chair, I got my hands up and deflected it completely. So far so good. I staggered off in retreat, making my way up the aisle as Terry grabbed a fistful of my hair and tossed me into a big, rolling canvas laundry bin that just happened to be sitting right there. With my legs hanging over the sides, I couldn't pull myself up into a better position. Terry spun it around and pushed it hard toward the ring. I braced myself by wrapping my arms around my head, but when I spilled out I whacked the back of my head on the heavy wooden lid of the cart, which made a sound like a dropped watermelon.

After the match, Terry felt terrible, but it wasn't his fault—I shouldn't have been in a hard-core match with a concussion in the first place. I gulped down another handful of Advils and didn't give it another thought, but I sure wished my horrible headaches would go away. And when I finally called Marcy, back in Calgary, to set up a doctor's appointment, it was because I thought I needed my sore neck looked at, not my head.

I filled in for Nash against Sid in Roanoke, Lowell and Utica. Each night I took a choke slam and a powerbomb. Sid did everything he could to set me down as lightly as he could, but it was nearly impossible. I took my lumps with little complaint.

In Utica, New York, I was needed to make a call to a radio station using the phone in an office across from the dressing room. I stripped down to my black singlet and left Doug Dillenger sitting outside my dressing room like a fat old sheriff to guard my stuff. Over the past year, Dillenger and his crack security team had allowed every one of my leather ring jackets to be stolen by fans until I stopped wearing them. After the call to the radio station, I returned to my dressing room to find Doug snoozing and all my wrestling gear stolen, except for one pink and white boot. Amazingly, the thieves never thought to grab my wallet, which was in the pocket of my jeans still hanging there, or my Rolex, which was tucked into my shoe.

On January 9, I worked in State College, Pennsylvania, wearing my work-out gear. That night I got a phone message from Martha letting me know that a judge had been picked and the trial date was set for February 5, 2001. She could at least see light at the end of the tunnel now.

I also got a message from Stu telling me that he and my mom agreed completely with everything I'd written in my column that Saturday in the *Calgary Sun*. I'd written an impassioned piece about the state of the business and how, when a fan asked me if wrestling is real, I realized that I didn't even know the answer to that question any more! It once bothered me when people thought wrestling was fake, and now it bothered me that they thought we were really hurting ourselves and one another: the sad part was that we were! In the column, I wrote that the colossal pulverizing that Goldberg gave me had been real, and so were Jerry Flynn's stiff kicks. When The Hitman tried to kill Sycho Sid with a monster truck, that was fake, but when I careened out of control and nearly crashed my rental car into the television truck, that was real. I'd written about how my match in Kansas City with Chris Benoit was the ghost of what wrestling used to be, but what I had always thought it was meant to be. And I asked myself, in the column, how far I could bend without breaking in order to help WCW beat Vince McMahon. Maybe I'd gone too far already. Maybe the whole wrestling business was fucked up now, including me.

I didn't know when I got up on January 10, 2000, that this would be the day I'd have the very last match of my twenty-three-year career. My head ached miserably and it was a long drive from State College to Syracuse, where I caught an early morning flight to Buffalo. I dropped my bags on the floor at the Avis car rental counter and made small talk with the lady working there. I happened to glance over my shoulder and caught Nasty Girl poking her head out from behind a cement pillar across the street. I was tired, fed up and sick of the threat of her doing God-knows-what to me. I matter-of-factly asked the Avis lady, "Have you ever seen a real-life stalker before?"

She couldn't help but notice this large girl poking her head out from behind the pillar over my shoulder, and she began taking me more seriously. "You're not kidding, are you?"

"No, I'm not."

She asked me if I'd mind if she called the airport police and I told her that not only would I not mind, I would greatly appreciate it. Within a few minutes, three policemen showed up and we had a brief chat. Two of the officers walked me to my car, while one headed over to ask Nasty Girl a few questions. I drove off to my hotel.

I called Julie when I got to the hotel, and we'd opened up our next round of peace talks when we were interrupted by a knock at my door. I set the phone down and found one of the policemen I'd just said goodbye to standing there. He looked a little rattled, and asked me if I'd come make a statement. Nasty Girl had attacked a cop with a knife. I told Julie I had to go, and I'd explain it all later.

Sitting at airport police headquarters, I couldn't help but hear loud wails from a not-too-distant holding cell, followed by the thuds of Nasty Girl's powerful kicks. The officers around me kept shaking their heads in amazement at the sheer power and volume of her rage. An exasperated cop finally came out of the holding cell, slamming the door behind her. She told her fellow officers, "If you want her wig off, you'll have to do it yourselves!" Apparently they'd needed to remove her wig to check whether she was carrying a concealed weapon in it! The cops then gathered in a circle and drew matchsticks to see who'd be the lucky one to take the wig off. Finally the cop who'd lost burst out of Nasty Girl's cell letting out his best war cry while shaking a long black mane above his head, "I got it! I got it!" I signed my statement: the policemen whom she'd attacked would ensure that she didn't bother me for a while.

When I arrived at the arena for *Nitro*, I found that Russo had concocted a storyline around me being forced by Terry Funk to wrestle a title match against my own nWo team member Kevin Nash. I'd hoped to be off that night, but instead I had to hurry away to buy black skater shorts, new running shoes and knee pads and change in time to air live clips of me and Kevin getting worked up and dressing for the match. With my head thick and thumping and that stabbing pain in my neck, I taped my ankles, wrapped my broken-down knees and smeared my lower back with gobs of Icy Hot. Just another day in my pain-filled life.

Kevin had read my last *Calgary Sun* column and told me: "You shouldn't be too hard on yourself, it's not your fault the business is so fucked up." He promised me we'd take it real easy and then he surprised me when he said, "The match I had with you back at *Survivor* in 1995 was the best damn match I ever had. You're the best worker this business ever knew. And that's the God's honest truth." I smiled and thanked him, wondering all the while why Kevin had put so many rocks in my path at WCW if that was the way he truly felt.

I made my way out to the ring, WCW champion of the world, with the big gold belt hung on my shoulder. I felt less than myself in a sleeveless nWo shirt and runners. If I'd been able to foresee the future, I would have strutted out there in my pink and black tights and my shades, and I'd have climbed all four turnbuckles taking in the faces of the fans who loved me in those final moments. I was Humpty Dumpty about to fall and never be put back together again. I'll forever imagine how it could have been, with fans, young and old, slowly rising, proudly standing and clapping and waving signs. In my mind's eye, I read them: HITMAN YOU WERE THE BEST; WE'LL MISS YOU. But I was the last one to know that this would be my last dance.

The bell rang, and Kevin and I worked hard and well together. He protected me as best he could. I chopped him down at the knees, and we let Russo's silly storyline unfold; it wasn't long before Kevin dropped me hard with a punishing sidewalk slam. I was rocked, and the next thing I saw was Arn Anderson on the floor cracking Kevin across the back with a rubber lead pipe, which was my cue. I forced myself up to fend Arn off with a steel chair, when suddenly Sycho Sid was behind me. As I turned, he mistimed his frontal kick, but somehow I still managed to clunk myself on the head with the chair anyway. Sid snatched me by the throat, hoisted me up over his head with one hand and held me, then drove me down into the mat with a choke slam. He pulled me right back up and proceeded to give me his powerbomb. I tucked my chin to protect myself as I floated to the mat in slow motion, but I landed flat and hard. Lying on my back staring up at the lights, I saw millions of tiny silver dots everywhere, a galaxy of stars. Like a TV falling from a high shelf, my tube smashed and I lay there not moving. I couldn't help but think, This must be what you see in the seconds before you die. I thought of Owen and tears filled my eyes. Then I managed to roll out of the ring to see Terry Funk racing out, brandishing a flaming branding iron and pretending to burn Kevin with it. By the time I sat down to unlace my boots, I'd already forgotten enough of what had just happened that I complained only about the pain in my neck.

The next day, in Erie, Pennsylvania, for *Thunder*, I told Russo again that I was hurt. He replied with a confident grin that I wasn't to worry—I didn't have to wrestle. Instead he had a storyline built around me turning babyface, appearing to be taken hostage by a hostile nWo, only to swerve everyone by the end of the show when I'd double-cross Funk and turn heel again. I hated it, but at that point I'd have done anything not to actually have to wrestle. I was so foggy it didn't occur to me that I could have just told them I was hurt and gone home, but maybe I stayed because it had always been so ingrained in me to keep going no matter what. Besides, Russo was on such thin ice I wanted to do whatever I could for him. I don't know why. It was just my nature, I guess. With hindsight, as soon as I told my WCW bosses I thought I had a concussion, they should have sent me home.

I opened the show coming out in a T-shirt and jeans for a heartfelt in-ring interview. I apologized to the fans for taking the wrong road and told them I was so disgusted with myself that I didn't deserve their respect. The camera cut to a fan holding a sign that read, RESPECT BRET HART! I saw one older woman in the bleachers cheering and jumping for joy, and I hated the thought of seeing their faces when I turned heel again at the end of the night. Then I challenged the nWo, and when they came out, Kevin declared, "Tonight, Hitman, your career will be finished, maybe even your life!"

All through the show there were clips of me being held hostage, choked and bullied with baseball bats by Nash, Steiner and Jarrett for my disloyalty to the nWo. They even burned some pink tights—not mine but they said they were—in effigy, setting them alight in a trash can. At the end, I made my escape, limping out into the ring holding a bat, and I again challenged the nWo to fight me. Seconds later, we were all taunting one another with bats and chairs. The three-to-one odds were too much for Terry Funk and a cavalry of WCW babyfaces to take, and they charged the ring to rescue me. I saw the old lady in the bleachers clapping and cheering like a school girl.

Then Arn tossed a pail of water in my face so everyone could see that my blackened eyes were only make-up. Unfortunately for Russo, nobody understood it. So I smashed Funk with a rubber bat to reveal the double-cross. I felt like a total piece of shit as the nWo beat all the babyfaces down with bats. And my heart filled with shame at the sight of the old woman in the stands now sobbing like a baby.

On Thursday, January 13, I sat in Dr. Meeuwisse's office in Calgary, telling him about Goldberg's ferocious kick to my neck while he felt around with his fingers. I told him about taking the choke slam and seeing silver dots. He noticed that I was slurring my words and asked me if I thought I had a concussion. I told him maybe a slight one. He probed me with questions and then recited some numbers and asked me to repeat them back to him backward. I couldn't. Then he gave me five random words that he'd ask me to remember in a few minutes. I couldn't. He studied me, then asked me again if I thought I had a concussion. I told him again, a slight one.

He asked me what I was taking for my headaches and when I told him, "Four Advils every three hours," he shook his head and told me they'd eat a hole in my stomach as he wrote me a proper script.

"I can feel a hole in the back of your neck the size of a quarter." He felt around the back of my skull. "This part here feels like hamburger."

"I have a pay-per-view on Sunday. I'm the main event."

With a dry smile, he said, "You're not going anywhere. The problem with people that have concussions is that you think you're okay, but you're not." He paused and crossed his arms, looking me in the eye. "I hate to be the one to have to tell you this, but your career is probably over."

"What happens if I don't stop?"

"The boxing world likes to pretend that Muhammad Ali's problems today are all related to Parkinson's disease, but the simple truth is Ali kept on boxing after being concussed. All those blows to the head cost him. You're no different than him, and I'm sure you don't want to end up like him. I don't want you doing *anything*. It could take up to a year before we can even determine how bad this is. No working out, no flying, no watching TV, no listening to loud music."

"When I call WCW, what should I tell them?"

"You tell them your doctor has diagnosed you with a *severe* concussion."

"Yeah, but who are you?" I meant, Why would WCW believe him?

"I'm the chairman of the NHL injury committee. Tell them to call me."

Driving home, tears came to my eyes as I thought about calling J.J. Dillon with the news. After twenty-three years, I didn't want to go out like this. What would I do now?

By that weekend, Vince Russo had been sacked and WCW rewrote their storylines without me; it was like I had never been there. I had been erased.

I sat home staring blankly at the walls with the TV off and the lights dimmed. I couldn't even read, my head hurt so much. Julie was pissed off and wasn't talking to me again. For comfort, I relied on the steadfast loyalty of a pug dog named Coombs, which Dallas had given me. He rested his head on my lap doing his best Jim Neidhart impression with a face that looked even sadder than mine.

I didn't want to lose myself to brooding, and Dr. Meeuwisse told me to find a hobby. When I was chosen by Calgary's Glenbow Museum as one of six guest curators to help design an exhibit paying tribute to Canadian heroes, I really put my heart into it. One of my choices was Tom Longboat, one of Canada's most famous long-distance marathon runners in the early 1900s. My mom surprised me with a story about how Longboat had run against her father, Harry. "My father impressed upon me that a marathon runner never, ever turns his head to look back," Helen said. "It's just not done. It throws off the timing. But in a big race one day, my father could hear footsteps behind him, always there, and so, for just a moment, he turned and his gaze was caught by the brown eyes of Tom Longboat, only a step behind him. Then Longboat edged past him! I don't know who won the race, but my father never forgot the speed and grace of that kid or the look in his eye."

WCW desperately needed me to make a tour of Germany in February: I was the headliner and it was sold out. I'd only step into the ring to say a few words to the fans. Reluctantly, Dr. M cleared me to fly, mostly because I was afraid I'd be fired if I didn't. Duggan, Sting, Knobbs and Liz all reached out to me with supportive arms. A big, young, white-haired kid from Philadelphia named Jerry Tuite, who worked as The Wall, insisted on carrying my bags for me. Still, I couldn't help but see that most of the other wrestlers didn't believe I was hurt. When I slurred my words, they grinned at me like I was putting them on, which hurt because I had never faked an injury in my "real" life or missed a match on purpose. But there were so many worked injuries in WCW that when somebody got hurt for real, hardly anybody believed it.

On the bus in Hamburg, I had a talk with Jeff Jarrett, who had been one of Owen's closest friends. He told me he was offended when Martha's lawyers pressed him about any possible philandering Owen might have been doing, and had refused to even call them back. I told him that they were just doing their job, checking out every aspect of Owen's life — and for the sake of Owen's kids, he needed to talk to them. He told me how he and Debra McMichael, his valet, had been up next after Owen's match in Kansas City and backstage everyone was running around in a panic, as Jeff stood at the Gorilla position. Owen's dead body was wheeled past him at the same time as two firm hands shoved him hard through the curtain, "Go! Go! Go!" He told me he was sorry he went out to the ring that night and that he bawled his eyes out the whole time, as he did again just telling me about it.

Terry Funk had been listening to us, and now he asked me how my family was doing. I told him how crazy things had got up at Hart house. Terry knew the Harts pretty well, and he gave it some deep thought before telling me: "Everybody's crazy. The whole world's crazy. You're crazy. I'm crazy. It's all about to what degree you're crazy." In my concussed state, Terry made a lot of sense.

Poor Davey was a case in point; he was a shell of his former self and still hooked on morphine. Being in no shape to wrestle, he hadn't lasted long in the WWF, but Vince still said he needed him, so he headed off to a rehab program in Georgia. In answer to my criticisms of the year-end show on *Stampede Wrestling*, that involved various non-wrestling members of the Hart family, Bruce ripped into me on the Stampede Wrestling website for taking shots at Davey in my column. He defended Davey, saying he was "a damn loyal and trusted trooper of the clan who'd been unjustly maligned and made to look bad." Bruce had as much right to express his opinion as I did, but he didn't know the truth.

I felt more and more estranged from so many people in my family because nobody stood shoulder to shoulder with me in defending Martha, except my mom. Keith, Wayne, Alison and Ross all steered clear of Ellie and Diana, supporting me only from behind the scenes. I understood why Georgia was on Ellie's side: she had spent her whole life defending Ellie and turning a blind eye to Ellie's actions, and she would never forget Ellie's support when she went through the loss of her son, Matt.

Struggling with my concussion, I'd begun ducking Martha's calls: it was too hard to listen to her rant about how Ellie and Diana were bullying my parents into settling with Vince like a heel tag team. Martha said, and I agreed, that Diana, Ellie and even Bruce thought that life is like wrestling in that they can just turn themselves heel and then turn back babyface over Christmas, expecting to be forgiven.

At the building in Hamburg, Terry Taylor handed me a five-page script and told me I had to cut a heel promo on my German fans. "I won't do it!" I said. "Just let me go out and say a few words." I walked out to chants of "Owen! Owen!" and explained that I'd suffered a concussion that might end my career and if I didn't get another chance I wanted to tell my German fans I'd never forget them. I talked about how much I loved Owen and how the last match we ever had was right here in Hamburg. The emotional outpouring from the crowd was powerful enough that it took me a long time to do my walk-around. When I finally came back through the curtain, Terry Taylor hung his head, ashamed that he asked me to rip into fans who loved me so much.

Each night after his hard-core matches, Brian Knobbs came back to the dressing room with a new ugly gash in his head. I couldn't help but draw him on the blackboard, showing the progression from day one of the tour, when he was smiling and happy, to days three and four, looking more bloodied and battered. In the last drawing, he was in a wheelchair with lumps on his head and the caption was STARTLING NEW EVIDENCE! PRO WRESTLING IS REAL! Brian laughed and hugged me when he saw it.

On the last night of the tour, in Leipzig, a four-year-old girl in a white dress climbed into the ring with flowers, ran up to me and jumped into my arms. She held me tight like she was taking care of me now. Everybody was crying and chanting for Owen. Every outstretched hand I touched around the ring empowered me like God's angels boosting my batteries.

I had one last bus ride with the boys. I have a vague memory of The Wall taking a handful of pills and of someone shaving his eyebrows. Ric Flair made the mistake of standing in the aisle and when the driver hit the brakes he took an ugly fall into the stairwell. When he got up, very slowly, I wondered how much longer he could keep going. I didn't tempt fate any more and was happy to have my seat belt on, tight.

WCW spared no expense, putting me on the Concorde to rocket to New York City for a toy fair. I was happy to have the chance to experience such sophisticated speed before they retired it. At the toy fair I met fellow Calgarian Todd McFarlane, creator of *Spawn*. I was a big fan of his comics and we joked about his old Aberhart high school beating Manning in basketball but never in wrestling!

At that convention I saw the coolest Hitman action figures ever created, but nobody would ever see them. Unbeknownst to anyone, and like the Concorde, WCW was almost out of business.

From the toy fair, I was beamed across America to Las Vegas for a signing at The Nitro Grill. I had some Hitman dolls in my overhead bag and every few minutes one of them would call out, "Ouch!" which got me a lot of strange looks for the whole flight. After the signing, I dashed off to make a flight home, but once we were in the air they announced that all flights were backed up and it didn't look like we'd land in Salt Lake City on time to make my connection. My head pounded, and every time I looked out the window at the clouds below the mountain peaks I thought of heaven and Owen. Soon my mind wandered to the thought of him lying on the mat like a dying bird after hitting a car windshield. I thought, I need to get home, Owen. Just then a woman passenger collapsed in the aisle right beside me, and the flight attendant feverishly worked on her. "We're losing her," she called out to another attendant. A runway was cleared at the Salt Lake City airport so we could land, the woman was met by paramedics and I raced across the terminal and squeezed through the doors of my plane home just as they were closing.

That night was a combination of heart-break and wonder. That's when I had a most powerful dream about Owen, who woke me from a deep sleep. He had tears in his eyes and was angry. "What is a life worth?" he said. "So is that all I'm worth? Fucking kill me and I'm worth $36 million? Is that it?" I told him, "Owen, it's not about the money. You know that." He was also seething about Ellie and Diana, and I didn't know how to comfort him as big tears slowly dripped down his cheeks. This dream haunted me enough that at the time I kept it to myself. But it didn't surprise me, afterward, when the next day Martha told me she had come up with a settlement number for Vince's lawyers — $32 million, close enough to my dream to spook me. I haven't dreamed of Owen since then.

I kept waiting for the headaches to fade and my life to return to normal, but every time I saw Dr. M, he told me it was going to take time. When I told him I couldn't feel the hole in my neck, he asked me to lay on a padded table in his office and told me to relax my head in his hands. As he poked around, he slipped his finger an inch deep into my neck.

I told him I cried all the time, and asked whether it was normal when even a shaving commercial could bring me to tears. He looked me in the eyes and said, "You're gonna start crying right now, aren't you?" I instantly blinked back tears, thinking, What the fuck is wrong with me?

Again, he told me it was all part of the concussion: my brain was like the squares on a soccer ball and the square that triggers pleasure had been bruised. He arranged for all kinds of brain tests with world-renowned specialists in Toronto and Montreal, and he even sent me to a psychologist. I was trying to take it easy, but simple things like carrying my groceries, tying my shoes or doing shoulder checks while I drove only aggravated the never-ending headache from hell. Steak tasted like liver and my libido disappeared. I was afraid I'd never get better.

I showed up to see my parents every other day, only to get into it with Ellie about *Survivor Series* yet again. Diana would join in, screaming at me that everything was my fault because I wouldn't drop the belt to Shawn Michaels. Diana, Ellie and even Bruce hated that Paul Jay's documentary, which had now been seen all over the world, portrayed me as some kind of Canadian hero: a whole new audience beyond the wrestling world now respected me for standing up for what was right.

Ellie left me a phone message demanding to know what options my parents had and that someone needed to enlighten her as to why this was the way things had to go. I wasn't even sure what she meant, and it was beyond me to understand why she kept calling me about the lawsuit when our parents and Martha made all the decisions having to do with it. In her message, Ellie said that she had no hard feelings and that she and Diana hadn't done anything wrong. But the truth was, unbeknownst to anyone at the time, they'd long since faxed Jerry McDivitt at the WWF a copy of Garry Robb's entire case file, which my mom had left on her desk. All I ever truly asked of Ellie and Diana was for them to stop making comments about Owen's case until we knew what happened. I kept saying, "Just do what Owen would want you to do," but they wouldn't listen. I knew that our confrontations would ultimately lead to the destruction of the Hart family and thought Vince must be laughing at how easy it was to play the Harts against one another.

Over the next few months, the only joy I got was when I took my parents to watch the real Hitmen, who were first in the Western Hockey League (WHL) and making another run for the Memorial Cup. The only time I ever saw my dad forget his broken heart after Owen died was one night when the Hitmen won a game in overtime, and he rose up to his feet jubilantly clapping as hard as he could.

One time, Stu asked me what it would take to make peace with Ellie and Diana. Maybe it was selfish of me, but I could only shake my head and tell him sadly, "Out of respect for Owen, I can't."

I kept myself busy doing promotional work for WCW in order to receive half—and then a quarter—of my salary. According to my contract, they could fire me any time after six weeks if I couldn't wrestle. If I did appearances, they kept paying me, but the longer I was out of the ring the less they paid. Dr. M told me that it'd be at least nine more months before we'd know anything. Despite my best efforts, it became more clear to me every day that I'd evolved into a wrestling tragedy, just as I'd feared. Thank God I had thought to take out an insurance policy from Lloyds of London to cover me.

It made little sense to me, or anyone else, when I was flown to *Nitro* in Denver on April 10 that year. But as I was asked, I charged into the ring, bashed Hogan with a chair and in an act of pathetic desperation, Hogan juiced big time.

Good guys don't last long in a wrestling office, especially when times are bad. Soon after that *Nitro*, Bill Bush was fired and replaced by Brad Segal, a TV exec who knew even less about the wrestling business than his predecessors. Bischoff and Russo were back and, ironically, the new storyline centred around two failed "experts" joining together to save WCW.

By the time I did *Thunder* in Memphis on May 2, every wrestler knew the WCW ship was sinking. It didn't surprise me to spot Lex and Liz openly sipping long-neck beers on the hood of their car at the back of the building. For some reason, Jarrett was called upon to smash a gimmicked guitar over my back. Things had got so bad that on May 7, Owen's birthday, a 150-pound actor named David Arquette won the WCW World title from Jarrett at the Kemper Arena.

That same day I was home in Calgary. I'd been scheduled to be in Kansas City to be deposed by Jerry McDivitt, but it was cancelled at the last minute, so I drove to Owen's grave for the first time in a while. I found myself telling the black marble monument, adorned with flowers and weathered cards and letters, that it was time for me to pick up the pieces. Just then two jackrabbits hopped right past me. I wondered if they were brothers. I wondered if Owen's death was some kind of colossal super rib that he was subjecting the whole family to in order to expose our shortcomings. It had ruined us and it would never, ever get better. I told Owen I loved him, that I'd fight to the end for him, and then broke down hard.

Diana had begun a serious romance with one of Bruce's novice wrestlers, a young kid named James. No one could blame her, but it didn't help things when she phoned Davey to tell him about it while he was dealing with the worst phase of rehab. He immediately checked himself out and flew home. There were several explosive clashes between Diana, Davey and Stu at Hart house, including one where Davey inadvertently knocked Stu down and hurt Stu's shoulder. The police were called and Davey made the front page of the *Calgary Sun*, being led away in handcuffs. Bruce kindly offered Davey a place to stay.

Before I got hurt, I'd promised to do some appearances to promote a Hitman photo book. Concussed or not, I did major talk shows where they'd invariably ask me about Owen. Inadvertently, I became the spokesperson for the rights of wrestlers and the wrongs of the business. I talked of the need for a wrestlers' union and wrestling schools, and I condemned the stupidity of backyard wrestling, a fad where young teens often put one another in the hospital because of real hard-core matches. I didn't feel comfortable being the voice of everything negative about the business because I still had a lot of friends making a living in it, but I still had a lot of passion for my art form. It was being killed off, and I felt the need to defend it.

A while before, I had taken on Bruce Allen as a manager. In June that year, he told me he'd always had his doubts that I was hurt. I was about to leave for Montreal to see Dr. Karen Johnston at McGill University to take comprehensive brain tests. Concussions are still largely misunderstood, and the medical world was only starting to see how broad-ranging their effects can be, from symptoms that last only a few minutes to those that change a person forever. I underwent various brain scans, X-rays and a functional MRI, which all left my head pounding like a drum.

Some of the tests were at Montreal General Hospital, where I met a young man of about nineteen by the name of Antoine. His girlfriend spotted me coming through the front door and then she and his brother loaded Antoine up in his wheelchair and found me in the radiology department. I felt kind of silly talking to them wearing only a little blue hospital gown and slippers, but Antoine was a huge fan of mine and was dying of cancer. His girlfriend told me that with three tumors in his brain he was in a lot of pain. He told me that I was his hero, how he cried after *Survivor Series*, and that wrestling wasn't the same after that. I said, yes, that was the day that wrestling died. Then he spoke about Owen and broke down crying in his wheelchair, and I changed my mind and thought, No, *that* was the day wrestling died.

But all of it seemed irrelevant in the face of the fact that Antoine only had a few days left to live. He'd bravely accepted it and smiled when he told me the first person he'd look for in heaven would be Owen. He joked about delivering any messages I might have and I told him, "Just tell Owen I miss him. Oh . . . and tell him I know it's him ribbing us all."

For three nights in a row, I visited Antoine in his hospital room until late in the evenings, talking about his girlfriend, the world and wrestling. When I told him stories about Owen's pranks, he laughed until he cried and it really filled my heart.

Everywhere I went, the people of Montreal apologized for what happened to me with Vince in their city, but they had nothing to apologize for. Montreal had always been very good to me.

Death and sadness weighed me down, and for no damn reason at all I ended up at a strip bar. Montreal's beautiful and skilful nude dancers were without a doubt the best in the world, and I lost myself in their moves. The boss welcomed me and played Tina Turner's "Simply the Best" as a compliment. I smiled at the memory of how Jim and I had hung our tag belts over the perfect breasts of two French beauties back in our old Hart Foundation days.

A few days later, back in Calgary, I got the call that Antoine had died. I was only privileged to know him for a short time, but I'll never forget him.

Ellie and Jim were making headlines of their own, with the police now breaking up their shouting matches; she had served him with a restraining order. Jim had been hired on by Vince as a talent scout, and sometimes we'd meet up to drink a few beers and I'd help him fabricate names for the scouting report he'd send on to Jim Ross. There were many who wondered why I never had any problems with Jim after Owen's death. Why would I have had problems? Jim never once made any comment about Owen's case, which is all that Martha ever asked of the family.

My mom, who'd only just recovered from a blood clot and an irregular heartbeat, told me that tragedy and greed are what made some of my siblings react irrationally. To my mind, the Hart family had turned into *The Jerry Springer Show*: Davey, whom Bruce had taken in, had just became involved with Bruce's wife, Andrea, who'd feuded with Diana for years. Poor Bruce was now having loud shouting matches with Davey, with the police never far behind.

The stress of it all took its toll on Stu. He was soon hospitalized with pneumonia. Then Davey overdosed on morphine. Then one of the grandkids accidentally burned Katie's place behind Hart house down! Even Lana, the old, crippled pit bull, keeled over dead. The Harts were simply drowning under waves of grief.

Martha was anxious to put all the heart-ache behind her and start a charitable foundation in Owen's name. Then Ellie admitted in her deposition in the lawsuit that she did, in fact, take legal documents from my mom and dad and faxed them right to Vince's lawyers, including the allocation agreement. No one knew what the ramifications of this would be, and there was concern that the trial could be delayed because of it.

Of course, this led to another furious meltdown between me and Ellie, especially when my mom tearfully told me that my dad had given $6,000 of the money I'd given to help them out to Ellie. My temper got the best of me and I hurled one of Stu's antique chairs into a wall, shattering it to pieces.

After that blow up, Ellie left me a phone message. "I haven't done anything, Bret. You won't get the satisfaction that you ultimately wanted from Vince over Montreal and a bunch of lawyers are getting the money. Mom and Dad should be able to get on with their lives. I don't know what makes you think that you're such a genius. Maybe you need to rethink things, Bret. I know it will never be right between me and you and I don't really care, but the one I do feel bad about is Martha, but I'm sure all of this will work out for Martha and I pray to God that it does. I haven't done anything except stand my ground and what I said right from the very start, that we should try and work this out, because the only ones that are going to win are a bunch of lawyers and it's going to rip the family apart, and it has. At least you know my point of view and respect it."

I was asked to show up at *Nitro* in Las Cruces on August 28, where I saw Bill Goldberg for the first time since he nearly cut his own arm off breaking that car window. He hugged me and told me how sorry he was about my concussion. I had no doubt about that—Bill was a good man. Unfortunately, he'd been pushed too fast and didn't understand his brute strength.

That night we both followed the insane booking angles: I hit Goldberg with a rubber shovel and pretended to bury him alive in the New Mexico desert. Maybe he should have been burying me for real: Dr. M called to tell me the verdict was in. It was official: I'd never wrestle again.

I went home and waited for Dr. Johnston to second Dr. M's opinion before I said anything to WCW. As Bob Dylan wrote, It's when you think you've lost everything that you find out you can always lose a little more. He was so right.

WCW had me show up on September 4 for Dallas *Nitro* just to slam Goldberg's head with a cage door. The following night at *Thunder*, a WCW angle reduced my very real concussion into a silly storyline when they had me go face-to-face with Goldberg in the middle of the ring. I was slurring my words for real, following the script to whine about how he hurt me, when a wave of emotion came over me as I realized that nobody was getting it: everyone, including all the fans, thought I was just acting like I was concussed. Then the big screen played the definitive camera angle of Goldberg's foot plowing into my head, one that I'd never seen before. The crowd laughed and jeered me as Goldberg dressed me down verbally. Afterwards, I felt like a whore as I remembered the devastating impact of Goldberg's foot connecting with my head, reinforced by what I'd seen up on the big screen. And I'd let them exploit it for ratings.

At the end of the month, I returned to Montreal for more brain injury tests. When I was done, Antoine's bereaved parents picked me up and had me over for a home-cooked meal.

46

PISSING GOD OFF

I'D BEEN A STEADY HORSE all these years. Since being hurt, I'd done everything WCW asked of me, yet they'd cut my pay, then cut it again. Now, like a limping circus pony, I waited for the end. It came on October 19, 2000, when J.J. Dillon called with the bad news. His voice cracked, and I knew it hurt him to tell me, though I could still feel the stick gently prodding me out the flap at the back of the circus tent. Twenty-three years and it's all over.

FedEx delivered my termination letter: "Based on your wrestling incapacity WCW is exercising its right to terminate your independent contractor agreement effective October 20, 2000. . . Your contributions to the wrestling business are highly regarded and we wish you only the best in the future."

Then I read a letter I'd just received from a young fan by the name of Rosalie. I'd received thousands of fan letters over the years, many similar to hers. Maybe it was the timing, but none quite touched me like this one did:

> I'm writing a letter to tell you how much you have meant to me. I want to tell you that you were the reason I first started watching wrestling and I basically grew up watching you. . . It's unbelievable how much of the Hitman character helped shape the person I am today. . . I saw how you never, ever gave up. . . What I learned from The Hitman was to work hard, to never give up and most importantly to have confidence in yourself. Those beliefs may sound corny but when you are a ten-year-old kid growing up in a broken home where you are constantly being told how worthless you are those beliefs can be a positive thing. I remember looking in the mirror as a teenager and saying, Rosalie, you are the best there is, the best there was and the best there ever will be and don't let anyone tell you otherwise. . .

I'm in third-year university, studying chemical engineering right now . . . The Hitman was the catalyst that has got me where I am today . . . I heard somewhere that celebrities shouldn't be a child's hero, that heroes should be people who are real. Well, sometimes the people in a child's life can't be heroes. The child may have to look elsewhere. I'm not ashamed to say that you were my hero. It just breaks my heart to hear the rumors about you retiring soon. I don't want to believe it because I don't want to let you go. I have been watching you wrestle for as long as I can remember and it'll be so strange when you're gone. Seeing you retire, letting you go, would be like saying good-bye to a very dear friend who I will never know if I will see again . . .

I plan to make enough money one day to buy a house, I'll hang my framed autographed picture of you and when friends and family come over I'll tell them about you. How much I respect you and when I'm old and gray I will still remember you and I'll tell my grandkids how you were my hero. Wrestling will never be the same without you but on a positive side, I wish you all the happiness in the world. You will always hold a special place in my heart. Yours Truly, Rosalie

On November 3, an elated Martha called to tell me that, after the many bumps in the road caused by Ellie, she had settled with Vince. I have to admit I was more than a little hurt when she told me she couldn't tell me the amount because she'd sworn an oath not to reveal it. When I asked her if she ever found out exactly what happened and who was responsible for Owen's death, she meekly offered up, "He just fell."

The more we talked, the more disappointed I became, especially when I remembered what she said in her eulogy. "There will be a day of reckoning and this is my final promise to Owen. I won't let him down."

I asked her if she and the lawyers at least tried to get back my photo and video archives from Vince. She told me Pam Fischer said the issue wasn't important enough even to bring up. When I hung up the phone, I called Marcy; she'd just heard the news through her media contacts that Martha settled for $18 million.

The next morning I read Martha's comments about the Harts in the paper. "These people worked against me . . . I am removing myself and my children from the family. I carry the last name, but I'm not related to them any more. People need to know that Owen was a white sheep in a black family."

After that, she called me again, and I told her point blank that I felt she'd completely used me and I didn't appreciate the way she painted us all with the same brush. I couldn't see why Martha had to hurt my whole family. While she'd been quick to praise me, she was quite venomous to my mother, who'd stood by her throughout all the family struggles. It didn't seem to matter to Martha that Owen was my mother's son. When Martha started to cry I forgave her, because I knew she felt she had no choice but to settle after Ellie had derailed the case, but what she had said was not about the money ended up being about the money.

Just before Christmas I was called to testify in a court proceeding on Smith's behalf. Over the years he'd fathered an unknown number of kids by different mothers, none of whom he took responsibility for. But he wanted custody of Chad, whose mother had died, and whom he was relying on Stu and Helen to raise. They were getting on in years and after twelve kids of their own, and forty-something grandchildren, they were burned out. My conscience told me it was more important to be a good uncle than a good brother, and sadly I couldn't endorse Smith as a responsible father. Smith took this as an unforgivable betrayal. So now I had one more estranged sibling out to get me.

Christmas that year was probably the worst one my mother ever lived through: everyone seemed hell-bent on making my ailing parents sorry they ever had twelve kids. Bruce had his problems; Davey, who was still with Andrea, managed to score more headlines when he supposedly made death threats to Diana. I, of course, had serious heat with Ellie, Diana, Bruce and now Smith. Ellie saw fit to blame the meltdown in the family on me, telling the media that she believed it was more important to me to make life unpleasant for Vince McMahon than to be loyal to them.

Then Carlo called to give me the big news that he had personally structured a WWF takeover of WCW. He laughed at how Vince got the organization, including the entire film library of not only WCW, but the NWA, for just half a million. I didn't let on to Carlo how much it bothered me that Vince now owned every inch of footage of my career, with the exception of Stampede Wrestling. But the wrestling war that broke out in 1984 was finally over, and for all intents and purposes Vince now monopolized the business.

The Governor General's office called on Valentine's Day with the much-needed good news that Stu would be invested as a Member of the Order of

Canada on May 31. My mom wanted me to accompany them to Ottawa for the ceremony, but when Stu's pneumonia landed him back in the hospital for much of April, we wondered if he'd be able to make it. I did my best to avoid any more confrontations with opposing family members. I'd spent the winter coming back from my concussion, watching Blade play hockey; I also started working on this book. Ever since I'd gone to work for the WWF I'd carried a tape recorder with me all over the world, recording a diary of my life. I just kept thinking, This will make a hell of a book some day, and it seemed to me that the time had come.

One night I had a dream that I had WWF's current world champion, Kurt Angle, in a tight headlock. In the dream, I asked myself if it was really happening, and to figure out if it was real or not, I stared at the sweat dripping off his head and then focused on the blue fabric of the ring canvas. In my dream I concluded it was not a dream, and when I woke up, for the first and only time I really missed working.

Carlo invited me to the WWF show in Calgary on May 28. I told him I'd like to meet Kurt Angle and Brock Lesner, but I wasn't comfortable going to *Raw* so close to the second anniversary of Owen's death. Why the WWF insisted on running shows in Calgary each May I'll never know. It infuriated Martha and lit a fuse to the powder keg at Hart house.

Carlo knew I was still extremely sensitive about what Vince had done to me, but he passed on the message that Vince wanted me to know that he didn't hate me: if I wanted to come down to the show he'd be more than happy to shake my hand. But the problem wasn't him hating me any more—it was me hating him. Aside from sticking it in my eye every chance he got, he'd destroyed the harmony of the Hart family, for which I was being blamed.

Carlo then asked me about Stu's health, saying that Ellie, Diana and Bruce desperately wanted Stu to be on TV to show the world that the Hart family had made peace with the WWF. He said that they had requested five hundred free tickets to the show—they didn't get them, of course—and didn't seem to see the absurdity of the situation. As soon as I hung up the phone, I drove down to Stu's. I was relieved when he told me through gritted teeth that he didn't want to go to *Raw*, but that he was being made to go.

"You don't have to do anything you don't want to do, and I'll be here to make sure of it!" I said. But Ellie, Diana and Bruce were more than determined to see that Stu should go. Meanwhile, in another chapter of our public soap opera, Martha told the media that she would be deeply offended if any of the family went to the WWF show, which only put added pressure on my parents to fix something that couldn't be fixed.

May 28, 2001. If the show is to start in the evening, the talent usually arrives at the building in the afternoon. When I got to Stu's house at ten that morning, I thought I was in more than enough time to spare him from going to the Calgary *Raw*. But I was too late: Ellie and Bruce had dragged him off at eight o'clock in the morning. I'd hear later that Diana and Bruce wheeled him into Vince's office like a battering ram, then commenced a heated argument over who could make their pitch to Vince first. But Vince was so busy with TV, he soon had them cleared out of his office.

As upset as I was, I told my mom that it would do Stu good to see the boys in the dressing room. But I thought it would break my heart if they paraded him out on *Raw*—the public would think that Stu had forgiven Vince for everything.

I didn't go down to the Saddledome. Tears came to my eyes as I watched the opening of the live show at home on TV: there was a clearly tired, deflated and demoralized Stu sitting in the front row with Ellie, Diana, Georgia, Bruce and Smith, who grinned as he held up a big sign that read, HA HA BRET.

At the end of the show, Vince stuck his big, fat, salty thumb in my eye as far as he could by re-enacting the *Survivor Series* screwjob finish, in Calgary, right in front of my father, as he played the corrupt promoter who rang the bell as Benoit had Stone Cold in my sharpshooter. I drove down to Stu's and burst into my mom's bedroom. Rage filled me as I denounced every single one of them for doing this to me—I was through with them all. I didn't know how to forgive any of them. I stomped down the stairs and took both Owen's and my childhood photos off the wall, leaving two white dusty blanks. I slammed the kitchen door as I left and burned rubber out of the yard, feeling every bit as betrayed as I did the day Vince ordered poor Mark Yeaton to ring the bell.

The next morning, Bruce drove an eighty-six-year-old Stu three hours north to the *Smackdown* taping in Edmonton and put him through the whole thing again. Both Benoit and Jericho called me, concerned about Stu's health and state of exhaustion.

Even though I'd looked forward to going to Ottawa to see Stu receive the Order of Canada, I was so offended by everything that had happened I chose not to go. As a result, I missed something that I had my heart set on. By June, I realized how it was wrong to punish my parents for being used by my brothers and sisters. Stu and Helen were both broken-hearted by my absence so, after a couple of weeks, I showed up and put the pictures back up on the wall. Then I went upstairs and wrapped my arms around my mom and, as I felt her shake with emotion, I silently loathed my brothers and sisters for doing this to her. I felt so sorry for all of us. I couldn't help but feel as though I was free-falling into a bottomless pit of despair. If I'd had to write a will, it would have been a few lines, but if I'd had to write a suicide note, it would have been a thousand pages long.

Throughout that summer, whenever I pulled into Stu's yard, Ellie and Diana would race out of the house and flee in their cars. But in a lot of little ways, I told myself, things hadn't changed too much. There was always a ring full of grandkids wrestling out in the yard, dogs and cats everywhere, a fresh pot of tea and five or ten young wannabe wrestlers taking bumps in the dungeon.

On a hot July afternoon, I opened my car door, my sidekick Coombs jumped out and together we went in search of my mom. I followed his snorts all the way into her office and gave her a big hug. She was never that crazy about dogs, but her mother, Gah-Gah, absolutely adored pugs. I soon had her laughing, and telling me stories. One of her favourites was about the time I lost my hug. One of her childhood friends from New York, who went by the name Little Helen (because she was even tinier than my mom, which wasn't that easy to be), came to visit when I was about three. She was getting hugs from everybody, but when it came to my turn, I was too shy to hug a stranger. She jokingly asked, "Where's my hug?" My eyes got big and I told her, "I lost it." For the whole week she was there, I pretended I was still looking for it. Luckily for her I found it on her last day!

Despite these attempts to cheer her up, I could tell my mom was really upset. Finally she told me that she'd read a draft of a tell-all book that Diana had coming out soon. Diana had got Stu to write the foreword without him reading the manuscript. My mom was so upset because, unbeknownst to Stu, he had endorsed a book that trashed his own family. She was trying desperately to cheer herself up, thinking of the reunion she was about to have with her sisters in California. I was thinking, Diana, what have you done?

In September, I was soon going to Australia to promote a tour for a fellow named Andrew McManus who had a new wrestling outfit called WWA. He asked me to help put them on the map by playing a non-wrestling role as their figurehead Commissioner. I enjoyed helping out the smaller promotions whenever I could, as a way of giving back to the business that'd given me so much. It did give me the opportunity to visit Australia, though; I'd never been there before, and I was having a great time

My concussion was finally beginning to clear, though I still wasn't allowed to lift weights or do any other form of exercise. On September 12, 2001, in Australia I'd just done a live night-time talk show with a host named Rove and was thrilled with how it had gone. I headed back to my hotel room and met some of the wrestlers from the tour in the elevator. They told me somebody had flown an airplane into one of the towers of the World Trade Center. When I got to my room I watched in horror, with the rest of the world, as the second plane hit. I stared at the TV all night with a deep sadness that heaped itself on the pain and hurt I already carried around.

I loved New York. She'd been good to me. I always thought of the New York skyline as a beautiful girl smiling at me. Now she had broken teeth; they'd really done a job on her. It was still hard for me to imagine a horror and sorrow beyond Owen, and I wondered what he'd have thought. I thought of home and how devastated my mom would be watching this on TV. She and Stu still remembered the impact of Pearl Harbor, and how out of that catastrophe and the war that followed, they met and fell in love on a beach in Long Island, New York.

Being in Australia made it all so surreal, as if it wasn't surreal enough already. I was stranded in Melbourne until there were flights to take me back to North America. I remember walking over to the Melbourne Aquarium, where I watched sharks and stingrays float over my head in giant glass tanks.

I couldn't help thinking that if anything ever happened to me, I'd still want it known that I wouldn't change anything about my life. A voice in my head kept telling me to live and live and live.

When I finally got back to Calgary, a week late, I learned that my poor mom had been delayed at LAX for an entire day because of the heightened security, and that her diabetes medicine had been in her checked luggage. The way I see it, Osama bin Laden also caused my mother's death. After getting home exhausted, she collapsed into a coma that she never really came out of. Poor Stu was distraught over not calling an ambulance for my mother as soon as she got sick. I don't think he ever got over that. He had been too weak and disabled to pick her frail body up from the floor.

Diana's book came out at the same time. The opening paragraph described Davey drugging and sodomizing her, and it went downhill from there. Diana told ridiculous stories about there being a wrestling alligator in the basement, about her friendship with André The Giant and her stardom in the WWF. She even ripped into close family friends such as Ed Whalen, saying he was no good at his job and stole Stu's thunder. When Diana hit the talk shows promoting her book, even the affable Mike Bullard, who referred to me as a Canadian hero, treated her with sarcasm. When I realized how truly clueless Diana was about the way people were reacting, I actually felt sorry for her. I'd later hear that Diana was misled by the woman who actually wrote the book, and embroidered

Diana's stories. Was I to assume that Diana was not even capable of reading her own book to approve its release?

Meanwhile in the ICU, my mom's baby sister, my aunt Diana, told my sister she didn't appreciate some of the remarks in the book. My sister snapped back at her, "My mother never even liked you!" Meanwhile, thirty feet away, my poor mom lingered on.

For days, the doctors pulled every trick in the book to bring her back to life. She suffered immeasurably with IV tubes in her arms and a respirator tube down her throat. She finally came out of it just enough to breathe on her own, barely. Too weak to talk, she could only squeeze my hand. One time she came around enough to faintly whisper, "How's Coombs?"

I knew she had to be hating all this, and was surely cursing the doctors for keeping her alive. At three-thirty in the morning of November 4, 2001, with Stu holding her hand, she slipped away and found the peace she so long deserved. At that very moment I was lying awake in bed. I said out loud, "I'm so sorry, Mom, that the light grew so dim at the end." I felt a soft breeze sweep over me and I just knew it was my mom saying goodbye.

Only weeks after Ed Whalen gave a heart-felt eulogy at my mom's funeral, he also passed away.

In January 2002, Tie Domi came to town for a game and we headed up to Hart house to visit my dad. Tie was a compact man with a head that looked like it was chiselled out of granite; he was generally regarded as the toughest guy in hockey. I called Stu to let him know we were coming, and when we got there, he was waiting for us all alone in his spot at the head of the dining-room table. Tie was dressed in a nice, neat suit. As we approached, Stu turned, stared at him and said, "You got an interesting head on ya." We all burst out laughing. If anybody had seen a lot of strange heads, it was Stu.

A few minutes later, Stu had Tie bent back over the table, trying to show him how he could pull another player in close and stick his chin into the guy's eye socket and trip him backward on the ice. Stu had Tie half twisted up with cat hair all over his nice slacks. After about an hour, I finally got Tie out of there. He told me later that the move Stu showed him would probably work in a hockey fight, if he dared take a chance on it.

On February 27, Carlo called me wanting me to do a trade off: if I'd referee at *Wrestlemania XVIII*, Vince would give me some pictures to use for this book. This was only the latest in a constant stream of attempts to get me back on Vince's TV shows. It was damage control; in the end, even guys who'd left on the worst possible terms always went back to Vince. I did want a truce with Vince, but I also wanted a public apology, one that Carlo told me I'd never get. I thought of my nephews, Harry and Ted, and even T.J. Wilson, who all dreamed about someday wrestling in the big time. I didn't want my animosity toward Vince to jeopardize everything they dreamed of, but I had no intention of showing up at *Wrestlemania* as a referee. I told Carlo all I really wanted was a meeting with Vince to clear the air between us.

The following day Carlo and Bruce Allen got me on a conference call and did their best to bully me into believing that it would be in *my* best interest to referee at *Wrestlemania*. They set up a meeting in New York City a few days later, but when I was packing to leave, Carlo called to say that if I wasn't going to agree to do *Wrestlemania* I shouldn't bother to show up—I'd only be wasting his and Vince's time. I asked him to tell me if he truly thought that refereeing at *Wrestlemania* was the right thing for me to do. He thought he had the hook in my lip as he went on about how this would be fantastic for me. Now I knew he was nothing but a company man. I refused.

On May 18 that year, the Grim Reaper of wrestling took Davey. He was vacationing in Invermere, British Columbia, with Andrea and died in his sleep of a heart attack at the age of thirty-nine. Andrea was Davey's girl at the end, even though she and Bruce were still married.

There were two funerals for Davey. Diana called to ask me to give a eulogy at the one she organized and I agreed, but first I attended the service Andrea put together. Poor Andrea was crying hard, and I was glad I made it there for her. I saw some of the old Stampede crew, including Ben Bassarab, who was one of Davey's closest mates, and his new wife, who was also very nice. But Bad News, Gerry Morrow and Gamma Singh snubbed me. They were all down and out, working security jobs together: none of them even talked to me. What did I ever do to them, I asked myself, and then I knew—I didn't go broke.

Diana timed her memorial service for Davey for May 29, the same day the WWF was in town. Vince, Hogan and others came. Ellie, who spoke just before me, ripped into poor Andrea with a vengeance. Wrong place, wrong time, awkward silence. Eventually one of the funeral home staff eased her away from the podium. I rose to clean up her mess and to give Davey a fitting send off, which left both Harry and his baby sister Georgia smiling with tears in their eyes. I loved Davey like a brother. His biggest mistake was letting bad people influence his innocent heart. I spoke of how I remembered him best as that shy, handsome kid with the big dimples.

I'm sorry, Bax, I thought, I should have been there for ya.

When I arrived at Hart house after the service, I was simmering with a lot of pent-up emotion. It was extremely hot in the kitchen. When I asked my dad how he felt, he told me he was tired and he didn't feel up to going to the WWF show. But then Ellie came in, and I could tell by the way he pursed his lips that she was dragging him down to the show.

I told Ellie, "He's tired. Clearly, he doesn't want to go. Look at him."

She snapped that Vince had invited him, like that was more important than his health.

In a flash, we had broken into a vicious yelling match, where I ripped into her for embarrassing the whole family at Davey's funeral. "We were supposed to pay our respects, not take shots," I said. Soon my sister Georgia and Ellie's eldest daughter, Jenny, took up for Ellie and while I was arguing with them, Ellie dragged Stu down the steps and zoomed off.

I felt terrible about the fight, realizing that the stress of everything was getting to me. Harry, now a strapping six-foot-five with Davey's dimples, came up to me then, thanked me for my words at the funeral.

I was carrying around anger, torment, regret and grief like a big bag of heavy rocks.

I'd been asked to dress like Mordecai Richler's character The Hooded Fang and deliver a monologue from his children's book, *Jacob Two-Two and the Hooded Fang*, on a CBC special celebrating Richler's life. On Thursday, June 20, I brought Julie to Montreal with me for the show. I was happy to be part of a cast including Richard Dreyfuss, Montreal Canadiens legend Jean Beliveau and several prominent stage and literary notables, but I'd let myself get really worried about how I'd do. I still had a thick, fuzzy head and concentration problems, and this show was live to tape. I studied the script for weeks.

I slipped a black wrestling mask over my head. When I looked in the mirror, it seemed like I was living my dream of working a crowd as my childhood cartoon wrestling character The Cool Cool Killer—or close enough anyway. Despite a last-second glitch with my mic as I walked on stage, I carried the role off. Halfway through my monologue I pulled off my mask and got a pleasant pop of recognition from the crowd. I bowed, and my smile was a dead giveaway of how proud I was of myself. Maybe my concussion was finally behind me.

Afterwards, I got slaps on the back from Dreyfuss and Beliveau. To top off the evening, I had a terrific time wining and dining Julie in old Montreal.

I flew home carefree and raring to go. This performance was going to mark my turnaround. I was going to get back on my feet, be me again, train and get my body back. Just maybe I could finally break free and clear of the heartaches and headaches of the last five years.

A day later, Julie was furious with me again. Jim had called me while I was riding my bike and he rode downtown to meet me. It was a beautiful, hot Saturday afternoon and we stopped to wet our whistles and catch up with each other. He had a big gut now, and a long red goatee. Both of us still agonized over Davey's death. It was like our lives had become this cartoon show, except in this cartoon all the characters were being killed off for real. Jim was drinking harder than ever and I was in the mood to celebrate after doing The Hooded Fang, so the beer went down easy. It was a long uphill ride back home, and it felt good sweating out the alcohol. But I was two hours late for dinner with Julie, and that was all it took to derail the progress we had been making.

On Monday, June 24, I woke up determined to make some serious changes. I called my divorce lawyer, who joked about my divorce taking the longest amount of time in the history of divorce negotiations. I told him I wanted to put the divorce papers through immediately. I'd had enough of the back-and-forth game with Julie. While I was at it, I didn't like how Bruce Allen had sided with Carlo, talking to him behind my back about how they could get me to take part in *WrestleMania XVIII* when he was supposed to be representing my best interests. So I penned Bruce a handwritten fax letting him know that I didn't need him any longer.

Since it was another beautiful sunny morning, I decided to ride my bike to the gym. I stopped at a bike shop to see if they could repair my helmet because one of my kids had monkeyed around with the clasp on the chin strap. They didn't have a piece to fix it and offered to sell me a new helmet instead. I decided to take my chances for one day.

Just before noon I was pedalling nice and easy along the Bow River. I realized I needed to relieve myself, so I veered off the bike path. I was coasting slowly toward a clump of trees when my front tire dropped into a grass-covered hole nearly stopping me cold. I bounced out, but the bike was off balance when the back tire hit the same hole. The bike wobbled and then tipped, sending me tumbling sideways. I got my hands up to protect myself, and I remember thinking that I didn't want to break my sunglasses or the cellphone in my pocket.

I tucked and rolled on the hard grassy field. The thought crossed my mind that anyone watching would probably get a good laugh. The second my head hit the ground, I'd be sorry for the rest of my life that I ever hit that hole.

I thought I'd get up red-faced and dust myself off. I was wrong. I lay there groaning and badly winded, writhing around in terrible agony like a speared fish. I saw those same silver dots again, but this time only in my left eye and they moved toward a cone-shaped point. For several minutes I couldn't get up. I desperately grabbed clumps of prickles to pull myself up to my knees and then struggled to do a right-legged squat to get to my feet. Using my bike for support I stood there, thinking, What the fuck happened to me?

A man jogged past and yelled to ask if I was okay. I waved him off, but seconds later I realized that my left arm was hanging by my side and refused to work. I finally grabbed my left hand with my right one and placed it on the handlebar, but it fell off and just hung there. With my weight on my right leg, I leaned my chest on the seat and, with my right hand, I somehow manoeuvered my bike back to that damn hole and stared at it, unable to comprehend what had happened. I couldn't believe that fucking hole had done this to me!

I tried to swing my left leg over the bike and keep going because I didn't want to be late for my work out, but I fell over in an embarrassing heap. As I lay there sweating and drooling taking in the smell of fresh-cut grass, the sun beat down on me as dragonflies and bumblebees buzzed by. I managed to reach Jade on my cellphone, only to find that my tongue and lips weren't working right and my speech was slurred. Having no idea what I was talking about, Jade put Julie on the phone. As best I could I explained what had happened and that I was a few feet from a little hill where we had sat down to read paperback novels one time.

About ten minutes later, Julie and Beans were racing up to me. I told them I was okay, that I'd just banged my head. "Just get me out of here!" Julie didn't tell me that the pupil of my left eye was big and black. I told them to pull me up to my feet and we'd all just walk to the car, but at my first step we all fell over. A roller blader raced off to call 911 while a nurse from Toronto who happened to be jogging by splashed me with cold water and told me to stay awake.

Soon paramedics were strapping me into a cervical collar. Beans rode with me in the ambulance while Julie followed behind in the car. I wondered what I did to piss off God.

Hours later, at the Foothills ICU, the nurses were trying to persuade me that I'd feel better if I peed. Every hour on the hour, they'd come by to tell me that if I didn't pee soon, they'd have no choice but to insert a catheter. I assured them they'd have to kill me first. I could hear them tell the same story to some guy behind the curtain in the bed next to me. He finally gave them permission, and his blood-curdling screams sounded as if they were amputating his leg with no anesthetic. The poor guy died the next morning.

I have blurry memories of Julie and my kids gathered around me, and of Blade holding my hand in tears telling me, "You're the best dad there ever was!"

At one point, a Dr. Watson showed up and asked me if I could move my fingers and toes. It took every ounce of strength I had to ever so faintly twitch the very tips of my toes and fingers. Dr. Watson flashed me a hopeful look, saying, "That's a really good sign."

I was wheeled away for an angiogram, where they rammed an ice-cold golf-ball-sized camera on a tube the size of a garden hose down my throat. My gag reflex was so extreme they ended up sedating me. When I came to, they did an MRI, using some sort of dye that I can only describe as making my head feel like my veins and arteries were carrying gasoline and somebody had lit a match. My ears got so hot that I thought they were going to melt off. On top of everything, I could barely breathe from the unrelenting pain in my back.

At three in the morning, Dr. Watson showed me the images of my brain. Pointing out a small jelly-bean-shaped spot on top of my head, he told me I had suffered a stroke. I wasn't quite sure what the ramifications of having a stroke were. Dr. Watson explained that nobody could make any promises about how much I'd recover, but if I was lucky and I worked very hard, I might get some of my mobility back.

But he told me that they couldn't give me the miracle drug TPA because they feared my brain was hemorrhaging. If they'd only known sooner that my stroke had been caused by a clot, TPA would have blasted through it and I might very well have got up and walked out of there.

In the wee hours of the morning, a kind young nurse finally wheeled me into a shower. I cried like a baby out of gratitude as this sweet girl washed me clean. It'd been about sixteen hours since I pulled off the bike path to relieve myself, and with the water running, I pissed for a very long time

47

GOING HOME SONG

AFTER MY STROKE, I woke up every day feeling sorry for myself, even though I knew I was lucky to be alive.

I was a wreck. I couldn't whistle any more so when the nurses doted over me, I hummed "Amazing Grace" in my head. My smile curved south on the left side and stayed that way, a cracked sneer. My left eye was stuck wide open, and my vision was poor. I couldn't stop having emotional meltdowns. Everything made me cry as I struggled every day to find my way back to where I had been. It got to be downright embarrassing, until I found out that emotional instability was common for stroke patients and that everyone on the ward was crying all the time.

I remembered when Shawn Michaels said he lost his smile. Well, I had lost my smile, my ability to wink and I was paralyzed on the entire left side of my body. At first, I kept waiting to make a Hitman-style comeback, but after about four days I asked Dr. Watson if I better get used to the idea that I wasn't just going to walk out of there. He told me I wouldn't be going anywhere for a long time. But I still didn't realize what I was dealing with.

I watched the Mordecai Richler special from my hospital bed, and seeing my big smile at the end, so relieved and happy to have beaten my concussion, when only a week later I would be paralyzed by a stroke, made me remember Vince's comment: "Life's not fair."

I couldn't pick up a toothpick. I choked all the time because my lips and tongue were only half working. I was told that the best part of my recovery would come in the first six months and that the first three were critical.

On July 1, Canada's first Olympic gold medalist in wrestling, my friend Daniel Igali, and his coach, Dave McKay, came to visit me. Just as I was being loaded into the ambulance in the park, Daniel had been leaving me a phone message inviting me to dinner with him, Kofi Annan and the African leaders who were attending a G8 summit in Kananaskis, near Calgary. Daniel was kind enough to wheel me down to the basement, where I sat parked in my wretched wheelchair listening to a sweet old gal named Miriam, also a stroke patient, telling me she was sure I was going to beat this thing.

My brother Bruce showed up unannounced in my room with a TV news camera crew. Luckily I was spared the humiliation of being seen at my lowest point because I was out of the room at a rehab session. After that episode, I made a short list of friends and family who I was comfortable seeing and gave Marcy the unenviable task of enforcing it; those who couldn't get in blamed her. She coordinated a uniformed security team than was posted at my door 24/7 and I felt safe knowing I was protected.

Ellie tried to use Stu to get in to see me, but was told by a guard that she wasn't on the list. Ellie then led Stu to believe that I didn't want to see him either, and she took him home. That evening Keith called to tell me how much this had upset Stu, and I was furious. I don't think Ellie could have done anything more hurtful at that time to me, and to Stu. Knowing how upset I was, first thing the next morning Marcy picked Stu up at Hart house and brought him to see me. When she wheeled him into the room, I used every ounce of strength I had to stand up out of my wheelchair and take three or four unsteady steps toward him to squeeze his big, fat hand. He smiled so huge he got tears in his eyes.

One day, after coming back from exhausting physio, I was slumped in bed ready for a nap when my phone rang. I couldn't have been more flustered at hearing Vince's voice. He gave me some kind words of encouragement while I resisted the urge to slam the phone down. My voice cracked as I struggled to tell him that I really wanted to clear the air with him, and that one of the most important things to me was that I didn't want my career to be erased.

We talked about resurrecting that anthology of my career that didn't happen because of *Survivor Series* and about the idea that maybe someday I'd be inducted into the WWF Hall of Fame. When I finally set the phone down, I broke down into tears because I realized at that very moment I'd just dropped one of the heaviest rocks I'd been carrying around.

Every morning, Julie brought me breakfast and a coffee. She helped me in ways I can never forget. I would never have recovered as well without her love and support

After Julie left, my orderly would come to get me for physio again. As he wheeled me down the hall past my fellow patients, all of whom couldn't stop crying, I'd have to remind myself that today I was going to gain some ground.

One morning, in the elevator going down, I couldn't help staring at a handsome little boy of about nine or ten. He was in a wheelchair with bloody, bandaged stumps where his legs used to be. Gaunt and sad, he wore a ball cap covering his bald head.

In seconds, I had flashed back to all the girls and all the places I'd seen, how the world had been mine. I had my doubts that this poor little guy would ever get his driver's licence or make love to a first girlfriend. The ride was only a few floors and I pulled my ball cap down over my face to hide my tears. The courage that flickered in his brooding eyes made me feel ashamed that I ever felt sorry for myself. It woke something up inside me.

After that elevator ride with that child, I prayed for my life. I slowly came back, one heart beat at a time. Time to be the hero I always pretended to be.

Eleven months later I was in Australia.

It was May 20, 2003, and the fourth anniversary of Owen's death was a few days away. I was glad to get the hell out of Calgary because May was such a depressing month for me. It'd been a long year. Not to mention Calgary's infamous weather, teasing a spring that was much closer to winter. The wet cold sapped my energy because it made my muscles stiff and it was much harder for me to get around. It'd been a long year.

I'd always seen myself as indestructible, and to be humbled beyond anything I could ever imagine had left me with little to do but cling to the hope that I would come out of it. I found myself digging deep to muster the courage to overcome the very real fear that I'd never walk again. I fought emotions that whispered to me that I'd never be the same man. I don't know how I would have managed if it hadn't been for all the TLC from my doctors, nurses and therapists—and that includes both Marcy and Julie, who stood by me through the worst of it. One friend after another came to see me and bolster my heart. One of the most inspirational phone calls came from "the even greater one," Walter Gretzky, who had suffered his own catastrophic stroke, and consoled me with the best advice: "Don't despair, my friend, and be patient!" I carried his words with me every day. But of all the wrestlers I'd known, only Roddy Piper came to Calgary to visit me.

Whatever you get back becomes a milestone. I started out not being able to lift a finger. I became exhausted from "just" trying to turn my hand over on a table. Although this might seem like a small feat, I would compare it to doing a one-handed five-hundred-pound bench press. A doctor compared one hour of physical therapy to an entire day of downhill skiing. At first I couldn't dress myself, feed myself or wash myself, and whenever I pushed too hard I only slowed my recovery.

I hated that the nurses needed to come with me to the bathroom in case I fell. Within a few days, I had taught myself to lean on the wall for support in order to get to and from the bathroom on my own. I couldn't believe how incredibly difficult this was and took it as my own private challenge. My stubbornness paid off, but when I got caught by the nurses they reprimanded me. They didn't want me even to attempt it because if I fell and broke my left arm, that would all but snuff out my chances for recovery.

I made a point of getting a lot of rest and recharging my batteries— especially since the batteries on my left side were almost dead. Every "little" step of the way was a huge goal to work toward, and it was all fueled by my fear of failure. Slowly—I couldn't believe how slowly—I began to turn a hand . . . lift an arm . . . stand . . . walk . . . lose the wheelchair.

Then came holding a coffee cup on my own and reading a newspaper.

When my stroke team felt I was ready, they let me have day and weekend passes. I wasn't allowed to drive, and whenever I was a passenger in a car I'd automatically flip the visor down to see if I could wink yet. I hated that I always bore the expression of a guy who'd been hit on the head with a sledgehammer.

On September 4, 2002, I winked back at myself in the visor mirror for the first time and tears filled my eyes. My smile started to show a little life too.

Two weeks after that, which was three months since I had my stroke, I managed to wobble my bike around the parking lot of Foothills Hospital. I only had about fifteen per cent power on the left side, but whether I realized it or not, my brain was making new pathways and I was very, very slowly getting better.

That fall, I dropped the puck at the Hitmen season opener. I even did a Hooded Fang voice-over for the *Jacob Two-Two* animated TV series. In December, I was in Miami at a dinner honouring the Hurricanes football team. I happened to look up and there was Muhammad Ali standing not ten feet away from me, staring at me with that penetrating gaze, those dumbbell-sized fists playfully challenging me. I stood up and as I struggled to limp my way toward him, a concerned look washed the challenging stare from his face. When we stood together, the whole place broke into cheers. I leaned into him and explained that I suffered a stroke back in June. Ali squeezed my hand hard and long and smiled as he looked deep into my eyes. The look said, Here I am, a fellow fighter also battling a challenge greater than any I ever faced in the ring.

Earlier that day, I stopped in to see Vince at his palatial condo in Boca Raton. We'd spoken regularly since that first call in the hospital and things were beginning to thaw out between us. Vince had a way of being fatherly, oddly enough. I missed it, even welcomed it, and somehow we buried the hatchet.

The Grim Reaper of wrestling took Curt Hennig in February 2003 and Miss Elizabeth in May, both from drug overdoses. Curt was one of my closest friends. Liz, like my mother, struck me as just too nice a person to have been mixed up in wrestling. After staring my own mortality in the eye, their deaths made me appreciate how lucky I was to be alive and regret everything about our business that had conspired to end their lives.

I wanted to try to put those feelings into words for a WWA show in Sydney, Australia, on May 21. I wasn't so eager to try it in front of a live audience. I'd made an appearance for wrestler Jacques Rougeau in Montreal only six weeks after my stroke, which turned out to be a nightmare. But he had invested everything he had in the show and it would have been a disaster for him and his family if I didn't show up. So I kept my promise that I'd be there no matter what. It was humbling to limp slowly out to the ring in front of five thousand fans, though they gave me one of the most heart-felt receptions I ever received. Even if I dragged my leg and slurred my speech, they were just happy I was alive. I wasn't ready yet and was far too overwhelmed to speak. I felt like a clubbed seal trying to flap his flippers and left the ring regretting that I'd come, even though I was proud of myself at least for having the balls to attempt it.

And now, here I was in Australia to try it again. One of the promises I made to myself when I was still in my wheelchair was that I'd bike along the Yarra River—and I did! By doing the WWA pay-per-view I showed the world—and myself—that whatever doesn't kill you only makes you stronger.

I enjoyed being around the wrestlers again, and I was touched that they didn't hide their concern. Sting gave me a deep talk about what finding Jesus had done for him. I appreciated his words because he meant them, but I didn't need to find God: I didn't feel as though I'd ever really lost Him. As I waited nervously to go out to the ring, the midgets, who were on after me, gathered around to show support. I was uncomfortable about people staring at me or feeling sorry for me, but the midgets lived their whole lives facing those two challenges.

Andrew McManus gave me a big introduction, and suddenly my old WWF theme music kicked in, surprising me as I slowly and stiffly limped my way down the aisle. As I'd feared, I had another meltdown. I fought it and tried to speak as the crowd chanted my name. I somehow managed to thank them briefly and wave goodbye. I did my walk around the ring and hated how pathetic I was. As I came back through the curtain, Teo, one of the midgets, patted me on the leg, gave me a big smile and told me I did good. Midget wrestlers had been nice to me for as long as I could remember. I thanked him and kept my head up, but when I made it around the corner I broke down.

By the time I got to Melbourne on May 23, I had something to prove to myself. I spent the afternoon telling stories to a couple of Greek guys I knew who ran a deli not far from my hotel. When I left, we joked about how if I could talk to them for hours, I could easily talk to my fans for a few minutes. That night, I was prepared to hear my music, and I walked out with a shaky but confident stride and spoke from the heart. This time when I came back through the curtain, three midgets—Teo, Puppet and Meatball—all greeted me with low-fives. I was elated.

When some of the wrestlers asked me if I wanted to meet them at a strip bar, I said why not. I had a limo to myself and arrived earlier than everyone else. The dancers were beautiful and topless, twirling around the poles and walking the runways like models. The clientele was upscale and struck me as surprisingly stuffy. Well-dressed couples stood around sipping cognac and puffing thin cigars like it was a classy event. Who was I to judge, maybe it was!

I surprised myself by sparking up a conversation with a pretty, petite black girl who came from Trinidad. I sipped my beer and impressed myself by nearly talking her into coming around to see me in my room later on that night. Just then a drunk but attractive blonde, who resembled Courtney Love, turned to me and pointed at a well-dressed man who was busy sucking the neck of a scantily clad dancer. "All men are pigs. Ya know that? That's me husband and he's a fooking pig. Look at 'em." So much for classy. While I was talking to her, the other girl disappeared. "I need something different," the blonde complained. Maybe she should turn lesbian, she wondered. "Maybe get a girlfriend or somebody to tie me up. Got any ideas?"

Just then I saw the midgets coming in the front door. I'm not sure what made me lean into her ear and say, "You know what might be really different? When was the last time you were gang-banged by a bunch of midgets?"

By the time she figured out what I said, three midgets who came up to her waist were standing beside me. She snapped at me angrily, "Who the hell do you think yer talking to?"

"I was only making a suggestion."

Late that night I lay in my bed, tipsy for the first time in too long a time. There was a faint knock at my door and the girl from Trinidad was standing there with a big smile. "I thought you might be lonely," she said. I closed the door behind her and thought, Yeah, the old Bret Hart is back.

The next day, New Zealand appeared outside my plane window as a lush emerald-green paradise in the middle of nowhere. It was chilly and damp with rain, and when I made my way past the fans waiting at the backstage gate one of them, a Maori, called me over. He gave me a long jade stone on a black string. He said that the High Chief of all the Maoris had blessed it with healing energy to help me in my recovery and he wanted me to have it. I put it on and to this day, I've never taken it off. I told him, "I'll take all the help I can get," and thanked him.

There was no heat in the building, and when I made my way to the ring, my walk was even stiffer than usual, but I was living and breathing. I wasn't so sure what I was going to say to the fans, but I realized that just being there was a triumph. So I told them life is short and death is long and that it'd been a tough year in the wrestling world. When I spoke of losing Owen, Davey, Curt and Liz, only then did I truly realize that I was a survivor.

I thought Stu might be more comfortable living somewhere where he could have professional care, but he stayed on at Hart house. Ellie and Georgia did their best to take care of him, along with Ellie's daughters Jenny and Nattie. He had to hate losing his independence. His hearing was too far gone for him to make out my deep voice, but whenever I stopped by to see him, he'd light up. At one point he looked at me with a warm smile and said, "Your mother, she was crazy about you." Then he added, "You were always one of my favourite people."

He had growing trouble recognizing people but there were times he had amazing recall. Smith did his part to make up for all the pain he'd put Stu through, taking out the garbage, answering the phone and making Stu dinner. Stu slept most of the time now, with pictures of his Tiger Belle piled up on her side of the bed. Oh, how he missed her! When he was awake he never stopped talking about her. He lingered a little less stubbornly every day. Helen was his life, and the only thing that mattered to him any more was that she'd be waiting for him on the other side.

Occasionally, when I caught him recharged after a nap, we would talk about everyone from Antonio The Great to Superstar Billy Graham. He'd come to life when I brought up old-time shooters such as Reb Russell, Toots Mondt, Wilbur Kneed and, in particular, one tough old bugger named George Tragos. While he talked on about the shooters he loved and respected, I could only think of the workers I loved and respected: Curt, Cowboy Bob, Leo, Steamboat. He'd talk about Scotty Steiner's arms, but sooner or later it always came back to him staring at me with a glint of pride. He'd say, "You were a good amateur, but so were most of my sons." Wrestling had always been Stu's mistress, but what he saw on TV didn't make him happy any more. He rarely watched pro wrestling, and when he did, he'd wince and shake his head. Pneumonia nearly took him a couple of times that spring, eventually landing him in Rockyview Hospital. Blade's peewee hockey team won the city championship, and I drove him right from the rink to the hospital so he could show Grampy his medal.

I took a break and went to the New Orleans Jazz Festival to visit Aaron Neville; all the Nevilles embraced me like a brother. One night Aaron introduced me to Bob Dylan, who was wearing a hoodie and clearly wasn't in the mood to meet anybody. But when Aaron said I was a friend, Bob offered me his hand. His fingers were soft and delicate, and I was careful not to squeeze them too hard. I'm grateful for the fame I got, but sometimes it can really suck to be *too* famous.

The next day I accompanied Aaron to the funeral of blues great Earl King. Musicians dressed in black carried open black umbrellas through the streets of New Orleans playing soulfully. It made me reflect on so many of my wrestling friends who'd gone.

Classy Freddie Blassie died on June 2. At least he lived to be eighty-five.

That summer of 2003, I took Blade along with me on a trip to Europe. We toured the battlefields of Verdun and then hit Paris, London and Milan. I let Blade be my seeing-eye dog because I still had limitations from my stroke, especially regarding my vision. I did an appearance in Monza, Italy. The promoters were just kids, but they pulled it off nicely, an action-packed small outdoor show on a beautiful night. They hired some American wrestlers and whatever workers were in Italy, wrapped it around a question-and-answer session with The Hitman, included a full buffet and got a nice turnout. Even Blade answered a few questions. I found myself staring at a beautiful girl with long dark hair and piercing blue eyes. When she came by for an autograph, she bent down and kissed me on the cheek. As she handed me a letter, I noticed her hand was shaking. I read her kind letter and asked the promoters to bring her to me and we talked for more than an hour. I promised to stay in touch and we swapped e-mail addresses. As I watched her walk away I thought, Well, I can dream, can't I?

When we got home to Calgary, Stu was back in Rockyview, and we all feared the worst. I allowed myself to be distracted by my lawyers, who'd been wrangling with Lloyds of London. It looked liked my disability claim could turn into a costly angle with some double-crossing heels, the likes of which even I'd never seen before. Lloyds became just another one of those heavy stones that I had to carry around. They were entitled to have me assessed by their own doctor, but they put it off until three and a half *years* after my concussion, during which time I'd suffered my stroke, so the exam was pointless, but still required.

I flew to Edmonton on September 10, 2003, for two days of neuropsychological testing with Dr. Michael Keegan. I believed that surely Dr. Keegan would concur with my doctors and tell Lloyds to pay me. An assistant administered the first half-day of concentration and memory tests and then, after a short lunch break, I sat down with Dr. Keegan in his office. He made a point of telling me that wrestlers are con men, professional liars and that I wasn't going to get away with lying to him because he was too smart to fall for such crap! He let me know that by the time he was through with me, he'd expose me for faking my injury and filing a false claim. I had nothing to hide, so I was direct and honest with him. I pointed out that there would be no logical reason for me to give up three years of great money at a time when I was WCW World Champion for an insurance payout that would be far less. He still said I was full of it. He claimed that I was derelict for not reporting a substantial number of previous concussions, based on being "hit" with baseball bats, chairs and cage doors, all of which I'd "reported" in my *Calgary Sun* columns. The doctor wanted it both ways: wrestling was all fake, but the worked injuries were all real! My Lloyds case was becoming less about my career-ending concussion and more about what's real and what's not in pro wrestling.

The truth was that, before Goldberg's kick, I'd never been diagnosed with a concussion in my life. I realized Dr. Keegan was simply trying to provoke me. When he referred to Stu as a coward and a bully who picked on anybody who was smaller than him, my hands balled up into fists. I wondered if I'd get mad enough to tip him and his desk over and snatch him by the throat. But I kept my cool. As I drove to the Edmonton airport, I was steaming over how he treated me and his ignorant comments about my dad, which struck me as even more reprehensible because he knew Stu was ailing in the hospital with pneumonia. (He told me he read about it in the newspaper.)

Stu was hard on us sometimes, but he did what he needed to do to keep order in a family of twelve kids. Fearing him is what kept me in line. My dad had his own way of doing things, and a good example of what kind of man he was came one winter's night when we were all awakened at two in the morning by the sound of spinning tires. Stu saw one of his cars stuck in a snowdrift by the Hart house gates and, thinking it was Smith, he went down to help push him out. I looked out the window and saw the car in the driveway with the door hanging open and the engine running . . . and Stu hauling someone up to the house. Dean, Ross, Owen and I could hear the pots and pans banging around all over the kitchen, punctuated by yells of agony. All the boys snuck to the top of the stairs and listened to hear which older brother was in trouble. But we soon realized we were all accounted for.

I didn't find out until the next morning that Stu had caught some guy in the act of trying to steal the car. Most people would have just phoned the police, but Stu's first instinct was to apply his own form of discipline. Being stretched by Stu is a humbling experience. My father taught humility, not humiliation. He eventually phoned the kid's parents to come pick him up, and later even gave him a job working as an usher at the matches. He got that kid a life, and a second chance, when others would have called the cops and washed their hands of him.

I don't remember my dad ever being afraid of anything. One time at the matches in Calgary when I was a teen, he broke up a knife fight between two Victoria Park kids, snatching the knife and cuffing the ruffian hard on the ear. The kid broke into tears. Minutes later Stu had the two of them shaking hands. Dr. Keegan calling my dad a coward made my blood boil.

I also remembered a time back in 1987 when I was trying to get a break in the WWF and my dad drove up to Edmonton with me. It was just him and me in the car, and he told me things about his life that I'd never heard before; how he'd been a bouncer at the Palace Garden Dance Hall in Yellowknife and how he'd take on all comers in the mining camps up there; how he'd had to hitchhike to Vancouver to win the Canadian amateur heavyweight championship. He told me, with a twinkle in his eye, about how he met my mom; how her dad, Harry, had loved him while Gah-Gah had it in for him. He told me how he and his sisters were saved from starving by the Salvation Army and that his father, Edward, was a better man than he got credit for. He gave me advice on saving my money, and told me stories about all three generations of McMahons. Time flew on that drive, and I didn't want it to end.

After Owen's death, my dad was never the same. His kids wore him out. I believe my mom died feeling more ashamed of herself than she was of any of her children, because she blamed herself for our failures. After Helen was gone, Stu let the fire in his heart die down to a flicker, and his friends and family knew that the only thing he wanted any more was to be with her.

On October 10, I stopped in to see my dad at the hospital. The sight of him asleep with an oxygen tube in his nose and IVs in his wrists didn't sit right with me. He seemed too humbled. To me, he'd always been invincible. The nurses needed to take Stu down for X-rays, so they asked me to wait out in the hall. There I met an old retired cop suffering from dementia. His wife told me how sorry she was about my dad's health, how they both loved Stu and the Hart family, adding that her husband never forgot working for my father down at the pavilion.

They wheeled Stu out into the hallway on a gurney; he was facing away from me with his big hands behind his head. For the first time since he'd been hospitalized, I felt tears sting my eyes when I realized that his forearms were now so thin that the skin was hanging loose. I'll always remember him as the man with legs like telephone posts, hands as big as telephones, built solid as a rock and square as a door with that strong chin and those cobalt eyes. Now, with his hair neatly combed by his nurses, he looked like a good-natured baby, quiet and grateful.

The next day I brought him my collection of old Stampede Wrestling programs, which spurred a brief but amazing recovery. The photos had him sitting up and pointing his finger with a twinkle in his eyes: "He was a tough bastard, this one!"

A few days later we had a family meeting with the doctors. They said that Stu was making progress and he might even see a couple more Christmases. After the way my mom had suffered, I dreaded the very thought of Stu withering away in a hospital for years. I felt like there were angels in the room thinking the same thing. I left sad and afraid.

Two days later, B.J. stopped by to tell me in person that Stu had suffered a stroke, and if I wanted to see him one last time, I'd better hurry. I asked Julie to come with me. Various family members had kept vigil all night, and we passed them in the hallway as they went to take a break.

Stu was propped up on his side with pillows, breathing hard. Julie gasped and put her hand over her mouth when we saw that somebody had written PISS OFF MARTHA PATTERSON on the blackboard in his room. I erased it, thinking there should be no hate in this room, only love and prayers.

Stu hung on for another day. When I headed over to the hospital the next morning with Julie, we drove slowly, talking about Stu and my mom. I'd feared this day for as long as I could remember.

Several local reporters were in the waiting room. Julie went to check on Stu while I shook the hand of an old Hutterite fan who'd driven ninety miles to pay his respects. She returned with a look of panic in her eyes, "Bret, you better come now." When I rushed into his room, Jenny was there, wishing she could do something for him. His breathing was shallow and I smoothed his hair with my hand, bending to kiss his head. I couldn't help but think of him doing the same to me the day I was born. I stared down at my dad. I loved him so much. He was my hero and a hero to all that knew him. Sometimes when a hero fails, it only makes him more human and real and you love him even more. My heart filled with love and pride. I saw the colour drain from his face and his big hands, and then I watched my father breathe his last breath.

Jenny frantically called for a nurse, but I knew he was gone. I kissed his head one last time. It was instantly cold and dry. I pinched his knobby, thick cauliflower ears. Nothing. He was at peace, and with my mom, Dean and Owen. Julie and Jenny wept in each other's arms. I was proud to be the son lucky enough to be there with him at that moment.

At my dad's funeral, I was asked to be the final speaker. Calgary loved Stu Hart and people showed him just how much that day, lining the streets, sombre and respectful. If my mom had been at the church, she'd no doubt have quipped that it was a good house. I have to admit, it felt like a big-time wrestling show, just the way Stu would have wanted it. As always, there were cowboys and Indians in the seats and the front row was filled with the biggest marks of them all—wrestlers.

The pastor called me to the podium, "And our last speaker today, Bret Hart, would you please come up . . ."

I knew as I slowly made my way to the front of the church that this was my biggest and final main event. I was more than afraid I'd have a meltdown and I did all I could to hold myself together. I swallowed hard and saw Vince staring back at me. All my brothers and sisters were leaning forward, almost in prayer. It was time to make my parents proud and help heal some of the wounds of recent times.

> We should all remember those times when it was late at night and the Hart house would grow still and quiet and the Hart kids would all be tucked in. My dad's feet would shuffle down the hall and as he'd pass each room he'd turn out the lights. It always seemed like there was so much on his mind, his heart weighed down with the worries that only a father of twelve children could understand. He'd click off the lights and it was in that black darkness that you could hear twelve little voices cry out one after another, Good night dad, I love you. The voices of your children that love you so much cry out in the dark, the lights are all turned out. Goodbye dad. I love you.

At the Eden Brook cemetery, respected elder Hal Eagletail, in his full headdress and a beautiful white buckskin coat, pounded his drum at graveside and in a mournful wail sang "The Going Home Song." I knew then that this was the day that wrestling truly died for me. Maybe it died for a lot of other people too. I'll always try to do right by my father and carry myself like him as much as I can. I saw the sun breaking through the clouds and I could feel the flood of a million memories. As the chief sang, I thought about what a great life my dad had given me. I closed my eyes and said goodbye to my father.

AFTERWORD

AFTER MY FATHER DIED, I said goodbye to The Hitman too. I couldn't help but feel that my Hitman character died out like Crazy Horse. I'd had my place and time in the world, but the little pink soldier only marched around in my head now.

Life is all about living fully before you die. When people are dying, they never want to feel like somehow they missed out. I never will. I've had a great life, an interesting life and I've got a long way left to go. I got into wrestling to meet girls, to see the world, stay in shape and make some money. I did. And I learned some things along the way. There was a price to pay for every dalliance, and I paid up in full. To quote Mark Helprin, "If you want to make it to the top, give yourself up to loneliness, fear nothing and work hard."

What goes around does come around. Life isn't always fair. Live every day like it might be your last because, good or bad, you never know what's waiting around the corner.

I was just a kid when I started out. I had big dreams and I lived through them. Twenty-three years later, I was finally home, not broke, not broken—but I had a lot of scars. I was called a young lion once and I'd also soared like an eagle. I feared after Julie and I finally divorced that I'd become a cold, lonely polar bear padding his way across the Arctic snow, lost and empty, but in September 2004, I married the beautiful Italian girl with the piercing blue eyes. Cinzia showed me her diary from 1995, when she was fourteen, where she'd written that someday she'd marry me. She did, but by the time I'd finished writing this book, we'd called it quits simply because she could never be so far away from her home country and family. After thirty years of being away from home I knew exactly how she felt. But polar bears never slow down, they move ever forward—and I have always been a survivor.

If I was a stallion, my heart called out to the rest of the ghost herd: Dean, Owen, Davey, Pillman, Curt, Rude, even Dynamite, who had all been so strong, swift and young. Although I can't rightfully declare myself a soldier,

I had a lot of white crosses in my life. I made a lot of sacrifices and I shared in a lot of glory, but for me, it was always about the brotherhood of the wrestlers. It was better to be respected than feared, and although I never pretended to be a tough guy, among the wrestlers I was always respected. In the dressing room I never lied about anything to anybody. If I said I was with two girls the night before, I was. If I said I benched 415 pounds, I did. I was never ribbed, except by Owen, and nobody ever shit in my crown.

I can't say there wouldn't have been pro wrestling without my father, but I can say it wouldn't have been nearly as good or as real. My father's generation was the one that made the work more important than one's hardness in a ring. They were the toughest men I ever knew.

As for Vince, I'll forever appreciate what he did for me. I wish I could say that we learned a lesson from our encounters that cheaters never prosper. Sadly cheaters do prosper and even become billionaires. The world's full of them, and maybe that's why we need heroes who don't gage success with dollars.

I did get inducted into the WWE Hall of Fame, and Vince gave me creative control over an anthology of my career—but it took *eight years* after the Montreal screwjob. Six years after Bill Goldberg blasted me in the head, Lloyds of London finally agreed that I have a permanent career-ending brain injury, and we settled out of court for the full amount.

I can look myself in the mirror and know that I never stabbed Shawn, Hunter, Hogan, Flair or anyone else in the back to get where I got. In 2005, Hogan made the preposterous comment that I was a wrestler that none of the other wrestlers could trust, that I wasn't one of the boys. I was always one of the boys. I never needed my own dressing room, fruit basket and flowers, or a manservant to carry my bags. And I never denied anyone the chance to make money.

Shawn Michaels found religion and settled down with an ex-*Nitro* girl. Over time he seems to have convinced himself that it was me who screwed him over at *Survivor Series*. To me, Shawn will always be a phony, a liar and a hairless yellow dog. The difference between Bret Hart and Shawn Michaels is that I'd have never done to him, or to any of the boys, what he did to me.

Hunter dumped Chyna, became famous as Triple H, married Vince's only daughter, Stephanie, and is poised to become the master and ruler of the wrestling world.

More wrestlers have died: Road Warrior, Hawk, The Wall, Bossman, Herc, Eddie Guerrero, Earthquake, Chris Candido, Bam Bam Bigelow, Ernie Ladd, Bad News, Sheri Martel, Chris Benoit, Brian "Crush" Adams—and more will die. When I got into the business, wrestling was all about trust and respect, and doing the honours meant something. I'll never forgive Shawn, or

Hunter, for killing the business that so many of us gave our lives for. Although pro wrestling will never truly die, but always morph into something else, the business that I knew and loved and gave all I had to is dead and gone forever.

I escaped with my head up and my conscience clear.

INDEX

KEY TO BRET'S CARTOON

1. Hitman
2. Wolfie
3. Sky Low Low
4. Davey Boy Smith
5. Owen Hart
6. Jim The Anvil Neidhart
7. Matilda
8. Terrible Ted
9. Bam Bam Bigelow
10. Big Daddy Crabtree
11. Cuban Assassin
12. Yokozuna
13. Stone Cold Steve Austin
14. Little Beaver
15. Rowdy Roddy Piper
16. Kamala
17. Ravishing Rick Rude
18. Duke Myers
19. One Man Gang
20. Sheik
21. Road Warrior Hawk
22. Road Warrior Animal
23. Vader
24. Inoki
25. Harley Race
26. Bad News Brown
27. Tiger Jeet Singh
28. Sergeant Slaughter
29. Hulk Hogan
30. Goldberg
31. Jake The Snake Roberts
32. Big Bossman
33. Curt Mr. Perfect Hennig
34. Rey Mysterio
35. Macho Man Randy Savage
36. Andre The Giant
37. Iron Sheik
38. King Kong Bundy
39. Abdullah The Butcher
40. Dynamite Kid
41. Tiger Mask
42. J.R. Foley
43. Mel Philips
44. Bushwacker Luke
45. Bushwacker Butch
46. Chief Jay Strongbow
47. Destroyer
48. Undertaker
49. Mankind
50. Archie The Stomper Gouldie
51. Stu Hart
52. Ed Whalen
53. Kendo Nagasaki
54. Sweet Daddy Siki
55. Ultimate Warrior